WHAT DO YOU SAY AFTER YOU SAY HELLO?

THE PSYCHOLOGY OF HUMAN DESTINY

Eric Berne's extraordinary new bestseller is a book about the scripts that people follow compulsively throughout their lives—as if they had no more choice than the characters in a tragedy, or a melodrama, or a farce.

YOUR LIFE SCRIPT—AND
WHAT IT DOES TO YOU

As a psychiatrist, Dr. Berne found that each person—under the powerful influence of his parents—writes in early childhood the script that will govern the general course of his life.

Your script dictates what kind of person you will marry . . . how many children you will have . . . even the kind of bed you will die in, and who will be present when you do. It determines whether you will be a winner or a loser, a spendthrift or a skinflint, a tower of strength or a doomed alcoholic.

Some people have scripts that call for them to fail in their professions, or to be repeatedly disappointed in love, or to be chronic invalids. Some have scripts that end in suicide.

WHAT DO YOU SAY AFTER YOU SAY HELLO? demonstrates how life scripts get written, and how to find out what kind of script you have. If your script is a bad one, it shows you how to break out—so that you may begin at last to live a life of true freedom and fulfillment.

What Do You Say After You Say Hello?

The Psychology of Human Destiny

Eric Berne, M. D.

BANTAM BOOKS
TORONTO · NEW YORK · LONDON

A NATIONAL GENERAL COMPANY

WHAT DO YOU SAY AFTER YOU SAY HELLO?
*A Bantam Book | published by arrangement with
Grove Press, Inc.*

PRINTING HISTORY
*Grove Press edition published June 1972
5 printings through January 1973
Bantam edition published May 1973*

*Bantam Books are published by Bantam Books, Inc., a National
General company. Its trade-mark, consisting of the words "Bantam
Books" and the portrayal of a bantam, is registered in the United
States Patent Office and in other countries. Marca Registrada.
Bantam Books, Inc., 666 Fifth Avenue, New York, N.Y. 10019.*

PRINTED IN THE UNITED STATES OF AMERICA

CONTENTS

TABLE OF FIGURES

PREFACE

This book is in direct succession to my previous ones on the transactional approach, and outlines the new developments in thinking and practice which have taken place during the last five years, chiefly the rapid advance in script analysis. During this period there has been a great increase in the number of trained transactional analysts. They are testing the established theories in many different fields, including industry, corrections, education, and politics, as well as in a variety of clinical situations. Many of them are making original contributions of their own, as mentioned in the text and footnotes.

That is primarily intended as an advanced textbook of psychotherapy, and professionals of different backgrounds should have no difficulty in translating into their own dialects the short and simple annals of transactional analysis. No doubt some nonprofessionals will read it too, and for that reason I have tried to make it accessible to them. It may demand thinking, but I hope it will not require deciphering.

Conventional psychotherapy ordinarily employs three different dialects: therapist-therapist, therapist-patient, and patient-patient, which are as different from each other as mandarin and Cantonese, or ancient Greek and modern Greek. Experience shows that eliminating these as far as possible in favor of a *kua-yu* or *lingua franca* of basic English increases the "communication" which many therapists so ardently court (and so diligently leave waiting at the altar, as the saying is). I have tried to avoid the fashion popular in the social, behavioral, and psychiatric sciences of masking uncertainty with redundance and vagueness with prolixity, a practice which has its origins in the Faculty of Medicine of the University of Paris in the fourteenth century.

This has led to charges of "popularization" and "oversimplification"—terms reminiscent of the old Central Committee accusations of "bourgeois cosmopolitanism" and "capitalist deviation." Given the choice between the arcane and the open, between over-complication and simplicity, I have thrown in with the "people," tossing in a big word now and then as a sort of hamburger to distract the watchdogs of the academies, while I slip in through the basement doors and say Hello to my friends.

It is quite impossible to thank everybody who has helped in the development of transactional analysis, since they now number in the thousands. The ones I know best are the Teaching Members of the International Transactional Analysis Association, and the members of the San Francisco Transactional Analysis Seminar, which is the one I attend regularly every week. Those who have been most actively concerned with script analysis include Carl Bonner, Melvin Boyce, Michael Breen, Viola Callaghan, Hedges Capers, Leonard Campos, William Collins, Joseph Concannon, Patricia Crossman, John Dusay, Mary Edwards, Franklin Ernst, Kenneth Everts, Robert Goulding, Martin Groder, Gordon Haiberg, Thomas Harris, James Horewitz, Muriel James, Pat Jarvis, Stephen Karpman, David Kupfer, Pamela Levin, Jack Lindheimer, Paul McCormick, Jay Nichols, Margaret Northcott, Edward Olivier, W. Ray Poindexter, Solon Samuels, Myra Schapps, Jacqui Schiff, Zelig Selinger, Claude M. Steiner, James Yates, and Robert Zechnich.

In addition, I want to thank my secretary in San Francisco, Pamela Blum, for keeping the Seminar running smoothly and contributing her own ideas; and also her successors, Elaine Wark and Arden Rose; and particularly my secretary in Carmel, Mrs. Mary N. Williams, without whose conscientiousness, skill, and application the physical manuscript, through all its drafts and changes, could never have come into being. My fifteen-year-old son, Terence, ably assisted me in collating the bibliography and drawings and other details of the manuscript, and my daughter, Ellen Calcaterra, read it and made many valuable suggestions. Finally, I want to thank my patients for being such good sports about revealing themselves, and for letting me go away on vacations so that I could think; and also the millions of readers in fifteen languages who encouraged me by their interest in reading one or another of my books.

SEMANTICS

As in my other books, *he* may refer to human beings of either sex, while *she* may be used if I think a statement applies more to women than to men; sometimes *he* may also be used for grammatical simplicity to distinguish therapist (male) from patient. I hope these convenient syntactic devices will not be taken amiss by emancipated women. *Is* means that I have a reasonably firm conviction about something, based on the clinical experience of myself and others. *Seems to be* or *appears to be* means that I am waiting for further evidence before making a firm commitment. The case histories have been drawn from my own experience and from those presented at seminars and supervisory sessions. Some are composites, and all have been masked from outside recognition, although significant incidents or dialogues are faithfully reported.

—*Eric Berne*

PART I

General Considerations

CHAPTER ONE

Introduction

A · WHAT DO YOU SAY AFTER YOU SAY HELLO?

This childlike question, so apparently artless and free of the profundity expected of scientific inquiry, really contains within itself all the basic questions of human living and all the fundamental problems of the social sciences. It is the question that babies "ask" themselves, that children learn to accept corrupted answers to, that teen-agers ask each other and their advisors, that grownups evade by accepting the corrupted answers of their betters, and that wise old philosophers write books about without ever finding the answer. It contains both the primal question of social psychology: Why do people talk to each other? and the primal question of social psychiatry: Why do people like to be liked? Its answer is the answer to the questions posed by the Four Horsemen of the Apocalypse: war or peace, famine or plenty, pestilence or health, death or life. It is no wonder that few people find the answer in their lifetimes, since most go through life without ever finding the answer to the question which precedes it: How do you say hello?

B · HOW DO YOU SAY HELLO?

This is the secret of Buddhism, of Christianity, of Judaism, of Platonism, of atheism, and above all, of humanism. The famous "sound of one hand clapping" in Zen is the sound of one person saying Hello to another, and it is also the sound of the Golden Rule in whatever Bible it is stated. To say Hello rightly is to see the other person, to be aware of him as a phenomenon, to happen to him and to be ready for him to happen to you. Perhaps the people who show this ability to the highest degree are the Fiji Islanders, for one of the rare jewels of the world is the genuine Fijian smile. It starts slowly, it illuminates the whole face, it rests there long enough to be clearly recognized and to recognize clearly, and it fades with secret slowness as it passes by. It can be matched elsewhere only by the smiles of an uncorrupted mother and infant greeting each other, and also, in Western countries, by a certain kind of open personality.*

This book discusses four questions: How do you say Hello? How do you say Hello back? What do you say after you say Hello? and, principally, the plaintive query, What is everybody doing instead of saying Hello? These questions will be answered briefly here. The explanation of the answers will occupy the rest of this psychiatric textbook, which is addressed first to the therapist, secondly to his patients as they get cured, and thirdly to anyone else who cares to listen.

1. In order to say Hello, you first get rid of all the trash which has accumulated in your head ever since you came home from the maternity ward, and then you recognize that this particular Hello will never happen again. It may take years to learn how to do this.

2. In order to say Hello back, you get rid of all the trash in your head and see that there is somebody standing there or walking by, waiting for you to say Hello back. It may take years to learn how to do *that*.

3. After you say Hello, you get rid of all the trash that is coming back into your head; all the after-burns of all the grievances you have experienced and all the reach-backs of all the troubles you are planning to get into. Then you will be speechless and will not have anything to say. After more years of practice, you might think of something worth saying.

4. Mostly, this book is about the trash: the things people are doing to each other instead of saying Hello.

---

*Oddly enough, in my experience, such smiles are most frequently seen in girls in their twenties, with long black hair.

It is written in the hope that those with training and talent for such things can help themselves and others to recognize what I am calling (in a philosophical sense) "trash," since the first problem in answering the other three questions is to see what is trash and what isn't. The way people speak who are learning to say Hello is called "Martian," to distinguish it from everyday Earth-talk, which, as history shows from the earliest recorded times in Egypt and Babylonia to the present, has led to wars, famines, pestilence, and death; and, in the survivors, to a certain amount of mental confusion. It is hoped that in the long run, Martian, properly learned and properly taught, will help to eliminate these plagues. Martian, for example, is the language of dreams, which show things the way they really are.

C · AN ILLUSTRATION

To illustrate the possible value of this approach, let us consider a dying patient, that is, a patient with an incurable disease and a limited time to live. Mort, a thirty-year-old man with a slowly developing form of cancer, incurable in the present state of knowledge, was given at worst two years, and at best, five. His psychiatric complaint was tics, consisting of nodding his head or shaking his feet for reasons unknown to him. In his treatment group he soon found the explanation: he was damming his fears behind a continuous wall of music which ran through his mind, and his tics were his way of keeping time with that music. It was established by careful observation that it was this way 'round and not the other, that is, that it was not music keeping time with tics, but body movements keeping time with mental music. At this point everyone, including Mort, saw that if the music were taken away by psychotherapy, a vast reservoir of apprehension would be released. The consequences of this were unforeseeable, unless his fears could be replaced by more agreeable emotions. What to do?

It soon became clear that all the members of the group knew they were going to die sooner or later, and that they all had feelings about it which they were holding back in various ways. Just as with Mort, the time and effort they spent covering up were blackmail payments made to death, which prevented them from fully enjoying life. Such being the case, they might do more living in the twenty or fifty years left to each of them than Mort could do in the two or five years left to him. Thus it was determined that it was not the duration of life, but the quality of living which was important: not a startling or novel discovery, but one arrived at in a more poignant way than usual because of the presence of the dying man, which had a deep effect on everyone.

It was agreed by the other members (who understood Martian talk, which they gladly taught Mort, and which he gladly learned) that living meant such simple things as seeing the trees, hearing the birds sing, and saying Hello to people: experiences of awareness and spontaneity without drama or hypocrisy, and with reticence and decorum. They also agreed that in order to do these things, all of them, including Mort, had to get tough about the trash in their heads. When they saw that his situation was, in a way, not much more tragic than their own, the sadness and timidity caused by his presence lifted. They could now be merry with him and he with them; he and they could talk as equals. They could get tough with him about his trash, because now he knew the value of toughness, and why they were being tough; in return, he had the privilege of getting tough with them about *their* trash. In effect, Mort turned in his cancer card and resumed his membership in the human race, although everyone, including himself, still fully realized that his predicament was more acute than anyone else's.[1]

This situation illustrates more clearly than most others the pathos and depth of the Hello problem, which, in Mort's case, went through three stages. When he first entered the group, the others did not know that he was a condemned man. They first addressed him in the manner customary in that group. Their approaches were basically set by each member's upbringing—the way his parents had taught him to greet other people, adjustments learned later in life, and a certain respect and frankness appropriate to psychotherapy. Mort, being a newcomer, responded the way he would anywhere else, pretending to be the ambitious, red-blooded American boy his parents had wanted him to be. But when he stated, during his third session, that he was a doomed man, the other members felt confused and betrayed. They wondered if they had said anything which would make them look bad in their own eyes and his, and especially in the eyes of the therapist. They seemed, in fact, angry at both Mort and the therapist for not telling them sooner, almost as though they had been tricked. In effect, they had said Hello to Mort in a standardized way, without realizing to whom they were speaking. Now that they knew he was a special person, they wished they could go back and start over, in which case they would treat him differently.

So they did start over. Instead of talking forthrightly, as they had before, they addressed him softly and cautiously, as though to say: "See how I'm going out of my way to be thoughtful of your tragedy?" None of them wanted to risk his good name now by speaking out to a dying man. But this was unfair, since it gave Mort the upper hand. In particular, nobody dared to laugh very long or very loud in such a presence. This was corrected when the problem of what Mort could do was solved; then the tension lifted and they could go back and start over for the third time, talking to him as a member of the human race, without restraint. Thus, the three stages were represented by the superficial Hello, the tense, sympathetic Hello, and the relaxed, real Hello.

Zoe cannot say Hello to Mort until she knows who he is and that can change from week to week, or even from hour to hour. Each time she meets him, she knows a little more about him than she did the last time, and she must say Hello to him in a slightly different way if she wants to keep up with their advancing friendship. But since she can never know all about him, nor anticipate all the changes, she can never say a perfect Hello, but only come closer and closer to it.

D · THE HANDSHAKE

Many patients who come to a psychiatrist for the first time introduce themselves and shake hands when he invites them into his office. Some psychiatrists, indeed, offer their own hands first. I have a different policy in regard to handshakes. If the patient proffers his hand in a hearty way, I will shake it in order to avoid being rude, but in a noncommittal fashion, because I am wondering why he is being so hearty. If he offers it in a way which merely suggests that he considers it good manners, I will return the compliment in such fashion that we understand each other: this pleasant ritual will not interfere with the job to be done. If he proffers it in a way which indicates that he is desperate, then I will shake it firmly and reassuringly to let him know that I understand his need. But my manner when I enter the waiting room, the expression on my face and the position of my arms, indicates clearly enough to most newcomers that this amenity will be omitted unless they insist upon it. This is intended to establish, and usually does establish, that we are both there for a more serious purpose than to prove that we are good fellows or to exchange courtesies. Mainly, I do not shake hands with them because I do not know them, and I do not expect them to shake hands with me, because they do not know me; also, some people who come to psychiatrists object to being touched, and it is a courtesy to them to refrain from doing so.

The ending of the interview is a different matter. By that time I know a great deal about the patient, and he knows something about me. Thus, when he leaves, I make a point of shaking hands with him, and I know enough about him to know how to do it properly. This handshake means something very important to him: that I am accepting* him even after he has told me all the "bad" things about himself. If he needs comforting, my handshake is such that it will comfort him; if he needs assertion of his masculinity, my handshake will evoke his masculinity. This is not a carefully thought out device to seduce the patient; it is a spontaneous and freely-given recognition of him as I now know him after talking for an hour with him about his most intimate concerns. On the other side, if he has lied to me out of malice rather than natural embarrassment, or tried to exploit or browbeat me, I will not shake hands with him, so that he knows he will have to behave differently if he wants me on his side.

With women, it is slightly different. If one needs a palpable sign that I accept her, I will shake hands in a way suitable to her needs; if (as I know by this time) another shrinks from contact with men, I will say farewell in a correct way but let her pass without a handshake. This latter case illustrates most clearly the reason for not shaking hands as a greeting: if I shake hands with her at the start, before I know with whom I am shaking hands, I awaken her abhorrence. I have, in effect, intruded upon and insulted her before the interview, by forcing her, out of good manners, and against her inclination, to touch me and let me touch her, however courteously.

In therapy groups, I follow a similar policy. I do not say Hello on entering, because I have not seen the members for a whole week, and I do not know to whom I am saying Hello. A light or cordial Hello might be quite out of place in the light of something that has happened to them in the interval. But I do make a very strong point of saying Good-by to each member at the end of the meeting, because then I know to whom I am saying Good-by, and how to say it in each case. For example, suppose one woman's mother has died since the last meeting. A genial Hello from me would seem

---

*"Acceptance" is not used here in its ill-defined, sentimental sense; it means, specifically, that I am willing to spend more time with him. This involves a serious commitment which may, in some cases, mean one or more years of patience, effort, ups and downs, and getting up in the morning.

out of place to her. She might forgive me for it, but there is no need to put that strain on her. By the time the meeting is over, I know how to say Good-by to her in her bereavement.

E · FRIENDS

Socially, it is different, since friends are for stroking. With them, Hello and Good-by range from an open handshake to a big hug, depending on what they are ready for or need; or sometimes it is josh and jive to keep from getting too involved, a "smile when you say that." But one thing in life is more certain than taxes and just as certain as death: the sooner you make new friends, the sooner you'll have old ones.

F · THE THEORY

So much for Hello and Good-by. What happens in between falls into the framework of a specific theory of personality and group dynamics, which is also a therapeutic method, known as transactional analysis. In order to appreciate what follows, it is first necessary to understand the principles of this approach.

REFERENCES

1 The advantages of coming back to life instead of waiting for death are shown in: (1) "Terminal Cancer Ward: Patients Build Atmosphere of Dignity." *Journal of the American Medical Association*. 208:1289, May 26, 1969. (2) Klagsbrun, S. C. "Cancer Emotions, and Nurses." *Summary of Scientific Proceedings*. 122nd Annual Meeting, American Psychiatric Association, Washington, D.C., 1969.

CHAPTER TWO

Principles of Transactional Analysis

The principles of transactional analysis have been described previously on numerous occasions. The most detailed account can be found in the writer's work on *Transactional Analysis in Psychotherapy;*[1] its application to group dynamics is outlined in *The Structure and Dynamics of Organizations and Groups;*[2] its use in analyzing games is described in *Games People Play;*[3] its application to clinical practice is found in *Principles of Group Treatment;*[4] and a summary of the theory is given in popular form in *A Layman's Guide to Psychiatry and Psychoanalysis.*[5] Hence, only a brief outline will be given here, for the benefit of those readers who do not have any of these works immediately to hand.

A · STRUCTURAL ANALYSIS

The basic interest of transactional analysis is the study of ego states, which are coherent systems of thought and feeling manifested by corresponding patterns of behavior. Each human being exhibits three types of ego states. (1) Those derived from parental figures, colloquially called the Parent. In this state, he feels, thinks, acts, talks, and responds just as one of his parents did when he was little. This ego state is active, for example, in raising his own children. Even when he is not actually exhibiting this ego state, it influences his behavior as the "Parental influence," performing the functions of a conscience. (2) The ego state in which he appraises his environment objectively, and calculates its possibilities and probabilities on the basis of past experience, is called the Adult ego state, or the Adult. The Adult functions like a computer. (3) Each person carries within a little boy or little girl, who feels, thinks, acts, talks, and responds just the way he or she did when he or she was a child of a certain age. This ego state is called the Child. The Child is not regarded as "childish" or "immature," which are Parental words, but as childlike, meaning like a child of a certain age, and the important factor here is the age, which may be anywhere between two and five years in ordinary circumstances. It is important for the individual to understand his Child, not only because it is going to be with him all his life, but also because it is the most valuable part of his personality.

Figure 1A, then, purports to be the complete personality diagram of any human being whatsoever, encompassing everything he may feel, think, say, or do. (Its more convenient abbreviated form is shown in Figure 1B.) A more detailed analysis does not yield new ego states, but only subdivisions within the primary ones. Thus, it is evident that careful study will

Structural Diagram
of a Personality

An Informal
Structural Diagram

Second Order
Structural Diagram

FIGURE 1A   FIGURE 1B   FIGURE 1C

show two Parental components in most cases, one derived from the father, the other from the mother; it will also uncover within the Child ego state the Parent, Adult, and Child components which were already there when the Child was fixated, as can be verified by observing actual children. This second-order analysis is represented in Figure 1C. The separation of one feeling-and-behavior pattern from another in diagnosing ego states is called *structural analysis*. In the text, ego states will be denoted Parent (P), Adult (A), and Child (C), capitalized, while parent, adult, or child, uncapitalized, will denote actual people.

There we will also encounter descriptive terms which are self-explanatory or which will be explained: the Natural or Nurturing Parent and the Controlling Parent, and the Natural, the Adapted, and the Rebellious Child. Where the "structural" Child is represented by horizontal divisions, the "descriptive" Child is shown with vertical ones, as in Figure 1 D.

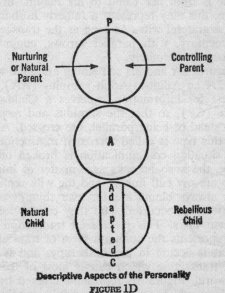

Descriptive Aspects of the Personality

FIGURE 1D

B · TRANSACTIONAL ANALYSIS

From the above, it is evident that when two people confront each other, there are six ego states involved, three in each person, as in Figure 2A. Since ego states are as different from each other as actual people are, it is important to know which ego state is active in each person when something takes place between them. What happens can then be represented by arrows drawn between the two "people" in the diagram. In the simplest transactions, the arrows are parallel, and these are called complementary transactions. It is evident that there are nine possible types of complementary transactions (PP, PA, PC, AP, AA, AC, CP, CA, CC) as shown in Figure 2B. Figure 2A represents, as an example, a PC transaction between two spouses, in which the stimulus is from the husband's Parent ego state to the wife's Child ego state, and the response is from her Child to his Parent. In the best situation, this may represent a fatherly husband taking care of a grateful wife. As long as the transactions are complementary, with parallel arrows, communication may proceed indefinitely.

In Figures 3A and 3B something has gone wrong. In Figure 3A an Adult-to-Adult stimulus (AA), such as a request for information, receives a Child-to-Parent response (CP), so that the stimulus and response arrows, instead of being parallel, are crossed. A transaction of this type is called a *crossed transaction,* and in such a situation communication is broken off. If, for example, the husband asks as a matter of information "Where are my cuff links?" and the wife replies "Why do you always blame me for everything?" a crossed transaction has occurred, and they can no longer talk about cuff links. This is crossed transaction Type I, which represents the common form of transference reaction as it occurs in psychotherapy, and is also the type of transaction which causes most of the troubles in the world. Figure 3B represents crossed transaction Type II, in which an Adult-to-Adult stimulus (AA), such as a question, receives a patronizing or pompous

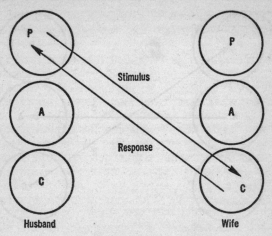

A Complementary Transaction PC-CP

FIGURE 2A

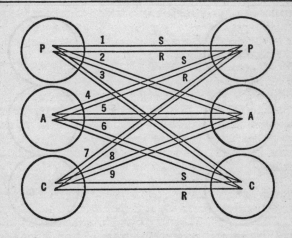

A Relationship Diagram
Showing Nine Possible Complementary Transactions

FIGURE 2B

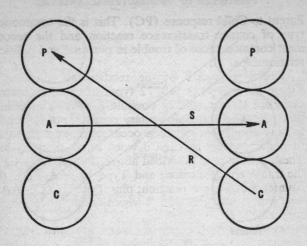

Crossed Transaction Type I AA-CP

FIGURE 3A

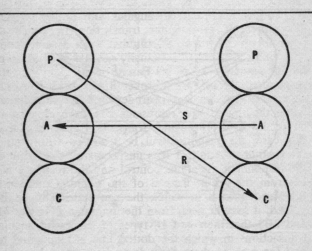

Crossed Transaction Type II AA-PC

FIGURE 3B

Parent-to-Child response (PC). This is the commonest type of counter-transference reaction and the second most common cause of trouble in personal and political relationships.

Careful inspection of the relationship diagram in Figure 2B will show that 72 types of crossed transactions are mathematically possible (9x9=81 combinations, less the 9 complementary ones),* but fortunately only about four of them occur often enough to be of major concern in clinical work or in everyday life. These are the ones described above, Type I (AA–CP), the transference reaction; and Type II (AA–PC), the counter-transference reaction; plus Type III (CP–AA), the "exasperating response," where someone who wants sympathy gets facts instead, and Type IV (PC–AA), "impudence," where someone who expects compliance gets what he considers a "smart aleck" response instead, in the form of a factual statement.

Complementary and crossed transactions are simple, one-level transactions. There are two types of ulterior or two-level transactions, angular and duplex. Figure 4A represents an angular transaction in which an ostensibly Adult-to-Adult stimulus, such as a rational-sounding sales appeal, is actually devised to hook some other ego state—either the Parent or the Child—in the respondent. Here the unbroken line, Adult-to-Adult, represents the social or overt level of the transaction, while the dotted line represents the psychological or covert level. If the angular transaction is successful in this case, the response will be Child-to-Adult rather than Adult-to-Adult; if it is unsuccessful, the Adult of the respondent maintains control and the response will be from the Adult instead of the Child. Considering the various ways in which the ego states can be involved, it may be seen from the diagrams (Figures 4A and 2B) that there are 18 types of successful angular transactions in which the dotted line is responded to, and for each of these there is an unsuccessful angular

---

*This can be verified by drawing each one separately or writing them out: PP–PA, PP–PC, PA–PP, PA–PC, and so on down to CC–CA, after which some of them can be matched with examples from clinical practice or daily life.

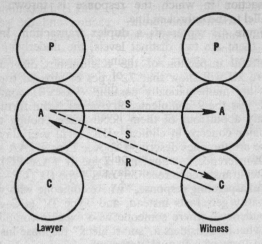

A Successful Angular Transaction (AA+AC) (CA)

FIGURE 4A

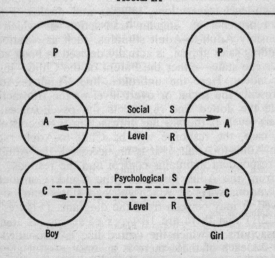

A Duplex Transaction (AA-AA) (CC-CC)

FIGURE 4B

transaction in which the response is thrown back parallel to the unbroken line.

Figure 4B represents a duplex transaction. In this case there are two distinct levels, the underlying psychological or covert level being different from the social or overt level. A study of the diagrams will show that there are 81^2 or 6561 different types of duplex transactions possible.* If we subtract those in which the social and psychological levels duplicate each other (which are, in effect, the 81 types of simple transactions) there are actually 6480 types of duplex transactions. Fortunately again, only about six of these are of common clinical or everyday significance.**

The reader may wonder why there are so many numbers in this section. There are three reasons. (1) The Child reason is that lots of people like to figure out numbers. (2) The Adult reason is to demonstrate that transactional analysis is more precise than most other social and psychological theories. (3) The Parent reason is to show that even though it is so precise, it does not fence people in. For example, if we engage in only three transactions, and each time we have a choice among 6597 varieties, then we can have our three transactions in 6597^3 ways. This gives us about 300 billion different ways of structuring our three exchanges with each other. That certainly gives us all the room we need to express our individualities. It means that the whole population of the world could pair off, and each couple have three exchanges 200 times in a row,

---

*This can be worked out as follows. Take the nine complementary transactions from Figure 2B, and add the 72 crossed transactions. For each one of these 81 possibilities at the social or overt level, there are the same 81 possibilities at the psychological or covert level. Again, many of these combinations can be found in clinical and personal situations by someone who has learned to recognize ego state in action.

**(AA–AA)+(CC–CC) (as in Figure 4B), (AA–AA)+ (PP–PP), (AA–AA)+(PC–CP), (PP–PP)+(CC–CC), (AA–AA)+(CA–CA), (AA–AA)+(PA–PA). Others enter in special situations such as child-rearing, teaching, or child psychiatry, where the overt level may be complementary (PC–CP, CC–CC) or crossed (AA–CP, Type I), for example, while the covert level may be any of the 81 possibilities. In order to visualize these, it is best to draw the transactional diagrams and then translate them into actual situations.

without any pair ever duplicating what any other pair did, or repeating anything they themselves had done before. Since most people engage in hundreds or thousands of transactions every day, each person has trillions and trillions of combinations at his disposal. Even if he has an aversion to 5000 of the 6597 possible types of transactions, and never gets into them, there is still plenty of room to maneuver in, and there is no necessity for his behavior to be stereotyped unless he himself sets it up that way. If he does so, as most people do, that is not the fault of transactional analysis, but of other influences that form the chief subject matter of this book.

Since this system as a whole, in all its branches, is referred to as transactional analysis, what has been described above, the analysis of single transactions, is called *transactional analysis proper,* which is the second step after structural analysis. Transactional analysis proper gives a rigorous definition of the system as a whole, which will be of interest principally to those trained in scientific methodology. A transaction consisting of a single stimulus and a single response, verbal or nonverbal, is the unit of social action. It is called a transaction because each party gains something from it, and that is why he engages in it.[6] Anything that happens between two or more people can be broken down into a series of single transactions, and this gives all the advantages which any science attains when it has a well-defined system of units.

Transactional analysis is a theory of personality and social action, and a clinical method of psychotherapy, based on the analysis of all possible transactions between two or more people, on the basis of specifically defined ego states, into a finite number of established types (nine complementary, 72 crossed, 6480 duplex, and 36 angular). Only about 15 of these commonly occur in ordinary practice; the rest are largely of academic interest. Any system or approach which is not based on the rigorous analysis of single transactions into their component specific ego states is not transactional analysis. This definition, in effect, purports to set up a model for all possible forms of human social behavior. This model is efficient because it follows the principle of scientific economy (sometimes known as "Occam's razor"), making only two assumptions: (1) that human beings can change from one ego state to another, and (2) that if A says something and B says something shortly thereafter, it can be verified whether or not what B said was a response to what A said. It is also very effective because, so far, no examples have been found among thousands or millions of interchanges between human beings which could not be dealt with by the model; and it is rigorous as well, because it is limited by simple arithmetical considerations.

The best way to understand the "transactional viewpoint" is to ask: "What would a one- or two- or three-year-old child do that would correspond to this grownup's behavior?"

C · TIME STRUCTURING

It is also possible to classify long series of transactions, extending even to a whole lifetime, so that significant human social behavior, both short term and long term, can be predicted. Such chains of transactions take place, even when they yield little instinctual satisfaction, because most people become very uneasy when they are faced with a period of unstructured time; hence, they find cocktail parties, for example, less boring than being by themselves. The need to structure time is based on three drives or hungers. The first is *stimulus* or *sensation hunger*. Far from trying to avoid stimulating situations, as some people have claimed, most organisms, including human beings, seek them out. The need for sensation is the reason why roller coasters make money and why prisoners will do almost anything to avoid solitary confinement. The second drive is *recognition hunger,* the quest for special kinds of sensations which can only be supplied by another human being, or in some cases, by other animals.[7] That is why milk is not enough for baby monkeys and human infants; they also need the sound

and smell and warmth and touch of mothering or else
they wither away, just as grownups do if there is no
one to say Hello to them. The third hunger is *structure
hunger,* which is why groups tend to grow into organizations, and why time-structurers are among the most
sought after and the most highly rewarded members of
any society.

An interesting example combining both stimulus
hunger and structure hunger is found among rats raised
in a state of sensory deprivation, that is, in complete
darkness, or in a constantly lighted white cage with no
variation. Later in the lives of these animals, after they
had been put in ordinary cages with "normal" rats, it
was found that they would go to food in a maze if it
was placed on a checkerboard, but they would not go
to food if it was placed on a simple background. Normally raised rats would go to the food regardless of the
background. This showed that the hunger of the deprived rats for a structured stimulus was more important than their hunger for food. The experimenters concluded that the need for structured stimuli (or as they
put it, for "perceptual experience") may involve
biological processes just as basic as food hunger, and
that the effects of early sensory deprivation may persist
throughout life in the form of a strong attraction to
complicated stimuli.[8]

There are four basic classifications for the short-term
structuring of time in human social behavior, with two
limiting cases. Thus, if two or more people are in a
room together, they have six possible kinds of social
behavior to choose from. At one extreme the limiting
case is *withdrawal,* in which the people do not overtly
communicate with each other. This may occur in such
diverse situations as a subway train or a therapy group
of withdrawn schizophrenics. Next to withdrawal, in
which each individual remains wrapped in his own
thoughts, the safest form of social action is
rituals. These are highly stylized interchanges which
may be informal or may be formalized into ceremonies
which are completely predictable. The transactions
which make up rituals convey little information, but

are more in the nature of signs of mutual recognition. The units of a ritual are called *strokes,* by analogy with the way in which infants are recognized by their mothers. Rituals are programed from outside by tradition and social custom.

The next safest forms of social action are called *activities,* what is commonly called *work,* in which the transactions are programed by the material that is being worked with, whether it be wood and concrete, or problems in arithmetic. Work transactions are typically Adult-to-Adult, oriented toward the external reality— that is, the subject of the activity. Next in order are *pastimes,* which are not as stylized and predictable as rituals, but have a certain repetitive quality and are in the nature of multiple-choice, sentence-completion interchanges, such as take place at cocktail parties where people do not know each other very well. Pastimes are largely socially programed by talking about acceptable subjects in acceptable ways, but individual notes may creep in, leading to the next form of social action, which is called *games.*

Games are sets of ulterior transactions, repetitive in nature, with a well-defined psychological payoff. Since an ulterior transaction means that the agent pretends to be doing one thing while he is really doing something else, all games involve a con. But a con only works if there is a weakness it can hook into, a handle or "gimmick" to get hold of in the respondent, such as fear, greed, sentimentality, or irritability. After the "mark" is hooked, the player pulls some sort of switch in order to get his payoff. The switch is followed by a moment of confusion or crossup while the mark tries to figure out what has happened to him. Then both players collect their payoffs as the game ends. The payoff, which is mutual, consists of feelings (not necessarily similar) which the game arouses in both the agent and the respondent. Unless a set of transactions has these four features, it is not a game—that is, the transactions must be ulterior so that there is a con, and the con must be followed by a switch, a crossup, and a payoff. This can be represented by a formula.

$$C + G = R \to S \to X \to P \quad \text{(Formula G)}$$

C+G means that the con hooks into a gimmick, so that the respondent responds (R). The player then pulls the switch (S), and that is followed by a moment of confusion or crossup (X), after which both players collect their payoffs (P). Whatever fits this formula is a game, and whatever does not fit it is not a game.

For example, the mere fact of repetition or persistence does not constitute a game. Thus, in a therapy group, if a scared patient repeatedly asks the therapist for reassurance every week ("Tell me I'll get better, doctor") and when he receives it, says "Thank you," that is not necessarily an ulterior transaction. The patient has stated his need frankly and has had it gratified, and does not take advantage of the situation in any way, but gives a courteous response. These transactions, therefore, do no constitute a game but an operation, and operations, no matter how often they are repeated, must be distinguished from games, just as rational procedures must be distinguished from rituals.

If another patient, however, asks the therapist for reassurance, and upon receiving it, uses the response to make the therapist look stupid, that constitutes a game. For example, a patient asked: "Do you think I'll get better, doctor?" and the sentimental therapist replied "Of course you will." At that point the patient revealed her ulterior motive in asking the question. Instead of saying "Thank you," as in a straight transaction, she pulled the switch with: "What makes you think you know everything?" This reply crossed the therapist up and threw him off balance for a moment, which is what the patient wanted to do. Then the game ended, the patient feeling elated at having conned the therapist, and he feeling frustrated; and those were the payoffs.

This game followed Formula G precisely. The con was the original question, and the gimmick was the therapist's sentimentality. When the con hooked into the gimmick, he responded in the way she expected. Then she pulled the switch, causing a crossup, after which each collected a payoff. So

$$C + H = R \rightarrow S \rightarrow X \rightarrow P$$

This is a simple example of the game called, from the patient's side, "Slug Him," or "Whammy," and from the therapist's side, "I'm Only Trying To Help You." Colloquially, the payoff is called a *trading stamp*. "Good" feelings are spoken of as "gold" trading stamps and distressing feelings are said to be "brown" or "blue" trading stamps. In this case the patient got a counterfeit-gold trading stamp for a counterfeit triumph or success, and the therapist got a brown one, which is not unusual.

Each game has a slogan or motto by which it can be recognized, such as "I'm Only Trying To Help You." This slogan is colloquially called a "sweatshirt." Usually the name of the game is taken from its slogan.

Beyond games lies the other limiting case of what can take place between people, which is called *intimacy*. Bilateral intimacy is defined as a candid, game-free relationship, with mutual free giving and receiving and without exploitation. Intimacy can be one-sided, since one party may be candid and freely giving, while the other may be devious and exploitative.

Sexual activities offer examples which cover this whole spectrum of social behavior. It is evident that they can take place in withdrawal, that they can be part of a ritualistic ceremony, or that they can be all in a day's work, a pastime for a rainy day, a game of mutual exploitation, or acts of real intimacy.

D · SCRIPTS

The above forms of social action are ways of structuring time with the object of avoiding boredom and at the same time getting the greatest possible satisfaction out of each situation. Each person, in addition, has a preconscious life plan, or script, by which he structures longer periods of time—months, years, or his whole life—filling them with ritual activities, pastimes, and games which further the script while giving him immediate satisfaction, usually interrupted by periods of withdrawal and sometimes by episodes of intimacy. Scripts are usually based on childlike illusions which may persist throughout a whole lifetime; but in more sensitive, perceptive, and intelligent people these illusions dissolve one by one, leading to the various life crises described by Erikson.[9] Among these crises are the adolescent reappraisal of parents; the protests, often bizarre, of middle age; and the emergence of philosophy after that. Sometimes, however, overly desperate attempts to maintain the illusions in later life lead to depression or spiritualism, while the abandonment of all illusions may lead to despair.

Time structuring is an objective term for the existential problem of what to do after saying Hello. What follows is the attempt to answer this question by observing what it is that people actually do after they say Hello, and by inserting a few hints of what might be. This can be profitably done by investigating the nature of life scripts and the course of their development.[10]

NOTES & REFERENCES

1 Berne, E. *Transactional Analysis in Psychotherapy*. Grove Press, New York, 1961.

2 Berne, E. *The Structure and Dynamics of Organizations and Groups*. J. B. Lippincott Company, Philadelphia, 1963. Grove Press (Paperback), New York, 1966.

3 Berne, E. *Games People Play*. Grove Press, New York, 1964; (Paperback) 1967.

4 Berne, E. *Principles of Group Treatment*. Oxford University Press, New York, 1966. Grove Press, New York (Paperback), 1968.

5 Berne, E. *A Layman's Guide to Psychiatry and Psychoanalysis*. Simon & Schuster, New York, 1968. André Deutsch, London, 1969. Grove Press (Paperback), New York, 1962, pp. 277–306.

6 "The transaction, or exchange, seems the central focus toward which various social scientists have been gravitating. I could hardly agree more with Blau's position that exchange is both the most obvious point of common reference for all social science and the most likely building block with which (by adding the cement of communications) we can put together the analysis of more complex social relationships and structures." From Alfred Kuhn's review

of Blau, Peter M. *Exchange and Power in Social Life*. Wiley, New York, 1964; in *Science* 147:137, January 8, 1965.

7 Szasz, K. *Petishism: Pets and their People in the Western World*. Holt, Rinehart & Winston, New York, 1968.

8 Sackett, G. P., Keith-Lee, P., and Treat, R. "Food versus Perceptual Complexity as Rewards for Rats Previously Subjected to Sensory Deprivation." *Science* 141: 518–520, August 9, 1963.

9 Erikson, E. H. *Identity and the Life Cycle*. International Universities Press, New York, 1959.

10 For a systematic critique of transactional analysis theory, see Shapiro, S. S. "Critique of Eric Berne's Contributions to Subself Theory." *Psychological Reports* 25: 283–296, 1969.

PART II

Parental Programing

CHAPTER THREE

Human Destiny

A · LIFE PLANS

The destiny of every human being is decided by what goes on inside his skull when he is confronted with what goes on outside his skull. Each person designs his own life. Freedom gives him the power to carry out his own designs, and power gives him the freedom to interfere with the designs of others. Even if the outcome is decided by men he has never met or germs he will never see, his last words and the words on his gravestone will cry out his striving. If by great misfortune he dies in dust and silence, only those who know him best will get the slogan right, and all outside the private chambers of friendship, marriage, and medicine will see him wrong. In most cases he has spent his life deceiving the world, and usually himself as well. We will hear more about these illusions later.

Each person decides in early childhood how he will live and how he will die, and that plan, which he carries in his head wherever he goes, is called his script. His trivial behavior may be decided by reason, but his important decisions are already made: what kind of person he will marry, how many children he will have, what kind of bed he will die in, and who will be there when he does. It may not be what he wants, but it is what he wants it to be.

MAGDA

Magda was a devoted wife and mother, but when her youngest boy got very sick, she realized to her horror that in the back of her mind was an idea, a picture, or perhaps even a wish that the much-loved son would die.

It reminded her of the time when her husband was overseas with the army and the same thing had happened. She was haunted by an eerie wish that he would get killed. In both cases she pictured herself in terrible grief and affliction. This would be her cross to bear, and everyone would admire the way she bore it.

Q. What would happen after that?

A. I never got that far. I'd be free, and then I could do what I wanted to. Start over.

When Magda was in grade school she had had many sexual adventures with her classmates, and the guilt of that had been with her ever since. The death of her son or husband would be a punishment or an expiation for this, and would free her from her mother's curse. She would no longer feel like an outcast. People would exclaim: "Isn't she courageous!" and acknowledge her as a fullfledged member of the human race.

Throughout most of her life she had had this tragic cinema planned out and pictured in her mind. It was the third act of her life drama, or script, as written in her childhood. Act I: Sexual Guilt and Confusion. Act II: Mother's Curse. Act III: Expiation. Act IV: Release, and a New Life. But in reality she was leading a very conventional life, in accordance with the teachings of her parents, and doing what she could to keep her loved ones healthy and happy. This was counter to the plot of her script—a counterscript—and was certainly not as dramatic or exciting.

A script is an ongoing life plan formed in early childhood under parental pressure. It is the psychological force which propels the person toward his destiny, regardless of whether he fights it or says it is his own free will.

It is not our intention in this book to reduce all human behavior or all human life to a formula. Quite the contrary. A real person may be defined as one who acts spontaneously in a rational and trustworthy way with decent consideration for others. One who follows a formula is a not-real, or unreal, person. But since these seem to constitute the bulk of humanity, it is necessary to try to learn something about them.

DELLA

Della was a neighbor of Magda's, in her late twenties, and led much the same kind of domestic life. But her husband, a salesman, traveled a lot. Sometimes when he was away Della would start out drinking and end up far away from home. She "blacked out" these episodes, and as is common in such cases, she knew what happened only because she would find herself in strange places with the names and telephone numbers of strange men in her purse when she came to. This not only horrified her, but terrified her, since it meant that she could ruin her life some day by picking up an indiscreet or evil man.

Scripts are planned early in childhood, so if this was a script, it must have had its origins there. Della's mother died when she was little and her father was away all day, working. Della didn't get along very well with the other kids in school. She felt inferior, and led a lonely life. But late in childhood she discovered a way to be popular. Like Magda, she offered herself for sexy play to a gang of little boys. She had never thought of the connection between those school days in the hayloft and her current behavior. But all along in her head she was carrying the outline of her life drama. Act I: The setup. Fun and Guilt in a Hayloft. Act II: An outbreak of script. Fun and Guilt While Drunk and Irresponsible. Act III: The payoff. Denunciation and Ruin. She loses everything—husband, children, and position. Act IV: The final release. Suicide. Then everybody feels sorry and forgives her.

Both Magda and Della lived in their peaceful counterscripts with a feeling of impending doom. The script was a tragic drama which would bring them release and reconciliation. The difference was that Magda was waiting patiently for an act of God to fulfill her destiny —salvation; while Della, propelled by the compulsion of an inner demon, was hurrying impatiently toward hers—damnation, death, and forgiveness. Thus, from the same beginnings ("sexual delinquency") these two women were moving by diverse means to different ends.

The psychotherapist is sitting in his office like a wise man and is getting paid to do something about all this. Both Magda and Della will be free if somebody dies, but his job is to find a better way to free them. He leaves his office and walks down the street past the stockbroker's, the taxi stand, and the saloon. Nearly everybody he sees is waiting for a Big Killing. In the grocery store a woman is shouting at her daughter: "How many times have I got to tell you not to touch that?" while somebody admires her little boy: "Isn't he cute!" When he gets to the hospital, a paranoid says: "How do I get out of here, doctor?" A depressive says: "What am I living for?" and a schizophrenic answers: "Don't diet, liveit. I'm not really that stupid." That's what they all said yesterday. They're stuck, while the ones on the outside are still hoping. "Shall we increase his dose of medication?" asks a medical student. Dr. Q turns to the schizophrenic and looks him in the eye. The schizophrenic looks back at him. "Shall we increase your medication?" asks Dr. Q. The boy thinks a while and then replies. "No." Dr. Q puts out his hand and says: "Hello." The schizophrenic shakes hands with him and says: "Hello." Then they both turn to the medical student, and Dr. Q says: "Hello." The medical student looks flustered, but five years later, at a psychiatric meeting, he walks up to Dr. Q and says : "Hi, Dr. Q. Hello."

MARY

"Some day I'm going to open a nursery school, get married four times, make a lot of money on the stock market, and become a famous surgeon," said drunken Mary.

This is *not* a script. First, she didn't get any of these ideas from her parents. They hated children, didn't believe in divorce, thought the stock market was too speculative, and that surgeons charged too much. Second, her personality was not suited to any of these things. She was up tight with children, frigidly cool

with men, scared of the market, and her hands shook
from drinking. Thirdly, she had long ago decided to be
a realtor during the day, and an alcoholic evenings
and weekends. Fourthly, none of those projects really
turned her on. They were more expressions of what she
couldn't do rather than of what she could. And fifthly,
it was obvious to anyone who heard her that she wasn't
ever going to do any of them.

A script requires (1) Parental directives. (2) A
suitable personality development. (3) A childhood decision. (4) A real turn-on to a particular method of
success or failure, and (5) A convincing attitude (or a
credible stance, as they say nowadays).

In this book we will consider what is known so far
about the script apparatus, and what can be done to
change it.

B · ON STAGE AND OFF STAGE

Theatrical scripts are intuitively derived from life
scripts, and a good way to start is to consider the connections and similarities between them.[1]

1. Both are based on a limited number of themes,
the best known of which is the Oedipal tragedy. The
others can likewise be found in Greek drama and
Greek mythology. Other people had the rude dithy-
rambs and lewd orgies of the ancient priestly dramas,
but the Greeks and Hebrews were the first to distill out
and record the more homely and recognizable patterns
of human living. Human life, it is true, is full of epic
Agon, Pathos, Threnos, and Theophany, as in the
Primal Rituals, but these are much easier to understand
and contemplate if they are played out in ordinary
language, Bam! and Wow! with a man and a maid in
the moonlight under the laurel tree when along comes
Bigmouth, whoever he or she may be. Reduced to this
level by the Greek poets, the life of every human being
is already charted in Bulfinch or Graves.* If the gods

---

*Personally, I prefer Lemprière's *Classical Dictionary* (Tenth edition, 1818).

smile on him, he will be a going concern. But if they frown he becomes something else, and if he wants to remove the curse or live more comfortably with it, he becomes a patient.

For the transactional script analyst, as for the play analyst, this means that if you know the plot and the character, you know what his outcome will be, unless some changes can be made. For example, it is clear to the psychotherapist, as to the drama critic, that Medea had her mind made up to kill her children, unless someone could talk her out of it; and it should be equally clear to both of them that if she had gone to her treatment group that week, the whole thing would never have happened.

2. Not only do certain life courses have predictable outcomes if they are allowed to go on as they are, but a certain dialogue of specific words spoken a certain way is necessary to establish the proper motivation for the outcome. In both the theater and in real life, the cues have to be memorized and spoken just right so that the other people will respond in a way that justifies and advances the action. If the hero changes his lines and his ego state, the other people respond differently. This throws the whole script off, and that is the aim of therapeutic script analysis. If Hamlet begins to use lines from *Abie's Irish Rose,* Ophelia has to change her lines, too, in order to make sense of it, and the whole performance will proceed differently. The two of them might then take off together instead of skulking around the castle—a bad play, but probably a better life.[2]

3. A script has to be rehearsed and rewritten before it is ready for the most dramatic performance. In the theater there are readings, rewrites, rehearsals, and try-outs before the big time. A life script starts off in childhood in a primitive form called the *protocol.* Here the other players are limited to parents and brothers and sisters; or in an institution or foster home, to table-mates and those in charge. These all play their roles rather rigidly because every family is an institution, and the child does not learn much flexibility from them. As he moves into adolescence, he begins to meet more people. He seeks out those who will play the roles his

script requires (they will do it because he plays some role their scripts require). At this time, he rewrites his script to take account of his new environment. The basic plot remains the same, but the action is a little different. In most cases (except for adolescent suicide or murder), this is rehearsal—something like a small-town tryout. Through several such adaptations, he gets it into final form for the biggest production of all—the farewell performance, the final payoff on the script. If it is a "good" one, it takes place at a farewell dinner. If it is a "bad" one, he says good-by from a hospital bed, the door of a prison cell or psychiatric ward, the gallows, or the morgue.

4. Almost every script has roles for "good guys" and "bad guys," and for "winners" and "losers." What is considered good or bad,[3] and what is a winner or a loser, is something peculiar to each script, but it is very clear that every script has these four characters, sometimes combined in two roles. In a cowboy script, for example, the good guy is a winner and the bad guy is a loser. Good means brave, quick on the draw, honest, and pure; bad may mean cowardly, slow on the draw, crooked, and interested in girls. A winner is someone who survives; a loser is someone who is hanged or gets shot. In a soap opera, a winner is a girl who gets a man; a loser is a girl who loses a man. In a paper-shuffle opera, the winner is the man who gets the best contract or the most proxies; a loser is a man who doesn't know how to shuffle papers.

In script analysis, winners are called "princes" or "princesses," and losers are called "frogs." The object of script analysis is to turn frogs into princes and princesses. In order to do this, the therapist has to find out who the good guys and the bad guys are in the patient's script, and also what kind of a winner he can be. The patient fights being a winner because he is not in treatment for that purpose, but only to be made into a braver loser. This is natural enough, since if he becomes a braver loser, he can follow his script more comfortably, whereas if he becomes a winner he has to throw away all or most of his script and start over, which most people are reluctant to do.

5. All scripts, whether in the theater or in real life, are essentially answers to the basic question of human encounter: "What do you say after you say Hello?" The Oedipal drama and the Oedipal life, for example, both hinge entirely on this question. Whenever Oedipus meets an older man, he first says Hello. The next thing he has to say, driven by his script, is: "Wanna fight?" If the older man says "No," Oedipus has nothing further to say to him, and can only stand dumbly wondering whether to talk about the weather, the conduct of the current war, or who is going to win in the Olympic games. The easiest way out is to mumble "Pleased to meetcha," *"Si vales bene est, ego valeo,"* or "Everything in moderation," and go on his way. But if the older one says "Yes," Oedipus answers: "Groovy!" because now he has found his man and he knows what to say next.

6. Life-script scenes have to be set up and motivated ahead of time, just like theatrical scenes. A simple example is running out of gas. This is nearly always set up two or three days in advance by looking at the gauge, "planning" to get gas "sometime soon," and then not doing it. In fact it is impossible to run out of gas "right now" except in a strange car with a broken gauge. It is nearly always an impending event, a pre-planned scene in a loser's script. Many winners go through a whole lifetime without ever running dry.

Life scripts are based on parental programing, which the child seeks out for three reasons. (1) It gives a purpose to life where it might otherwise be wanting. A child does most things for the sake of people, usually his parents. (2) It gives him an acceptable way to structure his time (acceptable, that is, to his parents). (3) People have to be told how to do things. Learning for oneself may be inspiring, but it is not very practical. A man does not become a good pilot by wrecking a few airplanes and learning by his errors. He has to learn through other people's failures, not his own. A surgeon has to have a teacher, rather than taking out appendixes one after the other to find out all the things that can go wrong. So parents program their children by passing on to them what they have learned, or what they think they have learned. If they are losers, they will pass on their loser's programing, and if they are winners, then they will pass on that kind of program. The long-term pattern always has a story line. While the outcome is determined for better or for worse by parental programing, the child is often free to select his own plot.

C · MYTHS AND FAIRY TALES

The first and most archaic version of the script, the primal protocol, is conceived in the mind of the child at an age when few people outside his immediate family are real to him. We assume that his parents appear to him as huge figures endowed with magic powers, like the giants and giantesses, ogres and gorgons of mythology, if only because they are three times as tall and ten times as big as he is.

As he grows older and becomes more sophisticated, he moves from this classical universe into a more romantic world. He devises the first palimpsest, or rewrite, of his script, to make it correspond with his new view of his surroundings. If conditions are right, he is helped here by fairy tales and animal stories at first read to him by his mother, and later read by himself in his leisure hours when he is free to let his imagination roam. There is magic in these, too, but less earth-shaking. They give him a whole new set of characters to play their roles in his fancies: all the personalities in the animal kingdom, which are familiar to him either as warm-blooded playmates and companions, or as fleeting figures of fear or fascination seen or heard in the distance, or as semi-imaginary creatures of unknown capabilities that he has only heard or read about. Or perhaps this comes to him from the television screen, where at that age even the commercials have a halo. Even in the worst case, without book or screen, or even mother, somewhere he knows there is a cow, or can imagine his own distorted beasts.

In the first stage he is dealing with magical people who can perhaps on occasion turn themselves into animals. In this second stage he is merely attributing to animals certain human characteristics, a tendency which persists in adult life to some degree in people associated with stables, kennels, and dolphin tanks.

In the third stage, in adolescence, he reviews his script once more to adapt it to the current reality as he hopes it will be, still romanticized and still golden, or sometimes gilded with the aid of drugs. Gradually, as the years go by, he moves closer to reality, which is the actual likelihood that the people and things around him will give the desired responses. In this way, through the decades, he prepares himself for his farewell performance. It is this farewell performance which, above all, it is the therapist's business to change.

Below are some examples to show the similarity between myths, fairy tales, and real people. These are best understood from the transactional viewpoint, the Martian one referred to earlier, which is based on its own myth—one devised by game and script analysts as a way of seeing human life more objectively. Here Mario the Martian comes to Earth and has to go back and "tell it like it is"—not like the Earth people say it is, or want him to think it is. He doesn't listen to big words nor tables of statistics, but watches what people are actually doing to, for, and with each other, rather than what they say they are doing. Here, then, is the story of Europa.

THE STORY OF EUROPA

Europa was Neptune's granddaughter. One day she was in a seaside meadow gathering flowers when a beautiful bull appeared and knelt at her feet. His eyes invited her to get on his back. She was so taken with his melodious voice and friendly manner that she thought it would be fun to ride around the dell. But the moment she mounted, he took off over the sea, for he was really Jupiter in disguise, and Jupiter would stop at nothing when he saw a girl he liked. Europa did not fare too badly, however, because after they landed in Crete she gave birth to three kings and had a continent named after her. All this is supposed to have happened in 1522 B.C. and the story can be found in the *Second Idyllium* of Moschus.

Jupiter, the abductor, came of a rather unusual family. His father, Saturn, according to Hesiod's *Theogony*, had six children. He ate the first five as soon as they were born, so when Jupiter, the sixth, came along, his mother hid him and put in his place a stone wrapped in swaddles, which his father gobbled. When Jupiter grew up, he and his grandmother forced Saturn to disgorge the stone and also the five babies he had eaten: Pluto, Neptune, Vesta, Ceres, and Juno. Now after Jupiter was through with Europa, she took up with Danaus, King of Egypt, and by him she had a daughter named Amymone. Amymone's father, the King, sent her to carry water to the city of Argos, and while she was doing that, Neptune saw her and was filled with love. He rescued her from a lecherous satyr, and carried her off for himself, he being her own great-grandfather, just as Jupiter, who carried off her mother, was her mother's granduncle.

Now let us list the significant transactions in this family saga by stimulus and response. Each response, of course, can become the stimulus for the next transaction.

1. Stimulus: A beautiful maiden gracefully gathers flowers. Response: An amorous god, her granduncle, turns himself into a golden bull.

2. Response: The maiden strokes his sides and pats his head. Response: The bull kisses her hands and rolls his eyes.

3. The maiden mounts his back. The bull abducts her.

4. She expresses fear and wonder, and asks him who he is. He reassures her, and all turns out well.

5. Stimulus: A father eats his children. Response: The mother feeds him a stone.

6. Response: The saved son forces the father to give up the eaten children and the swallowed stone.

7. Stimulus: A beautiful maiden is sent by her father to fetch water. Response: She gets into trouble with a satyr, what would nowadays be called a "wolf."

8. Stimulus: Her beauty excites her great-grand-

father. Response: He saves her from the satyr and carries her off.

To a script analyst, the most interesting feature of this series of mythical transactions (in Moschus's version) is that in spite of Europa's wild lamentations and protests, she never expressly says "Stop!" or "Take me back at once!" but instead quickly switches into trying to guess the identity of her abductor. In other words, while she makes loud token protests, she is careful not to abort the drama, but instead resigns herself to it and becomes curious about its outcome. Thus her lamentations have the ambiguous quality which in Martian is called "gamy" or "scripty." In fact, she is playing the game called "Rapo," which fits into her destined script of becoming the mother of kings, providing it happens "against her will." Taking a personal interest in her abductor is not the firmest way to discourage him; but her protests disclaim her own responsibility for having flirted with him in the first place.

There is a more familiar story which includes most of these transactions, though in a slightly different order. The following version is taken from Andrew Lang and Grimm. This tale is known from earliest years to nearly all literate children in English-speaking countries, and others as well, and is a common stimulus to their imaginations.

LITTLE RED RIDING HOOD

There was a sweet little maiden named Little Red Riding Hood (LRRH), and one day her mother sent her through the woods to bring food to her grandmother. On the way she met a seductive wolf who thought she was a nice morsel. He told her to turn on, tune in, drop out, and pick flowers, instead of looking solemn. While she dallied, the wolf went to her grandmother's house and ate up the old lady. When LRRH arrived, he pretended he was her grandmother and invited her to get into bed with him. She did so, and noticed many peculiar things about his appearance which made her wonder if it really was the old lady. He first tried to reassure her, and then ate her up (apparently without chewing her). A hunter came and rescued her by cutting the wolf open, and let her grandmother out alive as well. Then LRRH happily helped the hunter fill the wolf's belly with stones. In some versions, LRRH calls for help and the hunter kills the wolf with an ax and rescues her in the nick of time before the villain can eat her up.

Here again there is a seductive scene between an innocent maiden who likes to gather flowers and a crafty animal who betrays her. The animal likes to eat children but ends up with stones in his belly instead. Like Amymone, LRRH is sent on a helpful errand, gets into trouble with a wolf on the way, and gets chummy with her rescuer.

To a Martian, this story raises interesting questions. He takes it at face value, including the talking wolf, even though he has never met one. But given what happens, he wonders what it is all about and what kind of people it happens to. Here, then, are his thoughts on the matter.

A MARTIAN REACTION

One day LRRH's mother sent her through the woods to bring food to her grandmother, and on the way she met a wolf. What kind of a mother sends a little girl into a forest where there are wolves? Why didn't her mother do it herself, or go along with LRRH? If grandmother was so helpless, why did mother leave her all by herself in a hut far away? But if LRRH had to go, how come her mother had never warned her not to stop and talk to wolves? The story makes it clear that LRRH had never been told that this was dangerous. No mother could really be that stupid, so it sounds as if her mother didn't care much what happened to LRRH, or maybe even wanted to get rid of her. No little girl is that stupid either. How could LRRH look at the wolf's eyes, ears, hands, and teeth, and still think it was her grandmother? Why didn't she get out of there as fast as she could? And a mean little thing she was, too, gathering up stones to put into the wolf's belly. At any rate, any straight-thinking girl, after talking to the wolf, would certainly not have stopped to pick flowers, but would have said to herself: "That son of a bitch is going to eat up my grandmother if I don't get some help fast."

Even the grandmother and the hunter aren't above suspicion. If we now treat the *dramatis personae* of this story as real people, each with his or her own script, we see how neatly their personalities mesh from a Martian point of view.

1. The mother is evidently trying to lose her daughter "accidentally," or at least she wants to end up saying: "Isn't it awful, you can't even walk through the park nowadays without some wolf . . ." etc.

2. The wolf, instead of eating rabbits and such, is obviously overreaching himself, and he must know that he will come to a bad end that way, so he must want to invite trouble. He evidently read Nietzsche or someone similar in his youth (if he can talk and tie on a bonnet, why shouldn't he be able to read?), and his motto is something like "Live dangerously and die gloriously."

3. Grandmother lives alone and leaves her door unlatched, so she may be hoping for something interesting to happen, something which couldn't happen if she were living with her folks. Maybe that's why she didn't move in with them, or at least live next door. She was probably young enough to be ripe for adventure, since LRRH was still a little girl.

4. The hunter is obviously a rescuer who enjoys working over his vanquished opponents with sweet little maidens to help: quite clearly an adolescent script.

5. LRRH tells the wolf quite explicitly where he can meet her again, and even climbs into bed with him. She is obviously playing "Rapo," and ends up quite happy about the whole affair.

The truth of the matter is that everybody in the story is looking for action at almost any price. If the payoff at the end is taken at face value, then the whole thing was a plot to do in the poor wolf by making him think he was outsmarting everybody, using LRRH as bait. In that case, the moral of the story is not that innocent maidens should keep out of forests where there are wolves, but that wolves should keep away from innocent-looking maidens and their grandmothers; in short, a wolf should not walk through the forest alone. This also raises the interesting question of what the mother did after she got rid of LRRH for the day.

If all this seems cynical or facetious, let us now consider LRRH in real life. The crucial question here is that with such a mother, and after such an experience, what was LRRH like after she grew up?

A LITTLE RED RIDING HOOD SCRIPT

In the psychoanalytic literature, a great deal of attention is devoted to the symbolic meaning of the stones put into the wolf's belly. For the transactional analyst, however, the most significant items are the transactions between the people involved.

Carrie came for treatment at the age of thirty, complaining that she had headaches, depressions, didn't know what she wanted to do, and couldn't find a satisfactory boy friend. Like all the Little Red Riding Hoods in Dr. Q's experience, she had a red coat. She was always trying to be helpful in an indirect sort of way. One day she came in and said:

"There's a sick dog in the street down from your office. Do you want to call the SPCA?"

"Why don't you call the SPCA?" asked Dr. Q.

To which she replied: "Who, me?"

She herself never rescued anybody, but she always knew where rescuers could be found. This is typical of LRRH. Dr. Q then asked her if she had ever worked in an office where someone had to go out to get the refreshments for the coffee break, which she had.

"Who went out to get the refreshments?"

"Me, of course," she replied.

The scripty part of her story was as follows. During the time she was six to ten years old, her mother used to send her over to her (maternal) grandparents' house on errands and to play. Often when she got there her grandmother was out and she played with her grandfather, mostly him feeling under her dress. She never told her mother because she knew that her mother would get angry at her and call her a liar.

Nowadays she met men and "boys" frequently, and many of them dated her, but she always broke up with them after two or three dates. Each time she told Dr. Q about her latest breakup he would ask why it happened, and she would reply: "Ha! Ha! Ha! Because he's a junior wolf." Thus she spent years of her life trotting through the forests of the financial district bringing sandwiches to people, and continually brushing off junior wolves: a dull, depressing kind of existence. The most exciting event in her life, actually, was the affair with her grandfather. It now appeared that she was going to spend the rest of her days waiting for a repetition of that.

This tells us how LRRH spent her life after the story ended. The wolf affair was by far the most interesting thing that ever happened to her. When she grew up, she passed the time trotting through forests, bringing goodies to people, and eternally hoping to meet another wolf. But all she ran into were wolf cubs, whom she contemptuously brushed aside. Carrie's story also tells us who the wolf really was, and why LRRH was bold enough to get into bed with him: it was her grandfather.

The characteristics of a real-life LRRH are as follows:

1. Her mother used to send her on errands.

2. She was seduced by her grandfather, but didn't tell her mother. If she had, she would have been called a liar. Sometimes she pretended to be too stupid to know what was going on.

3. She doesn't often rescue people herself, but likes to arrange rescues, and is always looking out for such opportunities.

4. When she grows up, she is the one chosen to run errands. She often scurries or wanders like a little girl, rather than walking in a dignified way.

5. She is waiting for something really exciting to happen and is bored in the meantime, since all she meets nowadays are junior wolves, whom she looks down on.

6. She enjoys filling wolves' bellies with stones, or the everyday equivalent of that.

7. It is not clear yet whether the male psychiatrist is there to rescue her, or is merely a nice, nonsexual grandfather with whom she feels comfortable and slightly nostalgic, and whom she settles for because she can't have the real thing.

8. She laughs and agrees when he says she reminds him of LRRH.

9. Oddly enough, she nearly always owns and wears a red coat.

It should be noted that the scripts of a Little Red Riding Hood's mother, maternal grandfather, and maternal grandmother must be complementary in order to allow such sexual incidents to happen more than once. The happy ending of the tale is also suspect, and does not occur in real life. Fairy tales are told by well-meaning parents, and the happy ending is an intrusion of a benevolent but mendacious Parental ego state; tales made up by children themselves are more realistic, and do not necessarily have happy endings; in fact, they are notoriously gruesome.[4]

D · WAITING FOR *RIGOR MORTIS*

One object of script analysis is to fit the patient's life plan into the grand historical psychology of the whole human race, a psychology which apparently has changed but little from cave days, through the early farming and ranching settlements and the great totalitarian governments of the Middle East, up to the present time. Joseph Campbell, in *The Hero With A Thousand Faces,* which is the best textbook for script analysts, summarizes this as follows:

"Freud, Jung, and their followers have demonstrated irrefutably that the logic, the heroes, and the deeds of myth survive into modern times. . . . The latest incarnation of Oedipus, the continued romance of Beauty and the Beast, stand this afternoon on the corner of Forty-Second Street and Fifth Avenue, waiting for the traffic light to change." He points out that while the hero of myth achieves a world-historical triumph, the hero of the fairy tale achieves merely a small domestic victory. And patients are patients, we may add, because they cannot achieve the victories they aim for and still survive. Hence they come to the doctor, "the knower of all the secret ways and words of potency. His role is precisely that of the Wise Old Man of the myths and fairy tales whose words assist the hero through the trials and terrors of the weird adventure."

That, at any rate, is the way the Child in the patient sees it, no matter how his Adult tells the story, and it is quite evident that all children, since the beginning of humanity, have had to cope with the same problems, and have had about the same weapons at their disposal. When it comes to the cutting, life is the same old wine in new bottles: coconut and bamboo bottles gave way to goatskins, goatskins to pottery, pottery to glass, and glass to plastic, but the grapes have hardly changed at all, and there is the same old intoxication on top and the same old dregs at the bottom. So, as Campbell says, there will be found little variation in the shapes of the adventures and the characters involved. Hence, if we know some of the elements of the patient's script, we can predict with some confidence where he is heading, and head him off before he meets with misfortune or disaster. That is called preventive psychiatry, or "making progress." Even better, we can get him to change his script or give it up altogether, which is curative psychiatry, or "getting well."

Thus, it is not a matter of doctrine or necessity to find precisely the myth or fairy tale which the patient is following; but the closer we can come, the better. Without such a historical foundation, errors are frequent. A mere episode in the patient's life, or his favorite game, may be mistaken for the whole script; or the occurrence of a single animal symbol, such as a wolf, may lead the therapist to bark up the wrong tree. Relating the patient's life or his Child's life plan to a coherent story which has survived for hundreds or thousands of years because of its universal appeal to the primitive layers of the human mind, at least gives a feeling of working from a solid foundation, and at best may give very precise clues as to what needs to be done to avert or change a bad ending.

THE WAITING FOR *RIGOR MORTIS* SCRIPT

For example, a fairy tale may reveal elements of a script which are otherwise hard to dig up, such as the "script illusion." The transactional analyst believes that psychiatric symptoms result from some form of self-deception. But patients can be cured just because their lives and their disabilities are based on a figment of the imagination.

In the script known as "Frigid Woman," or "Waiting for *Rigor Mortis*" (WRM), the mother keeps telling her daughter that men are beasts, but it is a wife's duty to submit to their bestiality. If the mother pushes hard enough, the girl may even get the idea that she will die if she has an orgasm. Usually such mothers are great snobs, and they offer a release or an "antiscript" that will lift the curse. It is all right for the daughter to have sex if she marries a very important person, such as the Prince with the Golden Apples. But failing that, she tells her erroneously, "all your troubles will be over when you reach your menopause, because then you won't be in danger of feeling sexy any more."

Now it already appears as though we have three illusions: Orgathanatos, or the fatal orgasm; the Prince with the Golden Apples; and Blessed Relief, or the purifying menopause. But none of these is the real script illusion. The girl has tested Orgathanatos by masturbation, and knows it is not fatal. The Prince with the Golden Apples is not an illusion, because it is just possible that she might find such a man, just as she might win the Irish Sweepstakes or get four aces in a poker game; both of these things are unlikely, but not mythical; they do happen. And Blessed Relief is not something her Child really wants. In order to find the script illusion, we need the fairy tale which corresponds to WRM.

THE STORY OF SLEEPING BEAUTY

An angry fairy says that Briar Rose will prick her finger with a spindle and fall down dead. Another fairy commutes this to a hundred years of sleep. When she is fifteen Briar Rose does prick her finger, and immediately falls asleep. At the same moment everybody and everything else in the castle also fall asleep. During the hundred years, many princes try to get to her through the briars which have grown up around her, but none succeeds. At last, after the time is up, a prince arrives who manages to get through because the briars let him. When he finds the princess and kisses her, she wakes up and they fall in love. At the same moment, everybody and everything else in the castle take up exactly where they left off, as though nothing had happened and no time had passed since they fell asleep. The princess herself is still only fifteen years old, not 115. She and the prince get married, and in one version, they live happily ever after; in another, this is only the beginning of their troubles.[5]

There are many magic sleeps in mythology. Perhaps the best known is that of Brunhilde, who is left sleeping on the mountain with a ring of fire around her which only a hero can penetrate, and that is accomplished by Siegfried.[6]

In one way or another, with slight alterations, almost everything in the story of Sleeping Beauty could actually happen. Girls do prick their fingers and faint, and they do fall asleep in their towers, and princes do wander around in the forest and look for fair maidens. The one thing that cannot happen is for everything and everybody to be unchanged and unaged after the lapse of so many years. This is a real illusion because it is not only improbable, it is impossible. And this is just the illusion on which WRM scripts are based: that when the Prince does come, Rose will be fifteen years old again instead of thirty, forty, or fifty, and they will have a whole lifetime ahead of them. This is the illusion of sustained youth, a modest daughter of the illusion of immortality. It is hard to tell Rose in real life that princes are younger men, and that by the time they reach her age they have become kings, and are much less interesting. That is the most distressing part of the script analyst's job: to break up the illusion, to inform the patient's Child that there is no Santa Claus, and make it stick. It is much easier for both of them if there is the patient's favorite fairy tale to work with.

One of the practical problems of WRM is that if Rose does find the Prince with the Golden Apples, she often feels outclassed and has to find fault and play "Blemish" to bring him down to her level, so that he ends up wishing she would go back in the briars and fall asleep again. On the other hand, if she settles for less—the Prince with the Silver Apples, or even ordinary McIntoshes from the grocery store—she will feel cheated and take it out on him, meanwhile always keeping an eye out for the Golden One. Thus, neither the frigid script nor the magic antiscript offers much chance for fulfillment. Also, as in the fairy tale, there is his mother to contend with as well as her witch.

This script is important because a great many people in the world, in one way or another, spend their lives waiting for *rigor mortis*.

E · THE FAMILY DRAMA

Another good way to uncover the plot and some of the most important lines in a person's script is to ask: "If your family life were put on the stage, what kind of play would it be?" Such family dramas are usually named after the Greek Oedipus and Electra plays, in which the boy competes with father for his mommy and the girl wants daddy for her own.[7] But the script analyst has to know what the parents, called for convenience Supideo and Artcele, are up to meanwhile. Supideo is the other side of the Oedipus drama, and expresses the frank or disguised sexual feelings of the mother for her son, while Artcele is the other side of Electra and shows father's feelings for the girl. A close inquiry will nearly always reveal rather obvious transactions which demonstrate that these feelings are not imaginary, even though the parent tries to conceal them, usually by playing "Uproar" with the child. That is, the disturbed parent tries to cover up his Child sexual feelings for his offspring by coming on Parental and ordering the offspring about in a quarrelsome way. But on certain occasions they leak out, despite all efforts to disguise them by "Uproar" and other devices. Actually, the happiest parents are often those who openly admire the attractiveness of their children.

The Supideo and Artcele dramas, like Oedipus and Electra, have many variations. As the children grow older, they may be played out as mother sleeping with son's boyfriend or father sleeping with his daughter's chum. Farther out and even more "gamy" versions are mother sleeping with daughter's boyfriend or father sleeping with son's girl.* This compliment may be returned by the young Oedipus sleeping with father's mistress, or Electra with mother's lover. Sometimes the family script calls for one or several members to be homosexual, with corresponding variations in child sex play, incest between siblings, and later seductions of each other's partners. Any deviations from the standard Oedipus (son wondering or dreaming about sex with mother) or Electra (daughter wondering or dreaming about father) roles will undoubtedly influence the whole life course of the person.

In addition to, or beyond, the sexual aspects of the family drama, there are even more poignant ones. A jilted homosexual girl attacked her lover, held a knife to her throat, and cried: "You'll let me give you these wounds, but you won't let me heal them." This perhaps is the motto of all family dramas, the origin of all parental anguish, the basis for youthful rebellion, and the cry of couples not yet ready for divorce. The wounded flee, and the cry above is the Martian translation of the ad: "Mary, come home. All is forgiven." And that is why children stick with even the most miserable parents. It hurts to be wounded, but it feels so good to be healed.

---

*This may occur when mother has no son of her own to play Jocasta with, and similarly if father has no daughter of his own.

F · HUMAN DESTINY

It is incredible to think, at first, that man's fate, all his nobility and all his degradation, is decided by a child no more than six years old, and usually three, but that is what script theory claims. It is a little easier to believe after talking to a child of six, or maybe three. And it is very easy to believe by looking around at what is happening in the world today, and what happened yesterday, and seeing what will probably happen tomorrow. The history of human scripts can be found on ancient monuments, in courtrooms and morgues, in gambling houses and letters to the editor, and in political debates, where whole nations are talked down the righteous road by somebody trying to prove that what his parents told him in the nursery will work for the whole world. But fortunately, some people have good scripts, and some even succeed in freeing themselves to do things their own way.

Human destiny shows that, by diverse means, men come to the same ends, and by the same means they come to diverse ends. They carry their scripts and their counterscripts around in their heads in the form of Parental voices telling them what to do and not do, and their aspirations in the form of Child pictures of how they would like it to be, and among the three of them they put their shows on the road. There they find themselves entangled in a web of other people's scripts: first their parents, then their spouses, and over all of them, the scripts of those who govern the places where they live. There are also chemical hazards like infectious diseases, and physical ones, such as hard objects that the human body is not constructed to withstand.

The script is what the person planned to do in early childhood, and the life course is what actually happens. The life course is determined by genes, by parental background, and by external circumstances. An individual whose genes cause mental retardation, physical deformity, or early death from cancer or diabetes, will have little opportunity to make his own life decisions or to carry them through to completion. The course of his life will be determined by inheritance (or perhaps birth injury). If the parents themselves suffered from severe physical or emotional deprivation as infants, that may destroy their children's chances of carrying out a script, or perhaps even of forming one. They may kill their offspring by neglect or abuse, or condemn them to life in an institution from an early age. Diseases, accidents, oppression, and war may terminate even the most carefully thought out and best supported life plan. So can a walk or a drive through the script of an unknown person: an assassin, thug, or car-crasher. A combination of these—genes plus oppression, for example—may close so many avenues to members of a certain line that they have few choices in planning their scripts, and it may make a tragic life course almost inevitable.

But even with strict limitations, there are nearly always some alternatives open. An aerial bomb, an epidemic, or a massacre may leave no choice at all, but at the next level, the person may be able to choose between killing, being killed, or killing himself, and there his choice will depend on his script, that is, the kind of decision he made in early childhood.

The difference between life course and life plan can be illustrated by considering two rats used in an experiment to show that the early experiences of a mother rat can affect the behavior of her offspring.[8] The first animal was named Victor Purdue-Wistar III, or Victor for short. (Purdue-Wistar was the actual surname of the rats used in this experiment, and Victor and Arthur were the forenames of their godfathers, the experimenters.) Victor came from a long line of experimental subjects, and his genes suited him for this station in life. His mother, Victoria, had been handled and caressed when she was a pup. His distant cousin, Arthur Purdue-Wistar III (Arthur) was equally suited to being an experimental subject. His mother, Arthuria, had been left in her cage and was never handled or caressed when she was little. When the two cousins grew up, it was found that Victor weighed more, explored less, and dropped his excretions more often than Arthur did. What happened to them in the long run, after the experiment was over, is not stated, but it probably depended upon external forces, such as what the experimenters needed to use them for. Thus, their life courses were determined by their genes, their mothers' early experiences, and decisions made by stronger forces over which they had no control and to which there was no appeal. Any "scripts" or "plans" they wanted to carry out as individuals were limited by all of this. Thus Victor, who liked to vegetate, could so indulge himself; while Arthur, who wanted to explore, was frustrated in his cage; and neither of them, however strong the urge, could seek for immortality through reproduction.

Tom, Dick, and Harry, distant cousins of Victor and Arthur, had a different experience. Tom was programed to press a lever in order to avoid getting an electric shock, and as a reward he would get a pellet of food. Dick was programed the same way, except that his treat was a drink of alcohol. Harry was also programed to avoid the unpleasant shock, and his reward was a pleasant shock instead. Then they were switched around so that in the long run all three of them learned all three of the programs. After that, they were put in a cage with three levers: one for food, one for alcohol, and one for the pleasant shock. Then each one could make his own "decision" as to how he wanted to spend his life: eating, lying in a drunken stupor, or getting electric thrills, or any combination or alternation of these. Furthermore, there was a treadmill in the new cage, and each one could decide whether he wanted to take exercise along with his other rewards.

This was exactly like a script decision, for each rat could decide whether he wanted to spend his life as a gourmand, an alcoholic, a thrill-seeker, or an athlete, or whether he preferred a moderate combination. But although each could follow his "script decision" and take the consequences as long as he remained in the cage, the actual outcomes of their lives depended on an external *force majeure,* for the experimenter could interrupt the experiment and break up the "script" whenever he felt like it. Thus their life courses and their life styles were largely determined by their "life plans" up to the final outcome, which was decided by someone else. But these "life plans" could only be chosen from among the alternatives offered by their "parents," the experimenters who programed them. And even that choice was influenced by things that had happened to them earlier.

Although men are not laboratory animals, they often behave as though they are. Sometimes they are put in cages and treated like rats, manipulated and sacrificed at the will of their masters. But many times the cage has an open door, and a man has only to walk out if he wishes. If he does not, it is usually his script which keeps him there. That is familiar and reassuring, and after looking out at the great world of freedom with all its joys and dangers, he turns back to the cage with its buttons and levers, knowing that if he keeps busy pushing them, and pushes the right one at the right time, he will be assured of food, drink, and an occasional thrill. But always, such a caged person hopes or fears that some force greater than himself, the Great Experimenter or the Great Computer, will change or end it all.

The forces of human destiny are foursome and fearsome: demonic parental programing, abetted by the inner voice the ancients called the *Daemon;* constructive parental programing, aided by the thrust of life called *Phusis* long ago; external forces, still called Fate; and independent aspirations, for which the ancients had no human name, since for them such were the privileges mainly of gods and kings. And as a resultant of these forces there are four kinds of life courses, which may be mixed, and lead to one or another kind of final destiny: scripty, counterscripty, forced, and independent.

G · HISTORICAL

As a clinician, the psychiatrist or the clinical psychologist is interested in *everything* that may affect the patient's behavior. In the following chapters no attempt is made to discuss all the factors which might affect the life *course* of the individual, but only those which are known at present to have a strong influence on the life *plan*.

But before we go on to consider how scripts are chosen, reinforced, and put into operation, and to dissect out the elements which make them up, we should state that the idea is not entirely new. There are many allusions in classical and modern literature to the fact that all the world's a stage and all the people in it merely players, but allusions are different from a sustained and informed investigation into the matter. Such investigations have been carried on by many psychiatrists and their pupils, but they have been unable to go very far in a systematic way because they did not have at their disposal the powerful weapons of structural analysis (diagraming and classifying transactions), game analysis (uncovering the con, the gimmick, the switch, and the payoff), and script analysis (the script matrix with the dreams, sweat shirts, trading stamps, and other elements derived from it).

The general idea that human lives follow the patterns found in myths, legends, and fairy tales, is most elegantly elaborated in Joseph Campbell's book, previously referred to.[9] He bases his psychological thinking mainly on Jung and Freud. Jung's best-known ideas in this connection are the Archetypes (corresponding to the magic figures in a script) and the Persona (which is the style the script is played in).[9] The rest of Jung's ideas are not easy to understand or to relate to real people without very special training, and even then they are subject to different interpretations. In general, Jung is in favor of thinking about myths and fairy tales, and that is an important part of his influence.

Freud directly relates many aspects of human living to a single drama, the Oedipus myth. In psychoanalytic language, the patient is Oedipus, a "character" who exhibits "reactions." Oedipus is something going on in the patient's head. In script analysis, Oedipus is an ongoing drama that is actually taking place right now, divided into scenes and acts, with a build-up, a climax, and an ending. It is essential for others to play their parts, and the patient sees that they do. He only knows what to say to people whose scripts match or dovetail with his own. If his script calls for him to kill a king and marry a queen, he has to find a king whose script calls for him to be killed, and a queen whose script calls for her to be stupid enough to marry him. Some of Freud's followers, such as Glover, are beginning to recognize that Oedipus is a drama rather than merely a set of "reactions," while Rank, Campbell's chief predecessor, showed that most important myths and fairy tales come from a single basic plot, and that this plot appears in the dreams and lives of large numbers of people all over the world.

Freud speaks of the repetition compulsion and the destiny compulsion,[9] but his followers have not pursued these ideas very far to apply them to the entire life courses of their patients. Erikson is the most active psychoanalyst in making systematic studies of the human life-cycle from birth to death, and naturally, many of his findings are corroborated by script analysis. In general, it may be said that script analysis is Freudian, but it is not psychoanalytic.

Of all those who preceded transactional analysis, Alfred Adler comes the closest to talking like a script analyst.

If I know the goal of a person I know in a general way what will happen. I am in a position to bring into their proper order each of the successive movements made. . . . We must remember that the person under observation would not know what to do with himself were he not oriented toward some goal . . . which determines his life-line . . . the psychic life of man is made to fit into the fifth act like a character drawn by a good dramatist . . . every psychic phenomenon, if it is to give us any understanding of a person, can only be grasped and understood if regarded as a preparation for some goal . . . an attempt at a planned final compensation and a (secret) life plan . . . the life plan remains in the unconscious, so that the patient may believe that an implacable fate and not a long-prepared and long-meditated plan for which he alone is responsible, is at work. . . . Such a man concludes his account and reconciles himself with life by constructing one or a number of "if-clauses." "If conditions had been different . . ."

The only exceptions which a script analyst would take to these statements are (1) that the life plan is usually not unconscious; (2) that the person is by no means solely responsible for it; and (3) that the goal and the manner of reaching it (the actual transactions, word for word) can be predicted much more precisely than even Adler claimed.[9]

Recently, R. D. Laing, the British psychiatrist, has described in a radio broadcast a view of life which is amazingly similar, even in its terminology, to the theory discussed in this book. For example, he uses the word "injunction" for strong parental programing.[10] Since, at this writing, he has not yet published these ideas, it is not possible to evaluate them properly.

Far older than all these, however, are the script analysts of ancient India, who based their prognostications largely on astrology. As the *Panchatantra* very aptly says, about 200 B.C.E.:

> These five are fixed for every man
> Before he leaves the womb:
> His length of days, his fate, his wealth,
> His learning, and his tomb.[11]

We need only make some slight changes to bring this up to date.

> These five are taken from your sires,
> Six summers from the womb:
> Your length of days, your fate, your wealth,
> Your learning, and your tomb.

NOTES & REFERENCES

1 For a discussion of the use of transactional analysis in the theater, see Schechner, R. "Approaches to Theory/Criticism." *Tulane Drama Review* 10: Summer 1966, pp. 20–

53. Also Wagner, A. "Transactional Analysis and Acting." Ibid. 11: Summer 1967, pp. 81–88, and Berne, E. "Notes on Games and Theater," in the same issue, pp. 89–91.

2 Wagner, A. "Permission and Protection," *The Drama Review* 13: Spring 1969, pp. 108–110, incorporates some of the more recent advances. For the direct application of transactional script theory to dramatic scripts, see the same issue pp. 110–114: Steiner, C. M. "A Script Checklist," and Cheney, W. D. "Hamlet: His Script Checklist." Both articles are reprinted from the *Transactional Analysis Bulletin* (Vol. 6, April, 1967, and Vol. 7, July, 1968).

3 For a historical consideration of one aspect of "good guys" and "bad guys," see my article "The Mythology of Dark and Fair: Psychiatric Use of Folklore," *Journal of American Folklore* 1–12, 1959. This gives a bibliography of about 100 items, including a few of the early psychoanalytic articles on fairy tales.

Geza Roheim is the most prolific writer on the folk tales of primitive people. See Roheim, G., *Psychoanalysis and Anthropology*, International Universities Press, New York, 1950.

4 I do not pretend to be enough of a scholar to give a complete variorum or an authorized version of the stories of Europa, Amymone, Little Red Riding Hood, and Sleeping Beauty. Even the color of Europa's bull varies in different accounts between white and gold. The versions given above suffice for the present purpose. The sources of Europa and Amymone are as follows:

Bulfinch's *Mythology*, Graves' *The Greek Myths*, Hamiton's *Mythology*, Lemprière's Classical Dictionary (London, 1818), Hesiod and Moschus (Family Classical Library No. XXX, London, 1832), Ovid's *Metamorphoses*, and my mother's copy of Edwards' *Handbook of Mythology* with the title page missing (Eldredge & Brothers, date unknown).

LRRH comes out of Andrew Lang's *Blue Fairy Book*, *The Grimms' Fairy Tales* (Grosset & Dunlap edition), and Funk & Wagnalls' *Standard Dictionary of Folklore, Mythology, and Legend* (New York, 1950). In France she is known as "Petit Chaperon Rouge," or "Little Red Hood" (Perrault, 1697) and in Germany as "Rotkäppchen," or "Little Red Cap."

The psychoanalysts' tendency to focus on filling the wolf's belly with stones is irrelevant to the present purpose, and this episode sounds to me like an interpolation, anyway. The psychoanalytic literature on LRRH starts with two papers in 1912, one by O. Rank and the other by M. Wulff, followed by Freud's paper on "The Occurrence in Dreams of Material from Fairy Tales" (1913), most easily available in the paperback edition of his *Delusion and Dream* (Beacon Press, Boston, 1956). One of the best-known discussions is that of Erich Fromm in *The Forgotten Language* (Grove Press, New York, 1951). Fromm says: "Most of the symbolism in this fairy tale can be understood without difficulty. The 'little cap of red velvet' is a symbol of menstruation." He does not state by whom it can be understood without difficulty, or to whom it is a symbol of menstruation. A recent paper by L. Veszy-Wagner, "Little Red Riding Hood on the Couch" (*Psychoanalytic Forum* 1:399–415, 1966), at least gives case material, although it is not convincing. Probably the best suggestions are offered by Elizabeth Crawford in her paper "The Wolf As Condensation" (*American Imago,* 12:307–314, 1955).

In real life, wolves are not as bad as they appear in fairy tales. See "Wolves Social as Dogs . . . can be taught to be friendly to people," by P. McBroom, *Science News* 90:174, September 10, 1966. This summarizes the studies of G. B. Raab and J. H. Woolpy on the social lives of wolves, from which it appears that wolves also play transactional games. Specifically, outcast wolves play "Wooden Leg," limping as though to ask for special consideration.

5 "Sleeping Beauty" or "Briar Rose" again comes from Andrew Lang's *Blue Fairy Book* and the Grimms. There is an expanded version, with sinister illustrations by Arthur Rackham, which is also very popular.

6 For further information about the recent use of fairy tales in psychiatry, see Heuscher, J. *A Psychiatric Study of Fairy Tales.* C. C. Thomas, Springfield, 1963. This gives an existential symbolic interpretation. D. Dinnerstein's analysis of the story of "The Little Mermaid" (*Contemporary Psychoanalysis* 104–112, 1967), uses a "maturational" approach which involves some of the elements related to the evolution of a script.

Most directly connected with script analysis, however, is the work of H. Dieckmann, who relates fairy tales to the life patterns of his patients in a systematic way. See Dieckmann, H. "Das Lieblingsmärchen der Kindheit und seine Beziehung zu Neurose und Persönlichkeit." *Praxis der Kinderpsychologie und Kinderpsychiatrie* 6:202–208, August–September, 1967. Also *Märchen und Träume als Helfer des Menschen.* Bonz Verlag, Stuttgart, 1966.

7 Cf. Flugel, J. C.: *The Psychoanalytic Study of the Family.* Hogarth Press, London, 1921.

8 Denenberg, V. H. and Whimby, A. E.: "Behavior of Adult Rats is Modified by the Experiences Their Mothers Had as Infants," *Science* 142:1192–1193, November 29, 1963.

9 The bibliography for the historical background of the script concept is as follows:

Adler, A. "Individual Psychology" in *The World of Psychology,* ed. G. B. Levitas, George Braziller, New York, 1963.

Campbell, J. *The Hero With A Thousand Faces.* Pantheon Books, New York, 1949.

Erikson, E. *Childhood and Society.* W. W. Norton & Company, New York, 1950.

Freud, S. *Beyond the Pleasure Principle.* International Psychoanalytical Press, London, 1922.

Glover, E. *The Technique of Psycho-Analysis.* International Universities Press, New York, 1955.

Jung, C. G. *Psychological Types.* Harcourt, Brace & Company, New York, 1946.

Rank, O. *The Myth of the Birth of the Hero.* Nervous and Mental Disease Monographs, New York, 1910.

10 First used in this connection by C. M. Steiner (*Transactional Analysis Bulletin* 5:133, April 1966).

11 *Panchatantra,* trans. A. W. Ryder. University of Chicago Press, 1925, p. 237. Although these fables are dated back to 200 B.C.E., this version is from a manuscript of A.D. 1199, probably from the Hebrew codex. The five-book original is lost, but many of the tales are repeated in the four-book medieval *Hitopadesa.* Some date the Sanskrit original as late as A.D. 300.

CHAPTER FOUR

Prenatal Influences

A · INTRODUCTORY

The script scene began long ages past, when life first oozed out of the mud and began to transmit the results of its experiences chemically, through genes, to its descendants. This chemical branch culminated in the spider, who spins his strange circular geometry without instruction, the coiled spirals in his chromosomes supplying him with instant engineering drawings that will bridge any corner where the flies abound.[1] In his case, the script is written in fixed molecules of organic acids (DNA) bequeathed him by his parents, and he spends his life as an educated pen point, carrying out their instructions with no possibility of deviation or improvement except by drugs or some untoward accident beyond his control.

In man, too, the genes determine chemically some of the patterns he must follow, and from which he cannot deviate. They also set the upper limit for his individual aspirations: how far he can go as an athlete, thinker, or musician, for example, although because of psychological barriers great or small, few men reach their full possibilities even in these fields. Many a man with the chemistry of a great ballet dancer spends his time dancing with other people's dishes in a lunchroom, and others with the genes of a mathematician pass their days juggling other people's papers in the back room of a bank or bookie joint. But within his chemical limitations, whatever they are, each man has enormous possibilities for determining his own fate. Usually, however, his parents decide it for him long before he can see what they are doing.

As life broke free to some extent from rigid chemical patterns, other ways of regulating behavior gradually evolved to take up the slack. The most primitive of these is probably imprinting, which is barely one step beyond a reflex.[2] Imprinting assures that an infant organism will automatically follow a certain object and treat it like a mother, whether it is really his mother or merely a yellow card drawn past him on a string. This automatic response helps to insure his survival in moments of stress, but if it goes awry it can make trouble, too.

The next step came when some animals stayed with their mothers and learned through play; patterns too complex or variable to be transmitted through the genes could be taught with a playful bite or roll or a box on the ear.[3] Then came imitation and a response to voice signals, so that the young could do not only what their genes prompted them to, and what they learned at their mothers' breasts, but also what they saw and heard in the real living of the seas and plains and forests.

It is now known that almost every kind of living organism can be trained. Bacteria can be "trained" chemically to use one kind of sugar as a substitute for another. Almost all other animals, from worms on up, can be trained psychologically, by conditioned reflexes, to go through new and special patterns of behavior. This is probably, in the long run, chemical, too, and depends on more flexible kinds of DNA than are found in the genes. But training requires trainers, and they are something else. They have to be one cut or dimension above the organisms they are training. This means they must be tamed. Taming is as different from training as a cat is from a tiger. Taming, in animals, means that the animal obeys his master even when his master isn't there. This is different from training, because training requires an outside stimulus to start off a certain pattern of behavior, while taming assures the behavior because the stimulus is inside the animal's head. A trained animal will obey his master's voice when he hears it out loud; a tamed one doesn't need to hear the sound, because he carries it around in his brain. Thus, wild animals can be trained to do tricks at their trainer's command, but they cannot easily be house-broken. Tame animals go further than that; they can be taught to behave as their master wishes even when he is away. There are various degrees of tameness, and the tamest animals of all are human children.

The most intelligent animals—monkeys, apes, and people (and maybe dolphins too)—have another special capacity, and that is invention. This means that they can do things that none of their kind has ever done before: anything from piling one wooden box on another, to putting two rods together to form a longer one,[4] to shooting for the moon.

In order to account for this progression, we can assume that DNA is evolving into ever softer and more pliable forms. Starting out as the brittle molecules of genes, which cannot be molded, but only shattered, it thawed out enough so that it could be slightly altered by repeated gentle blows of conditioning, although it would spring back if these were not reinforced from time to time. Then it softened still more so that it could record the echoes of vanished voices and events, and keep them there for a lifetime, long after they were forgotten. In still more flexible form, it became the vehicle for memory and consciousness. And in its most sensitive form to date, it shifts and vibrates in the zephyrs of experience to give us thinking and invention. What will come forth when it becomes even more delicate in its responses none of us now living will ever know, but some day our descendants will be wondrous beings that only poets presently can dimly contemplate.

Human beings have all the capacities mentioned above. Their behavior patterns are determined by rigid reflex genes, primitive imprinting, infant play and imitation, parental training, social taming, and spontaneous invention. Scripts involve all of these. The typical human being, whom we will call "Jeder," represents nearly every member of the human race in every soil and clime. He carries out his script because it is planted in his head at an early age by his parents, and stays there for the rest of his life, even after their vocal "flesh" has gone forevermore. It acts like a computer tape or a player-piano roll, which brings out the responses in the planned order long after the person who punched the holes has departed the scene. Jeder meanwhile sits before the piano, moving his fingers along the keyboard under the illusion that it is he who brings the folksy ballad or the stately concerto to its foregone conclusion.

B · ANCESTRAL INFLUENCES

Some scripts can be traced back in a clinical interview to the great-grandparents, and if the family has a recorded history, as is often the case with kings and their courtiers, it may go back a thousand years in time. No doubt scripts began when the first manlike creatures appeared on earth,[5] and there is no reason to suspect that their scenes and acts and outcomes were different then than they are now. Certainly the life courses of the kings of Egypt, which are the oldest reliable biographies we have, are typical scripts. The story of Amenhotep IV, 3500 years in the past, who changed his name to Ikhnaton is a good example.[6] By this change he brought on both greatness and the fury of those who followed him. If information about remote ancestors, or the great-grandparents, can be obtained, so much the better for the script analysis, but in ordinary practice, in most cases, it starts with the grandparents.

It is common knowledge, even proverbial, how much grandparents, alive or dead, influence the lives of their grandchildren. For a good script, "To make a lady, start with the grandmother," and for a bad one, "From shirtsleeves to shirtsleeves in three generations." Many children at an early age not only want to imitate their forebears, but would like actually to *be* their own grandparents.[7] This desire may not only have a strong influence on their life scripts, but it may cause considerable confusion in their relationships with their parents.[8] American mothers in particular, it is said, favor their fathers over their husbands, and encourage their sons to take after grandfather instead of Dad.[9]

The most productive single question to ask in regard

to ancestral influences is "What kind of lives did your grandparents lead?" There are four types of reports commonly given in answer to this.

1. *Ancestral Pride*. A winner or "prince" will state in a matter-of-fact way, "My ancestors were kings of Ireland," or "My great-great-grandfather was the Chief Rabbi of Lublin." It is apparent that the speaker has "permission" to follow in the footsteps of these ancestors and become an outstanding personality. If the statement is made pompously or solemnly, however, the speaker is probably a loser or "frog," and is using his ancestry to justify his existence because he himself does not have "permission" to excel.

If the response is: "(My mother was always telling me that) my ancestors were Irish kings, ha, ha," or "(My mother was always telling me that) my great-great-grandfather was the Chief Rabbi, ha ha," it is usually given from a not-O.K. position; the speaker is allowed to imitate his illustrious ancestors, but only in their losing characteristics. These replies may mean: "I'm as drunk as an Irish king should be, so that makes me like an Irish king, ha ha!" or "I'm as poor as a Chief Rabbi should be, so that makes me like a Chief Rabbi, ha ha!" In such cases, the early programing was: "You're descended from Irish kings, and they were great drinkers," or "You're descended from a Chief Rabbi, and they were very poor." This is equivalent to a directive: "Be like your famous ancestor . . ." with the clear implication from mother ". . . so drink a lot, your father does," or ". . . so don't make money, your father doesn't."

In all these cases the ancestor is a family euhemerus,[10] a heroic model from the past who can be imitated but never surpassed, and these are different ways that people deal with euhemeri.

2. *Idealization*. This may be romantic or paradoxical. Thus, a winner may say: "My grandmother was a wonderful housekeeper," or "My grandfather lived to be ninety-eight and had all his teeth and no gray hair." There is a clear indication that the speaker would like to follow in the romantic grandparent's footsteps and is basing her or his script on that. A loser will express

paradoxical idealization: "My grandmother was a tough, down-to-earth woman, but she became senile in her old age." There is a clear implication that she may have been senile, but she was the smartest woman in the state hospital; and furthermore, that that is also the speaker's script: to be the smartest woman in the state hospital. Unfortunately, this setup is so frequent that the competition in state hospitals to be the smartest woman on the ward can become quite strenuous, turbulent, and discouraging.

3. *Rivalry.* "My grandfather dominated my grandmother," or "My grandfather was a weakling who let everyone push him around." These are often the "neurotic" responses interpreted by psychoanalysts as expressing the child's desire to be more powerful than his parents. "Grandfather is one person who can talk back to my mother—I'd like to be him," or "If I were my father's father I wouldn't be a coward, I'd show him." Karl Abraham's case report[8] shows the scripty nature of such attitudes, where the boy indulges in daydreams of being the prince of an imaginary kingdom whose king is like his father. Then along comes the king's father, who is far more powerful than the king. Once, when the boy was punished by his mother, he said "Now I'll marry granny." Thus, his secret (but not unconscious) planning at that time was based on a fairy tale in which he becomes more powerful than his parents by becoming his grandfather.

4. *Personal Experiences.* These concern actual transactions between children and their grandparents, which are strong influences in molding the child's script. A grandmother can send a little boy forth to be a hero,[11] or on the other hand, a grandfather can seduce a schoolgirl and turn her into a Little Red Riding Hood.

In general, grandparents, as mythology and clinical experience show, are regarded with awe or terror, just as parents can be regarded with admiration or fear. The more primitive feelings of awe and terror are influential in forming the child's picture of the world during the early stages of script-building.[12]

C · THE CONCEPTIVE SCENE

The context in which Jeder was conceived may have a strong influence in deciding his life plan and his ultimate fate. This context starts off with his parents' marriage, if there was one. Sometimes the young couple gets married with a strong urge to have a son and heir. This is particularly apt to happen if the marriage is arranged or encouraged by their families, especially if there is something to inherit, such as a kingdom or a corporation. The son is then reared in accordance with his station in life, and learns all the arts and crafts suitable for kings or presidents. Thus, his script is handed to him already written, and to abdicate from it may require an act of heroic renunciation. If the first-born in such cases is a girl instead of a boy, she may run into difficulties; this is often seen in the first-born daughters of bankers, who may be cast adrift to become homosexuals, strip-tease artists, or the wives of improvident and irresponsible Bohemians or trust-fund bums. In some situations, the father may even divorce the mother if she doesn't produce a boy, leaving the daughters with a keen sense of original guilt for having been born female.

On the other hand, the father may have no intention of marrying the mother, and flees the scene, never to be heard from again, as soon as she announces her pregnancy. This leaves the young hero to make his own way almost from the day of his birth. Sometimes it is the mother who runs away. But even grudging parents may accept an unwanted child because he is an income-tax deduction or a welfare claim. The teen-ager may be well aware of this, and when asked who he is, or what his script is, he will reply "I'm an income-tax deduction (a welfare claim)."

If the child is long in being conceived, his parents' longing may lead them to dedicate him before his birth, as is the case in many legends of famous people, and in fairy tales such as Rapunzel: another way in which real life resembles literature, or as Oscar Wilde put it, nature imitates art. This raises other interesting script questions running the whole gamut of tragedy and romance. What if Romeo had fathered a child, or Ophelia given birth, or Cordelia become pregnant? What would have become of these offspring? Medea's children, and the Little Princes in the tower of London, are the most celebrated examples of children being the victims of their parents' scripts, just as the little girls and boys sold as sodomistic slaves in certain Arab countries are the most obscure.[13]

The bedside manner of the actual impregnation may be called the conceptive attitude. Was it due to accident, passion, love, violence, deception, spite, or resignation? If any of these, what was the background and preparation for such an event? If it was planned, was it planned coldly or warmly, simply or bookishly, with lots of talk, or by strong, silent communion? The child's script may have the same qualities. Is sex regarded as dirty, casual, sacred, or fun? The offspring may be treated the same way. Was an abortion attempted? Were several attempts made? How many abortions or attempts were there during previous pregnancies? There is almost an infinite number of questions of varying degrees of subtlety possible here, and all these factors can influence the script of the still unborn baby. One of the most common situations is nicely summarized in a popular limerick:

> There was a young (fellow, lady) named Horn
> Who wished (he, she) had never been born.
> (He, she) wouldn't have been
> If (his, her) (father, mother) had seen
> That the end of the rubber was torn.

Even this homely genealogy is not of such somber simplicity as it seems, since there are several possibilities. For example, it is one thing if neither parent knew the condom was defective; another if the mother knew and didn't mention it to the father; and still a third if the father knew and didn't mention it to the mother.

On the cheerful side, there are the cases where both

parents want children and will take their genders as they come. If a woman who decided as a little girl that her ambition was to get married and raise children meets a man who made the same decision when he was little, then the offspring has a good start. Biological difficulties which arise here may make the child even more precious: if the woman has repeated miscarriages, or the man has a low sperm count so that impregnation is delayed through the years, then, as we have already noted, the infant may be regarded as a real miracle. On the other hand, the seventh girl in a row, or even the seventh boy, may be greeted with mixed feelings, and perhaps start life as a family joke.

D · BIRTH POSITION

The most important factor here is the parents' scripts. Does Jeder fit in, or is he the wrong sex, or badly timed? Does his father's script call for a scholar, and he turns out to be, instead, a football player? Or vice versa? Does his mother's script go along with his father's, or is it opposite in this respect? There are also traditions that he will hear about from fairy tales and real life. The youngest of three sons is supposed to act stupid until the showdown comes, and then he wins over his brothers. If he happens to be the seventh son of a seventh son, he is almost compelled to be a prophet. More particularly, the parents' scripts may call for them to be glorified or punished by one of their children, who must therefore turn out to be either a colossal success or a colossal failure. Often the first-born son is chosen for this honor.[14] If the mother's script calls for her to be a spouseless invalid in her declining years, then one of the children must be raised from birth to stay and care for her, while the others must be taught to wander off and fill the role of ingrates. If the forty-year-old bachelor son or spinster daughter decides to break the script by moving out of the house, or worse, by getting married, the mother will respond, understandably and pitiably, by having severe attacks of illness. The scripty nature of such setups is demonstrated by the frequent switch whereby mother "unexpectedly" wills the bulk of her money to the ingrates, cutting off the devoted one with a pittance.

The general rule is that, other things being equal, children will follow their parents' script regarding family constellation, and this is best shown by taking the simplest factors: number and spacing of children. (The sex of the children cannot be considered, since that is still beyond the parents' control—fortunately, since that is one way that scripts are broken up from generation to generation, so that some children, at least, get a new chance.) A careful inquiry among a number of families will reveal a surprising number of "coincidences" in this respect.

Figure 5 shows such a scripty family tree. There were three boys in the Able family: Cal, Hal, and Val. When Val was born, Hal was four and Cal was six, so that their spacing is 0–4–6. Their father, Don, was the oldest of three children spaced 0–5–7. Their mother, Fan, was the oldest of three girls spaced 0–4–5. Her two sisters, Nan and Pan, also had three children each. Fan's mother was the older of two girls spaced 0–6, with a miscarriage in between. It can be seen that all of these threesomes were spaced within five to seven fertile years.[15]

This type of family tree shows how some people tend to follow their parents' example in family planning as far as number and spacing of offspring are concerned. Let us consider some of the possible "script directives" that might have come from Gramp and Granny to Don and Fan in this particular case.

a. "When you grow up, have three children, and then you are free to do as you please." This is the most flexible, and involves no hurry or constraint. Fear of "script failure" and loss of mother's love can occur only if Fan approaches menopause without having produced the required three offspring. But note that Fan is not free *until* she has the third child. This is an "Until" script.

b. "When you grow up, have at least three children." There is no constraint here, but there may be a

A Scripty Family Tree
The Ables

FIGURE 5

sense of hurry, particularly if Gramp or Granny make jokes about Don and Fan's fertility. This is an "Open End" script, since Fan is free to have as many children as she likes after the third.

c. "When you grow up, have no more than three children." There is no hurry, but there is constraint, and Don and Fan may be uneasy about further pregnancies after the three children are born. This is an "After" script, since it implies that there will be trouble if there are any children after the third.

Now let us consider Fan's point of view if she should have a fourth child, Pedwar, under any of these directives. (a) means "The first three children belong to Granny, and must be brought up her way." Pedwar then becomes Fan's very own boy, and he may or may not be brought up the same as Cal, Hal, and Val. Fan can use her own autonomy with him, and he may grow up to be more free and autonomous than the others. Fan may treat him as she did her Raggedy Ann doll. Raggedy Ann was her own very special doll to love as she pleased when she was little, while her other dolls had to be cared for Granny's way. In other words, Raggedy Ann may have prepared a "script slot" for Pedwar which Fan could fill after she had done her duty by Granny. (b) is similar to (a) except that Granny has more hold over Pedwar than under plan (a) because he may be considered an extra bonus granted by Granny, rather than a free choice. Under (c) Pedwar is in trouble because Fan has disobeyed Granny in having him; he must therefore be raised as an "unwanted" child, defiantly, uneasily, or guiltily. In such a case, if our working principle is correct, the people around him will remark again and again how different he is from his three older brothers.

The next item to consider is the games parents play about the size of their families. For example, Ginnie was the oldest of eleven children, and her mother, Nanny, complained that the last five were unwanted. The naive assumption would be that Ginnie would be programed to have six children, but that was not so. She was programed to have eleven children and complain that the last five were unwanted. In that way she would be able to play "There I Go Again," "Harried," and "Frigid Woman" in her later years, just as her mother did. In fact, this example can be used as a test of psychological sophistication. Given the question: "A woman had eleven children and complained that five of them were unwanted. How many children will her oldest daughter most probably have?" the script analyst would answer "Eleven." People who answer "Six" will have difficulty in understanding and predicting human reactions, since this answer assumes that important behavior, like trivial behavior, is "rationally" motivated, which is not so. It is usually decided by the Parental directives of the script.

In investigating this aspect, the parents of the patient are asked, first, how many brothers and sisters they each have; second, how many children they want to have; and third (since as any obstetrician knows, there is many a slip 'twixt the cup and the lip), how many they actually expect to have. If the parents understand how to distinguish correctly between their ego states, a great deal more information can be gained by asking the second and third questions in structural form: "How many children does your (Parent, Adult, Child) (want, expect) to have?" This may bring out otherwise hidden conflicts among the three ego states, and between the two parents, which have an important bearing on the script directives they are giving the patient. An even more sophisticated version of this, with a corresponding increase in information gained (providing the parents are properly educated to understand the question), is to ask it in a twelve-barreled instead of a six-barreled form: "How many children does your (nurturing, controlling) Parent, Adult and (natural, adapted, rebellious) Child (want, expect) to have?"[16]

With the patient himself, the most profitable question to ask, since it is the one he is most likely to have the answer to, is: "What is your position in the family?" followed by "When were you born?" The exact birthdays of the next older and the next younger must be obtained so that the differences can be calculated in months, if the children came close together. If the speaker comes into a world which is already occupied by a sister or a brother, it will make a considerable difference in his script decisions whether that sibling is older by eleven months, thirty-six months, eleven years, or twenty years. This difference will depend not only on his relationship with that sibling, but also on his parents' attitude toward that particular spacing of children. The same two considerations apply concerning the next born: it is important to know the speaker's exact age—for example, eleven months, nineteen months, five years, or sixteen years, at the time the next child arrived on the scene. In general, all siblings born before the speaker reaches his seventh birthday will have a decisive influence on his script, and one of the important factors is the number of months' difference in age between them, since as noted above, this will affect not only his own attitude but that of his parents as well. Notable variations occur if the speaker is a twin, or came before or after twins.

In some cases, where the patient is interested in astrology, meteorology, or hagiology, the exact date of his own birth will have a strong script significance. This is especially important if his parents had a similar interest in the calendar.

E · BIRTH SCRIPTS

Otto Rank believed that the circumstances of birth itself, the "birth trauma," are imprinted on the psyche of the infant and often reappear in symbolic form in later life, particularly as a desire to return to the blissful peace of the womb, as described by his disciple Fodor.[17] If that were so, the fears and longings which arise from passing under that arch through which no man can ever pass again, nature's original one-way street, would certainly appear as important elements in the script. Perhaps they do, but there is no reliable way to check it, even by comparing Caesarean births with normal ones. Hence the influence of the "birth trauma" on the life script remains in the realm of speculation. As a matter of fact, real-life scripts said to be based on the actual occurrence of Caesarean birth, like their theatrical counterparts, are unconvincing. As in *Macbeth,* the event is exploited as a mere play on words or a conundrum, a *foetus ex machina,* rather than forming the serious basis for a script. It is quite likely, however, that a child who is *told later* that he was a Caesarean birth, and can understand what that means, might incorporate that fact somehow into his script and elaborate upon it further when he learns who his distinguished predecessors were. A decision on this point awaits the collection of some good case histories.

In practice, the two most common "birth scripts" are the "Foundling Script" and the "Torn Mother Script." The Foundling Script arises from the fantasies of adopted or even natural children about their "real" parents, and comes out as some version of the Myth of the Birth of the Hero described by Otto Rank in his book of that name.[18] The Torn Mother Script is also common, and in my experience occurs with about equal frequency in both sexes. The foundation for this script is the mother telling the child that she has been sickly ever since he was born; or in a more vicious form, that she was so badly torn by his birth that she has never been the same. His reaction, and his script, is based on his own observations in the matter. If mother has indeed been invalided or crippled all his life, then he feels compelled to take the full responsibility, and no amount of Adult reasoning will convince his Child that it is not his doing. If the impairment is not visible, however, and particularly if someone in the family, such as the father, implies or states that her illness is a fake, then the patient's script will be heavily loaded with ambiguity, hypocrisy, and exploitation. Sometimes the mother does not make the accusation, but leaves it to father, grandmother, or an aunt. The script which evolves is then a three-handed one, with important messages and announcements, usually "bad news," coming from a third party. It is easy to see that where the Foundling Script comes out as the Myth of the Birth of the Hero, the Torn Mother Script is the Myth of the Birth of the Villain, one saddled from birth with the horrendous crime of matricide, or, more precisely, matriclasty. "Mother died in childbirth (mine)" is almost too much for anyone to bear without good help. If mother was injured or has a cystocele, it is never too late to have it repaired, and the less said about it the better.

F · FORENAMES AND SURNAMES

Roger Price, in his book *What Not To Name The Baby,* lists some common American forenames and gives a one-sentence description of the kind of personality that goes with each. The uncanny accuracy, or at least plausibility of his descriptions are of great interest to script analysts. There is no doubt that in many cases given names, short names, and nicknames, or whatever praenomen is bestowed or inflicted on the innocent newborn, is a clear indication of where his parents want him to go; and he will have to struggle against such influences, which will be continued in other forms as well, if he is to break away from the obvious hint.[19] Names as script indicators are most likely to take hold in high school, where the boy or girl reads about famous namesakes in myth and history, or where his or her classmates bring home to them with more or less brutality the hidden meanings in their names. This is something parents have control over and should be able to foresee.

There are four ways in which a forename can become scripty: purposefully, accidentally, inadvertently, and inevitably.

1. *Purposeful.* The name may be a very specialized one, such as Septimus S. (who became a professor of classical philosophy), Galen E. (who became a physician),* Napoleon (who became a corporal), or Jesus, a common name in Central America. Or it may be a variant of a common name. Charles and Frederick were kings and emperors. A boy who is steadfastly called Charles or Frederick by his mother, and insists that his associates call him that, lives a different style of life from one who is commonly hailed as Chuck or Fred, while Charlie and Freddie are likely to be horses of still another color. Naming a boy after his father or a girl after her mother is usually a purposeful act on the part of the parents, and puts an obligation on the offspring which they may not care to fulfill, or may even actively rebel against, so that their whole life plan is permeated by a slight bitterness or an active resentment.

2. *Accidental.* A girl called Durleen or Aspasia, and a boy called Marmaduke, may get along smoothly in one state or country or high school, but if their parents chance to move elsewhere, they may be made acutely conscious of their names and be forced to take a position about it. Similarly with a boy called Lynn or a girl named Tony.

---

*The current editor of Gray's *Anatomy* is Charles Mayo Goss.

3. *Inadvertent*. Pet names such as Bub, Sis, and Junior may not be intended to stick, but quite often they do, so that the person remains Bub, Sis, or Junior for life, willingly or unwillingly.

4. *Inevitable*. Surnames are a different matter, since the parents have little option but to pass on what they got from grandfather. There are many honorable European names which become obscenities in English; as one man morosely remarked: "I'm so lucky. I've got only one dirty word in my name." This was brought to his attention most clearly in high school, where he suffered not only the indignities bestowed on immigrants, but in addition offered a ready-made handle for ribaldry. But he felt that his name was no asset in the business world either. Some people in this predicament feel that they are cursed by their ancestors from birth to be losers. On the other hand, Christ is a not uncommon surname, and this also poses a script problem, albeit of a different kind, especially for church-going boys. It is no wonder that H. Head and W. R. Brain both became well-known neurologists.

Besides being asked "Who chose your name?" and "Where does your surname come from?" the patient should also be asked in every case: "Have you ever actually read your birth certificate?" If he has not, he should be instructed to do so, or even better, bring it in for the therapist to see. About fifty per cent of people find surprises on their birth certificates when they read them carefully for the first time: omissions, misapprehensions, or information they were not aware of. Often the name on the certificate is different from what they have been called all their lives, much to their astonishment or chagrin. Almost all of these surprises will throw additional light on the scripts of the parents and the context of the patient's birth.

NOTES & REFERENCES

1 Witt, P.N. and Reed, C. F. "Spider-Web Building," *Science* 149:1190–1197, September 10, 1965.
2 Lorenz, K. Z. *King Solomon's Ring*. Thomas Y. Crowell Company, New York, 1933.

3 Bateson, G. "The Message 'This is Play.'" In *Group Processes: Transactions of the Second Conference*. (Bertram Schaffner, ed.) Josiah Macy, Jr. Foundation, New York, 1956.

4 Zuckerman, S. *Functional Affinities of Man, Monkeys, and Apes*. Harcourt Brace & Company, New York, 1933.

5 Simons, E. L. "Some Fallacies in the Study of Hominid Phylogeny." *Science* 141: 879–889, September 6, 1963.

6 Cf. Freud, S. *Moses and Monotheism*, Alfred A. Knopf, New York, 1939.

From the present point of view, this deals with the effect of Ikhnaton's script on Moses' script. In script language, it places Ikhnaton as the euhemerus or "grandparent" of all Israelites, and their script follows his: his temples were destroyed and his followers persecuted or killed. The Israelis of today have the correct antithesis to this script, which is to employ the necessary hardware to avert the tragic ending.

Amenhotep-haq-Uast's other name (besides Ikhnaton) was Nefer-kheperu-Ra-ua-en-Ra, whose hieroglyphs roughly translate as "Take your lute and your scarab and enjoy the sun," while according to the Ikhnaton cartouche, he has traded this in for a cake and a feather (Line Character #12 and Trees and Plants #33 in Holzhausen's classification of hieroglyphs). This is like a modern, hippie, script switch, either way: people with guitars get a yen for cake, or people with cake turn it in for a guitar.

7 Jones, E. "The Phantasy of the Reversal of Generations." *Papers on Psycho-Analysis*, Fifth edition. Beacon Press, Boston, 1961. Here Jones describes the "grandfather complex," the desire of children to become the parents of their own parents, based on the belief that as they grow bigger their parents will grow smaller.

8 Abraham, K. "Some remarks on the role of grandparents in the psychology of neuroses." *Clinical Papers and Essays on Psycho-Analysis*. Basic Books, New York, 1955. What Abraham describes here is exactly what is meant by a "script fantasy," where the boy plans his life on a fairy-tale level.

9 Erikson, E. *Childhood and Society. Loc. cit.*

10 Berne, E. *The Structure and Dynamics of Organizations and Groups. Loc. cit.*, pp. 98–101.

11 Helene Deutsch describes three types of "good grandmother" and the dreaded "wicked grandmother," or witch, in her chapter on the climacterium in *The Psychology of Women*, Volume Two. Grune & Stratton, New York, 1945.

12 Anthropologists, more than most other groups, are aware of the important influence of the grandparents on the child's career, an influence which is not only clearly recognized, but also highly ritualized in small primitive societies,

especially those which have totems. See, for example, Ashley-Montagu, M. F. *Coming Into Being Among the Australian Aborigines.* George Routledge & Sons, London, 1937, and Roheim, G. *Psychoanalysis and Anthropology Loc. cit.*

13 O'Callaghan, S. *The Slave Trade Today.* (Including a debate in the House of Lords, Thursday, July 14, 1960.) Crown Publishers, Inc., New York, 1961.

14 There is a considerable body of literature about birth position. The first systematic study was probably F. Galton's *English Men of Science* (1874). He found a preponderance of only sons and first-born sons in his population. Adler, on the other hand, in his paper on "The Family Constellation," states that "the youngest child is usually a peculiar type." (*Understanding Human Nature*) One of the most interesting discussions is that of W. D. Altus in *Science* 151:44–48, January 7, 1966. This was followed by a series of "Letters to the Editor," *Science* 152: 1177–1184, May 27, 1966.

15 It is difficult to get adequate census data to evaluate statistically the significance of the coincidences in the Able family. One set of figures, obtained by the President's Research Committee on Social Trends (1933) is quoted by Pressey, S. L., Janney, J. E., & Kuhlen, R. G. in *Life: A Psychological Survey* (Harper & Brothers, New York, 1939). In metropolitan Chicago at that time, only 42 per 1000 families consisted of a husband, a wife, and three children, so that the probability of the occurrence of six such sets in collateral and direct ascendancy, which (except for the miscarriage) is the import of Figure 5, is not great by chance alone. Excluding families with no children at all from the Chicago figures, the prevalence of the cited constellation rises to 90 per 1000, or about one in ten. On this basis, the crude probability that the family tree of Figure 5 is due to chance alone is therefore of the order of one in 10^6, while the actual occurrence of similar improbabilities in my own patient population is about one in five. This indicates that we are dealing here with the influence of "information" or programing, and it is just that kind of behavior programing that we are calling the "script." If we consider, in addition, the regular irregularity of the unusually short fertile periods in Figure 5, this indication is strongly reinforced.

16 This may seem far out, but students of family size are quite unable to come up with reliable projections by assuming a unified or "integrated" personality. They use terms like "ideal," "desired," and "intended" families in interviews. These roughly correspond to Parent, Child, and Adult ideas. But "many wives who said that they had not 'really wanted' another child before the last conception also said . . . that if

they could have just the number they wanted and then stop, they would have the same number they had and even more." The debate is whether "excess fertility" can be equated with "unwanted" pregnancies. But the transactional analyst knows that there are at least three different people in each person interviewed who may "want," "really want," or "not want" more babies, and they may all feel differently about it, so questionaires on this subject that do not take ego state into account are missing something of decisive importance. For a discussion of such questionnaires, see Barish, N. H. "Family Planning and Public Policy: Who is Misleading Whom?" *Science* 165:1203–1204, September 19, 1969.

17 Fodor, N. *The Search for the Beloved*. Hermitage Press, New York, 1949.

18 Rank, O. *The Myth of the Birth of the Hero. Loc. cit.*

19 Price, R. *What Not To Name the Baby*. New York, 1904. H. L. Mencken gives many revealing examples of "scripty" names in *The American Language*, Alfred A. Knopf, New York (1919), 4th edition, 1949, Chapter 10, especially pp. 518 ff.

CHAPTER FIVE

Early Developments

A · EARLY INFLUENCES

The first script programing takes place during the nursing period, in the form of short protocols which can later be worked into complicated dramas. Usually these are two-handed scenes between the baby and his mother, with little interference from the onlookers, if any, and with such breast-fed titles as "Public Performance," "It's Not Time Yet," "Whenever You're Ready," "Whenever I'm Ready," "Hurry Up," "He Who Bites Gets Brushed Off," "While Mother Smokes," "Pardon Me, the Phone Rang," "What's He Fussing About?," "There's Never Enough," "First One Then the Other," "He Looks Pale," "Let Him Take His Time," "Isn't He Amazing?," "Golden Moments of Love and Content," and "Lullaby."

Slightly more complicated are the corresponding bathroom scenes in the same families: "Come and See How Cute," "It's Time Now," "Are You Ready," "You Can Just Sit There Till You Do," "Hurry Up," "Naughty Naughty," "While Mother Smokes," "While Mother Is on the Telephone," "Enema Tube," "If You Don't I'll Give You Castor Oil," "Here's Your Laxative," "You'll Get Sick If You Don't," "Let Him Do It His Own Way," "That's a Good Boy," "That's a G-o-o-d Boy," and "I'll Sing While You're Doing It." Three-handed protocols are more frequent at this stage, including: "I Told You He Wasn't Ready," "Don't Let Him Get Away With That," "I'll Make Him Do It," "You Try," "You're Disturbing Him," "Why Don't You . . . Yes, But," and "He's Sure Coming Through This Time." The Phantom in the Bathroom, who will some day be the Phantom in the Bedroom, may begin to appear: "Dr. Spock Says," "Tessie Had

Hers Trained by the Time," and "Sister Mary Was Only." In later life these will become "Freud Says," "Nancy Always Has One," and "Helen Has It Every Night."

It is already fairly predictable who the winners and the losers will be. "Isn't He Amazing?" reinforced two years later with "That's a Good Boy" will usually do better than "What's He Fussing About?" reinforced one year later by "Enema Tube"; similarly, "Lullaby," first at nursing and later in the bathroom, will probably prevail over "While Mother Smokes." Already the feeling of O.K.ness or not-O.K.ness, which separates the now and future princes from the now and future frogs, is being implanted, and several types of frogs and princes (or for the ladies, goose girls and princesses) are being set up. "Isn't He Amazing?," the Forever Prince with the success script, is often but not always the first-born. The Conditional Prince, "Come and See How Cute," or "Hurry Up," for example, can remain a prince as long as he stays cute or hurries up. The Conditional Frogs, "He Who Bites," "Naughty Naughty," or "He Looks Pale, Needs a Laxative," can stop being frogs by not biting or not looking pale; the Doomed Frogs, on the other hand, will hardly ever make it with anybody. Touching are the frogs who try not to care "While Mother Smokes" or "Has a Highball." Only a disaster can turn the Forever Princes into frogs; only a miracle can transform the Doomed Frogs into princes.

B · CONVICTIONS AND DECISIONS

By the time he gets to "I Guess I'd Better Drive You, Dear" or "Getcher Ass Outa Bed" or even "I'll Beatcher Goddam Brains Out If You Don't," the child already has certain convictions about himself and the people around him, especially his parents. These convictions are likely to stay with him the rest of his life, and may be summarized as follows: (1) I'm O.K. or; (2) I'm not-O.K.; (3) You're O.K. or; (4) You're not-O.K. On the basis of these he makes his life decision. "It's a good world, some day I'll make it a better one"—through science, service, poetry, or music. "It's a bad world, someday I'll kill myself"—or kill someone else, go crazy, or withdraw. Perhaps it's a mediocre world, where you do what you have to do and have fun in between; or a tough world, where you make good by putting on a white collar and shuffling other people's papers; or a hard world, where you sweep or bend or deal, or wiggle or fight for a living; or a dreary world, where you sit in a bar hoping; or a futile world, where you give up.

C · POSITIONS—THE PRONOUNS

Whatever the decision is, it can be justified by taking a position based on the now deeply ingrained convictions, a position which involves a view of the whole world and all the people in it, who are either friends or enemies: "I'll kill myself because it's a lousy world where I'm no good and neither is anyone else, my friends are not much better than my enemies." In position language this reads "I'm not-O.K., You're not-O.K., They're not-O.K. Who wouldn't kill himself under such conditions?" This is a futility suicide. Alternatively, "I'll kill myself because I'm not-O.K. and everybody else is O.K."—the melancholic suicide. (Suicide here can mean anything from jumping off a bridge or car-crashing, to overeating or alcoholism.) Or "I'll kill them or turn them out because I'm O.K. and they are very not-O.K." Or "Since we're all O.K., I and you both, let's get the job done and then go out and have some fun."

"But," says someone, "I know we're O.K., but those other fellows aren't so hot." "Very well, then, I'm O.K., you're O.K., and they are not-O.K., so let's get the job done now and we'll attend to them later." In child language, this translates as "We're going to play house, but you can't play with us," which in its most extreme form and with more sophisticated equipment can be parlayed in later years into an extermination camp.

The simplest positions are two-handed, You and I, and come from the convictions which have been fed to the child with his mother's milk. Writing as shorthand + for O.K. and — for not-O.K., the convictions read: I + or I —; You + or You —. The possible assortments of these give the four basic positions from which games and scripts are played, and which program the person so that he has something to say after he says Hello.

1. I + You +. This is the "healthy" position (or in treatment, the "get well" one), the best one for decent living, the position of genuine heroes and princes, and heroines and princesses. People in the other positions have more or less frog in them, a losing streak put there by their parents, which will drag them down again and again unless they overcome it; in extreme cases they will waste themselves if they are not rescued by a miracle of psychiatric or self-healing. I + You + is what the hippies were trying to tell the policeman when they gave him a flower. But whether the I + is genuine or merely a pious hope, and whether the policeman will accept the + or will prefer to be — on this particular scene, is always in doubt. I + You + is something the person either grows into in early life, or must learn by hard labor thereafter; it cannot be attained merely by an act of will.

2. I + You —. I'm a prince, you're a frog. This is the "get rid of" position. These are the people who play "Blemish" as a pastime, a game, or a deadly procedure. They are the ones who sneer at their spouses, send their children to juvenile hall, and fire their friends and retainers. They start crusades and sometimes wars, and sit in groups finding fault with their real or imagined inferiors or enemies. This is the "arrogant" position, at worst a killer's, and at best a meddler's for people who make it their business to help the "not-O.K. others" with things they don't want to be helped with. But for the most part it is a position of mediocrities, and clinically it is paranoid.

3. I — You +. This is psychologically the "depressive" position, politically and socially a self-abasement transmitted to the children. Occupationally, it leads people to live by choice on favors large and small and enjoy it with a vengeance, that being the poor

satisfaction of making the other pay as much as possible for his O.K. stamp. These are melancholic suicides, losers who call themselves gamblers, people who get rid of themselves instead of others by isolating themselves in obscure rooming houses or canyons or by getting a ticket to prison or the psychiatric ward. It is the position of the "If Onlys" and "I Should Haves."

4. I — You —. This is the "futility" position of the Why Notters: Why not kill yourself, Why not go crazy. Clinically, it is schizoid or schizophrenic.[1]

These positions are universal among all mankind, because all mankind nurses at his mother's breast or bottle and gets the message there, and later has it reinforced when he learns his manners, whether in the jungle, the slum, the condominium, or the ancestral halls. Even in the small unlettered communities which anthropologists study for their "cultures," where everyone is raised according to the same long-established rules, there are enough individual differences between mothers (and fathers) to yield the standard harvest. For winners, there are chiefs and medicine men, captains and capitalists who own a thousand head of cattle or are worth a hundred thousand yams. The losers can be found in the mental hospital at Papeete or Port Moresby or Dakar, or perhaps in Her Majesty's Gaol at Suva. For each position already carries with it its own kind of script and its own kinds of endings. Even in this country, where there are ten thousand "cultures," there are only a few endings, none different, really, from any other country's.

Because each person is the product of a million different moments, a thousand states of mind, a hundred adventures, and usually two different parents, a thorough investigation of his position will reveal many complexities and apparent contradictions. Nevertheless, there can usually be detected one basic position, sincere or insincere, inflexible or insecure, on which his life is staked, and from which he plays out his games and script. This is necessary so that he can feel that he has both feet on solid ground, and he will be as loath to give it up as he would the foundation of his house. To take one simple example, a woman who thinks it

very important that she is poor while others are rich
(I — They +) will not give this up merely because
she acquires a lot of money. That does not make her
rich in her own estimation; it merely makes her a poor
person who happens to have some assets. Her classmate
who thinks it is important to be rich in contrast to the
underprivileged poor (I + They —) will not abandon
her position if she loses her money; this does not make
her a poor person, but merely a rich person who is
temporarily embarrassed financially.

This tenacity, as we shall see later, accounts for the
life led by Cinderella after she married her prince, and
it also accounts for the fact that men in the first position (I + You +) make good leaders, for even in
utmost adversity they maintain their universal respect
for themselves and those in their charge. Thus the four
basic positions, (1) I + You + (success); (2) I +
You — (arrogant); (3) I — You + (depressive);
and (4) I — You — (futility), can rarely be changed
by external circumstances alone. Stable changes must
come from within, either spontaneously or under some
sort of "therapeutic" influence: professional treatment,
or love, which is nature's psychotherapy.

But there are those whose convictions lack conviction, so that they have options and alternations between
one position and another; from I + You + to I —
You —, or from I + You — to I — You +, for
example. These are, as far as position is concerned, insecure or unstable personalities. Secure or stable ones
are those whose positions, good or deplorable, cannot
be shaken. In order for the idea of positions to be of
any practical use, it must not be defeated by the
changes and instabilities of the insecure. The transactional approach—finding out what was actually said
and done at a certain moment—takes care of that. If
A behaves at noon as though he were in the first position (I + You +), then we say that "A is in the
first position." If he behaves at 6:00 P.M. as though
he were in the third position (I — You +), then
we say "In the noon setup A is in the first position
and under 6:00 P.M. circumstances he is in the third."
From this we can conclude (1) that A is insecure in

the first position, and (2) that if he has symptoms they occur under special conditions. If he behaves under all circumstances as though he were in the first position, then we say that "A is stable in the first position," from which we predict (1) that A is a winner, (2) that if he has been in treatment, he is now cured, and (3) that he is game free, or at least that he is not under a compulsion to play games, but has social control—the option of deciding for himself at each moment whether or not he wants to play. If B behaves under all circumstances as though he were in the fourth position, we say that "B is stable in the fourth position" from which we predict (1) that B is a loser, (2) that it will be difficult to cure him, and (3) that he will be unable to stop himself from playing those games which prove that life is futile. All this is done by careful analysis of actual transactions engaged in by A and B.

Once the predictions are made, they are easily tested by more observation. If later behavior does not confirm them, then either the analysis was faulty or the theory of positions is wrong and will have to be changed. If it does confirm the predictions, then the theory is strengthened. The evidence so far supports it.

D · WINNERS AND LOSERS

In order to verify predictions, it is necessary to define success, that is, winners and losers. A winner is someone who succeeds in what he says he is going to do. A loser is someone who fails to accomplish what he sets out to do. A man who says: "I'm going to Reno and gamble," is only committed to getting there and betting, regardless of whether he wins or loses. If he says: "I'm going to Reno and this time I'm going to win," then he comes out a winner if he wins and a loser if he doesn't, depending upon how much money he has in his pockets when he gets back on the pavement. A woman who gets a divorce is not a loser unless she has said "I will never get a divorce." If she has declared: "Some day I'm going to quit my job and I'll never work again," then her alimony will signify that she is a winner, because she has accomplished what she set out to do. Since she made no statement as to how she would do it, no one can fault her with being a loser.

E · THREE-HANDED POSITIONS

So far we have dealt mainly with two-handed positions, "I" and "You." But the idea of position is like an accordion, and can expand enough to include a vast assortment of attitudes besides the basic four, almost as many different ones as there are people in the world. Thus, if we move on to consider three-handed positions, we have the following combinations:

1a. I + You + They +. This is the democratic community position of a neighborly family, a sort of ideal to be striven for in the eyes of many people, stated as "We love everybody."

1b. I + You + They —. This is the prejudiced snob- or gang-position of a demagogue, stated as "Who needs them?"

2a. I + You — They +. This is the position of the agitator or malcontent, and sometimes of missionaries of various kinds. "You people here are no good compared to the ones over there."

2b. I + You — They —. This is the position of the solitary, self-righteous critic, the arrogant position in pure form. "Everybody must bow before me and be as much like me as inferior people can."

3a. I — You + They +. This is the self-punishing saint or masochist, the melancholic position in pure form. "I am the most unworthy person in the world."

3b. I — You + They —. This is the servile position of people who choose to work for gratuities out of snobbishness rather than necessity. "I abased myself and you rewarded me well, not like those other inferior ones."

4a. I — You — They +. This is the position of

servile envy, and sometimes of political action. "They hate us because we are not as well off."

4b. I — You — They —. This is the pessimistic position of cynics or of those who believe in predestination and original sin. "We are none of us any good anywhere."

There are also three-handed positions which are insecure, and some which are flexible and give the other fellow a chance. For example:

1? I + You + They ? This is an evangelistic position. "I and you are O.K., but we don't know about them until they show their credentials or come over to our side."

2? I + You ? They —. This is an aristocratic class position. "Most other people are no good, but as for you, I'll wait until I see your credentials."

Thus we have four two-handed positions and eight three-handed ones, twelve in all, with a mathematical possibility of an equal number of flexible ones with one ?, six more with two ?? (I + You ? They ?, I — You ? They ?, etc.) and one with three ???, the last a person who would find it difficult to function in relation to other people. This gives a total of thirty-one possible types, quite enough to make life interesting. This variety is enormously multiplied when we start to consider the meanings of the +s and —s, which stand, we remember, for O.K. and not-O.K. Here we are immediately confronted with pairs of good-bad adjectives, qualities or combinations which were emphasized in the family, and which fill out the formulas and give them real-life meanings.

F · POSITIONS—THE PREDICATES

The simplest positions, the most difficult to deal with, and the most dangerous for society, are those which are based on a single pair of O.K.-not-O.K. adjectives: Black-White, Rich-Poor, Christian-Pagan, Bright-Stupid, Jew-Aryan, Honest-Crooked. Each of these pairs can be sorted in four ways, any one of which may be emphasized in a given family and set for life by early training. Thus, the Rich-Poor polarity sorts into four variants, depending on parental attitudes.

1. I Rich=O.K., You Poor=not-O.K. (Snobbish, Supercilious)

2. I Rich=not-O.K., You Poor=O.K. (Rebellious, Romantic)

3. I Poor=O.K., You Rich=not-O.K. (Resentful, Revolutionary)

4. I Poor=not-O.K., You Rich=O.K. (Snobbish, Servile)

(In a family where money is not a decisive standard, then Rich-Poor is not a polarity, and the above schedule does not apply.)

The more adjectives included in each + and —, the more complex and flexible the position becomes, and the more intelligence and discrimination is required to deal with it securely. Sets of adjectives may be added together for emphasis (not only, but also), subtracted from each other for softening (but at least he also), weighed for fairness (but which is more important?), and so on. Thus to some black people, Rich Crooked White may be very not-O.K. (he's all bad — — —) compared to Rich Crooked Black (at least he's Black — — +), or to Rich Honest White (at least he's honest — + —), or to Poor Crooked White (at least he's poor like us + — —). But in some cases, Crooked White may be worst of all if he is Poor, but tolerable if he is Rich. This is because of the intrusion of another pair: Gets Away with it +, Doesn't Get Away with it —. In this case, Poor Crooked White gets — — —, while Rich Crooked White gets + — —. In other cases, there may be a condition, as when Rich White (the Finance Company) may be O.K. unless he's Crooked, and then he is shifted to not-O.K. (+ + + → + + —).

It appears that his particular selection of pronouns, I, You, and They, + or — or ?, determines the ultimate fate of the individual, including the end of his script, regardless of what adjectives or predicates he uses for + and —. Thus I + You — They — (2b) will almost always end up alone, perhaps in a hermitage, prison, state hospital, or morgue, no matter what he is supercilious about: religion, money, race, sex, etc., while I — You + They + (3a) will nearly always end up feeling miserable and perhaps suicidal no matter what particular qualities he feels unworthy about. Hence the pronouns decide the ending of the script, the winners and the losers. The predicates decide what the script will be about, the life style: religion, money, race, sex, etc., but have nothing to do with the outcome.

It must be admitted that there is nothing in all this so far which cannot be understood by a six-year-old child, at least as far as it applies to himself. "My mommy says I'm not supposed to play with you because you're (dirty, common, bad, Catholic, Jewish, Italian, Irish, etc.)", is simply I + You —. "I'll play with you but I don't want to play with him because he cheats" is I + You + He —, to which the excluded one responds: "I wouldn't play with you guys anyway because you're sissies," = I + You — He —. It takes a great deal of sophistication, however—more than most people have—to understand the key principle of positions: the pronouns and the signs (+ —) are the only things that count; the predicates or adjectives are just there for convenience in structuring time. The predicates merely give people something to talk about after they say Hello, but have no bearing on what is going to happen, how well or badly their lives will be conducted, or what their final payoffs will be.

For example, many people are unable to understand how ardent Nazi policemen in East Germany could become equally ardent Communist policemen, since the two parties seem directly opposed. But all that is opposed are adjectives. The Nazi position was I + (Nazi), He — (Traitor), therefore, kill him. The Communist position is I + (Communist), He — (Traitor), therefore, kill him. In both cases, although the predicates are contrary, the position is the same: I + He —, therefore, kill him. The rule is that a change in predicates, no matter how radical, does not change the position, or the script: in both cases, the person will end up a killer, and that is what is important to him, not what kind of people he kills. For this reason nothing is easier then for a fanatic, under proper guidance, to change sides.

This example also illustrates the fact that positions are very important in everyday social encounters. The first things people sense about each other are their positions, and here, for the most part, like attracts like. People who think well of themselves and the world (+ +) usually prefer to be with others of their kind, rather than with people who are going to complain. People who feel superior (+ −) also like to congregate together in clubs and organizations. And if misery loves company, then people who feel inferior (− +) will also get together, usually in not-O.K. bars. The ones who feel futile (− −) gather in coffee-houses or on the street to deride the squares. In Western countries, clothing indicates like position even more clearly than it does social position. + + dresses neatly but not gaudily; + − likes uniforms, decorations, jewels, and special designs which flaunt his or her superiority; − + is threadbare or negligent, but not necessarily sloppy, or he may wear an "inferior" uniform; while − − tends to wear a "fuck you" uniform which shows his disdain of clothes and all that they stand for. The schizophrenic uniform, which combines threadbare with elegant, lumpy with svelte, purple with gray, the scuffed shoes with the diamond ring, falls into this class.

We have already mentioned the tenacity with which people cling to their positions when circumstances change—the rich woman who does not become poor if she loses her money, but remains a rich person who is merely embarrassed financially; or even more poignant, the poor girl who gets a lot of money, but does not thereby become rich. This fixity of position can come out in everyday life in a way that is exasperating and confusing: "I'm a good person (in spite of the fact that I do bad things)." Someone who takes this position expects to be treated at all times as though he were good, and feels insulted if he is regarded otherwise.

This is a common source of marital strife. Thus Marty Collins insists that he is a good husband in spite of the fact that he beats his wife every Saturday night when he is drunk. What is even more astounding is that his wife, Scottie, supports him, with the famous protest: "How can you be mad at a man who sent you flowers last Christmas?" On the other hand, Scottie is firmly convinced that she is a completely honest person, even though she lies openly and steals money from her husband's wallet. And he supports her in her position during the week. It is only on Saturday night that she calls him a bum and he calls her a liar. Since the marriage is based on a bilateral contract to overlook the discrepancies, each of them is indignant when the lapses are brought up, and if the threat to the O.K. position is too great, a divorce will result. The divorce happens because (1) one spouse can't stand being exposed, or (2) the other spouse can't stand the bald-faced lying that is necessary to avoid exposure.

G · SELECTION OF THE SCRIPT

The next step in the development of the script is to find a plot with the proper ending, an answer to the question: "What happens to someone like me?" The child knows, because he is so taught, whether he is going to be a winner or a loser, how he is supposed to feel about other people, and how other people are going to treat him, and that is what is meant by "someone like me." Sooner or later he hears a story about "someone like me," and that tells him what he is headed for. It may be a fairy tale read to him by his mother, an African Nancy story told to him by his grandmother, or a street-gang legend he hears on the corner. But wherever he hears it, when he hears it he knows it, and he says: "That's me!" That story will then be his script and he will spend the rest of his life trying to make it come to pass.

Thus, on the basis of early experience with the breast or the bottle, in the bathroom or outhouse, in the bedroom and kitchen and living room, the child acquires his convictions, makes his decision, and takes his position. Then from what he hears and reads, he chooses a prediction and a plan: how he will go about being a winner or a loser, on what grounds, and what the payoff will be; and that is the first clear version of his lifelong script. We are now ready to consider various forces and elements from which the script is constructed. In order to accomplish this he has to have a script apparatus to work with.

REFERENCES

1 See Berne, E. "Classification of Positions." *Transactional Analysis Bulletin* 1:23, July 1962, and *Principles of Group Treatment. Loc. cit.,* pp. 269–277. Compare Harris, T. *I'm OK—You're OK, A Practical Guide to Transactional Analysis.* Harper & Row, New York, 1969. Harris, however, numbers the positions in a different order. Our 1 is his 4, our 2 his 3, our 3 his 1, and our 4 his 2: 4-3-1-2.

CHAPTER SIX

The Plastic Years

A · PARENTAL PROGRAMING

By the time he is six, our typical human being has left kindergarten (in America at least), and is pushed into the more competitive world of first grade. There he will be on his own to deal with teachers and the other boys and girls. Fortunately by this time he is no longer a babe, thrust helpless into a world he never made. From the little suburb of his home, he ventures into the great metropolis of the bustling school with whole sets of social responses ready to offer the various kinds of people around him. His mind is all wired up with his own ways of getting along, or at least of surviving, and his life plan has already been made. This was well known to priests and teachers of the Middle Ages, who said: "Give me a child until he is six, and you can have him thereafter." A good kindergarten teacher can even predict what the outcome will be, and what kind of life the child will have: happy or unhappy, winning or losing.

Thus the comedy or tragedy of each human life is that it is planned by an urchin of pre-school age, who has a very limited knowledge of the world and its ways, and whose heart is filled mainly with stuff put there by his parents. Yet this wonder child is precisely who determines in the long run what will happen to kings and peasants and whores and queens. He has no way to tell the facts from the delusions, and the most everyday events are distorted. He is told that if he has sex before marriage he will be punished and that if he has sex after marriage he will not be punished. He believes that the sun sets, and it takes him ten or forty years to discover that he is running away from the sun; and he confuses his belly with his stomach. He is much too young to be deciding much beyond what he wants for dinner, but he is the Emperor of Life who determines how each person will die.

The plan he makes for the eternal future is drawn to the family specification. Some of the key ones can often be uncovered very quickly, perhaps in the first interview, by asking: "What did your parents tell you when you were very little?" or "What did your parents tell you about life when you were little?" or "What did your parents say to you when they were angry?" Often the answer will not sound like a directive, but with a little Martian thinking it can be stated in that form.

For example, many of the training slogans mentioned at the beginning of Chapter Five are actually parental commands. "Public Performance" is, in effect, a command to show off. The child soon learns that by observing his mother's pleasure when he does and her disappointment when he fails to do so. Similarly "Come and See How Cute" means "Put on a good show!" "Hurry Up" and "You Can Just Sit There Till You Do" are negative commands or injunctions: "Don't keep me waiting!" and "Don't talk back!" "Let Him Take His Time," however, is a license of permission. He understands these differences first from his parents' reactions, and later, when he has vocabulary, from their actual words.

The child is born free, but he soon learns different. During the first two years he is programed mainly by his mother. This program forms the original skeleton, or anlage, of his script, the "primal protocol," at first concerned with swallowing or being swallowed, and then, when he gets teeth, with tearing or being torn. It is being a hammer or being an anvil, as Goethe put it, the most primitive versions of being a winner or being a loser, as seen in Greek myths and Primal Rituals, where children are devoured and the limbs of the poet lie scattered on the ground. Even in the nursery, it is often already apparent who is in control, the mother or the baby. This may be reversed sooner or later, but echoes of the original situation can still be heard in times of stress or temper. But very few people can remember anything from this period, which in many ways is the most important, so it has to be reconstructed with the help of parents, relatives, nursemaids, and pediatricians, conjectures made about dreams, and perhaps the family album.

From two to six the ground is firmer, because nearly everyone remembers a few transactions, incidents, or impressions from that phase of script development, which parallels and is closely connected with the progress of the Oedipus complex. In fact, after weaning and toilet training, the directives which are most universal throughout the world and have the most lasting effects are those concerned with sexuality and aggression. The organism and the species survive by means of circuits which have been built in by natural selection. Since nursing, sex, and fighting require the presence of another person, they are "social" activities. These urges give character or quality to the individual: acquisitiveness, maleness and femaleness, and aggressiveness. Also built in are circuits which tone down such urges. These give rise to the opposite tendencies: renunciation, reticence, and restraint. Those qualities enable people to live together at least part of the time in reasonable tranquillity, a dull roar of competition rather than an unmitigated and unremitting bedlam of grabbing, copulation, and fighting. And in some way which is not clear, excretion becomes mixed up in this system of socialization, and the circuits built in for its control give rise to qualities of orderliness.

Parental programing determines how and when the urges are expressed, and how and when the restraints are imposed. It uses the circuits which are already built in, and sets them up in a certain way in order to get certain results or payoffs. As a result of this programing, new qualities emerge, which are compromises between urges and controls. From acquisitiveness and renunciation emerge patience; from maleness or femaleness and reticence emerge masculinity and femininity; from fighting and restraint emerge shrewdness, and from messiness and orderliness come tidiness. All these qualities: patience, masculinity and femininity, shrewdness, and tidiness are taught by the parents and programed in during the plastic years between two and six.

Physiologically, programing means facilitation, the establishment of a path of lessened resistance. Operationally, it means that a given stimulus will evoke, with a high degree of probability, an already established response. Phenomenologically, parental programing means that a response is determined by parental directives, sound tracks previously recorded, whose voices can be heard by listening carefully to what goes on inside one's own head.

B · THINKING MARTIAN

When parents interfere with or try to influence their children's free expression, their directives are interpreted differently by the parent, the onlookers, and the child himself. In fact there are five different viewpoints. (1) What the parent says he meant. (2) What a naive onlooker thinks he meant. (3) The literal meaning of what was said. (4) What the parent "really" meant. (5) What the child gets out of it. The first two are "square" or "Earthian," and the last three are "real" or Martian.

BUTCH

Let us consider the example of a high school boy who was a heavy drinker. His mother caught him sniffing the whiskey bottle at the age of six and said: "You're too young to be drinking whiskey."

(1) What the mother says she meant was: "I don't want my son drinking whiskey." (2) A naive onlooker, his uncle, concurred: "Of course she doesn't want the kid drinking whiskey. No sensible mother would." (3) What she actually said was: *"You're too young* to be drinking whiskey." (4) And that is what she meant: "Drinking whiskey is a man's job, and you're still a boy." (5) What Butch got out of it was: "When the

time comes to prove you're a man, you'll have to drink whiskey."

Thus, to an Earthian, the mother's rebuke sounded like "common sense." But children think Martian until they are discouraged from doing it by their parents. That is why their uncorrupted thoughts seem so fresh and new. A child's job is to find out what his parents really mean. This helps to maintain their love, or at least their protection, or in difficult cases, his mere survival. But beyond that, he loves his parents, and his chief aim in life is to please them (if they will let him), and in order to do that he has to know what they really want.

Hence, from each directive, however indirectly it is put he tries to extract the imperative essence or the Martian core. In this way he programs his life plan. Cats and pigeons can do it too, although it takes them longer. It is called programing because the effects of the directives are likely to be permanent. For the child, his parents' wish is his command, and will remain so for the rest of his life unless some drastic upheaval occurs. Only ordeal (war, prison) or ecstasy (conversion, love) can release him quickly, while life experience or psychotherapy may do it more slowly. The death of the parents does not always lift the spell; in most cases it only makes it more binding. As long as his Child is adapted rather than free, no matter what miserable tasks his Parent demands, the "script-driven" person will perform them, and no matter what sacrifices are required, the "script-ridden" one will make them. The parallel with the pimp and the prostitute is striking. She would rather be exploited and suffer with him, and get whatever satisfactions she can out of that, than venture into the unknown world without his protection.

Martian translates words into their true meanings according to their results, and judges people not according to their apparent intent, but from the "final display." Thus, many seemly parental protections are really unseemly assignments. A teen-age boy had bad luck with his car and ran up repair bills which distressed his father. The "good" father "communicated" with him from time to time on the subject, and on one occasion graciously grumped: "Well, it is tough on me, but don't worry too much about it." This genteel generosity was naturally taken by the son to mean: "Do worry some." But if the boy said he was worrying or did something unusual to try to remedy the situation, the father could rebuke him by saying "I told you not to worry *too much.*" The Martian translation of the "nice" attitude: "Don't worry too much!" is, "Keep worrying until I can tell you you are worrying too much."

An even more dramatic example concerns a skillful waitress who was able to maneuver between the tables and hurly-burly of a busy and crowded restaurant with her hands and arms loaded with plates of hot food. Her surefootedness excited the admiration of both the management and the customers. Then one day her parents came to eat there and admire her in their turn. When she flitted past their table with her customary load, her overly apprehensive mother cried: "Be careful!" whereupon for the first time in her career, the girl . . . Well, even the most Earthian reader can finish the story without a translation. In short, "Be careful!" too often means: "Make a mistake so I can tell you I told you to be careful," and that is the final display. "Be careful, ha ha!" is even more of a provocation. As a straight Adult instruction "Be careful!" may have some value, but Parental overconcern or a Child Ha Ha gives it a different turn.

In Butch's case, "You're too young to be drinking!" from a crapulent mother meant "Hurry up and start drinking so I can object," and that was the final display of that maneuver. Butch knew what he had to do sooner or later if he wanted his mother's reluctant attention, her poor substitute for love. Her wish, as he interpreted it, became his mission. He had a good example in his hard-working father, who drank heavily on weekends. By the time he was sixteen, Butch was getting drunk regularly. When he was seventeen, his uncle sat him down at a table with a bottle of whiskey between them and said: "Butch, I'm going to teach you how to drink."

His father used to say to him with a contemptuous smile: "You're so stupid." That was about the only time his father ever spoke to him, so Butch decided early that the thing to do was act stupid—another example of the value of Martian thinking, since his father made it clear that he didn't want any "smart asses" around the house. What he was really saying was: "You'd better act stupid when I'm around here," and Butch knew it. So much for Martian.

Many children are brought up in families where the father works hard and drinks hard. Working hard is a prescription for filling in time between drinks. But drinking can interfere with work, and drink is the curse of the working class. On the other hand, work interferes with drinking, and work is the curse of the drinking class. Drinking and working run counter to each other. If drinking is part of a life plan or script, then working is a counterscript.

Butch's script directives are shown in the "script matrix"[1] in Figure 6. On top, father's irritable Parent is saying: "Be a man, but don't act smart," while on the bottom his jeering Child is saying: "Act stupid, ha ha." On top, mother's doting Parent is saying: "Be a man,

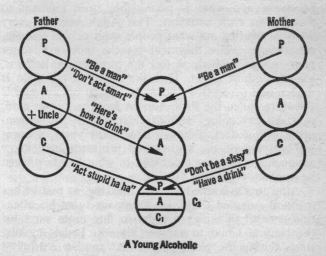

A Young Alcoholic

FIGURE 6

but you're too young yet," while on the bottom her Child is daring him: "Don't be a sissy, have a drink." In between, his father's Adult, with the help of his uncle, is showing him the proper way to drink.

C · THE LITTLE LAWYER

Martian thinking enables the child to find out what the parents "really" want, that is, what they will respond most favorably too. By using it effectively, he insures his survival and expresses his love for them. In this way he builds up the ego state known as the Adapted Child. The Adapted Child wants and needs to behave in an adapted way, and tries to avoid nonadaptive behavior or even nonadaptive feelings, which will get less than the best responses from those around him. Meanwhile his self-expressive or Natural Child must be held in leash. The balance between the two forms of behavior is held by the Adult in the child (AC in Figure 7, p. 116), which must behave like an exceedingly agile computer in order to decide what is necessary and what is permissible from moment to moment in each situation. This Adult becomes very adept at figuring out what people want or will tolerate, or at worst, what they will get the most excited or angry about, or perhaps feel the most guilty, helpless, scared, or hurt about. Thus the Adult in the child is a keen and perceptive student of human nature, and is therefore called the Professor. In fact, he knows more practical psychology and psychiatry than any grown-up professor does, although after many years of training and experience, a grown-up professor may know as much as thirty-three per cent of what he knew when he was four years old.

After he has learned Martian thinking, so that he has a sound Adapted Child, the Professor turns his attention to legal thinking, in order to find more ways for the Natural Child to express himself. Legal thinking starts during the plastic years, but reaches its fullest development in later childhood, and if encouraged by the parents may persist into maturity, giving rise to lawyers. Legal thinking is colloquially called cop-out thinking.* Cop out thinking is particularly common in personal sexual ethics. Thus a girl who is instructed by her parents not to lose her virginity may have mutual masturbation, or perform fellatio or a variety of other sexual acts which enable her to obey the letter of the parental law, although she may know that the parents "really meant" not to get sexy. If the parents warn her against "sex," she may have intercourse without orgasm. The classical sexual cop-out was that used by the prostitutes of Paris at the beginning of this century. (It may still be used, for all I know.) When they went to confession they were excused for their profession on the grounds that it was a matter of business, providing they didn't get turned on. Only if they enjoyed it was it treated as a sin.[2]

What parents do is give a prohibition which they think will cover the situation, not giving enough credit to the shrewdness which they themselves have usually taught to their offspring. Thus a boy who is told "Don't mess around with women" may take this as a permission to mess around with other boys, or in some cases with sheep or cows, and in a legal way of thinking he is in the clear, since he is not doing anything his parents have forbidden. A girl who was told "Don't let boys touch you," decided that meant it was all right to touch herself. By this cop-out her Adapted Child remained compliant to her mother's wishes, while her Natural Child enjoyed the pleasures of masturbation. A boy who was similarly told "Don't fool around with girls," took this as a permission to fool around with himself. Neither of these people was actually breaking a parental prohibition. Because the child treats such restrictions as a lawyer would, looking for the cop-out, they are often called in script analysis by the legal term "injunction."

Some children enjoy being compliant and do not look for cop-outs. Others have more interesting things to

---

*"Cop-out" has several meanings: to arrest, to settle for a lesser, sentence ("cop a plea"), to talk too much ("fink out"), and to find an alibi or a crooked way out. It is used here in the last sense.

do. But just as many people devote themselves to the problem of how to transgress without breaking the law, so many children are interested in the question of how to be naughty without actually disobeying their parents. In both cases, this kind of shrewdness is taught and encouraged by the parents themsleves, and is part of the parental programing. In some cases this may result in the formation of an antiscript, whereby the child succeeds in reversing the whole intent of the script, without actually disobeying any of the original script directions.

D · THE SCRIPT APPARATUS

Transactional analysts did not start out with the idea that human life plans are constructed like myths and fairy tales. They simply observed that childhood decisions, rather than grown-up planning, seemed to determine the individual's ultimate destiny. No matter what people thought or said they were doing with their lives, they seemed driven by some inner compulsion to strive for a final payoff that was often different from what they put down in their autobiographies or employment resumés. Many who said they wanted to make money lost it, while all around them others were growing rich. Some who claimed to be seeking love found hate even in the ones who loved them. Parents who declared they did everything to make their children happy ended up with addicts, convicts, and suicides. Righteous Bible students committed murders and child rapes. These were the contradictions which had existed since the beginning of the human race; they were the ones that operas sang about and that sold newspapers.

It gradually became clear that while none of this made Adult sense, it did make sense to the Child part of the personality. That was the part that liked myths and fairy tales, and believed that that was the way the world once was or could be. It was not surprising, therefore, to find that when children planned their lives they often followed the plot of a favorite story. The real surprise was that these plans persisted for twenty, forty,

or eighty years, and that in the end they usually prevailed over "common sense." Working backward from
a suicide, car crash, delirium tremens, jail sentence, or
divorce, and ignoring the "diagnosis" to find out what
really happened, soon showed that these outcomes were
nearly all planned before the age of six.[3] The plans or
scripts had certain elements in common, which formed
a "script apparatus." The same apparatus seemed to be
at work in good scripts: creators, leaders, heroes, vener-
able grandfathers, and people eminent in their professions. This apparatus had to do with how the life time
was structured, and turned out to be the same as the
apparatus used in fairy tales for that purpose.

In such stories, the programing is done by giants and
giantesses, ogres and witches, fairy godmothers and
grateful beasts, and sulky magicians of either sex. In
real life all these parts are played by the parents.

Psychotherapists know more about "bad" scripts than
about "good" ones because they are more dramatic and
people spend more time talking about them. Freud, for
example, cites innumerable case histories of losers, and
about the only winners in his works are Moses, Leonardo da Vinci, and himself. Only a few winners bother
to find out how they got that way, while losers are often
very anxious to know so that they can do something
about it. In the following sections, therefore, we will
deal first with losing scripts, where our knowledge is
quite precise. There, the script apparatus consists of
the following items, translated by the child into Martian
imperatives.

1. The parents tell the child how to end his life.
"Get lost!" and "Drop dead!" are death decrees. So is
"Die rich." "You'll end up like your (alcoholic) father," is a life sentence. Such a command is called the
script payoff, or curse.

2. They then give him an unfair negative command
that will keep him from lifting the curse: "Don't bother
me!" or "Don't act smart!" (= Get lost!) or "Stop
complaining!" (= Drop dead!"). This is the script injunction or stopper. Injunctions are given by a Controlling Parent or a crazy Child ego state.

3. They encourage behavior that will lead into the

payoff: "Have a drink!" or "You aren't going to let him get away with that!" This is called the script provocation, or come-on. It comes from a mischievous Child ego state, or demon, in the parent, and is usually accompanied by a "ha ha."

4. They also give him a prescription for filling in time while waiting for the action. This is in the form of a moral precept. "Work hard!" may mean "Work hard all week so you can get drunk on Saturday night." "Take care of every penny!" may mean "Take care of every penny so you can lose it all at once." This is the antiscript slogan, and comes from a nurturing Parent ego state.

5. In addition, they teach him what he has to know in real life to carry out the script: how to mix drinks, how to keep books, how to cheat. This is the pattern or program, a form of Adult instruction.

6. The child, on his part, has urges and impulses which fight the whole script apparatus that is laid on him by his parents. "Knock on the door!" (*vs.* Get lost), "Act smart!" "Take off!" (*vs.* Work hard), "Spend it all now!" (*vs.* Save every penny), "Do it wrong." These are called scripty impulses, or the demon.

7. Tucked away somewhere is a way to lift the curse. "You can succeed after you're forty." This spellbreaker is called the antiscript or internal release. But often the only antiscript is death. "You'll get your reward in heaven."

Exactly the same apparatus for structuring time is found in myths and fairy tales. The payoff or curse: "Get lost!" (Hansel and Gretel) or "Drop dead!" (Snow White and Sleeping Beauty). The injunction or stopper: "Don't be too curious!" (Adam and Eve, Pandora). The provocation or come-on: "Prick your finger with a spindle, ha ha." (Sleeping Beauty). The counterscript slogan: "Work hard until you meet the prince!" (Kari Woodengown), or "Be nice until she says she loves you!" (Beauty and the Beast). The pattern or program: "Be kind to animals and they'll help you in time of need." (Pretty Goldilocks). The impulse or demon: "I'll take just one look!" (Bluebeard). The antiscript or spellbreaker: "You can stop being a frog when she throws you against the wall." (The Frog Prince), or "You'll be free after twelve years of labor." (Hercules).

This is the anatomy of the script apparatus. The curse, the stopper, and the come-on form the script controls, and the other four items can be used to fight them. But the child lives in a fairy-tale world, beautiful, mediocre, or gruesome, and believes mainly in magic. Thus he seeks a magic way out, through superstition and fantasies. When that doesn't work, he falls back on the demon.

But the demon has one peculiarity. When the demon in the child says "I'm going to defy you, ha ha!" the demon in the parent says "That's exactly what I want you to do, ha ha." Thus the script provocation and the scripty impulses, the come-on and the demon, work together to bring about the loser's doom. The parent wins when the child loses, and the child loses by trying to win. All of these elements will be considered in more detail in Chapter Seven.

NOTES & REFERENCES

1 The script matrix was first described by Claude M. Steiner. See his article "Script and Counterscript." *Transactional Analysis Bulletin* 5:133–135, April 1966. (Counterscript is his term for our "antiscript.") See also Steiner, C. M. *Games Alcoholics Play*. Grove Press, New York, 1972.

2 Philippe, C. L. *Bubu of Montparnasse* (with preface by T. S. Eliot). Berkeley Publishing Company, New York, 1957.

3 A few dozen scripts have been gone over in some detail at the San Francisco Transactional Analysis Seminars. These, and those worked out in my own practice, are the ones I am most closely acquainted with. Many other script analysts accept the principles given here on the basis of their own experience, which includes altogether perhaps a few thousand cases in hospitals, clinics, schools and prisons, and private practice too.

CHAPTER SEVEN

The Script Apparatus

In order to understand how the script works and how to deal with it in treatment, it is necessary to have a detailed knowledge of the script apparatus as we understand it today. There are still a few gaps in our insight into its basic framework, and some uncertainties about its transmission, but our model has developed into quite a sophisticated one in the short space of ten years since the first description was written.[1] At that time it was like the one-cylinder Duryea of 1893, while now it is like a rather advanced Model-T Ford.

Summarizing from the brief examples just given, the apparatus consists of seven items. The payoff or curse, the injunction or stopper, and the provocation or come-on, together control the unfolding of the script toward its destiny, and are therefore called the script controls. These are all programed in before the age of six in most cases. So is the antiscript or spellbreaker, if there is one. Later, the counterscript slogans or prescription, and the parental behavior patterns and instructions, begin to take firmer hold. The demon represents the most archaic layer of the personality (the Child in the child), and is there from the beginning.*

A · THE SCRIPT PAYOFF

The payoffs that come up in clinical practice can usually be reduced to four alternatives: be a loner, be a bum, go crazy, or drop dead. Drug or alcohol addiction is the pleasantest way to accomplish any of these.

---

*The reader is once more reminded that Parent, Adult, and Child, capitalized, refer to ego states, while parent, adult, and child, without capitals, refer to actual people.

The child may interpret the decree in Martian or legal thinking, which is often to his advantage. In one case, where the mother told all the children they would end up in the state hospital, they all did. The girls ended up as patients, and the boys as psychiatrists.

Violence is a special kind of payoff, and occurs in "tissue scripts." Tissue scripts are different from all others because their currency is human flesh, blood, and bones. It is probable that a child who has seen, caused, or suffered mayhem or bloodshed is different from other children and can never be the same again. If the parents turn the child out at an early age to fend for himself, he is naturally much concerned with money, and that often becomes the chief currency of his script and his payoff. If they berate him and tell him to drop dead, then words may become the script currency. The script currency must be distinguished from the script theme. The chief themes of life scripts are the same as those which are found in fairy tales: love, hate, gratitude, and revenge. Any of the currencies can be used to express any of these themes.

The main question for the script analyst here is: "In how many ways can a parent tell a child to live forever, or to drop dead?" He can say it quite literally, "Long life!" in a toast or a prayer, or "Drop dead!" in a quarrel. It is difficult to realize or admit the almost incredible power which a mother's words have over a child (or a wife's over a husband, and vice versa). In my experience, a considerable number of legitimate hospital admissions have taken place shortly after the patient was told by a loved one (or even a hated one) to drop dead.

In many cases it is a grandparent who controls these payoffs, either directly or through the parent. Grandmother may save the patient from a father's death decree by offering a "life membership" instead. Or she may give mother a Medea script (or "overscript"), which forces her to drive her children to their deaths in one way or another.

All this is fed into the Parent of the little boy or girl, and is likely to stay there for life: someone's gentle hope that he will live forever, or a harsh voice urging him closer to his death. Sometimes there is no animosity in the death decree, but just futility or despair. But since he drinks her wishes in from the day he is born, it is usually mother who makes the decision for him. Father may join or contradict her later: add his weight to her curse, or commute it.

Patients can usually remember their childhood responses to payoff directives, things they didn't say out loud.

Mother: "You're just like your father." (Who got a divorce and lives in a room by himself.) Son: Good. Smart guy, father.

Father: "You'll end up like your aunt." (Mother's sister, who is in a mental hospital or committed suicide.) Daughter: If you say so.

Mother: "Drop dead." Daughter: I don't want to, but if you say so I guess I have to.

Father: "With your temper, you'll kill somebody some day." Son: Well, if it can't be you, it'll be somebody else.

The child is very forgiving, and only makes his decision to follow the directive after dozens or even hundreds of such transactions. One girl from a very confused family, where she got no support from her parents, described very clearly the day she made her final decision. When she was thirteen, her brothers took her out in the barn and put her through all kinds of sexual stunts, which she went through in order to please them. After they finished, they began to laugh at her and talk about her. They decided that now she would either have to become a hooker or go crazy. She thought about it very carefully for the rest of the night, and by morning she had decided to go crazy, which she did very effectively, and stayed that way for years afterward. Her explanation was very simple. "I didn't want to be a hooker."

While the script payoff is bestowed or decreed by the parents, it will not take effect unless it is accepted by the child. His acceptance speech will not have the fanfare and finish of a Madison Avenue presidential inauguration, but he will say it as clearly as he dares at least once. "When I grow up, I'm going to be like mommy" (= get married and have children), or "When I'm big, I'm doing to do what daddy did" (= get killed in a war), or "I wish I was dead." The patient should be asked: "What did you decide to do with your life when you were little?" If he gives a conventional answer ("I wanted to be a fireman"), this should be clarified with: "What I mean is, how did you decide you would end up?" Since payoff decisions are often first made earlier than he can remember, he may not be able to give the desired answer, but it can be inferred from some of his later adventures.

B · THE INJUNCTION

Real-life injunctions do not take effect by magic, but depend upon the physiological properties of the human mind. It is not enough to say once "Don't eat those apples!" or "Don't open that chest!" Any Martian knows that an injunction given in that way is really a challenge. For an injunction to be locked in solidly in the mind of a child, it must be repeated frequently and transgressions must be punished, although there are exceptional cases, as with battered children, where a single shattering experience may engrave an injunction for life.

The injunction is the most important part of the script apparatus, and varies in intensity. Hence, injunctions can be classified in the same way as games, into first, second, and third degrees. There is a tendency for each type to produce its own kind of person: winner, nonwinner, or loser. (These terms will be explained in more detail later. A nonwinner is someone who neither wins nor loses, but just manages to come out even.) First-degree injunctions (socially acceptable and mild) are straight directives reinforced by approval or discouragement. ("You've been nice and quiet." "Don't be too ambitious.") With these it is still possible to grow a winner. Second-degree (devious and tough) are crooked directives crookedly enforced by a kind of blackmail of seductive smiles and threatening frowns, which is the best way to raise a nonwinner

("Don't tell your father." "Keep your mouth shut.") Third-degree (very rough and harsh) are unreasonable stoppers enforced by fear. Words become screams, facial expressions become nightmarish distortions, and physical chastisement becomes viciousness. ("I'll knock your goddam teeth in.") This is one of the surest ways to produce a loser.

The injunction, like the payoff, is complicated by the fact that most children have two parents. Thus one may say "Don't act smart!" and the other "Don't act stupid." Such contradictory injunctions put the child in a difficult position. But most people who marry have compatible injunctions, such as "Don't act smart!" and "Keep quiet or I'll knock your goddam brains out!" which make a sad combination.

Stoppers are implanted at such a tender age that the parents look like magical figures to the little boy or girl. The part of the mother who gives out injunctions (her Controlling Parent or Child) is called colloquially "the fairy godmother" if she is benevolent, or "the witch mother" if she is not. In some cases, "mother's crazy Child" seems the most suitable label. Similarly, the Controlling Father is called "the jolly green giant," "the ugly troll," or "father's crazy Child," whichever is appropriate.[2]

C · THE COME-ON

Provocation or seduction is what makes lechers, addicts, criminals, gamblers, and others with losing scripts. For a boy it is the real Odyssey scene of a living Ulysses, mother as a Siren luring him to his doom, or as Circe turning him into a swine. For a girl it is father as the Dirty Old Man. In early years it starts out as a general invitation to be a loser: "He sure is clumsy, ha ha," or "She sure is a shit walker, ha ha." Then it moves on to more specific jeers and teases. "He's always banging his head, ha ha," or "She's always losing her pants, ha ha." In adolescence it is promoted into personal transactions. "Take a good look, baby!" (and maybe an accidental or on-purpose feel), "Have a drink," "Now's your chance," "Throw it all in, what's the difference," each accompanied by its ha ha.

The come-on is the Parent's voice whispering to the Child at the critical moment: not to stop thinking about sex or money, not to let them get away with that. "Come on baby. What've you got to lose?" This is the demon in the Parent, and the demon in the Child responds. Then the Parent does a quick switch, and Jeder falls flat on his face. "There you go again," says the gleeful Parent, and Jeder answers "Ha ha!" with what is colloquially called "a shit-eating smile."

The come-on is what promotoes hang-ups in children, and for that it must start early. The parent takes the child's yen for closeness and turns it into a yen for something else. Once this perverted love is fixed, it becomes a hang-up.

D · THE ELECTRODE

The come-on originates from the Child in the father or the mother, and is inserted into the Parent of the child, PC in Jeder in Figure 7. There it acts like a "positive" electrode, giving an automatic response. When the Parent in his head (PC) pushes the button, Jeder jumps to it, whether the rest of him wants to or not. He says something stupid, acts clumsy, has another drink, or puts it all on the next race, ha ha ha. The origin of the injunctions is not always so clear, but they, too, are inserted into PC, where they act like a "negative" electrode. This keeps Jeder from doing certain things such as talking or thinking clearly, or turns him off if he comes on too strong, as with sex or smiling. Many people know the instantaneous turn-off in the midst of sexual excitement, and have observed the smile which turns on and then instantaneously off as though someone in the smiler's head had pulled a switch. Because of these effects, PC, the Parent in the Child, is called the "electrode."

The electrode got its name from a patient named Norvil who sat very still and very tense during his group sessions, unless he was spoken to. Then he answered instantly with a string of careful clichés ("Norvil finally said something, ha ha"), after which he crunched up again. It soon became clear that it was a strict Father Parent in his head who controlled him with the "Sit Still" turn-off switch, and the "Talk" button that turned him on. Norvil worked in an experimental laboratory, and he himself was struck with the similarity between his reactions and those of an animal with an electrode in its brain.

Origin and Insertion of the Script Injunctions

FIGURE 7

The electrode is the decisive challenge for the therapist. He, together with the patient's Adult, must neutralize it, so that the Child can get permission to live freely and react spontaneously, in the face of the parents' programing to the contrary, and their threats if he disobeys. This is difficult enough with milder controls, but if the injunction is a demand made by a witch or giant whose features are distorted with rage, whose voice smashes through all the defenses of the child's mind, and whose hand is ever ready to strike humiliation and terror into his face and head, it requires enormous therapeutic power.

E · BAGS AND THINGS

If a child is boxed in by contradictory controls, there may be only one way out which allows him some measure of self-expression. He is then forced into that kind of activity or response no matter how inappropriate it may be. In such a case it is often evident to the people around him that he is responding to what is in his head rather than to the external situation, and he is then said to be in a bag. If his bag is backed up by some talent or ability, and by a winning payoff command, it may be a winner's bag, but in most cases people in a bag are losers because their behavior is nonadaptive. A person who breaks out of a bag (or "container," as it is sometimes called) will immediately proceed to do his thing, that is, whatever he has always wanted most to do. If that happens to be adaptive and is controlled with some Adult rationality, he may turn out to be a winner, but if he indulges too often and too well, he will end up being a loser. In fact, when a person starts to do his thing, after he breaks out of his bag, his payoff command will determine whether he does it judiciously so as to be a winner, or overdoes it like a loser. In some cases, however, he may be able to leave his payoff command in the bag along with the rest of his parentally programed script apparatus, and then he is really his own man and can decide his own destiny. But it is difficult for Jeder to know, without the appraisal of an objective outsider, whether he is really a maverick or liberated person, or is only an angry rebel, or maybe even a schizophrenic who has jumped out of his bag and into a bottle, with or without pulling the cork in after him.

F · THE PRESCRIPTION

The "natural" Parent in the mother and father (as distinguished from the controlling Parent) is biologically programed to some extent, and is naturally nurturing and protective. Both parents, whatever their inner problems, fundamentally wish Jeder well. They may be badly informed, but as "natural" parents they are well meaning, or at least harmless. They encourage Jeder in ways which, in their picture of the world and their theory of living, are meant to bring him well-being and success. They transmit to him, usually from the grandparents, prescriptions which are often the epitome of Earthian squareness: "Work hard!" "Be a good girl!" "Save your money!" and "Always be on time!" are common middle-class examples. But each family has its specialty: "Don't eat starches!" "Never sit on a public toilet seat!" "Take a laxative every day!" or "Masturbation will drain your spinal cord!"[3] are examples of this. "Never draw to an inside straight!" is one of the best because it has a Zenlike quality; used symbolically as well as literally, it becomes good Martian and may come in handy at unexpected times.

Since the prescription comes from a nurturing Parent, and the script controls from a controlling Parent or a crazy Child, there is plenty of room for contradictions. These are of two types, internal and external. An internal contradiction comes from two different ego states in the same parent. Father's Parent on top says "Save your money," and his Child on the bottom says "Put it all on the last roll." If one parent says "Save your money," and it is the other who gives the directive to gamble it away, that is an external contradiction.

The script controls are inserted and take effect early in life, while the counterscript slogans only become meaningful later. Jeder understands the prohibition "Mussentouchit!" when he is two, while he really doesn't understand the precept "Save your money!"

until he is a teen-ager and needs money to buy things with. Thus, his script controls are given by a mother who seems a magic figure to his youthful eyes, and have all the power and endurance of a witch's curse; his prescription is given by a benevolent, hard-working housewife, and is merely advisory.

This is an unequal contest in which the controls are bound to win if there is a head-on conflict, unless some other element can be introduced, such as a therapist. An added difficulty is that the script tells it like it is: people really do act clumsy, as the child well knows; while the counterscript is usually square as far as his experience is concerned: he may or may not have seen someone attain happiness by working hard, being a good girl, saving money, or being on time, not eating starches, avoiding public toilets, taking laxatives, and not masturbating.

The alternation between script and counterscript explains something that often puzzles patients when the therapist says that their confusion began in early childhood. "Then how come all through high school I was normal?" they will ask. The answer is that in high school they were following the counterscript, and then something happened which caused an "outbreak of script." This is an "at least" reply; it doesn't solve the problem, but it at least indicates where to look.

An attempt to satisfy a bad script and a well-meaning counterscript at the same time may lead to some strange behavior, as in the girl whose father's angry Parent frequently told her to "Drop dead!" while her mother's anxious Parent kept telling her to wear her rubbers so she wouldn't get her feet wet. So when she dropped off the bridge she wore her rubbers. (She survived.)

The counterscript determines the person's style of life, and the script controls his ultimate destiny. If they are harmonious, they may pass by unnoticed on the inside pages, but if they are in conflict they may bring surprises and make headlines. Thus, Hard-Working Church Deacon may end up President of Council, Retires After Thirty Years, or Jailed For Embezzlement, and Devoted Housewife comes out Mother of the

Year, Celebrates Golden Anniversary, or Leaps From Roof of Building. In fact it seems as though there are two kinds of people in the world: real people and plastic people, as the Flower Children used to say. The real people make their own decisions, while the plastic people are run by fortune cookies.

The Fortune Cookie Theory of human living says that each child gets to pull two cookies from the family bowl: one square and one jagged. The square one is a slogan, such as "Work hard!" or "Stick with it!" while the jagged one is a scripty joker, such as "Forget your homework," "Act clumsy," or "Drop dead." Between the two, unless he throws them away, his life style and his final destiny are written.

G · PARENTAL PATTERNS

To make a lady, you start with the grandmother, and to make a schizophrenic, you start with the grandmother, too. Zoe (as we will call Jeder's sister) can only be a lady if her mother teaches her what she has to know. She must learn very early how to smile and walk and sit by imitation, as most girls do, and later, by spoken instructions, how to dress, how to make herself agreeable to the people around her, and how to say "No" gracefully. Father may have something to say about these things, but handling father is also a matter for feminine instruction. Father may impose the controls, but it is mother who gives the pattern and the Adult instructions for carrying them out. The script matrix for a beautiful lady named Zoe is shown in Figure 8. Whether Zoe makes a career out of being a lady, or eventually rebels against the system and its restrictions, depends as much on what her script calls for as on her own decision. She may have permission for moderate sex or drinking, but if she suddenly becomes more active, is that breaking out of her script, or merely following a provocation to rebel? In the first case, her father would say (as the Martians put it): "No, no, not that shaggy!" and in the second (secretly, to himself): "Now she's showing some spirit, ha ha. Nothing stuffy about my little girl!"

On the other side, if Zoe's mother doesn't sit right, doesn't dress right, and is awkward in her femininity, Zoe is likely to be that way, too. This often happens to girls with schizoid mothers. It also happens to girls whose mothers died when they were very young, so that they have no pattern to follow. "When I get up in

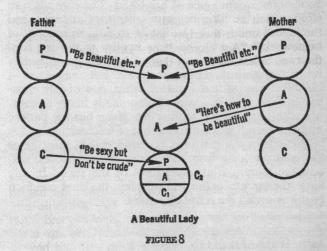

A Beautiful Lady

FIGURE 8

the morning, I can't even decide what to put on," said one paranoid schizophrenic whose mother died when she was four.

In the case of a boy, the script and the pattern are more likely to influence his choice of a working career. As a small child, Jeder may say: "When I grow up I want to be a lawyer (policeman, thief) like father." But this does not always come true. Whether it does or not depends on mother's programing, which reads: "Get (don't get) into something with plenty of risks and lots of fast action like (not like) your father." These controls, like all script controls, refer not so much to the choice of a particular profession, but rather to special types of transactions (in this case, straight or crooked, risky or safe, etc.).[4] But for or against, father is the one who offers the pattern.

Jeder may apparently go against his mother's wishes when he takes up his father's occupation. This may be a true defiance, or antiscript. On the other hand, there are three mothers: Parent, Adult, and Child. He may be going against the spoken wishes of her Parent or Adult, by complying with the unspoken but evident glee of her Child. The controls take effect when the little boy notes her rapt attention and fascinated smile while she listens to father's account of his latest adventure. The same applies to father's controls on Zoe. His Parent or Adult may continually warn her against getting pregnant, but may show a childlike interest and pleasure when one of her classmates does. This is a provocation she is likely to comply with, especially if mother has given her the pattern and Zoe herself was conceived out of wedlock.

Sometimes the matrix is reversed, but in most cases the controls come from the parent of the opposite sex, and the pattern from the parent of the same. In any case, the pattern is the final display, the final common pathway for all the script directives.

H · THE DEMON

The demon is the jester in human existence, and the joker in psychotherapy. No matter how well Jeder lays his plans, the demon can come in at the critical moment and upset them all, usually with a smile and a ha ha. And no matter how well the therapist plans his psychotherapy, the patient always has the upper hand. At the point when the therapist thinks he has four aces, Jeder plays his joker, and his demon wins the pot. Then he skips merrily off, leaving the doctor to leaf through the deck trying to figure out what happened.

Even if he is ready for it, there may be little he can do. The doctor may know ahead of time that just as Jeder gets his stone rolled up to the brow of the hill, the demon will distract his attention, and it will roll all the way down again. There may be others who know about it, too, but the demon is already at work, and sees to it that Jeder keeps away from anyone who would interfere. So the patient starts to miss appointments, or drifts away, and if anyone pressures him he just plain quits. He may return after he has Sisyphused out, sadder, but not much wiser, nor even aware of his glee.

The demon first appears in the high chair, when Jeder scatters his food on the floor with a merry glint, waiting to see what his parents will do. If they make friends with it, it will go on to later mischief, and then perhaps into humorous fun and jokes. If they beat it down, it will lurk surly in the background, ready to leap out at an unguarded moment and scramble his life as it originally scrambled his food.

I · PERMISSION

Negatives are usually said loud and clear, with vigorous enforcement, while positives often fall like raindrops on the stream of life, making little sound and only small ripples. "Work hard!" is found in copybooks, but "Stop loafing!" is more likely to be heard in the home. "Always be on time" is an instructive motto, but "Don't be late!" is heard more frequently in real life, and "Don't be stupid!" is more popular than "Be bright!"

So it turns out that most programing is negative. Every parent fills his children's heads with such restraints. But he also gives them permissions. Prohibitions hamper adaptation to circumstances (nonadaptive), while permissions give a free choice. Permissions do not cause the child trouble, since there is no compulsion attached. True permissions are merely permits, like a fishing license. A boy with a fishing license is not compelled to fish. He can use it or not as he wishes, and he goes fishing when he feels like it and when circumstances allow.

It should be said again that being beautiful (like being successful) is not a matter of anatomy, but of parental permission. Anatomy makes one pretty or photogenic, but only father's smile can make beauty shine from a woman's eyes. Children do things *for* someone. The boy is bright or athletic or successful *for* mother, and the girl is bright or beautiful or fertile *for* father. Or, on the other side, the boy is stupid or weak or clumsy for his parents, and the girl is stupid or ugly or frigid for hers, if that is what they want. It should be added that they have to learn *from* someone if they want to do it well. To do it for someone and to learn from someone is the real meaning of the script apparatus. As already noted, the children usually do it *for* the parent of the opposite sex and learn *from* the parent of the same sex.

Permissions are the chief therapeutic instrument of the script analyst because they offer the only chance for an outsider to free the patient from the curses laid on him by his parents. The therapist gives permission to the patient's Child by saying either "It's all right to do it," or "You don't have to do it." Both say to the Parent "Let him alone." Thus there are positive and negative permissions. In a positive permission, or license, "Let him alone!" means "Let him do it!" This cuts off the injunction. In a negative permission, or external release, it means "Stop pushing him into it!" This cuts off the provocation. Some permissions can be regarded either way. This is particularly true of antiscripts. Thus when the Prince kissed Sleeping Beauty in the Wood, he was offering her both a license to wake up and a release from the witch's curse.

One of the most important permissions is a license to stop acting stupid and start thinking. Many patients of advanced years have not had a single independent thought since early childhood, and have quite forgotten how it feels to think, or even what thinking means. With properly timed permission, however, they are able to come through, and are more than delighted when they say out loud at the age of sixty-five or seventy what may be the first intelligent observation of their adult lives. Often it is necessary to undo the work of previous therapists in order to give a patient permission to think. Some of them have spent years in mental hospitals or clinics where the slightest attempt on their part to think independently came up against powerful resistance from the staff. There they were taught that thinking is really a sin called "intellectualizing," to which they must confess promptly and promise never to indulge in again.

Many addictions and obsessions are based on parental come-ons. "Don't stop taking drugs (or you may stop coming home to ask for money)" says the mother of the heroin addict. "Don't stop thinking about sex," says the parent of a lecher or a nymphomaniac. And the whole concept of permissions as a therapeutic instrument was started by a gambler who said: "I don't need someone to tell me to stop gambling, I need someone to give me *permission* to stop, because somebody in my head says I can't."

A permission, then, allows Jeder to be flexible, instead of responding with fixed patterns frozen by slogans and controls. This has nothing to do with "permissive upbringing," since that is full of imperatives, too. The most important permissions are to love and to change and to do things well. A person with permission is just as easy to spot as one who is all tied up. "He sure has permission to think," "She sure has permission to be beautiful," and "They sure have permission to enjoy themselves," are Martian expressions of admiration.

(One of the frontiers of script analysis is the further study of permissions, primarily through observation of eye movements in very young children. Thus, in some situations the child glances sideways at his parents to see if he has "permission" to do something; in other cases, he seems to be "at liberty" to follow his own inclinations without consulting them. Such observations, carefully evaluated, may result in a significant distinction between "permissions" and "liberties.")

J · THE INTERNAL RELEASE

The spellbreaker, or internal release, is the element which lifts the injunction and frees the person from his script so that he can fulfill his own autonomous aspirations. It is a pre-set "self-destruct" which is obvious in some scripts but has to be hunted for or decoded in others, much like the pronouncements of the Delphic oracle which served the same function in Ancient Greece. Not much is known about it clinically, because people come for treatment just because they cannot find it by themselves; but the therapist doesn't wait for it or try it out. For example, in a "Waiting for *Rigor Mortis*" or "Sleeping Beauty" script, the patient thinks she will be freed of her frigidity when she meets the Prince with the Golden Apples, and may very likely feel that the therapist is that Prince. But he declines the honor, mainly for ethical reasons, but also because when her previous (unlicensed) therapist took on the job, his Golden Apples turned to dust.

Sometimes the spellbreaker is merely ironic. This is a common situation in losers' scripts: "Things will be better after you're dead."

The internal release may be event-centered or time-centered. "When you meet a Prince," "After you die fighting," or "After you have three children" are event-centered antiscripts. "When you pass the age at which your father died" or "After you've stayed with the company thirty years" are time-centered.

Here is an example of how the internal release comes up in clinical practice.

CHUCK

Chuck was a general practitioner in an isolated area in the Rockies. There was no other doctor for miles around. He worked day and night, but no matter how hard he worked there was never enough to support his large family and he was always in debt to the bank. For a long time he had advertised in medical journals for a partner to give him some relief, but he insisted that no one suitable had ever shown up. He operated in fields, homes, and hospitals, and sometimes at the bottom of a mountain crag. He was immensely resourceful and almost completely exhausted, but not quite. He came for treatment with his wife because they were having marital problems, and his blood pressure was going up.

In the end, he found a University Hospital not far away which had some fellowships for general practitioners who wanted to become specialists. This time he did find someone to take his place as a country doctor. He gave up his complex and lucrative practice and found that he had enough assets to keep his family going while he settled down as a surgical resident with a small stipend.

"I've always wanted to do this," he said. "But I never thought I'd get away from my driving Father Parent until after I'd had a coronary. But I didn't have a coronary, and this is the happiest time of my life."

It is evident that his spellbreaker was to have a coronary, and he thought that was the only way he would ever get off the hook. But with the help of the group he did manage to break out of his script in good health.

Chuck illustrates in a relatively simple and clear-cut way the action of the whole script apparatus, is illustrated in the "script matrix" in Figure 9. His counterscript came from both parents: "Work hard." His father than gave him the pattern of a hard-working doctor. His mother's injunction was "Never give up. Work hard until you drop dead." But his father gave him the spellbreaker: "You can relax if you have a coronary, ha ha." What his treatment did was get into that part of his brain or mind whence all these voices sent their directives. The injunction was then lifted by giving him permission: "You can relax without having a coronary." When this permission made its way through all the shells and devices protecting the script apparatus, it broke the curse.

Note that it was useless to say to him "If you keep on this way you'll have a coronary." (1) He was well aware of that threat, and telling him again only made him feel more miserable because (2) he wanted a coronary, which would free him one way or another. What he needed was not a threat, nor an order (he already had enough orders in his head), but a license that would liberate him from those orders, and that is what he got. Then he ceased to be a victim of his script, and became his own master to do his thing. He still worked hard, and he still followed his father's

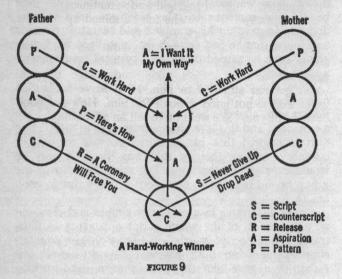

A Hard-Working Winner

S = Script
C = Counterscript
R = Release
A = Aspiration
P = Pattern

FIGURE 9

medical pattern, but he was no longer script-ridden to overwork nor script-driven to drop dead. Thus, at the age of fifty, he became free to fulfill the autonomous aspirations of his own choice.

K · THE SCRIPT EQUIPMENT

The script equipment is the nuts and bolts from which the script apparatus is built, a do-it-yourself kit partly supplied by the parents and partly by the child himself.

CLEMENTINE

Clementine was depressed by an unhappy love affair. She was afraid to be frank with her lover because she might lose him. On the other hand, she was afraid she might lose him if she weren't frank. There was nothing sinister in it, actually. It was just that she didn't want him to know how passionate she really was. The conflict sometimes made her frigid and sometimes panicky. When she talked about it she felt so mixed up that she clutched her head.

What would her parents say about it? Well, her father would say: "Take it easy. Don't lose your head." And her mother? "He's taking advantage of you. Don't get too attached to him. He'll leave sooner or later. You're not good enough for him. He's not good enough for you." She went on to tell an adventure.

When she was about five, an adolescent uncle had got sexy with her, and made her feel sexy, too. She never told her parents. One day when she was taking a bath, her father told her how cute she was. There were some visitors in the house and he had held her up naked for them to see. The sexy uncle was one of them. What were her reactions? "I want to hide. I want to hide." "My God, they'll find out what I've been doing." How did you feel toward your father for doing that? "I wanted to kick him in the penis. I knew what a penis looked like, too, from my uncle's erections." Was there any ha ha? "Yes, deep down, there was. I had a secret. And worst of all, I knew I liked it under all the other feelings."

From these reactions Clementine had constructed a script, which was to have passionate love affairs and then get left. Along with that, however, she also wanted to get married, stay married, and have children.

1. There were two counterscript slogans from her father: "Take it easy," and "Don't lose your head." These fitted in with her aspirations of getting married and raising a family.

2. There were five injunctions from mother, all telescoped into "Don't get attached to anyone."

3. There was a strong seduction to be passionate and sexy from her uncle, reinforced by the nude provocation from her father.

4. These seductions and provocations from Parental demons had reinforced her own demon throughout her life.

5. There was a strong implication of a built-in release: the familiar Prince with the Golden Apples—not like father; if she could only find one.

The interesting thing is that this whole bit came out in one session. As someone remarked, she was quite happy to hold it up for everyone to see.

L · ASPIRATIONS AND CONVERSATIONS

Caught in the mesh of his script apparatus, Jeder meanwhile has his own autonomous aspirations. These usually appear to him in day dreams in his leisure hours, or in hypnagogic hallucinations before he falls asleep: the brave deeds he should have done this morning, or the tranquil scenes he looks forward to in later years. All men and all women have their secret gardens, whose gates they guard against the profane invasion of the vulgar crowd. These are visual pictures of what they would do if they could do as they pleased. The lucky ones find the right time, place, and person, and get to do it, while the rest must wander wistfully outside their own walls. And that is what this book is about: what happens outside those walls, the external transactions that parch or water the flowers within.

What people want to do is shown in visual pictures, the home movies they make inside their skulls. What they *do* do is decided by voices, the skull-rapping of internal dialogue. Each sentence they say and each scripty decision is the result of such a dialogue: Mother says and Father says and Adult says You'd better, while Child, thus encircled, tries to break through to get what he wants. No one can know the enormous, amazing, and almost infinite amount of dialogue he has stored up in the dim-lit caverns of his mind. There are complete answers there to questions he never even dreamed of. But if the right button is pushed, sometimes they pour out in sheer poetry.

Grasp your right forefinger in your left hand. What

is your hand saying to your finger, and what does finger have to say for himself? If you do this right, you will soon find a lively and meaningful conversation going on between them. The amazing part is that it was there all the time, and so are hundreds of others. If you have a cold and an upset stomach, what is your churning stomach saying to your congested nose? If you are sitting with your foot swinging, what has your foot got to say to you today? Ask it and it will answer. The dialogue is right there in your head. All this was discovered, or at least brought into full light by the originator of Gestalt therapy, F. S. Perls.[5] Similarly, all your decisions are made by four or five people in your head, whose voices you can overlook if you are too proud to hear them, but they will be there next time if you care to listen. Script analysts learn how to amplify and identify these voices, and that is an important part of their therapy.[6]

The object of script analysis is to free Jeder and Zoe so that they can open the garden of their aspirations to the world. It does that by cutting through the Babel in their heads until the Child can say: "But this is what I want to do, and I would rather do it my own way."

M · WINNERS

Winners are programed, too. Instead of a curse, there is a blessing: "Long life!" or "Be a great man." The injunction is adaptive instead of constricting: "Don't be selfish!" and the come-on is "Well done!" With such benevolent controls, and all his permissions, there is still his demon to contend with, lurking in the murky caverns of his primal mind. If his demon is a friend instead of an enemy, then he will have it made.

N · DOES EVERYONE HAVE A SCRIPT?

At present, there is no way to answer this question with any degree of certainty, but it is certain that everyone is programed to some extent from early years. As previously mentioned, some people can become autonomous through drastic external circumstances, others by internal reorganization, and still others by applying the antiscript. The key lies in permissions. The more permissions Jeder has, the less he is bound by his script. On the other side, the more severely the script controls were reinforced, the more script-bound he is. It is likely that the human race as a whole forms a curve. At one end are those who become autonomous by one means or another, and at the other end are those who are script-bound, with most people in between, subject to changes in circumstances or outlook. Among the script-bound, there are two types. Script-driven people are those who have lots of permissions, but must fulfill the demands of their scripts before they can enjoy them. A good example is the hard worker who can have fun in his spare time. Script-ridden people are those who have few permissions, but must spend as much time as possible fulfilling their scripts at any cost. A typical example is the heavy drinker or drug addict who must speed toward his doom as quickly as he can. The script-ridden are the victims of tragic or "hamartic" scripts. On the other hand, it is a rare person who has not at one time or another heard the voice of the demon in his head, telling him to buy when he should sell, or stay when he should go, or speak when he should remain silent.[7]

O · THE ANTISCRIPT

But there are some people who rebel against their scripts, apparently doing the opposite of what they are "supposed" to. Common examples are the "rebellious" adolescent and the woman who says "The last thing I want to do is be like my mother." Such cases have to be evaluated very carefully, as there are several possibilities. (1) They may have been living on their counterscripts, and the apparent rebellion is merely "an outbreak of script." (2) Conversely, they may have been living on their scripts, and shifted to their counterscripts. (3) They may have found the spell-breaker, and be released from their scripts. (4) They may have different script directives from each parent, or from two different sets of parents, and are shifting from one set to another. (5) They may be merely following a special script directive that tells them to rebel. (6) The person may be a "script failure" who has despaired of carrying out his script directives and has simply given up. This is the cause of many depressions and schizophrenic breakdowns. (7) On the other hand, he may have freed himself and "got out of his script" through his own efforts or with the help of psychotherapy. (8) But this must be carefully distinguished from "going into an antiscript." These many alternatives emphasize how thorough the script analyst must be if he (and his patient) are to understand correctly the origin of certain changes in behavior.

An antiscript resembles closely what Erikson calls "identity diffusion."[8] If the script is compared to a computer punch card, then an antiscript is attained by turning the card around. This is a very rough analogy, but it makes the point. Where mother says "Don't drink," Jeder drinks. Where she says "Take a shower every day," he doesn't wash. Where she says "Don't think," he thinks, and where she says "Study hard," he drops out. In short, Jeder is meticulously defiant. But since he has to consult his programing to know precisely how and where to be defiant, he is just as surely programed by disobeying each instruction as he would be if he obeyed them all. Thus, where "freedom" is really defiance, it is only an illusion. Inverting his programing still leaves him programed. Such an inversion, turning the card around rather than tearing it up, is called an antiscript, and antiscripts offer a fertile field for further study.

P · SUMMARY

The script apparatus of a loser consists on one hand of injunctions, provocations, and a curse. These are the script controls, and are firmly implanted by the age of six. To combat this programing, he has an inner demon, and is sometimes supplied with an internal release. Later he comes to understand slogans, which give him a counterscript. Throughout, he is learning behavior patterns, which serve both the script and the counterscript. A winner has the same apparatus, but the programing is more adaptive, and he usually has more autonomy because he has more permissions. But in all human beings the demon persists, to bring sudden pleasure or grief.

It should be noted that the script controls are parameters or strictures, which merely set limits on what Jeder can do, while the behavior patterns he learns from his parents, including their games, tell him how he can actually structure his time. Thus, the script is a complete plan for living, offering both strictures and structures.

NOTES & REFERENCES

1 Berne, E. *Transactional Analysis in Psychotherapy. Loc. cit.*
2 The fairy godmother and witch-mother, "electrode-like" introjects, derived from transaction and introspective observations, will be easily recognized as allied to the good and bad introjected objects of Melaine Klein postulated on psychoanalytic grounds, and to the elaborations of her concepts by Fairbairn. In fact, Fairbairn is one of the best heuristic bridges between transactional analysis and psychoanalysis.

Klein, M. *The Psychoanalysis of Children.* Hogarth Press, London, 1932.

Fairbairn, W. R. D. *The Object-Relations Theory of Personality.* Basic Books, New York, 1954.

All this is disappointing from a literary point of view. It brings an unfortunate confrontation with Wordsworth, and Francis Thompson's line "each child has a fairy godmother in its soul" has to be modified, in this light, to include less benevolent mentors.

Cf. Sharpe, E. F. "Francis Thompson: A Psycho-Analytical Study," in her *Collected Papers on Psycho-Analysis.* Hogarth Press, London, 1950.
3 Cf. Berne, E. "The Problem of Masturbation." *Diseases of the Nervous System* 10:3–7, 1944.
4 Cf. Berne, E. "Concerning the Nature of Diagnosis." *International Record of Medicine* 165:283–292, 1952. The differences between the types of transactions engaged in by

mechanics, as compared with farmers, show in their faces. Since they were presumably born with the same assortment of facial muscles and nerves going to them, the differences must be due to some sort of "electrodes" in their central nervous systems. In one case the electrodes says "Look alert" and in the other "Wait and see," and these slogans describe the kinds of transactions they are engaged in.

5 Perls, F. S. *Gestalt Therapy Verbatim* (J. O. Stevens, ed.). Real People Press, Lafayette, California, 1969.

6 Cf. Shapiro, S. B. "Transactional Aspects of Ego Therapy." *American Journal of Psychology* 56:479–498, 1953.

7 The injunction, of course, has the same effect and the same origin as the Superego of psychoanalysis, and the counter-script slogan belongs here also. The demon is the same as the original concept of the Id. The situation seems to be this: the demon itself, the impulse, is an "id impulse." But phenomenologically, the demon is experienced as a living voice. This is the voice of the actual parent (or more precisely, the voice of the demon in the parent) implanted in the child. Speaking for the parent's Id, it also speaks for the Id of the still wordless child.

Re "mother's crazy Child," see Denenberg and Whimby, "Behavior of Adult Rats is Modified by the Experiences Their Mothers Had as Infants." *Loc. cit.*

8 Erikson, E. *Identity and the Life Cycle, Loc. cit.*

CHAPTER EIGHT

Later Childhood

A · PLOTS AND HEROES

Later childhood, from six to ten, is called by psychoanalysis the *latent period*. It is a "locomotor" phase,[1] when the child locomotes himself around the neighborhood to see what he can see. So far, he has only a sketchy idea, a protocol, as to how he is going to put his script equipment together to make himself into a person with a goal in life. He is ready to turn from animals who eat people or who act like people, to people themselves.

A child who starts out wanting to live forever or love forever can be made to change his mind in the course of five or six years[2] until he decides, quite appropriately in view of his limited experience, to die young or never to risk loving anyone again. Or he may learn from his parents that life and love with all their risks are worthwhile. Once the decision is made, he knows who he is, and begins to look at the outside world with the question: "What can happen to people like me?" He knows what the payoff is supposed to be, but doesn't really know what it means, how it will feel, or how to go about getting it. He has to find some sort of plot or matrix into which all his script equipment will fit, and some sort of hero to show him the path. He also looks wistfully for heroes with similar equipment who have followed different, and perhaps happier, paths, hoping to find a way out, or a way in.

The matrix and the hero are offered to him in stories which he reads in books or which are read to him or told to him by some reliable person: mother, grandmother, or children on the street, or perhaps a carefully indoctrinated kindergarten teacher. The telling of these tales is a story in itself—more real and fascinat-

ing than the tale that is told. What happens between
Jeder and his mother, for example, between the time
she says: "After you've brushed your teeth I'll read
you a story," and the moment when she smiles "That's
all!" and tucks him in? What is his final question, and
how does she tuck him in? Those times help form the
flesh of his life plan, while the tales told or the book
story give him the bones. What he ends up with, bone-
wise, are (a) a hero—someone he would like to be;
(b) a villain—someone he may find an excuse to be;
(c) a type—what he knows he has to be; (d) a plot—
a matrix of events which enables him to switch from
one to the other; (e) a cast—those others who will
motivate the switches; and (f) an ethos—a set of ethical standards which will justify him in feeling angry,
hurt, guilty, righteous, or triumphant. If external
events permit, his life course will then be the same as
the life plan he forms around this armature or matrix.
For this reason, it is important to know what his
favorite story or fairy tale was as a child, since this
will be the plot of his script, with all its unattainable
illusions and avoidable tragedies.

B · RACKETS

During this period, Jeder also makes a definite decision about what kind of feelings he will work for. He
has previously exprerimented with this, feeling by turns
angry, hurt, guilty, scared, inadequate, righteous, and
triumphant, and has discovered that certain of these are
treated with indifference or outright disapproval by
his family, while one of them is acceptable and gets
results. That is the one that becomes his racket. The
favored feeling becomes a sort of conditioned reflex
which may persist for the rest of his life.

In order to clarify this, we can use the roulette-wheel
theory of feeling. Suppose there is a housing development with 36 houses built in a circle around a central
plaza, and suppose that there is a baby waiting to be
born wherever it is that babies wait to be born. The
Great Computer in charge of such matters spins a

roulette wheel, and the ball falls in slot 17. The Great Computer then announces "The next baby will go to house 17." He makes five more spins, and comes up with 23, 11, 26, 35, and 31, so the next five babies go to the houses with those numbers. Ten years later, each of the children has learned how he is supposed to react. The one in house 17 has learned: "In this family, when the going gets rough, we feel angry." The one in house 23 has learned: "In this family, when the going gets rough, we feel hurt." The babies at 11, 26, and 35 have learned that when the going gets rough their respective families feel guilty, scared, or inadequate. The baby in 31 learns that "In this family, when the going gets rough, we find out what to do about it." It should be apparent that numbers 17, 23, 11, 26, and 35 are likely to be losers, and 31 is more likely to be a winner.

But supposing when the Great Computer made the spins, other numbers had come up, or the same numbers in a different order? Perhaps Baby A, instead of going to 17, would have gone to 11, and learned to cultivate guilt instead of anger, and Baby B, in 23, might have traded places with Baby F in 31. Then instead of Baby B being a loser and Baby F a winner, it would be the other way round.

This is another way of saying that aside from a doubtful influence of the genes, favorite feelings are learned from the parents. A patient whose favored feeling is guilt might go for anger if he had been born in a different household. Yet each will defend his favored feeling as the natural or even inevitable one in a given situation. That is one reason for having treatment groups. If those six babies were in such a group twenty years later, and Baby A related an incident, ending: "Naturally, I felt angry!" Baby B would say: "My feelings would have been hurt"; Baby C: "I would have felt guilty", Baby D: "I would have felt scared"; Baby E: "I would have felt inadequate"; and Baby F (who would presumably be the therapist by this time): "I would have found out what to do about it." Which of the babies is right? Each one is convinced that his is the "natural" reaction. The truth is that none of them is "natural," really; each one has been learned, or rather decided upon, in early childhood.

To put it in simpler terms, nearly all angers, hurts, guilts, fears, and inadequate feelings are rackets, and in any well-run group it is not difficult to distinguish the few such reactions which are genuinely appropriate. A racket, then, is a feeling, out of all the possible feelings, that is habitually turned on by a given person as his payoff in the games he plays. Group members soon recognize this, and can predict when a certain patient is going to collect an anger trading stamp, when another is going to collect a hurt trading stamp, and so on. The object of collecting such trading stamps is to turn them in for a script payoff.

Each person in the group is scandalized at the idea that his favored feeling is not a natural, universal, and inevitable response to the situations he meets. People in the anger racket, in particular, become very angry when their feelings are questioned, just as people in the hurt racket feel hurt.

C · TRADING STAMPS

Psychological "trading stamps" are called that because they are used the same way as the little blue, green, or brown stamps that people get as a premium when they buy groceries or gasoline. The following are some observations concerning commercial trading stamps.

1. They are usually obtained as a bonus in the course of legitimate business transactions; that is, the person has to buy groceries to get trading stamps.

2. Most people who collect them have a favorite color. If offered other colors, they may not bother to take them, or may give them away. Some people, however, will collect any type of trading stamp.

3. Some people paste them into their little "books" every day, and others at regular intervals, while still others leave them lying around until some day when they are bored and have nothing better to do, and then they paste them up all at once. Some neglect them until

they need something, and then count them in the hope that they have enough to get it free from the trading-stamp store.

4. Some people like to talk about them, look through the catalogue together, boast about how many stamps they have, or discuss which color offers better merchandise or better bargains.

5. Some people save only a few and then turn them in for trivial premiums; others save more, and get bigger bonuses; and still others become deeply involved in trying to collect enough stamps for one of the really large prizes.

6. Some people know that the trading stamps are not really "free" because their cost must be added to the cost of the groceries; some really do not stop to think about this; some know it, but pretend they don't, because they enjoy both the collecting and the illusion of getting something for nothing. (In some cases, the cost of the trading stamps is not added to the cost of the groceries; in such cases, the grocer has to take their cost as his own loss. But in principle, it is the customer who pays for the trading stamps.)

7. Some people prefer to go to "straight" grocery stores where they pay only for the groceries; with the money they save, they can then buy their own merchandise wherever and whenever they want to.

8. For those who are eager to get something "free," it is possible to buy counterfeit trading stamps.

9. It is usually hard for a person who seriously collects trading stamps to give them up. He may put them in a drawer and forget about them for a while, but if he suddenly gets a large fistful in some special transaction, he may pull them out again to count them and see what they are good for.

Psychological trading stamps are the currency of transactional "rackets." When Jeder is young, his parents teach him how to feel when things get difficult: most commonly, angry, hurt, guilty, scared, or inadequate; but sometimes stupid, baffled, surprised, righteous, or triumphant. These feelings become rackets when Jeder learns to exploit them and play games in order to collect as many as possible of his favorite, partly because in the course of time this favorite feeling becomes sexualized, or is a substitute for sexual feelings. For example, much "justified" grownup anger belongs in this category, and is usually the payoff in a game of "Now I've Got You, You Son of a Bitch." The patient's Child is full of suppressed anger, and he waits until someone does something to justify his expressing it. Justification means that his Adult goes along with his Child in saying to his Parent: "No one can reasonably blame me for getting angry under such conditions." Thus relieved of Parental censure, he turns on the offender and says in effect: "Ha! No one can blame me, so now I've got you," etc. In transactional language, he gets a "free" mad, that is, free of guilt. Sometimes it works differently. The Parent says to the Child: "You aren't going to let him get away with that, are you?" and the Adult sides with the Parent: "Anyone would get angry under such conditions." The Child may be only too happy to comply with these urgings; or on the other hand, he may be as reluctant to do battle as Ferdinand the Bull, but is forced to enter the fray.

Psychological trading stamps follow the same pattern as commercial ones.[3]

1. They are usually obtained as a by-product of legitimate transactions. Marital arguments, for example, usually start over some actual problem, which is the "groceries." While the Adult is carrying on its business, the Child is eagerly waiting to pick up bonuses.

2. People who collect psychological trading stamps have favorite "colors," and if offered other colors, they may not bother to take them. A person who collects angers will let guilts and fears go by, or let someone else pick them up. In fact, in a soundly structured marital game, one spouse will pick up all the angers while the other picks up all the guilts or inadequacies, so that they both "win" and add to their collections. There are some people, however, who will collect any kind of trading stamps. These are people who are starved for feelings and will play "Greenhouse," happily showing off any kind of feeling that comes along. Psychologists are especially prone to pick up windblown feelings

from the sidewalk, and if they are group therapists, to encourage their patients to do likewise.

3. Some people go over their hurts and angers every night before going to sleep; others do it less frequently; while still others only do it when they are bored and have nothing better to do. Some wait until they need one big justification, and then count up all their hurts and angers in the hope that they have enough to warrant an outburst of anger, a "free" sulk, or some other dramatic emotional display. Some people like to save them and some like to spend them.

4. People like to show their collections of feelings to others, and to talk about who has more or better angers, hurts, guilts, fears, etc. In fact, many saloons become showrooms where people can go to boast about their trading stamps: "You think *your* wife is unreasonable —well, listen to this!" or "I know what you mean. It takes even less than that to hurt (scare) me. Yesterday . . ." or "Embarrassed (guilty, inadequate)? I coulda sunk through the floor!"

5. The "store" where psychological trading stamps are redeemed has the same array of prizes as the commercial trading-stamp center: little ones, bigger ones, and really big ones. For one or two "books" the person can get a small prize, such as a free ("justified") drunk or sexual fantasy; for ten "books" he can get a toy (unsuccessful) suicide or an adultery, and for one hundred "books" he can get one of the big ones: a free quit (divorce, leave treatment, quit job), a free go to the mental hospital (colloquially known as a free crazy), a free suicide, or a free homicide.

6. Some people learn that psychological trading stamps are not really free, and that the collected feelings have to be paid for in loneliness, insomnia, raised blood pressure, or stomach trouble, so they stop collecting them. Others never do learn about this. Some know it, but continue to play games and collect payoffs because otherwise their lives would be too drab; since they feel little justification for their way of living, they have to content themselves with collecting small justifications for small outbursts of vitality.

7. Some people prefer to talk straight rather than

play games: that is, they will not act provocatively in order to get trading stamps, and will refuse to respond to the spurious provocative behavior of others. With the energy thus saved, they are ready when they meet the right person at the right time in the right place for more legitimate expressions of feeling. (In some cases, people collect psychological trading stamps painlessly and someone else pays the price. Thus a criminal may enjoy all the pleasures of robbing a bank without feeling bad about it or getting caught; apparently, some professional con men and card sharps can live very happily in this way if they do not get too greedy and push too hard. Some teen-agers enjoy dismaying their elders without feeling any remorse or other ill effects. But in principle, the person who collects trading stamps usually has to pay for them sooner or later.)

8. Some people, particularly paranoids, collect "counterfeit" trading stamps. If no one will provoke them, they imagine provocations. Then, if they are impatient, they can get a free suicide or a free homicide without having to rely on the natural course of events to supply enough irritations for a legitimate outburst. In this respect, there are two types of paranoids. The Child paranoid collects counterfeit wrongs and says "See what they did to me," while the Parent paranoid collects counterfeit rights, and says "They can't do this to me." In fact there are "check raisers" as well as true counterfeiters among paranoids. Those with delusions can pick up very small trading stamps here and there and raise each of them into a very large denomination so as to get a large payoff quickly. Those with voice hallucinations can manufacture trading stamps ad infinitum right out of their heads.[4]

9. It is just as hard for a patient to give up a lifelong collection of hard-earned psychological trading stamps as it would be for a housewife to burn her commercial ones. This is one factor hindering recovery, since, in order to be cured, the patient must not only stop playing games compulsively, but must also forgo the pleasure of using the stamps he has collected previously. "Forgiveness" of previous wrongs is not enough: they have to become truly irrelevant for the future

course of his life if he truly gives up his script. In my experience, "forgiveness" means putting the trading stamps away in a drawer, rather than disposing of them permanently; they will stay in the drawer as long as things go smoothly, but if there is a new offense, they will be pulled out and added to the new payoff in calculating the prize. Thus an alcoholic who "forgives" his wife will not go on just a little binge if she slips up again, but may throw in all the trading stamps he has got from all her slips or insults over the whole course of their marriage, and go on an epical bender perhaps ending in delirium tremens.

So far, nothing has been said about "good" feelings such as righteousness, triumph, and joy. Righteousness stamps are made of fool's gold, and will not pass as currency anywhere except in fool's paradise. Triumph stamps glitter, but they are not collected by people of good taste because they are only gilt. They can be turned in, however, for a free celebration, and can thus be used worthily to bring fun to a large number of people. Joy, like despair, is a genuine feeling, and is not the payoff of a game; thus we can speak of golden joy, just as we speak of black despair.

The important clinical point about "good" feelings is that people who save "brown" stamps, the "bad" feelings or "feeling bads" discussed above, are often reluctant to accept "gold" stamps when they are offered in the form of compliments or "strokes." They are quite comfortable with the familiar, bad, old feelings, but do not know where to put good ones, and so they will turn them away or ignore them by pretending not to hear. As a matter of fact, a zealous collector of "brown" stamps can turn even the most sincere compliments into veiled insults, so that instead of wasting them by refusing them or not hearing them, he will transform them into counterfeit browns. The most common example is: "My, you look good today!" bringing out the response: "I knew you didn't like the way I looked last week." Another is: "My, that's a beautiful dress!" eliciting: "So you didn't like the one I wore yesterday!" With a little practice, anyone can learn to transform compliments into insults, and by spraying a little feces over a pleasant gold stamp, turn it into an unpleasant brown one.

The following anecdote illustrates how easy it is for a Martian to understand the concept of psychological trading stamps. A woman came home from a group meeting one day where she had heard it for the first time, and explained it to her twelve-year-old son. He said "Okay, mom, I'll be back soon." When he returned, he had made a small roll of perforated paper stamps and a little dispenser to hold them, together with a paper book with the pages ruled off into squares. On the first page he had written: "This page when full of stamps entitles you to one free suffer." He understood perfectly. If people do not spontaneously provoke you, insult you, entice you, or frighten you, then you start a game in order to make them do it. In this way you collect a free mad, hurt, guilt, or fright, and a few of these add up to one free suffer.

There is another similarity between psychological trading stamps and commercial ones. They are both canceled once they are used, but people still like to talk nostalgically about the ones they turned in. The key word here is "recall." Real people, in ordinary conversation, say "Do you remember when . . ." whereas "Do you recall . . ." is usually used in referring to trading stamps that were used up and canceled long ago. "Do you remember the good time we had in Yosemite?" is reminiscence, whereas: "Do you recall what happened at Yosemite? First you dented the fender, and furthermore you forgot to . . . and then, as I recall, you . . . and in addition . . ." etc. is a worn-out reproach which is not good for a justified anger any more. Lawyers habitually use the word "recall" rather than "remember" in the exercise of their profession, when they bring out the plaintiff's often faded and sometimes counterfeit trading stamps to show the judge or jury. Lawyers are, in fact, philatelists, connoisseurs of psychological trading stamps; they can look over a collection, large or small, and estimate its current market value at the big redemption store in the courthouse.

Crooked spouses can con each other by pulling out

used or counterfeit trading stamps. Thus, Francisco discovered that his wife Angela was having an affair with her employer, and in fact rescued her when the employer threatened her with violence. After a tempestuous scene, she thanked him and he forgave her. But afterward, whenever he got drunk, which was often, he brought the matter up again, and there was another scene. In trading-stamp language, in the first scene he got a justified anger, she genuinely thanked him, and he generously forgave her. That was a decent settlement, and all the trading stamps were canceled.

But, as noted, "forgive" in practice means to put the stamps in the drawer until they are needed again, even though they have already been cashed in. In this case, Francisco pulled out the old canceled stamps every Saturday night and waved them in Angela's face. Instead of pointing out that they had already been used, Angela would hang her head and let Francisco have another free anger. In return, she would fob off on him some counterfeit thank-you stamps. The first time she thanked him, she gave him true stamps of golden gratitude, but after that her thanks were tired and spurious, "fool's gold" or iron pyrites, which he, in his drunken foolishness, cherished like the real thing. When he was sober, both of them could be honest and regard the matter as settled. But when he was drinking, they became crooked with each other. He blackmailed her with phony reruns, and she paid him off in kind.

Thus the analogy between commercial and psychological trading stamps is almost perfect. Each person tends to handle both kinds in the same way, according to his upbringing. Some people are raised to cash them in and forget it. Others are taught to save them and savor them; they keep their paper stamps and gloat over them as they mount up in anticipation of the day when they will be able to cash them in for a big prize; and they deal the same way with their angers, hurts, fears, and guilts, keeping them bottled up until they have enough for a really big payoff. Still others have permission to cheat, and use considerable ingenuity in doing so.

Psychological trading stamps exist as emotional memories, which probably take the form of molecular patterns in a continual state of agitation, or electrical potentials which go round and round in a circle of Jordan curve; and neither of them is completely exhausted until there is some kind of discharge of the piled-up energy. The rate at which the configurations or the potentials decay is probably based partly on genes and partly on "early conditioning" which in our terms falls into the category of parental programing. At any rate, if a person brings out the same old trading stamps again and again to exhibit to his audience, they begin to look more and more tired and shopworn, and so does the audience.

D · ILLUSIONS

Childhood illusions have mainly to do with rewards for being good and punishments for being bad. Good means mainly not being angry ("Temper, temper!") or sexy ("Nasty, nasty!") but it is all right to be frightened or ashamed. That is, Jeder is not supposed to express either his "instinct for self-preservation," whose expression can be quite satisfying, or his "instinct for preservation of the species," whose expression can be very pleasurable even at an early age; but he is allowed to have as many unsatisfying, unpleasant feelings as he wishes.

There are many systems which make formal rules about rewards and punishments. Besides legal systems, which exist everywhere, there are religious and ideological ones. Half the world are "true believers" (about one billion Christians and half a billion Moslems) for whom the rules regarding afterlife are most important. The "heathen" half are judged during their earthly sojourns by local gods or by their national governments. For the script analyst, however, the most important codes are the informal, hidden ones which are peculiar to each family.

For small children, there is usually some sort of Santa Claus who is watching their behavior and keeping the accounts. But he is for the "little kids," and "big kids" don't believe in him, at least not in Santa Claus as a man in a masquerade costume who comes on a certain day of the year. In fact, not believing in that kind of Santa Claus is what separates big kids from the little ones, along with the knowledge of where babies come from. But big kids, and grownups too, have their own versions of Santa, each one different. Some grownups are more interested in Santa Claus's family than in Santa himself, and firmly believe that if they behave properly they will sooner or later have their chance with either his son, Prince Charming, or his daughter Snegurotchka, the Snow-Maiden, or even with his Missis, Mrs. Menopause. In fact, most people spend their lives waiting for Santa Claus, or for some member of his family.

And then there is his opposite number down below. Where Santa himself is a jolly man in a red suit who comes from the North Pole bringing gifts, his opposite number is a grim man in a black cloak who comes from the South Pole carrying a scythe, and his name is Death. Thus the human race is split during later childhood into the Life Crowd, who will spend their lives waiting for Santa Claus, and the Death Crowd, who will spend their lives waiting for Death. These are the basic illusions on which all scripts are based: that either Santa Claus will come eventually bringing gifts for the winners, or Death will come eventually and solve all the problems for the losers. Thus the first question to ask about illusions is: "Are you waiting for Santa Claus, or Death?"

But before the Final Gift (immortality) or the Final Solution (death), there are meanwhile others. Santa can bestow a winning lottery ticket, a life pension, or prolonged youth. Death can bestow a permanent disability, a cessation of sexual desire, or premature old age, each of which relieves the person of some of his duties. For example, women in the Death Crowd are convinced that menopause will offer succor and surcease: that all sexual desire will vanish, to be replaced by hot flashes and melancholia which will excuse them forevermore from living. This sad myth, that

Mrs. Menopause will rescue them, is titled "Wooden Ovaries" in the language of script analysis. Some men also grab for this with "Wooden Testicles," the myth of the male menopause.

Every script is based on some such illusion, and it is the grievous but necessary task of script analysis to undermine it, hence the blunt titles which get this done with the most dispatch and the shortest pain. The transactional importance of the illusion is that it provides a cause, and a reason for saving up trading stamps. Thus people who are waiting for Santa Claus will save either compliments to show how good they have been, or "suffers" of various kinds to arouse his compassion, while those who are waiting for Death will save guilt or futility stamps to show that they are worthy of him or will welcome him with gratitude. But any kind of stamp may be offered to either Santa Claus or Death in the hope that with clever salesmanship the desired merchandise will be forthcoming.

The illusion, then, has to do with the store where the trading stamps are turned in, and there are two different stores, each with different rules. By doing enough good, or enduring enough suffering, Jeder can collect enough gold or brown stamps to turn in on a free gift from Santa's Store. By collecting enough guilts or futilities, he can get a free gift from the Death Shop. Actually, Santa and Death do not actually run stores. They are more like itinerant peddlers. Jeder has to *wait* for Santa or Death to come, and he never knows when they will. That is why he must save his trading stamps and always have them ready, because if he misses his opportunity when Santa or Death does pass by, he never knows when he will get another chance. If he is saving cheerios, then he must think positively at all times, because if he relaxes even for a moment, that might be the very moment of Santa's arrival. Similarly, if he is saving suffers, he must not risk ever looking happy because if Santa catches him off guard he will have lost his opportunity. It is the same with people in the Death Crowd. They cannot afford to risk even a single moment free of guilt or futility, for that might be the very moment of Death's visit, and then they would be condemned to live until the next round, which might be—well, only death knows how long the suspense might have to continue.

Illusions are the "if onlys" and "some days" upon which most people base their existence. In some countries, government lotteries offer the only possibility for Jeder to make his dreams come true, and thousands of men spend their lives, day after day, waiting for their numbers to come up. Now the truth of the matter is that there is a Santa Claus: at every drawing, somebody's number does come up and his dreams do come true. But oddly enough, in most cases, this does not bring happiness, and many people let their winnings slip through their fingers and return to their former state. This is because the whole system of illusions is a magical one: not only will the reward arrive magically, but it will be magic in itself. A proper child knows that the real Santa Claus will come down the chimney while he is asleep and leave him a little red wagon or a golden orange. But it will not be an ordinary little red wagon or orange; instead, a magical and unique one studded with rubies and diamonds. When Jeder discovers that the little red wagon or orange has indeed arrived, but that it is just an ordinary one like everybody else's, he is disappointed and asks: "Is that all?" much to the mystification of his parents, who thought they were giving him exactly what he wanted. Similarly, the man who wins the lottery finds that the things he buys are the same as the things other people have, so he often says: "Is that all?" and blows it. He would rather go back and sit under the tree hoping for magic than enjoy what he has. That is, illusions are more attractive than reality, and even the most attractive reality may be abandoned in favor of the most tenuous or improbable illusion.

Among the most remarkable examples of this are certain people with a "Never Give Up" script. One of the things they are reluctant to give up are their bowel movements, so that they suffer from chronic constipation. The illusion is that if they only hold on long enough Santa Claus will come, or if he doesn't at least they have something of their own to make up for the gifts they won't get. Some of these people are in an excellent position to enjoy a rewarding reality, but they would rather "sit" at home, waiting for they know not what or whom to come and rescue them. One such woman, even when she was lying flat on the analytic couch, would say: "I'm sitting here thinking." At home she spent a lot of constipated time doing just that. She found it hard to mingle with people, because wherever she went she carried a psychological toilet with her, and no matter what her Adult was doing, her Child was sitting on its favorite seat.

Actually, the Child almost never gives up its illusions. Some of them are universal, as Freud pointed out, and probably arise in the first few months of life, or even in the womb, which is a magical world man can only find later through love, sex, or drugs (or perhaps, with vicious people, through massacre). Freud names as the three earliest ones: "I am immortal, omnipotent, and irresistible." Of course these primal illusions do not last long in the face of infant reality: mother, father, time, gravity, unknown and frightening sights and sounds, and internal sensations of hunger, fear, and pain. But they are replaced by conditional illusions which are strong influences in the formation of scripts. There they appear as If Onlys: "If only I behave in the right way, Santa Claus will come."

Parents everywhere are the same in regard to illusions. If the child believes they are magicians, it is partly because they believe it themselves. There is no actual or conceivable parent who has not somehow conveyed to his offspring: "If you do what I tell you, everything will come out all right." To the child this means: "If I do what they tell me, I'll be protected by magic, and all my best dreams will come true." He believes this so firmly that it is almost impossible to shake his faith. If he doesn't make it, it is not because the magic has gone, but because he has broken the rules. And if he defies or abandons the parental directives, it does not mean that he has lost his belief in his illusions. It may only mean that he cannot stand the requirements any longer, or doesn't think he will ever meet them. Hence the envy and derision which some people direct at those who follow the rules. The inner Child still believes in Santa Claus, but the rebels are saying "I can get it from him wholesale" (drugs or revolution), while the futilists cry: "Who needs his sour grapes? The grapes of death are sweeter." But as they get older, a few people are able to give up the illusions themselves, and they seem to do so without the envy or derision of those who have not.

The Parental precept, at best, reads: "Do right and no harm can befall you!" a motto which has been the basis of ethical systems in every country throughout recorded history, starting with the oldest known written instructions by Ptahhotep, in ancient Egypt, five thousand years ago.[5] At worst it reads: "The world will be a better place if you kill certain people, and in that way you will attain immortality, become omnipotent, and acquire irresistible power." Oddly enough, from the Child's point of view, both of these are slogans of love, for they are both based on the same Parental promise: "If you do as I tell you, I will love and protect you, and without me you are nothing." This shows up clearly when the promise is given in writing. In the first case, it is the Lord who will love and protect you, as it is written in the Bible, and in the second it is Hitler, as it is written in *Mein Kampf* and other productions. Hitler promised the thousand-year Reich, which is practical immortality, and his followers did indeed acquire omnipotence and irresistible power over the Poles, Gypsies, Jews, painters, musicians, writers, and politicians whom they imprisoned in their extermination camps. While this was going on, however, reality took over in the Napoleonic form of infantry, artillery, and air support, and millions of Hitler's followers became mortal, impotent, and resistible.

It takes enormous power to shatter these primal illusions, and this occurs most commonly in wartime. When Tolstoy's Count goes into battle, he cries in outrage: "Why are they firing at me? Everybody likes me (= I am irresistible)."[6] The same applies to the conditional illusion: "If I do what my Parent tells me, everything will come out all right." The most horrifying example of smashing this almost universal belief by force is shown in the notorious picture of a little boy about nine years old standing in the middle of a street in Poland, alone and friendless despite the onlookers who line the sidewalk, while an armed Death's Head Trooper stands over him. The expression on his face says very plainly: "But mother told me if I was a good boy everything would be all right." The most brutal psychological blow that any human being can sustain is proof that his good mother deceived him, and that is the devastating torture which the German soldier is inflicting on the little boy he has cornered.

The therapist, with full humanity and poignancy, and with the patient's explicit and voluntary consent, may have to perform a similar task: not torture, but surgery. In order for the patient to get better, his illusion, upon which his whole life is based, must be undermined so that he can live in the world which is here today, rather than in his "If Only" or "Some Day." This is the most painful task which the script analyst has to perform: to tell his patients finally that there is no Santa Claus. But by careful preparation, the blow can be softened and the patient may, in the long run, forgive him.

One of the favorite illusions of later childhood is shaken when Jeder finds out where babies come from. In order to maintain the fiction of his parents' purity, he has to make the reservation: "All right, but *my* parents don't do that." It is difficult for the therapist to avoid seeming crass and cynical when he confronts Jeder with the fact that he was not a virgin birth, so they must have done it at least once, and if he has brothers and sisters, several times. This is equivalent to telling him that his mother betrayed him, something no man should tell another unless the other pays him to do just that. Sometimes he has the opposite task of restoring to some semblance of decency the picture which mother herself or external circumstances have smeared into degradation. And for millions of children, this illusion is an unattainable luxury, and they must exist in a bare state of psychological as well as material subsistence.

The beliefs in Santa Claus, Death, and mother's virginity may be regarded as normal because they are eagerly grasped and give spiritual nourishment to idealistic or weaker spirits whenever they are made available. On the other hand, confused people are confused because they have their own special illusions. These range from "If you take a colonic irrigation every day, you'll be healthy and happy" to "You can prevent your father from dying if you get sick. If he dies, it's because you didn't get sick enough." There are also private contracts with God, contracts God was never consulted about and which He never signed; and which He would in fact refuse to sign: "If I sacrifice my children, my mother will stay healthy" is a common example, or "God will send me a miracle if I don't have any orgasms." As already noted, the latter was institutionalized among the prostitutes of Paris as "No matter how many men I have sex with, or even knowingly infect with disease, I can still go to Heaven as long as it is done in the course of business and I don't enjoy it."[7]

In early childhood, then, magical illusions are accepted in their most romantic forms. In later childhood, they are tested against reality, and parts of them are reluctantly relinquished, leaving only a secret core to form the existential basis of life. Only the strongest can face the absurd gambles of living without any illusions. One of the hardest to give up, even in later life, is the illusion of autonomy or self-determination.

This is illustrated in Figure 10. The genuine autonomous area which represents true rational Adult functioning, free of Parental prejudices and wishful Child thinking, is marked A1. This aspect of the personality is actually free to make Adult judgments based on carefully gathered knowledge and observation. It may work efficiently in a trade or profession, where a mechanic or a surgeon uses good judgment based on previous education, observation, and experience. The area marked P is clearly recognized by the individual as Parental influence: ideas and preferences he got from his parents concerning food, dress, manners, and religion, for example. These he may refer to as his "up-

bringing." The area marked C he credits to wishful desires or early tastes, the things that come from his
Child. Insofar as he recognizes and separates these three
areas, he is autonomous: he knows what is Adult and
practical, what he accepts that came from others, and
what he does that is determined by early impulses
rather than by practical thinking and rational decisions.

The areas marked "Delusions" and "Illusions" is
where he lives in error. The delusions are things that
he treats as though they were his own ideas, based on
observation and judgment, whereas in reality they are
ideas imposed on him by his parents, which are so in-
grown that he thinks they are part of his Real Self.
The illusions, similarly, are ideas from his Child that he
accepts as Adult and rational and tries to justify as
such. Delusions and illusions may be called contamina-
tions. The illusion of autonomy, then, is based on the
erroneous idea that the whole area, A1, shown in Figure 10 is uncontaminated and autonomous Adult,
whereas it actually includes large areas that really belong

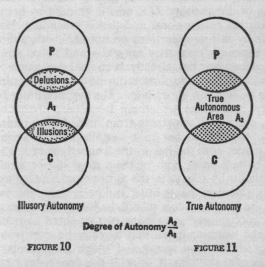

Illusory Autonomy   True Autonomy

Degree of Autonomy $\frac{A_2}{A_3}$

FIGURE 10   FIGURE 11

to the Parent and the Child. True autonomy is the recognition that the Adult boundaries are truly shown in

Figure 11, and that the shaded areas belong to the other ego states.

In fact, Figures 10 and 11 give us a measure of autonomy. The area of A in Figure 11, divided by the area of A in Figure 10, may be called "Degree of Autonomy." Where A-10 is large and A-11 is small, there is little autonomy and great illusion. If A-10 is small (though always bigger than A-11), and A-11 is large (though always smaller than A-10), then there is less illusion and more autonomy.

E · GAMES

During early infancy the child is straight, starting off in the first position, I'm O.K.—You're O.K. But corruption quickly sets in, and he discovers that his O.K. is not a completely undisputed automatic birthright, but depends to some extent on his behavior, and more particularly on his responses to his mother. In the course of learning his table manners, he may discover that his feeling of unblemished O.K.ness is granted by her only with certain reservations, and this is wounding. He responds by casting aspersions on her O.K.ness, although when dinner is over they may kiss and make up. But the groundwork has already been laid for game-playing, which begins to flower during his toilet training, where he has the upper hand. During mealtimes he is hungry, and wants something from her; in the bathroom, she wants something from him. At the table, he has to respond to her in a certain way to keep his O.K. grade; now she has to treat him right to keep her O.K. In rare cases both of them may still be straight, but usually by this time she is conning him by working his gimmicks just a little, and he is doing the same.

By the time he enters school, he has probably learned a few soft games, or perhaps two or three hard ones, or in the worst cases he may already be game-ridden. It depends on how smart and tough his parents are. The more they "play it smart," the crookeder he will be; and the tougher they are, the harder he will have to play in order to survive. Clinical experience shows that the most effective way to corrupt and tighten a child is to give him frequent enemas against his will, just as the most effective way to corrupt and disintegrate him is to spank him cruelly when he cries from pain.

In grade school he has a chance to try out, on the general population of other children and teachers, the games he has learned at home. He sharpens some up, tones others down, abandons some, and picks up new ones from the group. He also has a chance to test out his convictions and his position. If he thinks he is O.K., his teacher can confirm this or shake him up by putting him down, and if he is convinced he is not-O.K., she can confirm that (which is only what he expects) or try to build him up (which may make him uneasy). If he thinks the rest of the world is O.K., he will include her unless she has to prove she isn't. If he is convinced others are not-O.K., he will try to prove it by getting her angry.

There are many special situations which neither the child nor the teacher can foresee or cope with. The teacher may play the game called "Argentina." "What's the most interesting thing about Argentina?" she asks. "Pampas," says somebody, "Nooo." "Patagonia," says somebody else. "Nooooooo." "Aconcagua," offers another pupil. "Noooooooooo." By this time they know what's up. It's no use remembering what's in the book, or what they're interested in. They're supposed to guess what's in *her* mind, so she's got them in a corner, and they give up. "Nobody else wants to answer?" she asks in her phony gentle tone. "Gauchos!" she declares triumphantly, making them all feel stupid simultaneously. There is nothing they can do to stop her, and it is very hard for even the most charitable student to let her keep her O.K. On the other hand, even the most skillful teacher may have trouble keeping her O.K. with a pupil whose body is being violated with enemas at home. He may refuse to answer, and then if she tries to force him, she is raping his mind as well, and that proves that she is no better than his parents. But there's nothing she can do to help him, either.

Each of the lower positions has its own assortment of games, and by playing them with the teacher, Jeder can see which ones she falls for and sharpen his skill. In the second or arrogant position $(+ \, -)$ he may try "Now I've Got You," in the third or depressive one $(- \, +)$, "Kick Me," and from futility $(- \, -)$, "Making Teacher Sorry." He may give up the ones she declines or has an antithesis for. But he also tries them out on his schoolmates.

The fourth position is in many ways the hardest to deal with. But if the teacher keeps her cool and strokes Jeder with judicious words, neither marshmallows, rebukes, nor apologies, she may loosen his grip on the harsh rock of futility and float him part way up toward the sunshine of O.K.ness.

Thus, later childhood is the period that determines which games from the domestic repertoire become fixed favorites and which ones, if any, are given up. The most important single question here is: "How did your teachers get along with you at school?" and next to that, "How did the other kids get along with you at school?"

F · THE PERSONA

By the end of this phase, something else has come into full flower, something which answers the question: "If you can't talk straight and tell it like it is, what's the most comfortable way to be crooked?" Everything Jeder has learned from his parents, his teachers, his schoolmates, his friends, and his enemies, goes into answering this. The result is his persona.

Jung defines the persona as an *"ad hoc* adopted attitude," a mask which the person "knows corresponds with his conscious intentions, while it also meets with the requirements and opinions of his environment." Thus he "deceives others, and also often himself, as to his real character."[8] It is then a social personality, and the social personalities of most people resemble the personality of a child of the latent period, about six to ten years of age. This is because the persona is indeed formed by outside influences and the child's own decisions, at just that period. When he is on his social behavior, good, tough, likable, challenging, grown-up Jeder need not (though he may) come on as either Parent, Adult, or Child. Instead, he may behave like a grade school boy, adapting himself under the guidance of his Adult, and within Parental restrictions, to his social situation. This adaptation emerges as his persona, and that, too, fits in with his script. If he has a winning one, his persona will be attractive, and if a losing one, repulsive, except to his own kind. Often it is modeled on his hero. The real Child is hidden behind the persona, and may lurk there watching for an opportunity to spring if enough trading stamps can be collected to justify dropping the mask.

The question to ask the patient here is: "What kind of person are you?" or better: "What do other people think of you?"

G · THE FAMILY CULTURE

All culture is family culture, things learned as a knee baby. Details and techniques may be learned outside the home, but their value is determined by the family. The script analyst goes to the heart of the matter with a single pointed question: "What did your family talk about at the dinner table?" By this he hopes to ascertain the subject matter, which may or may not be important, and also the kinds of transactions which took place, which is always important. Some child-and-family therapists even have themselves invited to dinner at the patient's house, with the idea that this is the best way to get the greatest amount of reliable information in a short time.

One of the script analyst's slogans is, or should be, "Think sphincter!" Freud[9] and Abraham[10] were the first to elaborate the idea that character structure centers around bodily orifices. Both games and scripts do likewise, and the physiological signs and symptoms which form an important feature of every game and script usually center around a particular orifice or sphincter. The family culture, as shown at the dinner table, tends to revolve around the "family sphincter," and knowing which is the family's favorite is a great help in treating the patient.

The four external sphincters concerned are the oral, the anal, the urethral, and the vaginal, and perhaps more important are the internal sphincters related to these. There is also an illusory sphincter which may be called, as it is in psychoanalysis, the cloacal.

Although the mouth does have its own external sphincter, the *Orbicularis oris,* that is not usually the muscle "oral" families are concerned with, although some do have a motto, "Keep your mouth shut." What "oral" families mainly talk about is food, and the sphincters chiefly concerned are those of the throat, stomach, and duodenum. Thus, oral families are typically diet faddists and stomach worriers, and those are the subjects they talk about at dinner. "Hysterical" members of such families have spasms of the throat muscles, and "psychosomatic" members have spasms of the esophagus, stomach, and duodenum, or, conversely, they throw up or have fears of throwing up.

The anus is the sphincter par excellence. Anal families talk about bowel movements, laxatives, and enemas, or the more aristocratic colonic irrigations. Life for them is a round of poisonous matter that has to be got rid of promptly at any cost. They are fascinated by intestinal products, and proud of themselves or their children when these are large and firm and shapely. Diarrhea is judged by its copiousness, while mucous or bloody colitis is of eternal interest and can be worn with an air of modest distinction. The whole culture merges with sexuality (or anti-sexuality) in the motto "Keep a tight ass hole or you'll get screwed." This means keep a poker face as well, and the philosophy may pay off in making money.

Urethral families talk a lot, long streams of watered-down ideas with a few stutters at the end, although they are never really finished talking, as there are always some last drops left which can be squeezed out if there is time. Some of them are full of piss and vinegar, and when they get pissed off they piss on people, or so they say. Some of the children rebel against the system by tightening up their urethral sphincters and holding their urine as long as possible, getting considerable pleasure from the unpleasant sensations which result and even more pleasure when they finally let loose, sometimes at night in bed.*

Some families talk at mealtimes about the wickedness of sex. Their motto is "In our family, the women keep their legs crossed." Even when their legs are not crossed, they keep their vaginal sphincters up tight. In other families the vaginal sphincters are wide open and the legs loose, and the table talk is vulgar and pornographic.

These are common examples illustrating the theory of sphincters, or as it is usually called, the theory of infantile sexuality. This theory is most fully and clearly developed by Erikson.[11] He considers five stages of development, each centered around a particular anatomical zone (oral, anal, or genital). Each zone can be "used" in five different ways or modes, including Incorporative (1 and 2), Retentive, Eliminative, and Intrusive, so that he ends up with a basic matrix of twenty-five slots. He relates certain of these slots to particular attitudes and characteristics, and to particular lines of personal development, which are similar to scripty life courses.

Using Erikson's language, the parental injunction "Keep your mouth shut" is oral retentive; "Keep a tight ass hole" is anal retentive, and "Keep your legs crossed" is phallic retentive. Food fads are oral incorporative, vomiting is oral eliminative, and obscene talk is intrusive. Hence, a question about table talk can often place the family culture very precisely as to zone and mode. This is important because particular games and scripts, and their accompanying physical symptoms, are based in appropriate zones and modes. For example, "Schlemiel" is anal as to zone, and "I'm Only Trying to Help You" is intrusive as to mode, while "Alcoholic" is oral incorporative.

The mythical "cloacal sphincter" exists in the minds of confused people whose Child thinks that there is only

---

*But please do not beat bed wetters in an attempt to cure them.

one opening down below in both sexes, which opening can be closed off at will. This leads to scripts which are difficult for more realistic people to understand, especially if the mouth is also included. Thus a catatonic schizophrenic may close off everything at once: he keeps all his sphincters clamped down so that nothing can get in or out of his mouth, bladder, or rectum, and he may have to be tube-fed, catheterized, and clystered at regular intervals to insure his physical well-being and survival. Here the script slogan is "Better death than to let them in!" and this is taken literally by the Child who controls the sphincters and who, in such cases, is very confused about how they are assembled and how they work.

Most scripts, however, are centered mainly around one particular sphincter, and the psychology of the script is related to that physiological area. That is why the script analyst "thinks sphincter." The constant tightening of one sphincter can affect all the muscles of the body, and this muscle set is related to the person's emotional attitude and interests and also influences the way others respond to him. This works according to the model of the "infected splinter."

If Jeder has a small infected splinter in his right big toe, he will start to limp. This affects the muscles of his leg, and in order to compensate, the muscles of his back will tighten up. After a while, the muscles in his shoulders will also be affected, and pretty soon the muscles of his neck are involved. If he walks a lot, the disturbance in muscular balance progresses until eventually the muscles of his head and scalp are also affected; then he may get a headache. As walking becomes more difficult and his body is held more and more stiffly and the infection progresses, his circulation and digestion may become labored. At this point, someone might say: "This is a very difficult condition to cure, since it involves his internal organs and his head as well as all the muscles in his body. This is a disease of the whole organism." But along comes a surgeon, and says: "I can cure the whole thing, including his fever, his headache, and all his muscular tension." He pulls out the splinter, the infection subsides, Jeder stops limping, his scalp and neck muscles relax, and the headache vanishes; and as the rest of his body relaxes, everything returns to normal. Thus, even though the condition involves the whole body, it can be cured by looking in the right place for the splinter and removing it. Then not only Jeder, but all the people around him are relieved, and they can relax, too.

A similar chain of events happens when a sphincter is held tight. In order to give the sphincter traction and support, the surrounding muscles tighten up. To compensate for that, more distant muscles are affected, and eventually the whole body is involved. This is easily demonstrated. Suppose the reader, as he sits reading, tightens up his anus. He will immediately notice that this involves the muscles of his lower back and legs. If he now rises up out of his chair, keeping his anus tight, he will note that he has to purse his lips, which in turn affects the muscles in his scalp. In other words, keeping his anus tight changes the muscular dynamics of his whole body. That is exactly what happens with people whose script calls for them to "Keep a tight ass hole or you'll get screwed." Every muscle in their bodies becomes involved, including their muscles of facial expression. The facial expression influences the way other people respond to them, and in fact gives the come-on to the Child of the other person, the script antagonist, who is destined to bring about the script switch.

Here is how it works. Suppose we call the man with the tight anus Angus, and his opposite number, his script antagonist, Lana. Lana is looking for an Angus, and Angus is looking for a Lana. Lana knows instantly when she has found an Angus because of his facial expression. She confirms her Child's intuitive judgment in the course of their conversation as he reveals his attitudes and interests. Lana's role in the script of an Angus is to bring about the script switch. Angus's counterscript is to keep tight at all times, but his script is something else. No matter how hard he tries to keep tight according to the parental precept, sooner or later he drops his guard for a moment, and then his script takes over. In this moment of weakness he relaxes. That is just what Lana has been waiting for. She pulls the switch, and somehow or other, Angus "gets screwed" as she moves in to fulfill her mission. And as long as Angus tries to keep a tight anus, he is going to "get screwed" again and again. That is how the script works —unless it calls for him to be a winner, and then he is the one who will do the screwing, as in the case of some anal financiers.

Thus, the script analyst thinks sphincter so he will know what he is dealing with. The patient who gives up his script is much more relaxed in all the muscles of his body. The woman who formerly kept a tight anus, for example, will stop squirming in her chair, and the one who kept a tight vagina will no longer sit with her arms and legs tensely crossed and her right foot wrapped tightly around the inside of her left ankle.

With these remarks about the autocrats of the dinner table, who teach their children which muscles to anchor their bodies to for the rest of their lives, we conclude our survey of those influences which are most important in later childhood, and are now ready to consider the next stage in the development of the script.

NOTES & REFERENCES

1 Erikson, E. *Childhood and Society. Loc. cit.,* p. 81.

2 The time schedules given here, up to the age of puberty, are based mainly on memories of grown-up patients and reports of parents about their offspring, corroborated by reading, and only to a lesser extent by direct observation of children. Child psychiatrists and nursery and grade school teachers, such as those who attend the San Francisco Transactional Analysis Seminars, have for the most part found the dating acceptable.

3 The parallel between psychological trading stamps and commercial ones is truly amazing. See Fox, H. W. *The Economics of Trading Stamps.* Public Affairs Press, Washington, D.C., 1968. Almost every observation about household savers applies equally well to those who trade in psychological stamps.

4 Dr. Robert Zechnich (*Transactional Analysis Bulletin* 7: 44, April, 1968) first made the thought-provoking observation that there are Child paranoids and Parent paranoids, and Dr. Stephen Karpman pointed out that while hallucinations are truly counterfeit, delusions are not entirely so.

5 Breasted, J. *The Dawn of Conscience*. Charles Scribner's Sons, New York, 1933.
6 Tolstoy, L. *War and Peace*. The Modern Library, New York.
7 Philippe, C.-L. *Bubu of Montparnasse*. *Loc. cit.*
8 Jung. C. G. *Psychological Types*. *Loc. cit.*, p. 590.
9 Freud, S. *Three Contributions to the Theory of Sex*. E. P. Dutton & Company, New York.
10 Abraham, K. *Selected Papers*. Hogarth Press, London, 1948.
11 Erikson, E. *Childhood and Society*. *Loc. cit.*, Chapter 2.

CHAPTER NINE

Adolescence

Adolescence means high school and college days, driver's license, bar-mitzvah, initiation, having your own thing and your own things. It means hair here and there, brassières and menstruation, shaving, and maybe an undeserved affliction that blows your plans and your mind—acne. It means deciding what you are going to be the rest of your life, or at least how to fill in your time until you do decide. It means (if you really want to find out what it means) reading the three hundred or so books in print on the subject, as well as some of the very good ones that have gone out of print, and several thousand articles in magazines and scientific journals. For the script analyst it means a rehearsal, or a tryout before the show takes to the road. It means now you really are on the spot to answer the question, because if you don't you may not make it: "What *do* you say after you say Hello?" or "When your parents and teachers no longer structure your time completely, how do you structure your time?"

A · PASTIMES

Silences can be filled in by talking about things, cars or sports, usually a form of showing off, with points for the one with the most knowledge. The script comes into play by knowing more than anybody or less than anybody, by talking about triumphs or misfortunes, "I had a bigger time than you," or "I had a worse woe than you." Some people are such losers that even their misfortunes are trivial, and they can't win either way. Another topic with people you know better is ideas and feelings, comparing philosophies, "Me Too" or "With Me It's Different." A winner can be nobler or tougher, while a loser can produce bigger guilts and suffers; in between, a nonwinner may be stuck with merely mediocre feelings. A third area is PTA: "What do you do with delinquent teachers, or delinquent parents, or delinquent boy or girl friends?" This is the Life Crowd, waiting for Santa Claus, who will bring a better car, a better football team, better times, or better teachers, parents, boy or girl friends. The Death Crowd may despise all this and spend their time in more scripty ways, smoking marijuana, dropping LSD, going on "trips" together, and "really rapping." In any case, whichever crowd he runs with, Jeder learns what is acceptable and what is not acceptable to say and how to say it, and compares trading stamps with others of his ilk.

B · NEW HEROES

From such talk, from reading, and from what he sees, Jeder replaces the mythical or magical heroes of his script protocol with more workable figures, real live people or real dead ones whom he can emulate. He also learns more about real villains and how they work. At the same time he acquires a nickname, or a name form (Frederick, Fred, or Freddie; Charles, Charlie, or Chuck) which tells him how he looks to others and what he has to fight against or be. Fatso, Horseface, Blinky, or Meathead will have to work extra hard to have a happy ending. Busty and The Hairy Ape may find that sex comes easy, but what if they want something else?

C · THE TOTEM

A great many people have an animal or sometimes a vegetable which recurs again and again in their dreams. This is their totem. Thus there are bird-women, spider-women, snake-, cat-, and horse-women, rose- and herb- and cabbage-women, and many others, too. Among men, dogs, horses, tigers, large constrictor snakes, and trees are favorites. The totem appears in many forms.

Sometimes it is fearsome, as spiders and snakes almost always are, and sometimes it is benevolent, as cats and cabbages usually are. If a cat-woman has an abortion or miscarriage, it is quite likely that dead kittens will appear in her dreams.

In real life, the patient reacts to the totem animal very much as he does in dreaming. Negative totems are often connected with allergic reactions, and positive ones are highly favored as pets, although they may cause allergies, too. Some people envy their totems and try to be them. Many women would like to be cats, and say so frequently. Women's leg-and-arm movements are usually highly stylized in social situations, but their totem animals can often be surmised by watching movements of the head. They may imitate cats, birds, or snakes, which can be easily verified by watching cats, birds, or snakes. Men are freer with their limbs and bodies, and some stamp their feet like horses or throw out their arms like constrictors. This is not mere fancy on the part of the observer, since it can be confirmed by listening carefully to their metaphors and by hearing their dreams.

Totemism is usually given up by the age of sixteen. If it persists into later adolescence in the form of dreams, phobias, imitations, or hobbies, it should certainly be taken into account. If it is not that obvious, positive totemism is easily elicited by asking: "Which is your favorite animal?" or "Which animal would you like to be?" and negative totemism by: "Which animal are you most scared of?"

D · NEW FEELINGS

Masturbation is something of his own. He is not sure what to do with his new sex feelings or how to fit them into his plan, so he reacts to them with the earlier feelings he has become familiar with, his racket. Masturbation may also put him through the agony of a true existential crisis: it is something he does or does not do at a given moment, and it is (or should be) his decision alone; and once he has done it, he, and he alone, must take the consequences. These may be private feelings such as guilt (because masturbation is wicked), fear (because it will damage his health, he thinks), or inadequacy (because it will weaken his will power, he thinks). All these are "head transactions" between the Parent and the Child in his skull. On the other hand, he may have transactional feelings which depend on the reactions, real or imaginary, of his public: hurt, anger, or embarrassment, because now he thinks they have a real reason to make fun of him, hate him, or shame him. In any case, masturbation gives him a way of fitting the new sex feelings in with the old feelings he learned as a child.

But he also leans to be more flexible. From his schoolmates and teachers he gets "permission" to react with feelings other than those encouraged at home, and he also learns to cool it: not everybody takes seriously the things his folks worry about. This switch in his feeling-system gradually separates him from his family and draws him closer to people his own age. He adapts his script to the new situation and makes it more "presentable." He may even change his role from being a total failure to being a partial success, from being a loser to being merely a nonwinner and at least breaking even. If he has a winning script, he discovers that that requires a certain objectivity. He is now in a competitive situation and victories do not come automatically, but only after a certain amount of planning and work; and he learns to take a few losses without getting shaken up.

E · PHYSICAL REACTIONS

Under all this stress and change, and the need to keep cool in order to get what he wants, good or bad, he becomes more aware of his bodily reactions. His mother and father can no longer surround him with love and protection, or on the other hand, he is no longer inclined simply to cower before their rage, drunkenness, whining, or brawls. Whatever the situation at home, he is on his own outside. He must rise before his fellows and recite, and walk down long and often lonely corridors under the critical gaze of other boys and girls, many of whom already know his weaknesses. So sometimes he sweats aromatically, his hands shake, his heart pounds; girls blush, their clothes become moist, and their stomachs gurgle. In both sexes, there is an assorted loosening and tightening up of various internal and external sphincters, and this reorganization in the long run may determine which "psychosomatic" illnesses will play a major role in their scripts. Jeder becomes resphincterized.

F · THE FRONT ROOM AND THE BACK ROOM

What goes on in "the front room" and what goes on in "the back room" may be of two different colors, as the following anecdote shows. Cassandra was a clergyman's daughter who dressed in the sloppy but oddly erotic style of Loser Sex, and her life had the same quality: sloppy but oddly erotic. It was evident that her father had somehow instructed her to be seductive, while her mother had not taught her the conventional techniques for carrying this off. She agreed that her mother had not shown her how to dress or cultivate her body, but denied at first that her father had taught her to be sexy: "He was a very proper man, and very moral, as a clergyman should be." On further questioning by the therapist and the other group members concerning her father's attitude toward women, she said that it was very proper and approving, except that once in a while he sat in the back room with a few friends and they told sexy jokes, which were usually not to the credit of the female sex. Thus, her father was very proper in the "front room," but showed another side of his personality in the "back room." In other words, he showed his Parent or good little boy in the front room and his naughty Child in the room behind.

Children become aware very early in life that their parents have several sides to their characters, but they don't know how to evaluate that until they are adolescents. If they live in homes where there is "front room" behavior and "back room" behavior, they may resent this as part of the world's hypocrisy. A woman took her eighteen-year-old son to dinner when he came home from college for the holidays. She ordered a Martini for herself, but told him he couldn't have one, although she knew he liked liquor, and indeed, drank excessively. The group members had spent hours listening to her complaints about her son's drinking. Now they agreed that it would have been better if she had either not ordered a drink, or else allowed him to have one with her, but that the way she did it she was setting him up for an alcoholic script.

In script language, the front room represents the antiscript, where the parental precepts hold sway, while the back room represents the script, where the real action is.

G · SCRIPT AND ANTISCRIPT

Adolescence is the period when Jeder oscillates, or agonizes, between his script and his antiscript. He tries to follow his parents' precepts, then rebels against them, only to find himself following their script programing. He sees the futility of that and falls back on the precepts again. By the end of his adolescence, when he graduates from college, for example, or gets out of the army, he has made some sort of decision; he either settles down and follows the precepts, or breaks away and slides downhill toward his script payoff. He is likely to continue on this chosen course until he reaches forty, when he goes through his second agony. If he has followed his parents' precepts, he then tries to break out: he gets a divorce, quits his job, absconds with the profits, or at least dyes his hair and buys a guitar. If he has gone down with the script, he tries to reform by joining AA or going to a psychiatrist.

But adolescence is the period when he first feels that he can make an autonomous choice: unfortunately, this feeling of autonomy may be part of the illusion. What he often does is merely alternate more or less violently between the precepts of the Parent in his parents, and the provocations of the Child they put forth. Teen-age drug users are not necessarily rebelling against parental authority. They are rebelling against Parental slogans, but in so doing, they may simply be following the demonic come-ons, the "crazy Child," of the very same parents. "I don't want my son drinking," says mother as she takes a drink. If he doesn't drink, he is a good boy, a mama's boy. If he does drink, he is a bad boy, but he is still a mama's boy. "Don't let anybody up your skirt," says father to his daughter, looking at the waitress's skirt. Whichever way she plays it, she is still daddy's girl. She can either shack up in high school and then reform, or remain a virgin until she is married and then have affairs later. But somewhere in between, perhaps both the boy and the girl can make up their own minds and free themselves from their scripts and live life their own ways. Especially if they have permission to make up their own minds, and not "permission to make up your own mind (as long as you make it up my way)."

H · THE WORLD IMAGE

The child has a picture of the world which is quite different from the way it appears to his parents. It is a fairy-tale world, full of monsters and magic, and it persists all through his life and forms the archaic background for his script. A simple example is the night fear or night terror, where Jeder calls out that there is a bear in his room. His parents come in and turn on the light and show him that there are no bears there, or else become angry and tell him to hush up and go to sleep. Either way, his Child knows that there is, or was, a bear in the room nevertheless. Like Galileo, he cries: "Eppur se muove." The difference in the two ways of handling it does not change the fact of the bear. The reasoning approach means that when there is a bear your parents will come and protect you and the bear will go into hiding; the angry approach means that when there is a bear you are on your own. But the bear stays, either way.

By the time he grows up, Jeder's world image or script set has become much more elaborate and also much better hidden, unless it reappears with its original distortions in the form of delusions. Usually, however, there is no inkling of it until it appears in a dream, and then suddenly much of the patient's behavior becomes coherent and understandable. One woman was preoccupied with money troubles because her husband got into complex financial scrapes with various employers. But when the other group members questioned some of his actions, Wanda would angrily defend him. She was also much preoccupied with the quality of her family's diet. Actually she had no reason to worry, since her parents were well off and she could always borrow money from them. For about two years, the therapist was unable to construct a coherent picture in his own mind of what was going on, until one night she had a "script dream." She was "living in a concentration camp which was run by some rich people who lived up on the hill." The only way to get enough food was either to please these rich people or trick them.

This dream made her way of life easier to understand. Her husband was playing "Let's Pull a Fast One on Joey" with his employers, so that Wanda could play "Making Ends Meet." If he ever made any money, he was always careful to lose it at the first opportunity so that the games could continue. When things got really bad, Wanda pitched in and helped him pull a fast one on her parents. In the long run, much to their chagrin, his employers and her parents always managed to end up in control of the situation. She had to deny all this angrily in the group because it was so obviously unprofitable that, if she ever admitted it, the games would be broken up (which they eventually were). Thus, she was actually living much the way she did in her dream, her parents and her husband's employers being the rich people who lived up on the hill and ran her life, and whom they had to please or trick to survive.

Here the concentration camp was her world picture

or script set. She lived in reality as she would have to live if she lived in the camp of her dream. Her treatment up to that time was typical of "making progress." She had made a great deal of progress, but now it was clear that this progress meant merely "how to live better in a concentration camp." It had no effect on her script, but simply made her more comfortable while living it out. In order to get well, she had to get out of the concentration camp and into the real world, which for her was a comfortable one, or would be after the family affairs were in order. It is interesting to note how she and her husband selected each other on the basis of having complementary scripts. His script called for some rich people up on the hill to play tricks on, and a scared wife. Hers called for a trickster who would make her life easier in her enslavement.

The script set is usually so far removed from the reality of the patient's life that there is no way to reconstruct it by mere observation or interpretation. The best hope of getting a clear picture of it is through a dream. The "script-set dream" is recognizable because as soon as the patient tells it, many things fall into place. Pictorially, it has no resemblance to the patient's actual way of life, but transactionally, it is an exact replica. A woman who was always "looking for a way out" dreamed that she was being chased, and found a tunnel that sloped downward. She crept into the tunnel and the people chasing her could not follow. They just stood guard hoping she would come out again. She discovered, however, that there was another gang of dangerous people waiting for her at the other end of the tunnel. Thus she could go neither forward nor back; at the same time, if she relaxed, she would slide down into the arms of those who were waiting below. Therefore she had to press with her hands against the sides of the tunnel, and as long as she did that she was safe.

In script language, most of her life had been spent trapped in a tunnel in this cramped position, and it seemed clear from her attitudes and past history that the end of the script called for her to get tired of holding on and slide down into the arms of waiting death. She, too, had made considerable "progress" during her treatment up to that point. Translated, that progress meant "how to be more comfortable while holding on to the sides of a tunnel and waiting for death." A script cure meant to get her out of the tunnel and into the real world, which again was a comfortable one for her. The tunnel was her script set. There are, of course, many other interpretations of this dream, as any freshman who has taken Psychology 1 can readily see. But the script interpretation is important because it tells the therapist and the other group members, as well as the patient and her husband, what they are dealing with and what has to be done, and emphasizes that "progress" is not enough.

The tunnel scene had probably remained unchanged since early childhood, as the patient had had this dream many times before. The concentration-camp scene is evidently a later adaptation of a childhood nightmare which Wanda was unable to recall. It was clearly based on early experiences modified by reading and adolescent fantasies. Adolescence, then, is the period when the fearsome tunnels of infancy are given a more realistic and contemporary form to build the operative script set for the patient's life plan. Wanda's reluctance to probe into her husband's "tricks" shows how tenaciously people cling to their script scenes while complaining about how disagreeable they are.

One script set that can continue unchanged for a lifetime is the bathroom. In the last chapter, we gave an example of a woman whose Child spent her life sitting on the toilet, even when her body was lying on the couch. In her case, progress meant "how to have a richer social life and enjoy parties while carrying your toilet around wherever you go." Getting well meant that she had to get up and go out and leave her security tanklet behind, and this she was reluctant to do. Another girl who complained that she was ill at ease in company lived her script life crunched up on a small ledge on the face of a sheer cliff. She had a portable cliff that she carried with her wherever she went. She could make progress by being happier while crunched up on a cliff, or get well by coming down and dancing with the other people.

I · SWEATSHIRTS

All the items which have been discussed so far in this chapter are condensed into the patient's demeanor, the way he "comes on," and that is called his "sweatshirt." The sweatshirt, in an exceedingly creative, artistic, and economical phrase or two, indicates to the experienced eye the patient's favorite pastime, game, and feeling, his nickname, what he does in the front room and the back room, what kind of a mental world he lives in, what kind of ending his script calls for, and sometimes the critical sphincter, his hero, and his totem.

The sweatshirt is usually adopted in high school or early college years, the age when sweatshirts are popular. In later life it may be embroidered or the wording changed slightly, but the core of the meaning will remain unchanged.

All competent clinicians, of whatever school, have one thing in common: they are good observers. Since they are all observing the same thing—human behavior—there is bound to be a similarity in what they see and how they sort out and account for their observations. Hence the psychoanalytic idea[1] of "character defense" or "character armor," the Jungian concept[2] of "attitude," the Adlerian notion[3] of "life lie" or "life style," and the transactional metaphor of "sweatshirt" all describe very similar phenomena.*

An actual sweatshirt ("Hell's Angels," "The Losers," "Black Panthers," "Harvard Track Team," or even "Beethoven") states which gang a person belongs to, and gives some indication of his philosophy and how he is likely to respond to certain stimuli; but it does not indicate exactly how he will go about conning

---

*Many psychoanalysts consider that "transactional games" is merely a synonym for character defenses. This is not so. The sweatshirt is the character defense. Games belong to the open system of social psychology, and not to the closed energy system described by Freud.

someone and what payoff he expects. For example, it is clear that many members of the first three gangs mentioned above are riding on the "Fuck You" streetcar, but without knowing each member of the gang intimately (in the clinical sense) it is not possible to predict which ones want to be killed in order to become martyrs, which ones want merely to be manhandled so that they can cry "Police brutality!"[4] and which ones are straight. The sweatshirt indicates their collective attitude and the games they share in common, but each one is playing out his own script with its own individual payoff.

A transactional or script sweatshirt is an attitude which is clearly advertised by the person's demeanor, just as clearly as though he wore a sweatshirt with his script slogan printed on the front. Some common script sweatshirts are "Kick Me," "Don't Kick Me," "I'm Proud I'm an Alcoholic," "Look How Hard I'm Trying," "Buzz Off," "I Am Fragile," and "Need a Fix?" Some sweatshirts have a message on the front and a "kicker" on the back: for example, a woman comes on like "I'm Looking For a Husband," but when she turns her back it clearly says: "But You Don't Qualify." The man with "I'm Proud I'm an Alcoholic" on his forehead may have "But Remember It's a Sickness" on his back. Transsexuals wear particularly flamboyant ones with the front slogan "Don't You Think I'm Fascinating?" while on the back it says "Isn't That Enough?"

Other sweatshirts give a picture of a more "clubbish" way of life. "Nobody Knows the Trouble I've Seen" (NOKTIS) is a fraternity with many branches, one of which is the Melancholy Litvaks' Club. The Melancholy Litvaks' Club can be visualized by a Martian as a little wooden building, sparsely furnished with run-down furniture. There are no pictures on the wall, only a framed motto reading "Why Not Kill Yourself Today?" There is a small library consisting of statistical reports and books by pessimistic philosophers. The point of NOKTIS is not the total amount of trouble, but the fact that Nobody Knows. The NOKTIS makes sure that nobody ever finds out, either, because if any-body did know, then he couldn't say "Nobody knows," and his sweatshirt would lose its point.

The sweatshirt is usually derived from a favorite slogan of the parents, such as "Nobody in the world will love you like your father and mother do." This resigned, plod-ahead sweatshirt is disjunctive, and merely serves to separate the wearer from the people around him. By a simple twist it can be transformed into a conjunctive one which will attract other people instead of putting them off, and lead to appropriate "Ain't It Awful" pastimes and games: "Nobody loves me like my father and mother do." What attracts other people is the back of this sweatshirt, which reads: "How about you?"

We can now consider in detail two common sweat-shirts, and we shall try to demonstrate the usefulness of this concept in predicting significant items of behavior.

YOU CAN'T TRUST ANYBODY

There are certain people who quickly make it clear that they do not trust anybody. That is, they talk about life that way, but their behavior is not entirely con-sistent with what they say, because actually they are continually "trusting" people, but it usually turns out badly. The concept of sweatshirts has an advantage over the more naive approaches of "character defense," "at-titude," and "life style" because they tend to take things at face value, while the transactional analyst is accustomed to look first of all for the con or paradox, and is gratified rather than surprised when he finds it. That is what he looks for when he finds a sweatshirt, and that is what gives him his therapeutic advantage. To put it another way, character analysts analyze the front of the sweatshirt very effectively, but fail to look at the back where the game slogan or "kicker" is writ-ten, or at least it takes them a long time to get around to it, while the game analyst looks there right at the beginning.

The sweatshirt "You Can't Trust Anybody" (or

"You Can't Trust Anybody Nowadays," YOCTAN) is therefore not taken at face value. It does not mean that the wearer will avoid entanglements with people because he does not trust them. Quite the contrary. It means that he will seek entanglements for the express purpose of proving his slogan and reinforcing his position (I'm O.K.—They're not-O.K.). Hence the YOCTAN player picks untrustworthy people, makes ambiguous contracts with them, and then gratefully, or even gleefully, collects brown stamps when something goes wrong, thus confirming his position that "You Can't Trust Anybody." In extreme cases he may feel entitled to a "free" homicide, justified by repeated betrayals at the hands of people carefully chosen for their untrustworthiness. Once having collected enough brown stamps for such a payoff, the YOCTAN player may pick as his victim someone he has never met, perhaps a public figure whose murder rates the label of "assassination."

Other YOCTAN players may seize upon such an event to prove that the "authorities," such as the police who arrest the assassin, are untrustworthy. The police, of course, are paid for YOCTAN. It is part of their job not to be too trusting. Thus a tournament is started in which amateur or semi-professional YOCTAN players are pitted against professionals. The battle cries of such a tournament, "frame-up," "codes," and "conspiracy," may go on for years or even centuries, the object being to prove such propositions as: "Homer was not really Homer, but another man of the same name," "Raisuli loved Perdicaris," and "Gavrilo Princip was not really Gavrilo Princip, but another man of the same name."

The YOCTAN sweatshirt gives the following information about the wearer. His favorite pastime is discussing double-crosses. His favorite game is YOCTAN, proving that others are untrustworthy. His favorite feeling is triumph: "Now I've Got You, You Son of a Bitch." His nickname is Cagey, and the critical sphincter is his anus ("Keep a tight ass hole or you'll get screwed."). His hero is the man who proves that "the authorities" are untrustworthy. What he does in the front room is come on in a blandly righteous or ingenuous way, while in the back room he is scheming and untrustworthy (like the landlady who self-righteously said: "You can't trust any of your tenants nowadays. Only the other day I was going through the desk of one of them, and you'll never guess what I found!"). His mental world is a self-righteous one in which he is entitled to do all sorts of shady things, provided the aim is to uncover the untrustworthiness of others. His script calls for him to be done in by someone he trusts so that with his dying breath he can call out his slogan: "I knew it. You can't trust anybody nowadays."

Thus, the front of his sweatshirt, "You Can't Trust Anybody Nowadays," is a bland invitation to well-meaning people, such as unwary therapists, to prove that they are exceptions. If they don't take the trouble to look, ahead of time, it is only after the dust of battle settles down and the victorious player walks away, that they see what is written on the back: "Now Maybe You'll Believe Me." If the therapist is alert, however, he still must be careful not to move too soon, or the patient will say: "See, I can't even trust you." Then when he walks away, the kicker is still valid, so he wins either way.

DOESN'T EVERYBODY?

The thesis of this approach to life is: "It's all right to have measles, since everybody has it." Of course it isn't all right, since measles can be a dangerous disease. The classical example of "Doesn't Everybody?" occurred when a woman who was addicted to colonic irrigations came into a therapy group. She began to talk about her adventures at the colonic-irrigation parlor and everybody listened tolerantly until someone asked "What's a colonic irrigation?" The woman seemed surprised to learn that there could be so many people in one room who didn't take colonic irrigations. "Doesn't everybody?" Both her parents did, and most of her friendships were made at the irrigation parlor. The chief topic of conversation at her bridge club was comparing one irrigation parlor with another.

The "Doesn't Everybody?" sweatshirt is a favorite at high school, especially among cheer leaders, drum majorettes, and boys on the make, and even at that age it may have sinister connotations if it is reinforced by parents at home or teachers in the classroom. It is also good for business, where it is heavily exploited by undertakers, and in a lighter way by insurance salesmen. Interestingly enough, many stock salesmen, who are almost as conservative as undertakers, are wary of it. The key word, and the one that gives it its explosive political quality, is "Everybody." Who is Everybody? For the wearers of this sweatshirt, Everybody is "The people I say are O.K., including me, I hope." For this reason, they usually have two other sweatshirts that they wear on appropriate occasions. They put on "Doesn't Everybody?" when they go out among strangers. But when they are with the people they admire, they wear either "How'm I Doing?" or "I Know Prominent People." They are devotees of what Sinclair Lewis made into Babbittry[5] and what Alan Harrington satirically called "Centralism," the doctrine that the safest place to be is in dead center; Harrington's hero became such a thorough Centralist that he was able to sell an insurance policy every thirty seconds or so.[6]

The wearer of this sweatshirt has, for his favorite pastime, "Me Too," and his favorite game is "Come To Find Out" that actually "everybody" doesn't, as he knew all along. Thus his favorite feeling is being taken by (phony) surprise. His nickname is Creepy and his hero is someone who keeps everybody in line. In the front room he does what he thinks the O.K. people are doing and conspicuously avoids the not-O.K. ones, while in the back room he performs outlandish deeds, or even horrors. He lives in a world where he is misunderstood except by his cronies, and his script calls for him to be done in for one of his secret misdeeds. He does not protest much when the end comes, because he feels he really deserves it according to his own slogan: "He who breaks the rules of Everybody must suffer." And that is the kicker on the back of his sweat-shirt. "He's Different—Must Be a Kook or a Communist or Something."

Closely allied to the sweatshirt is the tombstone, which we shall consider in the next chapter.

REFERENCES

1 Reich, W. *Character Analysis*. Farrar, Straus & Company, New York, 3rd ed. 1949.
2 Jung, C. G. *Psychological Types. Loc. cit.*
3 Adler, A. *op. cit.*
4 Grier, W. H. & Cobb, P. M. *Black Rage*. Bantam Books, New York, 1969. This work contains many examples of antiscript strivings overtaken and undermined by losing scripts.
5 Lewis, S. *Babbitt*. Harcourt, Brace and World, New York, 1949.
6 Harrington, A. *Revelations of Dr. Modesto*. Alfred A. Knopf, New York, 1955.

CHAPTER TEN

Maturity and Death

A · MATURITY

Maturity can be defined in four different ways. (1) Trial by law. A person is mature when he is mentally competent and has reached the age of twenty-one. According to Hebrew law, a boy becomes a man when he reaches the age of thirteen. (2) Trial by Parental prejudice. A person is mature when he does things my way, and immature if he does them his way. (3) Trial by initiation. A person is mature when he has passed certain tests. In primitive societies these tests are tough and traditional. In industrial countries, he gets his maturity certificate when he passes his driving test. In special cases, he may be given psychological tests and his maturity or immaturity is then certified by the psychologist. (4) Trial by living. For the script analyst, maturity is tested by external events. The tests begin when the person is about to come out of a supervised and sheltered environment and the world moves in on him on its own terms. They start in the senior year at college, the final year of apprenticeship, at promotion or parole time, at the end of the honeymoon, or whenever the first opportunity offers itself in open competition or cooperation for script failure or success.

From this point of view, the common successes and failures in life depend on parental permissions. Jeder does or does not have permission to graduate from college, complete his apprenticeship, stay married, stop drinking, get promoted or elected or paroled, stay out of the mental hospital, or get well if he goes to a psychiatrist.

Through grade school and high school and the early years of college, it is possible to survive failures and even juvenile hall and reform school, especially in this country where minors are often given another chance. Nevertheless, there is a small number of suicides,[1] homicides, and addictions among adolescents, and a larger number of optional car crashes and psychoses. In less lenient countries, a failure to matriculate into college, or a criminal record, are for real, and one such mark is enough to set the individual's course for the rest of his life. For the most part, however, early failures are rehearsals rather than final performances, and playing for keeps does not begin until the twenties.

B · THE MORTGAGE

In order to play for keeps, put himself to the test, and know who he is, Jeder must take on a mortgage. In this country, he is not a man until he makes a down payment on a house, goes heavily into debt in business, or mortgages his working years to bring up his children. Those who have no mortgages are regarded as carefree, beautiful, or lucky people, but not as real people. The banker's television commercials show the great day in Jeder's life: the day he mortgages his earnings for the next twenty or thirty years to buy a house. The day he pays off the mortgage he is out of it and ready for the old people's home. This danger can be averted by taking on a bigger mortgage for a bigger house. In other parts of the world, he can mortgage himself for a bride. Just as the young man here, if he works hard, can become the "owner" or ower of a $50,000 house, so the young man in New Guinea can become the "owner" or ower of a 50,000-potato bride. If he pays that off too fast, he may be able to move up to a roomier 100,000-potato model.

Most well-organized societies, in one way or another, provide a way for young people to mortgage themselves and thus give meaning to their lives. Otherwise they might just spend their time enjoying themselves, as they do still in a few places. In that case, there is no easy way of telling the winners from the losers. With a mortgage system, the population readily divides itself. People who don't even have enough gumption to mortgage themselves are losers (according to those who run the system). People who spend their lives paying off the mortgage, so that they can never get much ahead, are the silent majority of nonwinners. The people who hold the mortgages are the winners.

People who are not interested in money-or-potato mortgages can do it another way—by becoming addicts. In that way there is a lifelong mortgage on their bodies which they can never pay off, so they are always playing for keeps.

C · ADDICTIONS

The simplest and most direct way to become a real loser is through crime, gambling, or drug addiction. Criminals are divided into two types: winners, who are professionals, and seldom if ever go to prison, and losers, who are following the injunction: "Don't have any fun!" The losers have what fun they can while they are at large, but then follow their scripts by spending drab years in prison. If they are released by discharge, parole, or legal technicality, they soon manage to get back in again.

Gamblers can also be winners or losers. The winners play carefully and save or invest their money. They like to quit when they are ahead. The losers play luck and hunches, and if they win by chance, get rid of their winnings as soon as they can, perhaps by following the famous slogan: "It may be crooked, but it's the only game in town." If they have permission to be winners, they win; otherwise they are compelled to lose. What a gambling addict needs is not an analysis, which is seldom successful, of why he gambles, but permission to stop being a loser. If he gets it, he will either stop gambling, or continue and win.

The mother's influence is most clearly shown in certain types of drug addicts. As previously noted, these are encouraged with the slogan: "Heroin, shmeroin, what's the difference as long as he loves his mother?" What such people need is permission to stop taking drugs, which means permission to leave their mothers and strike out for themselves, and that is exactly what the highly successful Synanon movement provides. Where mother's script injunction says "Don't leave me!" Synanon says "Stay here instead."

This also applies to alcoholics and Alcoholics Anonymous. Claude M. Steiner[2] discovered that almost all alcoholics had been analyzed, cajoled, or threatened concerning their drinking, but that none of his cases had ever been told simply: "Stop drinking!" Their previous jousts with therapists were based on such slogans as: "Let's analyze why you drink," "Why don't you stop drinking?," or "If you keep on drinking you'll injure yourself." Each of these is quite different in effect from the simple imperative "Stop drinking!" The "Alcoholic" player is quite willing to spend years analyzing why he drinks or explaining regretfully how he backslid, providing that in the meantime he can keep on drinking. The threat that he will injure himself is the most naive and ineffectual of all, because that is exactly what he is trying to do, following his script injunction "Kill yourself!" The threats merely add to his satisfaction by providing the gruesome details of exactly how he is bringing about his death, and by assuring him that he will be successful in fulfilling the destiny demanded by his mother. What the alcoholic needs is first permission to stop drinking, if he can take it, and then a clear and unqualified Adult contract to desist, if he can give it.

D · THE DRAMA TRIANGLE

During the period of maturity, the dramatic nature of the script is brought into full flower. Drama in life, as in the theater, is based on "switches," and these switches have been neatly summarized by Stephen Karpman[3] in a simple diagram he calls "The Drama Triangle," which is shown in Figure 12. Each hero in a drama or in life (the protagonist) starts off in one of the three main roles: Rescuer, Persecutor, or Victim, with the other principal player (the antagonist) in one of the other roles. When the crisis occurs, the two players move around the triangle, thus switching roles. One of the commonest switches occurs in divorces. During the marriage, for example, the husband is the persecutor and the wife plays the part of the victim. Once the divorce complaint is filed, these roles are reversed: the wife becomes the persecutor, and the husband the victim, while his lawyer and her lawyer play the part of competing rescuers.

Reproduced by permission
of S. B. Karpman, M.D.
© 1968 by the Transactional
Analysis Bulletin

The Drama Triangle

FIGURE 12

In fact, all struggles in life are struggles to move around the triangle in accordance with the demands of the script. Thus the criminal persecutes his victims; the victim then files a complaint, and becomes the plaintiff or persecutor with the criminal now the victim. If he is caught, the police also become his persecutors. He then hires a professional rescuer, a lawyer, who persecutes the policeman. In an interrupted rape, there is a race around the triangle. The criminal who is persecuting the girl victim becomes the victim of the rescuing policeman. The criminal's lawyer tries to rescue him by persecuting the girl victim and the policeman as well. Fairy tales, treated as dramas, show exactly this feature. Little Red Riding Hood, for example, is a victim of the persecuting wolf until the hunter rescues her, when she suddenly becomes the persecutor, putting stones in the belly of the now victimized wolf.

Minor roles in script dramas are the Connection and the Patsy, who are available to all three of the main characters. The Connection is the person who supplies what is needed for the switch, usually for a price, and is fully aware of his role: the man who sells liquor, drugs, influence, or guns. A gun, for example, often called an "equalizer," turns a coward (victim) into a braggart (persecutor), or switches the defensive into the offensive. The Patsy is there to be conned into preventing the switch, or speeding it up. The classical Patsies are juries, and the most poignant are mothers who pay to keep their sons out of jail. Sometimes the Patsy is passive and merely acts as bait for the switch, like Little Red Riding Hood's grandmother. It should be noted that the switch referred to here is the same switch that is included in the formula for games given in Chapter Two.

Karpman has many interesting variables in his fully developed theory, besides role switches. These include space switches (private-public, open-closed, near-far) which precede, cause, or follow role switches, and script velocity (number of role switches in a given unit of time). Thus, his thinking reaches far beyond the original roles as described for the game of "Alcoholic,"[4] and brings fascinating insights into numerous aspects of life, psychotherapy, and the theater.

E · LIFE EXPECTANCY

A recent study of causes of death concluded that many people die when they are ready to, and that coronary thromboses, for example, can be brought about almost by an act of will.[5] It is certainly true that most people have in their life plans a certain life span. The key question here is: "How long are you going to live?" Usually the life span has an element of competition. The Child of a man whose father died at the age of forty, for example, may not have permission to live longer than his father did, and will exist in a state of vague apprehension throughout most of his fourth decade. He becomes more and more aware that he fully expects to die before he is forty, and the most trying period will be the year between his thirty-ninth and fortieth birthdays, after which his way of living may change in one of four ways: (1) He settles down to a more relaxed way of life because he has passed the dangerous age and survived it. (2) He goes into a state of depression because by surviving he has disobeyed his script injunction and therefore loses his mother's love. (3) He begins to live a more hectic life because now he is living on borrowed time and death can strike at any moment. (4) He withdraws because his reprieve is conditional and will be withdrawn if he is caught enjoying himself. It is evident that (1) has permission to live longer than his father if he can make it, (2) does not have permission, (3) has permission to get away with what he can, and (4) has permission to make deals. In fact, (4) is an excellent example of the one-sided contract with God previously referred to, since (4), without consulting God, thinks he knows how to placate Him.

A more competitive person, however, will determine to live longer than his father did and will probably succeed in doing so. He then has to pass the hazard of living longer than his mother did, which is more difficult, since few men care to compete with their own mothers. Similarly, a daughter will competitively outlive her mother, but if her father died at an older age, she may find it difficult to live longer than he did. At any rate, a person who lives longer than both his parents did often feels uneasy in his later years. The next hurdle may be to outlive his script hero. For example, a physician came for treatment at the age of thirty-seven because his father had died when he was thirty-seven and he was afraid of dying. He withdrew from treatment shortly after his thirty-eighth birthday, because then he was "safe." By that time he had become more competitive, and his goal now was to live to be seventy-one. For a long time he was unable to account for this choice of date. Since his hero was Sir William Osler, in whose footsteps he wanted to follow, the therapist took the trouble to find out that Sir William had died at the age of seventy. The patient had read several biographies of his hero, and now recollected that many years previously he had determined to outlive him.

The treatment of such life-span neuroses is very simple. The therapist merely has to give the patient permission to live longer than his father. Psychoanalysis may be successful in such cases not primarily because of the conflicts which are resolved, but merely because the analytic situation offers protection during the critical year. Indeed, there is no conflict to resolve, since it is not pathological for the Child to feel bad about living longer than his father. That is merely a special example of "survival neurosis" which occurs to some degree in everyone who survives where others die. This is one of the principal influences in "war neuroses," and "Hiroshima neuroses," and "concentration-camp neuroses." The survivors almost always feel guilty because they have survived while others have died "in their place."[6] This indeed is what makes "the person who has actually seen someone else killed" different from other human beings. The Child will not "recover" or "be cured" of this feeling. The best that can be done is to put the feeling under Adult control so that the person can carry on a normal life and get permission to enjoy himself to some extent.

F · OLD AGE

Vitality in old age depends on three factors: (1) constitutional robustness; (2) physical health; (3) type of script. The onset of old age is determined by the same three factors. Thus some people are vital at eighty and others start vegetating at forty. Constitutional robustness is a *force majeure,* that is, it cannot be changed by Parental programing. Physical disability is sometimes a *force majeure,* and sometimes a script payoff. In the "Cripple" Script it is both. The crippling itself may occur because of unavoidable physical illness, but it is welcomed because it is part of the script and fulfills mother's injunction to end up disabled. This occurs occasionally in cases of poliomyelitis in young adults, where the man in the wheel chair says: "When I knew I had polio I almost welcomed it, as though I had been waiting for something like that." If his script called for him to be a cripple, and Nature did not help him out, he might have crashed a car. Nature's solution is simpler to deal with.

Older people may similarly welcome a stroke or a coronary occlusion, but for a different reason: not because it is part of the script, but because it relieves them of the compulsion to carry on with their script strivings. For the Child in them, these catastrophes become "Wooden Leg" or "Wooden Heart," so that they can say to the Parent in their heads: "Even you can't expect a man with a Wooden Leg or a Wooden Heart to carry on your witch's curse." Faced with a blood clot in Jeder's brain or heart, only the most ruthless parent does not concede defeat.

If a disability occurs early in life, it may fit very well into mother's script, or may throw it off completely. If it fits, the child will be raised as a professional cripple, sometimes with the help of outside organizations devoted to helping Crippled Children (as long as they stay crippled) or Mentally Retarded Children (as long as they stay mentally retarded). (The drag is due to the fact that the government subsidy usually stops if the child recovers.) In such cases, the mother learns to "face it," and teaches the child to do likewise. If it does *not* fit the mother's script, however, she does *not* learn to face it. She keeps trying, and the child learns to do likewise, so that he ends up as a one-legged jitterbug, a clubfooted broad-jumper, or a brain-damaged orthopedic specialist (all these examples exist or have existed in real life). The Crippled Children's organization and the Mentally Retarded organization pitch in here, too, and are delighted if one of their protégés makes it (with outside help). If the mother's script does not call for a physically or mentally disabled child, and the disability is so severe that it is necessarily permanent, then her life becomes a script-frustrated tragedy. If her script does call for a disabled child, and the disability is borderline, and possibly remediable, then the child's life becomes an unnecessary, script-inflicted tragedy.

Now to return to old age. Even people with robust constitutions and no physical disabilities (or only minor or hypochondriacal ones) can begin to vegetate at an early age if they have "Open-Ended" Scripts. These are commonly people living on pensions. The Parental precept is: "Work hard, and don't take any chances," and the payoff is "After that, give up." Once Jeder has put in his twenty or thirty years, and Santa Claus has come and given him his retirement banquet and gold watch, he doesn't know what to do. He is accustomed to following his script directives, but now they are exhausted, and he has no further programing in his head. Therefore he is content to sit and wait until something turns up: Death, for instance.

This raises an interesting question. What do you do after Santa Claus comes? With an "Until" Script, he comes down the chimney and brings a Freedom Certificate. Jeder has fulfilled the requirements of his script, is freed of the curse by the antiscript, and is now at liberty to do what he always wanted to do since he was a little boy. But going his own way is full of dangers, as many Greek myths attest. While he is free of his witch parent, he is also unprotected, and can easily come to grief. This is shown in fairy tales as well. A curse gives protection as well as trial and tribulation. The same witch that laid on the curse sees that the victim continues to live while he is under it. Thus, Sleeping Beauty was protected by the briar forest for a hundred years. But the moment she woke up, and could tell the witch to buzz off, her troubles began. A handy situation is to have a double script: an "Until" Script from one parent and an "After" Script from the other. In the commonest case this reads "You can't be free until you have raised three children" (from mother), and "After you are free you will become creative" (from father). Thus in the first half of her life Zoe is controlled and protected by her mother and in the second half by her father. In the case of a man, the double-script directive may be the same as above, but the control and protection are reversed: Father during the first phase and Mother during the second.

The vegetating aged are divided into three classes, and in this country the insignia are financial. Those with losers' scripts live alone in rooming houses or rundown hotels, and are called old men and old women. Those with nonwinning scripts own and live in small houses where they are free to develop their idiosyncrasies and eccentricities, so that they are known as old characters. Those with winning scripts live in retirement homes run by financial promoters, and are called Senior Citizens, or Mr. and Mrs. Taxpayer, which is how they sign their Letters to the Editor.

The cure for the scriptless aged is permission, but they seldom use it. There are thousands of older men living in small rooms in every large city, each of them wishing there was someone to cook for him, talk to him, and listen to him. At the same time, there are thousands of older women living under the same circumstances, wishing they had someone to cook for, talk to, and listen to. Even if the twain do happen to meet, they rarely take advantage of it, each preferring to remain in his or her familiar drab surroundings hunched over a glass or a TV set, or sitting with folded hands, waiting for a riskless, sinless death. Those were mother's directives when they were little, and these are the directives they are following seventy or eighty years later. They never took chances before, beyond a small bet at the racetrack or the stadium, so why should they jeopardize everything now? The script has vanished by its own fulfillment, but the old slogan lingers on, and when death comes they will greet him gladly. And on the front of the tombstone they will carve: "Gone to rest with his forebears," and on the back it will say: "I lived a good life, and never took any chances."

They say that in the next century, children will be grown in bottles, according to specifications laid down by the state and the parents, and there they will be genetically programed. But everybody is already raised in a bottle according to specifications laid down by the state and his parents, and there he is script-programed. Script-programing is easier to shake off than genetic programing, but few people exercise the privilege. For the ones who do, there can be a more inspiring tombstone. Nearly all pious epitaphs, translated into Martian, come out "Raised in a bottle, and stayed there, too." And so they stand, row after row of crosses and other symbols in the graveyard, all with the same motto. Only here and there is a surprise: "Raised in a bottle— but I jumped out." Many people refuse to do that, even when there is no cork.

G · THE DEATH SCENE

Death is not an act, nor even an event, for the one who dies. It is both for those who survive. What it can be, and should be, is a transaction. The physical horror of the Nazi death camps was compounded by the psychological horror, the prevention of dignity, self-assertion, or self-expression in the gas chamber. There was no brave blindfold and cigarette, no defiance, no famous last words: in sum, no death transaction. There were transactional stimuli from the dying, but no response from the killers. Thus, *force majeure* takes from the script its most poignant moment, the deathbed scene, and in one sense the whole human purpose of life is to set up that scene.

In script analysis, this is brought out by the question: "Who will be there at your deathbed, and what will your last words be?" An added question is: "What will *their* last words be?" The answer to the first query is usually some version of "I showed them"—"them" being the parents, especially mother in the case of a man and father in the case of a woman. The implication is either "I showed them I did what they wanted me to," or "I showed them I didn't have to do what they wanted me to."

The answer to this question is, in effect, a summary of Jeder's life goal, and can be used by the therapist as a powerful instrument in breaking up the games and getting Jeder out of his script:

"So your whole life boils down to showing them you were right to feel hurt, frightened, angry, inadequate, or guilty. Very well. Then that will be your greatest accomplishment—if you want to keep it that way. But maybe you would like to find a more worthwhile purpose in living."

The deathbed scene may be part of the hidden, or

script contract in marriage. The husband or wife may have a very clear image of the other partner dying first. In such cases, the spouse often has the complementary script, and is obligingly planning to do so. Thus, they get along well and pass contented years together. But if they each have the image of the other dying first, so that the scripts are crossed in this respect, those years will be contentious instead of contented, even though the scripts are complementary in other ways, as they must be for the marriage to take place. The difficulties will come out most clearly when one or the other is ill or in pain. A common script based on the death scene is found in the marriage of a younger woman to an older man. Even if the cynics say she marries him for his bread, the script scene is equally important, and she will always be at his side in time of danger, on the good side to take care of him, but also so as not to miss the final payoff transaction. If he is intuitively aware of this, the marriage may have only a very narrow margin of safety, since it is not easy to get along with someone who is waiting for you to die. The same situation, with the double payoff, may arise in the marriage of a younger man to an older woman, although these are less common. It is evident that the original script protocol has father in place of the aging husband, or mother in place of the aging wife.

H · THE GALLOWS LAUGH

Actual death scenes result from either *force majeure* or script directives. The untimely death due to ineluctable forces of fate—disease or violence in time of peace or war—is always a stark and simple tragedy. Scripty deaths are usually marked by the gallows smile or gallows humor. The man who dies with a smile on his face or a joke on his lips is dying the death his script calls for, and the smile or the joke says: "Well, mother, I'm now following your instructions, ha ha. I hope you're happy." The criminals of London in the eighteenth century were true disciples of gallows humor, often entertaining the admiring crowd with a final epigram as the trap was sprung,[7] because their deaths followed their mothers' injunction: "You'll end on the gallows as your father did, my boy!" The last words of many famous men were also jokes because they were likewise at peace with their mothers: "You'll die famous, son." Deaths due to human *force majeure* are not accompanied by such levity, because they may be in direct contradiction to mother's injunction: "Live long!" or "Die happy!" There are no stories of gallows humor in German concentration camps (as far as I know). There is also a special injunction "Enjoy death as you enjoyed life!" which permits a deathbed joke even if death comes sooner than mother could tolerate. Such a joke is, in fact, an attempt to ease the mother's bereavement.

All this means that in most cases the witch parent plans Jeder's life span and the manner of his death, and barring internal or external upheavals, he will, by his own decision, carry out the parental decree.

I · THE POSTHUMOUS SCENE

In success scripts, this is usually visualized with good reality sense. Jeder has built up a large organization, or left a large body of work, or a lot of children and grandchildren, and he knows that his life production will survive him and that those connected with it will see him to his grave.

Those with tragic scripts, however, have a pathetic fallacy about what will happen after their deaths. The romantic suicide, for example, says: "They'll be sorry," and imagines a sad, sentimental funeral which may or may not come to pass. The angry suicide says: "I'll fix them," and may be equally misguided, since they may be glad to have him out of the way. "I'll show them" may fail by not getting his name in the papers much beyond the obituary file. On the other hand, the futility or frustration suicide, who tries to kill himself unobtrusively with the fantasy that nobody will really notice or care, may make the front-page headlines due to some unforeseen complication. Even the man who kills himself so his wife can have the insurance money may be foiled if he has neglected to read his policy carefully.

In general, the consequences of killing oneself are no more predictable than the consequences of killing someone else. Except for soldiers and gangsters, death, either suicide or homicide, is a poor way to try to solve life's problems. Certainly, prospective suicides should be firmly told the two inviolable rules of death: (1) No parent is allowed to die until all of the children are over eighteen. (2) No child is allowed to die while either of his parents is still living.

The cases of people who have no minor children and no living parent have to be considered on their individual merits, but every patient who is accepted for treatment must make a firm commitment not to violate either of the two rules, if one or both apply. A similar commitment required of certain patients is that they will never use for improper purposes (including suicidal attempts) any medications prescribed by the therapist.

J · THE TOMBSTONE

The tombstone, like the sweatshirt, has two sides. The questions here are: "What will they put on your tombstone?" and "What will you put on your tombstone?" A typical answer is: "They'll say 'She was a good girl,' and I'll say: 'I tried hard but I didn't make it.'" Once more, "they" usually means the parents, or parental people. "Their" epitaph is the antiscript, while the patient himself writes his script injunction on his tombstone—in the case above: "Try hard but be sure not to make it." Thus the tombstone speaks nothing but good of the dead, for one side says that he fulfilled the precepts of his antiscript, while the other indicates that he was also an obedient child who followed his mother's script instructions, however encouraging or discouraging they might have been.

If the patient tries to avoid reading his tombstone by saying there won't be one, that answer has its own meaning. Whoever cops out on death is also copping out on life. But the therapist should then insist on getting the two epitaphs with the question: "What would be on it if there was one?" or "Here you've got to have one."

K · THE TESTAMENT

Whatever the person's fantasies about what will happen after his death, his will or his posthumous papers offer the last chance for a payoff. His whole life may have been based on a falsehood or a concealed treasure which is only revealed as a triumph after his death— a trick which he plays on posterity. There are many historical examples of this: hidden talents which only come to light when the manuscript or the canvases are found hidden in a closet, or works out of character which are found concealed among the papers. Hidden wealth and hidden poverty are commonly revealed during the probate of wills. Wills are also favorite vehicles for switch tricks. The commonest has already been mentioned: mother leaves the bulk of her property to the "faithless" daughter and cuts the devoted one off with a pittance. Sometimes bigamy only comes to light after the will is read. The question here is: "What is going to be the most important item in your will? What is going to be the biggest surprise for those you leave behind after you die?"

We have now followed Jeder in his script from before birth until after death. But there are many more interesting things to consider before we go on to talk about treatment.

NOTES & REFERENCES

1 The suicide rate increases roughly with age, and is lower for females than for males at all ages save early adolescence.
2 Steiner, C. M. "The Alcoholic Game," *Transactional Analysis Bulletin* 7:6–16, January, 1968.
3 Karpman, S. "Fairy Tales and Script Drama Analysis." *Transactional Analysis Bulletin* 7: 39–43, April, 1968.
4 Berne, E. *Games People Play. Loc. cit.*
5 Cf. early deaths following bereavement as described by

W. D. Rees & S. G. Lutkins in *British Medical Journal* 4:13, October 7, 1967, and summarized in *Current Medical Digest,* March, 1968.

6 Lifton, R. J. *Death in Life*. Random House, New York, 1968.

7 Cf. Grose, F. *A Classical Dictionary of the Vulgar Tongue.* Digest Books, Northfield, Illinois, 1971 (facsimile of 1811 edition).

PART III

The Script in Action

CHAPTER ELEVEN

Types of Scripts

A · WINNERS, NONWINNERS, AND LOSERS

Scripts are designed to last a lifetime. They are based on childhood decisions and parental programing which is continually reinforced. The reinforcement may take the form of daily contact, as with men who work for their fathers, or women who telephone their mothers every morning to gossip, or it may be applied less frequently and more subtly, but just as powerfully, through occasional correspondence. After the parents die, their instructions may be remembered more vividly than ever.

In script language, as noted, a loser is called a frog[1] and a winner is called a prince or a princess. Parents want their children to be either winners or losers. They may want them to be "happy" in the role they have chosen for them, but do not want them to be transformed, except in special cases. A mother who is raising a frog may want her daughter to be a happy frog, but will put down any attempts of the girl to become a princess. ("Who do you think you are?") A father who is raising a prince wants his son to be happy, but often he would rather see him unhappy than transformed into a frog. ("How can you do that to us? We've given you the best of everything.")

The first thing to be decided about a script is whether it is a winning one or a losing one. This can often be discovered very quickly by listening to the person talk. A winner says things like: "I made a mistake, but it won't happen again," or "Now I know the right way to do it." A loser says "If only . . ." "I should've . . ." and "Yes, but . . ." There are also near misses, nonwinners whose scripts require them to work very hard, not for the purpose of winning, but just to stay even. These are "at leasters," people who say "Well, at least I didn't . . ." or "At least, I have this much to be thankful for." Nonwinners make excellent members, employees, and serfs, since they are loyal, hard-working, and grateful, and not inclined to cause trouble. Socially, they are pleasant people, and in the community, admirable. Winners make trouble for the rest of the world only indirectly, when they are fighting among themselves and involve innocent bystanders, sometimes by the millions. Losers cause the most grief to themselves and others. Even if they come out on top they are still losers, and drag other people down with them when the payoff comes.*

A winner is defined as a person who fulfills his contract with the world and with himself. That is, he sets out to do something, says that he is committed to doing it, and in the long run does it. His contract, or ambition, may be to save $100,000, run the mile in less than four minutes, or get a Ph.D. If he accomplishes his goal, he is a winner. If he ends up in debt, sprains his ankle in the shower, or flunks out in his junior year, he is clearly a loser. If he saves $10,000, comes in second at 4:05, or goes into industry with an M.A., he is an at-leaster: not a loser, but a nonwinner. The important thing is that he sets the goal himself, usually on the basis of Parental programing, but with his Adult making the final commitment. Note that the man who goes for 4:05 and makes it is still a winner, while the one who goes for 3:59 and only makes 4:05 is a nonwinner, even though he beats the one whose ambition is lower. On a short-term basis, a winner is one who becomes captain of the team, dates the Queen of the May, or wins at the poker game. A nonwinner never gets near the ball, dates the runner-

---

*All this (and much of what follows) may sound familiar to some readers because it is reduced to simple terms and I have said it elsewhere[2] in much the same way, since this particular section was written several years ago.

up, or comes out even. A loser doesn't make the team, doesn't get a date, or comes out broke.

Furthermore, the captain of the second team is on the same level as the captain of the first team, since each person is entitled to choose his own league and is judged by the standards which he himself sets up. As an extreme example, "living on less money than any-one else on the street without getting sick" is a league. Whoever does it is a winner. One who tries it and gets sick is a loser. The typical, classical loser is the man who makes himself suffer sickness or damage for no good cause (like Della in Chapter Three). If he has a good cause, then he may become a successful martyr, which is the best way to win by losing.

A winner knows what he'll do next if he loses, but doesn't talk about it; a loser doesn't know what he'll do if he loses, but talks about what he'll do if he wins. Thus, it takes only a few minutes of listening to pick out the winners and losers at a gambling table or a stockbroker's, in a domestic argument or in family therapy.

The basic rule seems to be that a winning script payoff comes from the nurturing Parent through the counterscript slogans. A nonwinner gets his payoff from the controlling Parent through injunctions. A loser is led down the path to a bad payoff by the provocations and seductions of his parent's crazy Child, which tempts his self-destructive demon.

B · SCRIPT TIME

Winning or losing, the script is a way to structure the time between the first Hello at mother's breast and the last Good-by at the grave. This life time is emptied and filled by not doing and doing; by never doing, always doing, not doing before, not doing after, doing over and over, and doing until there is nothing left to do. This gives rise to "Never" and "Always," "Until" and "After," "Over and Over," and "Open-Ended" scripts. These are best understood by reference to

Greek myths, since the Greeks had a strong feeling for such things.

"Never" scripts are represented by Tantalus, who through all eternity was to suffer from hunger and thirst in sight of food and water, but never to eat or drink again. People with such scripts are forbidden by their parents to do the things they most want to, and so spend their lives being tantalized and surrounded by temptations. They go along with the Parental curse because the Child in them is afraid of the things they want the most, so they are really tantalizing themselves.

"Always" scripts follow Arachne, who dared to challenge the Goddess Minerva in needlework, and as a punishment was turned into a spider and condemned to spend all her time spinning webs. Such scripts come from spiteful parents, who say: "If that's what you want to do, then you can just spend the rest of your life doing it."

"Until" or "Before" scripts follow the story of Jason, who was told that he could not become a king before he had performed certain tasks. In due time he got his reward and lived for ten years in happiness. Hercules had a similar script: he could not become a god until he had first been a slave for twelve years.

"After" scripts come from Damocles. Damocles was allowed to enjoy the happiness of being a king, until he noticed that a sword was hanging over his head, suspended by a single horse-hair. The motto of "After" scripts is "You can enjoy yourself for a while, but after that your troubles begin."

"Over and Over" scripts are Sisyphus. He was condemned to roll a heavy stone up a hill, and just as he was about to reach the top the stone rolled back and he had to start over again. This is the classical "Almost Made It" script, with one "If only" after another.

The "Open-Ended" script is the nonwinner or "Pie in the Sky" scenario, and follows the story of Philemon and Baucis, who were turned into laurel trees as a reward for their good deeds. Old people who have carried out their Parental instructions don't know what to do next after it is all over, and spend the rest of their lives like vegetables, or gossiping like leaves rustling in the wind. This is the fate of many a mother whose children have grown up and scattered, and of retired men who have put in their thirty years of work according to company regulations and their parents' instructions. As already noted, "Senior Citizen" communities are filled with couples who have completed their scripts and don't know how to structure their time while waiting for the Promised Land where people who have treated their employees decently can drive their big black cars slowly down the left-hand lane without being honked at by a bunch of ill-bred teen-agers in their hot rods. "Was pretty feisty myself as a teen-ager," says Dad, "but nowadays." And Mom adds: "You wouldn't believe what they . . . And we've always paid our . . ."

C · SEX AND SCRIPTS

All of these script types have their sexual aspects. "Never" scripts may forbid either love or sex, or both. If they forbid love but not sex, they are a license for promiscuity, a license which some sailors and soldiers and wanderers take full advantage of, and which prostitutes and courtesans use to make a living. If they forbid sex but not love, they produce priests, monks, nuns, and people who do good deeds such as raising orphan children. The promiscuous people are continually tantalized by the sight of devoted lovers and happy families, while the philanthropists are continually tempted to jump over the wall.

"Always" scripts are typified by young people who are driven out of their homes for the sins which their parents have prompted them to "If you're pregnant, go earn your living on the streets" and "If you want to take drugs, you're on your own" are examples of these. The father who turned his daughter into the storm may have had lecherous thoughts about her since she was ten (ten? eight?), and the one who threw his son out of the house for smoking pot may get drunk that night to ease his pain.

The parental programing in "Until" scripts is the loudest of all, since it usually consists of outright commands: "You can't have sex until you're married, and you can't get married as long as you have to take care of your mother (or until you finish college)." The Parental influence in "After" scripts is almost as outspoken, and the hanging sword gleams with visible threats: "After you get married and have children, your troubles will begin." Translated into action now, this means "Gather ye rosebuds while ye may." After marriage, it shortens to "Once you have children your troubles will begin."*

"Over and Over" scripts produce always a bridesmaid and never a bride, and others who try hard again and again, and never quite succeed in making it. "Open-Ended" scripts end with aging men and women who lose their vitality without much regret and are content with reminiscing about past conquests. Just as women with such scripts wait eagerly for the menopause, with the hope that that will solve their "sexual problems," so the men wait until they have put in their time on the job with a similar hope of relief from sexual obligations.

At the more intimate level, each of these scripts has its own bearing on the actual orgasm. The "Never" script, of course, besides making spinsters and bachelors and prostitutes and pimps, also makes frigid women who never have one, not a single one in their whole lives, and also produces impotent men who can have orgasms providing there is no love, the classical situation described by Freud of the man who is impotent with his wife but not with prostitutes. The "Always" script produces nymphomaniacs and Don Juans, who spend their lives continually chasing after the promise of an orgasm.

The "Until" script favors harried housewives and tired businessmen, neither of whom can get sexually

---

*Part of this section follows the language of my previous work, referred to above,[2] but I don't know any better way to say it. I have been saying it this way in lectures for a long time now, as is well known to many script analysts.

aroused until every last detail of the household or the office has been put in order. Even after they are aroused, they may be interrupted at the most critical moments by games of "Refrigerator Door" and "Note Pad," little things they have to jump out of bed to take care of right now, such as checking the refrigerator door to make sure it is closed, or jotting down a few things that have to be done first thing in the morning at the office. "After" scripts interfere with sex because of apprehension. Fear of pregnancy, for example, keeps the woman from having an enjoyable orgasm and may cause the man to have his too quickly. Coitus interruptus, where the man withdraws just before he comes as a method of birth control, keeps both parties in a jumpy state right from the beginning, and usually leaves the woman stranded high and wet if the couple is too shy to use some way for her to get her satisfaction. In fact the word satisfaction, which is usually used in discussing this particular problem, is a giveaway that something is wrong, since a good orgasm should be far more substantial than the pale ghost called satisfaction.

The "Over and Over" script is one which will ring a bell for many women losers, who get higher and higher during intercourse, until just as they are about to make it, the man comes, possibly with the woman's help, and she rolls all the way down again. This may happen night after night for years. The "Open-End" script has its effect in older people who regard sex as an effort or an obligation. Once over the hill, they are "too old" to have sex, and their glands wither away from disuse, along with their skins and often their muscles and brains as well. Now they have nothing to do but fill in time until their pipes rust away. In order to avoid such vegetating, a script should not have a time limit on it, but should be designed to last a whole lifetime, no matter how long that lifetime may be.

The sexual potency, drive, and power of a human being are to some extent determined by his inheritance and his chemistry, but they seem to be even more strongly influenced by the script decisions he makes in early childhood, and by the parental programing which brings about those decisions. Thus, not only the authority and frequency of his sexual activities throughout his whole lifetime, but also his ability and readiness to love, are to a large extent already decided at the age of six. This seems to apply even more strongly to women. Some of them decide very early that they want to be mothers when they grow up, while others resolve at the same period to remain virgins or virgin brides forever. In any case, sexual activity in both sexes is continually interfered with by parental opinions, adult precautions, childhood decisions, and social pressures and fears, so that natural urges and cycles are suppressed, exaggerated, distorted, disregarded, or contaminated. The result is that whatever is called "sex" becomes the instrument of gamy behavior. The simple transactions of Greek myths, the pows, bams, and kazams that took place on Mount Olympus, which form the basis for the original version of the script, are elaborated into the trickery and subterfuges of folk tales, so that Europa becomes transformed into Little Red Riding Hood, Proserpina into Cinderella, and Ulysses into the stupid prince who is changed into a frog.

D · CLOCK TIME AND GOAL TIME

The ways of filling in short periods of social time were discussed in Chapter Two, the available options being withdrawal, rituals, pastimes, activities, games, and intimacy. Each of these has a beginning and an ending called a switch point. Over a longer period, the script also has its switch points, which usually mean that the players switch from one role to another in the drama triangle.

Richard Schechner has made a careful and scholarly analysis of time patterns in the theater[3] which also applies to the dramaturgy of real-life scripts. The two most important types he calls "set time" and "event time." Set time runs by a clock or calendar. The action begins and ends at a certain moment, or a certain time is given for its performance, as with a football game.

For script analysis, we can call this clock time (CT). In event time, the activity is to be completed, like a baseball game, no matter how long or short a time it takes by the clock. We will call this goal time (GT). There are also combinations of these. A boxing match can terminate either when all the rounds are completed, which takes a set time or clock time, or when there is a knockout, which is event time or goal time.

Schechner's ideas are useful to the script analyst, particularly in dealing with "Can" and "Can't" scripts. A child doing his homework can be given five different instructions. "You need plenty of sleep, so you can stop at nine o'clock." This is called Clock Time Can. "You need plenty of sleep, so you can't work after nine o'clock." This is called Clock Time Can't. "Your homework is important, so you can stay up and finish it." This it Goal Time Can. "Your homework is important, so you can't go to bed until you finish it." This is Goal Time Can't. The two Cans may relieve him, and the two Can'ts may irritate him, but none of them box him in. "You have to finish your homework by nine o'clock so you can get to sleep." Here Clock Time and Goal Time are combined, which is called a "Hurryup." It is evident that each of these instructions can have a different effect on his homework and on his sleep, and when he grows up, on his working habits and his sleeping habits. From a Martian point of view, the effects on the child's script may be quite different from what the parents say they meant. For instance, Clock Time Can't may end up with insomnia, and Goal Time Can't may throw in the sponge some day. (Chuck in Chapter Six was on Goal Time Can't and threw in with psychotherapy instead of with a coronary occlusion. Others prefer the coronary.)

This list is important because it helps to explain how people choose to fill in their time while following their script injunctions. "You can live until you're forty" (CT Can) is usually busy trying to get done what he wants to do; "You can live until your wife dies" (GT Can) is likely to spend more time worrying about how to postpone the event and keep his wife alive. "You can't do it until you meet the right men"

(GT Can't) may spend a lot of time looking for men, where "You can't do it until you're twenty-one" (CT Can't) has time for other things. It also explains why some people are run by the clock while others are goal oriented.

REFERENCES

1 Young, D. "The Frog Game." *Loc. cit.*
2 Berne, E. *Sex in Human Loving.* Simon & Schuster, New York, 1970.
3 Schechner, R. *Public Domain.* The Bobbs-Merrill Company, New York, 1969, Chapter 2.

CHAPTER TWELVE

Some Typical Scripts

Scripts are artificial systems which limit spontaneous and creative human aspirations, just as games are artificial structures which limit spontaneous and creative intimacy. The script is like a piece of decorated, frosted glass which Jeder's parents place between him and the world (and themselves), and which he then secures and keeps in good repair. He peers at the world through it, and the world peers back, hoping to see at least a flicker, and perhaps a burst, of his true humanity. But since the world is peering through its own frosted glass, the visibility is no better than that between two skin divers with cloudy face pieces at the bottom of a muddy river. The Martian has rubbed his face piece with No-Fog, so he can see a little better. Here are some examples of what he sees, which may help to explain how the script gives an answer in each case to the question: "What do you say or do after you say Hello?"

A · LITTLE PINK RIDING HOOD, or THE WAIF

Little Pink Riding Hood was an orphan, and she used to sit in a clearing in the forest waiting for someone who needed help to pass by. Sometimes she would wander down the paths in case anyone needed her in another part of the woods. She was very poor and could not offer very much, but whatever she had she shared freely. She could hold things when people needed an extra pair of hands, and her head was full of wise precepts which she had learned from her parents while they were still alive. She was also full of merry quips, and she liked to cheer up men who were scared of getting lost in the forest. In this way she made many friends. But she was nearly always alone on weekends because then everybody went on picnics in the meadows and left her alone and a little scared herself to be in the forest. Sometimes they invited her to go along, but as she got older this happened less and less often.

She led a different life from Little Red Riding Hood, and in fact the one time they met they did not get along well together. Little Red Riding Hood was hurrying through the forest and passed by the clearing where Little Pink Riding Hood sat. She stopped to say Hello, and the two of them looked at each other for a minute, thinking they might become friends because they looked a little bit like each other except that one wore a pink cloak and the other a red one.

"Where are you going?" asked Pink. "I've never seen you around here before."

"I'm taking my grandmother some sandwiches my mother made," replied Red.

"Oh, how nice," said Pink. "I don't have any mother."

"Furthermore," said Red proudly, "when I get to my grandmother's, I'm going to be eaten by a wolf—I think."

"Oh," said Pink. "Well, a sandwich a day keeps the wolf away. And it's a wise child that knows her own wolf when she meets him."

"I don't think those merry quips are funny," said Red. "So good-by."

"How stuck-up can you get?" asked Pink. But Red had already departed. "She has no sense of humor," thought Pink to herself, "but I think she needs help." So Little Pink Riding Hood struck out into the forest to find a hunter who would protect Little Red Riding Hood from the wolf. Eventually she found one, an old friend of hers, and she told him that Little Red Riding Hood was in trouble. She followed him to the door of the hut where Red's grandmother lived and saw everything that happened there. Little Red in bed with the wolf, the wolf trying to eat her, the hunter killing the wolf, and he and Little Red laughing and joking as they cut the wolf open and put stones in his belly. But Red didn't even bother to thank Pink, which made Pink sad. And after it was all over, the hunter was better friends with Red than he had been with Pink, which made Pink even sadder. She was so sad that she began to eat peppy berries every day, and then she couldn't sleep, so she would eat sleepy berries at night. She was still a cute kid and still liked to help people, but sometimes she thought the best thing to do would be to take an overdose of sleepy berries.

CLINICAL ANALYSIS

Thesis: Little Pink Riding Hood is an orphan, or has reason to feel like one. She is a cute kid, full of wise precepts and merry quips, but she leaves it to others to do the real thinking, organize things, and carry them through. She is conscientious and always ready to help people, and has many "friends" as a result, but somehow she usually gets left out in the end. She then begins to drink and take stimulating drugs and sleeping pills, and often thinks of suicide. After she says Hello, she makes some merry quips, but that is only to pass the time until she has a chance to ask: "Can I help you with anything?" Thus she could have a "deep" relationship with a loser, but didn't do so well with winners after the quips were over.

CLINICAL DIAGNOSIS:	Chronic-depressive reaction.
FAIRY TALE:	Little Pink Riding Hood.
ROLES:	*Helpful Child,* Victim, Rescuer.
SWITCHES:	Rescuer (advising, nurturing Parent) to Victim (sad Child).
PARENTAL PRECEPT:	"Be a good helpful girl."
PARENTAL PATTERN:	"Here's how to help people."
PARENTAL INJUNCTION:	"Don't have much, don't get much, and wither away."
CHILDHOOD SLOGAN:	"Do your duty and don't complain."
POSITION:	"I'm not-O.K. because I complain." "They're O.K. because they can have things."

DECISION:	"I'll punish myself for complaining."
SCRIPT:	Wither away.
ANTISCRIPT:	Learn how to help people.
SWEATSHIRT:	Front—"I'm a Cute Kid." Back—"But I'm an Orphan."
GAME:	"No Matter How Hard I Try."
TRADING STAMPS:	Depressions.
FINAL PAYOFF:	Suicide.
EPITAPHS:	"She was a Good Kid." "I Tried."
ANTITHESIS:	Stop being a cute kid.
PERMISSION:	To use her Adult to get something worthwhile.

CLASSIFICATION

Little Pink Riding Hood is a loser's script, since everything she gets she loses. It is a Goal-Structured Can't script, with the standard slogan: "You can't make it unless you meet a Prince." It is based on a "Never" plan, "Never ask for anything for yourself." After she says Hello she proves she is a helpful, cute kid.

B · SISYPHUS, OR THERE I GO AGAIN

This is about Jack and his Uncle Homer. Jack's father was a war hero who got killed in battle when Jack was a little boy, and his mother died soon after. He was raised by his Uncle Homer who was a poor sport, a boaster, and not above cheating. He taught Jack all sorts of athletic and competitive games. But if Jack won, Homer would fly into a rage and say: "You think your shit don't stink?" If Jack lost, his uncle would laugh at him in a contemptuous, friendly way. So after a while Jack began to lose on purpose. The more he lost, the happier and more friendly his uncle became. Jack wanted to be a photographer, but his uncle said that was for sissies, and told him he should be an athletic hero instead. So Jack became a professional baseball player. What Homer really wanted was for Jack to try to be an athletic hero and fail.

With his uncle for a friend, it was not surprising that just as Jack was on his way up into the big leagues, he sprained his arm and had to retire from the game. As he said later, it was hard to explain how an experienced player like himself could get such a bad sprain in spring training, when everybody was taking it easy so as not to get injured before the beginning of the season.

Jack then became a salesman. He always started off very well, and got bigger and bigger orders until he became a favorite of the boss. At that point he felt a compulsion to goof off. He would sleep late and neglect his paper work, so that his deliveries were late. He was such a good salesman that he didn't even have to go out and sell, the customers would call him; but he would forget to put in their orders. As a result of all this, he had to have long, helpful dinners with the boss to discuss his problems in a personal way. After each dinner he would perk up a little, but after a while things would start to slide again. Sooner or later there would be a final dinner during which he would be fired in a friendly way. Then he would look for another job and start the whole cycle over. One difficulty was that he felt salesmen always had to lie and cheat a little, and that bothered him.

As a result of his treatment, Jack broke loose from his uncle and decided to go back to school and become a social worker.

CLINICAL ANALYSIS

Thesis: Sisyphus works very hard and gets right to the brink of success. At that point he gives up, stops working, and loses everything he has gained. Then he has to start over from the bottom, and repeats the cycle.

CLINICAL DIAGNOSIS:	Depressive reaction.
MYTH:	Sisyphus.
ROLES:	*Deserted Child,* Persecutor, Rescuer.
SWITCHES:	Hero (success) to Victim (failure) to Rescuer.
PARENTAL PRECEPT:	"Be a tough hero, not a sissy."

PARENTAL PATTERN:	"Cheat a little."
PARENTAL INJUNCTION:	"Don't succeed."
CHILDHOOD SLOGAN:	"I am the son of a hero."
POSITION:	"I'm not-O.K. because I'm really a sissy."
	"They're O.K. because they're successful."
DECISION:	"I've got to be a hero."
SCRIPT:	Don't make it.
SWEATSHIRT:	Front—"I'm a Super-Salesman."
	Back—"But Don't Buy Anything from Me."
GAMES:	"There I Go Again," "Schlemiel."
TRADING STAMPS:	Depressions and guilts.
FINAL PAYOFF:	Impotence and suicide.
EPITAPHS:	"He Tried Hard."
	"I Didn't Make It."
ANTITHESIS:	Stop listening to your uncle.
PERMISSION:	To go back to school and be a social worker for deserted children.

CLASSIFICATION

Sisyphus is a loser's script, since every time he gets near the top he rolls all the way down again. It is a Goal-Structured Can't Script, with the slogan: "Without me you can't make it." It is based on an "Over and Over" plan, "Try as often as you want to." The time between Hello and Good-by is structured with a game of "There I Go Again."

C · LITTLE MISS MUFFET, or YOU CAN'T SCARE ME

Muffy sat on a bar stool night after night, drinking whiskey sours. One evening a rather rough character sat down beside her. He frightened her, but she didn't run away. Eventually she married him in order to take care of him so that he could write better novels. When he was drunk he beat her physically and when he was sober, he humiliated her verbally, but still she didn't run away. The group members were at first sorry for her and horrified at her husband's behavior, but as the months elapsed, their attitude changed.

"How about getting up off your tuffet and doing something about it?" they would say. "You seem real happy when you have a sad story to tell us, so you're really playing a hard game of 'Ain't It Awful.' "

One day Dr. Q asked her what her favorite fairy tale was.

"I don't have one," she replied. "But I have a favorite nursery rhyme, 'Little Miss Muffet.' "

"So that's why you sit on your tuffet."

"Yes, I was sitting on one when he met me."

"So why doesn't he frighten you away?"

"Because when I was little, my mother told me if I ever ran away from home I would get into worse trouble than I was in already."

"Well, what about the original tuffet?" someone asked.

"Oh, you mean the potty? Well, they certainly made me sit there, and they frightened me with their threats, but I was too scared to get up and run away."

Thus her script was like Miss Muffet's, only she wasn't allowed to run away, and didn't know where she could run to. Meanwhile, instead of whey she drank whiskey. The group gave her permission to get up off her tuffet, throw away her whey, and strike out for herself. Previously, she had always looked sour, but now she began to smile.

What her husband knew was that after you said Hello to Miss Muffet, you said Boo! and she was supposed to run away. Most girls did, but Muffy didn't. If you say Boo! to Miss Muffet and she doesn't run away, the only thing to do is say Boo! again, and that is what he did. In fact, one way or another, that was about all he ever said to her, except maybe Pooh!

CLINICAL ANALYSIS

Thesis: Little Miss Muffet sits on a tuffet feeling curdy and waiting for a spider, which is all she can hope for. When he comes he tries to frighten her, but she decides that he is the most beautiful spider in the world and stays with him. He continues to frighten her periodically and she refuses to run away. But when he says that she frightens him, that really scares her. She looks around for another spider, but can't find one as beautiful as her own, so she sticks with him as long as she can help him spin.

CLINICAL DIAGNOSIS:	Character disorder.
NURSERY RHYME:	Little Miss Muffet.
ROLES:	*Rescuer,* Victim.
SWITCHES:	Victim (of circumstances) to Rescuer (of men) to Victim (of men).
PARENTAL PRECEPT:	"Don't give up."
PARENTAL PATTERN:	"Here's how to endure it—drink."
PARENTAL INJUNCTION:	"Don't leave, or you'll get into worse trouble."
POSITION:	"I'm O.K.—if I help him produce." "He's O.K.—he's producing."
DECISION:	"If I can't produce, I'll find someone who can."
SWEATSHIRT:	Front—"I Can Handle It." Back—"Kick Me."
GAMES:	"Kick Me," "Ain't It Awful."
ANTITHESIS:	Stop sitting on your tuffet and stop drinking.
PERMISSION:	To strike out on her own.

CLASSIFICATION

Little Miss Muffet is a nonwinner's script. She is not ever going to get ahead, but at least she has a spider to sit down beside her. It is a Goal-Structured Can Script with the slogan: "You can help him produce." It is based on an "Until" plan, "Sit by yourself until you meet a spider prince, then you can start living." The time between Hello and Good Night is structured with quarrels and drinking and loving and work.

D · OLD SOLDIERS NEVER DIE, or WHO NEEDS ME?

Mac was a brave soldier and took good care of his men. But one day through ignorance or disobedience a lot of them got killed, and Mac blamed himself. That, along with malaria, malnutrition, and a few other things, caused him to break down. When he recovered he worked and worked and worked so he wouldn't think, but no matter how hard he worked he never seemed to get ahead, and there was always more work to be done if he wanted to get out of debt. Mac was a caterer and went to all sorts of weddings and other celebrations, but he never had anything to celebrate himself. He was always an onlooker, helping other people feel good with food, drink, comfort, and advice, and that made him feel needed, as much as he could feel that way. The worst time was at night when he was alone and his thoughts went round and round. The best times were on Saturday night, when he got drunk and could forget and was almost one of the crowd.

This started long before he went into the army. His mother ran away with a soldier when he was six, and when he knew she was gone for sure, he fell into a raging fever and tried to die, because that meant she didn't need him. He began to work hard very early in high school, but whenever he got a little ahead, his father would somehow trick him out of the money. If he bought something for himself, his father would sell it. He was jealous of the other boys at school because they had mothers, and got into lots of fights. He didn't mind bloody noses in the schoolyard, but he couldn't stand the sight of dead bodies in the war. He was a good marksman, but he always felt sorry for the enemies he killed, nor did he hold it against them that his own men got killed. Because he blamed himself for that, he felt that his dead buddies were watching from somewhere, so he was very careful not to add insult to injury by having a good time. Except when he was drunk, and that didn't count—or did it? He could never be sure. Once or twice he tried to crash his car, and did get badly banged up, but survived. His chief way of trying to kill himself was by smoking heavily even when he had bronchitis. After a long period of treatment, he made friends with his mother, and that made him feel better again.

CLINICAL ANALYSIS

Thesis: The old soldier wasn't good enough for his mother and failed his friends. As a result, he is condemned to work hard forever without getting ahead. He is a spectator in life and cannot join in the fun. He is always willing to help others, and that means more work, but it makes him feel needed. Death will be his only release, but he can't hurt the ones who love him by actual suicide. All he can do is slowly fade away.

CLINICAL DIAGNOSIS:	Compensated schizophrenia.
SONG:	Old Soldiers Never Die.
ROLES:	*Failed Rescuer,* Persecutor, Victim.
SWITCHES:	Victim (of mother and father) to Rescuer (of men) to Victim (of circumstances).
PARENTAL PRECEPT:	"Work hard and help people."
PARENTAL PATTERN:	"Here's how to endure it—drink."
PARENTAL INJUNCTION:	"Don't get ahead."
POSITION:	"I'm not-O.K." "They're all O.K."
DECISION:	"I'll work myself to death."
SWEATSHIRT:	Front—"I'm a nice guy." Back—"Even if it kills me."
PASTIME:	Reminiscing about the war.
GAME:	"I'm Only Trying to Help You."
ANTITHESIS:	Stop killing yourself.
PERMISSION:	Tune in and get ahead.

CLASSIFICATION

Old Soldier is a nonwinner's script because it is a point of honor with old soldiers not to get ahead. It is a

Goal-Structured Can't Script with the slogan: "You can't get ahead until they need you again." It is based on an "After" plan, "After the war is over you can only fade away." The waiting time is filled by helping people and soldier talk.

E · THE DRAGON-SLAYER, or DADDY KNOWS BEST

Once upon a time there was a man named George, who was equally celebrated for slaying dragons and for fertilizing barren women. He wandered around the countryside as a completely free spirit—or so it seemed. Cantering through the meadows on a summer's day, he saw columns of smoke and forks of flame shooting upward in the distance. As he approached the scene, he heard a terrible roaring, mingled with the shrill screams of a maiden in distress. "Aha!" he cried, couching his lance. "This is my third dragon and maiden in less than a week. I will slay the dragon, and no doubt my bravery will be richly rewarded." A moment later he cried to the dragon: "Avast, lubber!" and to the maiden: "Have no fear!" The dragon drew back and began to paw the ground in anticipation not only of a double meal, but also of what he loved best, a good fight. The maiden, whose name was Ursula, threw her arms out and cried: "My hero! I am saved." She was delighted, not only in anticipation of being saved and watching a good fight, but also (since she was not really a maiden) at the prospect of showing gratitude to her rescuer.

George and the dragon backed off from each other, preparing for the charge, while Ursula cheered them both on. At that moment, another figure appeared on the scene, richly accoutered with a silver-mounted saddle and fat alforjas filled with golden coins.

"Hey boy!" cried the new arrival. George turned and said in surprise: "Father! How nice to see you!" He turned his back on the dragon, dismounted from his horse, and went to kiss his father's foot. A lively conversation ensued, with George saying "Yes, father.

Certainly, father. Whatever you say, father." Neither Ursula nor the dragon could hear father's side of the conversation, but it soon became apparent that it was going to go on indefinitely.

"Oh, for Christ's sake!" said Ursula, stamping her foot in disgust. "Some hero! As soon as his old man appears, he's right over there bowing and scraping, and he has no time for poor little me."

"You said it," said the dragon. "This is going to go on forever." So he turned off his flame thrower and rolled over and fell asleep.

But eventually the old man rode off, and George was ready to return to the fray. He couched his lance again, and waited for the dragon to get up and charge and Ursula to cheer him on. Instead Ursula said: "Jerk!" and walked away. The dragon got to his feet and said: "Crumb!" and he, too, walked away. When George saw that, he yelled: "Hey dad!" and galloped after his father. Ursula and the dragon both turned at the same moment and both shouted after him: "Too bad he's so old, or I'd take him on instead of you."

F · SIGMUND, or IF YOU CAN'T DO IT ONE WAY, TRY ANOTHER

Sigmund decided to be a great man. He was a hard worker, and tried to get into the Establishment, which would have been Heaven for him, but they wouldn't let him in. So he decided to look into Hell instead. There was no Establishment there, and no one was paying any attention to it. So he became an authority on Hell, which in this case was the Unconscious. He was so successful that after a while he became the Establishment.

CLINICAL ANALYSIS

Thesis: Jeder decides to be a great man. People put all sorts of obstacles in his way. Instead of spending his life fighting them head on, he goes around them to find a challenge worthy of his mettle, and becomes a great man.

CLINICAL DIAGNOSIS:	Phobias.
HEROES:	Hannibal and Napoleon.
ROLES:	*Hero,* Opponents.
SWITCHES:	Hero, Victim, Hero.
PARENTAL PRECEPT:	"Work hard, and don't give up."
PARENTAL PATTERN:	"Use your intelligence and find out what to do about it."
PARENTAL INJUNCTION:	"Be a great man."
POSITION:	"I'm O.K.—if I produce." "They're O.K.—if they think."
DECISION:	"If I can't get to Heaven, I'll move Hell."
SWEATSHIRT:	None visible.
TRADING STAMPS:	Not a collector.
GAME:	No time for games.
ANTITHESIS:	None necessary.
PERMISSION:	Already has enough.

CLASSIFICATION

This is a winner's script because Jeder is script-driven and does what he has to do. It is a Goal-Structured Can Script with the slogan "If you can't do it one way you can try another." It is based on an "Always" plan, "Always keep trying." After Hello, the next thing is to get to work.

G · FLORENCE, or SEE IT THROUGH

Florence's mother wanted her to marry well and settle down to a life in high society, but God's voice came to Florence and told her that her destiny was to serve the human race. For fourteen years everyone around her fought her decision, but at last she prevailed and began her career as a nurse. By tremendous efforts and still against opposition from those around her, she gained the favor of the Establishment and even of the Queen. She dedicated herself completely to her work and would have no part of intrigue or public acclaim. She revolutionized not only nursing, but also public health throughout the British Empire.

CLINICAL ANALYSIS

Thesis: Florence's mother wants her to be socially ambitious, but somewhere inside her a voice says she is destined for greater things. She fights her mother vigorously to gain her way. Other people put obstacles in her way, but instead of spending her time playing games with them, she goes around them to find more challenges, and becomes a heroine.

CLINICAL DIAGNOSIS:	Adolescent crisis with hallucinations.
HEROINE:	Joan of Arc.
ROLES:	*Heroine,* opponents.
SWITCHES:	Victim, Heroine.
PARENTAL PRECEPT:	"Marry rich."
PARENTAL PATTERN:	"Do as you're told."
PARENTAL INJUNCTION:	"Don't talk back."
HALLUCINATED INJUNCTION (presumably father's voice):	"Be a heroine like Joan of Arc."
POSITION:	"I'm O.K.—if I produce." "They're O.K.—if they let me."
DECISION:	"If I can't serve humanity one way, I'll serve it another."
SWEATSHIRT:	Front—"Take care of the soldiers." Back—"Do it better than before."
TRADING STAMPS:	Not a collector.
GAME:	No time for games.
ANTITHESIS:	None necessary.
PERMISSION:	Already has enough.

CLASSIFICATION

This is a winner's script and is classified the same as the one above. In both these cases, the subjects have taken losing scripts (Hannibal, Napoleon, Joan of Arc) and turned them into winning ones despite all external opposition. This was accomplished by leaving alternatives open so that they could go around the opposition instead of meeting it head on. This is the quality of flexibility, which in no way diminishes determination or effectiveness. Thus, if Napoleon and Joan of Arc had made conditional decisions, their script payoffs would have been quite different: for example, "If I can't fight the English, I'll fight disease."

H · TRAGIC SCRIPTS

There is still considerable debate as to whether winners are winners because they have winning scripts, or because they have permission to be autonomous. But there is little doubt that losers are following the programing of their parents and the urgings of their own inner demons. Tragic scripts (which Steiner calls "hamartic" ones[1]) may be either noble or ignoble. The noble ones are a source of inspiration and of noble dramas. The ignoble ones repeat the same old scenes and the same old plots with the same drab cast, set in the dreary "catchment areas" which society conveniently supplies as depots where losers can collect their payoffs: saloons, pawnshops, brothels, courtrooms, prisons, state hospitals, and morgues. Because of the stereotyped outcomes, it is easy to see the scripty elements in such life courses. Thus, books on psychiatry and criminology which give numerous and extensive case histories are excellent sources for studying scripts.[2]

A bad script is laid on the child by the Fascist Sneer, and he clings to it on the principle of the Nostalgic Prisoner. The Fascist Sneer is as old as history, and works as follows. The people are told that the enemy king or leader is filthy, incoherent, debased, and brutish, more animal than human. When he is captured, he is put in a cage with a few rags, no toilet facilities, and no eating utensils. After a week or so he is exhibited to the people, and sure enough, he is filthy, incoherent, debased, and brutish, and gets more and more so as time goes on. Then the conquerors smile and say: "I told you so."

Children are essentially captives of their parents, and can be reduced to any state the parents desire. For example, a girl is told that she is a hysterical, self-pitying crybaby. The parents know her weak spot and can torment her in front of visitors until she finds it intolerable and is reduced to tears. Since this is labeled "self-pity," she tries hard not to cry, and so when she does give way, it is like an explosion. Then the parents can say: "What a hysterical reaction! Every time we have visitors she does that. What a crybaby," etc. The key question of script analysis research is: "How would you raise a child so that when she grew up, she would react the way this patient does?" In answering this question, the script analyst more and more frequently is able to describe the patient's upbringing accurately before he is told about it.

Many people who have spent long years in prison find the outside world cold, difficult, and frightening, and commit an offense in order to be sent back to prison. It may be miserable, but it is familiar, they know the rules so as to keep out of serious trouble, and there are old friends there. In the same way, when a patient attempts to break out of his script cage, he finds it cold "out there," and since he no longer plays the old games, he loses his old friends and has to make new ones, which is often scary. Therefore he slides back into his old ways, like a Nostalgic Prisoner.

All this may make the script and its effects a little more understandable.

NOTES & REFERENCES

1 Steiner, C. M. *Games Alcoholics Play. Loc. cit.* Liddell and Scott give several variants of which the most relevant in *hamartetikos* (prone to failure), from Aristotle, Eth. N.2, 3, 7.

2 One of the most recent, and most enlightening and convincing studies of a particular kind of loser is *Another Look at Sex Offenders in California*, by Louise V. Frisbie. (California Department of Mental Hygiene, Sacramento, 1969.) While there is reason to believe that the author knows at least of the existence of script analysis, characteristically (of

criminologists) she ignores it, while offering many clear examples of scripty behavior. E.g., a man was put on three years' probation and committed no known offenses until two weeks before his probation expired. He could offer no explanation for becoming involved, but managed to get arrested for "perversion" with a prostitute (p. 60). Ben Karpman's two-volume *Studies in Criminal Psychopathology* (Medical Science Press, Washington, D.C., 1933 and 1944) offer fascinating examples of *hamartia* with full case histories. The first volume was published in the midst of the first wave of "bottom dog" books during the Great Depression, heralded by Edward Dahlberg's novel of that name (*Bottom Dogs*, 1930) and was far more interesting and convincing than most of the fiction published during that period. The current wave of bottom-dog literature (dating perhaps from William Burroughs' *Naked Lunch* [Grove Press, New York, 1962]) is more sophisticated, but no less dreary and stereotyped. From the script point of view, nothing has changed during the past thirty years, not even the style, which, after all, goes back to Joyce's *Ulysses* (1922) or at least to his *Work in Progress* (*Finnegans Wake*) and other things published in *transition* of the late twenties. Joyce even wore dark glasses, like many of his current imitators. (Dr. Stephen Karpman, incidentally, originator of the Drama Triangle described in Chapter 10, is Dr. Ben Karpman's son.)

CHAPTER THIRTEEN

Cinderella

A · CINDERELLA'S BACKGROUND

For the script analyst, the story of Cinderella has everything. It includes a large variety of interlocking scripts, innumerable nooks and crannies where delightful new discoveries can be made, and millions of real-life counterparts for every role.

Cinderella in this country usually means "The Little Glass Slipper." This is a translation of the French version of Charles Perrault, first published in 1697, and first Englished by Robert Samber in 1729.[1] In his dedication to the Countess of Granville, Samber makes it clear that he understands very well the scripty influence of such stories. He says that Plato "desires Children might suck in those Fables with their Milk, and recommends it to Nurses to teach them to 'em." Perrault's Morals to the tale of "Cinderilla" were, of course, Parental Precepts.

> But that thing, which we call good grace,
> Exceeds by far a handsome face;
> Its charms by far surpass the other,
> And this was what her good Godmother
> Bestow'd on Cinderilla fair,
> Whom she instructed with such care,
> And gave her such a graceful mien,
> That she became thereby a Queen.

The last three lines describe the Parental pattern which Cinderilla received from her godmother, and which exactly parallels the pattern described for the "lady" in Chapter Six. Perrault also draws a second moral, which stresses the need for Parental permission if a child is ever to amount to anything.

A great advantage 'tis, no doubt, to man,
To have wit, courage, birth, good sense and brain . . .
But none of these rich graces from above,
In your advancement in the world will prove
Of any use, if Godsires make delay,
Or Godmothers your merit to display.

Samber's translation was slightly changed by Andrew Lang for his *Blue Fairy Book,* which is one of
the most popular fairytale books read to and by children, and that is whence they get their first picture of
Cinderella. In this kindly French version, Cinderella
forgives her two stepsisters, and finds rich husbands
for them. *Grimm's Fairy Tales,* which are also very
popular in this country, contains the German version,
called "Ashenputtel." This is a bloody tale ending with
the sisters' eyes being systematically pecked out by
doves. Cinderella stories are found in many other nations.[2]

With this background, we are ready to consider a
Martian view of Cinderella, patterned after Perrault,
which is the version most English-speaking children
have in mind, and discuss the various scripts involved,
many of which will be easily recognizable in real life.
What Martian and real life tell us, as in the case of
Little Red Riding Hood, is something very important:
what happens to the characters *after* the book story
ends.

B · THE STORY OF CINDERELLA

According to Perrault, there was once upon a time
a gentleman who married for his second wife a widow,
the proudest and most haughty woman that ever was
known. (No doubt, as is usually the case with such
brides, she was also frigid.) She had two daughters
who were exactly like her in all things. He also had a
daughter by his first wife who was good and sweet
which she took from her mother, who was the best
creature in the world.

As soon as the wedding was over, the stepmother

began to treat Cinderella most cruelly. She could not bear the qualities of this pretty girl because they made her own daughters so much the more hated and despised. The poor girl bore all patiently, and dared not tell her father, who would have rattled her off, for his wife governed him entirely. When the girl had done her work, she used to go into the chimney corner and sit down upon the cinders, so they called her Cinderarse, or, more politely, Cinderella.

Now it happened that the King's son gave a ball, and invited all persons of quality to it, including the two sisters. Cinderella helped them do their hair and get dressed. Meanwhile they teased her because she was not invited, and she agreed that such a glamorous occasion was not for the likes of her. After they left, she started to cry. But her fairy godmother came along and promised that she should go, too. She instructed Cinderella: "Go into the garden and bring me a pumpkin." She then scooped out the pumpkin and turned it into a golden coach. There were mice for horses, a rat for a fat jolly coachman with fine whiskers, and lizards for footmen. Cinderella got a fine dress to wear, and jewels, and little glass slippers. Her godmother warned her not to stay at the ball after the clock struck twelve.

Cinderella made a sensation at the dance. The Prince gave her the most honorable place, and the King himself, old as he was, could not help looking at her, and whispering about her to the Queen. At a quarter to twelve, she left. When her sisters came home, she pretended that she had been asleep. They told her about the beautiful strange Princess. Cinderella smiled, and said: "Oh, she must be very handsome indeed. How I would like to see her! Lend me some of your clothes, so I can go there tomorrow night." But they said they wouldn't lend their clothes to such a Cinderarse, and Cinderella was glad, because she wouldn't have known what to do if they had agreed.

The next night Cinderella was having such a good time that she forgot to leave until the clock started to strike twelve. As soon as she heard it, she jumped up and fled, nimble as a deer. The Prince chased her, but he could not catch hold of her, even though in her haste she lost one of her glass slippers, which the Prince took up very carefully. A few days later, the Prince caused it to be proclaimed, by sound of trumpet, that he would marry her whose foot this slipper would just fit. He sent men around to try the slipper on all the women in the kingdom. After the two sisters had tried to thrust their feet into it without success, Cinderella, who knew the slipper, said laughing: "Let me try it." Her sisters laughed, too, and began to make fun of her. The gentleman who was sent to try the slipper said that he had orders to let everybody do so. He told Cinderella to sit down, and found that the slipper fitted her as if it had been made of wax. The astonishment her two sisters were in was very great; but much greater when Cinderella pulled out of her pocket the other slipper and put it upon her foot. Then her godmother came in, and with her wand changed Cinderella's clothes into rich and magnificent garments.

When they saw that she was the beautiful Princess, the two sisters threw themselves at her feet and said: "Sorry," whereupon Cinderella embraced them and forgave them. Then she was taken to the Prince, and a few days later he married her. Cinderella gave her two sisters lodgings in the palace, and married them the same day to two great lords of the court.

C · INTERLOCKING SCRIPTS

There are so many interesting features in this story, that it is difficult to know where to begin the discussion. First of all, the cast is much larger than it appears at first sight. In order of appearance, the persons are as follows:

Father	Godmother	(Queen)
Stepmother	(Coachman,	(Guards)
Daughter A	Footmen)	A Gentleman
Daughter B	(People at the ball)	Two Lords
Cinderella	Prince	
(Mother)	King	

This comprises nine principal characters, a few silent parts and one-liners, and lots of extras. The most interesting thing about the cast is that almost all of them are crooked, as we shall see shortly.

Another feature is the clarity of the switches, which is common to most stories intended for children. Cinderella starts out as an O.K. person, then becomes first a Victim, later a teasing Persecutor, and finally a Rescuer. The stepmother and her daughters are changed from Persecutors into Victims, much more so in the German "Ashenputtel" version, where the two stepsisters cut off parts of their feet in an attempt to make the slipper fit. The story also introduces the other two classical roles, as found in the "Alcoholic" game. The Connection in this case is played by the godmother, who supplies Cinderella with what she needs, while the Patsies are the lords who were chosen to marry the wicked sisters.

Let us now consider the scripts of the people involved. It takes a little time to realize how many of the characters have their scripts revealed in this apparently simple tale.

1. *Cinderella.* She has a happy childhood, but then must suffer until a certain event happens. The crucial scenes, however, are time structured: she can enjoy herself as much as she pleases until the stroke of midnight, and then she must return to her former state. Cinderella apparently avoided the temptation to play "Ain't It Awful," even with her father, and is simply a melancholy, forlorn figure until the action begins with the ball. Then she plays "Try and Catch Me" with the Prince, and later, with a scripty smile, "I've Got a Secret" with her sisters. The climax comes with a smashing game of "Now She Tells Us," as Cinderella, with a teasing laugh, gets the payoff for the winning script.

2. *Father.* Father's script calls for him to lose his first wife and then cast off his daughter and marry a bossy (and presumably frigid) woman who will make him and her suffer. But he has a trick up his sleeve, as we shall soon see.

3. *Stepmother.* She has a loser's script. She, too,

plays "Now She Tells Me," seducing the father into
marrying her and then revealing her true, wicked self
immediately after the wedding. She lives through her
daughters, and hopes to get a princely payoff for them
from her mean behavior, but ends up the loser.

4. *The Stepsisters*. Their counterscripts are based on
their mother's precept "Take care of yourself first and
don't give a sucker an even break," but the outcome is
based on the injunction "Don't succeed." Since that is
also the script injunction for their mother, it was evidently transmitted from their grandparents. They play
a hard game of "Schlemiel," first getting Cinderella (or
Cinderarse, as they called her) thoroughly messed up,
and then apologizing and obtaining her forgiveness.

5. *Godmother*. Actually, she is the most interesting
of all the characters. What were her motives in out-
fitting Cinderella for the ball? Why didn't she just
have a nice talk with her and comfort her, instead of
sending her out into all the glitter? The situation was
that stepmother and stepsisters were gone for the evening, and only Cinderella and her father were left in
the house. Why was godmother so anxious to get rid
of Cinderella? What was going on "back at the
ranch," where godmother and father were alone for the
evening, while everyone else was away at the ball?
Her telling Cinderella not to stay after midnight was a
good way to insure that Cinderella would stay out that
long, and also to insure that she would be the first to get
home. This avoided the risk of the other females finding godmother there, since Cinderella's approach gave
her warning to take off in good time. From a cynical
point of view, the whole story sounds like a setup to
allow father and godmother to spend the evening together.

6. *The Prince*. The Prince was a jerk, and no doubt
got what he deserved after he was married. He lets the
girl get away twice in a row without getting any clue as
to her identity. Then he is unable to catch her in a foot
race, even though she is limping along with only one
shoe. Instead of finding her himself, he sends a friend
to do the job for him. And finally, he marries this girl
of dubious upbringing and questionable family less

than a week after he meets her. In spite of the superficial impression that he wins her, all this points to a loser's script.

7. *The King.* The King has an eye for the girls, and is a bit of a blabbermouth. Nor does he protect his son from his own impulsiveness.

8. *The Gentleman.* He is the straightest of all the characters in the story. Instead of being sloppy or supercilious, and laughing at Cinderella as her sisters were doing, he gets his job done with a fine sense of justice. Nor does he run off with Cinderella himself, as a lesser man might have done, but brings her safely to his employer. He is honest, efficient, and conscientious.

9. *The two lords,* of course, are patsies to allow themselves to be married off to two very uncool girls whom they know nothing about, having only met them on their wedding day.

D · CINDERELLA IN REAL LIFE

The important thing is that all these characters can be picked out in real life. Here, for example, is the story of a Cinderella.

Ella's parents got divorced when she was little, and she stayed with her mother. Shortly afterward, her father remarried. He had two daughters by his second wife, who was jealous of Ella when she came to visit, and also begrudged the money her father sent for her support. A few years later, her mother also remarried, and then Ella had to go to live with her father because her mother and new stepfather were more interested in drinking than in taking care of her. Ella wasn't at all happy in her new home because her stepmother made it clear that she didn't like her, and her father did little to protect her. She always had the last choice in everything, and her sisters teased her. She grew up very shy and had few dates when she was a teen-ager, while her sisters led an active social life in which she was not invited to share.

Ella had one advantage, however. She knew something the others didn't know. Her father had a mistress, a divorcée named Linda, with a Jaguar, who wore very expensive hippie-type necklaces and sometimes smoked marijuana. Ella and Linda secretly became good friends, and used to have long talks about their problems with dad. In fact, Linda gave Ella advice about many different things, and was like a godmother to her. She was particularly concerned because Ella did not have much social life.

One afternoon Linda said: "Your mother is away, and your sisters are going out on dates, so why don't you go out, too? It's no fun sitting at home all by yourself. I'll lend you my car and some clothes, and you can go to the Rock-and-Roll Ballroom where there are lots of boys you can meet. Come over to my place about six and we'll eat and I'll fix you up." Ella figured Linda and her father were going to spend the evening together, and she agreed.

Linda thought Ella looked very nice all dressed up. "Don't hurry back," she said, as she handed Ella the keys to her beautiful car.

At the dance, Ella met a nice boy named Roland, and started to go out with him. But a poor guitar-player friend of his was much more interested in Ella than he was, and soon she was going out secretly with Prince, the guitar-player. She didn't want Prince to call at her house because she knew her mother wouldn't approve of his unkempt appearance, so Roland would come and pick her up with his date and then they would meet Prince and the four of them would go somewhere together. Meanwhile, her father and stepmother and sisters thought she was dating Roland, and Ella and he had lots of fun over that.

Prince was not really poor. He came from a well-to-do family and had a good education, but he wanted to make it on his own as an entertainer. He began to get more and more famous. After he was well known, he and Ella decided to tell her family the real story before they found out from someone else. It came as a complete surprise to her sisters, who adored Prince's records, and they were very jealous when Ella announced that she had won such a rich prize for a husband. But she didn't bear them any grudge for their ill-treatment, and often got them free tickets to Prince's concerts. She even introduced them to some of his square friends.

E · AFTER THE BALL IS OVER

We have already seen that Little Red Riding Hood's childhood adventure with the wolf (her grandfather) had a profound effect on her life when she grew up.

Knowing what real people do, it is not hard to surmise also what happened to Cinderella after she married. She found that being a Princess was lonely. She wanted to play "Try and Catch Me" with the Prince some more, but he was not much fun. She teased her sisters when they came to visit her, but that didn't amuse her for long either, particularly since they were not very good sports about it now that she had the upper hand. The King sometimes looked at her oddly, and he wasn't as old as he pretended to be, but he wasn't as young as he pretended to be either; in any case, she didn't want to think about things like that. The Queen was nice to her, but very proper as a Queen had to be. As for the rest of the people at court, Cinderella had to be very proper to them. In due time, she did have the son that she and everybody else were waiting for, and there was much joy and celebration. But she did not have any other children, and since the little Duke was taken care of by nursemaids and governesses as he grew up, Cinderella was soon as bored as before, particularly during the day when her husband was out hunting, and in the evening when he sat with his gentlemen friends losing money at cards.

After a while, she made an odd discovery. The people who interested her most, although she tried to keep it a secret, were the scullery maids and the cinder maids who cleaned the fireplaces. She would find all sorts of excuses to be around while they were working.

Pretty soon she was making suggestions to them from her own long experience with these matters. Then she found, riding around the little kingdom in her carriage, sometimes with her son and his governess and sometimes without them, and strolling through the poorer parts of the towns and villages, something she had known all along: all over the kingdom there were thousands of women doing scullery work and cleaning out hearths. She would stop and gossip with them and talk about their work.

Soon she got into the habit of making regular rounds to some of the poorest homes where the women had to work the hardest. She would put on old clothes and sit in the cinders with them talking, or help them in the kitchen. Word soon got around in the kingdom about what she was doing, and the Prince even quarreled with her about it, but she insisted that that was what she wanted to do more than anything else, and kept on doing it. One day, one of the ladies of the court, who was also bored, asked permission to go with her. As time went on, others got interested. Pretty soon, dozens of noble ladies were putting on their oldest clothes every morning and going into town to help poor housewives with their meanest work, meanwhile gossiping with them and hearing all sorts of interesting tales.

Then the Princess had the idea of all the helping ladies getting together to talk about the problems they encountered, so she organized them into the Ladies' Cinder and Scullery Society, with herself as President. Now, whenever foreign chimney sweeps, vegetable-peddlers, woodcutters, scullery maids, or trash-collectors passed through town, they were invited to the palace to talk to the Society about what was new in their trades and how things were done in their countries. In this way Cinderella found her place in life, and she and her new friends contributed much to the welfare of the kingdom.

F · FAIRY TALES AND REAL PEOPLE

Looking around in society or in one's clinical practice, it is not difficult to find examples of every character in the Cinderella story, from Cinderella herself, and her immediate family, through the ineffectual Prince and the King, and even down to the jolly, whiskered coachman who never said a word and who started out life as a rat. There are also shoe-fitters who Come To Find Out that what looks like a sow's ear is really a silk purse.

While the therapist can listen to the patient and search around in his head for a fairy tale which may match what he hears, or leaf through Stith Thompson's motif-index when he gets home, a simpler way is to ask the patient himself to tell his life story as a fairy tale. An example of this was Drusilla, who was not a patient, but obliged during a seminar on fairy tales.

An ancestor of Drusilla's, many generations back, invented a widely used device, so that his name is still a household word. The story starts with Drusilla's mother Vanessa, who was a descendant of this patriarch. Vanessa's father died when she was quite young and she went to live in the home of her great-uncle, Charles. Charles lived on a large ranch near Los Angeles, complete with swimming pool, tennis courts, private lake, and even a golf course. Vanessa grew up in these surroundings and met people from many countries. She was not too happy, however, and when she was seventeen she eloped with a man from the Philippines, named Manuel. Their two daughters, Drusilla, and her sister Eldora, were raised on a plantation there. Drusilla was her father's favorite. Eldora was something of a tomboy and became very athletic, an expert horsewoman, archer, and golfer. Her father used to beat her, but he never laid a hand on Drusilla. One day when Eldora was about eighteen her father wanted to punish her. By this time Eldora was as tall as he was and much stronger. As he advanced on her she cowered, as she had always done, but suddenly Drusilla observed a strange transformation. Eldora drew herself up, flexed her muscles, and said to her father, "Don't you dare ever lay a hand on me again." She looked him fiercely in the eye and her father in his turn now cowered and backed away. Shortly after this, Vanessa divorced him and went with her two children to live on Uncle Charles' estate.

Drusilla in her turn now lived on her great-uncle's ranch and met a man from a faraway country, whom she married. By him she had two children. But she always liked to make things so she became a weaver, and finally a teacher of weaving. It was because of her interest in weaving that she came to the seminar on fairy tales.

Drusilla was asked to tell her story in the form of a fairy tale, using the script analyst's language of frogs, princes, princesses, winners and losers, witches and ogres. Here is the way she told it:

"Once upon a time there was a king who conquered many lands, which his oldest son inherited. The kingdom was passed on from generation to generation. Since the oldest son inherited the kingdom, the younger sons got very little. One of the poor younger sons had a daughter Vanessa, but he died while on a hunt. Vanessa's uncle, the king, then took her to live with him at the palace and there she met a prince from a strange and faraway land. The prince took her away from the kingdom to his own kingdom by the sea, where many strange flowers and forests grew. After a while, however, she found that her prince, Manuel, was really a frog. Manuel was equally surprised when he discovered that the beautiful bride whom he had married because he thought she was a princess turned out to be a witch. Manuel and Vanessa had two daughters. The oldest, Eldora, was a frog like her father and he did not like her at all and used to scold her and beat her when she was little. The younger daughter, Drusilla, was a princess, and Manuel treated her like one.

"One day a fairy came to Eldora and said to her, 'I will protect you. If your father ever tries to beat you again you must tell him to stop.' So the next time

Manuel tried to beat Eldora she suddenly felt very strong and told him that he must never beat her again. Manuel was very indignant and thought it was his wife Vanessa who had caused Eldora to turn on him, so Vanessa decided to move away. She and her two daughters left the faraway kingdom and went back to the kingdom of Uncle Charles where the two girls lived happily until one day a prince came and fell in love with Drusilla. They were married with great pomp and had two beautiful daughters and Drusilla lived happily ever after, raising her children and weaving beautiful tapestries."

Everybody at the seminar thought that was a fine story.

NOTES & REFERENCES

1. Samber's book is entitled *Histories or Tales of Past Times: With Morals. By M. Perrault*. It was printed for J. Pote, at Sir Isaac Newton's Head, and R. Montagu, the Corner of Great Queen Street, 1729.

2. Thompson, Stith. *Motif-Index of Folk-Literature*. Indiana University Press, Bloomington and London, 1966. Cinderella-type tales are classified by Thompson under "Unpromising heroine. Usually, but not always, the youngest daughter." Some of the sources he gives are: Irish, Breton, Italian, Tuamotu, and Zuñi. He also includes "Unpromising heroes" as male Cinderellas. He refers back to "Victorious younger daughter," which gives a large number of references from all over the world, including India and China. There are also "Abused youngest daughter" and, most widespread of all, "Cruel Stepmother." Other common roles and transactions are "Prince in love with lowly girl," "Girl sends sign message to prince," and "Little girl bribes prince to marry her." Ashes as the abode of an unpromising heroine are found in French, Spanish, Italian, Icelandic, Chinese, and Micmac Indian lore, among others. The "Slipper Test" is also fairly widespread. The original French *Cendrillon* wore slippers of squirrel fur (*vair*, as it is called in heraldry), which was taken for *verre* and mistranslated as glass. Ashenputtel's slippers were gold. Cinderella, as we know her, probably originated in Naples as *La Gatta Cenerentola*. In French she is Cu Cendron, Ash Bottom or Cinderarse, and in English, Cinderbreech, at times. There is an opera by

Rossini called *La Cenerentola,** and two ballets. In the ballet by d'Erlanger and Fokine the two sisters are played by male dancers, which is supposed to be comic, as comedy goes in the Russian ballet. The most famous ballet on this subject is by Prokofiev.

Cf. Barchilon, J. and Pettit, H. (eds.) *The Authentic Mother Goose*. Alan Swallow, Denver, 1960.

---

*Performed by the San Francisco Opera in 1969, and in New York in 1958, and in April, 1970. Rossini calls the sisters Clorinda and Tisbe.

CHAPTER FOURTEEN

How Is the Script Possible?

Jeder sits at a player piano, his fingers wandering over the keys. The roll of paper, punched out long ago by his forebears, turns slowly as he pumps away. The music pours forth in a pattern that he cannot change, at times melancholy, at times gay, now jarring, and now full of melody. Occasionally he strikes a note or a chorus whose sound may blend with what is written, or disturb the smooth flow of the fateful song. He pauses to rest, for the roll is thicker than the whole scroll of the law in the temple. It contains the law and the prophets, the songs and the lamentations, an old testament and a new: a truly magnificent, a mediocre, a dreary, or a miserable gift given to him piece by piece by his loving, indifferent, or hateful parents. He is under the illusion that the music is his own, and has for his witness his body, slowly wearing out from hour after hour and day after day of pumping. Sometimes, during the pauses, he rises to take a bow or a boo from his friends and relatives, who also believe that he is playing his own tune.

How is it that the members of the human race, with all their accumulated wisdom, self-awareness, and desire for truth and self, can permit themselves to remain in such a mechanical situation, with its pathos and self-deception? Partly it is because we love our parents and partly it is because life is easier that way, but partly also it is because we have not yet evolved far enough from our apelike ancestors to have it otherwise. We are more aware of ourselves than apes are, but not really very much. Scripts are only possible because people don't know what they are doing to themselves and to others. In fact, to know what one is doing is the opposite of being scripted. There are certain aspects of bodily, mental, and social functioning which happen to man in spite of himself, which slip out, as it were, because they are programed to do so. These heavily influence his destiny through the people around him, while he still retains the illusion of autonomy. But there are also certain remedies which can be applied.

A · THE PLASTIC FACE

It is, above all, the plasticity of the human face which makes life an adventure rather than a controlled experience. This is based on an apparently trivial biological principle which has an enormous social power.[1] The human nervous system is so constructed that the visual impact on the onlooker of small movements of the facial muscles is greater than the kinesthetic impact on the subject. A two-millimeter movement of one of the small muscles around the mouth may be quite imperceptible to Jeder but quite obvious to his companions. This can be easily verified in front of a mirror. The extent to which the subject is unaware of what he looks like is easily demonstrated by the commonplace act of picking the front of the teeth with the tongue. Jeder may do this with what seems to him extreme discretion and delicacy. As far as he can judge from his kinesthetic or muscular sensations, he is hardly moving his face at all. But if he does it in front of a mirror, he sees that which feels like a minor movement of the tongue actually brings about a gross distortion of his features, especially the chin and including the neck muscles. If he pays more attention than he usually does to his muscular sensations, he will also notice that the movement is affecting his forehead and temples.

In the heat of a social encounter, this phenomenon may occur dozens of times without him being aware of it: what seems to him like a small excursion of his muscles of expression causes a major change in his appearance. On the other hand, the Child in Zoe, the onlooker, is watching (as much as good manners permit) for signs which will give her an indication of Jeder's attitude, feelings, and intent. Thus Jeder is always giving away far more than he thinks he is, unless he is one of those people who habitually keep their features immobile and inscrutable and are careful not to reveal their reactions. The importance of facial plasticity, however, is shown by the fact that such an inscrutable person makes others uneasy, since they get no clues as to how to adapt their behavior.

This principle clarifies the origin of the almost uncanny "intuition" of babies and young children about people. Since babies have not yet been taught that they must not look too closely at people's faces, they are free to do so, and see much that others miss and that the subject is not aware he is giving away. In everyday life, Zoe's Adult is politely careful not to look too closely at what happens to other people's faces while they talk, but meanwhile her Child is rudely "peeking," as it were, all the time, and thus forming judgments, usually accurate, of what the other is really up to. This is particularly apt to occur in the "first ten seconds" after meeting a new person, before he has a chance to figure out how to present himself, and thus he tends to give away things he later hides. That is the value of first impressions.

The social effect of this is that Jeder never knows how much he is giving away by his facial plasticity. Things which he tries to hide even from himself are quite apparent to Zoe, who reacts accordingly, much to Jeder's surprise. He is continually giving out script signals without being aware of it. Others respond ultimately to these signals, instead of to Jeder's persona or presentation of himself. In this way the script is kept going without Jeder having to take the responsibility for it. He can keep his illusion of autonomy by saying: "I don't know why she acted that way I didn't do anything to bring it on. People sure are funny." If his behavior is odd enough, others may react in a fashion which is quite beyond his comprehension, and in this way delusions can be established or reinforced.

The remedy for this is simple. If Jeder studies his facial expressions in the mirror, he will soon see what he is doing to make people react the way they do, and he will then be in a position to change the situation if he wants to. Unless he is an actor, he will probably not want to. In fact, most people are so intent on keeping their scripts going that they will find all sorts of excuses not even to study themselves in the mirror.[2] They may claim, for example, that this procedure is "artificial," which means that the only thing that is "natural" is to let the script proceed to its mechanical, foreordained conclusion.

Clara, a well-bred Latin-American woman, offered a poignant example of the profound effect that the plastic face has on human relationships. She came to the group because her husband was about to leave her, and she said she had "no one to talk to," although she had three grown children living at home. Her husband refused to come to the group, but her twenty-year-old son readily accepted the invitation.

"I hesitate to talk to my mother," he said, "and it's hard for me to talk about her here, because her feelings get hurt easily and sometimes she has a martyr attitude. I always have to think before I say anything to her about how she'll take it, and so I really can't speak frankly."

While he enlarged on this subject for a few minutes, his mother sat next to him with her body tense and her hands folded gracefully in her lap as she had been taught from childhood, so that the only parts of her that moved visibly were her face, head, and neck. As she listened to what her son said, she first raised her eyebrows in surprise, then frowned, then shook her head slightly, then pursed her lips, then bowed her head sadly, then looked up again, and then tilted her head to one side in a martyred attitude. All the time he talked, these plastic movements of the head and face continued, a veritable cinema of emotional expression.

When her son had finished his report, Dr. Q asked her:

"Why were you moving your face all the time he was talking?"

"I wasn't doing that," she objected in surprise.

"Then why were you moving your head around?"

"I didn't know I was."

"Well, you were," said Dr. Q. "All the time he was talking, your face was reacting to what he said, and that's exactly why he feels uneasy when he talks to you. You tell him he can say anything he wants, but since your reactions to what he says are quite clear, even when you don't say a word, he hesitates. And you don't even realize that you're reacting. Now if it has that effect on him after he's grown up, imagine what it does to a three-year-old, who's carefully watching his mother's face all the time to see how he affects her. That's why he thinks before he speaks to you, and why you feel you have nobody to talk to."

"Well, what can be done about it?" she asked.

"When you get home, you could stand in front of a mirror while he's talking to you so you can see how it works. But right now, what do you think about what he said?" suggested Dr. Q, and the conversation went on from there.

In this case, Clara's Parent was listening to her son with motherly respect, and that was her active Self at the moment. Meanwhile, her Child was reacting to what he said in quite another way, but neither her Parent nor her Adult was aware of her facial movements because she couldn't "feel" them. Her son, however, was fully informed of her Child's reactions because they were right in front of his eyes. Her Parent was sincere but out of touch, and everybody in the group except herself could see why he hesitated to talk frankly to her.

The plastic-face principle is related both to "mother's smile" as previously described, and to the "gallows laugh." Mother may be quite unaware of what her face is doing, and of the powerful effect it has on her children.[3]

B · THE MOVING SELF

Along with the biological principle of the Plastic Face, the psychological principle of the Moving Self is equally important in keeping the script going, and is based on a similar defect of awareness. The feeling of

"Self" is a mobile one. It can reside in any of the three ego states at any given moment, and can jump from one to the other as occasion arises. That is, the feeling of Self is independent of all other properties of ego states and of what the ego state is doing or experiencing. It is like a charge of electricity that is free to jump from one capacitor to another, regardless of what the capacitors are used for; the *feeling* of Self is carried along with this "free cathexis".[4]

Whenever one of the ego states is fully active, that ego state is experienced at that moment as the real Self. When Jeder comes on with his angry Parent, he feels that that is really he, himself. A few minutes later, in his Adult ego state, when he wonders why he did it, he experiences the Adult as his real Self. Still later, if he is feeling ashamed in his Child ego state because he was so mean, his Child is felt as his real Self. (All this, of course, assumes that the incident is part of his real living, and that he is not merely playing the role of an angry Parent or of a contrite Child. Role-playing is the Child being phony, and is not real Self.)

To illustrate the effect that the mobile Self has in everyday life, let us take the homely example of a nagging wife. Ordinarily Zoe is good-natured, sociable, and adaptable, but at certain times she becomes very critical of her husband. This is her nagging Parent. Later, she brings out again her fun-loving, sociable, adapted Child, and forgets what she has said to him in her Parent ego state. But he does not forget, and remains wary and detached. If this sequence is repeated again and again, his wariness and detachment become permanent, which she fails to understand. "We have so much fun together," says her charming Child. "Why is it that you withdraw from me?" When her Child is her real Self, she forgets or overlooks what she said while her Parent was her real Self. Thus one ego state does not keep a very good record of what the other ego states have done. Her Parent overlooks all the fun they have had, and her Child forgets all the criticism she has offered. But Jeder's Child (and Adult as well) remembers what her Parent said, and he lives in a continual state of apprehension that it will happen again.

Jeder, on the other hand, may take very good care of her in his Parent ego state, but his Child may complain about her and whine. His Parent, overlooking or forgetting what his Child has done, may then reproach her with ingratitude "after all he has done for her." She may appreciate what he has done, but lives in apprehension of his Child's next sallies. His Parent thinks that he himself, his real Self, has always been considerate of her, which is true. But it is also true that when his whining Child is active, that is also he himself, his real Self. Thus by one ego state or real Self forgetting what the others have done, Jeder can again keep his script going without having to take responsibility for it. His Parent can say: "I've always been so nice to her, I don't know why she acts this way. I didn't do anything to bring it on. Women sure are funny." His Parent forgets how his Child has provoked her, but she, being the victim, doesn't. These two examples explain the tenacity of the O.K. positions described in Chapter 5, Section F.

Now that the principle is clear, a more lively example is in order. Such a heedless or irresponsible shift from one ego state to another might be called an "ego trip," but since that term is hippies' slang for boasting, it might be more courteous to let them keep it and find another name for shifting ego states. We shall therefore call the following anecdote "Aminta and Mab, or A PAC Trip Through the Psyche."

Mab and her mother made each other so nervous that Mab took off for the weekend to visit a girl friend in another city. Her mother tracked her down by telephone and said: "If you aren't home by Sunday morning, I'll lock you out of the house." So Mab came back Sunday evening. Her mother refused to let her in and told her she would have to find her own apartment. Mab spent that night at the home of a neighboring girl friend. On Monday morning her mother called and forgave her. Mab told this episode to Dr. Q, along with other examples of her mother's inconsistency. Some of the stories weren't at all clear, so Dr. Q decided to talk to Mab and her mother together to see if he could find out what was really going on.

As soon as they sat down, Aminta, the mother, came on with a strong Parent, righteously criticizing Mab for her sloppiness, her irresponsibility, her marijuana smoking, and other matters not uncommonly disputed between mothers and their eighteen-year-old girls. During the recital, Mab first sat with a slight smile, as though to say: "There she goes again!" Then she looked away, as though to say: "I can't stand it any more." After that she stared at the ceiling, as though to say: "Is nobody up there going to rescue me?" Aminta paid no attention to Mab's responses, but went ahead with her tirade.

When this was exhausted, Aminta changed her tune. She began to talk about what a hard time she was having; not in a whining Childlike way, but giving a realistic Adult appraisal of her marital problems, which were well known to Dr. Q. At this juncture Mab turned and looked directly at her mother with an entirely new expression, as though to say: "After all, she is a real person." As Aminta went on, Dr. Q was able to trace her shifts in ego state from moment to moment, based on his detailed knowledge of her background and experiences. At one stage she went through the same sequence as she had during the "lockout" episode, first coming on with her angry Father Parent (turning Mab out of the house), and then relenting as her tender Mother Parent took over (worrying about her "little girl" wandering around the town with no place to lay her head). This was followed by more Adult, then helpless Child, and after that angry Father again.

These wanderings can be traced by a line drawn through Aminta's ego states as in Figure 13. Starting with FP (Father Parent), we move on to MP (Mother Parent), then down to A (Adult), followed by C (Child), then returning to FP. Listening further, the line took the course shown in the diagram, FP to A to C and back to MP. In this way we can follow Aminta's PAC Trip as she moves from one circle to another.

The question is, what does this line represent? It

represents Aminta's feeling of Self, a feeling which does not reside in any one ego state, but can move freely from one to another, carried along by the "free cathexis." No matter which circle she was in at any moment, she still felt that it was her "real Self" talking.

A PAC Trip Through the Psyche

FIGURE 13

The course or locus of the free cathexis is a continuous line Aminta is not aware that "she" is changing or that her behavior is changing from moment to moment, because the feeling "This is really me" stays the same throughout. Thus, when we say that "she" moved from one ego state to another, we mean her free cathexis did, carrying with it a continuous feeling of real Self. To "herself" she seemed the same consistent person all along, but she changed so much from one phase to the next, that to someone else it seemed as though there were several different people there (in her head), each taking its turn in talking. That is the way it seemed to Mab, and that is why she could not cope with her mother. She was unable to get any feeling of consistency that would enable her to predict how Aminta would behave or respond from one moment to the next, so that she could adapt herself to her mother's mood. And Mab's behavior at times seemed just as arbitrary to her mother.

Since both Aminta and Mab understood their own ego states, it was not difficult to clarify the situation for them, and they got along better after that.

The behavior of Clara, as described in the previous section, illustrates another way in which the lack of recognition between the different ego states has a profound effect on the whole life course of the person, and the spouse and children as well. There two ego states were active simultaneously, one listening sympathetically and the other grimacing, while they studiously ignored each other like suspicious strangers, although they had been cooped up in the same inner space ship for forty-five years.

Another interesting variant occurs when the person refuses to acknowledge his own behavior even to himself. (This, too, was mentioned toward the end of Chapter Five.) Thus, a man may continue to say sincerely that he is a good driver, even though he has at least one serious accident every year, and a woman may maintain that she is a good cook even though she burns the dinner regularly. The sincerity comes from the fact that the Adult in each case is a good driver or a good cook, and the accidents are caused by the Child. Because such people have a thick and rigid boundary between the two ego states, the Adult pays no heed to what the Child has done, and can truthfully say that "I (my Adult Self) have never made a mistake." The same can happen to people who are less up tight and behave well when they are sober (with the Adult in charge) but make mistakes when they are drinking (when the Child takes over). Some of these even black out when they drink so that the Adult is completely unaware of what they have done in their intoxicated state, and in this way they can maintain the fiction of righteousness in a watertight, alcoholic way. This can happen the other way round with a person who is ineffectual in the Adult state, but has a productive Child. Just as the "bad" people don't understand the reprimands or criticisms they get for their follies, so these "good" people are unable to accept compliments for what they produced, or do so only out of politeness. The Adult really doesn't know what people are talking about when they say that the Child's creations are worthwhile or valuable, since the Adult was out of commission when they were created.

We have also previously discussed the rich woman who doesn't become poor when she loses her money, and the poor man who doesn't become rich when he gets some. In those cases, the Child knows from his script directives whether he is rich or poor, and mere money isn't going to change his position. Similarly, the man's Child knows whether he is a good driver or not, and the woman's whether she is a good cook, and a few accidents or spoiled meals are not going to change the Child's mind.

The position after a PAC trip is usually one of bland disclaimer. "I'm O.K. My own Parent didn't notice me doing anything, so I don't know what you're talking about." In these cases there is a clear implication that the other person is not-O.K. for reacting to any objectionable behavior. This is an emergency sweatshirt that reads "I forgive myself" on the front, and "Why can't you forgive me?" on the back.

There is a simple remedy for this common lack of awareness, in one ego state, for what the other ego states have done. That is for the Adult to remember and to take full responsibility for the actions of all the real Selves. This will stop the cop-outs ("You mean to tell me I did that? I must have been out of my mind!") and replace them with face-ups. ("Yes, I remember doing that, and it was really I myself who did it," or even better, "I'll see that that doesn't happen again.") It is apparent that this suggestion has many legal implications, since it would tend to eliminate the cowardly and convenient insanity cop-out. ("Wooden Brain," or "You can't blame the *me* for what the *I* did.")

C · FASCINATION AND IMPRINTING

These are best illustrated by considering the difficulties of Neville and his wife, Julia. Neville had a mole on his left cheek which exerted a morbid fascination on Julia's Child. During their courtship she succeeded in suppressing the slight repulsion aroused by this blemish, but as time passed it became increasingly troublesome, so that by the end of the honeymoon it was almost impossible for her to look straight at his face. She did not mention this uneasiness to him for fear of hurting his feelings. She did think of suggesting that he have it removed, but she decided that this would merely replace the mole with a scar, which she might find even more troublesome, so she said nothing.

Neville, on his side, was a pimple-picker, and whenever they were lying naked together he would inspect her body, and if he found any sort of minute bulge on her skin, he would feel a strong urge to pick it out with his fingernail. Julia found this a very disagreeable intrusion on her person. Sometimes his urge was so great and her objections so vehement, that they would end up turning away from each other in ill-humor.

In the course of time they also discovered that they had an unfortunate difference in their sexual tastes, which at first seemed trivial, but later became a serious bone of contention. Neville, who had been raised by a nursemaid in the West Indies, was turned on by smocks and sandals, while Julia, following the examples of her mother and sister, liked to dress more fashionably and wear high heels. Neville had, in fact, what amounted to a fetish for sandals, while Julia had a "counterfetish" for high heels; she wanted men to be excited by the way she dressed. Hence, when she complied with Neville's desires and wore sandals, she was turned off, while if she went about the house in high heels, he was turned off. Thus, although from the outside they seemed to be happily mated, their union was seriously disturbed by seeming trivialities based on very early experiences. This was particularly distressing because they themselves had thought they would make an ideal couple, well matched by all the conventional social and psychological computer standards.

Fascination occurs in lower animals, and also in infants at a certain age. The Child parts of both Neville and Julia continued to be fascinated (positively in his case, negatively in hers) by minor skin blemishes after they grew up. Imprinting has been mainly studied in birds, who will mistake for their mothers whatever objects are shown to them during the early days of their existence outside the egg. Thus ducks can be "imprinted" or turned on by a piece of colored cardboard, and will follow it around a track as though it were their mother. Sexual fetishes, which also develop very early in life, exert a similar influence on men, while women may become devoted to counterfetishes which they discover are sexually exciting to the men around them.

Fascinations and fetishes are very deep-seated, and may seriously disturb the smooth course of living in those who are afflicted with them, very much as drug addiction does. In spite of all attempts at rational Adult control, the Child is almost irresistibly repulsed by or attracted to the specific object, and as a result may make sacrifices all out of proportion to the situation in order to avoid or attain it. Hence, fascinations and fetishes may play an important part in determining the outcome of a script, particularly in the selection of those destined to play the principal roles. This is another factor which lessens the individual's ability to decide for himself what his fate will be.

The remedy for fascinations is to become aware of them, to talk them over, and to decide whether they can be lived with. The last part can be "skulled out" in "head transactions"—internal dialogues between the Adult and the Child, in this case keeping the Parent out of it until the other two understand each other clearly. After that the Parent can be allowed its say. If the person decides in his head that he can live comfortably with a negative fascination—such as a girl with a physical defect—well and good. If not, then either a remedy must be sought or he should look for a new companion. He cannot realize, without considerable analysis of his thoughts and feelings, how much such a single item may be affecting his reactions, usually as a result of his own early experiences. On the other hand, a positive fascination may enslave him beyond the bounds of reason, and should be just as carefully considered. Exactly the same applies to women who are fascinated by blemishes in their men.

The remedy for fetishes is similar. But since here another person is actively involved, there are other helpful possibilities as well. There can be an agreement for mutual indulgences, and the fetish may be happily "lived out" with the lapse of time.

D · THE ODORLESS SMELL

In addition to the biological peculiarities of the human organism described above (the plastic face, the moving self, fascination and imprinting), there are more elusive possibilities which could have an equally profound effect on human living. The first of these is extrasensory perception. If Dr. Rhine's[5] cards are sending out signals which cannot be detected by the present generation of physical instruments, but can be received by a properly attuned human mind, that is obviously a matter of considerable, though not necessarily decisive, importance. If such signals exist, their objective detection would be of interest at first mainly for sensational reasons, and there would be a field day in the Sunday supplements. The later developments of such a discovery cannot be foreseen until it occurs. No doubt it would interest the military, which is already doing research in this field, especially if the target could be selected, just as it would be in the case of the long-distance atomic- and hydrogen-bomb detonator which could be flown over the factories and depots of a potential enemy.

Telepathy would be of considerably more significance if it existed. If one human mind can send readable messages to another, and an objective means for controlling and recording such messages could be devised, that would help to understand many things about human behavior. This is the second possibility. "Telepathic phenomena," when they are reported, seem to occur most often and most poignantly between intimately related people such as husbands and wives, or parents and children, who are presumably more closely attuned to each other than to other members of the human race. Telepathy would offer an ideal medium for hovering parents to exert control over their children's behavior, and would certainly be of prime interest to the script analyst if it existed. Intuition, which is a function of the Child ego state,[6] often verges on telepathy, in that rather obscure facts about other people can be intuited with a minimum of sensory clues.[7]

When telepathy has been claimed to occur, it is very fragile and easily broken, and depends a great deal upon the frame of mind of the agent and the percipient. Extraneous factors, such as challenges by scientists, seem to diminish its accuracy or abolish it altogether, according to the published results of such challenges.[8] This does not necessarily mean that telepathy does not exist, but rather gives us an indication of its nature if it does exist. I would propose the following hypothesis, which explains with only one major and one minor assumption, all the scientifically established (mostly negative) findings. If telepathy occurs, then the young infant is the best percipient; as he grows older, this faculty becomes corrupted and progressively more unreliable, so that it occurs only sporadically and under special conditions in grownups. In structural language, the hypothesis reads: If telepathy exists, it is a function of the very young Child, and soon becomes corrupted and impaired by interference from the Parent and the Adult.

Third, just as interesting and important, although more materialistic, is the question of odorless smells. It is well known that the male of the Bombyces moth can detect downwind the presence of a freshly emerged female as far as a mile away, and large numbers of males will fly against the wind and assemble around a caged female.[9] We have to assume that the female gives off an odorous substance which attracts the males through something like the sense of smell. The question at issue here is: Does the male "know" that he is "smelling" something, or does he respond "automatically" to the chemical? It is probable that he is not "aware" of what happens, but simply responds, and flies toward the female. That is, he is attracted through his olfactory system by an "odorless" smell.

With a human being, the situation regarding smells is this: (1) If he smells certain odors, such as the perfume of flowers, he is aware of them and is consciously attracted to them. The experience may leave memory traces and that, as far as we know, is all there is to it. (2) If he smells other odors, such as feces, two things commonly occur: (a) he is aware of them and is consciously repelled by them; and (b) without any volition on his part, his autonomic nervous system is affected by them, and he may gag or throw up. (3) We can postulate a third situation: in the presence of certain chemicals, his nervous system is affected in a subtle way without his smelling anything or being aware of it. I am not speaking here of toxic matter such as carbon monoxide, but of substances which stimulate specific receptors and leave specific traces or engrams in the brain.

Several facts should be noted in this connection. (1) The olfactory area of the rabbit contains 100,000,000 olfactory cells, each with six or twelve hairs, so that the olfactory receptor area is equal to the total skin area of the animal.[10] (2) It can be presumed that electrical discharges occur in the olfactory system long after adaptation to a given odor occurs; that is, although the odor can no longer be smelled, it continues to affect the electrical activity of the nervous system. The experimental evidence for this is not decisive, but is strongly suggestive.[11] (3) Smells can affect dreams without being perceived as smells. (4) The perfumes most sexually provocative to human beings are chemically related to the sex hormones. (5) The odor of the breath and of the sweat can change with a change in emotional attitude. (6) The olfactory nerves lead into the rhinencephalon, a "primitive" part of the brain which is probably heavily involved in emotional reactions.

The hypothesis here then would be: the human being is continually stimulated by a variety of subtle chemical stimuli of which he is not aware, but which affect his emotional responses and his behavior toward various people in various situations. While there may be special (so far unknown) receptors for this, the structure of the olfactory tract itself is sufficient to deal with these effects. Such stimuli can be called odorless smells. There is no firm evidence that odorless smells actually exist; but if they did exist, they would conveniently account for many behavioral phenomena and responses which are otherwise difficult or impossible to understand in the present state of our knowledge. Their influence on the script would be durable, as in the case of fascination, fetishism, and imprinting. Newborn kittens may "smell" their mother's teats without being "aware" of it, and the "memory" of this odorless smell, or something like it, evidently affects their behavior for the rest of their lives.

E · THE REACH-BACK AND THE AFTER-BURN

The reach-back and the after-burn are similar to transactional "rackets" in that they are developed mainly, although not entirely, under instructions from the parents. They differ from rackets because they are triggered internally rather than by specific stimuli from other people.

Reach-back is defined as that period of time during which an impending event begins to have an independent influence on the individual's behavior. It is most dramatically seen in people with phobias, whose whole functioning may be disturbed for days ahead at the prospect of getting into a feared situation, such as a medical examination or a journey. Actually, however, phobic reach-back is less damaging than the reach-backs of everyday life, which may in the long run (I think) result in "psychosomatic" physical diseases.

In Dr. Q's case, when he had to give a professional lecture on Tuesday in a distant city, reach-back began when the impending trip started to interfere with his everyday activities. The preceding Thursday, he lay awake for a while planning what he had to do before he left. To make up for the lost working days, he would have to go to the office on Saturday, which day he usually took off. He made a mental list of the things he would have to take care of on Friday, such as picking up his tickets, since that was the last business day before he took the plane on Monday. Friday's schedule was slightly disturbed by the errands he had to do, and his appointments with his patients were not as relaxed or as productive as usual because he had to prepare them for his absence. Friday night at home was not as relaxed as usual either because he had to go to bed earlier than was his custom in order to get up earlier than he usually did on Saturday. Saturday evening was slightly off because he had not had his usual weekend exercise nor seen his family that day, and he was also distracted by plans for packing on the morrow. Although making an outline for the lecture itself would take less than fifteen minutes, he was preoccupied with that during Saturday's dinner. Sunday afternoon he spent at the beach, but this was not as relaxing as usual because he had to get home early to pack, which disturbed his peaceful Sunday evening. On Monday he took the airplane and that night he went to bed early at his hotel. Tuesday morning he gave the lecture and returned home.

The most frequently occurring expression in the above account is "not as usual," and it is interspersed with qualifying words such as "since," "because," and "but." All these, especially the first, are reach-back words. In summary, in order for him to give a one-hour lecture on Tuesday, which required only fifteen minutes of preparation at home, he, his family, and his patients were tensed up for several days in advance: not seriously, but enough to affect their behavior perceptibly.

Reach-back must be distinguished from Adult planning and preparation. What Dr. Q did Thursday night before he fell asleep was planning, and of itself was an Adult procedure. If he had been able to plan during his waking hours without disturbing his normal schedule, that would not be called reach-back. But because of his busy day, he did have to lose some sleep Thursday night, and *that* was reach-back. Some of the errands he went on on Friday were preparation and not reach-back, since he did them on his lunch hour, but others interfered with his usual schedule, including one phone call that came while he was talking to a patient, which disturbed his train of thought. The repeated disturbances of his train of thought were part of the reach-back. Thus, planning and preparation are Adult activities as long as they do not conflict with the person's usual patterns, but if they do, they become part of the reach-back, particularly if they disturb the Child (with apprehension, for example) or the Parent (by making him neglect his usual duties).

Each impending event influences the individual's behavior in some way, but it need not have an effect *independent* of his usual patterns. For example, most people are waiting for Santa Claus, as discussed in Chapter Ten, but this expectation is integrated into their ways of life and their usual ways of behaving. Again, impending puberty reaches far back into the life of the child, and in a certain sense its influence extends back into the womb. It is often quite evident that the approaching onset of puberty influenced what a twelve-year-old girl or boy did yesterday, but it did not do independently of everything else that happened, so it does not meet the definition of reach-back.

It is manifest that the remedy for reach-back is Adult organization: to arrange one's time as far as possible so that planning and preparation can be carried on without disturbing normal patterns of behavior. It is also necessary to look ahead. After Dr. Q learned that a one-hour lecture in a distant city had a reach-back of five days, he no longer accepted such engagements, except on one occasion when it fitted in with his vacation plans to take five days off in order to give a one-hour lecture.

After-burn is defined as that period of time during

which a past event has an independent influence on the individual's behavior. In some way, each past event does influence behavior, but after-burn refers only to those occasions when it disturbs normal patterns for an appreciable period rather than being assimilated into them or excluded from them by repression and other psychological mechanisms.

After he returned from giving the lecture, Dr. Q had to face a clean-up. He had to answer the mail and telephone calls which had piled up during his absence, and take care of the accumulated problems brought to him by his family and patients. He also had to balance the accounts and fill out the vouchers connected with his trip. Most of this clean-up was an Adult procedure, and he managed to fit it in without disturbing his normal schedule. But when one of the vouchers was returned three weeks later because he had submitted it in duplicate instead of in triplicate, he became irritated, and this distracted him slightly during his next hour with a patient. There was also the matter of the black militant. In the question period after the lecture, a black militant (who shouldn't have been there anyway because he was not a professional therapist) had asked some questions and brought out some points which troubled Dr. Q for several days afterward. Here, the paper work (so long as it did not interefere with business as usual) was an Adult clean-up job, while his irritation about the vouchers and his conflicts about the black militant were part of the after-burn, in which his Parent and Child were involved.

All in all, the Adult activities, including the planning, the preparation, the task itself (the lecture), and the clean-up, extended over a period of twelve days or so. The reach-back and the after-burn, which involved his Parent and Child, lasted somewhat longer. The after-burn, as it often is, was reactivated much later when he got the letter about the voucher, which he had to do over and then grumble about at home.

The remedy for after-burn is to prepare oneself in advance to tolerate trivial upsets, and then forget them.

The lecture episode is an example of normal reach-back and after-burn. With encouragement from the parents, however, both of these can become seriously disturbing and can contribute to the outcome of the script, particularly if it is a tragic one. Either of them, in an exaggerated form, can lead to alcohol addiction, psychosis, suicide, or even homicide. Thus, both examination reach-back, and impotence after-burn, can contribute to adolescent suicide, and stage-fright reach-back contributes to excessive drinking in actors and salesmen. The following is an example of scripty after-burn.

A twenty-three-year-old executive named Cyril came for treatment, with diarrhea as one of his chief complaints. One day he mentioned in the group that he had difficulty falling asleep at night. He would lie awake reviewing his decisions and his transactions with his staff, picking faults in what he had done, and counting the day's collection of guilt, hurt, and anger trading stamps. From his early history, it was clear that this was all done under a script directive from his mother. This after-burn lasted an hour or so, or on special occasions, two or three hours, before he could fall asleep. The therapist and the other members of the group gave him permission to end his working day without any after-burn, and go right to sleep when he wanted to, against the opposition of his nagging critical Parent, and the insomnia stopped. Soon after that, for reasons which never became clear, his diarrhea stopped also, and two months later he terminated his treatment.

Although reach-back and after-burn can each alone cause trouble in people with hard scripts, in most cases one or the other can be tolerated without serious consequences. It can be dangerous for almost anyone, however, if the after-burn of the last event overlaps the reach-back from the next one. This is most commonly seen in "overwork" syndromes; in fact, this is a good definition of overwork. No matter how great the burden, as long as the work can be done without such an overlap occurring, there is no (mental) overwork. If such an overlap does occur, then the person is overworked, no matter how small his burden actually is. After yesterday, his Parent harasses him with guilts and doubts: he shouldn't have done *that,* what will they think of him, why didn't he do it the other way; and while all this is going round in his head like stale beer, his Child is worried about tomorrow: what mistakes he might make, what they might do to him, what he would like to do to them. These vinegary thoughts slosh into the others to form an unappetizing, depressing mixture. An example:

Pebble, the accountant, works far into the night preparing the annual report. The figures do not balance, and after he gets home he lies awake worrying about it some more. When he finally falls asleep, figures still float before him in uneasy dreams and visions. When he gets up the next morning, nothing has been settled, and the after-burn of last night's work is still with him. Now he starts worrying about what he is going to do at the office today, for meanwhile his regular tasks must go on, and they reach back with a powerful grip as he tries to talk to his family at breakfast. And underneath these urgencies, on a longer time scale, is the after-burn of the mistakes he made on last year's report, for which he was rebuked by his boss; and the apprehensive reach-back of what might happen at this year's annual meeting is already churning in his stomach. Meanwhile, with his mind in the pincers of these overlaps, he has no time, energy, or motivation left for his personal life, and things start to go bad at home. His relationships there are not helped by his irritability, his neglect, and his pessimism.

In most such cases, the outcome will be determined by the balance between Pebble's harsh driving Parent and his angry depressed Child. If his Parent is stronger, he will get the job done and then collapse and be hospitalized with an agitated depression. If his Child prevails, he will start to act oddly and give up before the task is finished, and come out with a schizoid or schizophrenic state. If his Adult is stronger than both, he may sweat it out and then lapse into a state of fatigue until he is restored by a few days' rest or a vacation. Even in such favorable cases, however, if the strain goes on year after year, he may end up with a chronic physical disability. According to the information available at present, he will be a good candidate for an ulcer or high blood pressure.

The menace in Pebble's position lies in the way his time is structured. As we saw in Chapter Ten, there are two ways of scheduling a task. One is Goal Time, "I'll work until I get this finished (no matter how long it takes)." The other is Clock Time, "I'll work until midnight (and then stop no matter what)." Pebble could neither finish nor stop. He was on "Hurryup" Time. He had to complete a certain task by a certain time, and this forced combination of Goal Time and Clock Time often imposes an almost impossible problem. This occurs in the fairy tale where the girl has to separate the grain from the chaff before dawn. She could do it all given enough time, or she could do a certain amount of it by working until dawn, but in order to do all of it within the time limit, she required magic help from the fairy or the elf or the birds or the ants. Pebble doesn't have any elves or ants or other magic help, so he pays the penalty the girl would have paid if she had failed: he loses his head.

The remedy for overlaps is a matter of arithmetic. Each person has a sort of standard "reach-back time" and "after-burn time" for various kinds of situations. The kinds of situations should be listed: domestic quarrels, examination or hearings, work deadlines, travel, visits from or to relatives, etc. The two worry times should be estimated from experience with each type of situation. With the information at hand, the prevention of overlap reduces to a simple calculation. If the estimated after-burn for situation A is x days, and the anticipated reach-back for situation B is y days, then the date set for B must be at least $x+y+1$ days after the date of A. If both events can be foreseen, this is easy to arrange. If A is unforeseen, the date of B must be postponed. If that is not practical, the second choice would be to hurry up with B so as to get both A and B over with in the shortest possible interval of overlap, hoping for the best. If B is immovable, the only alternatives left are to shape up or ship out.

Mothers of small children, for the most part, are the

best examples of people who manage to shape up rather than ship out. With amazing resilience, they assimilate numbers of little after-burns and dozens of daily reach-backs in their everyday living. If they fail to do so, they become harried, and the feeling of being harried is the first sign of unmanageable overlap, and the first indication that a vacation is needed. Overlap interferes with sexual activity in both sexes, acting as an anaphrodisiac. Conversely, sex is an excellent antidote for overlaps, and for many couples a week or even a weekend away from the children restores sexual desire and power, and replaces after-burn and reach-back with warm-up and afterglow. Most normal after-burns and reach-backs run their courses in about six days, so that a two-week vacation allows the superficial after-burns to burn out, after which there are a few days of carefree living before the reach-backs begin to creep in in unguarded moments and clutter up the situation again. For the assimilation of more chronic after-burns and deeper, repressed reach-backs, however, a vacation of at least six weeks is probably necessary. This formerly proceeded much more peacefully when the month in Europe was bracketed by restful six- or seven-day Transatlantic crossings, than it does now with jet planes and their time lags, which are in themselves strenuous experiences.

Dreaming is probably the normal mechanism for adjusting after-burn and reach-back. Thus it happens that people who are deprived experimentally or punitively of the opportunity to dream eventually go into a state resembling psychosis.[12] Hence, normal sleep is important in preventing overlap and its bad effects. Since sedatives such as barbiturates reduce the amount of REM dream sleep in favor of other stages of sleep, they do not encourage the assimilation of after-burn and reach-back; the effect may be to "deposit" the unassimilated overlap in some part of the body, leading to a "psychosomatic" disorder.[13] That, however, may sometimes be preferable to the effects of prolonged and extensive insomnia.

Many philosophers of living have recommended "living day by day." This should not mean living only for the moment, or living without organization or without planning for the future. Many of these same philosophers, such as William Osler,[14] were highly organized people with surpassingly successful planned careers. In the present language, living day by day means living a well-planned and organized life, and sleeping well between each day, so that the day ends without reachback, since tomorrow is well planned, and begins without after-burn, since yesterday was well organized. This is an excellent way to overcome the disabilities which might otherwise arise from a bad script, and an equally good way to bring a good one to its happy fulfillment.

F · THE LITTLE FASCIST

Every human being seems to have a small fascist in his head. This is derived from the deepest layers of the personality (the Child in the Child). In civilized people it is usually deeply buried beneath a platform of social ideals and training, but with proper permissions and directives, as history has shown again and again, it can be liberated into full bloom. In the less civilized portion of the population, it is openly exposed and nurtured, and awaits only proper opportunities for periodic expression. In both cases it is a strong force in advancing the script; in the first case, secretly, subtly, and denied; in the second case, crudely or even proudly acknowledged. But it may be said that whoever is not aware of this force in his personality has lost control of it. He has not confronted himself, and cannot know where he is headed. A good example of this occurred at a meeting of "conservationists," where Conservo remarked how much he admired a certain tribe in Asia for taking such good care of their natural resources, "much better than we do." A humanist countered, "Yes, but they have a terrible infant-mortality rate." "Ho, ho," said Conservo, and several others joined in. "That's all to the good, now, isn't it? There are too many babies as it is."

A fascist may be defined as a person who has no respect for living tissue and regards it as his prey. This arrogant attitude is no doubt a relic of the prehistory of the human race, still surviving in the gusto of cannibalism and the joys of massacre. For carnivorous anthropoids on the hunt, ruthlessness meant efficiency and greed was motivated by hunger. But as the human mind and brain evolved through natural selection, these qualities were not bred out. After they were no longer necessary for survival, they became detached from their original goal of bringing down the dinner meat and degenerated into ends in themselves, luxuries often indulged in and enjoyed at the expense of other human beings. Ruthlessness developed into cruelty, and greed into exploitation and theft. Since the prey—the flesh itself, and especially human flesh—was largely replaced by more compliant stomach-filling commodities, it began to be used to satisfy psychological hungers. The pleasures of torture replaced or preceded the pleasures of eating, and "He He" took over from "Yum Yum." It became less important to kill him (or her) than to hear and watch him (or her) scream and grovel. This became the essence of fascism—a roving band seeking male or female prey to torment or deride—whose art lay in probing for the victim's weakness.

There are two by-products of the grovel, both of them advantageous to the aggressor. The biological effect is sexual pleasure and excitement, with the victim available to indulge even the most ingenious perversions the favorite of record being anal rape. Torture brings about a peculiar intimacy between the torturer and the victim, and a profound insight into each other's souls, an intimacy and insight which is often otherwise lacking in both their lives. The other by-product is a purely commercial one. The victim always has valuables which can yield a profit. For cannibals it may be strength derived from magic organs such as the heart or the testicles, or even the ear. For advanced peoples, the fat can be used to make soap, and golden tooth fillings can be salvaged. These yields are exploited after the furor of personal encounter has subsided, and they are "melted down" into anonymity.

As the human embryo grows, it relives the whole evolutionary tree. Sometimes it gets hung up and is born with relics of ancient stages, such as gill clefts. As children grow, they relive the prehistory of the human race and go through hunting and planting and manufacturing stages, and they may get hung up at any of these. But everyone retains some vestiges of all of them.

The small fascist in every human being is a little torturer who probes for and enjoys the weakness of his victims. If this comes out openly, he is a cripple-kicker, a stomper, and a rapist, sometimes with some excuse or other such as toughness, objectivity, or justification. But most people suppress these tendencies, pretend they are not there at all, excuse them if they show their colors, or overlay and disguise them with fear. Some even try to demonstrate their innocence by becoming the purposeful victims instead of the aggressors, on the principle that it is better to shed their own blood than that of others, but blood they must have.

These primitive strivings become interwoven with the injunctions, precepts, and permissions of the script, and form the basis for third-degree or "tissue" games that draw blood. He who pretends that these forces do not exist becomes their victim. His whole script may become a project to demonstrate that he is free of them. But since he is most likely not, this is a denial of himself and therefore of his right to a self-chosen destiny. The solution is not to say, as many do, "It's frightening," but rather "What can I do about it and what can I do with it?" It is better to be a martyr than to be a troglodyte, that is, a man who refuses to believe he has ascended from an apelike creature because he hasn't yet, but to know oneself is better than both.

It is important to realize that certain "genocidal" aspects of human nature have remained unchanged during the past five thousand years regardless of any genetic evolution which has taken place during this period; they also remain immune to environmental and social influences. One of these is the prejudice against darker people which has persisted unchanged since the dawn of recorded time in ancient Egypt, whose "miserable people of Cush" are still represented in oppressed

Negro populations throughout the world.[15] The other is "search and destroy" warfare. For example:

"234 Viet Cong ambushed and killed" and "237 villagers slaughtered in Viet Nam." (Both from U.S. Army reports, 1969.)

Compare: "800 of their soldiers by my arms I destroyed; their populace in the flames I burned; their boys, their maidens, I dishonored. 1000 of their warriors' corpses on a hill I piled up. On the first of May, I killed 800 of their fighting men, I burned their many houses, their boys and maidens I dishonored etc. (From the Annals of Assur-Nasir-Pal, Column II, about 870 B.C.E.)

Thus for at least 2800 years there have been willing and eager corpse-counters. The good guys end up as "casualties"; the bad guys as "bodies," "dead," or "corpses."

G · THE BRAVE SCHIZOPHRENIC

Besides the biological and psychological characteristics of the human organism which allow the preprogramed script to become the master of personal destiny, societies are set up in such a way as to encourage this lack of autonomy. This is done by means of the transactional social contract, which reads: "You accept my persona or self-presentation, and I'll accept yours." Any abrogation of this contract, unless it is one specifically permitted in a given group, is regarded as rudeness. The result is a lack of confrontation: confrontation with others and confrontation with oneself, for behind this social contract lies a hidden individual contract between the three aspects of the personality. The Parent, Child, and Adult agree among themselves to accept each other's self-presentation, and not everyone is courageous enough to change such a contract with himself when it is advisable.

Lack of confrontation is seen most clearly in the case of schizophrenics and their therapists. The majority of therapists (in my experience) say that schizophrenia is incurable. By this they mean: "Schzophrenia is incurable by my kind of psychoanalytic therapy, and I'm damned if I'm going to try anything else." Hence they settle for what they call "making progress," and like the well-known electrical manufacturer, progress is their principal product. But progress means merely making the schizophrenic live more bravely in his crazy world, rather than getting him out of it, and so the earth is full of brave schizophrenics living out their tragic scripts with the help of not so brave therapists.

Two other slogans common among therapists are also common among the general population: "You can't tell people what to do," and "I can't help you, you have to help yourself." Both of these are outright falsehoods. You *can* tell people what to do, and many of them will do it and do it well. And you *can* help people, and they don't have to help themselves. They merely have to get up, after you have helped them, and go about their business. But with slogans such as those, society (and I don't mean Arsisiety, I mean *all* societies) encourages people to stay in their scripts and carry them through to their often tragic endings. A script merely means that someone told the person what to do a long time ago and he decided to do it. This demonstrates that you can tell people what to do, and are in fact telling them all the time, especially if you have children. So if you tell people to do something other than what their parents told them, they may decide to follow your advice or instructions. And it is well known that you can help people get drunk, or kill themselves, or kill someone else; therefore, you can also help them stop drinking, or stop killing themselves, or stop killing other people. It is certainly possible to give people *permission* to do certain things, or to stop doing certain things which they were ordered in childhood to keep doing. Instead of encouraging people to live bravely in an old unhappy world, it is possible to have them live happily in a brave new world.

Thus we have listed above seven factors which make the script possible and encourage its continuation: the plastic face, the moving self, fascination and imprinting, silent influences, the reach-back and the after-burn, the little fascist, and the acquiescence of other people. But we have also listed a practical remedy for each one.

H · THE VENTRILOQUIST'S DUMMY

As psychoanalysis came into its own, it pushed aside much valuable work that had been done previously. Thus, free association replaced the centuries-long tradition of introspection. Free association was concerned with the contents of the mind, leaving it to the psychoanalyst to figure out from this how the mind worked. This could only be done when it did not work smoothly. There is no way to figure out how a closed machine (a "black box") works as long as it works perfectly. This can only be found out if it makes mistakes, or is induced to make a mistake by throwing a monkey wrench into it. Thus, free association is only as good as the psychopathology behind it: the switches, the intrusions, the slips, and the dreams.

Introspection, on the other hand, takes the cover off the black box, and lets the Adult of the person peer into his own mind to see how it works: how he puts sentences together, which direction his images come from, and what voices direct his behavior. Federn was the first psychoanalyst, I think, to revive this tradition, and to make a specific study of internal dialogues.

Almost everyone has said "to himself" at some time: "You shouldn't have done that!" and he may even have noticed that he answers "himself": "But I had to!" In this case, it is the Parent saying "You shouldn't have done that!" and the Adult or Child saying: "But I had to!" This exactly reproduces some actual dialogue of childhood. Now what is really happening? There are three "degrees" of such internal dialogue. In the first degree, the words run through Jeder's head in a shadowy way, with no muscular movements, or at least none perceptible to the naked eye or ear. In the second degree, he can feel his vocal muscles moving a little so that he whispers to himself inside his mouth; in particular, there are small abortive movements of the tongue. In the third degree, he says the words out loud. The third degree may take over in certain disturbed conditions so that he walks down the street talking to himself, and people turn their heads to watch and are likely to think he is "crazy." There is also a fourth degree, where one or other of the internal voices is heard as coming from outside the skull. This is usually the voice of the parent (actually the voice of his father or mother) and these are hallucinations. His Child may or may not answer the Parental voices, but in any case they affect some aspect of his behavior.

Because people who "talk to themselves" are thought to be crazy, nearly everyone has an injunction against listening to the voices in his head. This is a faculty which can be quickly recovered, however, if the proper permission is given. Then almost anyone can listen in on his own internal dialogues, and that is one of the best ways to find out the Parental precepts, the Parental pattern, and the script controls.

A sexually excited girl started to pray in her head so that she would be able to resist her boy friend's seduction. She clearly heard herself directed by the Parental precept: "Be a good girl, and when you are tempted, pray." A man got into a fight in a bar and was very careful to fight skillfully. He clearly heard his father's voice saying: "Don't telegraph your punches!" which was part of his father's pattern: "Here's how to fight in a bar." He got into the fight because his mother's voice said provocatively: "You're just like your father, some day you'll get your teeth smashed in a bar fight." At the critical moment, a stockmarket speculator heard a demonic whisper telling him: "Don't sell, buy." He abandoned his carefully planned campaign, and lost his entire capital—"Ha ha," he said.

The Parental voice exerts the same kind of control as a ventriloquist. It takes charge of the person's vocal apparatus, and he finds himself saying words which come from someone else. Unless his Adult steps in, he then follows the instructions given by this voice, so that his Child acts exactly like a ventriloquist's dummy. This ability to suspend one's own will, usually without realizing what has happened, and to let someone else take charge of the vocal muscles and the other muscles of the body, is what enables the script to take over at the appropriate time.

The remedy for this is to listen to the voices in one's head, and let the Adult decide whether to follow their instructions or not. In this way the person frees himself from the control of the Parental ventriloquist, and becomes master of his own actions. In order to accomplish this, he requires two permissions which he can give himself, but which may be more effective coming from someone else, such as a therapist.

1. Permission to listen to his internal dialogue.
2. Permission not to follow the directives of his Parent.

There is some peril in this undertaking, and he may require protection from someone else if he dares to disobey the Parental directives. Thus, one job of the therapist is to give his patients protection if they act independently of their ventriloquist Parents and try to be real people instead of dummies.

It should be added that while *Parental voices* tell him what he can or cannot do, it is *Child pictures* that tell him what he wants to do. Desires are visual, and directives are auditory.

I · MORE ABOUT THE DEMON

All the items mentioned so far are helpful in making the script possible, and most of them are matters beyond the person's awareness. Now we come to the key item, which not only makes the script possible, but gives it the decisive push. That is the demon who sends Jeder naked on roller skates down the hill to his destruction just when he is on the verge of success, before he even knows what is happening to him. But looking back, even if he has never heard the other voices in his head, he will usually remember that one, the voice of the demon prompting irresistibly: "Go ahead and do it!" Which he does, in the face of all the other forces warning him against it and vainly trying to call him back. This is Daemon, the sudden supernatural push that determines a man's fate, a voice from the Golden Age, lower than the gods but higher than humanity, perhaps a fallen angel. That is what the historians tell us, and perhaps they are right. For Heraclitus, the Daemon in man was his character. But this Daemon, according to those who have known him or her, the losers who are just picking themselves up from their falls, speaks not in a loud command like the ghost of a mighty god, but in a seductive whisper, like a beckoning woman, like an enchantress: "Come, do it. Go ahead. Why not? What have you to lose but everything? Instead you will have me, as you once did in the Golden Age."

This is the repetition compulsion which drives men to their doom, the power of death, according to Freud, or the power of the goddess Ananke. But he places it in some mysterious biological sphere, when after all it is only the voice of seduction. Ask the man (or woman) who owns one and knows the power of his demon.

The remedy against demons has always been cantrips and cantraps, and that is the case here. Every loser should carry it in wallet or purse, and whenever success looms in sight, that is the moment of danger. That is the time to pull it out and read it aloud again and again. Then when the demon whispers "Stretch out your arm—and put the whole wad on one last number, or have just one drink, or now is the time to pull your knife, or grab her (him) by the neck and pull her (him) toward you," or whatever the losing movement is, pull the arm back and say it loud and clear: "But mother, I'd rather do it my own way and win."

J · THE REAL PERSON

The converse of the script is the real person living in a real world. This real person is probably the real Self, the one which can move from one ego state to another. When people get to know each other well, they penetrate through the script into the depths where this real Self resides, and that is the part of the other person they respect and love, and with which they can have moments of real intimacy before Parental programing takes over again. This is possible because it has happened before in the lives of most people, in the most intimate and script-free relationship of all: that between the mother and her infant. The mother can usually suspend her script during the nursing period if left to her own instincts, and the infant does not yet have one

As for myself, I know not whether I am still run by a music roll or not. If I am, I wait with interest and anticipation—and without apprehension—for the next notes to unroll their melody, and for the harmony and discord after that. Where will I go next? In this case my life is meaningful because I am following the long and glorious tradition of my ancestors, passed on to me by my parents, music perhaps sweeter than I could compose myself. Certainly I know that there are large areas where I am free to improvise. It may even be that I am one of the few fortunate people on earth who has cast off the shackles entirely and who calls his own tune. In that case I am a brave improviser facing the world alone. But whether I am faking on a player piano, or striking the chords with the power of my own mind and hands, the song of my life is equally suspenseful and full of surprises as it rolls off the pulsating sounding board of destiny—a barcarole that either way will leave, I hope, happy echoes behind.

NOTES & REFERENCES

1 Berne, E. *Principles of Group Treatment. Loc. cit.*, p. 66f.
2 Harding, D. C. "The Face Game." *Transactional Analysis Bulletin,* 6:40–52, April, 1967.
3 Cf. Spitz, R. A. *No and Yes: On the Genesis of Human Communication.* International Universities Press, New York, 1957. See also Crossman, P. "Position and Smiling." *Transactional Analysis Bulletin,* 6:72–73, July, 1967.
4 For a more detailed discussion of the construct of free cathexis, see Berne, E. *Transactional Analysis in Psychotherapy. Loc. cit.*
5 Rhine, J. B. *Extra-Sensory Perception.* Bruce Humphries, Boston, 1962. Cf. Churchman, C. W. "Perception and Deception," review of C. E. M. Hansel's *ESP: A Scientific Evaluation* (Scribner, New York, 1966) in *Science,* 153:

1088–1090, September 2, 1966, and the interesting "thought coincidence" calculations of L. W. Alvarez in "A Pseudo Experience in Parapsychology," Ibid., 148:1541, June 18, 1965.

6 Berne, E. "Intuition VI: The Psychodynamics of Intuition." *Psychiatric Quarterly*, 36: 294–300, 1962.

7 Berne, E. *A Layman's Guide to Psychiatry and Psychoanalysis, Loc. cit.* Third edition, Appendix: "Beyond Science."

8 *Fifty Years of Psychic Research.*

9 McKenzie, D. *Aromatics and the Soul.* Paul B. Hoeber, New York, 1923. For a review of the anatomy and physiology of olfaction in insects, see Schneider, D. "Insect Olfaction: Deciphering System."

10 This is a well-known fact of rabbit biology.

11 Schneider, D. and Seibt, U. "Sex Pheromone of the Queen Butterfly." *Science*, 164: 1173–74, June 6, 1969.

12 Luce, G. G. and Segal, J. *Sleep.* Coward-McCann, Inc. New York, 1967.

13 At present this is merely an interesting hypothesis from my own observation, and I am unable to give any convincing evidence to validate it as yet. But compare Kales, et al. "Psychophysiological and Biochemical Changes Following Use and Withdrawal of Hypnotics." In *Sleep: Physiology and Pathology* (A. Kales, ed.). J. B. Lippincott & Company, Philadelphia, 1969. Also Rubin, R. T. and Mandell, A. J. "Adrenal Cortical Activity in Pathological Emotional States." *American Journal of Psychiatry*, 123: 387–400, 1966. And others.

14 Osler, W. *Aequanimitas and Other Papers.* W. W. Norton & Company, New York, 1963.

15 Berne, E. "The Mythology of Dark and Fair." *Loc. cit.*

CHAPTER FIFTEEN

Transmission of the Script

A · THE SCRIPT MATRIX

The script matrix is a diagram designed to illustrate and analyze the directives handed down from parents and grandparents to the current generation. An enormous amount of information can be compressed very elegantly into this relatively simple drawing. Script matrices were drawn for some of the cases given in Chapters Six and Seven (Figures 6, 8, and 9) as accurately as the information given would permit. The problem in practice is to separate the decisive parental directives and the decisive patterns of behavior, the script theme, from the "noise" or foreground confusion, which is made doubly difficult because not only the person himself, but all the people around him, contribute as much as they possibly can to these distractions. This tends to conceal the steps leading up to the script's payoff, the happy or tragic ending, which in the language of biologists[1] is the "final display." In other words, people take great pains to conceal their scripts from themselves and from others. This is only natural. To return to a previous metaphor, a man sitting in front of a player piano and moving his fingers under the illusion that he is making the music himself does not want somebody telling him to look inside the piano, and the audience, which is enjoying the spectacle, doesn't want it either.

Steiner, who devised the script matrix,[2] follows the original scheme proposed by the writer, that usually the parent of the opposite sex tells the child what to do, and the parent of the same sex shows him how to do it (Cf. Butch). Steiner made important additions to this basic scheme. He carried it much further by specifying what each ego state in the parents does. He postulates that it is the Child in the parent who gives the injunctions and the Adult in the parent that gives the child his "program" (which we have also called his pattern). And he added a new element, the counterscript, coming from the Parent of the parents. Steiner's version of the matrix is derived mainly from work with alcoholics, addicts, and "sociopaths." These all have third-degree, hard, tragic scripts (what he calls "hamartic" scripts). His matrix therefore deals with harsh injunctions from a "crazy Child," but it can be extended to include seductions and provocations, as well as injunctions that seem to come from the Parent in the parent rather than from the parent's crazy Child. (Cf. Butch's matrix, Figure 6.)

While there are several questions to be settled in the light of further experience, the setup shown in Figure 8 has been accepted by many people as an interim model, and is certainly of great value in clinical work, as well as in developmental, sociological, and anthropological studies, as will be shown shortly. This "standard" matrix shows the injunctions and provocations coming from the Child of the parents, most commonly from the parent of the opposite sex. If this turns out to be universally true, it will be a crucial discovery concerning human destiny and the transmission of destiny from one generation to another. The most important principle of script theory could then be stated as follows "The parent's Child forms the Child's Parent," or "The child's Parent is the Parent's Child."[3] This should be easy to understand with the aid of the diagram, remembering that "Child" and "Parent" with capital letters refer to ego states in the head, while "parent" with a small "p" and "child" with a small "c" refer to actual people.

A blank script matrix, such as that shown in Figure 14, can be painted on a blackboard and put to good use during group-treatment meetings and in teaching script theory. In analyzing an individual case, the parents are first labeled according to the sex of the patient, and then the slogans, patterns, injunctions, and provocations can be filled in with chalk along the arrows. This gives a clear visual representation of the decisive script transactions, and results in a diagram similar to Figures 6, 8, and 9. With the help of such a device, it will soon be found that the script matrix says things that have never been said before.

People with good scripts may be interested in script analysis only in an academic way, unless they are going to be therapists. But with patients, in order to get them well, it is necessary to dissect out the directives in as pure a form as possible, and drawing an accurate script matrix is a useful tool in planning treatment.

The most likely way to elicit the information for filling in the script matrix is to ask the patient the following four questions: (a) What was your parents' favorite slogan or precept? This will give the key to the antiscript. (b) What kind of life did your parents lead? This will best be answered by a long association with the patient. Whatever his parents taught him to do,

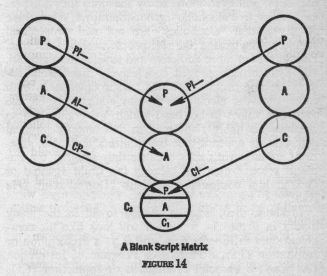

A Blank Script Matrix

FIGURE 14

he will do again and again, and the patter will give him his ordinary social character: "He's a heavy drinker." "She's a sexy girl." (c) What is your Parental Prohibition? This is the most important single question for understanding the behavior of the patient and for planning the decisive intervention which will free him to live more fully. Since his symptoms are a substitute for the prohibited act, and also a protest against it, as demonstrated by Freud, freedom from the prohibition will also tend to cure his symptoms. It takes experience and subtlety to pick out the decisive parental injunction from the "background noise." The most reliable clues are offered by the fourth question, (d) What did you have to do to make your parents smile or chuckle? This gives the come-on, which is the alternative to the prohibited behavior.

Steiner believes that the prohibition in the case of "alcoholics" is "Don't think!" and that drinking heavily is one program for not thinking.[4] The absence of thinking is well shown in the drinking platitudes common among "Alcoholic" players and their sympathizers, and even more so by the ones they foist on each other in "alcoholic" group therapy.[5] What these all say is that "alcoholics" are not real people and should not be treated like real people, which is not true. Heroin is even more addictive and sinister than alcohol, and Synanon has proved conclusively that heroin addicts are real people. The real person emerges in both cases after the alcohol or heroin addict cuts off the seductive voices in his head which are urging him to continue his habit, reinforced in due time by physical demands. It appears that tranquilizers and phenothiazines are effective partly because they smother the Parental voices which are keeping the Child agitated or making him confused with their "Don'ts" and "Ha Ha's."

In short, then, what is needed to fill in the blank matrix in Figure 14 so that it will look like the completed ones in Figures 6, 8, and 9, is a Prescription or Inspiration (PI), a Pattern or Program of Instruction (AI), and a Parental Prohibition or Injunction (CI), along with whatever Provocations (CP) can be elicited.

The most forceful script directives are given during the family drama (Chapter Three), which in some respects reinforces what the parents have been saying, and in others demonstrates that they are hypocritical impostors. It is these scenes which bring home in the most poignant way what the parents want the child to learn about his script. And it should be remembered that loudly spoken words have just as profound and enduring an effect as so-called "nonverbal communication."[6]

B · THE FAMILY PARADE

The script matrices in Chapter Six and Seven show how the main elements of the script apparatus—the Parental precepts, the Adult patterns, and the Child script controls—were transmitted from the two parents to their offspring. Figure 7 shows in more detail how the most important element, the injunction, is transmitted to Jeder from one of his parents, usually the parent of the opposite sex. All this is good preparation for studying Figure 15, which shows how an injunction may be transmitted from one generation to another. Such a series is called a "family parade." Here five generations are linked by the same injunction.

The situation shown in Figure 15 is not at all uncommon. The patient has heard or seen how grandmother was a loser; she knows very well that her father was a loser; she is in treatment because she is a loser; her son is going to the clinic because he is a loser; and her granddaughter is already showing signs at school that she is going to be a loser, too. Both the patient and the therapist know that this five-generation chain must be broken somewhere or it may go on indefinitely for more generations. This is a good incentive for the patient to get well,* since if she does she can withdraw her injunction to her son, which she is prob-

---

*Through the family parade it was possible to trace the games and script of a woman patient (whose great grandmother lived to a very advanced age with her memory unimpaired) back to the Napoleonic Wars, and to project them forward through her grandchildren to the year 2000.

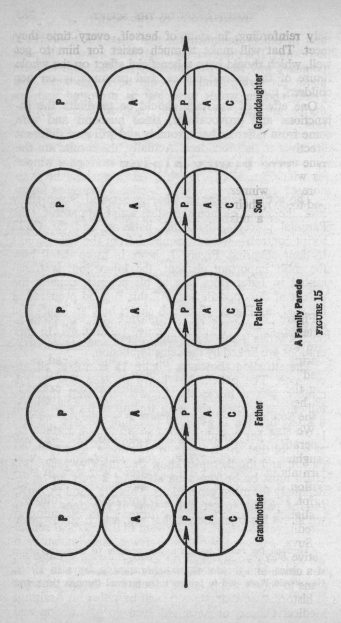

Grandmother   Father   Patient   Son   Granddaughter

A Family Parade

FIGURE 15

ably reinforcing, in spite of herself, every time they meet. That will make it much easier for him to get well, which should have a beneficial effect on the whole future of the granddaughter, and presumably on her children, too.

One effect of marriage should be to dilute the injunctions and provocations, since husband and wife come from different backgrounds and will give different directives to their children. Actually, the results are the same as with their genes. If a winner marries a winner (as winners tend to do), their offspring may be even more of a winner. If a loser marries a loser (as losers tend to do), their offspring may be even more of a loser. If there is a mixture, the result will be mixed. And there is always the possibility of a throwback either way.

C · CULTURAL TRANSMISSION

Figure 16 illustrates the transmission of precepts, patterns, and controls through five generations. In this case we are fortunate enough to have the information bearing on a "good" or winning script instead of a "bad" or losing one. This life plan may be called "My Son the Doctor," and we have taken as our example the hereditary medicine man of a small jungle village in the South Seas. The explanation is as follows:

We start off with a father and a mother. Father, in generation 5, was born about 1860, and married the daughter of a chief. Their son, generation 4, was born about 1885, and did likewise. Their son, in generation 3, was born in 1910, and followed the same script. His son, in generation 2, born in 1935, followed a slightly different pattern. Instead of becoming a hereditary medicine man, he went to the medical school in Suva, Fiji, and became what was then known as a Native Medical Assistant. He, too, married a daughter of a chief, and their son, in generation 1, born in 1960, plans to follow in his father's footsteps, except that due to historical developments he will be called an Assistant Medical Officer, or he might even go to London and

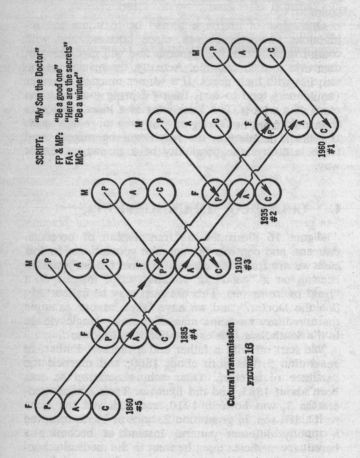

SCRIPT: "My Son the Doctor"

FP & MP: "Be a good one"
FA: "Here are the secrets"
MC: "Be a winner"

Cultural Transmission

FIGURE 16

become a fullfledged Medical Officer. Thus the son in each generation becomes the father (F) of the next generation, and his wife becomes the mother (M).

Each father and mother give the same precept or inspiration from the Parent in them to the Parent in their son: "Be a good medicine man." The father's Adult transmits to his son's Adult the secrets of his trade, which of course are not known to the mother. But the mother does know what she wants her son to do; in fact, she knew from her earliest years that she would want her son to be either a chief or a medicine man. Since he is obviously going to be the latter, she transmits from her Child to his Child (from her early childhood decision to him in his early years) the benevolent come-on, "Be a winner as a medicine man."

In this case (Figure 16) the family parade of Figure 15 is shown in a more complete form. It can be seen that father's precepts and father's program of instruction form two parallel lines going straight down the generations from 1860 to 1960. Mother's precepts and mother's injunctions ("Don't fail") are also parallel, and come in from the side in each generation. This neatly demonstrates the transmission of "culture" over a period of one hundred years. Similar diagrams could be drawn for any element of "culture" or any "role" in the village society.

In a family parade of daughters, whose roles might be "mothers of successful medicine men," the diagram would look exactly the same except that the M's and F's would switch places. In a village where uncles or mothers-in-law were important influences on the children's scripts, the diagram might be more complicated, but the principle would be the same.

It should be noted that in this parade of winners, the scripts and antiscripts coincide, which is the best way to insure a winner. But if mother 3, for example, happened to be the daughter of an alcoholic chief, she might give her son a bad script injunction. Then there would be trouble, since there would be a conflict between his antiscript and his script. While her Parent was telling him to be a good medicine man, her Child might show fascination and glee when she told the boy stories about the stupidity and drinking prowess of his grandfather. Then he might get thrown out of Medical School for drunkenness, and spend the rest of his life playing "Alcoholic," with his disappointed father playing "Persecutor" and his nostalgic mother playing "Rescuer."*

D · THE INFLUENCE OF THE GRANDPARENTS

The most intricate part of script analysis in clinical practice is tracing back the influence of the grandparents. This is illustrated in Figure 17, which is a more detailed version of Figure 7. There it can be seen that PC in mother is split into two parts, FPC and MPC. FPC represents the influence of her father when she was very little (Father Parent in her Child) and MPC represents the influence of her mother (Mother Parent in her Child). This split may look complicated and impractical at first sight, but it is not so to anyone accustomed to thinking in terms of ego states. For example, it does not take very long for patients to learn to distinguish between FPC and MPC in themselves. "When I was little, father liked to make me cry, and mother dressed me in a sexy way," said the weepy, pretty prostitute. "Father liked me to be bright and mother liked to dress me up," said the bright, well-dressed psychologist. "Father said girls were no good and mother dressed me like a tomboy," said the frightened beatnik in her boyish clothes. Each of these women knew very well when her behavior was guided by father's early influence (FPC) or mother's (MPC). When they were weepy, bright, or frightened, they were doing it for father, and when they looked sexy, well dressed, or tomboyish, they were following mother's instructions.

Now remembering the tendency for the script con-

---

*Actually, the family parade described above is partly based on anthropological and historical material, and partly on the family trees of some American doctors.

trols to come from the parent of the opposite sex, FPC
in mother is her electrode, and MPC in father is his
(Figure 10 again). Thus, mother's script commands to
Jeder come from her father, and so it can be said that
"Jeder's script programing comes from his maternal
grandfather."³ Father's commands to Zoe come from
his mother, so Zoe's script programing comes from her
paternal grandmother. The electrode, then, is mother
(grandfather) in Jeder's head, and in the case of Zoe,
father (grandmother) in her head.⁴ Applying this to the
three cases above, the prostitute's grandmother married
and divorced several mean husbands, the psychologist's
grandmother was a well-known writer, and the tomboy's grandmother was a crusader for women's rights.

It can now be understood why the family parade
diagramed in Figure 15 alternated generations between
the sexes—grandmother, father, female patient, son,
and granddaughter. Figure 16, on the other hand, illustrates how such a diagram can be adjusted to follow

MPC = Mother's Parent's Child
= Maternal Grandfather
FPC = Father's Parent's Child
= Paternal Grandmother

The Child of ♂ or ♀

Transmission From The Grandparents

FIGURE 17

straight down the line with either male descendants or female descendants. It is just because of this kind of versatility that the script-matrix diagram is such a valuable instrument. It has properties which even its originator did not suspect. Here it offers a simplified method for helping to understand such complex matters as family histories, the transmission of culture, and the psychological influence of grandparents.

E · OVERSCRIPTING

There are two requirements for the transmission of the script. Jeder must be able, ready, and willing or even eager to accept it, and his parents must want to pass it on.

On Jeder's side, he is able because his nervous system is constructed for the purpose of being programed, to receive sensory and social stimuli and organize them into patterns which will regulate his behavior. As his body and his mind mature, he becomes readier and readier for more and more complex types of programing. And he is willing to accept it because he needs ways to structure his time and organize his activities. In fact he is not only willing, he is eager, because he is more than a passive computer. Like most animals, he has a craving for "closure," the need to finish what he begins; and beyond that, he has the great human aspiration for purpose.

Starting off with random movements, he ends up knowing what to say after he says Hello. At first he is content with instrumental responses, and they become goals in themselves: incorporation, elimination, intrusion, and locomotion, to use Erikson's terms. Here we find the beginnings of Adult craftsmanship, his pleasure in the act and its successful completion: getting the food safely off the spoon and into his mouth, walking on his own across the floor. Initially his goal is to walk, then it is to walk *to* something. Once he walks to people, he has to know what to do after he gets there. At first they smile and hug him, and all he has to do is be, or at most, cuddle. They expect nothing from him beyond getting there. Later they do expect something, so he learns to say Hello. After a while, that is not enough either, and they expect more. So he learns to offer them various stimuli in order to get their responses in return. Thus, he is eternally grateful (believe it or not) to his parents for giving him a pattern: how to approach people in such a way as to get the desired responses. This is structure hunger, pattern hunger, and in the long run, script hunger. So the script is accepted because Jeder is script hungry.

On the parents' side, they are able, ready, and willing because of what has been built into them through eons of evolution: a desire to nurture, protect, and teach their offspring, a desire which can only be suppressed by the most powerful inner and outer forces. But beyond that, if they themselves have been properly "scripted," they are not only willing, but eager, and derive great enjoyment from child-rearing.

Some parents, however, are overly eager. Child-rearing for them is neither a drag nor a joy, but a compulsion. In particular, their need to pass on precepts, patterns, and controls far exceeds the children's needs for such parental programing. This compulsion is a rather complex affair, dividing roughly into three aspects. (1) A desire for immortality. (2) The demands of the parents' own scripts, which may range from "Don't make any mistakes," to "Mess up your children." (3) The desire of the parents to get rid of their own script controls, and pass them on to someone else so as to be free themselves. Of course this extrajection doesn't work, and so the attempt has to be made over and over.

These continuous assaults on the child's psyche are well known to child psychiatrists and family therapists, who call them by various names. From the point of view of script analysis, they are a form of "over-scripting," and the excessive directives which are laid on the child, and surfeit him far beyond the cravings of his script hunger, may be called his episcript or over-script. Usually his reaction is to ward them off by some form of repudiation, but he may follow his parents' policy and attempt to pass them on to someone else.

For this reason, the episcript has been described by Fanita English[7] as a Hot Potato, and the continual attempts to pass it back and forth she calls the Hot Potato Game.

As she points out in her original paper on this subject, all sorts of people play this game, including therapists, and she gives the example of Joe, a psychology student, whose script payoff from his mother was: "Get locked up in a madhouse." Thus, he was in the habit of picking for his inept therapeutic attempts people who were good candidates for the state hospital, and he managed to help them along the way. Fortunately his supervisor observed his scripty smile whenever one of his patients verged on a breakdown, and put a stop to the whole procedure by persuading him to give up psychology, go into a business career, and seek treatment for himself. His script payoff was an episcript or "hot potato" of his mother's, who had spent her life trying "to stay out of the madhouse," as she frequently said. She received the directive to get locked up from one of her parents, and tried to get rid of it by passing it on to Joe, who in turn tried to pass it on to his patients.

Thus the parents transmit the script as part of their normal parenting, to nurture, protect, and encourage their children by showing them, to the best of their ability, how to live life. Overscripting may arise from various causes. The most pathological is an attempt to get rid of an episcript by passing it on to one of the children. The episcript, especially if it is a "hamartic" or tragic one, becomes a hot potato which no one wants to hold on to. As English points out, it is the Professor, the Adult in the Child, who says: "Who needs it?" and decides that it can be got rid of, like a curse in a fairy tale, by passing it on to someone else.

F · BLENDING OF THE SCRIPT DIRECTIVES

As the years go by and the script becomes adapted by experience, the controls, patterns, and prescriptions become blended so that it is hard to distinguish one from the other in the person's behavior, and to determine which is a "final common pathway." He adopts a program or routine which synthesizes them all. The major script payoffs occur in the form of a "final display." If the payoff is a bad one, the script elements may be quite apparent to an experienced observer, as in cases of psychosis, delirium tremens, car-crashing, suicide, or murder. With good payoffs, it is more difficult to dissect out the script directives, partly because in such cases there are usually extensive permissions granted by the parents, which may obscure the directives.

Consider the following real-life romance, taken from a news item in a small town newspaper:

ROMANTIC HISTORY IS REPEATED IN THE X FAMILY

Fifty years ago an Australian soldier went to England to serve in the First World War. His name was John X, and he met and married Jane Y. After the war was over, they came to America to live. Twenty-five years later, their three children were vacationing in England. Tom X, their son, married Mary Z, of Great Snoring, Norfolk, and his two sisters married Englishmen. This fall, Tom and Mary X's daughter, Jane, who spent her vacation in Great Snoring with an aunt, announced her engagement to Harry J, also of Great Snoring. Jane is a graduate of our local high school. After their marriage, the couple plan to live in Australia.

It is an interesting exercise to try to dissect out the probable precepts, patterns, controls, and permissions that were passed down from John X and his wife Jane, through Tom and Mary, to the granddaughter, Jane.

It should be noted that script programing is a natural happening like the growth of weeds and flowers, and takes place without regard to morals or consequences. Sometimes script and antiscript feed into each other with the most dire results. The Parental directives may give the Child a license to inflict enormous damage on other people. Historically, such unfortunate combinations have given rise to leaders of wars, crusades, and massacres, and on a more individual level, to political assassinations. Mother's Parent is saying "Be good!" and "Be famous!" while her Child is directing: "Kill everybody!" Father's Adult then shows the boy how to kill people, by teaching him how to handle guns, in civilized countries, and knives, in uncivilized ones.

Most people spend their lives comfortably embedded in their script matrices. It is a bed which their parents made for them and to which they have added a few trimmings of their own. It may have bugs in it and be lumpy, too, but it is their very own and they have been accustomed to it since their earliest years, and so, few people are willing to trade it in for something better built and more adapted to their circumstances. Matrix, after all, is just Latin for mother's womb, and the script is as close and cozy as they can get once they have forever left the real thing. But for those who do decide to strike out for themselves, and say "Mother, I'd rather do it my own way," there are several possibilities. If they are lucky, mother herself may have included a reasonable release or spellbreaker in the matrix, in which case they may do it on their own. Another way is for their friends and intimates and life itself to help, but this is rare. The third way is through competent script analysis, from which they may get permission to put their own shows on the road.

G · SUMMARY

The script matrix is a diagram designed to illustrate and analyze the directives handed down from the parents and grandparents to the current generation. These will, in the long run, determine the person's life plan and his final payoff. Current information indicates that the most decisive controls come from the Child ego state of the parent of the opposite sex. The Adult ego state of the parent of the same sex then gives the person a pattern which determines his interests and life course while he is carrying out his life plan. Meanwhile, both parents, through their Parental ego states, give him prescriptions, inspirations, or slogans which set up his counterscript. The counterscript occupies lulls in the forward movement of the script. If he makes appropriate moves, it may take over and suppress the script. The following table (from Steiner's findings[4]) illustrates the elements in the case of one man with an "Alcoholic" script. The first column gives the active ego state in each parent. The letters in parentheses give the receiving ego state in the protagonist, and the next two show the type of directive. The last two columns are self-explanatory.

Mother's Child (C)	Injunctions and Come-ons	Script	"Don't Think, Drink."
Father's Adult (A)	Program (Pattern)	Life Course	"Drink and Work."
Both Parents (P)	Prescription (Slogans)	Counterscript	"Work Hard."

Even if the origins (but probably not the insertions) of the script directives vary in individual cases, the script matrix nevertheless remains one of the most useful and cogent diagrams in the history of science, compressing, as it does, the whole plan for a human life and its ultimate destiny into a simple, easily understood, and easily checked design, which also indicates how to change it.

H · RESPONSIBILITY OF THE PARENTS

The dynamic slogan of transactional and script analysis is "Think sphincter." Their clinical principle is to observe every movement of every muscle of every patient at every moment during a group meeting. And their existential motto is "Transactional analysts are healthy, happy, rich, and brave, and get to travel all over and meet the nicest people in the world, and the same when they are home treating patients."

In the present connection, the bravery consists of attacking the whole problem of human destiny and finding its solution by the use of the dynamic slogan and the clinical principle. Script analysis is then the answer to the problem of human destiny, and tells us (alas!) that our fates are predetermined for the most part, and that free will in this respect is for most people an illusion. For example, R. Allendy[8] points out that for each individual who faces it, the decision to commit suicide is a lonely and agonizing and apparently autonomous one. Yet whatever vicissitudes it goes through in each individual case, the "rate" of suicide remains relatively constant from year to year. The only way to make (Darwinian) sense of this is to consider human destiny to be the result of parental programing, and not of individual "autonomous" decision.

What, then, is the responsibility of the parents? Script programing is not their "fault," any more than an inherited defect is, such as diabetes or clubfoot, or an inherited talent for music or mathematics. They are merely passing on the dominants and recessives they got from their parents and grandparents. The script directives are being continually reshuffled, just as the genes are, by the fact that the child requires two parents.

On the other hand, the script apparatus is much more flexible than the genetic apparatus and is continually being modified by outside influences, such as life experience and the injunctions inserted by other people. It is only rarely possible to predict when or how an outsider will say or do something that alters a person's script. It may be a casual remark accidentally overheard at a carnival or in a corridor, or it may be the result of a formal relationship such as marriage, school, or psychotherapy. It is a common observation that spouses gradually influence each other's attitudes toward life and people, and that these changes are reflected in the tonus of their facial muscles and their gestures, so that they come to look alike.

A parent who wishes to change his script so that he will not lay on his children the same directives that were laid on him should first of all become familiar with the Parent ego state and the Parental voices he carries around in his head, and which the children learn to "cathect" by appropriate trigger behavior. Since the parent is older and presumably wiser in some ways than his offspring, it is his duty and responsibility to control his Parental behavior. Only if he brings his Parent under the control of his Adult can he accomplish this. Beyond that, he is just as much the product of his Parental upbringing as his children are.

One difficulty is that children represent facsimile and immortality. Every parent is openly or secretly delighted when his children respond the way he does, even when they follow his worst characteristics. This delight is what he must forgo under Adult control if he wishes his children to adapt to the solar system and all its ramifications better than he himself did.

And now we are ready to consider what happens when Jeder, who is Everyman and any man, wants to change that design, the tapes in his head, and the program they dictate, and becomes a special kind of man —Pat the patient.

NOTES & REFERENCES

Hendricks, S. B. "Metabolic Control of Timing." *Science*, 141:21–27, July 5, 1963.

2 The script matrix in its present form was devised by Dr. Claude M. Steiner, of the San Francisco Transactional Analysis Seminar, and first appeared in print in his article "Script and Counterscript," *Loc. cit.* In my estimation, its value cannot be overestimated, containing as it does the programing for a whole human life, as well as indicating how to change it. It is such an important invention that, without detracting from Dr. Steiner's perceptiveness, ingenuity, and creativity, I would like to claim a part in it. Its predecessors were the more primitive diagrams to be found on pages 201 and 205 of my book *Transactional Analysis in Psychotherapy* (*loc. cit.*). The above article also marks the first appearance in print of the concepts of counterscript and injunction, which are further products of Dr. Steiner's insights.

3 Johnson and Szurek went as far as "superego lacunae" in accounting for "acting out." That is, children "act out" because there is something "missing" in the parents. This was one of the first theoretical statements of how parents influence their children to "bad" behavior. (Johnson, A. M. and Szurek, S. A. "The Genesis of Anti-Social Acting Out in Children and Adults." *Psychoanalytic Quarterly*, 21:323–343, 1952.) We have broadened the problem from "acting out" to real living, and have tried to include all forms of behavior, whether "anti-social" or not. Erikson approaches the script concept very closely but veers away. (Erikson, E. *Identity*

and the Life Cycle. Loc. cit.) As already mentioned, Freud speaks of the "destiny compulsion" as a biological phenomenon, without specifying its psychological origin; while Adler talks of life style. The injunction principle stated in the text, therefore, may be regarded as supplementing the observations of all these writers. Cf. Jackson, D. D. "Family Interaction, Family Homeostasis and Some Implications for Conjoint Family Psychotherapy." In *Individual and Familial Dynamics* (J. H. Masserman, ed.). Grune & Stratton, New York, 1959.

4 Steiner, C. M. "The Treatment of Alcoholism." *Transactional Analysis Bulletin,* 6:69–71, July, 1967. Also "The Alcoholic Game." *Quarterly Journal of Studies on Alcohol,* 30:920–938, December, 1969, with discussion by six eminent authorities on alcoholism. Dr. Steiner's book on this subject, *Games Alcoholics Play,* has recently been published (Grove Press, 1971).

5 Karpman, S. "Alcoholic 'Instant Group Therapy.' " *Transactional Analysis Bulletin,* 4:69–74, October, 1965.

6 Berne, E. "Concerning the Nature of Communication." *Psychiatric Quarterly,* 27: 185–198, 1953.

7 English, F. "Episcript and the 'Hot Potato' Game." *Transactional Analysis Bulletin,* 8:77–82, October, 1969.

8 Allendy, R. *Le problème de la destinée, étude sur la fatalité intérieure.* Librarie Gallimard, Paris, 1927. L. du Nouy, on the other hand (*Human Destiny.* Signet Books, New York, 1949), puts more weight on external forces as seen by a religious scientist.

PART IV

The Script in Clinical Practice

CHAPTER SIXTEEN

The Preliminary Phases

A · INTRODUCTORY

Since the script influences begin before birth, and the "final display" or ultimate payoff occurs at death or later it is only rarely that the clinician will have an opportunity to follow a script through from beginning to end. Lawyers, bankers, family doctors, and clergymen, especially those who practice in small towns, are the people most likely to know all the secrets of someone's life over such a long period. But since psychiatric script analysis itself is only a few years old, there is in fact not a single example of clinical observation of a complete life course or script. The best way at present to get a long term view is by means of biographical books, but these are usually lacking in many important respects; few of the questions mentioned in the previous sections can be answered from the usual academic or literary biographies. The first attempt at something approaching script analysis was Freud's book on Leonardo da Vinci.[1] The next landmark is Ernest Jones' biography of Freud himself,[2] and Jones had the advantage of knowing his subject personally. Erikson has studied the life plans and life courses of two successful leaders, Martin Luther and Mahatma Gandhi.[3] Leon Edel's continuing biography of Henry James,[4] and Zeligs' study of the Hiss-Chamberlain relationship[5] also reveal many of the script elements. But in all of these cases, most of the early directives can only be guessed at.

The closest approach to a scientific study of scripts comes out of the work of McClelland.[6] He studied the relationship between stories heard and read by children, and their motives in living. His work was followed up by Rudin[7] many years later.

Rudin studied the causes of death among those who were motivated by such stories. Because "achievers" have to be "good," they tend to keep their feelings under careful control, and they often suffer from ulcers or high blood pressure. He contrasted this group with those who had a desire for "power" and expressed themselves freely in action in order to attain it; they had a high death rate from what we could call "scripty" causes: suicide, homicide, and cirrhosis of the liver from drinking too much. The "achievers'" scripts were based on success stories, while the "power" people's scripts were based on tales of risk, and Rudin tells us what kinds of deaths they were courting. This is a twenty-five-year survey and easily fits into the framework of script analysis as given here.

Even with studies such as this, script analysis cannot attain the precision and certainty of mouse psychology, or bacteriology. What script analysts have to do in practice is read biographies, keep track of their friends' successes and their enemies' failures, see large numbers of patients with various types of early programing, and project backward and forward in the lives of people they are clinically acquainted with for a reasonably long period. A clinician who has been in practice for twenty or thirty years, for example, and keeps in touch with his former patients either by periodic visits or even through Christmas cards, begins to feel more and more secure in his script analyses. With such a background, he knows better what to do with the patients he is currently seeing, and how to get the maximum amount of information as quickly as possible with new patients. The more quickly and accurately the script can be understood in each case, the more quickly and effectively its antithesis can be applied by the therapist, thus avoiding a waste of time, energy, lives, and new generations.

Psychiatric practice, like all branches of medicine, carries with it a certain mortality rate and a certain disability rate, and the first aim of the therapist must be to reduce those, whatever else he accomplishes besides. Overnight suicide by drugs, and long-term suicide by alcohol or high blood pressure have to be averted. His slogan must be "Get better first and analyze it later," otherwise he will have some of his most "interesting" and "insightful" patients either the smartest people in the morgue or the smartest people in the state hospital or penitentiary. The first problem, then, is: what are the "script signs" that occur during treatment? He should know what to look for, where to find it, what to do about it after he finds it, and how to tell whether he is doing it effectively, and that is what we shall take up in the next chapter. The second problem is to check his observations and impressions and put them into some sort of systematic order so that he can talk about them to others. For those purposes the Script Check List beginning on page 417 should be of some help.

Many of the patients who come to transactional analysts do so after going to other kinds of therapists. If not, they go through, with the transactional analyst, the phases they would otherwise go through in "preliminary" therapy. It is therefore convenient to consider two phases in clinical script analysis: the preliminary phase, and the phase of script analysis. Whatever form of therapy is used, similar phases will occur, and they are not peculiar to script analysis. The script analyst may see the failures of other therapists, but he does not see their successes. Conversely, other therapists see the failures of script analysis and do not usually see the successes.

In the previous section we considered the development of human beings in general, trying to pick out universals, and the subject was called Jeder. We will continue to call him that except when he is actually in the office or on the ward, and then we will call him Pat, and his therapist Dr. Q.

B · THE CHOICE OF THERAPIST

Nearly every therapist likes to think that the patient chose him and his profession because in this choice at least he was rational, intelligent, and discriminating, no matter how confused he might be about everything else. This feeling of being chosen on merit—the merit of one's profession and personal merit as well—is a healthy one, and is one of the rewards of our vocation. Every therapist, therefore, is entitled to bask in it and to enjoy it to the utmost—for about five or seven minutes. After that, he should put it on the shelf with his other trophies and his diplomas, and forget it permanently if he wants to get the patient well.

Dr. Q may be a very good therapist, and he may have the diplomas and the reputation and the patients to confirm it. He may think that is the reason the patient comes to him, or the patient may tell him so. He should be sobered, however, by the thought of all the patients who do *not* choose him. According to the available statistics, forty-two per cent of troubled people go first to their clergyman, and not to a psychiatrist, and nearly all the rest go to their family doctors.[8] And only about one patient out of five who needs psychiatric care is getting it, either in a hospital, in a clinic, or in private practice.[9] In other words, four out of every five disturbed people do *not* choose psychiatry as their treatment, even though in almost all cases it is available at the state hospital, if nowhere else. In addition, a very large percentage of patients who have a choice deliberately choose the second best therapist rather than the best, and a quite large percentage choose the *worst*. The same thing happens in other branches of medicine. It is also well known that a large number of people spend more money destroying themselves with liquor, drugs, and gambling, than they would on the psychotherapy which might save them.

Given a free choice, the patient will choose a therapist according to the needs of his script. In some places, he has no choice, but has to go to the local witch doctor, shaman, or angakok.[10] In other places, he has a choice between a traditional doctor and a modern one,[11] and will choose the magic of tradition or the magic of science according to local custom[12] and political pressure. In China and India, traditional and modern approaches are often combined, as in the mental hospital in Madras[13] where Ayur-Vedic medicine and Yoga exercises were used in conjunction with modern treatments for psychoses. In many cases his choice is forced by financial considerations.

In America, most patients do not have a free choice of therapists, but are referred or assigned by various "authorities" to one type or another: psychiatrists, psychologists, psychiatric social workers, psychiatric nurses, counselors, and even sociologists. A patient in a clinic, social agency, mental hospital, or government hospital may be assigned to any of these professions. A schoolboy is sent to the school counselor, and a person on probation is sent to a probation officer who may have no therapeutic training at all. If the patient has no prior knowledge or fantasies about psychotherapy and he likes his first therapist, he will often favor that therapist's profession if he seeks treatment elsewhere.

It is in private practice where free choice does exist that the "scripty" selections begin to emerge, particularly in the choice between psychiatrists, psychoanalysts, psychologists, and psychiatric social workers, and between the competent and the incompetent members of these professions. Christian Scientists, for example, if they do go to a medical therapist, often choose a less competent one, since their scripts prohibit them from being cured by a medical person. There are also subdivisions and schools in these professions to choose among. Among psychiatrists, for example, there are types colloquially called "shock treaters," "drug-givers," "shrinks," and hypnotists, and if the patient makes his own choice among these, as he often does, he will choose the one that suits his script. If he is referred by the family doctor, the doctor may well choose the one that fits in with his own script. This is most clearly seen when the patient seeks or is referred to a hypnotist. If he calls a psychiatrist to request hypnosis and that psychiatrist does not use hypnosis, the ensuing conversation becomes very scripty as the patient insists that he must be put to sleep before he can get better. Some people automatically (i.e., by script directive) go to the Mayo Clinic and others to the Menninger Clinic. Similarly, in choosing a psychoanalyst, some, for script reasons, select the most orthodox one possible, others prefer more flexibility, and still others go to "analysts" belonging to splinter schools. Sometimes the age or sex of the therapist is important for scripty reasons, such as a need to seduce or a fear of seduction. Rebels often go to rebellious therapists. People with failure scripts pick the worst possible therapists, such as chiropractors or outright quacks.[14] H. L. Mencken once remarked that the only relics of Darwinian natural selection left in America, where everyone is "taken care of," are chiropractors, because the more widely they are allowed to practice, the more quickly will unfit members of the human race be eliminated by their treatment.

There are clear indications that three factors are determined by the patient's script directives. (1) Whether he seeks help at all, or just lets things run their course; (2) the choice of therapist, where there is a choice; (3) whether or not the therapy is destined to be successful. Thus a person with a loser's script will either not go to a therapist, or may choose an incompetent one. In the latter case, when the treatment fails, he not only remains a loser, as his script calls for, but also has various other satisfactions from his misadventure; for example, he can blame the therapist, or obtain a Herostratic[15] satisfaction from being the "worst" patient, or boast that he had ten years of therapy with Dr. X at a cost of Y thousands of dollars with no benefit.

C · THE THERAPIST AS A MAGICIAN

To the patient's Child, the therapist is a magician of sorts. He is likely to choose the same kind of magical figure that he knew in childhood. In some families, the revered figure is the family doctor, a medical man; in others the revered is the clergyman. Some doctors and clergymen are serious figures out of tragedy, like Tiresias, who will tell them the bad news and perhaps give them a cantrap, amulet, or draught for salvation; others are jolly green giants who protect children from harm by comforting them and reassuring them, and flexing their giant muscles. When Jeder grows up, he will usually look for help from a similar person. If his experience was unhappy, however, he may rebel and find some other kind of magic. One puzzle is why people choose psychologists to fill this role in their scripts, since comparatively few people so far have had a friendly neighborhood psychologist as the family magician in early childhood. From a fairy-tale point of view, the therapist is the dwarf, the witch, the fish, the fox, or the bird who gives Jeder the magic means to attain his ends: the seven-league boots, the cloak of invisibility, the magic chest that produces on command gold or tables laden with cakes and dainties; or some *apotropaion* to ward off evil.

Roughly speaking, the patient can choose between three kinds of magic in selecting a therapist, and he can select each one for success or for failure. He can also play one against the other if his script requires that. These are known as "science," "chicken soup," and "religion." Any profession can offer all three, but typically a certain type of psychologist offers "modern science," a certain type of psychiatric social worker offers "chicken soup," and a certain type of pastoral counselor offers "religion." A well-trained therapist in each of these professions is prepared to offer any of them if occasion demands, and some offer two in combination. Science and religion, chicken soup and science, or religion and chicken soup, are common farragoes for the patient who seeks more than one kind of magic. The practical difference between "science," "chicken soup," and "religion" on the one hand, and a scientific, a supportive, and a religious approach to therapy is in knowing when to stop. The therapists who use the first three do not know when to stop, since each one's brand of magic is part of his own script, while those who use the last three do know when to stop, because they know what they are doing. The first group, is playing "I'm Only Trying to Help You," while the others are helping people.

D · THE PREPARATION

In his preliminary ventures into therapy, the patient gets "couch-broken," which means that he learns to play his own games lying down, literally or figuratively,[16] and he also learns to play the therapist's games well enough to keep the doctor happy. This is best seen on psychiatric in-patient wards, where the patient is taught the rules of mental illness well enough so that he can choose at will between (1) staying on indefinitely (or as long as the family finances hold out), (2) being transferred to a less demanding environment such as a state hospital, or (3) going home whenever he is ready. He also learns how to behave in order to be read-mitted.

After several stays in the hospital, such patients become adept at "training" younger therapists and psychiatric residents. They know how to cater to the doctor's hobbies, such as dream interpretation, and how to indulge in their own particular hobbies, such as "producing interesting material." All this confirms the basic assumption that patients are good sports. There are a few exceptions, however. Some refuse to play the ward games or the doctor's games by maintaining that they are innocent of mental illness. Others stubbornly or sulkily refuse to get well even though they admit that there is something wrong or actively complain about it. Some of these can be placated by allowing them to rest up for a week or two before demanding that they get better. There is a small number of unfortunates who would like to be good sports, but are helpless in the grip of organic conditions such as Pick's disease, or quasi-organic illnesses like "process" schizophrenia, agitated melancholia, or mania. Once the latter receive adequate doses of medication such as phenothiazines, dibenzazepines, or lithium, however, they usually become as tractable as need be. Some hospitals, deplorably, use shock treatment to whip headstrong patients into shape.

In any case, the first stage in the hospital treatment of psychiatric patients should be to discuss the various aspects of tractability in ward meetings attended by patients, staff, and visiting clinicians. Any of these may offer valuable suggestions if they understand that the object of psychotherapy is not to get patients out of the hospital, but to get them well. If such meetings are conducted with the proper attitude, not only are numerous games short-circuited very quickly, but "making progress" may be given up in favor of getting well and staying well, with the exceptions mentioned above. Furthermore, almost all the patients are grateful for this frank approach. After the meeting nearly always some of them come up to shake hands with the therapist and perhaps remark: "This is the first time a doctor has treated me like a real person and talked straight to me." This happens because hospital games are by no means "unconscious." The patient knows very well what he is doing and why he is doing it, and appreciates an understanding therapist who is not taken in by it. Even if he does not admit this on the first try, the patient is grateful because this approach relieves the tedium of conventional psychotherapy.

For those who are more comfortable thinking that their patients have "weak egos," I should say that I would not hesitate to read the above paragraph at my very first encounter with a group of psychiatric inpatients, even very disturbed ones, after only a very short period of preparation and getting acquainted (say thirty minutes), and I would have no doubt of its beneficial effects, since I have said just those things on many occasions under such circumstances.[17]

When a patient who has previously been to one or more therapists or psychiatric hospitals comes to a transactional analyst, as an out-patient or a private patient, the proper procedure is as follows. During the first interview the therapist makes sure he gets the script background, unobtrusively as far as possible, swinging along with the patient's conversation; but later, if there are omissions, making a clear point of filling them in. First, he gets a medical and psychiatric history. In the course of this, he asks for a dream—any dream, because that is the quickest way to get a picture of the patient's script protocol and his world view. Then he inquires about each of the previous therapists: why the patient went to him, how he selected him, what he learned from him, why he left, and under what circumstances. From these inquiries, the script analyst gets many clues. He follows some of them up by asking about other activities: how Pat selects jobs or spouses, and why and *how* he quits or gets a divorce. If this is done competently, the patient will not terminate therapy prematurely, as he often does if the therapist is apprehensive about the transference and hides his fear behind a poker face, a ritualistic courtesy, or a tape recorder. Nothing is as reassuring as competence.

A common situation is where the patient is obviously collecting failures in therapy and elsewhere in order to justify a psychotic or suicidal script payoff, and quits with "Now He Tells Me": that is, by springing some major surprise without previous discussion, and quitting without notice. At the end of the thirtieth session, for example, when everything appears to be going well and Pat is making "progress," he may say casually as he rises to leave: "By the way, this'll be my last visit because I'm going to commit myself to the State Hospital this afternoon"—something he has not previously brought up. If Dr. Q has taken a careful history, he will abort this in the third session by saying: "Now what I think you're heading for is to come here for six months or a year, and then quit suddenly." If Pat objects, Dr. Q responds: "But that's what you did on your two last jobs, and with three of your former therapists. It's all right with me if you want to go through with it, because I can always learn something meanwhile, but if you really want to get well, that's the first thing we have to talk about. Otherwise you'll just waste six months or a year of your life. But if we can thrash it out right now, you'll save that much time and we can go ahead." Alcoholics who crave absolute control or complete surrender are most likely to take umbrage at this abortion of their games, while patients who want to get well will be grateful. If the patient nods or laughs, the prognosis is very good.

E · THE "PROFESSIONAL PATIENT"

Patients who have had a long term of previous therapy, or who have been to several previous therapists, usually come on like "professional patients." There are three criteria which give the diagnosis of "professional patient." One is that Pat uses long words and diagnoses himself, the second is that he refers to his pathology as "Childish" or "immature," and the third is that he looks solemn throughout the interview. By the end of the second visit, he should be told that he is a professional patient, if he is one, and instructed to stop using long words. Since he is well aware of the situation, it is only necessary to say: "You're a professional patient, and I think you should give it up. Stop using long words and speak English." If this is done properly, he will stop using long words very quickly and start to speak English, except that now he will talk in clichés. He is then told to stop using clichés and talk like a real person. By this time he will have stopped looking solemn and will smile or even laugh occasionally. He can then be told that he is no longer a professional patient, but a real person with some psychiatric symptoms. He should also understand by this time that his Child is here to stay, and is not "childish" or "immature" in the stuffy senses of the words, but is confused, and that beneath the confusion is all the charm and spontaneity and creativity of an actual child. The progression here should be noted: from couch-broken precocious Child to cliché-throwing Parent to straight-talking Adult.

F · THE PATIENT AS A PERSON

In script-analysis terms, the patient is now, we hope, "out of his script" during his treatment hours and behaves like a real person, called colloquially "a card-carrying member of the human race." If he relapses, the therapist in individual therapy, or the other group members in group treatment, will so inform him. As long as he can stay out of his script he can examine that script objectively and the script analysis can proceed. The chief difficulty to be overcome is the pull of the script, something like the "Id resistance" of Freud. Professional patients adopt that role because they decided when they were very young, with encouragement from their parents, to be mental cripples, and may have been helped along by their previous therapists. This is usually a family script, and the brothers and sisters and parents may also be in treatment. A typical example is where a brother or sister is in a psychiatric hospital, where he or she continually "acts out" (as the staff calls it), or "acts crazy," as Pat now learns to call it. Pat is a little huffy, and will soon say quite frankly that he is jealous of his brother or sister, because he or she is in a hospital while Pat has to be contented with out-patient therapy. As one man put it, "How come my brother is in a nice plushy mental hospital on the East Coast while I have to be contented with this lousy little therapy group? I was enjoying it much more when I was a professional patient."

While such things are said jokingly, they are the core of the resistance against getting well. First of all, Pat is losing all the advantages of being in a hospital and all the fun of acting crazy. But more than that, he says quite frankly (after he begins to understand his script), his Child is scared to get well and cannot accept the permission offered by the therapist and the other group members to do so, because if he does his mother (in his head) will desert him. No matter how miserable he is with all his fears, anxieties, obsessions, and physical symptoms, he is still better off, he thinks, than being out in the world on his own without his Parent to protect him. At this point there is a phase where script analysis becomes almost indistinguishable from psychoanalytic probing. The protocol of his script becomes the subject of investigation, and the early influences which led him to decide on a not-O.K. position and way of life come under scrutiny. Here his pride at being a neurotic, a paranoid schizophrenic, an addict, or a criminal will begin to emerge, and he may bring in his diary or talk about his plans for writing an autobiography, as so many of his predecessors have done. Even people who are cured of "mental retardation" may have some nostalgia for their previous condition.

NOTES & REFERENCES

1 Freud, S. *Leonardo da Vinci: A Study in Psychosexuality.* Vintage Books, New York, 1955.

2 Jones, E. *The Life and Work of Sigmund Freud.* Basic Books, New York, 1953–1957.

3 Erikson, E. *Young Man Luther.* W. W. Norton & Company, New York, 1958. *Gandhi's Truth.* W. W. Norton & Company, New York, 1969.

4 Edel, L. e.g., *Henry James: The Untried Years.* J. B. Lippincott Company, Philadelphia, 1953.

5 Zeligs, M. *Friendship and Fratricide.* The Viking Press, New York, 1967.

6 McClelland, D. C. *The Achieving Society.* D. Van Nostrand Company, Princeton, 1961.

7 Rudin, S. A. "National Motives Predict Psychogenic Death Rate 25 Years Later." *Science* 160: 901–903, May 24, 1968.

8 Gurin, G., Veroff, S., & Feld, S. *Americans View Their Mental Health.* Basic Books, New York, 1960.

9 Gorman, M. in *Mental Health Statistics,* National Institute of Mental Health, Washington, D.C., January, 1968.

10 Carpenter, E. *The Intermediate Sex.* George Allen & Unwin Ltd., London, 1908.

11 Penfield, W. "Oriental Renaissance in Education and Medicine." *Science,* 141: 1153–1161, September 30, 1963.

12 An interesting confrontation in this respect can be found in *Black Hamlet,* by Wulf Sachs (Geoffrey Bles, London, 1937), where a modern psychotherapist has an African witch doctor as his patient.

13 Berne, E. "Some Oriental Mental Hospitals." *American Journal of Psychiatry,* 106: 376–383, 1949.

14 Steiner, L. *Where Do People Take Their Troubles?* Houghton, Mifflin & Company, Boston, 1945.

15 The trick about Herostratus, or Eratostratus, is to ask "Have you ever heard of him?" I hadn't, and was introduced to him by Dr. Paul Federn. He burned down the Temple of Diana at Ephesus (now a ruin outside of Kushadasi, Turkey) on the same night that Alexander the Great was born, when Diana was too busy officiating at the confinement to take proper care of her shrine. He did this solely for personal publicity. As a punishment fitting the crime, it was decreed that his name should be totally erased from all records. But somehow Plutarch got wind of it neverthe-

less, and so the name of Herostratus became a symbol of gruesome notoriety.

16 Berne, E. *Games People Play. Loc. cit.*

17 Berne, E. "The Staff-Patient Staff Conference." *American Journal of Psychiatry,* 125: 286–293, September, 1968.

CHAPTER SEVENTEEN

The Script Signs

The first duty of a group therapist, whatever theoretical approach he is using, is to observe every movement of every muscle of every patient during every second of the group meeting. In order to accomplish this, he should limit the size of his group to no more than eight patients, and take whatever other measures are necessary to insure that he will be able to carry out this duty with the greatest possible efficiency.[1] If he chooses as his approach script analysis, the most powerful instrument known for effective group treatment, what he is looking for and listening for primarily are those specific signs which indicate the nature of the patient's script and its origins in past experience and parental programing. Only if the patient gets "out of his script" can he emerge as a person capable of autonomous vitality, creativity, fullfilment, and citizenship.

A · THE SCRIPT SIGNAL

For each patient there is a characteristic posture, gesture, mannerism, tic, or symptom which signifies that he is living "in his script," or has "gone into" his script. As long as such "script signals" occur, the patient is not cured, no matter how much "progress" he has made. He may be less miserable, or happier, living in his script world, but he is still in that world and not in the real world, and this will be confirmed by his dreams, his outside experiences, and his attitude toward the therapist and the other members of the group.

The script signal is usually first perceived intuitively by the therapist's Child[2] (preconsciously, not unconsciously). Then one day it comes into full awareness and is taken over by his Adult. He immediately recognizes that it has been characteristic of the patient all along, and he wonders why he never really "noticed" it before.

Abelard, a middle-aged man who complained of depression and slowing up, had been in the group for three years and had made reasonably good "progress" before Dr. Q had more than a vague idea of what his script signal was. Abelard had Parental permission to laugh, which he did with great vigor and enjoyment at every opportunity, but he did not have permission to speak. If addressed, he went through a complicated, sluggish routine before he answered. He slowly pulled himself up in his chair, took hold of a cigarette, coughed, hummed as though collecting his thoughts, and then began: "Well . . ." Then, one day when the group was discussing having babies, and other sexual matters, Dr. Q "noticed" for the first time that there was one other thing Abelard did before he spoke: he slid his hands under his belt quite far down. Dr. Q said: "Get your hands out of your pants, Abel!" at which everyone, including Abelard, began to laugh, and suddenly they realized that he had been doing this all along, but no one had ever "noticed" it before, neither the other members, Dr. Q, nor Abelard himself. It then became clear that Abelard was living in a script world where the prohibition against talking was so severe that his testicles were in jeopardy. No wonder, then, that he never talked unless someone gave him permission to by asking him a question! As long as this script signal was present he could not be free to talk spontaneously, nor to decide other matters that were bothering him.

A more common and similar script signal occurs among women, and may also be perceived intuitively for a long time before it comes into full awareness; from experience, however, the therapist soon learns to see and evaluate it more quickly. Some women sit relaxed until a sexual subject comes up, and then they not only cross their knees, but wind the upper instep around the lower ankle, often simultaneously crossing their arms over their chests and sometimes also leaning forward. This posture forms a triple or quadruple protection against a violation which exists only in their script worlds and not in the real world of the group.

Thus, it is possible to say to a patient: "It's nice that you're feeling better and making progress, but you can't get well until you stop . . ." and the script signal is inserted. This is the opening statement of an attempt to get a "cure contract" or a "script contract" instead of a "making progress" contract. The patient may then agree that he is coming to the group to get out of his script, rather than to get companionship and handy household hints as to how to be happy while living in fear or misery. Clothing is a fertile field for script signals: the woman who is well dressed except for her shoes (she will be "rejected" as her script calls for); the Lesbian who wears "dikey" clothes (she will probably play "Making Ends Meet" with money, be exploited by her girl friends, and attempt suicide); the male homosexual who wears "queenie" clothes (he will get mixed up with women who put their lipstick on crooked, get beaten up by his lovers, and attempt suicide); and the woman who puts her lipstick on crooked (she will often be exploited by male homo-sexuals). Other script signs are blinking, tongue-chewing, jaw-clamping, sniffing, hand-wringing, ring-turning, and foot-tapping. An excellent list can be found in Feldman's book on mannerisms of speech and gestures.[3]

Posture and carriage are also revealing. The tilt of the head in "Martyr" and "Waif" scripts is one of the commonest script signals. An extensive discussion can be found in Deutsch,[4] and a psychoanalytic interpretation, particularly of signals given while lying on the analytic couch, is given by Zeligs.[5]

The script signal is always a reaction to some Parental directive. In order to deal with it, the directive must be uncovered, which is usually easy to do, and the precise antithesis must be found, which may be more difficult, particularly if the signal is a response to an actual hallucination.

B · THE PHYSIOLOGICAL COMPONENT

The sudden onset of symptoms is also usually a script sign. Judith's script called for her to "go crazy," as her sister had done, but she was resisting this parental command. As long as her Adult was in charge she was a normal healthy American girl. But if someone around her acted "crazy" or said he felt "crazy," her Adult would drain away and her Child would be left with no protection. She would immediately get a headache and excuse herself, thus getting away from the scripty situation. On the couch, a similar sequence would occur. As long as Dr. Q would talk to her or answer her, she was in good shape, but if he remained silent, her Adult would fade out, her Child would begin to come on with crazy thoughts, and she would get an instant headache. With some patients, nausea occurs in exactly the same way, only here the parental directive is "get sick" instead of "go crazy," or, in grownup language, "be neurotic" instead of "be psychotic." Anxiety attacks with palpitation, or sudden outbreaks of asthma or hives are also script signals.

Allergic outbreaks when the script is threatened may be quite severe. For example, Rose had been a hiker all her life, and had not suffered from poison oak since childhood. But when her psychoanalyst told her to get a divorce, she got such a severe attack that she had to be hospitalized, and terminated her analysis. He was not aware that her script called for her to get a divorce, but forbade it until her children were grown up. Severe attacks of asthma can also occur at such junctures, requiring hospitalization in an oxygen tent. A full awareness of the patient's script can (I think) prevent such serious outbreaks. Ulcerative colitis and perforated gastric ulcer also come under suspicion here at times. In one case a paranoid gave up his script world and started to live in the real world without sufficient preparation and "protection," and less than a month later sugar appeared in his urine, marking the onset of diabetes. This brought him back to the "safety" of his "Fail Sick" script in a modified way.

The slogan "Think sphincter" also refers to the physiological component of the script. The man with a tight mouth, and the person who eats, drinks, smokes, and talks simultaneously (as far as possible) are typical "script characters." The man addicted to laxatives or enemas may have an archaic "bowel" script. Women with violation scripts may keep their *Levator eni* and *Sphincter cunni* muscles tightened up, resulting in painful intercourse. Premature and retarded ejaculation, and asthma, may also be regarded as sphincter disturbances of a scripty nature.

Sphincters are the organs of final display or payoff. The actual "cause" of sphincter disturbances is of course nearly always in the central nervous system. The transactional aspects, however, do not arise from the "cause" but from the effect. For example, whatever the "cause" of premature ejaculation in the central nervous system, the effect is on the relationship between the man and his mate, and thus premature ejaculation arises from, or is a part of, or contributes to his script, which is usually a "failure" script in other areas besides sex.

The importance of "thinking sphincter" lies in the way the sphincters can be used transactionally. The Child in Mike intuitively senses very quickly in what way various people want to use sphincters against him. He knows that this man wants to urinate on him, that one wants to defecate on him, that a woman wants to spit on him, and so forth.[6] And he is almost always right, as he finds out in the long run if he engages with any of these people.

What happens is this. When Mike first meets Pat (in the first ten seconds or at most, ten minutes, after they first set eyes on each other), Mike's Child senses exactly what Pat's Child is up to. But as quickly as possible, Pat's Child, with the assistance of his Adult and Parent, generates a thick smoke screen which, like a jinn, gradually takes on a human form as Pat's persona, or disguise. Mike then starts to ignore and bury his Child's intuitive perception in favor of accepting Pat's persona. Thus Pat cons Mike out of his accurate perception and offers his persona instead. Mike accepts Pat's persona because Mike is just as busily throwing up a smoke screen to con Pat, and he is so intent on this that he forgets not only what his Child knows about Pat, but also what he knows about himself. I have discussed the first ten seconds in more detail elsewhere. People ignore their intuitive perceptions and accept each other's personas instead because that is the polite thing to do and plays along with the needs of their games and scripts. This mutual acceptance is called "the social contract."[7]

The script significance of sphincters is that each person seeks, and intuitively spots, someone who has a complementary script. Thus, to put it in the most basic terms, the person whose script calls for him to eat shit will seek out someone whose script calls for him to shit on people. They will hook into each other in the first ten minutes, spend more or less time disguising the sphincter basis of their attraction for each other, and if they continue beyond this point, eventually they will satisfy each other's script needs.

If this does not sound credible, consider the more flagrant cases where there is an immediate satisfaction of script needs. A male homosexual can go into a men's room or bar, or even walk down the street, and in ten seconds he can unerringly spot the man he is looking for, one who will not only give him the kind of sexual satisfaction he wants, but do it in the way his script calls for: in a semi-public place where the thrills of a game of "Cops & Robbers" are added to the sexual satisfaction, or in a quiet place where they may form a longer-lasting liaison which may (if the script calls for it) end in murder. An experienced heterosexual man walking down the right street in any large city can usually pick out unerringly just the woman he wants: one who will not only give the desired type of sexual satisfaction, but will also play the games that fit into his script. He can get rolled, paid, drunk, high, killed, or married, whichever one his script calls for.

Many civilized or well-brought up people learn to ignore or suppress their intuitions, although these abilities can be unmasked and developed under proper conditions.

C · HOW TO LISTEN

In the first section we described some of the visual script signals. We now turn to the art of listening. The therapist can either listen to the patients with his eyes closed, assuring them at some point that he is not asleep, and rewarding them for their indulgence by telling them what he has heard, or listen to a tape recording of a group meeting, again preferably with his eyes closed so as to shut out visual distractions. One of the scripty things taught to almost all children, along with not looking at people too carefully, is not to listen with their eyes closed, lest they hear too much. This injunction is not always easy to overcome—mother wouldn't like it.

Even if he has never seen the patients, and initially knows nothing about their previous histories, an experienced script analyst can learn an enormous amount from a ten- or twenty-minute tape run of a treatment group. Starting with zero information he should, merely by listening to an unknown patient talk for a while, be able to give a quite detailed account of his family background, favorite games, and probable destiny. After thirty minutes, the returns diminish because of fatigue, and no tape ought to be played for more than a half-hour at one sitting.

There is always room for improvement in knowing how to listen. This is a kind of Zen proposition, since for the most part it depends on what is going on in the listener's head, rather than on what is taking place outside. The useful part of the listening is done by that aspect of the personality known as "The Professor," the Adult in the Child (see Figure 7). The Professor commands the power of intuition,[8] and the most important aspect of intuition concerns transactional sphincter behavior: What sphincter does the other fellow want to use on me, and which one does he want me to use on him? Where do these desires come from, and where are they headed for? By the time this archaic or "primal" information filters through to the Adult of the listener, it may be elaborated into something more specific: information about the patient's family background,[9] his instinctual strivings,[10] his occupation, and his script goal. What is necessary, then, is to know how to free the Professor to do his job most effectively. The rules for this are as follows:

1. The listener should be in good physical condition, having had a good night's sleep,* and should not be under the influence of alcohol, medications, or drugs which impair his mental efficiency. This includes both sedatives and stimulants.

2. He must free his mind of outside preoccupations.

3. He must put aside all Parental prejudices and feelings, including the need to "help."

4. He must put aside all preconceptions about his patients in general and about the particular patient he is listening to.

5. He must not let the patient distract him by asking questions or making other demands, and should learn harmless ways of warding off such interruptions.

6. His Adult listens to the content of what the patient says, while his Child-Professor listens to the way he says it. In telephone language, his Adult listens to the information, and his Child listens to the noise.[11] In radio language, his Adult listens to the program, and his Child listens to how the machine is working. Thus, he is both a listener and a repairman. If he is a counselor, it is enough for him to be a listener, but if he is a therapist, his most important job is making repairs.

7. When he begins to feel tired, he stops listening and starts looking or talking instead.

---

*This probably means REM sleep. Often a therapist who has lain awake tossing all night will find his intuition sharper than usual the next morning. The hypothesis would be that his Adult is tired from lack of NREM sleep while his Child is in extra-good shape from plenty of REM sleep.

D · BASIC VOCAL SIGNALS

After he has learned how to listen, he must learn what to listen for. From the psychiatric point of view there are four basic vocal signals: sounds, accents, voices, and vocabulary.

1 · BREATHING SOUNDS

The commonest breathing sounds and their usual meanings are as follows: coughs (nobody loves me), sighs (if only), yawns (buzz off), grunts (you said it), and sobs (you got me); and various kinds of laughs such as jollies, chuckles, snickers, and titters. The three most important types of laughs, known colloquially as Ho Ho, Ha Ha, and He He, will be discussed further on.

2 · ACCENTS

Culture has very little to do with scripts. There are winners and losers in every layer of society and in every country, and they go about fulfilling their destinies in much the same way all over the world. For example, the prevalence of mental illness in any large group of people is pretty much the same all over,[12] and there are suicides everywhere. Every large group in the world also has its leaders and its rich men.

Nevertheless, foreign accents do have some meaning for the script analyst. First, they make possible educated guesses about early Parental precepts, and that is where culture does come in: "Do as you're told" in Germany, "Be quiet" in France, and "Don't be naughty" in Britain. Secondly, they indicate the flexibility of the script. A German who has been in this country for twenty years and still speaks with a thick accent probably has a less flexible life plan than a Dane who speaks good American after only two years. Thirdly, the script is written in the native language of the Child, and script analysis is swifter and more effective if the therapist can speak that language. A foreigner living out his script in America is the equivalent of putting on *Hamlet* in Japanese in the Kabuki theater. A great deal is going to be lost or misunderstood if the critic does not have the original at hand.

Native accents are also informative, particularly if they are affected. A man who speaks with a Brooklyn accent but throws in a few Boston or Broadway broad *a*'s clearly shows the influence of a hero or a parental person he is carrying around in his head, and that person must be tracked down, because his influence is probably widespread, even if the patient denies it. "She passed a remok, or I should say an epigram," or "We left oily, but didn't get to the game until hof time," clearly indicates a split in the Parental directives.

3 · VOICES

Each patient has at least three different voices, Parent, Adult, and Child. He may keep one, or even two of them carefully hidden for a long time, but they will slip out sooner or later. Usually a careful listener can hear at least two of them in any fifteen-minute period. The patient may say a whole Parental paragraph with only one Child whine, or a whole Adult paragraph with only one Parental scold, but an alert listener will pick up the key phrase. Other patients change voices from one sentence to another, or even use two or three voices in a single sentence.

Each of the voices reveals something about the script. A Parental voice, speaking to another person, uses Parental slogans and precepts, and duplicates what father or mother would have said in the same situation: "Doesn't everybody?," "Look who's talking," "You've got to keep your mind occupied," "Why don't you try harder?," "You can't trust anybody." An unswerving Adult voice usually means that the Child is being suppressed by Parental command in favor of some humorless pedantic pattern perhaps loaded with a few "official" or anal jokes. This indicates that the Child will therefore find devious ways of expression or periodically explode, giving rise to the nonadaptive behavior and waste of energy which makes a loser. The Child voice indicates the script role: "Cute Kid," "Little Old Me," "Clinging Whine," for example. Thus, the Parental voice tells the counterscript, The Adult voice gives the pattern, and the Child voice takes the script role.

4 · VOCABULARY

Each ego state may also have its own vocabulary. Parental words, such as "bad," "stupid," "coward," and "ridiculous," tell what Jeder is most afraid of being, and tries hardest to avoid. A persistent Adult technical vocabulary may be simply a way of avoiding people, as is common in engineering, aviation, and finance, under a script directive of "Do great things but don't get involved personally." The Adult "helpnik" vocabularies (PTA, psychology, psychoanalysis, social science) may be used in an intellectual Rite of Spring, where the victim's dismembered psyche is left scattered over the floor on the theory that he will eventually join himself together and be more fertile afterward. The story line of this script reads: "I'll tear you apart, and remember I'm only trying to help you. But you'll have to put yourself together, since nobody else can do it for you." Sometimes the patient is his own favorite Ritual victim. The Child vocabulary may be the obscene words of revolt, the clichés of compliance, or the sweet phrases of charming innocence.

A typical triad often found in the same person is Parental marshmallow-throwing, Adult dissection, and Child obscenity. For example: "We all have our ups and downs; I think you're handling it beautifully. Of course you have to split off your autonomous ego from your identification with your mother. After all, it's a shitty world." This script comes right out of Dante's *Inferno:* "How to keep smiling while reading a textbook when you're up to your neck in sewage."

E · CHOICE OF WORDS

Sentences are constructed jointly by the Parent, Adult, and Child, and each one reserves and exercises the right to insert words and phrases according to its needs. In order to understand what is going on in the patient's head, the therapist must be able to break the finished product down into its significant components. This is called transactional parsing and is somewhat different from grammatical parsing.

1 · PARTS OF SPEECH

Adjectives and abstract nouns are name-calling. The correct response to a person who says that he suffers from "passive dependency" or that he is "an insecure sociopath" is "What names did your parents call you when you were little?" Action euphemisms such as "aggressive expression" or "sexual intercourse" should be eliminated by asking "What did you call that when you were little?" "Expressive aggression" is a pure artifact and means that Pat has gone to a modern dance class or been wrestled by a Gestalt therapist, while "intercoursal sex" means that he attends meetings of the Sexual Freedom League.*

Adverbs are a little more intimate. Thus "I sometimes feel sexual excitement" is over there in the vague distance, while "I sometimes get sexually excited" is over here. The precise psychological significance of adverbs, however, remains to be clarified.

Pronouns, verbs, and concrete nouns are the most real parts of speech, and "tell it like it is." Telling it like it is may mean that the patient is ready to get well. Thus, a woman who is afraid of sex often stresses adjectives and abstract nouns: "I had a satisfactory sexual experience." Later on, she may emphasize pro-

---

*"Noun adjectives" ending in "ic," such as hysteric, sociopathic, psychopathic, are usually put-downs applied to patients. "Verb adjectives" ending in "ive," like punitive and manipulative, are more neutral, and can be applied to patients and staff members alike.

nouns and verbs: "We really turned on." One woman went to the hospital the first time to have "an obstetrical experience." The second time, she went to have a baby. Patients "express hostility against authority figures." When they become real people, they just swear or tear up the papers. On the therapist's side, the one who reports: "We initiated the interview by exchanging positive greetings. The patient then related that he had expressed hostility by performing an act of physical aggression against his wife," is having a harder time than the one who says: "The patient said Hello and told me that he hit his wife." In one case the therapist maintained that a boy "attended a residential school setting in the private area," while the boy said that he merely "went to boarding school."

The most important single word in script language is the particle "but," which means "According to my script, I don't have permission to do that." Real people say: "I will," or "I won't," or "I won," or "I lost," while "I will but . . ." "I won't but . . ." "I won but . . ." or "I lost but . . ." are all scripty.

2 · O.K. WORDS

The rule for listening to tape recordings is: If you can't hear what the patient is saying, don't worry about it, because usually he isn't saying anything. When he has something to say, you'll hear him, no matter how noisy or poor the recording is. Sometimes a poor tape recording is better than a good one for clinical purposes. If every word can be heard, the listener may become distracted by the content, and lose the more important script indices. For example: "I met a man at a bar and he made a pass at me. So after he got too fresh I said to him, I said 'Whom do you think you are anyhow, so he could see I was a lady, but he kept on so after a while I told him off.' " This is a rather dull, uninstructive, and commonplace tale. It is much more revealing on a poor recording, where it comes out: "Mumble mumble mumble PASS AT ME mumble mumble FRESH mumble mumble mumble SEE I WAS A LADY mumble mumble TOLD HIM OFF." Here the audible words are "the O.K. Words." This patient is under instructions from her mother to TELL MEN OFF, thus proving that SHE IS A LADY, providing she can collect enough trading stamps or PASSES to justify herself (as a lady) in becoming angry. The instruction reads "Remember LADIES get angry when men make passes at them." Father throws in helpfully: "There are lots of FRESH guys at bars. I ought to know." So she goes to bars and sets about proving that she is a lady.

After she has been in psychoanalytic therapy for a while, her tape goes: "Mumble mumble mumble SADISTIC MAN mumble mumble mumble MY MASOCHISTIC SELF mumble mumble. Mumble mumble mumble EXPRESSING MY USUAL HOSTILITY mumble mumble." She has replaced the old O.K. Words with some new O.K. Words. If she transfers to a transactional analyst, the tape goes: "Mumble mumble HIS CHILD mumble mumble mumble MY PARENT mumble mumble played 'RAPO.' " But a month later there are no more mumbles even on a poor and noisy tape, and what comes through clearly is "I've met some awfully nice men since I stopped going to bars."

O.K. Words tell the story much better than the story itself. It might take months of conventional therapy to unravel the details of a hard-luck story told in the clear by a female graduate student, but if the tape goes "Mumble mumble mumble STUDIED HARD mumble mumble GOOD GRADES BUT mumble mumble TERRIBLE AFTERWARD," the loud O.K. Words that come through tell the story of her life right there: "You're supposed to work hard and succeed except that something is supposed to go wrong so you'll end up feeling terrible." The O.K. Words state her script directives loud and clear.

The O.K. Words referred to in the last section come from the Parental precepts, patterns, and threats. Precepts such as "Be a lady," "Study hard," give Lady and Study as O.K. Words. The threat "Otherwise something awful will happen" gives Something Awful as an O.K. Word. When a patient gets couch-broken, the therapist's vocabulary becomes O.K. Words, and indeed, this is one of the signs that the patient is couch-broken. She says masochism, hostility, Parent, Child, etc., because at this stage the therapist becomes a substitute parent, and his O.K. vocabulary replaces the original one learned in childhood. O.K. Words are those approved by the Parent part of the patient's father, mother, therapist, or other parental person.

3 · SCRIPT WORDS

We remember, however, that many of the script controls are given by the Child part of the father or mother, and these rely on a whole other vocabulary of Script Words and Phrases, which are usually quite different from the O.K. Words. Some of them, indeed, may be in direct contradiction. A woman who uses very lady-like O.K. Words when she is in her antiscript may use very foul language when she is in her script. Thus, she may call her children "my lovely teen-agers" when she is sober, and "those shitfaces" when she is drunk. Script words give important information regarding script roles and script scenes, both of which are important in trying to reconstruct the script world, or the kind of world the patient's Child is living in.

In men's scripts, the commonest roles for females are girls, ladies, and women. In women's scripts, males becomes kids, men, and old men. More specialized are "little girls" and "dirty old men." These two attract each other, especially in bars. The man refers to the women he meets as "nice little girls." The woman refers to the men she meets as "dirty old men." He needs a little girl for his script and she needs a dirty old man for hers, and when they meet the action begins and they know what to say to each other after they say Hello. Various women live in worlds populated by wolves, beasts, charmers, cats, creeps, suckers, and pricks, and their menfolk see them as dishes, bitches, grooves, chicks, broads, whores, and cunts. All these are script words which emerge in the course of conversation or group treatment.

The script scenes are usually centered around one or

other room of the house: the nursery, the bathroom, the kitchen, the living room, and the bedroom, and these are located in such expressions as "plenty to drink," "all that crap," "a regular feast," "all those people," and "sock it to them" Each of these rooms has its own vocabulary, and the person stuck in any of these chambers will use the appropriate expressions over and over. Equally common is the workroom, signified by "Get your ass over there."

Counterscript words can also be detected in people who are fighting their scripts. Jack, the Sisyphus mentioned in Chapter Twelve, became a professional baseball player, partly because it was his thing and partly because he was boxed into it by his uncle. As Dr. Q listened to him one day, he noticed for the first time a tremendous power behind the word "not," which Jack said frequently, and a lesser but still striking impact whenever Jack said "something else." He immediately sensed intuitively the meaning behind these two terms. Whenever Jack said "not," he was pitching, and whenever Jack pitched his Child was saying "not"—"You're *not* going to hit it!" Whenever he said "something else," he was throwing to first base, and whenever he was throwing to first base, he was saying "something else" —"If I can't strike you out we'll try something else." Jack not only confirmed these intuitions, but related how a pitching coach had told him the same thing in different language. "Relax! If you throw every pitch that hard, you're going to get a bum shoulder!" Which Jack eventually did. Like Dr. Q, the coach had perceived, on the basis of his intuition and experience, that Jack was pitching in anger, and he knew that was no good.

Jack's antiscript was to succeed as a baseball player, and behind his professional pitching was a great rage against his father and uncle for commanding him to be a loser. Thus, every time he threw the ball he was fighting his script and trying to smash his way out of his bag into success. This gave him tremendous speed, and his antiscript gave him superb control. The only thing he lacked was the ability to cool it and fit his pitches into the context of the batting order and the state of the game. In the end, his nonadaptive rage brought about just the payoff he was trying to avoid, and he had to quit the game. The intuitive perceptiveness of the Adult in the therapist's Child, The Professor, is his most valuable therapeutic instrument. The acute sensitivity of a properly attuned Professor is demonstrated by the fact that Dr. Q knew all this in spite of the fact that he had only been to one professional baseball game in his whole life, although he had pitched in many sandlot softball games.

4 · METAPHORS

Closely allied to script words are metaphors. Thus, Mary had two different and separate vocabularies of metaphors. In one, she was all at sea, couldn't fathom anything, could hardly keep her head above water, had stormy days, and waves of feelings. At other times, life was a feast, she could eat her words, she had lots of goodies, or she might feel sour or bitter because that was the way the cookie crumbled. She married a sailor and complained of obesity. When she felt at sea, all her lingo was maritime, and when she was overeating, it was culinary. Thus she fell from the ocean to the kitchen and back again, and the therapist's problem was to get her feet on the ground. Metaphors are an extension of the script scene, and a change in metaphors means a change of scene. In her case, the stormy waters turned out to be a sea of anger.

5 · SECURITY PHRASES

Some people have to go through certain rituals or make certain gestures before they begin to talk, in order to protect themselves or apologize for speaking. These rituals are addressed to their Parents. We have already cited the case of Abelard, who always slid his hands under his belt before he began to talk. It was evident that he was protecting his testicles from some inner assailant who was scheduled to attack him when he was off guard because he was speaking to somebody, so he always took care of that danger before he ventured to speak. In other cases these security measures are incorporated into the sentence structure. There are various degrees of protection in answering a question like: "Did you ever get mad at your sister?" "*Maybe* I did" implies a Parental order "Never commit yourself." "I *think maybe* I did" implies two Parental orders: "How can you be sure?" and "Don't commit yourself." The first usually comes from father, the second from mother. "I *think maybe* I *might* have" contains a triple protection. Security phrases are chiefly of prognostic value. It is much easier for the therapist to penetrate one layer of security measures than three "I think maybe I might have" is similar to the Berkeley Subjunctive, and is likewise designed to protect and conceal a very young and very apprehensive Child who is not going to let anybody in very easily.

6 · THE SUBJUNCTIVE

The subjunctive, or as it is called colloquially, the "Berkeley Subjunctive," comprises three items. First, the phrases "if" or "if only"; secondly, the use of subjunctives or conditionals such as would, should, and could; and thirdly, the noncommitment words such as "toward." The Berkeley Subjunctive is most highly developed on college campuses. The classical phrase is "I should, and I would if I could, but . . ." Variants are "If only they would, I could, and I think I probably should, but . . ." or "I should, and I probably could, but then they would . . ."

This subjunctive attitude becomes formalized in the titles of books, theses, papers, and student assignments. Common examples are "Some Factors Involved In . . ." (=if only), or "Toward a Theory of . . ." (=I would if I could, and I know I should). In the extreme case, the title reads: "Some Introductory Remarks Concerning Factors Involved in Gathering Data Toward a Theory of . . ." —a very modest title indeed, since it is plain that it will take about two hundred years before the theory itself will be ready for publication. It is obvious that this man's mother told him not to stick his neck out. His next paper, presumably, will be: "Some Intermediate Remarks Concerning . . . etc." and then "Some Final Remarks Concerning . . . etc." Having disposed of Remarks, presumably the titles of his succeeding papers will get shorter and shorter. By the time he is forty, he will have the prolegomena shaved off and will come out with number six, "Toward a Theory Of . . ." but the actual theory is rarely forthcoming. If it is, and the seventh paper is the theory itself, then there will be an eighth entitled: "Oops, Sorry. Back to the Old Computer." He is always on the way, but never gets to the next station.

This is not amusing for the therapist who undertakes to treat a man who is writing a paper with such a title. Pat will also be complaining of not being able to finish his thesis, inability to concentrate, sexual and marital problems, depression, and suicidal impulses. Unless the therapist can find a way to change the script, the treatment will follow exactly the eight stages outlined above, each phase taking six months to a year or more, with the therapist writing the final paper (the Oops one) instead of the patient. In script language, "toward" means "don't get there." Nobody asks "Does this airplane go toward New York?" nor would many people want to travel with a pilot who says: "Yes, we're going toward New York." He either goes *to* New York or you take another airplane.

7 · SENTENCE STRUCTURE

Besides the subjunctivists there are other people who are forbidden to finish anything or come to the point, so when they talk they "run off at the mouth." Their sentences are strung out with conjunctions: "Yesterday I was sitting at home with my husband and . . . and . . . and then . . . and . . . and then . . ." Often the directive is "Don't tell any of the family secrets!" so they go all around the secret and play with it as long as they can without giving it away.

Some speakers are careful to balance everything: "It's raining, but the sun will come out soon." "I have a headache, but my stomach is better." "They're not very nice, but on the other hand, they look cheerful."

The directive in this case seems to be "Don't look at anything too closely." The most interesting example of this type was a man who had been a diabetic since the age of five, and had been taught to balance his diet with the utmost care. When he spoke, he weighed every word with similar care, and balanced each of his sentences very cautiously and precisely. These precautions made him very difficult to listen to. All his life he had been in a rage against the unfair restrictions imposed on him because of the disease, and his speech became very unbalanced when he was angry. (The implications of this for the psychology of diabetes must await further study.)

Another type of sentence structure is the dangling point, with free use of "and so forth" and "et cetera." "Well, we went to the movies and so forth, and then I kissed her and so forth, and then she stole my wallet and so forth." Unfortunately, this often conceals a deep anger against the mother. "Well, I'd like to tell her what I think of her, et cetera." "What is 'et cetera?' " "What I'd really like to do is cut her to pieces." "Et cetera?" "No, no more 'et cetera.' That's the et cetera." Sentence structure offers a fascinating field for study.

F · THE GALLOWS TRANSACTION

Jack: I stopped smoking. I haven't had a cigarette for over a month.

Della: And how much weight have you put on, heh, heh, heh?

Everyone smiled at this sally except Jack and Dr. Q.

Dr. Q: Well, you really are getting well, Jack. You didn't fall for that one.

Della: I want to get well, too. I could have bitten my tongue off for saying that. That was my mother talking. I was trying to do to Jack exactly what she does to me.

Don (a new member): What's so terrible about that? Just a little joke.

Della: My mother came to see me the other day and

she tried to do it to me again, but I wouldn't let her. It sure made her mad. She said "You're sure putting on weight again, ha ha." I was supposed to laugh, too, and say "Yeah, I'm overeating, ha ha." But instead I said "You're kind of heavy yourself." So then she changed the subject and said "How can you live in a run-down shack like this?"

It is pretty clear from this that for overweight Della, keeping mother happy = putting on weight and laughing about it, the tragedy of her life, and that not laughing about it is impudent and makes mother unhappy. She is supposed to hang herself while they have a good chuckle over it.

The gallows laugh is the dying man's joke, or famous last words. As already noted, the crowds of spectators at the Tyburn or Newgate hangings in the eighteenth century used to admire people who died laughing: "I was the capper, see," says Daniel Then. "We had the cull all set up and then something went wrong. The others got away but I got nabbed, ha ha ha!" And "Ha, ha, ha," roars the crowd in appreciation of the jest as the trap is sprung, "the damber died game." Danny seems to be laughing at the wry joke fate played on him, but deep down he knows who is responsible, and he is really saying: "Well, mother (or father), you predicted I'd end up on the gallows, and here I am, ha ha ha." The same thing happens in a minor way at almost any group-treatment session.

Danny Now was one of four children, none of whom had permission to succeed. The parents were both a little dishonest in socially acceptable ways, and the children each carried this tendency a little further. One day Danny told about his troubles at college. He was falling behind in his work, so he had paid a ghost writer in advance to do his thesis. The group listened with interest as he described his negotiations with this man, and told how the ghost writer had also undertaken to write theses for some of Danny's friends, all of whom had paid in advance. The other members asked questions here and there, until finally Danny came to the point. The writer had absconded to Europe, taking all the money he had collected, and without leaving any theses behind. At this, the group broke into uproarious laughter in which Danny joined.

The others said they thought the story was funny for two reasons: first, the way Danny told it, as though he expected them to laugh, and would be disappointed if they didn't; and second, because it was the sort of thing they expected, or perhaps even hoped, would happen to Danny because of the complicated way he went about doing things instead of carrying out his obligations in a straightforward, honest way. They all knew that Danny was supposed to fail, and it was amusing to see how much effort he put into it. They joined in Danny Now's laughter the same way the crowd had joined in Danny Then's. Later they would all be depressed about it, Danny most of all. His laugh said "Ha, ha, ha, mother, you always loved me when I failed, and here I go again."

The Adult in the Child, The Professor, has had the task from earliest years of keeping mother contented so that she will stay with him and protect him. If she likes him and expresses the liking with a smile, he feels safe even when he is actually in trouble or even in dire peril of death. Crossman[13] discusses this in more detail. In normal mothering, she says, mother's Parent and Child both like kids. So when mother smiles both her Parent and her Child are pleased with her offspring, and things will proceed smoothly between them. In other cases, mother's Parent smiles at her son because she is supposed to, while her Child is angry at him. He can get on the good side of her Child, and get a smile that way, by behavior which her Parent might disapprove of. For example, by demonstrating that he is "bad," he may get a Child smile because he has proven that he is not-O.K., and that pleases the Child in mother—what we have previously called "the witch mother." From all this, Crossman concludes that both script and antiscript can be considered attempts to evoke mother's smile: the antiscript for the approving smile of mother's (and father's) Parent, the script for the smile of mother's Child, who enjoys the baby's pain or discomfiture.

The gallows laugh, then, occurs when Danny "finds himself" with the rope around his neck, and his Child says: "I didn't really want to end up this way. How did I get here?" Then Mother (in his head) smiles, and he realizes that she has conned him into it. He then has the choice of either going crazy, killing her, killing himself, or laughing. At such moments he may envy the brother who chose instead to go to the mental hospital, or the sister who elected to kill herself, but he is not ready for either of those—yet.

The gallows laugh or the gallows smile occurs after a special kind of stimulus and response called the "gallows transaction." A typical example is an alcoholic who has not had a drink for six months, as everyone in the group knows. Then one day he comes in and lets the others talk for a while. When they have gotten all their troubles off their chests, so that he has the stage to himself, he says: "Guess what happened over the weekend?" One look at his slightly smiling face and they know what happened. They get ready to smile, too. One of them sets up the gallows transaction by asking: "What happened?" "Well, I took one drink and then another, and the next thing I knew" —by this time he is laughing and so are they—"I went on a three-day bender." Steiner,[14] who first described these phenomena clearly, says it thus: "In the case of the Alcoholic, White tells the audience about last week's bender while the audience (including, perhaps, the therapist) beams with delight. The smile of the Children in the audience parallels and reinforces the smile of the witch mother or ogre who is pleased when White obeys the injunction ('Don't think— drink'), and in effect tightens the noose around White's neck."

The gallows laugh (which results from a gallows transaction) means that if the patient laughs while recounting a misfortune, and particularly if the other group members join in the laughter, that misfortune is part of the catastrophe of the patient's script. When the people around him laugh, they reinforce the payoff, hasten his doom, and prevent him from getting well.

In this way, the parental come-on is brought to fruition, ha ha.

G · TYPES OF LAUGHTER

It can be fairly said that script analysts and their groups have more fun than anybody, even though they do refrain from laughing at the hanging or when someone gets his feet dirty. There are several kinds of laughs which are of interest in script analysis.[15]

1 · SCRIPTY LAUGHS

a. "Heh Heh Heh" is the Parental chuckle of the witch mother or ogre father who is leading someone, usually his own offspring, down the primrose path of derision and defeat. "How much weight did you put on, heh heh heh?" (Sometimes written "ha ha.") This is the scripty laugh.

b. "Ha Ha Ha" is the Adult's chuckle of rueful humor. As in Danny's case, it signifies a superficial insight. From his recent experiences, Danny had learned not to trust ghost writers, but he had not learned much about himself and his own weaknesses, which would again and again lead him into similar traps until the final one was sprung. This is the gallows laugh.

c. "He He He" is the Child's laugh when he is going to pull a fast one. He is really getting into a game of "Let's Pull a Fast One on Joey," a true con game where he is enticed into thinking that he is going to fool somebody, but he himself ends up being the victim instead. For example, Danny Now said "He He He!" when a ghost writer explained how they could pull a fast one on the English professor, but then Come to Find Out, Danny ended up as the victim. This is the gamy laugh.

2 · HEALTHY LAUGHS

d. "Ho Ho Ho" is the Parent's laugh at the Child's struggle to succeed. It is patronizing, benevolent, and helpful, at least as far as the immediate problem is concerned. It usually comes from people who are not too heavily involved and can turn over the final responsibility to someone else. It demonstrates to the child that there are rewards for nonscripty behavior. This is the granddad or Santa Claus laugh.

e. There is another kind of "Ha Ha Ha" which is much more hearty and meaningful. This signifies true insight on the part of the Adult as to how he has been conned, not by external figures, but by his own Parent and Child. It is similar to what psychologists call an "aha experience" (although I personally have never heard anyone except a psychologist say "aha" on such occasions). This is the laugh of insight.

f. "Wow Wow" is the Child laugh of sheer fun or the belly laugh of older people who have bellies. It only comes to people who are script free or can put their scripts aside for the occasion. This is the spontaneous laugh of healthy people.

H · GRANDMOTHER

No one who has ever known his grandmother is an atheist, even if she herself was one, for all grandmothers, good or evil, are watching somewhere out there, usually on pass from Heaven. During group meetings (and often during poker games as well) she hovers in the corner of the room by the ceiling. If a patient's Child does not have complete confidence in his Parent, in time of need he usually feels that he can still trust grandmother, and he will gaze up at the ceiling in her direction to get protection and guidance from her invisible presence. It should be remembered that grandmothers are even more powerful than mothers, although they may appear but seldom on the scene. But when they do, they have the final say. This is well known to readers of fairy tales, where the old crone can put a blessing or a curse on the baby prince or princess, and the bad fairy or the fairy godmother cannot take it away, but can only tone it down. Thus, in "Sleeping Beauty" the old crone condemns the princess to die. The good fairy modifies this to sleeping for one hundred years. That is the best she can do, for as she says: "I have no power to undo entirely what my elder has done."

Thus grandmother, for good or evil, is the court of last appeal, and if the therapist succeeds in breaking the curse put on the patient by her mother, he still has grandmother to reckon with. A good therapist, therefore, must learn how to deal with antagonistic grandmothers as well as with mothers. In therapeutic situations, grandmothers always think they are right, and justified. The therapist has to talk firmly to them: "Do you really want Zoe to be a failure? Do you really think your complaint will be well received at Headquarters if you tell them the truth? The truth is that I am not seducing your granddaughter into bad ways, but I am actually giving her permission to be happy. Whatever you tell them, remember that psychiatrists come from Headquarters, too, and will also be heard there. Zoe cannot speak for herself against you, but I can speak for her."

In most cases, it is grandmother who decides which cards Jeder will get when he plays poker. If he keeps in good with her he will certainly not lose, and will usually win. If he offends her by thought or deed, he is bound to lose. But he must remember that the other players have grandmothers, too, and they may be just as powerful as his. In addition, they may be in better standing with their grandmothers than he is with his.

I · TYPES OF PROTEST

The main types of protest are anger and weeping. These are highly regarded by the majority of group therapists as "expressing real feelings," while laughter is for some reason not so highly thought of, and is sometimes lightly dismissed as not expressing a "real feeling."

Since about ninety per cent of anger is a "racket" encouraged by the Parent, the real question is "What good does it do to get angry?" It seldom accomplishes anything that cannot be done better without it, and the price is hardly worth paying: four to six hours of disturbed metabolism, and possibly several hours of insomnia. The crucial point in the after-burn of anger occurs when Jeder stops saying to himself or his friends: "I should have . . ." (using the past tense) and switches into "I'd like to . . ." (using the present tense). This staircase anger is nearly always misguided. The rule for staircase anger is the same as the rule for staircase wit. "If you didn't say it on the spot, don't go back to say it afterward, as your intuition was probably right in the first place." The best policy is to wait until the next occasion, and then if you are really ready to do better, you will.

The phase of the present tense ("I'd like to . . .") is usually short lived, and the future tense soon takes over: "Next time I'll . . ." This signifies a shift from Child to Adult. I am firmly convinced (without any chemical evidence) that the shift from past to future coincides with a shift in metabolic chemistry, and is merely a slight change in some small radical of some complex hormonal substance—a simple process of reduction or oxidation. This is another assault on the illusion of autonomy. As the person shifts from past to future in his indignation, he thinks "I am calming down," or someone says: "Now you are being more sensible." But in fact he is neither "calming" nor "being" and is simply reacting to a trivial chemical change.

Nearly all anger is part of a game of "Now I've Got You, You Son of a Bitch" (NIGYSOB). ("Thank you for giving me an excuse to get angry.") Jeder is in fact pleased at being wronged, since he has been carrying around a bag of anger since early childhood and it is a relief to vent some of it legitimately. ("Who wouldn't get angry under such conditions?") The question here is whether abreaction is beneficial. Freud long ago said it didn't do the job. Nowadays, however, for most group therapists it is the mark of a "good" group meeting, and leads to lively staff conferences. Everybody is delighted and exhilarated and relieved when a patient "expresses anger." Therapists who encourage patients to do this, or even demand it from them, feel very supercilious toward their less trippy colleagues and have no hesitation in saying so. The *reductio ad absurdum* of this attitude is in the following statement by an imaginary patient: "I took public transportation toward my occupational area and resolved that today I would really communicate with authority figures by expressing real feelings. So I screamed at my boss and threw my typewriter through the window. He was very happy, and said 'I'm glad that we're finally communicating and that you're freely expressing your hostility. That's the kind of employee we like to have around here. I note that you have liquidated a fellow employee who happened to be standing under the window, but I hope this will not arouse hampering guilt feelings in you that will interfere with our interpersonal interaction.' "

The distinction between racket anger and genuine anger is often easy to make. After NIGYSOB anger the patient may smile, whereas genuine anger is usually followed in the group by weeping. In any case, the patients should understand that they are not permitted to throw things, or assault or strike each other in the group. Any attempt to do so should be physically restrained, and, except in special cases, a patient who does either of these things should be dropped from the group. There are, however, some therapists who contract to let patients express their anger physically, and have proper facilities and personnel for handling the possible complications.

Weeping is also a racket in most cases, or may even be a dramatic put-on. The response of the other group members is the best way to judge this. If they feel annoyed or overly sympathetic, the tears are probably spurious. Genuine weeping usually results in a respectful silence and genuine responses of Aristotelian tragic pity.

J · THE STORY OF YOUR LIFE

One of the most instructive tales ever written for the script analyst is *The Strange Life of Ivan Osokin,* by P. D. Ouspensky, the well-known mystic. Ivan Osokin is given a chance to relive his life, and the prediction is that he will make the same mistakes all over again, and that he will repeat all the behavior he regrets. The hero replies that this will be no great wonder, since he will be deprived of the memory of what he has been through and will therefore have no way of avoiding his errors. He is told that quite to the contrary, and against the usual policy in such cases, he will be permitted to remember everything and will still make the same mistakes. On these terms he accepts, and sure enough, even though he can foresee each disaster that he brings on himself, he does repeat his previous behavior, as Ouspensky skillfully and convincingly demonstrates. Ouspensky attributes this to the force of destiny, and the script analyst will agree with him, adding only that that destiny was programed into him in his early years by his parents, and did not come from a metaphysical or cosmic force. The script analyst's position, then, is the same as Ouspensky's: every individual is compelled by his script to repeat again and again the same patterns of behavior no matter how much he regrets their consequences. In fact, the regret is itself a motive for repeating them, and they are repeated, in fact, just in order to collect regrets.

This picture can be rounded out by including another tale: "The Strange Case of M. Valdemar," by Edgar Allan Poe. M. Valdemar is hypnotized just before his death, and survives for a long time. Eventually, he is brought out of his hypnotic trance, and immediately, before the gaze of the horrified onlookers, he turns into a putrefying corpse, in just the state he would have been in if he had died on the day he was hypnotized. That is, he "caught up with himself." In script terms, this is also an everyday occurrence. The child is, in effect, hypnotized by his parents into carrying out a certain life pattern. He will show all the signs of vitality as long as it is humanly possible for him to continue, until his script destiny is completed. After that he may fall apart very rapidly. In effect, many people are "propped up" by their scripts, and as soon as the script is completed, they deteriorate. That is the fate of many old or "retired" people all over the world, as I have noted. (Not only in "our society," as is commonly claimed.)

The script itself is under the protection of the Greek Goddess of Necessity, "the sublime *Ananke*," as Freud calls her. In psychoanalytic language, it is driven by the repetition compulsion, the compulsion to do the same thing over and over. Thus, a short script may be repeated over and over in the course of a lifetime (a woman marries one alcoholic after another, on the premise that each time it will be different; or a man marries one invalid wife after another, thus undergoing a whole series of bereavements). Furthermore, in a diluted form, the whole script may be repeated every year (Christmas depressions due to disappointment) within the larger framework of the lifetime script (eventual suicide due to a very big disappointment). Also, it may be repeated every month within the year (menstrual disappointments). And beyond that, it may also be repeated every day in a smaller version. Even more microscopically, it may be run through in an hour: for example, the whole script, in watered-down form, may occur in the course of the weekly group meeting, week after week, if only the therapist knows where to look. Sometimes a mere few seconds of activity may reveal the "story of the patient's life." I have given an example elsewhere of the commonest form of that, which may be called "Rush and Stumble"—and "Quick Recovery."[16]

"Mrs. Sayers stretched her arm out across Mrs. Catters's chest to reach for an ash tray on the end table. As she drew her arm back she lost her balance and almost fell off the settee. She recovered just in time, laughed deprecatingly, muttered 'Excuse me!' and settled back to smoke. At this moment, Mrs. Catters took her attention away from Mr. Troy long enough to murmur: 'Pardon me!' "

Here, condensed into a few seconds, is the story of Mrs. Sayers's life. She tries to be careful but does things in an awkward way. She almost comes to grief but is rescued just in time. She apologizes, but then someone else takes the blame. One could almost visualize her ogre father telling her to fall over, or pushing her (script), and her mother rescuing her in the nick of time (counterscript). After that, she apologizes politely for being clumsy. (She learned in childhood that it paid to be clumsy if she wished to keep her father's love, because that was the way he wanted it; furthermore, it gave her an excuse to apologize, and that was one of the few times when he listened to her and acknowledged her existence.) Then comes the script twist, which makes the whole episode into a drama rather than a mere catalogue of misfortune: someone *else* takes the final blame and apologizes even more sincerely. Here we have a classical illustration of the Karpman triangle[17] for categorizing scripts and theatrical dramas (Figure 12, Chapter Ten).

K · THE SCRIPT SWITCHES

According to Karpman, all dramatic action can be summarized as switches between three main roles: Victim, Persecutor, and Rescuer. Those switches occur at varying speeds and may go in either direction. In the drama Rush and Stumble—and Quick Recovery, we have a very rapid set of switches. Mrs. Sayers starts off with Father (in her head) as Persecutor ("pushing" her), Mother in her head as Rescuer ("rescuing her from falling"), and herself as Victim. That is the way the triangle stands in her head, the skull script. In the action script, she makes herself the Persecutor by brushing against Mrs. Catters, who thus becomes her Victim. She apologizes for this, but Mrs. Catters in turn (in accordance with the needs of *her* script) pulls a very quick switch, and instead of behaving like a Victim, apologizes as though *she* had done something wrong, thus taking the role of Persecutor.

In this condensed set of transactions we learn a great deal about the story of two lives. Mrs. Sayers ordinarily came on like a plaintive victim; it is now clear that she can switch into the role of Persecutor providing it is "accidental" and she apologizes for it. The goal of the Rush and Stumble script is to be relieved of responsibility by getting the Victim to apologize. She has found a complementary script figure in Mrs. Catters, whose script is evidently called something like "Hit Me and I'll Apologize," or "I'm Sorry My Face Got in the Way of Your Fist"—the typical script of the wife of an alcoholic.

Danny, the young man without a thesis, also ran through the drama story of his life in recounting his experience. As already noted, the name of his favorite game, which is also the title of his script, is "Let's Pull a Fast One on Joey." Danny meets a friendly neighborhood Rescuer who offers for a fee to help him pull a fast one on his Victim, the professor. Danny ends up holding the bag as the Victim, and his friendly Rescuer turns out to be a better crook or Persecutor than Danny is. The professor, who, unknown to himself, was originally slated to be the Victim, now has to play the part of Rescuer to Danny who comes to him for help in order to graduate. That is the story of Danny's life. He gets outsmarted in his attempts to pull a fast one, and ends up being a martyr; but since everyone can see that he arranged his own downfall, instead of sympathy he gets laughter. He not only fails to accomplish his task, he even fails at being a martyr. That is one thing that keeps him from attempting suicide. He knows that if he tries, he will either bungle it in some laugh-provoking fashion, or if he succeeds, something will happen that will make the whole sacrifice seem humorous. Even his attempts at psychosis are unconvincing and just make the other group members laugh. What his mother has given him is a benevolent trap for a script. "Look," she has instructed him, "you're going to fail in everything. It's no use beating your head against the wall, because you'll even fail at going crazy or killing yourself, so go on out there and try it for a while, and when you're convinced, come back to me like a good boy and I'll take care of everything for you."

This is one reward for the group therapist if he watches every movement of every patient at every moment during the session. He may observe one of his patients going through his script in condensed form in the space of a few seconds. Those few seconds may break the case wide open by telling him the story of the patient's life, which he might otherwise have to spend laborious months or years in digging out and clarifying. Unfortunately, there is no rule to pass on about how to know when this is happening. It probably happens with every patient at every group meeting in some form or other, more or less heavily disguised or coded. Its detection then depends on the therapist's readiness to understand what is happening, and that depends on his intuition. When his intuition is ready not only to understand what the patient is doing, but also to communicate that understanding to his Adult, then he will be able to recognize the patient's script when he sees it, including the roles he and the other group members play. Since these roles are essential to know in order to carry on the treatment successfully, that will be the subject of the next chapter.

NOTES & REFERENCES

1 Berne, E. *Principles of Group Treatment. Loc. cit.*
2 The Child's perceptions often occur in dreams as day residues, caricatures, or symbols: perceptions which the Adult was not aware of but which nevertheless registered. Such perceptions are the basis for intuitive judgments. See Berne, E. "Concerning the Nature of Diagnosis." *Loc. cit.* Also refs. 6, 8, 9, 10, and 11.
3 Feldman, S. S. *Mannerisms of Speech and Gestures in Everyday Life.* International Universities Press, New York, 1959.
4 Deutsch, F. "Analytic Posturology." *Psychoanalytic Quarterly*, 21: 196–214, 1952.

5 Zeligs, M. "Acting In: Postural Attitudes Observed During Analysis." *Journal of the American Psychoanalytic Association,* 5:685–706, 1957.

6 Berne, E. "Primal Images and Primal Judgments," *Psychiatric Quarterly,* 29: 634–658, 1955.

7 Berne, E. *The Structure and Dynamics of Organizations and Groups. Loc. cit.*

8 Berne, E. "Intuition VI. The Psychodynamics of Intuition." *Loc. cit.*

9 Berne, E. "The Nature of Intuition." *Psychiatric Quarterly* 23: 203–226, 1949.

10 Berne, E. "Intuition V. The Ego Image." *Psychiatric Quarterly,* 31: 611–627, 1957.

11 Berne, E. "Concerning the Nature of Communication." *Loc. cit.*

12 Cf. Berne, E. "Difficulties of Comparative Psychiatry: The Fiji Islands." *American Journal of Psychiatry,* 116: 104–109, 1959.

13 Crossman, P. "Position and Smiling." *Loc. cit.*

14 Steiner, C. M. "A Script Checklist." *Loc. cit.*

15 Grotjahn, M. *Beyond Laughter.* McGraw-Hill Book Company, New York, 1957.

16 Berne, E. *Transactional Analysis in Psychotherapy. Loc. cit.,* pp. 123 ff.

17 Karpman, S. "Fairy Tales and Script Drama Analysis." *Loc. cit.*

CHAPTER EIGHTEEN

The Script in Treatment

A · THE ROLE OF THE THERAPIST

We have already discussed how the patient comes to choose a particular therapist, if he has a choice. If he has no choice, he will attempt to maneuver the therapist he is assigned to into fulfilling the role required by his script. Once he gets past the preliminary phase, he will try to make the doctor fit the childhood slot reserved for the "magician" in order to get from him the type of magic he needs: "science," "chicken soup," or "religion." While the patient's Child is setting up the games and script scenes required to accomplish this, his Adult will try to get whatever insight he can from the treatment. The sooner the therapist recognizes the role he is expected to play, and can foresee the script drama which the patient, in his own good time, will try to bring to a climax, the sooner he can do something about it, and the more effective he will be in helping the patient out of his script world and into the real one, where he can be cured instead of merely making progress.

B · GAME DOSAGE

The "neurotic," many clinicians have said, does not come for treatment in order to get better, but to learn how to be a better neurotic.[1] The game analyst says something similar: the patient comes not to learn how to be straight, but to learn how to play his games better. Hence he will quit if the therapist declines to play entirely, and also if the therapist is a pigeon and can be too easily conned. In this respect, transactional games are like chess: an enthusiastic chess player is not interested in people who do not want to play at all, nor in people who do not offer any real opposition. In a treatment group, a confirmed "Alcoholic" player will get angry if no one offers to rescue or persecute him, or play the patsy or the connection, and will soon leave. He will also leave if the rescuers are too sentimental, or the persecutors too vehement, because there is no fun if he hooks them too easily. Like other game players, he prefers a little finesse and some reticence on the part of his partners or opponents. If they come on very strong, like the Salvation Army, he may not stay long.

He may also resign from Alcoholics Anonymous if he feels it does not offer any real challenge with its claim of "It's Not You, It's a Disease," and its threats of "Wooden Liver." Only if he stays on past that stage will he begin to appreciate its real value. Synanon does better by playing it tough and saying: "It's not a disease, it's your own responsibility that you're a dope fiend." Hence the "Alcoholic" player may move out of AA and try the family doctor, who is not so sure it is a disease. If he is a real sport he will take on a psychotherapist, even one who says it isn't a disease at all. If he is ready to get well, he may look for a script analyst, or stumble on one accidentally, and then if things go right he may find himself quitting the game.[2]

"If It Weren't For Them" players, particularly the Arsisiety Type, behave similarly. A therapist who will not play at all and demands individual responsibility rather than Arsisiety will soon lose them. If the therapist believes too strongly in Arsisiety, the treatment degenerates into a pastime of "Ain't It Awful" between him and the patient. Most such patients become bored with this after a while and transfer to someone else who will put up at least a token argument for psychodynamics or self-appraisal. This often happened in the 1930's when young "Communists" went to "Communist" therapists, but soon broke off in favor of more conventional ones. If the therapist feels guilty about Arsisiety, he will form an alliance with the patient instead of treating him, which may be all to the good, but it should not be called treatment.

The Board, The Establishment, and The Man really do exist, but Mr. Arsisiety, upon whom so much is blamed, is a myth. Each person has his own society, with friends as well as enemies. Psychiatry cannot fight The Board, The Establishment, or The Man, it can only fight what is in the patient's head. The patient and the therapist both have to face that sooner or later. Psychiatric treatment, like all medical treatment, can only be effective under reasonably decent conditions. In cases where "If It Weren't For Them" is an empty stomach, the chair or couch has no place, but where it is a game it must be stopped sooner or later, and the skill of the therapist lies in doing that without driving the patient away. Dusay[3] gives an excellent summary of the ways games can be handled in treatment.

Thus game dosage, properly chosen and timed for each patient, will decide whether or not he continues in treatment.

C · MOTIVES FOR THERAPY

Usually the patient comes to therapy for two reasons, neither of which places the script in jeopardy. His Adult comes in order to find out how to be more comfortable living in his script. The most forthright example of this is the homosexual of either sex, who usually makes an honest declaration in this respect. The male homosexual, for example, does not want to leave his script world which is populated by women who are either dangerous and hateful schemers, or else innocent and occasionally amiable weirdos. All he wants is to live more comfortably in that world, and only rarely does he wish to see women as real people. Other therapeutic goals of a similar nature are: "How to live more comfortably while bashing your head against a stone wall," "How to live more comfortably while holding on to the sides of a tunnel," "How to keep other people from making waves when you're up to your chin in Shit Creek," and "How to outcrook the crooks when the whole world is Crooksville." Any vigorous attempt to change the script world itself must be postponed until after the patient is firmly established in therapy and understands how it fits into his script.

Besides the rational Adult desire to live more comfortably, there is a more urgent Child reason why the patient comes to therapy, and that is to advance his script through transactions with the therapist.

D · THE THERAPIST'S SCRIPT

The seductive female patient is the most common example of this. As long as she can seduce him, no matter how subtly or spiritually, he is playing his part and will be unable to cure her. Under these conditions, she may make all sorts of "progress" in order to please him, and to gratify or even help herself, but he will not be able to get her to "flip out" of her script and "flip in" to the real world. This fact is the legitimate basis for the "analytic reticence" or the "analytic frustration" which Freud spoke of. By remaining independent of the patient's maneuvers, and sticking strictly to his job of analyzing her resistances, her instinctual vicissitudes, and when necessary, the transference, the analyst avoids the possibility of being seduced physically, mentally, or morally. Countertransference means that not only does the analyst play a role in the patient's script, but she plays a role in his. In that case, both of them are getting scripty responses from each other, and the result is the "chaotic situation" which analysts speak of as making it impossible for the analysis to proceed to its proper goal.

A simple way to avoid most of these difficulties is to ask the patient right at the beginning, when the contract has been set up, "Are you going to let me cure you?"

At the end of the line there is the therapist who has actual sexual relations with his patients, which may give both of them considerable script pleasure as well as sexual pleasure, but makes it impossible for either of them to benefit from the treatment. In between is the pernicious technique of the therapist telling the patient that she excites him sexually, on the grounds that this will make their "communication" better. It certainly will, and if properly timed can prolong the treatment if it does not scare her away, but it is no help in getting her out of her script, since it is merely an admission on the part of the therapist that she fits into his life plan. In the commonest case, if the patient sits with her knees apart, the proper procedure is not to have a "frank discussion" about the therapist's sexual fantasies, but to tell her to pull her skirt down. With that come-on out of the way, the treatment can proceed on its useful course without being adulterated with a crude game of "Rapo." Similarly, if the patient sits with her hands clasped behind her head, thrusting her breasts out at the therapist, he can say "Amazing!" or "Stupendous!" and that will usually put things back in their proper perspective. If a homosexual man sits with his legs wide apart to exhibit his basket, the therapist can say: "Tremendous basket you've got there. Well, to get back to your diarrhea . . ." etc. If the patient replies "Fuck you!" the answer is "Not me. I'm here to cure you. What about the diarrhea?"

E · PREDICTING THE OUTCOME

The therapist's first task is to find out what role he fits in the patient's script, and what is supposed to happen between them. A good example is the patient whose script directive is "You can go to a psychiatrist as long as you don't get cured, because you have to kill yourself in the end." The patient gets what fun he can out of this grim destiny by playing "Now He Tells Me." This game can usually be anticipated from the patient's history, particularly if he has been to other therapists. The events leading up to the termination of previous therapy should be gone over in detail. When the therapist is sure of his ground, he can then use the antithesis previously described, which consists simply of giving a straight prediction of the outcome: "What you're going to do is come here for six months or a year, and then at the end of a session you're going to say 'By the way, I won't be back any more.' We can both save six months of our lives by breaking that up right now. Or if you'd rather go through with it, it's all right with me, since I can always learn something by your coming here."

This is much better than waiting until the patient does turn in his resignation, and then saying (somewhat prissily): "Perhaps you had better come in and talk it over before making such a serious decision," or something like that. By that time it is too late, and the therapist has already demonstrated his stupidity, so why should the patient continue to come to someone he can con so easily? The therapist's job is to see it coming before it happens, and not to try to pick up the pieces afterward.

A simple way to avoid many of the difficulties mentioned in the last four sections is to ask the patient right at the beginning, as soon as the contract has been set up: "Are you going to let me help you find the cure?"

Briefly, there are three possible outcomes to therapy.

1. The therapist can play out an act or scene in the patient's script, after which the patient leaves, "not improved," "improved," or "much improved," as it is commonly stated on statistical tables. But in no such case will the patient be cured.

2. The patient may have an "until" script: "You can't succeed until you meet certain conditions." The commonest spellbreaker or internal cutout is the one discussed earlier: "—until you have lived to be older than your father (mother, brother, sister) was when he died." This is a "clock time" release. Once the patient meets this condition, he has "permission" to get well, so that no matter how many unavailing therapists he has been to previously, the fortunate one who takes him on at this time will be able to chalk up a success (unless he makes an outright error). Since the patient is now "ready for therapy" and "ready to get well," almost any reasonably competent and discreet therapist can cure him. Similarly, when Sleeping Beauty was "ready" to wake up, almost any prince would do, since this release was built into her script. The "until" script with a "goal time" release may be more of a challenge. E.g., "You can't get well until you meet a therapist who can outwit you (or who is smarter than I, your father)." Here the

therapist may have to answer a riddle ("You're supposed to guess that.") or perform some other magic task. The patient may run through many therapists before she finds one who knows the key. The therapist is then in the position of the prince who must guess the riddle or perform the task that wins the princess, or lose his head. If he does find the secret, the patient is delivered from the power of her father's (or her witch mother's) spell. This means that she is then permitted to get well, and will, because that spellbreaker is built into the script just as it is built into the fairy tale.

3. The third case is where the script decrees that the patient must never get well, but the therapist manages to overthrow this curse. This takes enormous potency and skill on his part. He must win the complete trust of the patient's Child, since success depends entirely upon the Child having more confidence in him than in the original parent who dictated the script. In addition, he must have a sound knowledge of script antitheses or cutoffs, and how and when to apply them.

The difference between the spellbreaker (the internal release or cutout) and the script antithesis (the external release or cutoff) can be illustrated as follows. Sleeping Beauty was condemned to sleep for a hundred years, after which, providing a prince kissed her, (apparently) she could resume her life. The prince kissing her was the internal release or cutout: the remedy written into the script to lift the curse. If a prince had come along after only twenty years and said: "You really don't have to lie there," that would be a script antithesis or cutoff (if it worked): something from outside, not provided for in the script, which can break it up.

F · THE SCRIPT ANTITHESIS

All that has been said up to now is merely a preparation for answering the question "What can be done about it?" Psychiatric treatment boils down to three main ingredients: (1) "Being there"; (2) "Handy household hints"; and (3) "Flipping in."

"Being there" means that the patient knows there is

somewhere he can go, someone he can talk to, someone he can play his games with to cover up his anxieties and relieve his depressions, and someone who will encourage him, forgive him, prescribe penances, or feed him cookies—all of these being a kind of priestly function which is of value mainly to a lonely Child. Patients who lacked an effective parent in early life, patients whose mothers or fathers died before they were ten, five, or two, or who were deserted, ignored, or cast out, must have the vacuum filled by someone who will "be there" before any other kind of treatment will be effective.

"Handy household hints" is advice given by the therapist, telling the patient how to be happy or less miserable in his script world. "Hold on tighter." "Don't give your grandmother's address to a wolf." "Get her telephone number before midnight." "Don't take candy from strangers." Such hints are of value mainly to the confused schizoid Child, Little Red Riding Hood, Cinderella's Prince, Hansel and Gretel.

"Flipping in" means getting the patient out of his script and into the real world. In its most elegant form, it requires the therapist to think of the one single intervention which will do the most to break up the script: the most effective script antithesis. The following case history will illustrate the kind of probing, intuition, and professional confidence required to accomplish this.

AMBER

Amber McArgo came a very long distance to see Dr. Q, whom she had heard of from some friends. Back in her native city of Bryneira, she had gone to three different "psychoanalysts" who had been unable to help her. Dr. Q knew that these people were not really psychoanalysts, but were among the poorer therapists in Bryneira, who had confused her, one after the other, by using long words like "identification," "dependence," "masochism," etc. She told Dr. Q that she would have to fly back home that same night to take care of her children, so that he had the interesting challenge of trying to cure her in one visit.

She had complained of apprehensiveness, palpitation, insomnia, depression, and inability to get her work done. She had had no sexual desire and no sexual intercourse for the past three years. Her symptoms had begun when her father was found to have diabetes. After taking a psychiatric and medical history, Dr. Q encouraged her to talk more about her father. At the end of forty minutes, it appeared to him that the purpose of her illness was to keep her father alive. As long as she was sick, he had a chance to survive. If she got better, he would die. In fact, this was only her Child's script illusion, since the diabetes was mild and well controlled, and he was in no danger of dying, but she preferred to think that she had the sole power to keep him alive.

The Parental precepts were: "Be a good girl. We live only for you." Her father's injunction appeared to be "Don't stay healthy, or you'll kill me!" but Dr. Q decided that there was something more to it. Her "nervous" mother had given her an example of how to be sick, and that was the pattern she was following.

Dr. Q now had to find out whether she had something to replace her script with if she gave it up. Everything hinged on that. If he attacked the script and she had nothing to put in its place, she might get worse. It appeared that she had a rather solid counterscript based on the precept "Be a good girl," which at this point in her life meant "Be a good wife and mother."

"What would happen if your father did die?" he asked.

"Then I'd get worse," replied Amber.

This indicated that her script was not an "until" script, but a tragic one, which in this case made Dr. Q's task easier. If her instructions had been "Stay sick until your father dies!" she might have chosen to do that rather than risk the consequences of getting better, which in her Child's mind might cause his death. But evidently the script actually read: "You have made your father sick, so you must get sick also to keep him alive. If he dies, you must suffer the consequences." This gave Amber a much more clear-cut decision to make: "Either get better now, or continue to suffer now and suffer more later until your own death!"

With the way now prepared, Dr. Q said:

"It sounds to me as though you're staying sick to save your father's life."

This statement was carefully worded and timed so as to reach her Parent, Adult, and Child simultaneously. Both her Mother Parent and her Father Parent could not help but be pleased that she was such a "good girl" as to suffer for her father's sake. The Child in her Father would be additionally gratified that she was following his instructions to get sick (evidently he liked nervous women, since he had married one). The Adult in her Mother would be pleased that Amber had learned her lesson well and knew how to be a good invalid. How the Child in her Mother would react Dr. Q had no way of knowing, but he would watch out for that. So much for the different parts of Amber's Parent. Amber's own Adult, he thought, would agree, since his diagnosis was probably correct. Amber's Child would also be agreeable, because he was in effect telling her that she was a "good girl" and was obeying all the instructions of both her parents. The test would be in her reply. If she said "Yes, but . . ." there was going to be trouble, but if she accepted his diagnosis with no "ifs" or "buts," things might turn out well.

"H'm!" said Amber. "I think you're right."

With this answer, Dr. Q now felt free to proceed with the antithesis to the script, which meant getting Amber to "divorce" her father. The watchwords here were the three "P's" of script antithesis: potency, permission, and protection.

1. Potency. Was he powerful enough to prevail at least temporarily over her father? There were two things in his favor there. First, she actually did seem tired of being sick. Perhaps she had gone to her other therapists to play games or to learn how to live more comfortably with her symptoms, but the fact that she had planned such a long journey to see Dr. Q indicated that perhaps she was really ready to flip in and get well. Secondly, since she had actually made the trip (rather than saying she was much too fearful to do it), that probably meant

that her Child had a high regard for his magical potency as a curer.*

2. Permission. He had to word the permission very carefully. Like the pronouncements of the oracle at Delphi, his words would be twisted to her own needs. If she could find exceptions, she would, since as already noted, under such conditions the Child behaves like a smart lawyer looking for loopholes in a contract.

3. Protection. This was the most serious problem in the present situation. Because Amber was leaving immediately after the interview, she could not return to Dr. Q for protection if she disobeyed the injunction to be sick. Her Child would be exposed to her Parent's wrath with no one to reassure her in her panic. The telephone might help, but not very much after seeing him in person only once.

Dr. Q proceeded as follows. First he hooked Amber's Adult.

"Do you really think you can save him by getting sick yourself?" he asked.

To which Amber's Adult could only reply: "I guess not."

"Is he in danger of dying?"

"Not in the near future, according to what his doctors tell me."

"But you're under some sort of curse that requires you to get sick and stay sick in order to save his life, and that's what you're doing."

"I think you're right."

"Then what you need is permission to get well." He looked at Amber and she nodded.

"Then you have my permission to get well."

"I'll try."

"Trying won't do it. You have to decide. Either divorce your father and let him go his own way and you go yours, or don't divorce him and leave things as they are. Which do you want to do?"

There was a long silence. Finally she said:

---

*A doctor's duty is to exploit every possible means for the patient's cure. Or, stated in practical terms: "The patient's health is more important than what the pursed lips will say at the staff conference."

"I'll divorce him. I'll get well. You're sure I have your permission?"

"Yes, you do."

Then he had another idea. He invited her to stay over after lunch and come to a group meeting, to which she agreed.

As the interview terminated, he looked her in the eyes and said: "Your father won't die if you get well," to which she made no reply.

Two hours later, Dr. Q explained to his group that Amber had come a long distance to see him and had to leave that evening. He asked if they would agree to having her attend the group meeting, which they did. She fitted in well because she had read a book about transactional analysis and understood what they meant when they talked about Parent, Adult, Child, games, and scripts. After she told her story, they quickly got the point, as Dr. Q had.

"You're staying sick in order to keep your father from dying," said one of them.

"What's your husband like?" asked another.

"He's like the Rock of Gibraltar," replied Amber.

"So you came all the way out here to consult the Great Pyramid," said a third, meaning Dr. Q.

"He's not the Great Pyramid," objected Amber.

"He is to your Child," said someone, and she had no reply to that.

Dr. Q said nothing, and just listened. As the discussion proceeded, someone asked:

"Have you given her permission to get well?"

Dr. Q nodded.

"Why don't you give it to her in writing, if she's leaving?"

"Maybe I will," he said.

Finally he heard what he had been waiting for. When they asked her about her sex life, Amber volunteered that she had had frequent sexual dreams about her father. As the meeting drew to a close, Dr. Q wrote out the permission, which read:

"Stop having sex with your father.

"Amber has permission to have sex with other men

besides her father. Amber has permission to get well and stay well."

"What do you think he means?" asked someone.

"I'm not sure. Does he mean I should have an affair?"

"No, he doesn't. He means you have permission to have sex with your husband."

"Oh. One of the other doctors said I should have an affair. It scared me."

"That's not what Dr. Q means."

She put the paper in her purse, and then someone got suspicious.

"What are you going to do with that paper?"

"She's going to show it to her friends, I bet."

Amber smiled. "That's right."

"A written message from the Great Pyramid, eh? That'll make you famous at home."

"You won't get better if you show it to your friends. That's a game!" said another.

"I think they're right," said Dr. Q. "Maybe you shouldn't have it in writing."

"You mean you want it back?"

Dr. Q nodded, and she handed it back to him. "Do you want me to read it out loud to you?" he asked.

"I can remember."

Dr. Q did give her something in writing, which were the names of two real psychoanalysts in Bryneira. He was sorry there were no transactional analysts there. "When you get home, go and see one of these men," he advised her.

A couple of weeks later he got a letter from her.

"I want to thank everybody for giving me their time. When I left, I felt 99% cured. Things went well, and I had overcome some major problems. I felt I could solve the others by myself. My father no longer had the same hold over me, and I no longer feared his death. My sex life was back to normal for the first time in three years. I looked well and felt well. I had a few low periods, but I recovered very quickly. Then I decided to see Dr. X as you advised me."

This story is offered as an example of how a script

analyst thinks. The results were quite satisfactory for a single interview and a single group meeting, since the patient took advantage of the specific permission that was offered to her, and got whatever advantages she could out of that.

G · THE CURE

It is evident that Amber was not permanently cured. Nevertheless, the script antithesis offered to her did have a well-defined therapeutic effect and is likely to be of some permanent benefit. But however gratifying, these are only by-products. The real aim of the script antithesis is to gain time so that the patient can dig further into his script apparatus with the object of changing his original script decision. Thus the patient with a Parental voice urging "Kill yourself," and a discouraged Child replying "Yes, mother," is told "Don't do it!" This simple antithesis is given in such a way that the therapist's voice will be heard at the critical moment in opposition to the suicidal provocation, so that the patient may be held back on the very brink of death. The reprieve so gained is put to good advantage in the treatment. Pat is there because of the script decision he made in childhood, and he has now borrowed enough time to rescind that by making another, different decision.

As he cuts loose from his Parental programing, his Child becomes more and more free. At a certain point, with the help of the therapist and his own Adult, he is capable of breaking out of his script entirely and putting his own show on the road, with new characters, new roles, and a new plot and payoff. Such a script cure, which changes his character and his destiny, is also a clinical cure, since most of his symptoms will be relieved by his redecision. This can happen quite suddenly, so that the patient "flips in" right before the eyes of the therapist and the other group members. He is no longer a sick person or a patient, but a well person with some disabilities and weaknesses which he can now deal with objectively.

This is analogous to what happens after a successful abdominal operation. For the first few days, the patient is a sick person who is making progress, walking a little farther each day, and sitting up a little longer. Then on the fifth or sixth day or so, he wakes up in quite a different capacity. He is now a well person with some bothersome disabilities: weakness and a sore belly perhaps. But he is no longer content merely to make progress. He wants to get out, and his disabilities are no longer crippling, but merely bothersome afflictions that he wants to get rid of as quickly as possible so that he can resume his life in the great world outside. And all this happens overnight, in a single dialectical switch. That is the way it is with "flipping in" in script analysis: one day a patient, and the next a real person raring to go.

Nan lived at home with her parents. Her father was a professional patient who was paid a monthly salary by a government agency for being depressed. She was raised to follow in his footsteps, but when she got to be eighteen, she was tired of missing all the fun. She made progress in the group for about six months, until one day she decided to get well.

"How do I get well?" she asked.

"Mind your own business," replied the therapist.

The following week she came back dressed differently and in quite a different frame of mind. It was a struggle for her to take care of her own emotional business instead of her father's, but she learned to do it better and better. Instead of getting sick when he did, she let him get sick by himself. She also cut out her mother's programing, which in summary read: "Life is a struggle, stay home with Dad." She made a whole new set of autonomous decisions. She took off her "daughter of a schizophrenic"* uniform and began to dress like a woman. She went back to college, had lots of dates, and was elected Queen of the student body. All that remained to tell her was "It isn't true that your

---

*I don't know enough about women's clothes to describe this accurately, but I know it when I see it. It is a kind of negating of the body, where the "I am a schizophrenic" uniform makes a caricature of the body.

life is a struggle unless you make it so. Stop struggling and start living." She succeeded in doing that, too.**

REFERENCES

1 Lorand, S. *Technique of Psychoanalytic Therapy.* International Universities Press, New York, 1947.
2 Steiner, C. M. *Games Alcoholics Play. Loc. cit.*
3 Dusay, J. M. "Response in Therapy." *Transactional Analysis Bulletin,* 5: 136–37, April, 1966.

**This was not an accident, since another patient in the same group flipped in on the same day and made much the same set of redecisions. Both of these women could easily have become chronic patients, whose main contribution to humanity through the years might have been thick, complicated charts in the clinic file.

CHAPTER NINETEEN

The Decisive Intervention

A · FINAL COMMON PATHWAYS

What happens in the patient's head is unknown to the therapist unless it is expressed in some outward sound or movement. Each ego state, in principle, finds its own final pathway for such outward expression. In the classical example, Bridy is asked: "How is your marriage?" and replies pompously: "My ma-ridge; is perf-ict." As she says this, she takes hold of her wedding ring with the thumb and forefinger of her right hand and simultaneously crosses her legs and begins to swing her right foot. Someone then asks: "That's what you say, but what is your foot saying?" upon which Bridy looks down at her foot in surprise. Another member of the group then inquires: "And what was your right hand saying to your wedding ring?" whereupon Bridy begins to weep and ends up telling them that her husband drinks and beats her.

When Bridy becomes more sophisticated in transactional analysis, she is able to tell them the origin of her three replies to the question. The sentence "My marriage is perfect" was said or dictated by a pompous, unyielding Mother Parent, who took over Bridy's talking apparatus as a final common pathway. Her right hand was taken over by her Adult to verify that she was really and possibly permanently married to a scoundrel. Her legs were crossed by her Child, to keep him out, and she then offered him a few tentative kicks. The use of the passive voice in this paragraph signifies that the various parts of her body were merely instruments at the service of her ego states for final common pathways.

There are three principal ways in which the final common pathway is selected: by dissociation, by exclusion, or by integration. If the ego states are dissociated from each other and do not "communicate," then each will find its own pathway for expression, independently of the others, so that each one is "unconscious" of what the others are doing. Thus, Bridy's talking Parent was not aware of her fingering Adult or her kicking Child, nor were the other two aware of each other. This reflects the situation as it was in real life. As a child, Bridy could not speak freely to her parents, and had to do things behind their backs. If she was caught, she tried to evade taking responsibility for her actions by claiming that she (her Adult) didn't know what she (her Child) was doing. Clinically, this is a hysterical situation, where the Child can do all sorts of complex things while the Adult disclaims knowledge of them, and the Parent is out of it.

Exclusion means that one ego state is much more highly "cathected" than the others, and takes over at will regardless of their strivings. In groups, this is most dramatically seen in religious or political fanatics, where the excluding Parent takes over all the pathways of expression (except for an occassional "unconscious" lapse), and rides roughshod over the Child and Adult as well as all the other members of the group. This also occurs in a milder degree in compensated schizophrenics, where the Parent takes over and excludes the "bad" or unreliable Child, and the ineffectual, poorly "cathected" Adult as well, in order to keep out of the hospital or the shock-treatment room. This again reflects the actual childhood situation, where the child was left to his own devices and self-development, providing he did not dare to take the initiative when the parents were around.

A "normal" type of exclusion occurs in well-organized personalities, where one ego state takes over with the consent of the others. The Child and the Parent, for example, let the Adult take over during working hours. In return for this cooperation, the Child is allowed to take over at parties, and the Parent at other appropriate times, as at PTA meetings.

Integration means that all three ego states express

themselves at once, as in artistic productions and professional dealings with people.

Voice and posture are both good examples of final common pathways. The voice is particularly valuable in detecting compromises. Thus, many women say intelligent things in a little girl voice with considerable assurance. Here the compromise is between a Parent who is saying: "Don't grow up," an Adult who is offering counsel, and a Child who enjoys being protected. This can be called an "Adult-programed Child," or a "precocious Child." Many men say intelligent things in a grown-up voice lacking in assurance. Here the Parent is saying "Who do you think you are?" the Child is saying "I want to show off," and the Adult is saying "I've got something you can try out." This can be called a Child-programed Adult. Parent-programed Child ("Mommy said to.") and Adult-programed Parent ("Do it just this way.") are also common.

Posture indicates not only the principal ego states, but also their different aspects. Thus, the Critical Parent sits upright and points his finger straight ahead, while the Nurturing Parent opens up and forms a receptive circle with her body. The Adult posture is flexible, alert, and mobile. The Adapted Child withdraws by curling up (emprosthotonos), and may ultimately end in a fetal position with as many muscles as possible in flexion. The Expressive Child opens up (opisthotonos) with as many muscles as possible in extension. Emprosthotonos occurs with weeping, and opisthotonos with laughing. Even curling up one finger, such as the forefinger, can give a feeling of insecurity and withdrawal, while extending it gives a feeling of confidence and openness. Pointing it stiffly ahead gives the Parental feeling of putting up an impenetrable obstacle against the approach of anyone else's person or ideas.

Put in another way, the Child retains more or less complete control over the involuntary muscles, the Adult usually controls movements of the voluntary muscles, especially the larger ones, and the Parent controls the attitude, or the balance of the tonus between the flexor and extensor muscles.

It is apparent from all this that final common pathways are selected or apportioned after a kind of dialogue in the head. There are four dialogues possible between simple ego states: three duologues (P–A, P–C, A–C), and one triologue (P–A–C). If the Parental voice splits up into Father and Mother, as it usually does, and if other Parental figures chime in, the situation is more complicated. Each voice may be accompanied by its own set of "gestures" expressed by a chosen set of muscles or a special part of the body. But whatever the nature of the dialogue, its outcome will be expressed through final common pathways, or more precisely, there will be one final common pathway by dominance, agreement, or compromise, while the frustrated ego states will find subsidiary pathways for expression.

B · VOICES IN THE HEAD

How real are the voices referred to above? Breuer[1] discovered ego states (separate states of consciousness) almost one hundred years ago, but did not follow up his discovery. His colleague, Freud, at about the same time, became convinced that visual imagery expressed wishes, and spent the greater part of his life involved with that idea. As a result he neglected the auditory aspect of the psyche. Even Federn,[2] who first developed the idea of "a mental duologue between two parts of the ego," overlooked the question of actual voices and spoke of the duologue as being visually represented (in dreams, for example). Freud's main contribution here was his statement that voices and words heard in dreams represent voices and words that had actually been heard in waking life.[3]

The clinical rule derived from experience with transactional analysis has already been noted. The Child expresses his wishes in visual images; but what he does about them, the final display through the final common pathway, is determined by auditory images, or voices in the head, the result of a mental dialogue.* This dialogue between Parent, Adult, and Child is not "unconscious," but preconscious, which means that it can easily be brought into consciousness. Then it is found that it consists of sides taken from real life, things which once were actually said out loud. The therapeutic rule is a simple derivative of this. Since the final common pathway of the patient's behavior is determined by voices in his head, this can be changed by getting another voice into his head, that of the therapist. If this is done under hypnosis, it may not be effective, since that is an artificial situation. But if it is done in a waking state, it may work better because the original voices were implanted in the patient's head also in the waking state. Exceptions occur when a witch or ogre parent shouts the child into a state of panic, which is essentially a traumatic fugue.

As the therapist gets more and more information from different patients as to what the voices in their heads are saying, and becomes more and more experienced in relating this to their behavior as expressed through final common pathways, he develops a very acute ability and judgment in this regard. He begins to hear the voices in a patient's head very quickly and accurately, usually before the patient can clearly hear them herself. If he asks a loaded or sensitive question which she takes a little time to answer, he can observe a twitch here, a contraction there, and a shift of expression, so that he can follow the "skull dialogue" almost as though he were listening to a tape recording. An illustration of this was given in the case of Mab as she listened to her mother's tirade in Chapter Fourteen (B).

Once he understands what is going on, his next task is to give the patient permission to listen, and to teach her how to hear the voices which are still there in their pristine force from childhood. Here he may have to overcome several kinds of resistance. She may be for-

---

*The situation must be different with deaf children, and also with the blind, but so far nothing is known about how scripting occurs under such handicaps.

bidden to listen by Parental directives, such as: "If you hear voices, you're crazy." Or her Child may be afraid of what she will hear. Or her Adult may prefer not to listen to the people governing her behavior in order to maintain her illusion of autonomy.

Many "actionistic" therapists become very skillful at bringing these voices to life by special techniques, where the patient finds himself carrying on the dialogue out loud, so that both he and the audience can plainly see that what he says has been in his head all along. Gestalt therapists often use "the empty chair," where the patient moves from one chair to the other, playing two parts of himself.[4] Psychodramatists supply trained assistants who play one role while the patient himself plays another.[5] Watching or reading about such sessions, it soon becomes clear that the sides for each role come from different ego states or different aspects of the same ego state, and consist of dialogue which has been running in the patient's head since his early years. However, almost everybody mutters to himself at some time or another, so every patient has a good start toward unearthing his mental dialogue without such special techniques. As a general rule, phrases in the second person ("You should have," etc.) come from the Parent, while those in the first person ("I must," "Why did I?" etc.) come from the Adult or Child.

With some sort of encouragement, the patient soon becomes aware of his most important script directives as spoken in his head, and can report them to the therapist. The therapist must then give Pat the option of choosing between them, discarding the nonadaptive, useless, harmful, or misleading ones, and keeping the adaptive or useful ones. Even better, he may enable Pat to get a friendly divorce from his parents and make a fresh start altogether (although often the friendly divorce will be preceded by an angry phase, as most divorces are at the beginning, even if they eventually end up friendly). This means he must give Pat permission to disobey the Parental directives, not in rebellion, but rather in autonomy, so that he will be free to do things his own way and not have to follow his script.

An easier way to handle this is to give the patient

drugs such as meprobamate, phenothiazines, or amitriptyline, all of which mute the Parental voices. This relieves the Child's anxiety or depression and thus "makes the patient feel better." But there are three disadvantages. First, these drugs tend to dumb down the whole personality, including the voice of the Adult. Some physicians, for example, advise the patient not to drive a car while he is taking them. Second, they make psychotherapy more difficult precisely because the Parent's voices cannot be heard clearly, and so the script directives may be masked or de-emphasized. And third, therapeutic permission given under such conditions may be freely exercised, since the Parental prohibitions are temporarily out of commission, but if and when the drug is discontinued, the Parent usually comes back in full force, and may even take revenge on the Child for the liberties he took while the Parent was decommissioned.

C · THE DYNAMICS OF PERMISSION

Transactional analysis as a therapeutic method is based on the assumption that words and gestures can have a therapeutic effect without any bodily contact with the patient beyond a handshake. If a transactional analyst considers that bodily contact is desirable for a certain patient, he refers her to a dance class, sensory-awareness group, or a "permission class." Permission classes differ from the other two because they are run by people trained in transactional analysis who follow the prescription of the therapist rather than imposing their own theories or needs on the patient. Thus, a transactional analyst may decide: "This patient needs hugging, but I can't hug him and still do well-planned therapy, so I'll refer him to a permission class with a prescription for hugging." Or: "This patient needs loosening up through dance and informal touch contact with people, but I'm not running a dance class, so I'll refer her to a permission class with a prescription for dancing."

Permission classes are run as groups, so that the

patient does not get individual hugging or individual dancing exercises. All the patients do the same things at the same time, but the teacher is aware of each one's special needs and devotes some attention to them. (The patients do not *have* to do the same things at the same time. The teacher merely makes the suggestion, but each person is free to do as he wishes—that is part of the permission derived from the class. Usually, however, they enjoy the participation with other people, something they may have missed in childhood.)

Dr. Q attended a permission class in order to find out how it felt and what he could learn. When the instructor suggested: "Everybody sit on the floor," the voices in his head said: "My Child and my Adult agree to accept your suggestion to sit on the floor," and he did so. Where was his Parent? His Adult and Parent had previously agreed that the Parent would leave the Child free to do as he pleased, under some Adult control, unless things "went too far," i.e., got too sexy. His Child did get slightly aroused but there was no need for the Parent to come out, since his Adult was quite able to handle the situation. This gives some clue as to how permission takes effect.

Since permission is the decision intervention for script analysis, it is worth having as clear as possible an understanding of how it works, and every opportunity should be taken to learn about it by observing this in different situations.

When Jeder already has permission from his Parent to do something, no internal dialogue is necessary. This corresponds to the literal meaning of permission, which is a license. Once a person has a license to do something, he does not have to report back each time he wants to do it. Only if he abuses the license and goes too far will he hear from the authorities under ordinary circumstances. Some parents, of course, are "inspectors" by nature, and even after they give a license they want to oversee everything. People who have such Parents in their heads will be very inhibited and edgy.

When there is a prohibition against doing something, a dialogue will result whenever the person starts to do it. The Parent becomes active and says "no!" in a hard script, "Watch out!" in a threatening one, or "Why do you want to do that?" in a soft one—usually whatever the actual parent would say in real life. The energy which the Child had mobilized to do it is then taken over by the Parent, and is used by him to restrain the Child. The more energy the Child had mobilized to put into it, the more energetic can the Parent become by appropriating this energy. Under these conditions, how can the Child be given permission to do something? If an outsider says: "Let him do it!" the Parent becomes alarmed, and his prohibitions become even more energetic, so that the Child alone does not have a chance. The outsider, however, can seduce the Child by supplying "energy" in the form of encouragement or pressure. The Child may then go ahead and do it. But after it is done, the still active and energetic Parent moves in and causes the "hangover" phenomenon, as in alcoholic hang-overs, guilt feelings, and manic-depressive depression following too much Child freedom.

This is the state of affairs with a weakly "cathected" or inactive Adult. In fact, the Adult is the only force which can effectively intervene between the Parent and the Child, and all therapeutic interventions must take account of that. It appears that the Adult can get permission from the outside to mobilize its own energy, or can be charged up by an outside source. It is then in a position to intercede between Parent and Child. It takes on the Parent, thus leaving the Child free to go ahead. If the Parent later objects, the Adult remains "cathected" and can oppose him.

The relationship between the Parent and the Child also applies in reverse. Not only can the Parent grab energy from the Child to oppose it, but it can transfer energy to the Child to goad it on. Thus a "bad" Parent makes a "bad" Child not only by directing, but also by energizing the Child to do "bad" things.[6] This is well known to schizophrenics who have been cured by transactional analysis through re-parenting.[7] In re-parenting, the Adult also performs its function by getting turned on enough to argue with the discarded Parent if he becomes active again.

We have noted that there are positive permissions or

licenses, where the therapist or the Adult says "Let him do it!" and negative permissions or releases, where the argument is "Stop pushing him into it!"

Hence, the decisive factor in therapy is to hook the patient's Adult first. If the therapist and the Adult can agree and form an alliance, this alliance can be used against the Parent to give the Child permission: either to do something forbidden, or to disobey a Parental provocation. After the crisis is over, Pat's Child still has to confront a fully charged Parent. In the case of a positive permission ("You may have an orgasm with your husband if you want to."), the Child may be drained of energy and too weak to resist the punishing Parent. After negative permission ("You don't have to get drunk to prove you're a man."), the Child is tense and edgy and perhaps resentful against whomever gave him the permission to resist. In this frustrated and vulnerable state, he has no defense against the Parent's taunts. In both cases, this is the point at which the therapist must be available to protect the Child against the Parent's retribution or jeers.

Now we can speak with some assurance of the "three P's" of therapy, which determine the therapist's effectiveness. These are potency, permission, and protection.[8] The therapist must give the Child permission to disobey the Parental injunctions and provocations. In order to do that effectively, he must be and feel potent: not omnipotent, but potent enough to deal with the patient's Parent. Afterward he must feel potent enough, and the patient's Child must believe he is potent enough, to offer protection from the Parental wrath. (The word "potency" is used here in a sense which applies to female therapists as well as male ones.)

Della (Chapter Three) offers a simple illustration. Della had blackouts when she drank and was in danger of ruining herself during these episodes.

(1) "If I don't stop doing that," she said (Adult), "I'm going to ruin myself and my children."

(2) "That's right," replied Dr. Q (Adult), thus hooking into her already active Adult. (3) "So you need permission to stop drinking."

(2) "I certainly do." (Adult.)

(6) "Right! (4) So stop drinking." (Parent to her Child.)

(5) "What shall I do when I get all tensed up?" she asked. (Child.)

(5) "Telephone me." (Adult procedure.)

Which she did, with good results. Here the transactions are: (1) Hook the Adult, or wait until it is active. (2) Form an alliance with the Adult. (3) State your plan and see if the Adult agrees with it. (4) If everything is clear, give the Child permission to disobey the Parent. This must be done clearly and in simple imperatives, with no ifs, ands, or buts. (5) Offer the Child protection from the consequences. (6) Reinforce this by telling the Adult it is all right. It should be mentioned that this was Dr. Q's second attempt to give Della permission. The first time her Child answered instead of her Adult: "But what'll I do if I get tensed up and want to drink?" As soon as he heard the Child's "but," "if," and "and," Dr. Q knew that the permission would not take hold, so he aborted the maneuver and went on to something else. This time she said: "What shall I do when I get all tensed up?" Since there were no ifs, ands, or buts in this sentence, he thought she was ready to make it. The permission was a potent one because Dr. Q did not use any ifs, ands, or buts either. It will be noted that he did not follow the steps in numerical order, but adapted them to what was going on.

In summary: (1) Permission means a license to give up behavior which the Adult wants to give up, or a release from negative behavior. (2) Potency means power to confront. "If" and "but" do not signify potency to a Child. Any permission which contains an "if" in the form of a condition or a threat, is no good, and if it is conditioned, qualified, or reduced by a "but" it is no good either. (3) Protection means that during this phase the patient can call on the therapist to exercise his potency again in time of need. His protective power resides as much in the timbre of his voice as in what he says.

Figure 18 shows the three steps in giving effective permission. The first vector, AA, represents hooking the Adult. The second vector, PC, is the permission itself. The third vector, PC, represents the therapist

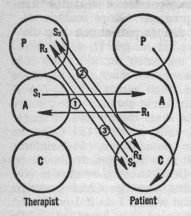

1   Potency
S₁ Th (A):   I can give you permission
R₁ Pt (A):   I need it

2   Permission
S₂ Th (P):   I give it
R₂ Pt (C):   I accept

3   Protection
S₃ Pt (C):   I'm scared
R₃ Th (P):   You're OK

4   Reinforcement (not shown)
S₄ Pt (A):   I am?
R₄ Th (A):   Yes, you are

Therapist   Patient

The Permission Transaction

FIGURE 18

giving protection to the patient's Child against an aroused Parent.

A timid therapist is as out of place trying to tame an angry Parent as a timid cowboy is trying to ride a bucking bronco. And if the therapist gets thrown, he lands right on the patient's Child.

D · CURING PATIENTS vs. MAKING PROGRESS

Herbert O. Yardley[9] describes the long, drawn-out, and excruciating task of breaking one of the Japanese codes during World War I—without knowing Japanese. One of his assistants had the following dream:

"I am walking on a beach with a heavy sack of pebbles which I have to carry and which tires me out. I can get some relief as follows: whenever I find a pebble on the beach that matches one of the pebbles in my load, I can get rid of the one I am carrying."

This beautiful dream shows how the laborious task of solving the code, one word at a time, was translated into visual images. It is also a parable of what it is like for the patient to "make progress." Script analysis attempts to cut the straps so that the patient can drop the whole load at once and feel free as quickly as possible. Undoubtedly the slower "pebble by pebble" system of therapy gives the therapist a great feeling of confidence that he knows what he is doing, but script analysts are getting a greater feeling of confidence, too, and more and more often they are finding where to cut so as to relieve the patient of his burden all at once. Nothing is lost by this, since it is quite possible to go through the now discarded sack pebble by pebble and do the same job as the psychoanalytic therapist, *after* the patient gets better. The slogan of "Making-Progress Therapy" is "You can't get better until you are fully analyzed," while the slogan of "Curing-Patients Therapy" is "Get well first, and we'll analyze it later if you still want to." This is similar to the problem of the Gordian Knot. Many people tried to unravel the knot, since it was prophesied that whoever did would become the master of Asia. Alexander came along and cut through it with his sword. The others complained loudly that that was not the way he was supposed to do it, that he was taking the easy way out, oversimplifying the problem. But he did get the job done, and he did get his reward.

To put it another way, a therapist can be either a botanist or an engineer. A botanist goes into the underbrush and looks at each leaf and flower and blade of grass to find out what is happening there. Meanwhile the hungry farmer says: "But we need that land for crops." "Takes a long time," says the botanist. "You can't hurry a project like this." The engineer says: "How come all that underbrush is growing there? Let's change the drainage, and that'll clear the land. Just find the creek and build the right dam, and all your troubles will soon be over. No sweat." But if the "hungry farmer" is a patient starving for affection, he says: "Oh, but I love all that underbrush, so I'd rather starve until we go over every leaf and flower and blade of grass." The botanist makes progress, and the engineer fixes it up—

if the patient will let him. That's because botany is a science and engineering is a method for changing things.

NOTES & REFERENCES

1 Breuer, J. and Freud, S. *Studies in Hysteria*. Nervous and Mental Disease Monographs, New York, 1950, pp. 14–32.

2 Federn, P. *Ego Psychology and the Psychoses*. Basic Books, New York, 1952, Chapter 4.

3 Freud, S. *The Interpretation of Dreams*. The Macmillan Company, New York, 1915.

4 Perls, F. S. *Gestalt Therapy Verbatim. Loc. cit.*

5 Moreno, J. L. "Psychodrama." In *American Handbook of Psychiatry*, Vol 2, Basic Books, New York, 1959.

6 Psychoanalysis accepts the idea that energy can be transferred from the Id into the Superego, and that the Superego is in fact a split-off part of the Id. It is less enthusiastic about the idea that the energy can be transferred back from the Superego into the Id, but that is what takes place in active schizophrenia, so this phenomenon must be studied energetically. Psychoanalysis, in practice at least, discourages the Adult by abuse of the term "intellectualizing." That is why "transference cures" are the bane of "psychoanalytic therapy." Little possibility is left for anything else. Only in the terminal phase of formal psychoanalysis is the Adult allowed full expression, and when that happens the patient is regarded as "cured." Put in another way, a psychoanalytic patient is cured when the analyst finally gives him permission to think for himself. In transactional analysis, the Adult is enlisted as an ally as soon as possible and proves it worth. Protection does not imply a transference cure, it is merely a way of passing through a shaky phase to self-confidence. A person learning horseback riding or skin-diving or flying needs similar protection at first, but that does not mean in any reprehensible sense that he is "dependent" on his instructor. When he is ready, he takes off by himself (in those sports, perhaps after ten weeks). Anybody learning to face a powerful force of nature needs ten weeks of protection, perhaps more in some cases.

7 Schiff, J., *et al*. "Reparenting in Schizophrenia." *Transactional Analysis Bulletin*, 8:45–75, July, 1969.

8 Crossman, P. "Permission and Protection." *Transactional Analysis Bulletin*, 5:152, July, 1966.

9 Yardley, H. O. *The American Black Chamber*. Bobbs-Merrill Company, New York, 1931.

CHAPTER TWENTY

Three Case Histories

A · CLOONEY

Clooney was a thirty-one-year-old housewife whom Dr. Q had known since she was eighteen years old, long before he knew very much about script analysis. When she first came to him she was scared, lonely, awkward, and blushing. She gave the impression that an angel spirit had come down from Heaven looking for a body to travel around in, and after settling in Clooney's, felt that she had made a slight error. She had few acquaintances and no friends. She reacted to the boys at school by being supercilious and sarcastic, which effectively chased them away. She was also overweight.

Her first course of therapy was based mainly on structural analysis, with only a few rudimentary ideas about games and scripts, but it was effective enough so that she got married and had two children. She returned about five years later because she was having difficulties with her outside social life, and thought that was unfair to her husband. One thing that bothered her was that she drank a lot at parties in order to loosen up, and then she did crazy things like taking off all her clothes on a dare. She improved enough at that time so that she could go to parties without drinking to excess. Although she was still unhappy on such occasions, she was able to talk to people, and thought that was good enough.

About five years after that, she returned again, this time determined to get well instead of just making progress. After five group meetings and two individual sessions, she requested another individual session. On that occasion, she sidled into the office, made a half-hearted gesture at closing the door behind her, and sat down. Dr. Q shut the door and sat down, too. The following exchanges then took place.

C: I've been thinking about what you told me last week—you said I should grow up. You told me that before, but I wasn't able to listen. My husband has given me permission to grow up, too.

Q: I didn't say grow up. I don't think I've ever said that to anybody. I said you had permission to be a woman, which is quite a different thing. Growing up is making progress, but being a woman means that your Adult takes over and you get well.

C: Well, my husband said that when we first got married he needed me to be dependent on him, but now he doesn't need that any more, so I have his permission to become a woman.

Q: How did your husband get so smart?

C: He's been here, too, in spirit at least. We talk over what happens here and he's learned a lot about it, so he understands.

Q: Your mother was like your husband. She needed you, too.

C: That's exactly right. She needed me to be dependent on her.

This puzzled Dr. Q, because that was mother's Parent giving directives to Clooney, telling Clooney to be dependent on her, a directive which Clooney carried into her marriage. But if the script theory was correct, it seemed there should also be an important script control coming from mother's Child. While Dr. Q was pondering this, Clooney changed the subject.

C: Then you always talk about my bottom, and we know there was something that happened in the bathroom that I've never been able to remember.

Q: Well, the scene I'm thinking of is a very common one. The little girl goes into the living room where mother is with her friends, and her diapers fall off and everybody says "Isn't that cute!"

C: Yes, that happened to me.

Q: And then the little kid gets very embarrassed and blushes, and maybe her bottom blushes, too, and that makes it worse because then everybody gets really interested and says: "Now look at that! That really is cute, ho ho ho."

C: That's really the way I feel.

Q: That has something to do with your taking your clothes off at a party. That's one way you know of making contact with people.

At this point Dr. Q drew on the blackboard the diagram in Figure 19A. (It is the custom among transactional analysts to have a blackboard on the wall for the purpose of drawing such diagrams when occasion calls for them.)

Q: This diagram shows the relationship between your Child and your husband's Parent. It was the same when you were growing up. Your mother's Parent needed you to depend on her, and your Child went along with that. So you see as far as that part of your marriage goes, your husband really fills in for your mother.

C: That's right. I married him because he's like my mother.

Q: Yes, but somehow your mother's Child must come into it, too.

C: Oh, yes. She always smiled when something embarrassing happened or when one of us girls did something she thought was naughty. Then she would say: "But isn't it awful?"

Q: It's very important to know whether she laughed or smiled first and then said "Isn't it awful?" or said "Isn't it awful?" first and then smiled.

C: Oh, you mean if she let her Child out first and then apologized to her Parent, or talked with her Parent first and then let her Child out.

Q: That's right.

C: I see what you mean. Well, she smiled first.

Q: Oh, then she wanted you to do the things she couldn't do, and that really tickled her Child, but then she had to apologize to her Parent. That's exactly what you do: you're always apologizing to your Parent. You go ahead and do your mother's naughties for her, and then you keep saying: "What do I do about guilt feelings?" Like after your mother's Child encourages you to do something, her Parent moves in and clamps down on you.

C: Yes, I know. But what do I do about the guilt feelings?

Q: You get a divorce from your mother. Mind your own business. Take care of your own problems instead of being a stooge for her. Let her do her own naughties, and if that upsets her, then it's her problem.

C: My aunt was the same way.

Q: So now we put an arrow in the diagram where your mother's Child is encouraging your Child to act up. (Figure 19B.) Then her Child is pleased and smiles, and after that her Parent comes out with "Isn't it awful?" But there's still something missing, because your father should come into it.

C: I know how he came into it. He always said I was a coward and couldn't do it. He said he was a coward, too. When he was sick and in pain he would moan and then say: "I'm a coward, I can't stand it."

Q: Oh. Then we can fill in your script diagram with that. (Figure 19C.) Up above, I imagine his Parent was telling you to be brave, but down below his Child was telling your Child that in the end you'll both be cowards. What did your mother tell you up above?

C: Be a good girl so people will like you.

Clooney's main complaint is being scared of people. Since she doesn't know how to talk to strangers, she would rather stay home with her children than go to parties. Both her parents are likewise socially anxious and awkward. The script matrix (Figure 19C) takes account of all these factors.

1 PP: Mother's Parent saying "Be a good girl." (Precept)

2 CC: Mother's Child saying "Do naughty embarrassing things." (Provocation)

3 AA: Mother's Adult showing her how to be an awkward social coward. (Pattern)

4 PC: Mother's Parent rebuking her for being naughty. (Prohibition)

5 PP: Father's Parent saying "Be brave." (Precept)

6 CC: Father's Child saying: "We'll both be cowards." (Seduction)

7 AA: Father's Adult showing her how to be a coward. (Pattern)

8 PC:Father's Parent rebuking her for being a coward. (Prohibition)

Here the script directives seem to be equally distributed between both parents. Both of them are showing her how to be a coward, and both of them are making her feel guilty. So she has no one to support her when she is afraid, and no one to appeal to when she feels remorse. That's why she feels lonely. But her mother's Child is spunky, so Clooney has permission to do impulsive spunky things like taking her clothes off, since she knows mother really thinks (or once thought) that to be cute. Then she suffers for it later when both Parents move in on her.

C: You know this is the first time I've really seen what my father did in this picture, although we've talked about it before. But now I really get it.

Q: There's an awful lot here for one session.

C: Yes, I understand part of it, but the rest I'll have to think about.

Q: Yes, you may not understand it all by next week, but don't get flustered, we'll go over it again.

There's one more thing I want to say. We can see how your Child acts up and your Parent makes you feel guilty. And you can see that actually your mother kept you in the Child position, and so did your husband, because they both needed you to be like that. In that way you were just a puppet in their scripts. But I guess you contributed your fifty per cent in continuing that kind of relationship. The question is, where is your Adult in all this?

One of the things that happened today is that when you came in, you half shut the door. You didn't either leave it open for me to shut, or shut it yourself.

C: But it's your door.

Q: But it's your interview. Why do I have a door?

C: So someone in the waiting room won't overhear me.

Q: Well, do you want them to overhear you?

C: He, he, he. Maybe I do.

Q: Well, it's your session, so in that sense it's your door.

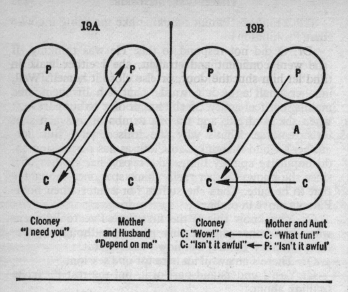

19A

Clooney
"I need you"

Mother
and Husband
"Depend on me"

19B

Clooney
C: "Wow!"
C: "Isn't it awful"

Mother and Aunt
C: "What fun!"
P: "Isn't it awful"

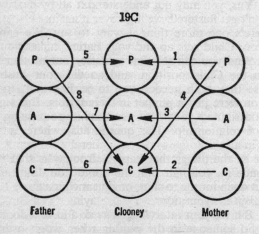

19C

Father

Clooney

Mother

Clooney's Script Matrix (for explanation see text)

FIGURE 19

C: Yes, but I wouldn't dare take over a thing like that.

Dr. Q did not respond to this. He was thinking. If she were confident and straight, she'd either walk in and let him shut the door, or else close it herself. Well, she had half an Adult, so she shut it halfway. At the social level, she didn't feel enough of a lady to leave it up to him, but she was afraid or embarrassed to shut it completely herself, so she compromised. As a Good Little Girl she made the gesture, and as an almost woman, she let him finish the job. At the psychological level it was different. She was shy about speaking up in the group, but her Child was willing or even hoping to be "overheard" through a half-open door, especially when there was really nobody in the next room to overhear her. That all came under the heading of "exposing herself," but these games would have to be dealt with later. She had had enough for one day. Finally he said:

Q: Anyway, that's where your Adult comes into the picture: what you decide to do, like close the door or leave it open. Well, I'll see you next week at the same time.

This interview was the culmination of many years of work. When Clooney first came, the doctor knew very little about scripts. Now he knew a great deal more and had a lively interest in the subject. Clooney knew a great deal more, too, and was ready to get well, with some assistance from her husband, who was now an amateur but shrewd script analyst at second hand. Sessions with Clooney were generally difficult and unproductive. She was usually droopy and plaintive, demanding reassurance from the doctor, asking him unanswerable questions, getting annoyed when he did not give the right answers, and playing "Yes But" if he tried. This time she was animated and receptive and thoughtful. She leaned forward in her chair instead of drooping, and so did he. They both talked in a quick and lively way. Her Child had given up moaning and making progress in favor of getting well, so her Adult was free to listen and think. She was willing to look at her own father instead of seeing Dr. Q as a father. That freed her to listen to his Adult, instead of hearing him as a critical Parent. She was transformed from a patient with a "Wooden Brain" into a real person with some problems (such as "expressing herself") to be solved. All her life she had been flipped out, and this was the week she flipped in.

She was now in a good position to consider objectively the body aspects of her script, where her buttocks played an important role. Through her blushing Child, they controlled how she sat, how she walked, what she was afraid of, what she wanted to do, and how the Child in other people reacted to her. This level was the Child in her Child, much of which is what psychoanalysis calls "the unconscious." It remained, therefore, to dig up the long forgotten transactions with her parents which focused her fears, desires, and attention on this part of her body. And that had to be done under careful Adult and therapeutic control so that she would be able to handle the confusing and dangerous feelings usually connected with blushing buttocks.

B · VICTOR

When Victor came for treatment, he was heavily involved in games with his superior, an aging elephant who played "Now I've Got You." Victor responded with "Look How Hard I've Tried," "There I Go Again," and "Kick Me." When Victor was about to leave for a new job, his wife said to a friend: "He's going to try it and see how it works out."

"I'm not going to try it," said Victor. "I'm going to do it."

"So you've finally given up that trying stuff!" said the friend.

"Well, so now you've got permission to succeed," said Dr. Q, when Victor related this anecdote.

"It's not that I've got permission to succeed," replied Victor. "What I've got is permission to stop 'trying.'"

"How does that work?" asked Dr. Q.

"My mother used to say: 'Keep trying, and if it doesn't work, it'll be all right anyway.' Now that I know Martian, I can see that my Child translated that into 'Don't succeed, it's better to go home to mother.' So I need to be released from trying, so I can just do it. I'm a big boy now. Well, can you give me the names of some people in New York?"

Something made Dr. Q hesitate, but since it was customary to give patients the names of some people when they were moving to another city, he looked in his psychiatric directory and gave Victor the names and addresses of two doctors back East.

"Will you send them my chart, or whatever your records are?"

This time Dr. Q listened to his intuition, and replied:

"Not unless they ask."

"How come?"

"Well, now you're well, you're supposed to have left all that behind. If something goes wrong, you can tell them about it yourself." Now he knew what was wrong. Victor had freed himself from the elephant and also from Dr. Q, but in his Child mind, he was already under the protection of the two psychiatrists back East, and to that extent had given up some of his newly won, and hard-won, autonomy. "I'll tell you what. Burn that paper with the two names on it."

"But I'll remember them anyway, so I might as well just carry it in my wallet."

"Burn it."

"A ritual," said Victor.

"That's right. It's your Adult telling your Child you can sacrifice them and make it on your own."

Victor looked at him, and Dr. Q knew what he was thinking. ("I'll try.")

"Burn it," he repeated.

Victor smiled. The session was over. They rose and shook hands, and that was the end of Victor's treatment.

C · JAN AND BILL

Jan and Bill came to Dr. Q with a request for group therapy. They had been in transactional analytic groups (or "TA groups," as they called them) for about a year with several different therapists who worked together, and they had also been in four or five "marathons." They both felt grateful for these experiences, which had brought them closer together, and also had other beneficial results. It was evident that they were very much in love after three years of marriage, and that they were very fond of their two babies.

"How long is it since you've been in a group?" asked Dr. Q.

Bill looked at Jan. She smiled at him and replied:

"We stopped about a year ago."

"Well, why do you want to start again?"

"There are a lot of things that could be improved," said Bill. "I feel good most of the time, but I'd like to feel good all the time."

"That's a pretty tough assignment," said Dr. Q.

"Well, I can be more specific than that," Bill continued. "My job of selling rare books is really a matter of relating to people. Before I went into TA, I would never have thought that I could be a salesman, but now I am, and a good one. But I could do better if my Adult stayed in control even under stress. For instance, I think I'm due for a raise. I make about eight hundred dollars a month now, which is the most I've ever earned in my life, and it's the first time we've ever been able to get the things we wanted instead of living on the edge all the time.

"But asking for a raise is not easy in a small establishment with only two or three employees, and I think my boss would rather not give me one. But I know the business well enough and I'm effective enough to deserve one. I could never have said something like that two years ago, but now I really believe it. The problem is to keep my Adult on the ball and not let my Child take over at the critical moment and start some games going. I've also got to know what my boss is up to, because he has some games of his own. So I can either flub it by asking for it in such a way as not to get it, and then get mad, which would be dangerous and unnecessary, or I can cut through his games and get him to sit down with me and figure out how much I'm worth. So I need a little help right now to do that.

"I think what I really want and need is a little more work on my script. My father was an alcoholic and my mother went along with it, so I have a failure script always lurking in the background. That's why I still goof up occasionally, and I want to stop it. So I need some more understanding of my script and some good permissions. Is that a good enough contract for us to work with?"

"I'm not sure yet," said Dr. Q. "Is there anything more specific?"

"I still do drink more often than I think I should to do the best job," said Bill.

"How about an anti-'Alcoholic' contract to start with?" suggested Dr. Q. "That'll help us get at your script and strengthen your Adult, too."

"That sounds fine for a start," said Bill.

"What do you want to get out of it, Jan?"

"I want my Child to be freer and more creative. I'm a lab technician and I still work part-time at that, but I started writing after I got into Dr. X's group and I'm doing well at it. I just want to do better. I have a lot of witch instructions from my mother that my Child is still scared of, and that interferes. Also, I need regular stroking to keep happy, and I could do better at getting it."

"Tell me a dream," requested Dr. Q.

"I used to have the most horrible nightmares. You see I spent a couple of years in my childhood being bombed and running for air-raid shelters in London, and I only saw my father once, when he was on leave, during that period. But now I have beautiful dreams, soaring and flying and beautiful colors."

"Dr. X seems to have done an awfully good job for both of you," said Dr. Q. "Why do you want to come into my groups?"

"He certainly did a lot for us," said Bill. "But toward the end we seemed to have reached a plateau, and we think you might have some fresh ideas for us. We're still far from perfect. We both started out as frogs, and now Jan is certainly a princess and I think I can learn to be a prince."

Jan smiled when he said that, a beautiful smile that certainly belonged to a princess. But she still had some remnants of her war neurosis. She no longer panicked when she heard loud sounds, but they did disturb her train of thought. So in her case they agreed on a contract to cure her vestiges of apprehension. That should release her creative Child still further, which was her main goal, and also make her more comfortable with the children and them more comfortable, too. Dr Q had no doubt that Dr. X would be agreeable to these undertakings, so he proceeded to take a psychiatric and medical history from each of them as a preparation for coming into one of his groups.

This case illustrates the convenience of transactional analysis. Jan and Bill and their therapists all spoke the same language, so the couple could transfer from one therapist to another anywhere along the line without noticeably retarding their rate of improvement. Although Dr. Q was a stranger to both of them, they had no difficulty in explaining to him what they had accomplished so far and what more they hoped to do. They also knew where the difficulties lay and were able to explain that in simple language that all three of them understood.

When they started in the group, they were able to explain to the other patients exactly where they stood, and the other patients knew what they were talking about. And by listening to the others, Jan and Bill could soon see how far along each one was and where he was headed. This took up their first meeting. After that, they were ready to engage in more personal transactions with the other patients, who were soon able to find traces of Bill's alcoholic Father Parent, Jan's Witch Mother, and other significant items. All this was possible because everyone spoke the same simple language and meant the same thing when he used the same word.

And the most useful words were basic English ones, which could be understood by a kindergarten child out of his own experience: parent, adult, child, games, permission, and script. (Children who don't understand "Script" can understand "what you're going to do with your life.")

PART V

Scientific Approaches to Script Theory

CHAPTER TWENTY-ONE

Objections to the Theory of Script

Many people object to the theory of scripts, each from his own point of view. The more satisfactorily these objections can be answered, the stronger the inference that script theory is valid.

A · SPIRITUAL OBJECTIONS

Some people feel intuitively that the theory of scripts cannot be valid because it is contrary to the destiny of man as a creature of free will. The whole idea arouses in them a kind of revulsion, since it appears to reduce mankind to a mechanism without a vitality to call his own, very much as, in its extreme form, conditioning theory does. These people are also, and for the same humanitarian reasons, uneasy about psychoanalytic theory, which in one form constricts man into a closed-off, cybernetic energy system with only a few restricted input and output channels, and leaves no room for his godhead. These are the moral descendants of people who felt the same way about the Darwinian theory of natural selection, which in their minds reduced the processes of life to mechanics and left no room for Mother Nature's creativity. They, in turn, are the descendants of those who found Galileo intolerably impudent. Nevertheless, such objections, arising as they do from a philanthropic regard for human dignity, must be treated with proper consideration. The answer, or apology if you will, is as follows:

1. Structural analysis does not pretend to answer *all* questions about human behavior. It states certain propositions about observable social behavior, and

about inner experiences, and these propositions are valid. It does not deal, formally at least, with the essence of being, the Self. It deliberately provides a concept which is beyond its province, the construct of free cathexis, wherein that Self resides, and thereby sets aside a whole field, in many respects the most crucial one, for philosophers, metaphysicians, theologians, and poets to deal with as they see fit. It in no way attempts to encroach on this well-defined area, and expects the same courtesy in return from those who do deal with the problem of man's essence or Self. It has no desire to intrude into either the ivory tower, the cathedral, the minstrel's pad, or the courtroom, but on the other hand, neither does it expect to be dragged into any of them against its will.

2. Script theory does not pretend that *all* human behavior is directed by the script. It leaves as much room as possible for autonomy, and indeed, autonomy is its ideal. It only states that relatively few people attain it completely, and then only on special occasions. Its whole purpose is to increase the distribution of that invaluable commodity, and it offers a method for doing so. But the first requirement is to separate the spurious from the genuine, and that is its whole task. It does forthrightly call a chain a chain, however, and this should not be taken as an insult by those who love their chains or choose to ignore them.

B · PHILOSOPHICAL OBJECTIONS

These are both transcendental and existential. Script analysis sees imperatives as directives from the parents, the purpose of most existences being to carry out those directives. If the philosopher says: "I think, therefore I am," the script analyst asks: "Yes, but how do you know *what* to think?" The philosopher answers: "Yes, but that's not what I'm talking about." Because they are both saying "Yes, but" it appears that they will get nowhere. But this is a misapprehension that can be easily clarified.

1. The script analyst deals *only* with phenomena,

and does not intrude on the territory of the transcendentalist. What he says is: "If you stop thinking the way your parents ordered you to think, and start thinking for yourself, you will think better." If the philosopher objects that he is already thinking for himself, the script analyst may have to tell him that that is to some extent an illusion, and furthermore, that it is the one illusion he cannot afford. The philosopher may not like that, but the script analyst has to stick to what he knows. Thus, the conflict, as is the case with the spiritual objectors, is between something the philosopher doesn't like and something the script analyst knows, and there the matter must rest until the philosopher is willing to take himself more seriously.

2. When the script analyst says: "The purpose of most existences is to carry out the parental directives," the existentialist objects: "But that is not really a purpose in the sense I use the word." To which the script analyst replies: "If you find a better one, let me know." What he means is that the individual cannot even begin to think of finding a better purpose as long as he is content to follow his parental directives. What he offers is autonomy. The existentialist then says: "Yes, but my problem is what do you do with autonomy after you have it?" The script analyst replies: "I don't know any more than you do about that. All I know is that some people are less miserable than others because they have more options in life."

C · RATIONAL OBJECTIONS

The rational objection is: "You yourself said that the function of the Adult is to make rational decisions, and that everybody has an Adult to make them with. How then can you also say that the decisions have already been made by the Child?"

A good point. But there are hierarchies of decisions, and the highest level is the decision to follow or not to follow a script, and until that decision is made, all other decisions will not avail to change the individual's ultimate destiny. The hierarchy goes as follows: (1) To follow or not to follow a script. (2) If a script, which one? If not a script, what to do instead? (3) "Permanent" decisions: to get married or not, to have children or not, to commit suicide, to kill somebody, to go crazy, to resign or get fired, or to succeed. (4) "Instrumental" decisions: which girl to marry, how many children to have, how to commit suicide, etc. (5) "Temporal" decisions: when to get married, when to have children, when to commit suicide, etc. (6) "Expedient" decisions: how much money to give your wife, which school to send your children to, etc. (7) "Urgent" decisions: whether to go to the party or stay home and have sex, whether to spank your son or scold him, whether to visit the prospect today or tomorrow, etc. Each level in this hierarchy is subject to all the higher ones, and each lower level is trivial compared to the ones above it. Yet all levels contribute directly to the final outcome, and are designed to bring it about more effectively, whether that is script directed or autonomously chosen. Therefore, until the first decision is made, no other decisions are "rational" in an ultimate existential sense, but are "directed" decisions rationalized on spurious grounds.

"But," says the rational objector, "there is no script."

Since this is a rational objector, and he is not saying that merely because script theory makes him nervous, we take the trouble to answer him. This is our chance to make a very strong inference. First we ask him if he has read this book carefully, and then we offer him some of our strongest arguments, which may or may not convince him.

Suppose then that there is no script. In that case (a) People do not hear voices in their heads telling them what to do, or if they do hear them, they always act independently (i.e., neither in compliance nor rebellion) of these voices; (b) People with many different voices telling them what to do (e.g., people raised in a series of foster homes) are as sure of themselves as people raised in one stable home; (c) People who shoot drugs or overdrink or move their bowels on the floor (hippies of a certain type) will not usually feel that they are being pushed by inner forces beyond their control toward a well-defined destiny, but instead regard each such act as an isolated, autonomous decision. Or alternatively, the "inner forces" are irreversible and not subject to change by psychological methods.

If all, or perhaps even any, of these hypotheses are true, then perhaps there is no script. But the clinical evidence is that they are all false, therefore there is a script.

D · DOCTRINAL OBJECTIONS

Doctrinal objections fall into two main classes: religious and psychoanalytic. From a religious point of view, the script question is one of predestination or something like it, vs. free will: Presbyterians vs. Jews, Roman Catholics vs. Christian Scientists, etc. Such differences in viewpoint, as they are usually stated, are beyond the province of scientific inquiry.

The psychoanalytic objections are Jesuitical ones. As a doctrine, script analysis is not independent of or irrelevant to psychoanalysis, it is an extension of it, and hence is regarded by some as anti-analytic, and as, in effect, not paganism, but a heresy within the doctrine itself. Thus, the Monophysite heresy was merely an extension of Roman Catholic doctrine, and it made the Church much more uneasy than did paganism, for which the penalty was only conversion, rather than decapitation.

In order to discuss the objections raised by some psychoanalysts (usually when confronted by a living staff member who actually wants to do script analysis in a psychoanalytically oriented clinic or hospital), it is necessary to find the meaning of "anti-analytic."

Script analysts subscribe to the doctrines of Freud in their entirety, and only wish to add something in the light of further experience. The differences between the orthodox view and that of script analysis is one of emphasis. Actually, script analysts are "better Freudians" than orthodox analysts. The writer, for example, besides having repeated and confirmed the conventional observations of Freud, also believes right down the line with him concerning the death instinct, and the pervasiveness of the repetition compulsion. For this, he has been called "anti-Freudian." He also believes that short words can express what we know about the human mind more concisely, cogently, and intelligibly than long words, and that Freud's terminology has been misused for a purpose which Freud himself would decry—to obscure the facts. He has been called "anti-analytic" for this; not for doing anything about it, but merely for expressing the idea.[1] Script analysts believe in the unconscious, but they emphasize the conscious when dealing with patients for whom orthodox psychoanalysis is more or less unsuitable, according to Freud's own statement.[2] Furthermore, script analysts do not pretend that what they do is psychoanalysis, since it isn't. (Most therapists who do psychoanalytic therapy, which is *not* psychoanalysis, attempt to follow the rules laid down for psychoanalysis, which are of course inappropriate and hinder the treatment.) Hence, script analysis may be called "para-Freudian" (by someone who has private reasons for making an issue of it), but cannot rightly be called anti-analytic, and certainly not anti-Freudian.

Another doctrinal objection to script theory is that it is nothing new; it is merely Adler's life style in more fashionable clothes, or an archer version of Jung's archetypes, etc. The fact is that the facts were always there, and they were observed by many keen observers, and whether script theory corroborates what others have said, or they corroborate script theory, is immaterial. Freud takes seventy-nine pages (in my edition) to summarize the observations of his precursors in dream theory, many of whom made "psychoanalytic" statements; Darwin takes only nine, but he quotes many "evolutionary" statements made by others before him. But statements, however accurate and numerous, do not make a theory. The crux of script theory lies in structural analysis. Without the theory of ego states, and specifically Parent, Adult, and Child ego states, there can be an infinite number of pertinent observations and statements, but there can be no script theory. To be worthy of the name, any theory in any branch of science has to be based on structural elements, and without them it will fall like a house of cards, which may be pretty to look at, but has nothing to support it under the slightest adversity, and cannot bear anything but its own weight.

Script theory has the same advantages over its predecessors as the Arabic system of numerals has over the Roman system, and for the same reason: the elements are better to work with. Imagine the task of a Roman builder who has to bill you for fifty items, beginning with MCMLXVIII building blocks at LXXXVIII oboli each. A modern contractor could do the whole thing in less than half an hour by using better number elements, and he could use the time saved to think about architecture, without the irrelevant distractions imposed on his Roman colleague.

In practice, most doctrinal objections result from what Freud calls "the aversion characteristic of scientific men to learning something new." This is no longer as prevalent as it was in his day, when he noted the reaction to his dream theory: "naturally least attention has been bestowed upon it by the so-called 'investigators of dreams' . . . my only possible answer to my critics would be to read this book over again. Perhaps also the request should be that they read it as a whole." An improvement on psychoanalysis is no more antianalytic than an improvement on airplanes is a slur on the Wright brothers.

E · EMPIRICAL OBJECTIONS

We shall consider here only the commonest of the empirical objections to script theory, since that can be dealt with most concisely: "If people's destinies are determined by parental programing, how come children from the same family turn out so differently?"

The first comment is that children from the same family do not always turn out differently. In some families they do, in others they don't. There are many cases where all the siblings are uniformly successful, uniformly alcoholic, uniformly suicidal, or uniformly schizophrenic. Such outcomes are often attributed to heredity, leaving the geneticists in a sophistical position when the siblings turn out differently: they can then argue, somewhat unconvincingly, from an adulterated Mendelianism, which amounts to little more than mumbling. The self-determinists are in the converse position: they argue vigorously for the cases where the siblings turn out differently, but are reduced to muttering when faced with uniformity. Script theory can take both situations in its stride.

The script at issue here is the parent's script, of which the offspring's script is a derivative. Children turn out differently for the same reason that Cinderella turned out differently from her stepsisters. The stepmother's script was to have losers for daughters and a winner for a stepdaughter. In the other well-known fairy-tale motif, the two clever older brothers turn out in the long run to be stupid, while the stupid younger brother turns out to be the cleverest (as their mother secretly knew all along, since she set it up that way). On the other hand, both of the Roman Gracchi boys were equally talented and equally devoted to the interests of the people, and both of them came to the same end by assassination; while the five or ten or fifteen or twenty children of Niobe (depending upon who counted them), all came to the same end as part of her (Niobe's) "Pride and Fall" script. The mother's script may call for her to raise ten policemen (Glory be!) or ten robbers (Get 'em, boys!), or five policemen and five robbers (Let's you and him fight!), and a shrewd woman will have no difficulty in realizing any of these projects if she has the ten boys to raise.

F · DEVELOPMENTAL OBJECTIONS

Developmental objections to script theory center around infantile psychosexual crises and adolescent identity crises.

1. In regard to the first, a script does not negate instinctual strivings, or prevail over early traumata. On the contrary, it goes along with them. It offers an on-

going social matrix for acting out sexual fantasies, whatever their origin. It says that instinctual strivings, or sexual fantasies, can be given free play, or become repressed, distorted, or sublimated, but that in the long run they are in the service of a higher principle which directs the timing, force, and mode of their expression in accordance with the requirements of the script, or what Freud would call the destiny compulsion. At this level, the script directive reads: "Do what you like, as long as meanwhile you collect enough trading stamps to justify the outcome." Hence, script theory is not behaviorism. It does not postulate that everything, or even very much, of what most people do is the result of "conditioning." All it requires is that the person follow orders at certain critical moments; for the rest, he is free to go wherever and do whatever his fancy dictates.

2. It is true that some adolescents shake off their scripts completely and become autonomous. Others, however, merely rebel (following a parental directive to rebel), thus fulfilling their scripts in a kind of *Appointment in Samarra* tragedy: the faster they think they are running away from their parents' programing, the closer they are to following it. Others shake off the script temporarily, and then subside into suburban desperation. The "identity diffusion" of this period is merely a bad script. In Erikson's view, it is a struggle against mother in which she loses. But script analysts take the opposite position: it is a struggle with mother in which she wins. Her son becomes a bum not in spite of her, but because of her, because he cannot get permission to succeed against her orders. The therapy then is not directed toward bringing him back to mother so that he can be a good boy, but to divorcing him from mother so that he can have permission to do things right.

G · CLINICAL OBJECTIONS

The commonest clinical objection to script theory is that a patient cannot be cured in the psychoanalytic sense by dealing with conscious material alone. This is correct. But:

1. The unconscious has become fashionable, and hence grossly overrated. That is, by far the larger percentage of what is called unconscious nowadays is not unconscious, but preconscious. The patient, however, will oblige the therapist who is looking for "unconscious" material by advancing preconscious material with a spurious label. This is easily verified by asking the patient "Was it really unconscious, or was it just vaguely conscious?" True unconscious material (for example, the original castration fear and the original Oedipal rage) is truly unconscious, and not vaguely conscious. Therefore the script analyst dealing with conscious material is engaged with a far larger area of the psyche than many people would suppose. In any case, there is no proscription against the script analyst dealing with unconscious material (that is, some of the primal derivatives of the original castration fear and the original Oedipal rage) if he is equipped to do so. And he will do so, because, of course, it is these very experiences which form the basic protocol for the script.

2. It is commonly assumed that there is some sort of legislation which gives psychoanalysts the irrevocable right to define a cure. This is not so. Even if there were such legislation, they would be in a difficult position, because their definitions (which are almost synonymous with the termination of treatment) are not clearly stated or unanimously accepted among themselves. Their criteria can usually be boiled down to a pragmatic statement which applies equally well to those therapies which are not psychoanalysis: e.g., "The patient is cured when he is symptom-free and can work and love effectively." Script analysis can accomplish that at least as frequently as psychoanalysis can.[3]

In conclusion, it should be mentioned that there are two kinds of people who have objections to script theory. The first are theoreticians and clinicians, who can be met courteously on their own debating ground, wherever it may be, and who will show script analysts the same consideration that script analysts show them, which mainly consists of reading each other's literature with reasonable care and objectivity. The second are those in administrative positions who can and sometimes do block the intellectual and professional development of younger clinicians, especially psychiatric residents, by actually and overtly forbidding them to use script theory in their work. Some of these are just poorly educated, grumpy, or unreasonably prejudiced people, and to them there is nothing to be said. But there are also some highly educated, benevolent, and more open-minded administrators and supervisors who have done the same thing. These are mostly well-trained psycho-analysts. For their benefit, it may be pointed out that Freud himself was a script-ridden person, a fact which he openly acknowledged. His heroes were military ones, and he passionately admired Bonaparte. His metaphors were often taken from the battlefield, and so was some of his vocabulary. His slogan is given in the epigraph to his book on dreams, which in my edition reads: *"Flectere si nequeo Superos, Acheronta movebo,"* roughly translated as "If I can't bend the Heavens, I'll raise Hell," which he did. His "mysterious" and "ob-sessional" idea that he would die precisely at the age of fifty-one is a typical scripty prophecy. Freud's father's motto was: "Something will turn up," and that was a precept Freud devoutly believed in, as his letters show. His hero, Napoleon, whose very words he quoted in referring to his own "court" (Abraham, Ferenczi, Rank, and Sachs, *"Un parterre des rois"*), died at the age of fifty-one.[4]

NOTES & REFERENCES

1 Giovacchini, P. L. "Characterological Aspects of Marital Interaction." *Psychoanalytic Forum* 2: 7–29, Spring, 1967, with discussion by E. Berne and reply by Giovacchini.

2 Freud, S. *New Introductory Lectures on Psycho-Analysis.* W. W. Norton & Company, New York, 1933, p. 212.

3 Cf. Hamburg, D. A. *et al., loc. cit.,* 1967. About half the patients in that study "completed treatment" and were judged by their therapists to be improved in "total function-ing." Figures reported at meetings by transactional analysts (as well as individual case reports) compare very favorably with this. (It must be said that there are as yet no *published*

figures for transactional analysis, in general, although there are some for special populations, as when it is used in prisons.)

4 Robert, M. *The Psychoanalytic Revolution*. Harcourt, Brace & World, New York, 1967, p. 94. For an even scriptier scene, see p. 215f. Jones, E. *The Life and Work of Sigmund Freud. Loc. cit.*, Volume 1, p. 342, gives the Napoleonic quotation.

CHAPTER TWENTY-TWO

Methodological Problems

A · MAP AND TERRITORY

If we say that the script follows or is matched by a fairy tale, there is a danger of Procrustes. The therapist picks out a fairy tale prematurely, and then stretches the patient or cuts him down so that he will fit it. Procrustes is very common in all the behavioral sciences. The scientist has a theory, and then stretches, cuts down, or weighs the data to match it, sometimes by overlooking hidden variables, sometimes by ignoring items that do not fit, or even at times manipulating the data with flimsy excuses so that they will fit better.

Procrustes is most active at clinical staff conferences, where there is no control match at all, so that the situation is wide open for speculations, bright ideas, orthodoxy, and authoritative pronouncements *ex cathedra*. In order to cut down on the casuistry and sophistry of such conferences, each one should include two cases with similar histories, preferably one without any apparent pathology along with that of the patient. It is amazing how closely the "case history" of many a well-functioning, productive person can resemble the "case history" of a psychiatric patient. That is to say, for every schizophrenic with a certain kind of upbringing, there appears to be a nonschizophrenic with the same upbringing. It should be noted that most staff conferences are based on an unstated but ever present assumption: "The patient is sick, and our job is to prove it and then find out why he is." Staff meetings can become much more interesting by reversing this to read: "The patient isn't sick, and our job is to prove that and then find out why he isn't."

In Procrustes, the information is stretched or cut down to fit the hypothesis or diagnosis. In The Unicorn,[1] the hypothesis or diagnosis is stretched or cut down to fit the recalcitrant data. Thus, in ESP experiments, if the subject's percentage of correct hits is unsatisfactory, his guesses on this try can be matched against the way the cards turned up on the last trial, or two, five, or ten trials earlier, or on the next trial, or is found somewhere which matches his guesses on this trial. Then a claim can be put in, rightly or wrongly, but certainly unsoundly, for delayed telepathy or premature clairvoyance. The same plan is followed by the fortuneteller who predicts that one of the greatest earthquakes in history will take place in 1969. When it does not occur, he says that he may have transposed a digit, so the earthquake is really due in 1996; or maybe it was just a reincarnation memory trace of the great earthquake of 1699. Which great earthquake of 1699? The one in Rabaul, of course. Well, there are earthquakes in Rabaul nearly every day, and every year there is bound to be one which is greater than the others. Or maybe it was the great Italian earthquake of 1693 that he was re-experiencing? So he went back 300 years and was only six years off, and who could quarrel over a mere two per cent error?

Now if script analysts are going to approach the subject with any degree of scientific objectivity and true curiosity, they have to avoid both Procrustes and The Unicorn, and that is hard to do. In fact there is no doubt that both of them have appeared in this book, although I have tried my best to prevent it. With such a complex concept, in its early stage of development, it is difficult to avoid them completely. They are still making frequent appearances in psychoanalytic theory almost a century after Bertha Pappenheim (Anna O.) discovered the cathartic method.[2] And Procrustes is still the patron saint of sociology, as The Unicorn is of psychology.

What then is the best way to proceed? This was outlined by a dentist with a clinical interest in transactional analysis, Dr. Rodney Pain,[3] who is also an aviator. He compared the problem of validating script theory to the Map-Ground problem. A flyer looks at his map and sees a telephone pole and a silo. He looks at the ground and sees a telephone pole and a silo. He says: "Now I know where we are," but he is actually lost. His friend says: "Wait a minute. On the ground are a telephone pole, a silo, and an oil derrick. Find those on the map." "Well," says the flyer, "the pole and the silo are there, but the derrick isn't. Maybe they left it out." So his friend says: "Lend me the map." He looks over the whole map, including sections that the flyer ignored because he thought he knew where he was. The friend finds, twenty miles off their charted course, a pole, a silo, and a derrick. "We're not here," he says, "where you had your pencil mark, but away over there." "Oh, sorry," says the pilot. The moral is, look at the ground first, and then at the map, and not vice versa.

In other words, the therapist listens to the patient and gets the plot of his script first, then he looks in Andrew Lang or Stith Thompson, and not vice versa. In that way he will get a sound match, and not just a bright idea. *Then* he can use the fairy tale to predict where the patient is headed, verifying from the patient (not from the book) all the way.

B · THE CONCEPTUAL GRID

Transactional analysis is such a rich mesh of intertwined concepts, all consistent with each other, that it is possible to wander around in any direction and come up with something interesting and useful. But that is quite different from the logical approach to a theory.

Consider the following brief excerpt of a case which was presented at the San Francisco Transactional Analysis Seminar as a focus for discussion of script theory.

A woman who came for treatment for frigidity proposed that the therapist have intercourse with her. Her mother had taught her how to dress and act sexy, and her father had encouraged this.

The purpose of the discussion was to try to show that the script matrix, as presently constructed, is inaccurate. According to Figure 7, which shows the second-order structure of the Child, the Parent in the Child (PC) functions like an implanted electrode, while the Adult in the Child (AC) is the intuitive Professor who is an expert judge of other people. Dr. Z, who presented the patient, maintained that in her case PC functioned like an Adapted Child, and AC functioned like an electrode. He offered developmental data from her childhood to support this. Others chimed in with logical arguments on both sides, drawing from their clinical experiences. They talked about games, scripts, and the patient's Natural Child. Would the standard script matrix stand up against this deliberately planned assault? The arrows drawn by Dr. Z between the patient, her father, and her mother, took quite a different course from those shown in Figure 7. Apparently a good case had been made to overthrow it. But on closer scrutiny, the arguments turned out to have grave defects.

First of all, when Dr. Z, with help from the audience, tried to define what he meant by PC, AC, Adapted Child, and electrode, he and they talked at one moment from a developmental point of view, then from a behavioral point of view, at times using logic and at other times empiricism. Some of them brought in transactions, others, games and scripts. It turned out that there were four different frameworks being used, each with its own language and approach, and the definitions wandered unsystematically from one to the other. The first framework was structural and transactional, with four key ego terms: states, transactions, games, and scripts. The second was validating, again with four key terms. They could talk about her behavior, which offered operational criteria; her mental processes, which included voices in her head giving her directives; her developmental history, which showed the origins of her behavior patterns; and the kind of social responses she elicited by her behavior. The third language dealt with naming her ego states. They could be named according to psychobiological principles: the Parent in her Child, the Adult in her Child, etc., or described functionally by adjectives: Adapted Child, Natural Child, etc. The arguments themselves could be termed logical on the one hand, or empirical on the other.

If all these frameworks are tabulated, the result is a terminological grid, as shown below, classified into transactional terms, validating terms, modifying terms, and methodological terms.

TERMINOLOGICAL GRID

TRANSACTIONAL	VALIDATING	MODIFYING	METHODOLOGY
Ego States	Operational	Structural (Biological)	Logical
Transactions	Phenomenological	Functional (Descriptive)	Empirical
Games	Historical		
Scripts	Social		

If we draw lines across this grid to include one term from each column, it is apparent that there will be $4 \times 4 \times 2 \times 2 = 64$ possible paths for discussion. (We do not count the words in parentheses.) Unless everybody follows the same path, the various discussions cannot be correlated without an enormous amount of labor and definition: essentially an impossible task in a limited amount of time (such as one long evening) if twenty discussants take twenty different paths. If one goes Ego States–Historical–Descriptive–Empirical, while another follows Games–Social–Biological–Logical, they may both make sense, but they are following such different lines of reasoning that they cannot really settle anything between them.

In the simplest example, if one argument takes a structural or biological approach to the Child ego state, and another takes a functional or descriptive approach, it is impossible to reconcile the two. This is demonstrated in Figure 20. In Figure 20A the structural division of the Child into its main aspects is represented by horizontal lines separating the second-order Parent, Adult, and Child components. In Figure 20B, vertical lines are used to indicate its functional aspects: in this case, Adapted, Rebellious, and Natural Child. Whichever scheme is used, the lines have to go in different directions to indicate that the approaches are different. One uses structural nouns, the other uses functional adjectives as modifiers, and the nouns and adjectives do not belong to the same framework or come from the same viewpoint. Similar considerations apply to the other columns in the grid.

The only way to have a well-reasoned and decisive argument is to choose one path through the grid and stick to that. Dr. Z was given this option, and chose Ego States–Social–Descriptive–Empirical: not a promising path for the job in hand, but it was his presentation, and his privilege to choose. Thus committed, it became apparent that his arguments were not nearly as convincing as they seemed at first when he was free to jump from one path to another. The same applied to his supporters when they tried to follow his selection. In other words, what had seemed plausible and well organized when all sorts of jumps and distractions were permitted, did not stand up so well when closer reasoning was required. On this basis, the original script matrix retained its supremacy, at least until a better-prepared assault could be launched.

FIGURE 20A

Psychobiological Structure

Parent

Adult

Child

FIGURE 20B

Descriptive Functions

Adapted | Rebellious | Natural

The Child Ego State from Two Points of View

It is necessary, then, for any argument about transactional analysis, including script analysis, to state its choices from the above grid before it can be considered valid. If it wanders from its self-chosen path, it becomes invalid by reason of looseness, sophistry, or obfuscation. Therefore, anyone proposing to engage in such an argument should select one term from each column as a framework for his definitions, and adhere rigorously to that. Otherwise the argument is open to methodological question and will not stand up under objective criticism, no matter how convincing it appears from a rhetorical point of view.

C · SOFT DATA AND HARD DATA

The data of script analysis are mostly soft. Because scripts are existential commitments, they cannot be investigated in artifical situations experimentally. The payoff must have overriding significance for the protagonist. As an example, there is no such thing as a reliable experimental poker game. A player will play one way when the stakes are trivial and another way when they are significant. A good high-stake player may lose in penny ante, and a good penny-ante player may panic in a high-stake game. Scripts can only be tested in high-stake situations, and these are not available under ordinary civil conditions. There is but one way to find the answer to the question: "Would you throw yourself on a land mine to save the lives of your comrades?" It can only be tested existentially on a battlefield, and all simulations are trivial.

The data of script analysis can be sorted roughly in order of increasing hardness as follows: historical, cultural, clinical, logical, intuitive, developmental, statistical, introspective, experimental, and blind matching. This may seem a strange array to scientists accustomed to studying trivialities of human behavior, such as the ones commonly tested in the psychological and social sciences. It will seem less strange to psychotherapists, and least strange to psychoanalysts, since both of them deal with hard games and hard payoffs such as divorce, suicide, and homicide. There can hardly be such a thing as an experimental suicide or homicide in a decent society.

1. Historical. Since the beginning of mankind, man has suspected that his destiny is not autonomously determined, but is controlled by some outside force. The very universality of this belief requires that it be critical-

ly examined rather than summarily dismissed by calling it metaphysical.

2. Cultural. This same belief is the foundation of most human cultures, which requires that it also be taken seriously, just as economic motives are taken seriously for the same reason.

3. Clinical. Clinical data is not rigorous because it can be subject to different interpretations. But the investigator who wishes to minimize or deny the influence of the script on clinical phenomena must have adequate training in script analysis, and give it an adequate clinical trial before he is competent to pass judgment on it. Exactly the same statement can and has been made about psychoanalysis. Similarly, a man who looks through a microscope or a telescope and says: "I don't see anything," is hardly a competent critic of bacteriology or astronomy unless he has had a thorough training in how to use the instrument.

4. Logical. We have previously noted that people can be told what to do and not do. They can be effectively encouraged to drink or commit suicide by means of words, and they can be effectively restrained from doing either of those things by means of words, providing they are the right words. Therefore, it follows that it is quite possible to raise a child to do either of those things when he grows up. This is tested by the following question: "How would you raise a child to turn out the way you have?" People with "good" scripts are quite willing to answer this question, and their answers are often credible. People with "bad" scripts are reluctant to make the attempt, but if they do, their answers are equally credible.

5. Intuitive. An experienced script analyst will make intuitive judgments which can subsequently be tested. E.g., "Since you often try to do two things at once but don't do either of them well, I infer that your parents had different goals for you and they never quite got together on how you could attain both of them. That is, your parents did not clarify their differences." "That is exactly how it was." If the answer is negative, in my experience this probably means that the diagnostician is

not competent, or else that in the particular case some personal consideration has interfered with his intuition.[4]

6. Developmental. Hearing children state their scripts is one of the most convincing pieces of evidence, especially if the children can be followed over a long period to see whether they carry them out. This does not refer to choice of a career ("I want to be a fireman."), but to payoff transactions ("I wish I were dead.").

7. Statistical. The most relevant statistical work is the study of the effects of fairy tales on subsequent careers and mode of death, previously cited from the work of Rudin.[5]

8. Introspective. This is the most convincing criterion of all. As soon as a person becomes accustomed to hearing the voices in his head which he has suppressed or repressed since early childhood, and confirms that these voices speak the actual words spoken by his parents during that period, he realizes the extent to which his most significant behavior is programed.

9. Experimental. For reasons given above, experimental validation of script theory is not possible with human beings, although certain elements can be examined in this way. But animal experimentation can be extrapolated into the framework of script theory, as has been done with the rat experiments cited in Chapter Three.

10. Blind Matching. In a few cases, where a supervisor had inferred the script of a student, but had not brought the subject up with him, and the student then transferred to a therapist, both supervisor and therapist inferred the same script, and when this was communicated to the student, he agreed. In these cases, the two script analysts had been acquainted with the subject over a long period and had a wide range of behavior to survey. This can be considered hard data. Applied systematically, it would require several script analysts to listen to a taped interview and thence infer the script of the subject. These inferences could then be matched against the subject's life course, with a five-year follow-up. A pilot study would first test three types of tape interviews, autobiographical, free association, and use of

the script check list, to see which type yielded the most solid data pertaining to the script. This procedure offers the best opportunity for obtaining hard data.

Present indications are that script theory is softer than learning theory, harder than social and economic theory, and is approaching the hardness of psychiatric diagnosis, as far as predicting human behavior is concerned.

REFERENCES

1 Cole, L. C. "Biological Clock of the Unicorn." *Science,* 125: 874, May 3, 1957.
2 Jones, E. *The Life and Work of Sigmund Freud. Loc. cit.,* Vol. 1, p. 223.
3 Pain, R. "A Parable." *Transactional Analysis Bulletin,* 7:69, July, 1968.
4 Berne, E. "Intuition VI." *Loc. cit.*
5 Rudin, S. A. *op. cit.*

CHAPTER TWENTY-THREE

The Script Check List

A · DEFINITION OF A SCRIPT

In order to tell whether or not a certain set of transactions is a game, we look for certain special features. If there is a con, a handle or gimmick, a switch, and a payoff, then we have *identified* a game. If, in addition, we can do a structural analysis showing which ego states are active during each transaction, and a clinical analysis, which clarifies the advantages gained from playing it and how they got started, then we can say that we have not only identified the game, but that we *understand* it. The items required for such an understanding can be put down as a "check list," and the formal analysis of a game is based on such a check list. The game check list describes the anatomy of a game, which is a small segment of life.

The anatomy of a script, which deals not with a small segment, but with the whole course of a human life from birth or even earlier until death or even later, is naturally more complicated. A game may be compared to a flip of the wrist, which contains eight bones and involves seven others; a script may be compared to a mountain-climbing expedition, which involves the complete human skeleton of 206 bones. Thus the "check list" for a script contains many more items than does the check list for a game, but such a check list is the easiest way to understand how a script is put together.

The first problem is to define a script so that it can be identified when it appears. Any definition will be subject to alteration with advancing knowledge in the field. Game theory is now like a well-made bicycle which will travel reliably and without hesitation over short distances; but script theory is like a one-cylinder automobile of 1900 which may or may not work when it is most needed, so skeptics can still cry: "Get a horse!" (or at least a couch), and perhaps demand that a more conventional therapist with a red flag walk ahead of the script analyst to warn timid people to keep out of the way.

The following definition, based on the current state of knowledge, will serve for the present to distinguish what is a script from what is a "not-script." A script is an ongoing program, developed in early childhood under parental influence, which directs the individual's behavior in the most important aspects of his life.

The terms used in this definition can be defined as follows, using standard dictionaries, with some additional explanation.

Ongoing = continually moving forward (Webster). This implies irreversibility, a one-way street. Each move approaches closer to the termination.

Program = a plan or schedule to be followed (Random House). This means that there is a plan, which is a scheme of action, project, design; the way in which it is proposed to carry out some proceeding (Oxford), and also a schedule. The anlage or skeleton of the plan can be found in a specific fairy tale.

Parental influence = actual transactions with the parents or their equivalents. This means that the influence was exerted in a specific, observable way at a specific moment of time.

Directs = the person must follow directives, but has free choice in matters where the directive does not apply. In some cases there is a special directive that says: "Turn the card over," which means "In this area do the opposite of what I say." Thus "rebellion," when it occurs, is really part of the script, and is not the same as "throwing the card away," which is autonomy.

Important aspects = at least marriage, child-rearing, divorce, and manner of death, if that is chosen.

We can test this definition by seeing how well it defines "not-script." "Not-script" would then be reversible behavior, with no particular time schedule, developed later in life, and not under parental influence. This is a fairly good description of autonomy, which is, in fact, the opposite of script. For example, the autonomous person can reverse his guilts, fears, angers, hurts, and inadequacies and start over without being in a hurry to bring things to a head, instead of following his parents' directive to collect trading stamps and use them with reasonable speed to justify his behavior in marriage, child-rearing, divorce, and death.

Hence, the definition is exclusive: that is, by defining script it also defines "not-script," and that makes it worthwhile. If, then, we find that an individual's behavior in the most important aspects of his life is directed by an ongoing program developed in early childhood under parental influence, we can say that we have *identified* a script. This can be reduced to a formula, as in the case of games, and the script formula will read:

$$EPI \rightarrow Pr \rightarrow C \rightarrow IB \rightarrow Payoff \text{ (Formula S)}$$

where EPI = Early Parental Influence, Pr = Program, C = Compliance, and IB = Important Behavior. Whatever behavior fits in with this formula is part of a script, and whatever behavior does not fit in with it is not part of a script. Every script will fit this formula, and no other behavior will fit it.

For example, a simple reflex is programed by the nervous system, and not by early parental influence (no EPI); the individual may comply with a blow on his knee tendon, but this is not important behavior (not IB). If an individual learns to drink socially, late in life, that may be social compliance, but if it is not part of his program (not Pr) to become an alcoholic, the drinking will not be important behavior (not IB), and will not be an important influence on his payoff— his marriage, child-rearing, or manner of dying. If a boy is heavily programed by his parents to be a trust-fund bum when he grows up, but does not comply (no C), then his important behavior is not "scripty." If a child is moved from one foster home to another, his EPI may be spotty, and his program will be poorly organized (no Pr); he may comply as best he can, but never marry, raise children, stake his life on anything, or make any important decision (no IB). These examples illustrate how each item in the formula applies in actual practice. The tendon reflex is not based on EPI, the social drinking is not part of Pr, the non-bum has EPI and Pr but does not have C; and the orphan avoids IB.

Formula S, then, serves to identify a script in the same way that Formula G (Chapter Two) serves to identify a game. It should be noted that the formula only applies to "scripty" people; the behavior of an autonomous person cannot be reduced to a formula because such a person is making his own decisions on his own grounds from moment to moment. In the same way, inbred laboratory mice can be programed by conditioned reflexes, and their behavior can be directed by the experimenter. Thus, they act like machines run by a trained operator, just as "scripty" people act like machines operated by their parents. But wild mice do not respond in the same way; they act like "real" people, and make their own decisions. They refuse to accept the experimenter's program when they are put in the laboratory;[1] they do not rebel, they simply act independently and autonomously.

B · HOW TO VERIFY A SCRIPT

If the script is properly diagnosed, then it should be possible to find some elements which can be treated quantitatively. For example, what percentage of all women own red coats? How many Rapunzels actually have long blond hair? These are mostly of the nature of incidence-and-prevalence studies, and their real value is to dissect out the essential elements of scripts in order to make their diagnosis more rigorous. In the case of LRRH, the diagnostic criteria as they are understood at present read as follows:

1. Her mother must have sent her on errands to grandmother's house when she was a little girl.

2. Her grandfather must have played with her sexually during those visits.

3. She must be the one most likely to be chosen to run errands in later life.

4. She must be contemptuous about men her own age and curious about older men.

5. She must have a naive kind of courage, confident that there will always be someone to rescue her if she gets into trouble.

If, and only if, all five of these criteria are present, then the diagnosis of an LRRH script is justified. If it is, then it can be predicted that the patient will put herself in the way of older men, will complain that older men ("dirty old men") are making passes at her, will look for someone to rescue her from them, and will laugh when they are discomfited. But many questions come to mind. Do all women who meet these criteria actually spend time in the woods picking flowers? And do they all own red coats? How many other items could be added to the list? How many of the items are redundant—that is, how many of them could be eliminated without affecting predictive accuracy, and what is the smallest number of essential ones which would predict all the others and script outcome as well? What is the correlation between the items? Do all women who were seduced in childhood by their grandfathers like to pick flowers in the woods? Are women who spend time picking flowers in the woods also the ones most likely to be chosen to run errands? Do all women who meet the five criteria end their lives as spinsters, or after a relatively brief marriage, as divorcées? This kind of factor analysis would greatly help to test the validity and usefulness of script analysis.

The LRRH criteria are largely "subjective," but then there are other variables which are objective. One of these is family constellation. The most reliable way to study this from a script point of view is to find "scripty" families. One indication in this regard is the naming of children after their parents or after living members of their families, since this is a clear indication that the parents expect the offspring to be like their namesakes, and also implies "I am bringing you up (programing you) to be like your namesake." If a person

who meets this namesake requirement comes to a psychiatrist, that strengthens the assumption that he is
saddled with a script, since this is regularly the case
with psychiatric patients; it also offers an opportunity
to investigate whether the script is related to the name.
If it is, then the patient is a proper subject for study in
this connection. The following is an example of such a
scripty family.

The Baker family consisted of three girls: Dona,
Mona, and Rona. The mother's family consisted of
two girls: Dona and Mona. Thus Dona was named after
her mother, and her younger sister Mona was named
after her mother's younger sister. When Rona was born,
they had run out of script names on the mother's side,
so she was named after her father's younger sister. The
two Donas, mother and daughter, were repeatedly arrested together for the same offenses and shared the
same jail tank. The two Monas, aunt and niece, both
got married to men who deserted them and were left
to raise children by themselves with no support from
the fathers. The two Ronas both hated men, led them
on, and then drew away. Thus the Donas played "Cops
and Robbers" together, the Monas played "Who Needs
Him?" and the Ronas played "Rapo." When Mona and
Rona (the daughters) came for treatment, it was evident that they were headed for the same kind of endings as their respective aunts, and neither of them liked
the prospect, but they felt helpless, by themselves, to
break up their scripts.

Another "scripty" development is repeated marriages
and divorces, which can not only be objectively verified, but are accurately numerable. One or two divorces
may be considered independently of mother's script, but
as the number of divorces rises, the clinician cannot
help but be struck by the fact that the greater the
number of the mother's divorces, the more likelihood
there is that the daughters will follow in her footsteps.
A similar relationship is frequent with arrests or
alcoholic hospitalizations of the mother. Sociologists
claim that such events may be dependent on social and
economic factors, but if we consider arrests and hospitalizations separately, the case is harder to make: that

is, it may be that arrests and alcoholic hospitalizations, taken together, are affected by "social and economic factors" in some independent way, but it is important that where there is a choice, some families choose one, other families the other.

We are not concerned here with whether the patient breaks the law or drinks, since such acts may not necessarily be central to his script. What we want to know is whether he is "scripty" about stealing or drinking and plays games with them: "Cops and Robbers" or "Alcoholic." The question is whether he steals or drinks enough to be, or in order to be, arrested or hospitalized. A professional thief or a drinking man may play the games he favors and be a winner and retire rich, honored, and happy; that is one kind of script. Another may be a loser and end up in an institution. That is quite a different one. What is important in script analysis is not the act, but the ultimate response and payoff which it yields, since that is what is important for the individual and the people around him.

Another "scripty" area is death. The most frequent script indicator here is when the person expects, or feels that he is expected, to die at the same age as the parent of his own sex did. It seems that the death of the father at a certain age sentences the son (in his own mind) to die before or at the same age, and the same applies to mothers and daughters. While this is subjective, it does involve numbers, and has the added advantage of being easy to check. More objective is the age at which suicide or homicide is attempted or committed, and the relationships of these to deaths of ancestors or near relatives. Regarding causes of death, as already noted, Rudin studied the relationships between stories told to children ("achievement" stories or "power" stories) and those causes of death which would here be called "scripty," and finds many interesting correlations between the types of stories read in childhood in seventeen countries and later causes of death.[2]

All the relationships mentioned above between parents and their children can be scored categorically. A person named after a family member either does or does not follow the script of his namesake; the patient either does or does not follow the parental script in regard to marriage, divorce, jail, or hospitalization; and he either does or does not expect to die at the same age as his deceased parent. The script problem is a decisive one for human living; the whole meaning of life depends on whether or not script theory is valid. If we are free agents, that is one thing; if we spend most of our time, and our most decisive moments, following instructions received in infancy and childhood, with the pathetic illusion of free will, that is quite another story. It will take at least ten thousand cases to give a feeling of conviction one way or another about such a fundamental matter. Any confidence extended to a study of fewer than that number will really be a scientific courtesy rather than a valid conviction. Kinsey, as a taxonomist, worked with sets as high as 100,000 specimens of wasps; his books on sexual behavior are based on twelve thousand cases and still leave room for extensive controversy.[3] Since many clinicians see one hundred new patients a year, ten thousand cases is not an unattainable goal, and is well worth the effort. I have seen more than ten thousand games being played in the last ten years (five hundred weeks, about fifty patients seen each week) and a series of such size gives me a feeling of unshakable confidence in transactional game theory. What is needed is a similar series for script theory.

In regard to the questions above, the correlations will either be consistent with and reinforce script theory, or they will be inconsistent with it and weaken it. It will be necessary to find these correlations for different parts of the country and for different countries of the world, as well as making historical studies, in order to determine whether script theory is in truth "a fact about human nature" or a mere regional impression derived from and confined to a selected population (psychiatric patients); or worse, merely a bright idea with no solid backing in reality.

What is required is what Platt[4] calls "strong inference." It is impossible in a finite time to test the universality of script theory by interviewing every human being, but it can easily be disproven, if it is erroneous, by a relatively small sample (say ten thousand cases). The script analyst, in order to maintain his position that script programing by the parents is a universal directive for all human beings everywhere, and is thus "a fact about human nature," would require, for the strongest possible inference, that all the above correlations should come out very highly positive in every large series.

As an aid to the clinician, wherever he may be, we shall now give a "script check list," consisting of questions which are designed to elicit the maximum of information for each of the numerous items required for a clear understanding of a script.

C · INTRODUCTION TO THE SCRIPT CHECK LIST

In order to understand a script clearly, we should understand each aspect, the history of that aspect, and its articulations with all other aspects. This can be most conveniently done by taking the items in chronological order. For each item, a single question is given which is most likely to elicit the maximum amont of relevant information. Other questions are included, which will help if more elaboration is desired about certain specific items. Alternative questions are given where the main question is often found to be inapplicable or unanswerable.

Script analysis in its present form was mainly developed at the San Francisco Transactional Analysis Seminar during the years 1966–1970, and it is almost impossible to dissect out the originator of many of the ideas, since more than one hundred clinicians took part in the weekly discussions during the period. Specific contributions have been published in the *Transactional Analysis Bulletin* by Pat Crossman, Mary Edwards, Stephen Karpman, David Kupfer, I. L. Maizlish, Ray Poindexter, and Claude Steiner. The original stimulus came from the present writer in a chapter in *Transactional Analysis in Psychotherapy*,[5] later elaborated in other books and at the Seminar.

The idea of a check list was first proposed by Claude Steiner (Berkeley), and Martin Groder and Stephen Karpman (both of San Francisco). It was designed to be used as a shortcut in treatment, giving a quick way of finding the active elements in a patient's script so that its tragic progress could be headed off as quickly and effectively as possible. Their list included seventeen of the most decisive items.[6] The comprehensive list given below includes those items, along with many others derived from the material in Parts II, III, and IV of this book. It is intended for teaching, research, and other specialized purposes, and contains about 220 items. It is followed by a more manageable, condensed version for everyday use.

D · A SCRIPT CHECK LIST

Questions are given in chronological order as far as it is convenient to do so, with clinical observations put last, thus following for the most part the order in the text. Each stage of development is numbered in sequence, and the questions dealing with that stage are given its key number. The number of the chapter dealing with each stage is given in parentheses. The letter in the key number refers to the section in the corresponding chapter. For example, Stage 1, Prenatal, is discussed in Chapter Four. Its heading therefore reads 1. Prenatal Influences (Chapter 4). The question, number 1F.4 indicates that this is a Stage 1, or "Prenatal" question, that is discussed in Section F of Chapter Four, and that it is the fourth question referring to that section. 2A.3 means Stage 2 (Chapter Five), the third question referring to Section A of that chapter. A "P" after the key number means that the question is intended to be asked of the patient's parents. Thus 2A.3P gives the same location as 2A.3 but means that this time the question is for the parents, not for the patient. This system sorts out the text so that the questions themselves occur in numerical order and can be used separately from the text.

1 · PRENATAL INFLUENCES
(CHAPTER 4)

1.B.1   What kind of lives did your grandparents lead?

1C.1   What is your position in the family?
    a. What is the date of your birth?
    b. What is the birthday of your next oldest sibling?
    c. What is the birthday of your next youngest sibling?
    d. Have you any special interest in dates?

1C.1P   How many brothers and sisters do you have?
    a. How many children do you (does your Parent, Adult, Child) (want, expect) to have?
    b. How many children did your parents want to have?
    c. Do you have any special interest in dates?

1D.1   Were you wanted?

1D.1P   Did you want him?
    a. Was he planned?
    b. Where and when was he conceived?
    c. Was an abortion attempted?
    d. How do you feel about sex?

1E.1   How did your mother feel about your birth?

1E.2   Who was there when you were born?
    a. Was it a Caesarean or a forceps delivery?

1F.1   Have you ever actually read your birth certificate?

1F.2   Who chose your name?

1F.3   Whom were you named after?

1F.4   Where does your surname come from?

1F.5   What did they call you as a child?
    a. What is your Child's name?
    b. Did you have a nickname as a child?

1F.6   What did the other kids call you in high school?

1F.7   What do your friends call you now?

   a. What does your mother, father, call you
   now?

2 · EARLY CHILDHOOD (CHAPTER 5)

2A.1   How did your mother and father teach you
       table manners?
           a. What does your mother say when she is
           feeding a baby?
2A.1P What happened during his nursing period?
           a. What did you used to say to him then?
2A.2   Who gave you your toilet training?
2A.3   How did they train you and what did they
       say?
           a. What do your parents say about toilet
           training?
2A.3P How and when did you toilet-train him?
           a. What did you used to say to him then?
2A.4   Did you get lots of enemas or laxatives as a
       child?
2B.1   How did your parents make you feel when you
       were little?
           a. How did you feel about yourself when
           when you were little?
2B.2   What did you decide about life when you
       were little?
2C.1   How did the world look to you when you were
       little?
           a. How did you feel about other people?
2C.2   Do you remember as a child ever deciding
       that never again would you do a certain thing
       or show a certain feeling?
           a. Did you decide always to do a certain
           thing, no matter what?
2C.3   Are you a winner or a loser?
2C.4   When did you decide that?
2D.1   What was your interpretation of what went on
       between your parents when you were little?
           a. What did you feel like doing about it?
2E.1   What kind of people did your parents look
       down on?

a. What kind of people do you dislike most?

2E.2   What kind of people did your parents look up to?

      a. What kind of people do you like best?

2F.1   What happens to people like you?

3 · MIDDLE CHILDHOOD (CHAPTERS 6 & 7)

3A.1   What did your parents tell you to do when you were little?

      a. What did they say to you when you were very little?

3A.2   What was your parents' favorite slogan?

3A.3   What did your parents teach you to do?

3A.4   What did they forbid you to do?

3A.5   If your family were put on the stage, what kind of a play would it be?

4 · LATER CHILDHOOD (CHAPTER 7)

4A.1   What was your favorite fairy tale as a child?

      a. What was your favorite nursery rhyme as a child?

      b. What was your favorite story as a child?

4A.2   Who read it to you or told it to you?

      a. Where, when?

4A.3   What did the reader say about it?

      a. How did she react to the story?

      b. What did her face say about it?

      c. Was she interested in it, or was she just reading it for your sake?

4A.4   Who was your favorite character as a child?

      a. Who was your hero?

      b. Who was your favorite villain?

4B.1   How did your mother react when things got tough?

4B.2   How did your father react when things got tough?

4C.1   What kind of feelings bother you the most?

4C.2   What kind of feelings do you like best?

4C.3   What is your most frequent reaction when things get tough?

4C.4   When a storekeeper gives you trading stamps, what do you do with them?

4D.1   What are you waiting for in life?

4D.2   What is your favorite "if only?"

4D.3   What does Santa Claus look like to you?
        a. Who or what is your Santa Claus?

4D.4   Do you believe in immortality?
        a. What were your parents' favorite games?

4E.1   What kind of hassles did your parents get into?

4E.1P   What games did you teach the patient when he was little?
        a. What games did you play with your parents when you were little?

4E.2   How did your teachers get along with you at school?

4E.3   How did the other kids get along with you at school?

4F.1   What did your parents talk about at the dinner table?

4F.2   Did your parents have any hang-ups?

5 · ADOLESCENCE (CHAPTER 8)

5A.1   What do you talk about with your friends?

5B.1   Who is your hero nowadays?

5B.2   Who is the worst person in the world?

5C.1   How do you feel about people masturbating?

5C.2   How would you feel if you masturbated?

5D.1   What happens to your body when you get nervous?

5E.1   How do your parents behave when there is company around?

5E.2   What do they talk about when they are alone or with their buddies?

5F.1   Have you ever had a nightmare?
        a. What kind of a world do you see in your dreams?

5F.2   Tell me any dream you ever had.

5F.3   Have you ever had any delusions?

5F.4   How do people look to you?

5G.1   What is the best thing you can do with your
        life?

5G.2   What is the worst thing you can do with your
        life?

5G.3   What do you want to do with your life?

5G.4   What do you expect to be doing five years
        from now?
            a. Where do you expect to be ten years
               from now?

5H.1   What is your favorite animal?
            a. What animal would you like to be?

5I.1   What is your life slogan?
            a. What would you put on your sweatshirt
               so people would know it was you com-
               ing?
            b. What would you put on the back of it?

6 · MATURITY (CHAPTER 9)

6A.1   How many children do you expect to have?
            a. How many children does your (Parent,
               Adult, Child) want to have?
        (This should be correlated with 1C.1 and
        1C.1P)

6A.2   How many times have you been married?

6A.3   How many times has each of your parents been
        married?
            a. Did they have any lovers?

6A.4   Have you ever been arrested?
            a. Has either of your parents ever been
               arrested?

6A.5   Have you ever committed any crimes?
            a. Has either of your parents done like-
               wise?

6A.6   Have you ever been in a mental hospital?
            a. Has either of your parents?

6A.7   Have you ever been hospitalized for alcohol-
        ism?
            a. Has either of your parents?

6A.8   Have you ever attempted suicide?
            a. Has either of your parents?

6B.1   What will you do in your old age?

7 · DEATH (CHAPTER 10)

7B.1   How long are you going to live?

7B.2   How did you pick that age?

       a. Who died at that age?

7B.3   How old was your father, mother (if not living) at death?

       a. How old was your maternal grandfather when he died? (For males.)

       b. How old were your grandmothers when they died? (For females.)

7B.4   Who will be at your deathbed?

7B.5   What will your last words be?

       a. What will their last words be?

7C.1   What will you leave behind?

7D.1   What will they put on your tombstone?

       a. What will it say on the front of your tombstone?

7D.2   What will you put on your tombstone?

       a. What will it say on the back?

7E.1   What surprises will they find after you are dead?

7F.1   Are you a winner or a loser?

7G.1   Do you prefer time structure or event structure? (Explain terms.)

8 · BIOLOGICAL FACTORS (CHAPTER 13)

8A.1   Do you know how your face looks when you react to something?

8A.2   Do you know how other people respond to your facial reactions?

8B.1   Can you tell the difference between your Parent, your Adult, and your Child?

       a. Can other people tell the difference in you?

       b. Can you tell the difference in other people?

8B.2   How does your real self feel?

8B.3   Does your real self always control your actions?

8C.1   Do you have any sexual hang-ups?

8C.2   Do things go round and round in your head?

8D.1   Are you conscious of odors?

8E.1   How far ahead do you begin to worry about things before they happen?

8E.2   How long do you worry about things after they are over?
        a. Do you ever lie awake at night planning revenge?
        b. Do your feelings interfere with your work?

8F.1   Do you like to show that you are able to suffer?
        a. Would you rather be happy than prove yourself?

8G.1   What do the voices in your head tell you?

8G.2   Do you ever talk to yourself when you are alone?
        a. When you are not alone?

8G.3   Do you always do what the voices in your head tell you?
        a. Does your Adult or Child ever argue with your Parent?

8H.1   What are you like when you are a real person?

9 · THE CHOICE OF THERAPIST (CHAPTER 15)

9B.1   Why did you choose my profession?
        a. What do you think about being assigned to one of my profession?
        b. Which profession would you prefer?

9B.2   How did you choose me?

9B.3   Why did you choose me?
        a. What do you think of being assigned to me?

9B.4   Who was the magician in your childhood?

9B.5   What kind of magic are you looking for?

9C.1   Have you had any previous psychiatric experience?

9C.2   How did you choose your previous therapist?
      a. Why did you go to him?
9C.3   What did you learn from him?
9C.4   Why did you leave?
9C.5   Under what circumstances did you leave?
9C.6   How do you select a job?
9C.7   How do you quit a job?
9C.8   Have you ever been in a psychiatric hospital or ward?
      a. What did you have to do to get there?
      b. What did you have to do to get out?
9C.9   Can you tell me any dream you ever had?

10 · THE SCRIPT SIGNS (CHAPTER 16)
(Questions the therapist asks himself)

10A.1   What is the script signal?
10A.2   Is he having hallucinations?
10B.1   What is the physiological component?
10C.1   What is the most frequent respiratory expression?
10C.2   What causes voice switches?
10C.3   How many vocabularies are there?
10C.4   What is the favorite part of speech?
10C.5   When is the subjunctive used?
10C.6   Where do the O.K. words come from?
10C.7   What are the script phrases?
10C.8   What is the metaphor scene?
10C.9   How are the sentences constructed?
10C.10   What are the security phrases?
10D.1   When does the gallows laugh occur?
10D.2   What is the gallows transaction?
10E.1   Is he consulting his grandmother?
10.F1   What is the story of his life?
10F.2   What is his favorite drama switch?

11 · THE SCRIPT IN TREATMENT (CHAPTER 18)

11A.1   How do you think your treatment will end?
11B.1   Do you think I am smarter than you are?

11B.2   Who is causing your trouble?

11B.3   How well do you want to get?

11B.4   What would you like to happen here?

11B.5   Are you ready to get well now?

          a. What has to happen before you can get well?

11B.6   What keeps you from getting well?

11C.1   Do you think I could handle your parents?

          a. Were your parents very powerful?

11D.1   Would you rather get well or be completely analyzed?

          a. Would you rather get well or get out of the hospital?

          b. Would you rather get well or stay in the hospital?

E · A CONDENSED CHECK LIST

The following list includes only those items related specifically to script analysis, and is intended as an adjunct, and not as a replacement, for psychiatric history-taking. The fifty-one questions chosen are more "natural" and less intrusive, and in most cases will promote rapport rather than challenge it.

1B.1   What kind of lives did your grandparents lead?

1C.1   What is your position in the family?

1E.2   Who was around when you were born?

1F.3   Whom were you named after?

1F.4   Where does your surname come from?

1F.5   What did they call you as a child?

1F.6   Do you have any nicknames?

2A.4   Were you constipated as a child?

2F.1   What happens to people like you?

3A.1   What did your parents say to you when you were little?

4A.1   What was your favorite fairy tale as a child?

4A.3   What did the reader say about it?

4B.1   How did your parents react when things got tough?

4C.1	What kind of feelings bother you the most?
4F.1	What did your parents talk about at the dinner table?
4F.2	Did your parents have any hang-ups?
5F.2	Tell me any dream you ever had.
5F.3	Have you ever had any delusions?
5G.4	What do you expect to be doing five years from now?
5I.1	What would you put on your sweatshirt so people would know it was you coming?
6A.8	Have you ever attempted suicide?
6B.1	What will you do in your old age?
7B.1	How long are you going to live?
7B.2	How did you pick that age?
7D.1	What will they put on your tombstone?
7D.2	What will you put on your tombstone?
7F.1	Are you a winner or a loser?
8A.1	Do you know how your face looks when you react to things?
8B.3	Does your real self always control your actions?
8C.1	Do you have any sexual hang-ups?
8D.1	Are you conscious of odors?
8E.1	How far ahead do you begin to worry about things?
8E.2	How long do you worry about things after they are over?
8F.1	Do you like to show that you are able to suffer?
8G.1	What do the voices in your head tell you?
9B.2	How did you choose me?
9C.3	What did you learn from your previous therapist?
9C.4	Why did you leave him?
9C.9	Can you tell me any dream you ever had?

(Questions the therapist asks himself)

10A.1	What is the script signal?
10A.2	Is he having hallucinations?

10C.1   What is the most frequent respiratory expression?
10C.6   Where do the O.K. words come from?
10C.8   What is the metaphor scene?
10C.10   What are the security phrases?
10D.1   What is the gallows transaction?
10E.1   Is he consulting his grandmother?
10F.1   What is the story of his life?

11A.1   How do you think your treatment will end?
11B.5   What has to happen before you can get well?
11D.1   a. Would you rather get well or be completely analyzed?
             b. Would you rather get well or leave the hospital?

F · A THERAPY CHECK LIST

This is a list of forty items which indicate that the patient has come out of his script. He may be considered completely cured when the answer to all these questions is Yes. This gives a quantitative way of estimating how effective his treatment has been up to any given point. So far there is no convincing way of weighing the items, so for the present they may be given equal weight. The list is designed to test the theory that a script cure and a clinical cure are identical. It is primarily intended to be used when the patient terminates treatment. It is best used in a treatment group, and the patient's responses are considered valid if the therapist and the other group members concur with him, and questionable if they do not, making due allowance for possible ulterior motives on the part of all concerned.

The questions are keyed in the same way as the script check list.

1F.7   Do your friends now call you by the name you like?

2B.1	Are you an O.K. person?
2C.1	Does the world look different to you now?
2C.2	Are you free of delusions?
2C.3	Have you changed your childhood decision?
3A.1	Have you stopped doing destructive things your parents ordered you to do?
3A.4	Can you now do constructive things your parents forbade you to do?
4A.4	Do you have a new hero, or see the old one differently?
4C.1	Have you stopped collecting trading stamps?
4C.3	Do you react differently than your parents did?
4D.1	Are you living right now?
4D.2	Have you given up saying "if only" or "at least"?
4E.1	Have you given up playing the games your parents played?
4I.1	Have you taken off your sweatshirt?
5F.1	Has your dream world changed?
6A.6	Have you given up your script payoff: prison, hospital, suicide?
7B.1	Are you going to live longer than you used to think?
7B.5	Have you changed your last words?
7D.1	Have you changed your epitaph?
8A.1	Are you aware of how your facial reactions affect other people?
8B.1	Do you know which ego state is in charge at a given moment?
8B.3	Can your Adult talk straight to your Parent and Child?
8C.1	Can you get turned on sexually without artificial stimulation?
8D.1	Are you aware of how odors affect you?
8E.1	Have you cut down your reach-back and afterburn so they do not overlap?
8F.1	Are you happy rather than just brave?
9B.5	a. Have you changed your reason for coming to therapy?
	b. Have you stopped doing what used to get you into the hospital?
10A.1	Is your script signal gone?

10A.2   Are you free of hallucinations?

10B.1   Are your physical symptoms gone?

10C.1   Have you given up coughing, sighing, and yawning for no apparent reason?

10C.4   Do you use verbs, instead of adjectives and abstract nouns, when talking about people?

10C.8   Do you use a wider variety of metaphors?

10C.9   Are your sentences crisper?

10C.10 Have you stopped hedging when you say something?

10D.1   Have you stopped smiling and laughing when you describe your own errors?

11A.1   Do you see your therapist differently?

11B.1   Have you stopped playing games with him?

11C.1   Are you able to stop playing games before they begin?

11D.1   Do you think you have gotten cured rather than just made progress?

REFERENCES

1 Kavanau, J. L. "Behavior of Captive White-Footed Mice." *Science,* 155: 1623–1639. March 31, 1967.

2 Rudin, S. A., *op. cit.*

3 Kinsey, A. C. *et al. Sexual Behavior in the Human Male.* W. B. Saunders Company, Philadelphia, 1948.

4 Platt, J. R. "A Strong Inference." *Science,* 146: 347–353, October 16, 1964.

5 Berne, E. *Transactional Analysis in Psychotherapy. Loc. cit.*

6 Steiner, C. M. "A Script Checklist." *Loc. cit.*

Appendix

WHAT *DO* YOU SAY
AFTER YOU SAY HELLO?

There is a simple rule here: the harder the script, the easier it is to know what to say. We have already mentioned Oedipus, who got by with two one-liners: "Wanna fight?" for men, and "Wanna make it with a kid half your age?" for women. Criminals use one-liners too: "Where's the dough?" for robbers, and "Shut up!" for rapists. Similarly with addicts: "Have a drink!" or "Got a fix?" Some criminals and schizophrenics don't even bother to say Hello.

For others, there are six possible situations. (1) Where talking is obligatory and the situation is highly structured, as in the courtroom or the doctor's office. This is easy because of the professional structure. (2) Where talking is obligatory and the structure is social. The possibilities here range from the banal "Warm enough for you?" to "Is that an Ethiopian necklace?" (3) Where talking is obligatory and the situation is unstructured, as in certain kinds of "encounter" groups This is a more or less new invention of the human race and presents difficulties for certain people. The most impersonal "personal" remark that is possible in such situations is "Nice shoes you have on." (4) Where talking is permissible but not obligatory. This is often the case at outdoor concerts, marches, etc. "Groovy!" is a universal second line here. The third line should be a throw-off, e.g.: "Hello." "Hello." "Groovy." "Yeah." "The lighting, I mean." "Oh, I thought you meant the music," and from then on it's all gravy. (5) Where talking is not customary and requires some courage. This is the most difficult, since rejection is legitimate and the talker is always working on a probability basis.

Ovid, *The Art of Love,* Book 1, is the man to consult here. His suggestions are just as good for New York, San Francisco, London, or Paris of today as they were for Rome two thousand years ago. If you make it with Book I, you will be ready to go on to the more advanced stages in Book II, and if that works out you will be ready for home plate, which is Book III. (6) Where talking is forbidden, as on the New York subway. Except under the most unusual circumstances, only people with very hard scripts will try it.

The classical joke here concerns the man whose conversation with women ran as follows: "Hello." "Hello." "Would you like to go to bed?" A friend advised him that it would be better to make some conversation before he asked the question. So the next time he was introduced to a girl, he said: "Hello. Have you ever been to Ethiopia?" "No." "Then let's go to bed." Actually that is not a bad line. Here are some possibilities.

Wistful: "Hello."

"Hello."

"Have you ever been to Ethiopia?"

"No."

"Neither have I. I'd sure like to travel though. Have you traveled much?"

Naive: "Hello."

"Hello."

"Have you ever been to Ethiopia?"

"No."

"It's a beautiful country. One time when I was there I saw a man eat a lion."

"Man eat a lion?"

"Barbecue. Have you eaten yet? Do you like barbecues? I know a little place . . ." etc.

These few suggestions are offered out of courtesy, in order to make good on the title of this book, and are intended only to stimulate the reader's ingenuity.

GLOSSARY

Antiscript	The inverse of the script. The defiant opposite of what each directive calls for.
Adult	An ego state oriented toward objective, autonomous data-processing and probability-estimating.
After-Burn	The period of time before a past event is assimilated.
Button	An internal or external stimulus which turns on scripty or gamy behavior.
Child	An archaic ego state. The Adapted Child follows parental directives. The Natural Child is autonomous.
Clock-Time	A period measured by clock or calendar.
Come-on	A provocation or seduction into nonadaptive behavior.
Commitment	An operationally ratified decision to follow certain principles of action in order to attain a certain goal.
Contract	An explicit agreement between a patient and a therapist which states the goal of the treatment during each phase.
Conviction	A firm opinion about the O.K.ness or not-O.K.ness of oneself on the one hand, and the rest of the world on the other.
Counterscript	A possible life plan based on parental precepts.
Curse	The script injunction.
Cut-off	A script release from without.
Cut-out	A script release from within.
Death Decree	A fatal script payoff.
Decision	A childhood commitment to a certain form of behavior, which later forms the basis of character.
Demon	(a) Urges and impulses in the child which apparently fight the script apparatus, but in reality often reinforce it. (b) The whispering voice of the Parent urging the Child on to nonadaptive impulsive behavior. The two usually coincide in their aims.
Depression	The failure of a dialogue between the Child and the Parent.
Drama Triangle	A simple diagram showing the possible switches of roles in a game or script. The three major roles are Persecutor, Victim, and Rescuer.

Earthian   One whose judgments are based on pre-conceptions rather than on what is actually happening. A square.

Earthian Viewpoint   One which is obscured by preconceptions learned from other people, usually in early childhood.

Ego State   A consistent pattern of feeling and experience directly related to a corresponding consistent pattern of behavior.

Electrode   The Parent in the Child. When activated, it brings about an almost automatic response.

Family Culture   The chief interest of the family, particularly in regard to bodily functions.

Family Drama   A dramatic series of events which occurs repeatedly in each family, and which forms the protocol for the script.

Gallows Laugh   The laugh or smile which accompanies a gallows transaction, and which is usually shared by the others present.

Gallows Transaction   A transaction which leads directly toward the script payoff.

Game   A series of transactions with a con, a gimmick, a switch, and a crossup, leading to a payoff.

Game Formula   The sequence of events occurring in a game, expressed as a formula by means of letter symbols:
$$C + G = R \to S \to X \to P.$$

Gamy Behavior   Behavior which seems more calculated to get an eventual trading-stamp payoff than to accomplish its declared purpose.

Gimmick   A special attitude or weakness which makes a person vulnerable to games or scripty behavior.

Goal Time   A period terminated by the attainment of a goal.

Illusion   An unlikely hope which the Child clings to and which influences all his decisive behavior.

Injunction   A prohibition or negative command from a parent.

Intimacy   A game-free exchange of emotional expression without exploitation.

Life Course   What actually happens.

Life Plan   What is supposed to happen according to the script.

Life Sentence   A negative but not fatal script payoff.

Loser	Someone who does not accomplish a declared purpose.
Martian	One who observes Earthly happenings without preconceptions.
Martian Viewpoint	The naivest possible frame of mind for observing Earthly happenings.
Mortgage	An optional obligation undertaken to structure long periods of time.
Nonwinner	Someone who works hard just to break even.
Ogre Father	The Child ego state of the father, which forms the Parent of his daughter's Child ego state and directs the tragic script. In a productive script, this is called the Jolly Giant.
O.K. Words	Words rewarded by parental approval.
Overlap	When reach-back begins before afterburn has subsided.
Palimpsest	A later version of a script arising from new potentialities as the child enters later phases of development.
Parent	An ego state borrowed from a parental figure. It may function as a directing influence (the Influencing Parent), or be directly exhibited as parental behavior (the Active Parent). It may be nurturing or controlling.
Pattern	A style of life based on parental instruction or example.
Permission	(1) A parental license for autonomous behavior. (2) An intervention which gives the individual a license to disobey a parental injunction if he is ready, willing, and able, or releases him from parental provocations.
Persona	A masked presentation of self. It usually is at an eight- to twelve-year-old level.
Position	A concept of O.K.ness and not-O.K.ness which justifies a decision; a position from which games are played.
Prescription	A set of precepts offered by a nurturing parent.
Program	The life style which results from all the elements of the script apparatus taken together.
Protocol	The original dramatic experiences upon which the script is based.
Provocation	Nonadaptive behavior encouraged or demanded by a parent.

Racket	The sexualization and transactional seeking and exploitation of unpleasant feelings.
Reach-Back	The period of time during which an impending event influences behavior.
Release, External	An outside intervention which releases the individual from the demands of his script. A cut-off.
Release, Internal	A condition built into the script whereby the individual is released from it. A cut-out.
Re-Parenting	Cutting off early Parental programing and substituting a new and more adaptive program through regression, especially in schizophrenics.
Role	A set of transactions played out in any of the three ego states according to the demands of the script.
Santa Claus	The illusory source of the illusory gift which the Child spends his life waiting for.
Script	A life plan based on a decision made in childhood, reinforced by the parents, justified by subsequent events, and culminating in a chosen alternative.
Antithesis	A command which directly contradicts the parental injunction; a therapeutic intervention which brings about temporary or permanent release from the demands of the script. An external release.
Apparatus	The seven elements that make up a script.
Can Script	One stated in positive terms.
Can't Script	One stated in negative terms.
Check List	A list of questions carefully selected and worded so as to get the greatest amount of information, with the least ambiguity, concerning the script.
Controls	The payoff, the injunctions, and the provocations which control the individual's scripty behavior.
Currency	The medium that leads to the script payoff: words, money, or tissues are examples.
Directives	Controls, patterns, and other script equipment.
Driven	Of a person who has to accomplish

what his script calls for at any cost, but may have fun on the side.

Episcript An excess of parental programing. *See* Overscript.

Equipment Parental stimuli and responses out of which the individual constructs his script apparatus.

Failure If the script cannot be carried through, it leads to despair.

Formula The sequence of events essential to the progress of a script, expressed in a formula by means of letter symbols: EPI → Pr → C → IB.

Hamartic One with a self-destructive, tragic ending.

Matrix A diagram showing the parental directives which form the basis of the script.

Outbreak (or Outbreak of Script) shifting from more or less rationally controlled behavior into a scripty scene.

Overscript An excess of parental programing which is passed from one person to another, as from parent to child. Whoever has this "hot potato" at any given moment is overscripted. An episcript.

Payoff The ultimate destiny or final display that marks the end of a life plan.

Primal The earliest version of the script, based on the infant's interpretation of the family drama.

Ridden Of a person who must concentrate on his script at the expense of everything else.

Set The dreamlike setting in which the Child plays out the script.

Sign A special item of behavior which gives a clue to a patient's script.

Signal A movement or mannerism which marks scripty behavior.

Space The space within which the decisive transactions of a script take place.

Theme Love, hate, revenge, or jealousy are the commonest.

Velocity The number of role switches occurring in a script in a given unit of time.

World The distorted world in which the script is played out.

Scripty Behavior	Behavior which seems more motivated by a script than by rational considerations.
Spellbreaker	An internal release, built into the script.
Slot	A place in a script to be filled by any person who will respond according to its demands.
Stopper	A script injunction or prohibition.
Stroke	A unit of recognition, such as "Hello."
Structural Analysis	Analysis of the personality, or of a series of transactions, according to Parent, Adult, and Child ego states.
Sweatshirt	A life motto which is apparent from the person's demeanor.
Switch	1. A switch from one role to another in game or script. 2. A maneuver which forces or induces another person to switch roles. 3. An internal or external stimulus which turns off adaptive behavior.
Therapeutic Hypothesis	A hypothesis concerning the value of a planned therapeutic operation.
Totem	An animal which fascinates the individual and influences his behavior.
Trading Stamp	A feeling "collected" as the payoff in a game.
Transaction	A transactional stimulus from a certain ego state in the agent plus a transactional response from a certain ego state in the respondent. A transaction is the unit of social action.
Transactional Analysis	(1) A system of psychotherapy based on the analysis of transactions and chains of transactions which occur during treatment sessions. (2) A theory of personality based on the study of specific ego states. (3) A theory of social action based on the rigorous analysis of transactions into an exhaustive and finite number of classes based on the specific ego states involved. (4) The analysis of single transactions by means of transactional diagrams; this is transactional analysis proper.
Winner	Someone who accomplishes his declared purpose.
Witch Mother	The Child ego state of a mother, which forms the Parent of her son's Child ego state and directs the tragic script. In a

productive script, this is called the Fairy Godmother.

World View   The Child's distorted view of the world and the people around him, upon which his script is based.

INDEX

ABOUT THE AUTHOR

DR. ERIC BERNE, as the originator of transactional analysis, has attained recognition for developing one of the most innovative approaches to modern psychotherapy, but it wasn't until his *Games People Play* became an international bestseller that his method achieved wide popularity. In his writings and teachings, until his death in 1970, Dr. Berne laid the groundwork for a rational method for understanding and analyzing human behavior which is gaining increasing application in modern therapy as one of the most promising new developments in the mental health field. A prolific author, Dr. Berne outlined the principles of transactional analysis in such works as *Transactional Analysis in Psychotherapy* (1961); its application to group dynamics in *The Structure and Dynamics of Organizations and Groups* (1963); its use in analyzing games in the celebrated bestseller *Games People Play* (1964); its application to clinical practice in *Principles of Group Treatment* (1966); and a summary of the theory in popular form in *A Layman's Guide to Psychiatry and Psychoanalysis* (1968).

Dr. Berne came to the United States from Canada soon after his graduation from the McGill University Faculty of Medicine in Montreal. He studied at the New York Psychoanalytic Institute and served three years in the Army Medical Corps, practicing psychiatry and neurology in several large hospitals in the West. After the war he was appointed Consultant in Psychiatry and Neurology to the Surgeon General of the United States Army, and attending psychiatrist at the Veterans Administration Mental Hygiene Clinic in San Francisco.

Before his death, Dr. Berne was a practicing psychiatrist in Carmel, California, and a Fellow of the American Psychiatric Association, as well as a diplomate of the American Board of Psychiatry and Neurology. He was also adjunct psychiatrist at Mount Zion Hospital and a lecturer in group therapy at the Langley Porter Neuro-psychiatric Institute, both in San Francisco, where he was also a consultant in group therapy at the McAuley Clinic. Dr. Berne was also chairman of the San Francisco Social Psychiatry Seminars, a visiting lecturer at the Stanford Psychiatric Clinic in Palo Alto, and editor of the TRANSACTIONAL ANALYSIS BULLETIN.

EUROPE, YOUR WAY!

These three helpful, matter-of-fact guides give you everything you need to know **before** you go! Whether it's your first trip or your fifty-first, these three guides tell you how to get the most out of Europe, your way!

THE REAL EUROPE AND THE MEDITERRANEAN (B7724/$2.25)

From what to see to where to shop, from where to sleep to what to eat, this is the MOST COMPREHENSIVE, UP-TO-DATE, all-inclusive guide to Europe and the Mediterranean, 1973!

THE REAL ECONOMY GUIDE TO EUROPE (Y7721/$1.95)

From how to stay in London for less than $5.00 a night to how to live in an Italian villa absolutely FREE! Here are hundreds of money-saving secrets to seeing Europe on **your** budget!

THE REAL RESTAURANT GUIDE TO EUROPE (Y7723/$1.95)

From the most elegant Parisian restaurants to enchanting inexpensive hideaways—here is the handiest, most complete guide to more than 200 great restaurants.

Bantam On Psychology

IN AND OUT THE GARBAGE PAIL by Frederick S. Perls, M.D., Ph.D. (DM7299—$1.65)

GESTALT THERAPY VERBATIM by Frederick S. Perls, M.D., Ph.D. (DM7292—$1.65)

BLACK RAGE by William Grier & Price Cobbs. Two Negro Psychiatrists examine the Negro mentality in this brilliant bestseller. (N3931—95¢)

BEYOND THE PLEASURE PRINCIPLE by Sigmund Freud. (NM5381—95¢)

THE REVOLUTION OF HOPE by Erich Fromm analyzes the problems and hopes of mankind in a mechanized society. (N4187—95¢)

PSYCHOANALYSIS AND RELIGION by Erich Fromm. (NM5558—95¢)

THE FIFTY-MINUTE HOUR by Robert Lindner. The brilliant study of psychosis and violence. (NM4388—95¢)

We Deliver!
And So Do These Bestsellers.

QUALITY CIRCLES

A GUIDE TO
PARTICIPATION AND PRODUCTIVITY

by

OLGA L. CROCKER
*Professor, Faculty of Business Administration,
University of Windsor
Adjunct Professor, Institute for Personal and Career Development,
Central Michigan University*

CYRIL CHARNEY
Management Consultant, Thorne, Stevenson and Kellogg

and JOHNNY SIK LEUNG CHIU

A MENTOR BOOK

MENTOR
Published by the Penguin Group
Penguin Books USA Inc., 375 Hudson Street,
New York, New York 10014, U.S.A.
Penguin Books Ltd, 27 Wrights Lane,
London W8 5TZ, England
Penguin Books Australia Ltd, Ringwood,
Victoria, Australia
Penguin Books Canada Ltd, 10 Alcorn Avenue,
Toronto, Ontario, Canada M4V 3B2
Penguin Books (N.Z.) Ltd, 182–190 Wairau Road,
Auckland 10, New Zealand

Penguin Books Ltd, Registered Offices:
Harmondsworth, Middlesex, England

This is an authorized reprint of a hardcover edition published by Facts on File.

First Mentor Printing, February, 1986
11 10 9 8 7 6 5 4 3

 REGISTERED TRADEMARK—MARCA REGISTRADA

Library of Congress Catalog Card Number: 85-62119

Printed in the United States of America

To our families

NATHAN, KEVIN, GERRI, TERENCE, and GINGER

MR. and MRS. SHU-CHONG CHIU

and

RHONA, DANEAL, THALIA, and DAVIN

PREFACE

The purpose of this book is to introduce the reader to the concept of quality circles and to compare quality control circles in Japan with those in the United States (and by projection, those in Canada). It is hoped that through an identification of the differences between these two countries and an analysis of the reasons behind these differences, an isolation of the effects that quality circles have on productivity and on worker motivation can be made. The study is important for another reason. At present, literature is replete with articles emphasizing the desirability of introducing Japanese-type quality circles to North American industry; no analysis of the differences and similarities between the two countries, however, is usually given.

The book is written for five types of audiences. First it is written for the practitioner—that man or woman who is participating or is trying to decide whether or not to participate in quality circles. It is hoped that both blue- and white-collar circle members will find the book a useful and complete guide.

Second, it is written for my students and those of other professors. Many have taken courses in innovative methods of resolving labour–management conflict and are expected to apply in the "real world" what they have learned or should have learned. The book answers an often-heard plea of many of them: How do I start and what do I do?

The third audience is those students who are still in the

classroom and have aspirations of becoming employed in areas in which they can use their knowledge of team processes and productivity improvements. Perhaps a book such as this will help in teaching the fundamentals and will serve as a useful everyday reference when these students leave their academic institutions.

Fourth, it is written for facilitators and coordinators who have been trained in group processes but have not been trained in quality circles processes. This group may obtain ideas and assurance that they are on the right track.

The fifth audience is the managerial one—those people who want a quick overview of what their personnel are doing, and who must be knowledgeable in spite of the fact that time is at a premium.

To the extent that the book meets the needs of any and all of these groups it is a success.

Many people have participated in bringing this book to completion. Special thanks are extended to those people who read the book and provided many useful comments: Dr. Pierre DuBois of the consulting firm of Woods Gordon; L. M. Galicinski, Qualitran Professional Services, Stroud, Ontario; Prof. Kevin B. Crocker of College-University of Cape Breton, Sydney, Nova Scotia; and Ginger Grant. And to Ginger, many thanks for the technical assistance.

Thanks also go to: Mr. and Mrs. Dan Connor; Mr. and Mrs. Tse; Brenda Butler, Manager, General Planning, Aetna Canada; Donna M. Hornsby, Secretary–Director of Maintenance, Air BC; Peter R. Leslie, Supervisor, Employee Relations, Allis-Chambers Canada Inc.; Anne S. Connor, Meeting Planner Program Manager, AMR International, Inc; R. H. Bettinger, Supervisor, Reliability Programs, American Airlines, Maintenance & Engineering Centre; Yvonne Horvath, Administrative Assistant, American Society for Quality Control; Zenon Onufryk, Bonar Packaging Ltd.; J. W. Cormier, Specialist, Union Relations, Canadian General Electric; Nestor Chyz, The Canadian Salt Company Limited; Jacquie Taylor, Coordinator, Cariboo Management Centre, Cariboo College; Joseph H. Martin, President, Conestoga College; Jan Shuckard, Assistant Vice President Corporate Services, Constellation Assurance Company; Laurie A. Hirsch, Corporate Quality Circle Facilitator, Continental Illinois Bank and Trust Company of Chicago; E. L. Marr, Crush Canada Ltd.; Garry S. Kissuk,

Manager, Human Resource Planning, Dome Petroleum Limited; Linda Lehtonew, QC Coordinator, Dominion Life Assurance Co. Ltd.; K. McCullough, Manager, Engineering, Dover Elevator; G. J. Peterson, Human Resources Manager, Esso Chemical Canada; Philip C. Hassen, Executive Vice President, Foothills Hospital.

Cam Prymak; Gary Lesperance, El Program Coordinator, Windsor Operations; Rudy Orgis, Processing Engineer; Gary H. Blevins, Forward Planning and Analysis Department, Labour Relations Staff; William Johnston, Manager of Labour Relations and Hourly Personnel, Windsor Operations (all of the Ford Motor Co. of Canada Ltd.); Jerry W. Dillard, Manager, Corporate Safety, Ford Motor Co.; and Stephen Barney, World Headquarters, Ford Motor Co.

Michael Nastanski of General Dynamics; Ed J. Taylor, Associate Manager, Productivity Services, Great West Life; John T. Rooney, Commercial Services Manager, National Quality Team/Steering Committee Chairman, Hewlett Packard Canada Ltd.; S. Cairns, Vice President Operations, Hostess Food Products Ltd.; J. Al Spence, President, Hussman Store Equipment Limited; Larry S. Kacher, Manager, Organization Development, Corporate Human Resource Development Department, Honeywell, Inc.; S. Takeda, Publicity, Hotel Okura, Tokyo, Japan; Robert Collier, Executive Director of International Association of Quality Circles; J. E. Vereshack, Senior Information Representative, Information Department IBM (Canada) Ltd.; Tsunetaka Irei, Okinawa, Japan; Joji Arai, Director, Japan Productivity Center; Japan Trade Centre Office; W. Alan Lewis, Vice-President and General Manager, Knape & Vogt Canada Inc.; Audrey LaPointe, Controller, *Mainland* Magazine; Dr. Stanley Stark, Professor, Department of Management, Michigan State University; Jack Germain, Vice-President and Director of Quality, Motorola, Inc.; Don L. White, Vice President Operations, Motorways Limited; J. J. Zeyen, Vice President–Manufacturing, Nashua Canada Ltd.; R. M. Cuddy, Vice-President, Manufacturing, Northern Telecom Canada Limited, Islington, Ontario; Robert I. Patchin, Director of Productivity Improvement Programs, Northrup Corporation, Aircraft Division; Bob Ackerman, Omark Canada Ltd., Guelph, Ontario; Art Van Pelt, Employee Relations Manager, Overwaitea Foods; Bruce Fuller, Vice-President Corporate Affairs, the Jim Pattison Group; Rober J. Shaw,

PREFACE

Principal, Peat, Marwick, Mitchell & Co.; Stan Jarovi, Price Waterhouse Limited.

Donald Young, PSI Coordinator and Director of Governmental Affairs; Bob Brown; John Olaja, Director of Advertising; and Derek Millet, Engineer and Team Captain; all of Vickers World headquarters.

R. C. Sinclair, Coordinator, Quality Programme Project, Toronto-Dominion Bank; Ed Artuso, QCC Facilitator, Tridon Limited; Ray Wakeman, Curtis Davidson, Frank Morand, and members of UAW Local 200 for their help in the completion of the Ford Motor Co. survey; Dr. Vedanand, Faculty of Administrative Studies, Department of Marketing, University of Manitoba; Dr. Robert E. Cole, Professor, University of Michigan; Dr. Akira Kubota, Political Science Department, University of Windsor.

Guy Cassady, Clara Chai, Patrick Chee, Albert Pak Choong, Garry Swee Foo, Thomas Ho, Vincent Lam, Thomas Ng, Shih Yuan Wong, Marianne Wylupek, and Alfred Yau, all students at the University of Windsor, and Jo Ann Sokkar, Senior Associate Librarian, Graduate School of Business Administration Library, University of Windsor.

K. B. Nisbet, Director, Corporate Affairs, Westinghouse Canada, Inc.; Ralph J. Barra, Director of Corporate Quality, Westinghouse Electric Corporation; Dean J. Alex Murray and Dr. Hans J. Bocker, Wilfred Laurier University; and Dr. Charles J. McMillan, Professor, Faculty of Administrative Studies, York University.

Special thanks are given to the Faculty typists and the women at the Word Processing Centre who helped bring this work to a readable conclusion: Catherine Walker, Suzanne Patterson, Sandra Van Zetten, Pat Awid, Barbara Faria, Lucia Brown, Roni Burleigh, Carmela Papp, Lyn LaPorte and Nancy Dawid.

Last, but not least, Dr. Eric West, Dean, Faculty of Business Administration, University of Windsor, and Methuen's executive editor, Herb Hilderley, and assistant editor, Catherine Munro, without whose support and assistance this project would have been much more difficult.

CONTENTS

CONTENTS

CONTENTS

CONTENTS

PART I

JAPAN AND NORTH AMERICA

ONE

THE CONCEPT OF QUALITY CIRCLES

The 1970s have been riddled with one crisis after another—wars, political problems and the energy crisis. Not the least was the economic crisis created by the enormous influx of Japanese goods on the Canadian and American markets. North America in the 1980s is in a period of record high inflation and record high unemployment.

Many analysts argue that high unemployment is attributable to a "productivity crisis." On the surface, the solution appears simple—increase employee productivity. Productivity can be defined as the ratio of what goes into the production process (inputs) to what comes out (outputs). But the inputs and outputs of even the most simple production process are many. As a consequence, many different approaches are suggested to accomplish increased productivity.

Some analysts attribute high unemployment and low productivity to the gap in wage rates between North American workers and workers in other parts of the world, particularly Japan. The figure depends on who does the calculation, but generally it is estimated that North American workers cost about $25 per hour whereas Japanese workers cost about $12 per hour, a substantial difference of $13 per hour. Therefore, some claim, the answer to productivity problems is to slash labour costs drastically.

This measure, of course, would be easier than tackling the productivity problems that exist. Labour costs could be reduced to the level of those in Japan if, as a society, Ameri-

3

cans were prepared to allow their standard of living to regress to that of the Japanese. Some other issues also must be considered. If the United Auto Workers (UAW; the union which represents automotive industry blue-collar employees) is typical of North American unions, it is doubtful that, over the long term, American workers would be prepared to tolerate "clawbacks." Nor would American workers and unions accept the ramifications associated with a labour cost-cutting contest with workers in other parts of the world. It appears, then, that this solution is impractical.

Labour's answer to the problems facing the domestic market is to avoid the question of productivity but invoke protectionist measures. This could take the form of stringent import quotas or content legislation or both. However, there could be a price to pay for such a move.

First, invoking protectionist legislation would invite retaliation from countries that import North American goods. For Canada, which exports more to Japan than it imports, such a move would have a net negative effect. This also would go against world pressures to ease import restrictions and promote fair trade between countries.

Second, protectionism, over time, tends to make the protected industry inefficient. Economists argue that with protectionism there is a substitution of legislation for natural market forces. This in turn puts the economy and the marketplace, which are in delicate balance, into a state of disequilibrium. If this is so, in the long run protectionism would do more harm than good to the economy.

The government's answer to the problem includes wage or price controls or both, nationalization, government grants, loans and subsidies. But these partial solutions have also been very inefficient in the long run and are expensive or politically unacceptable.

Within industry, in the past, the answer has been increased job specialization. But it is probable that very little further increase in productivity can be accomplished by breaking down jobs into tasks that are even simpler and more repetitive. Too, it is doubtful that the better-educated workers of the 1980s and '90s will be willing to do more menial tasks merely to increase productivity. This partial solution is ineffective and unacceptable.

The Japanese have utilized robots to increase productivity

and to do the more repetitive, dangerous and less desirable jobs. But in North America, it has been argued that the application of such technology would result in the loss of jobs, and that robots do not buy cars and other consumer goods. It is probably true that the use of robots in production processes can displace workers. The development, manufacture and servicing of robots, however, will create many more new jobs and preserve existing ones. In any case, the introduction of robots to industry in North America has met with considerable resistance, and their application here has been slower than in Japan.

It appears that workers in North America will not work for Japanese wages. Protectionist legislation would be a step in the wrong direction and, like government grants, loans and subsidies, would be very inefficient and unacceptable. Breaking existing jobs down into more simple repetitive tasks also would be counterproductive. Lastly, the introduction of robots to industry has been and will probably continue to be slower in North America than in Japan. A remaining possibility, however, is the human factor in productivity. Can employees be managed in such a manner that they are more satisfied, more motivated and more productive? The key may be the involvement of employees at all levels within the organization in the decision-making process. One such approach is quality circles.[1]

The words "quality circle" or "quality control circle" mean different things to different people. Additionally, they

---

Possible answers to productivity problems:
• lower wages
• protectionist measures
• wage and price controls
• increased job specialization
• more robots

These ideas are impractical, politically unwise or inefficient.

The answer: more motivated and more productive workers through quality circle programs.

---

suggest that quality control (the improvement of quality within an organization) and quality circles (participative decision-making groups) are one and the same. Although quality circles generally do focus on quality control, the two concepts are not synonymous.

In Japan, quality control circles are organized within a department or work area for the purpose of studying and eliminating production-related problems. They are problem-solving teams which use simple statistical methods to research and decide on solutions to workshop problems. Similar types of activities are known by many names, such as: *Ai* (chemical industry—all members' ideas) movements; big brother or big sister groups; JK (*jishu kanri*, in the steel industry); level-up movements; management by objectives; mini-think tanks; new-life movements; no-error movements; productivity committees; safety groups; suggestion groups; workshop involvement groups; workshop talk groups; and ZD (zero defect) movements.[2]

Presently, in Japan, quality circles and other small group activities have expanded beyond the manufacturing sector, especially into the sales and marketing fields. They focus on more than quality and productivity improvement. Employee development and the improvement of communication and morale among co-workers also are important.

Quality circles in North America are similar to Japanese circles in spite of the fact that each may emphasize a particular function such as problem solving, team building or quality control. In many cases, each company (and representative union) has its own unique name for the circle activity. For example, Ford Motor Co. and the United Auto Workers have EI (Employee Involvement); Vickers, Inc. has PSI (People Seeking Improvement); and American Motors Corporation and the United Auto Workers have PIP (Partners in Progress) and JEEP (Joint Effort Employing People); the Toronto-Dominion Bank's circles are EWG (Employee Work Groups). Frequently an individual circle within a particular company will give its team a name. Ford Motor Co. and the United Auto Workers in Windsor, Ontario, for example, has SOS (Save Our Stampings) and TOPP (Total Opportunity for Plant Participation).

Canadian and U.S. quality circles, although concerned with quality and productivity, also study the improvement of life at the job site. It is not unusual for QC members to tackle such issues as carpooling, busing, absenteeism and child care. Also, the idea has expanded beyond the manufacturing sector into the service sector, particularly into retailing, finance, education and transportation.

The quality circle concept is the result of the interaction between the American statistical method of quality control and Japanese organizational practices. The Japanese adopted the concept of quality control, which originated in the United States, and developed it pragmatically into quality control circles. In the Japanese reinterpretation, each and every person in the organizational hierarchy, from top management to rank-and-file workers, receives training on statistical quality control concepts and techniques. Workers and supervisors participate jointly in small groups to upgrade quality control practices. In this context, quality control shifts from being the prerogative of a minority of engineers with limited shop experience to being the responsibility of each employee. As Norihiko Nakayamo, manager of Fujitsu subsidiaries, stated recently at a seminar in New York City:

> Quality Control is not just a little room adjacent to the factory floor, whose occupants make a nuisance of themselves to everyone else. It is a state of mind and a matter of leadership with everyone from the president to production trainee involved.[3]

Underlying the QC concept is the assumption that the causes of quality or productivity problems are unknown to workers and to management. It is also assumed that shop-floor workers have hands-on knowledge, are creative, and can be trained to use this natural creativity in job problem solving. Quality circles, however, are a people-building, rather than a people-using, approach. They aim at making every worker a decision maker concerning his or her own work.

CHARACTERISTICS OF QUALITY CIRCLES

Quality circles are a formal, institutionalized mechanism for productive and participative problem-solving interaction among employees.[4] Small groups of workers engage in a continuing cooperative study process to uncover and to solve work-related problems. Each circle also acts as a surveillance mechanism which assists the organization in adapting to its environment and in monitoring opportunities. It "scans the environment for opportunities, does not wait to be activated by a problem, and does not stop its activities when a problem has been found and solved."[5] It follows that, for greatest organizational benefit, quality circles should function continuously and be independent of the production process.

The number of members within any one circle differs depending on the policies of the organization. Usually the number is in the three-to-twenty-employee range, with the average circle having eight to ten members. Members get together regularly to learn interpersonal skills and statistical methods associated with problem solving and to select and solve real problems. Meetings are conducted both during regular working hours, with the approval of supervisors, and outside of regular working hours, on the workers' own initiative. Membership in circles is voluntary.

Meetings are chaired by a group leader. In most cases, the role is assumed by the first-line supervisor. In the context of the circle, the leader is not in an authority position over the other members but is a discussion moderator who facilitates the problem-solving process. It is this person's task to keep the group directed toward accomplishing its agenda and to ensure that everyone participates. In the words of one manager, the task is one of "complementing one another's work rather than managing it." In this sense, a circle leader has no authority but is a coordinator in the real sense of the word.

Most organizations also employ a facilitator. The facilitator develops training programs, provides continuing training and guidance to team leaders and, on request, offers training programs for team members. When the number of circles becomes large, some organizations also use a coordinator. This individual acts as a liaison between the facilitators and the quality circle steering committee and middle management.

Each circle is formally independent but may meet with other circles in the company to work jointly on common problems. At each meeting, all members are given assignments which they are expected to complete, on company and non-company time, by the next meeting. These assignments commonly involve first-hand observation of specific phenomena in the workplace and the collection and analysis of data. At the quality circle meeting itself, the brainstorming approach operates; each member is encouraged to participate and put forward ideas. A more detailed summary of the characteristics of quality circles is given in Table 1–1.

TABLE 1-1
Typical Characteristics of Quality Circles

Objectives
- To improve communication, particularly between line employees and management.
- To identify and solve problems.

Organization
- The circle consists of a leader and eight to ten employees from one area of work.
- The circle also has a coordinator and one or more facilitators who work closely with it.

Selection of Circle Members
- Participation of members in circle is voluntary.
- Participation of leaders may or may not be voluntary.

Scope of Problems Analyzed by Circles
- The circle selects its own problems.
- Initially, the circle is encouraged to select problems from its immediate work area.
- Problems are not restricted to quality, but also include productivity, cost, safety, morale, housekeeping, environment and other spheres.

Training
- Formal training in problem-solving techniques is usually a part of circle meetings.

Meetings
- Usually one hour per week.

Awards for Circle Activities
- Usually no monetary awards are given.
- The most effective reward is the satisfaction of the circle members from solving problems and observing the implementation of their solutions.

THE MYTHS AND FACTS OF QUALITY CIRCLES

A number of myths have grown up around quality circles and act as obstacles to utilizing worker creativity on the job. Among the most common are that quality circles are used solely to solve product quality problems, that there is a need to train only shop-floor employees because managers and supervisors already have the needed training, that the quality circle concept requires copying of every detail of the Japanese practice, and that workers in successful quality circle projects must be compensated by large financial rewards. Juran (1980) has analyzed a number of these myths and identified the associated factual situation (Table 1–2).

TABLE 1–2
The Myths and Facts about Quality Circles

Myths	Facts
The QC is to be used solely to solve problems in product quality.	QCs can be used (and are being used) to solve problems in productivity, safety and cost as well as quality. The original preoccupation with quality was for reasons unique to Japan during the 1960s.
The QC concept is applicable anywhere provided the workers are trained in problem solving.	The QC concept involves a significant amount of worker participation in decision making on matters previously regarded as solely the responsibility of supervisors. Managers must be willing to accept such participation.

The need is to train only the workers. The managers and supervisors already have all the training needed.	The training of managers and supervisors must precede that of the workers. This training is not only in the techniques but in the entire idea of how to work with QCs.
The QC is the only way ever invented to make use of the education, experience and creativity of the worker.	Nonsense. Pride in crafts and skills dates back many centuries to the days of the guilds. Even in Taylor system-type factories, ways were found to secure worker participation before the QC concept was invented, for example, the "Scanlon Plan."
Adoption of the QC concept requires copying the Japanese practice on details of application; for example, should training be done outside or during working hours; what amount of payment should be made for time spent working on projects, etc.	The need is to establish practices which are compatible with the culture. The Japanese practice evolved in response to the nature of their unique culture.
Workers associated with successful QC projects must be rewarded specially, just as in the case of useful employee suggestions.	The rewards, if any, whether financial or non-financial, must be responsive to the cultural realities.
The QC can make a major contribution to solution of the company's quality problems.	The contribution can be significant but not major. Most of the company's quality problems must be solved by the managers, supervisors and professional specialists.

Source: Adapted from J.M. Juran, "International Significance of the QC Circle Movement," *Quality Progress* 13 (November 1980): 21.

If there is only one thing that can be learned from Juran's work, it is that the Japanese quality control circles concept cannot be transplanted to other countries without modification. In fact, it requires significant modification to ensure its applicability.

In summary, quality circles are not a new panacea to cure all industrial ailments. They are a mechanism for creating the type of organization and the type of people-oriented philosophy that is needed if North American corporations are to compete successfully in world markets in the future.

Quality circle definition:
- Small group of workers.
- Group has a leader.
- Organized by work area.
- Solves problems of that area.

Assumptions underlying quality circles:
- Causes of quality or productivity problems are unknown to workers and management.
- Workers can help to solve these problems.
- Must be a people-building, not a people-using, approach.

Characteristics:
- Formal mechanism for participation of employees in problem solving.
- Helps organization to adapt to its environment.
- Eight to ten members in each circle.
- Meets regularly.
- Leader is not in an authority position.
- Facilitator assits in training and coordination.

Myths corrected:
- Not a panacea.
- Can be used to solve all types of problems.
- Training of managers and supervisors must precede that of workers.
- Only one of the many methods available that can be used to tap the creativity of the worker.
- Quality circle practices must be compatible with the culture.

TWO

QUALITY CONTROL CIRCLES IN JAPAN

This chapter explores the development of the quality control circle (QCC) movement in Japan, its salient characteristics and particularly the underlying factors that have contributed to its success.

Since the late 1950s, Japanese companies have expended considerable effort in formulating small group teams among their workers. These have played a vital role in raising productivity, creating a workplace which is fulfilling to workers, and improving labour-management relations. Quality control circles have been one of these informal small group team concepts. Other circle activities have dealt with such objectives as zero defects, suggestions, safety and recreation. Presently 77 percent of Japanese companies with more than 10,000 employees have some type of small group team activities.[1]

Before discussing Japanese QCCs, it would be wise to remember that postwar Japan was a country which had been virtually destroyed and which had a reputation for producing cheap, poor quality products. The government was determined to change the countryside and the image: to rebuild the country into a strong nation (by reconstructing the economy based on industrial production) and to secure a competitive edge in international markets through uniformly high-quality products. This conviction, shared by some influential industrialists with foresight, was to become the driving force behind the QCC movement. Seven events made the quality control circles concept the workable and pragmatic idea that it is today:

1. The introduction of statistical quality control methods.
2. The founding of the Japanese Union of Scientists and Engineers (JUSE).
3. The Industrial Standardization Law.
4. The consulting work of Dr. W.E. Deming (see Deming's principles in Chapter 4).
5. The lectures of Dr. J.M. Juran.
6. Publication of the *Gemba* (Supervisor's Guide) to Quality Control.
7. The first International Conference on Quality Control was held in Japan.

The QC movement began during the Allied occupation years. W.G. Magil of the Civilian Telecommunications Section of the office of the Supreme Commander for the Allied Powers (SCAP) introduced statistical quality control concepts to manufacturers in the electrical communication section. The idea caught on and other members of SCAP continued to promote wide-scale adoption of quality control practices.[2]

In 1946, the Japanese Union of Scientists and Engineers (JUSE) was founded. JUSE was, and is, dedicated to studying foreign technology, launching research studies and implementing training programs. Today, it continues to be the major organizational instrument for diffusing quality control practices in Japan. It also serves as a major liaison between the manufacturing and academic sectors.

Also, under the Allied occupation, Walter Shewhart, one-time head of technical staff, Bell Telephone Laboratories, Inc., and Dr. W.E. Deming, Harvard professor and chief statistician for the U.S. Bureau of Census, were called in as consultants to assist in the reconstruction of Japanese industries. Deming's work is well cited in other publications and will not be repeated here. Suffice it to say that the Deming Prize was instituted by JUSE to commemorate Dr. Deming's contribution.[3]

The Japanese government strongly supported the quality movements. As a result, The Industrial Standardization Law was passed in July 1949. Under this law, companies that are successful in meeting quality requirements prescribed by the Minister of International Trade and Industry are authorized to use a special label on their products. Also, because of this law, the Japanese Standards Association, a strong force for quality control, was established.[4]

A short time later, in 1954, Dr. J.M. Juran, international consultant and lecturer, visited Japan to give lectures on the managerial aspects of quality control. He emphasized management's role in quality control. Influenced by his teachings, Japanese companies adopted a new orientation. Quality control became an integral part of the management function and was practised throughout the entire organization. In effect, quality control mobilized ordinary workers into participating in the operational decision-making process.

In 1962, JUSE published the *Gemba* to Quality Control (*Quality Control for Foremen*). The publication put particular emphasis on using case studies to train supervisors. The event was significant in that it coincided with a pan-industrial[5] move for the adoption of the QCC concept. In the same year, JUSE set up the QCC head office and named its founder, Dr. Kenichi Koyanagi, as the first director. Currently, the head office administers eight chapters in eight regions and sponsors QCC conferences, seminars and company visits to promote nation-wide activities.

Significant too was the first International Conference on Quality Control, held in 1969 in Tokyo. It led to the inauguration, in 1970, of the Japanese Society for Quality Control, which had as one of its prime responsibilities the strengthening of cooperation between the industrial and academic sectors. Gradually, through this society, the foundation for the organized movement was solidified, and the number of QCCs registered with JUSE grew phenomenally (from a total of 1,000 in 1964 to 115,254 in December 1980.[6] (See Table 2–1.) Indeed, in 1982 it was estimated that as many as one out of every eight Japanese employees was participating in a QCC or some small-group activities.

QCCs in Japan have not only proliferated but have also been fruitful. The QCC movement has significantly improved product quality and spurred productivity. Juran (1980) summarizes the results thus:

> Collectively, the millions of improvement projects have saved enormous sums of money, running into many billions [milliards] of dollars. These same projects have significantly improved the saleability of Japanese product

15

[sic] by removing numerous sources of customer dissatisfaction. Through such great saleability, the companies become more competitive, which makes the workers' jobs more secure.[7]

TABLE 2–1
Number of Members and Quality Control Circles in Japan (By Selected Years)*

	Circles		Participants	
Year	Number	Percent Increase Over Previous Three-Year Period	Number	Percent Increase Over Previous Three-Year Period
1962	23			
1965	4,930	21,334.8	70,920	
1968	17,416	253.3	212,134	199.1
1971	42,366	143.3	472,421	122.7
1974	65,477	54.6	664,458	40.6
1977	86,189	24.0	836,448	25.9
1980	115,254	33.7	1,062,759	27.6

*Note: Data are as of December. Raw figures have been provided by Japanese trade consulate.

People, Organizations, and Events Which Have Made QCCs Workable
• Introduction of quality control methods
• Japanese Union of Scientists and Engineers (JUSE)
• Industrial Standardization Law
• Dr. W.E. Deming
• Dr. J.M. Juran
• *Gemba*
• First International Conference on Quality Control

This achievement is reflected in the Japanese world-wide industrial trade surplus of over $76 billion in 1981. During the same year, the U.S. had a deficit of $28 billion.[8] Japan has succeeded because there is an all-out effort to seize world leadership in quality, and this, in no small measure, is attributable to the QCC movement.

THE CHARACTERISTICS OF JAPANESE QUALITY CONTROL

The preceding section has examined briefly the development of quality control and quality control circle activities in Japan following the war. This section will examine the unique characteristics of the concept. Ishikawa, founding father of the quality control circle movement, describes six salient features of Japanese quality control. These are: (1) company-wide quality control, (2) emphasis on education and training, (3) QCC activities, (4) application of statistical methods, (5) the quality control audit, and (6) nation-wide quality control promotion activities.[9] Each of these concepts is described in more detail below.

Company-Wide Quality Control and Total Quality Control

Total Quality Control (TQC), proposed in 1961 by V.A. Feigenbaum, Secretary, Quality Control Coordinating Committee of General Electric, is "religion" in Japanese firms. As one Japanese executive commented: "QCC are not effective without TQC; 'circles' must be a way of life, not something extra." Unlike traditional statistical quality control, the TQC concept posits the overall management of quality control. Thus TQC embraces product design and development, sales and after-sale servicing. In fact, the proper objective of TQC is to eliminate quality control, that is, to have quality control "built in" and not "inspected in."[10]

To meet this objective, quality control policies are specified as corporate strategy. They are reflected in the way top management policies are transmitted and implemented throughout the organization. . . . Once top management policies are established . . . the policy is deployed down to the lowest level, and its progress is checked, on a regular basis, again using the common statistical and factual data.[11]

In other words, quality control involves all facets of design and production and all employees in upgrading quality and maximizing corporate resources. Japanese companies train workers to do the quality control checks. The training is given by company instructors. The in-house training sessions are specifically aimed at different company echelons such as middle management, engineers, supervisors and operators. As an example, Appendix 2 illustrates a breakdown of a quality control training program in Toyota Motor Company.

JUSE, the Japanese Standards Association, the Japanese Management Association, the Japanese Productivity Center, and several other organizations conduct seminars on quality control. In addition to regular technical training and education, some companies sponsor trips and sessions whereby supervisors, senior workers and new employees participate in exchanging views and examining new ideas.

An Emphasis on Training

Japanese companies place particular emphasis on training supervisors. The content of these training programs (as summarized by Ishikawa, 1968) includes:

- administrative training (an integral part of the in-company training program which is given to all employees)
- simple statistical methods for analyzing and carrying out shop improvements
- an emphasis on practical (as opposed to academic) training and the study of real cases
- teaching that is tied closely to the given firm's own technology
- participative management techniques.[12]

The absence of professional quality control experts in Japan makes training extremely important. Since quality control is not an established profession, it is very difficult, if not impossible, to assign experts to all departments actually involved in the implementation of quality control. Furthermore, most companies refrain from using experts to solve work group problems because work groups are regarded as independent social entities and are endowed with considerable autonomy in decision making. The use of experts would be regarded as outside interference and would undermine employee morale and leadership. All employees therefore are taught quality control methods. This, in turn, diminishes the need for specialists or industrial engineers.

Quality Control Circle Activities

A large number of Japanese workers have had twelve years of formal education (nine are compulsory). No real differences exist, therefore, in the basic skills of employees among the major Japanese companies. How adequately a firm can draw on the capabilities of workers depends on the personnel policy of that organization and upon the leadership exhibited by management. QCC activities make employee motivation and commitment a reality at the actual working level. This is achieved through company-wide instruction and training of employees at all levels within the organization.

Most Japanese companies organize quality control circles as shown in Figure 2–1. There is a quality control circle committee which is headed by the president or vice-president, a plant-wide promotional committee, a care-takers group, advisers and trainers. Supervisors are generally quality control circle team leaders. It is not unusual to have mini-circles working on one specific aspect of a problem nested within sub-circles which work on some broader aspect, nested within the QCC as a whole, which works on the total problem. For example, the circle may be working on rust prevention of a particular area on a car, the sub-circle may decide to examine the corrosibility of the various metals used, and the mini-circle may be studying the impact of a particular acid on one metal.

An example, Sankyo Seiki Manufacturing Company, is given in Figure 2–2. This company sets up a formal hierarchy to administer small group activities. The hierarchy is composed of four committees—the standardization committee, the rust-prevention committee, the training committee and the qual-

FIGURE 2–1
Typical Quality Circle Organization in Japan

Source: Sud Ingle, *Quality Circles Master Guide* (Englewood Cliffs, NJ: Prentice-Hall, 1982): 19.

ity control circle offices. Each division has its quality control organization which is chaired by the divisional manager and which is under the overall supervision of the quality control circle office. Further, each division forms its own QCC, which is supervised by a section chief.

Application of Statistical Methods

To minimize quality problems, it is necessary to observe the relevant phenomena closely and to analyze objectively the relationship between the numerous factors affecting product quality and any changes in that quality. For this purpose, statistical methods can be used extensively as an analytical

FIGURE 2–2

Q C C Organization of Sankyo Seiki Manufacturing Company

At present, a company-wide Standardization Conference is being formed outside the Q C C.

Source: Toshiharu Yokosawa, "The QC Circle Movement Applied to Shop Requirement," in *Japan Quality Control Circles* (Tokyo: Asian Productivity Organization, 1982): 192.

tool and therefore are included in quality control training programs. (According to the authors of Toyota's and JUSE's training programs, for example, statistical methodology is one of the most important parts of quality control training.)

Like quality problems, other job-related troubles may be caused by managerial ignorance, misunderstanding or faulty analysis. Statistical methods are again crucial in the diagnosis of symptoms and identification of problems. Highly sophisticated statistical methods are not needed. In fact, most Japanese companies use comparatively simple methods like the "seven basic tools of quality control"—(1) Pareto diagrams, (2) cause-and-effect diagrams, (3) histograms, (4) check sheets, (5) graphs, (6) scatter diagrams, and (7) control charts—to solve workshop problems.

Quality Control Audits

In Japan it is quite usual for top management, especially the presidents and general managers, to provide leadership in quality aspects of production. Accordingly, large Japanese companies normally establish a quality control audit committee at the strategic apex to review comprehensively policy matters such as:

- What should be the quality mission of the company?
- What are the key product qualities (as seen by clients?)
- As to these key qualities, what is the company's competitive position?
- What opportunities does the company have for quality improvement and reduction of quality-related costs?
- What can be done to make better use of the human resources within the company?
- What competitive threats are developing?[13]

In the structural sense, the committee is simply an integrating mechanism designated to coordinate QC activities, to scan environmental opportunities and threats, and finally to promote liaison contacts within the organization. As a result, the company can achieve synergistic effects in production.

Nation-Wide Quality Control Promotion

Japan is not endowed with natural resources. It also is harassed by typhoons, earthquakes and tidal waves. The Japanese see themselves as a ''ship at sea'' and feel that they must work together to keep the ship afloat. Both government and enterprise recognize that the improvement of productivity is the key to survival in international competition. Indeed, John McAllister (staff executive for product quality at General Electric), who participated in a Technology Transfer Institutes exchange in 1979, claims:

> The only way it [Japan] can survive is by importing its food and resources and exporting high contributed-value goods. To do that, its products have to be regarded as of high quality. . . . [This] is a strategic requirement for national as well as business success.[14]

This urge for international survival is an instigating factor in forcing Japan to make an all-out effort to seize world leadership in quality. Quality control circles are a key activity in this effort.

CHARACTERISTICS OF JAPANESE QUALITY CONTROL

Total company commitment to quality.

Promoted nation-wide.

Emphasis on training:
• All workers learn to perform quality control checks.
• Supervisors are especially important.

All workers learn statistical control methods.

Management performs frequent quality audits.

QCC activities are well organized.

FACTORS CONTRIBUTING TO QCC SUCCESS

What is the secret of QCC success? Many factors are involved: (1) the culture, (2) the national and organizational structure, (3) the industrial relations and personnel systems, (4) the extensive educational and training programs, and (5) the technology. Figure 2–3 uses an Ishikawa diagram to illustrate these factors.

Japanese Culture and Society

Japan has been characterized as collectively-oriented or group-minded (*Bonsai*). Traditionally, the individual and the contribution of the individual have been deemphasized. This is founded on the conviction that the energy produced by the collectivity brings the most effective results. Because the overriding principle of teamwork is *Bonsai* (harmony), employees share *Gemeinschaft* (group values) and strive for *Ikiga* (a worthwhile life) while achieving company goals.[15]

Japan is also a paternalistic society. The nature of this paternalism can be more fully expressed by two Japanese expressions—*Kigyō ikka* (one family enterprise) and *Kigyō wa unmei kyodotai de aru* (the enterprise and its employees share a common destiny). Japan's culture is built on the teachings of Confucius—respect for parents and ancestors, kindliness, faithfulness, intelligence and proper behaviour—and the philosophy of *amae*, a nurturance and dependency relationship between superiors and subordinates. Thus large organizations are concerned about the welfare of all employees.[16]

These paternalistic practices mean committed employees. Workers develop a company spirit, identify with the company, and are loyal to it. As Reischauer observes:

> There is little of the feeling, so common in the West, of being an insignificant and replaceable cog in a great machine. In other words, there is no loss of identity but rather a gaining of pride for both workers and executives through their company, particularly if it is large and famous.[17]

The company is a familial social group to which employees have total emotional and psychological commitment.[18] It is this culture, this collectivism and this commitment and loyalty to the organization that sustain and expand the QCC movement.

The National and Organizational Structure

National structures exist which encourage quality control and quality circles. There is a nationwide promotion of the concepts. The Japanese Union of Scientists and Engineers awards the Deming and other prizes for outstanding company achievement. Among companies, including competitors, there is a sharing of information regarding new techniques and methods.

FIGURE 2–3
Factors Which Contribute to Success of the Japanese QCC Movement

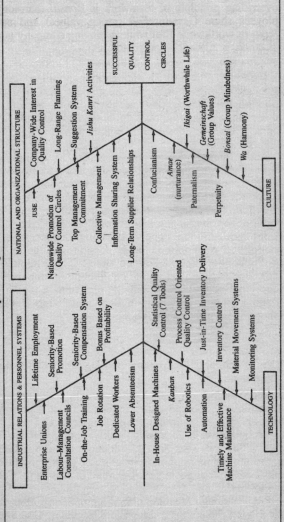

| INDUSTRIAL RELATIONS & PERSONNEL SYSTEMS | NATIONAL AND ORGANIZATIONAL STRUCTURE |

SUCCESSFUL
QUALITY
CONTROL
CIRCLES

Lifetime Employment
Company-Wide Interest in Quality Control

Seniority-Based Promotion
Long-Range Planning

Labour–Management Consultation Councils
Nationwide Promotion of Quality Control Circles
Suggestion System

Seniority-Based Compensation System
Top Management Commitment
Jishu Kanri Activities

On-the-Job Training
JUSE

Bonus Based on Profitability
Collective Management

Job Rotation
Information Sharing System

Dedicated Workers
Long-Term Supplier Relationships

Lower Absenteeism
Confucianism

Enterprise Unions

Amae (nurturance)

Paternalism
Ikigai (Worthwhile Life)

Perpetuity
Gemeinschaft (Group Values)

Bonsai (Group Mindedness)

Wa (Harmony)

CULTURE

Statistical Quality Control (7 Tools)

In-House Designed Machines

Process Control Oriented Quality Control

Kanban

Use of Robotics
Just-in-Time Inventory Delivery

Automation
Inventory Control

Material Movement Systems

Timely and Effective Machine Maintenance
Monitoring Systems

TECHNOLOGY

For most large companies, a long-term relationship with suppliers exists. Suppliers are expected to meet specific standards but, in exchange, have a guaranteed long-term commitment. At the organizational level, there is company-wide interest in quality control. This results in quality circles, *jishu kanri* and other small group activities, and in the promotion of various types of employee suggestion systems. [19]

The *ringi* system of decision making is utilized: consensus is sought among all those who are affected by a decision prior to its implementation. Once consensus occurs implementation of a change is very quick. [20] In North America, on the other hand, it takes a considerable length of time to introduce a change.

Senior managers also are committed to quality control. They ensure that long-range planning and the enforcement of quality control practices occur on a company-wide basis. Support is not of a token nature. In fact, no money or effort is spared in this cause. The efforts, commitment and experiences of top management are translated into daily activities. At Meindensha, for example, both the president and board chairperson took part in study sessions on the subject of quality control circles before the concept was instituted. Their attitude clearly showed to the entire body of employees what the company was doing and the direction in which it was heading. Similar leadership of QCC movements is shown by other top Japanese executives.

The Industrial Relations and Personnel Systems

Japan has unique industrial relations and personnel systems. There is no inherited class-conscious union militancy, like that which is found in the United Kingdom. Unions generally are cooperative in promoting quality control and quality circles within the work setting. Although they have very little input into the decision-making process, union leaders seldom adopt adversarial positions. A number of factors may contribute to this.

First, although Japanese unions are patterned after those in the United States, there are some differences. One important difference is that Japanese unions are enterprise unions, that is, they are organized by company rather than around crafts or industries. Each business enterprise has its own union. Larger industrial federations do exist; their activities, however, are mostly limited to distributing information and coordinating the bargaining policies of their affiliated unions for the Spring Wage Offensive (*Shunto*).[21]

Second, in order to moderate the labour movement, management encourages foremen,[22] supervisors, and white-collar workers below the managerial level to join unions. This has narrowed the gap between management and the rank-and-file worker, and thereby the gap between management and union.

The Japanese style of ''bottom-up management'' where decisions are made primarily by employees and junior managers and handed up the hierarchy, instead of being made by top management and handed down, is another key factor. Union members are not as removed from the source of decision-making power. In fact, managers may have been union members just a few years previously and therefore are much better able to understand the union's situation. Additionally, there are fewer levels within the hierarchy than in most large North American corporations.

A fourth important factor that affects the union-management relationship is the nature of Japanese management philosophy. A key part of this philosophy is a concern for the welfare of employees. As Jiro Tokuyama, Director of Nomura Research Institute, commented, ''Japanese management is more personalized. On many occasions, management will do more for the employees than it has to do—more than the contract requires.''[23]

A key aspect of this philosophy is the lifetime employment system. Layoffs or dismissals of permanent employees are rare. When business slows, permanent employees are kept on the job. If necessary, companies obtain monetary assistance from the government. Also, employees displaced by new technology are retrained for new jobs.[24]

Japan's personnel policies might seem strange to North Americans. In addition to lifetime employment, there is seniority-based promotion and seniority-based remuneration in the early years of an employee's career. Wages depend not only on level within the organization and seniority but also on need. A married man who has a large family to support receives, at least in theory, more financial remuneration than one with no family, even if they are both at the same hierarchical level and have equivalent seniority.[25] (In reality, the dependency allowances are likely to be small.)[26] There is also a bonus system which is based on the profitability of the company. The Japanese believe in training generalists rather than specialists. Job rotation, therefore, is frequent. As a consequence of these personnel policies, employees are more committed and absenteeism is low.

This job security has other important implications. It is possible that in return for lifetime employment and other benefits, workers generally do not insist as strongly on other rights. Other observers of the Japanese environment argue that this kind of commitment to the worker has earned the trust and loyalty of employees, and that this trust consequently is the reason why unions do not insist on a greater role in decision making As Bryon (1981) notes, "The workers trust their bosses to make the right decisions because there is a pervasive sense that both labor and management are working together."[27]

The feelings of cooperation and trust and the lack of alienation among employees may be attributable to the relatively homogeneous and classless society that exists. According to opinion polls conducted by the Prime Minister's office in 1980, 90 percent of Japanese consider that they are middle class. Four percent identify themselves as upper class; and around 6 percent feel they belong to the lower class.[28] Much of the cooperation and trust in labour relations may be associated with this social stability.

Also, there is little class consciousness in Japanese labour management relations. This is reflected in the fact that the union leaders often become executives in later years. Indeed, a position as a union officer is seen by many as a way to demonstrate the leadership ability needed to become a good manager. As the 1981 Nikkeiren report, based on a survey of 313 corporations, shows, one out of six Japanese executives once served as a leader of an employees' union. Of the 6,121 executives, 992 or 16.2 percent were previously union leaders.[29]

In summary, the structure of unions and union membership, together with paternalistic management and personnel practices, tend to lessen the militancy of unions. Second, cultural homogeneity and bottom-up decision making have helped diminish the feelings of powerlessness and alienation that could lead to employee demands for a larger role in the decision-making process.

Extensive Educational and Training Programs

In Japan, it is widely believed that the success of small group activities has been achieved through the improvement of the educational level of the workforce (94 percent have graduated from senior high school; 36 percent from colleges and universities).[30] Both government and enterprises have expended considerable effort in providing training courses. For example, the Japan Productivity Center has been conducting "productivity seminars" for youth leaders. Some unions even use productivity seminars as part of their training programs for union executives.

Japanese companies also concentrate on training junior leaders. Every year, the Junior Executive Council of Japan conducts a "sea cruise training session." Fumio Imamura, managing director of the Council, explains why such training is important:

> A good piece of fabric is always made of two threads—the warp and the woof, the horizontal and vertical threads. Similarly, a healthy organization must have both formal and informal threads. The vertical threads are the managerial hierarchy. . . . The informal or horizontal are represented by voluntary participation in the numerous small groups of which the company is comprised. It is at this level that corporate policy is discussed and implemented. That is why we need to develop junior leaders who can induce participation and commitment from other members.[31]

Furthermore, Japanese workers often take the initiative to participate in training programs. For instance, several hundred workers of Matsushita gave up a day of their own time, without being paid, to attend lectures sponsored by Kanto Subdivision on how to improve quality control.

The massive training effort is not only a salient characteristic of Japanese quality control circle movements, but also is a decisive factor in making them successful.

Technology

The use of technology is important to Japanese industrial success. Four approaches contribute to this technological effectiveness: attitudes toward robots; machine design and upkeep; inventory delivery and control; and statistical controls.[32]

First, machines are designed in-house. Quality control circles suggest required tolerances and the necessary capabilities of robots and other automated equipment. They also request that robots replace workers so that more effective production can occur.

Every member is responsible for minor machine maintenance and for ensuring that major problems are corrected quickly. Timely and effective maintenance of all equipment is key.

The inventory delivery and control system is very different. Suppliers bring raw materials and parts to the plants three or four times per day, that is, through a *kanban*[33] re-order system just in time to be used within the production process. Parts are perfect or near perfect; little allowance is made for variance from the required tolerance levels. (Defects are measured in parts per million.) The movement of materials within the plant is watched closely to ensure that shortages or product build-up do not occur.

Circles are involved in these activities and in the correction of malfunctioning processes.

OTHER ADVANTAGES OF QUALITY CIRCLES

Small group activities have other advantages, namely:
1. Setting group objectives creates a sense of teamwork.
2. Group members share and coordinate their respective roles better.
3. Communication is improved between labour and management, as well as between workers of different ages.
4. Morale is greatly improved.
5. Workers can acquire new skills and knowledge and develop more cooperative attitudes.
6. The group is self-initiating and undertakes problem-solving tasks which would otherwise be left up to management.

7. Labour-management relations are greatly improved.[34]
QCC management also achieves the following effects:
• People grasp the real issues more rapidly.
• More emphasis is placed on the planning phase.
• A process-oriented way of thinking is encouraged.
• People concentrate on the more important issues.
• Everybody participates in building the new system.[35]
To assist members to perform their duties, workers learn process control and monitoring and the seven tools of statistical control. Skills are reinforced within the circles.

WHY ARE QCCs SUCCESSFUL IN JAPAN?

Culture
• Collectivism
• Paternalism

Nation-wide promotion of concept

Unions
• Company, not craft or industry.
• Include supervisors and white-collar workers.
• Participate in decision making.
• Union leaders often become managers.

Management philosophy

Practice of lifetime employment

Training of junior leaders

Members involved in technological decisions

AND THE SHORTCOMINGS?

No business endeavour is perfect, and the Japanese QCC approach does have shortcomings. In principle, participation in a circle is voluntary, but in many companies, peer and management pressure pushes participation rates for workers to 90 percent or more. Cole, commenting on this problem, states:

> [I]t is known that there is tremendous variation among companies and industries in how voluntary those activities are; in most companies with circles, there is strong pressure on all workers to belong to quality circles. Not to do so would suggest to management a lack of commitment to corporate goals and thereby damage one's promotion prospects. There are companies that have quota systems—so many suggestions per circle, so many suggestions per month—which are hardly models of voluntarism.[36]

When this occurs, QCCs become a burden rather than a motivational scheme. There is a lack of spontaneity; the circle becomes unproductive and inactive.[37]

Other problems also exist. In some companies, QCC participants complain that the involvement of quality control or production engineers is excessive. Moreover, some companies place greater emphasis on productivity than they do on the development of worker potential.

Another significant problem is that participation tends to become ritualistic once it loses its spontaneity. As time passes, it becomes more difficult for group members to identify new problems to attack. As a solution, some Japanese companies, such as Suzuki Motor Company, have introduced evaluation systems to revitalize QCC activities and to promote worker participation (see Chapter 11).[38]

The last problem is that unions have not become involved in the group activities. In most instances, unions act only as monitors of the movement. Thus, in the future, as QCCs become more established and as the results of their efforts are more difficult to quantify, activities may need to be monitored more closely or promoted with the positive participation of company unions.

This chapter has presented a study of how the Japanese have skilfully woven modern Western industrial methods into the technical fabric of quality control and quality circles. From all these movements, a pattern of industrial strategy has emerged which is uniquely Japanese.

SHORTCOMINGS IN SOME ENTERPRISES

Participation is not always voluntary in every firm.

Involvement of production engineers may be excessive.

Participation becomes ritualistic.

Unions are not involved.

THREE

QUALITY CIRCLES IN NORTH AMERICA

During the past ten years in North America, companies have been plagued with problems of stagnating productivity, unemployment and job insecurity, consumer dissatisfaction, worker alienation and low morale. On the surface, none of these problems seems to be directly related to product quality. So why a quality control circle movement?

The "catching up with the Japanese" syndrome serves as one of the major catalysts of the movement. As North American industries lag in productivity, especially in the automobile industry, American managers search for clues by looking at the techniques used by their Japanese competitors. They focus upon Japanese-style management with its stable labour-management relations, high labour productivity, superb quality control and the like. In this sense, American managers recognize the underlying benefits of involving workers in the workplace and the implications of involvement for motivation. On the surface, it becomes sensible to emulate Japan's productivity tour de force.

Other American observers are still skeptical about the practicability of quality circles in U.S. industries. They speculate that the quality circle (QC) movement is only a fad. As Edgar H. Schein explains:

> One of the greatest strengths of U.S. society is our flexibility, our ability to learn. When we see a problem, we tinker with it until we have it solved, and we seem to be

willing to try anything and everything. One of our greatest weaknesses, on the other hand, is our impatience and short-run orientation. This leads to fads, a pre-occupation with instant solutions, a blind faith that if we put in enough effort and money anything is possible.

Institutionalization of QCs requires long-term commitment, resolute implementation and patience. In this chapter, an examination of the development of quality circles in North America is made. The history and salient features are described and the basic reasons that have led to these conditions are examined. The chapter also indicates some of the problems that might be encountered when companies install quality circles.

THE DEVELOPMENTAL PATTERN OF QUALITY CIRCLES

Although quality circles are rapidly gaining momentum in U.S. industries, the literature tends to be more popular than documentary. The first U.S. firms to adopt the full QC concept were Lockheed Missile & Space Co. Inc., a Sunnyvale, California division of Lockheed Aircraft Corporation,[2] and Honeywell Corporation.[3]

At Lockheed, after learning about the concept from a visiting Japanese team and consulting with Dr. J.M. Juran, international consultant, Missile System Division Manufacturing Manager Wayne Ricker arranged for a number of employees to tour eight Japanese firms. They were impressed and reported that quality circles were effective in motivating workers by enriching their jobs and increasing their sense of participation. The report also noted the strong support which senior management gave to the program and the involvement and commitment of workers in the plant. As a result, Lockheed established the first circle in October 1974. By the end of 1975, there were fifteen circles, and by 1977, thirty were to be found in production, research and development, machine, electronic and composite shops.

Although some managers and workers were reluctant to participate, those who did were generally enthusiastic. The results were impressive. By 1977, Lockheed estimated that circles had saved them $3 million. The number of defects per 1,000 hours caused by the manufacturing process declined by two-thirds. Late in 1976, the firm conducted a survey of members of two circles. They found that morale and job satisfaction had improved.

Honeywell too established its first circle in 1974. Since 1974, about 400 such groups have operated—mostly in an effort to improve quality of working life. The results indicate that both financial and human gains have occurred. An extensive 1982 study of seven divisions of the company found that there is improved communication between employees and supervisors, an interest in working toward organizational goals, a commitment to the organization, and an increased sense of individual self-worth. The study also suggests that professional quality circles tend to be less successful and that participants who have experienced failure tend to be more reluctant to participate in additional circles.[4] On the whole, QCs at Honeywell have worked well.

Since that time, other companies of different sizes, industries, and technologies have accepted the circle idea. Among the early pioneering companies were Metaframe Corporation, Smithline Instruments Inc. and the United States Envelope Company. Growth of the circle movement in America started slowly; only about twenty-five companies were involved in 1978. The rate of growth increased, and the number of organizations that were exploring circles leaped (see Appendix 3). By 1980, there were at least 6,000 circles in the United States and signs that many people were viewing circles as a panacea (which they are not). In Canada, the institution of quality circles is just beginning (see Appendix 4).

In truly American fashion, a variety of consultants has sprung up to implement quality circles, and the circle philosophy is now a regular feature of seminars offered by leading management organizations. The International Association of Quality Circles was set up exclusively to promote the spread of the concept. It is currently being restructured to carry out these activities in a more professional manner, with a Board of Directors composed primarily of company representatives from user organizations. As of winter 1982, the Association has some 5,400 members who represent individual member companies and seventy-three chapters. Its various training programs, conferences and publication activities have provided a major source of information to those who want to learn about quality circles.

The American Society of Quality Circles (ASQC) and the Technology Transfer Institute (TTI) are also rapidly moving toward a stronger commitment in supporting quality circle activities. In particular, TTI serves to facilitate the exchange of technical information and professional skills between Japanese and American businesses, and also sponsors international study missions to Japan to provide Americans with first-hand information on quality control and quality circle activity. In short, the publicity campaigns which diffuse quality circle practice are beginning to develop and accumulate momentum.

As the movement is still in a developmental stage, it is too soon to try to determine its significance. Despite numerous reports that quality circles are beneficial, it is felt, in view of the short time that has elapsed, that the findings are incomplete and perhaps even inconsequential. Any conclusions could be premature, controversial and misleading.

HISTORY OF QUALITY CIRCLES IN THE U.S. AND CANADA

1974—Lockheed Missile & Space Co. sets up its first quality circle.

1974—Honeywell Corporation establishes its first quality circle.

1980—There are over 6,000 circles in the United States.

1984—In Canada, nation-wide spread of idea is just beginning.

Organizations committed to spreading the concept:
• American Society of Quality Circles
• Technology Training Institute
• International Association of Quality Circles

THE CHARACTERISTICS OF NORTH AMERICAN QUALITY CIRCLES

Americans have "reborrowed" the Japanese quality control concept and have adapted it to fit the unique business environment in North America. During the adaptation process, some notable features have evolved. These are; (1) QC organization and structure, (2) the use of facilitators, (3) union involvement, (4) voluntary participation, (5) extensive use of external consultants and (6) white-collar circles.

QC Structure vs. the Formal Hierarchical Structure

In the developmental phase, in order to ensure that resistance to change will not develop, management may introduce few major changes. There may be no radical organizational or managerial innovations. Quality circles are established as a number of committees or task-forces. Although orientation and training in the concept increases, these activities generally are perceived as a normal function of all organizations. As the process evolves, however, a separate organizational structure is required if the program is to be responsive and if it is to maintain its vitality and continuity. What emerges is a formal quality circle organization which exists alongside the formal bureaucractic structure (Figure 3–1).

The typical hierarchical organization has a series of functional leadership levels which range from presidential to unit supervisor ranks. Each level is assigned authority, and has responsibility, for work performed by employees at levels subordinate to it. The quality circle organizational structure, on the other hand, is much flatter. It is administered and coordinated by a steering committee whose members include middle management (directors, functional managers and departmental managers), union leaders and, in a liaison position, at least one facilitator or coordinator. At the second hierarchical level are facilitators who, as the name implies, assist but have no authority over, or responsibility for, the core people in quality circles—the circle leaders and the circle members.

The contrast between the two can be better understood

through an examination of Stein and Kanter's parallel-structure concept (Figure 3–2). The hierarchical bureaucratic structure is geared to routine operations, that is, it focuses primarily on functional mass-production activities in which employees perform fixed job assignments according to objectives established by senior management. They are competent for these jobs prior to assignment. For this, they are provided with limited developmental and promotional opportunities but receive reasonably generous compensation in the form of pay and benefits. Leadership in this organization is based on level within the organization.

By contrast, the parallel structure is that adopted by quality circles. It is, ideally, a

---

FIGURE 3–1

Quality Circle Structure Compared to the Formal Hierarchical Structure of a Typical North American Company

---

vehicle for creating new ways of flexibly grouping people providing the possibility of challenge, learning and growth [opportunity] and for opening access to resources, support, and recognition.[5]

It focuses on the non-routine and on high uncertainty. Circle members have flexible job assignments and identify, develop and solve those problems that are important to them and their work tasks. Ideally, objectives or specifications are also bottom-up; there is little or no chain of command. The assignment has expandable learning opportunities and the circle members are able to increase their competencies as the situations demand. Rewards are both extrinsic (financial incentives) and intrinsic (recognition, visibility by more senior management, an ability to learn new skills, personal growth and development, and self-fulfillment). Leaders are those who have the expertise or who have been chosen or recognized by the group.

It must be pointed out that the quality circle organization is not an ad hoc committee. It exists as part of the total organization, yet operates independently and continuously to achieve its designated goals and purposes. Furthermore, it is organic in nature; workers temporarily group together to study work-related problems. Participants are not limited by their positions and occupations. Circles may be dissolved or organized at any time. In an effort to encourage dialogue between management and workers, a new set of organizational relationships and a new reporting system is established. The communication structure is modified so that information flows up as regularly and freely as it does down; power is redistributed to give workers more decision making in areas which concern them. In sum, the quality circle organizational structure is designed to be adaptive and responsive to both internal and external environments.

The Organization of Quality Circles

North American companies normally organize quality circles in the manner depicted in Figure 3–3. This usually includes a steering committee, coordinator, facilitators, leaders and circle members. The *steering committee* is the focal point or

FIGURE 3–2
Characteristics of Bureaucratic and Parallel Organizations

Bureaucratic Organization	*Parallel Organization*
routine operations; low uncertainty	problem-solving; high uncertainty
focused primarily on "production"	focused primarily on "organization"
limited opportunities (e.g., promotion)	expandable opportunities [e.g., decision making within the quality circles]
fixed job assignments	flexible [job assignments] —problem identification and [problem] prevention
competency established before assignment	developmental assignment [assignment develops competency]
long chain of command	short chain of command
objectives usually top-down	objectives also bottom-up
rewards: pay and benefits	rewards: recognition, visibility, personal growth, development learning new skills, financial incentives, self-fulfillment
functionally specialized	diagonal slices—mix functions
leadership is a function of level	leadership drawn from any level

Source: B. A. Stein and R.M. Kanter, "Building the Parallel Organization: Creating Mechanisms for Permanent Quality of Work Life," *The Journal of Applied Behavioral Science* 16 (1980): 385.

FIGURE 3–3
Quality Circles Organization

Circles
Three to thirteen members:
identify, analyze and resolve
work-related problems;
implement solutions

Leaders
Direct Circles

Facilitators
Make integration of Program
easier at all levels

Coordinator
Supervises Facilitators and
directs administration
of Program

Steering Committee
Five to fifteen members:
oversee and direct Program

Source: Joseph Hanley, "Our Experience with Quality Circles," *Quality Progress* 13 (February 1980): 24.

central hub. Under its direction, policies and procedures for the program are established and implemented. The committee then oversees the operation period. The committee is normally composed of management and union. For example, at Cordis Dow, the steering committee includes two department managers, a union leader, group leaders, production workers and an engineer.[6]

The *facilitators* are the liaison between the steering committee and circle leaders. They oversee and keep abreast of all activities within the circle for which they are responsible. The number of facilitators within the company depends on the number of circles within the plant.

Circle leaders are responsible for conducting meetings and coordinating the activities of the individual circle. In most cases, under the facilitator's supervision, leaders conduct the training of circle members to ensure that they are knowledgeable in the various methods of identifying, analyzing and resolving problem situations brought before them.

The *coordinator's* position is generally the last to be added. Most companies omit this position, especially if their programs are limited. The coordinator normally supervises the facilitators and provides administrative backing.

Industrial engineers and plant managers continue to have a dominant role in production planning, quality control and coordination. The quality circle organization and the quality control department work together closely in an effort to ameliorate conflict and to attain synergistic results.

The quality circle organization of the Toronto-Dominion Bank, in Toronto, is an excellent example (Figure 3–4). The president, R. W. Korthals, personally oversees the overall activities of the T.D. quality program. The Employee Work Groups (EWG) are coordinated through the steering committee. A full-time coordinator, Ron Sinclair, has been added to assist in the administration of the program. The division support team serves as the in-house consulting team, which is responsible for promoting EWG among management and bank employees. Each branch (such as Bathurst and Steels of the Metro West Division) has a full-time facilitator to provide training, information and resources needed by the groups. Each EWG is made up of six to ten volunteer members who meet, with the group leader, for one to one-and-a-half hours every week.[7]

More detailed studies of two other successful quality circle organizations, Ford Motor Co. of Canada and Vickers, Inc., appear in Chapters 12 and 14.

FIGURE 3–4
Toronto-Dominion Bank Quality Program Organizational Chart

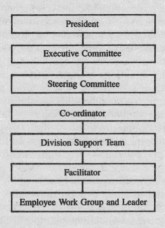

Source: *Toronto-Dominion Quality Programme Introductory Kit* (Toronto: Toronto-Dominion Bank of Canada, 1982): 10.

Involvement of the Union

Because the relationship between companies and unions has been traditionally adversarial, most management teams do not proceed with the implementation of quality circles without consulting and getting the support of the union. To do so would defeat the participative principles which the program is attempting to promote and invite a confrontational approach on cooperative issues. The consultation and involvement begins with the planning phase. Union leaders are invited to encourage their members to join the circles. The majority of union executive officers also provide valuable contributions to make the endeavour successful. Some union officials, however, are cautious about endorsing the plan. They feel that, historically, management almost always has been concerned with increasing productivity and net output. New ideas have been used as gimmicks to trap workers into greater productivity. Management and unions alike, however, do see the importance of a cooperative effort to meet foreign competition, especially that of the Japanese. Because their welfares are intimately intertwined, both groups are more willing to work together. Generally, there is agreement that "something must be done to close the chasm between management and labor in this country. It is an adversarial and counter-productive atmosphere. . . ."[8] Essentially these joint efforts help institutionalize quality circles and protect against their discontinuity.

In a number of companies, management installed circles with only a bare minimum of consultation with unions. When this occurred, union leaders put pressure on workers not to cooperate, and the circle either did not get off the ground or collapsed soon after it had started. On this point, Widtfeldt of Honeywell notes: ". . . we never go into a plant without explaining thoroughly to everyone, union and rank-and-file workers, what QC are all about. There really is nothing about QCC that impinges on the negotiating process in any case."[9] Union participation is critical in making the program successful.

Voluntary Participation

Worker membership in most American quality circles usually is voluntary, but supervisors who appear to have potential as circle leaders are encouraged to participate. In some companies, during pilot runs, management invites selected workers to become members to ensure that the first few circles are successful. Generally there are more than enough initial and new volunteers. At the present time, there is seldom peer pressure to join, as there is in Japan.

Extensive Use of Consultants

In forming quality circles, many American companies ask external management consultants to help in planning, in designing training packages and in providing training for circle facilitators and leaders. Sometimes consultants may act as the "buffer" between management and union in establishing communication and facilitating reconciliation. In a recent survey by the American Management Association, 65 percent of companies surveyed had employed consultants to help on a portion or on all of the circle activity.[10]

White-Collar Circles

A number of firms are experimenting with quality circles for staff, office and professional personnel. Others are establishing union-management circles. Westinghouse. for example, has set up ten white-collar quality circles under the construction group in which controllers, personnel directors and marketing directors discuss common problems with their counterparts in other units. The details of an engineering quality circle at Vickers Inc. are given in Chapter 14.

The concept is even being used in banks. Continental Illinois National Bank and Trust Company of Chicago established a management circle or "horizontal team circle" for managers of eleven divisions to address problems on a departmental scale. These management circles have four main advantages. They:

1. Serve as a model to demonstrate management support.
2. Provide managers with a problem-solving structure.
3. Address problems that cannot be resolved at lower circle levels.
4. Communicate corporate-level goals.[11]

CHARACTERISTICS OF THE QUALITY CIRCLES PROGRAM

Both a quality circle structure and a formal hierarchical structure exist side by side.

Quality circle structure:
• flat
• flexible job assignments
• short chain of command
• bottom-up objectives

- leadership drawn from any level
- rewards are intrinsic

Is part of the total organization but operates independently.

Is organic.

Organization includes
- steering committee
- facilitator
- circle leader
- circle members
- perhaps a coordinator if there are many circles

Union must be involved.

Participation is voluntary.

External consultants are used frequently.

Staff, office and professional circles function in North America.

FACTORS CONTRIBUTING TO PROBLEMS

If there is only one lesson which companies using quality circles have learned, it is that Japanese methods do not work in North America. In order to make the concept workable, adaptation is required. Problems generally occur for one or more of the following reasons: lack of senior management commitment, lack of support of middle management, an adversary relationship between union and management, a poor implementation process, an inadequate clarification of objectives and roles, and inadequate feedback to employees.

Lack of Senior Management Commitment

To every manager who is judged by the bottom line, the idea of improving profits and productivity is tremendously appealing.

Companies too frequently seek an elixir. Success stories regarding quality circles suggest that they may be a magic potion which need only be imbibed. So, a management announcement states that Jason Williams will be in charge of the quality circle program. A bewildered but pleased Williams searches the literature and phones his more knowledgeable friends and acquaintances. The anticipated or fantasized results fail to materialize. Management blames Williams and the program is allowed to die a slow death.

This situation recurs far too frequently. Commitment is more than the budgeting of monies, establishment of committees or recruitment of people to oversee and participate in the meetings. It involves time, interest, a specific management philosophy regarding the worth of employees, and last, but most important, patience.

Many writers have suggested that the key is Theories X and Y versus Theory Z. Theory X and Theory Y are two different beliefs about human nature that *influence* managers to adopt one strategy of managing people rather than another. Theory Z is a management strategy.

Theory X assumes that human nature is basically evil. Employees therefore are indifferent, irresponsible, lazy, untrustworthy and incapable of self-direction and self-control. The manager who subscribes to this theory persuades, rewards, punishes and controls subordinates. McGregor (1960), the originator of the concept, argues that this is the philosophy of most American managers.

Theory Y is a very different philosophy (but not the opposite to Theory X). The assumption is that human nature is basically good. This means that if employees are provided with the right type of opportunities, they will respond in positive and constructive ways and will blend their personal goals with those of the organization.[12]

Basic to Theory Z are three concepts: the collective work ethic, trust and loyalty. At the organizational level, this translates into teamwork, the merging of individual and organizational goals, collective decision making, group sacrifice in times of adversity, and implicit group control of each employee (see Figures 3–5 and 3–6). Theory Z philosophy can be and is practised in North American companies, namely IBM, Intel, Procter and Gamble, and Hewlett-Packard.[13]

To implement Theory Z philosophy throughout a company

requires money, executive time and executive interest. If the program is important at the executive level, it will be important down the hierarchy. If it is not, that message also is transmitted quickly. One of the best methods of transmitting the message is by the assignment of funds—for training, for materials, for learning to use the process, for release time and perhaps to make some mistakes.

Last, but most important, patience is required. An individual must learn to crawl, walk and run before becoming an award-winning athlete. So, too, circle members need time—to absorb the techniques and skills, to learn to work together, to decide on a problem to study, to analyze the issues, to reach a satisfactory consensus, to implement the decision, for the "bugs to be ironed out" and for visible results. This process may take two or three years. If the groundwork is properly laid, subsequent projects will show results after a short time.

What about a pilot project? Pilot projects either do not work, or work too well for all the wrong reasons. When a company begins with a pilot project, it is communicating that it doesn't feel this activity is going to be successful. Such lack of confidence generally is the kiss of death. Sometimes employees, enjoying the attention and limelight which they are receiving, ensure that the experiment is perceived by senior management as a success. That, after all, is what management wants!

What is needed, of course, is the opportunity, every hour of every day, for employees to collaborate in problem-solving situations with the knowledge that they will succeed. What then is in doubt is not whether success will occur but the extent of that success.

Lack of Middle Management Support

For most American managers, the quality circle concept involves an extensive delegation of authority to rank-and-file employees. This delegation means that there is a diffusion of the prerogatives to which management has clung tenaciously in the past. Middle management and industrial engineers especially dislike the idea because they fear a loss of job security. Other managers believe that they have the responsi-

FIGURE 3–5
Douglas McGregor's Theory X and Theory Y Assumptions

Two Sets of Assumptions or Propositions Concerning Management's Task of Harnessing Human Energy to Organizational Requirements

Conventional View: Theory X   A New View. Theory Y

1. *A Proposition Common to Theories X and Y.* Management is responsible for organizing the elements of productive enterprises—money, materials, equipment, people—in the interest of economic ends.

2. With respect to people, this is a process of directing their actions, modifying their behavior to fit the needs of the organization.

2. People are *not* by nature passive, or resistant to organizational needs. They have become so as a result of experience in organizations.

3. Without this active intervention by management, people would be passive—even resistant—to organizational needs. They must therefore be persuaded, rewarded, punished, controlled—their activities must be directed. This is management's task. We often sum it up by saying that management consists of getting things done through people.

3. The motivation, the potential for development, the capacity for assuming responsibility, the readiness to direct behavior toward organizational goals are all present in people. Management does not put them there. It is a responsibility of management to make it possible for people to recognize and develop these human characteristics for themselves.

4. The average man is by nature indolent—he works as little as possible.

4. The essential task of management is to arrange organizational conditions and

methods of operation so that people can achieve their own goals best by directing *their own* efforts toward organizational objectives.

5. He lacks ambition, dislikes responsibility, prefers to be led.
6. He is inherently self-centered, indifferent to organizational needs.
7. He is by nature resistant to change.
8 . He is gullible, not very bright, the ready dupe of the charlatan and the demagogue.

Source: Douglas McGregor, *The Human Side of Enterprise* (New York: McGraw-Hill, 1960).

FIGURE 3–6
Theory Z Management

Comparison of American-Style Management and Japanese Management Using Theory-Z Philosophy

Japanese Organization	*American Organization*
1. Lifetime employment	1. Short-term employment
2. Slow evaluation and promotion	2. Rapid evaluation and promotion
3. Non-specialized career paths	3. Specialized career paths
4. Implicit control mechanisms	4. Explicit control mechanisms
5. Collective decision making	5. Individual decision making
6. Collective responsibility	6. Individual responsibility
7. Holistic concerns	7. Segmented concerns

(cont'd)

Making Theory Z Work

1. Managers should understand Theory-Z organization and individual roles.
2. Periodic audits of company philosophy should be made.
3. The desired philosophy should be defined clearly.
4. The desired philosophy should be implemented by creating both structures and incentives.
5. Employees must be encouraged to develop interpersonal skills. Managers must also develop interpersonal skills.
6. The union should be encouraged to become involved.
7. Stabilize employment through the use of temporary employees. The majority of the work force should be permanent employees.
8. Evaluate employees over a lengthy period of time. No one can perform at one hundred percent level all of the time.
9. Employees should be encouraged to have broad career paths.
10. Managers should seek out areas to implement employee participation.
11. Managers should permit the development of a holistic relationship.

Source: Based on William Ouchi, *Theory Z: How American Business Can Meet the Japanese Challenge* (Reading, MA: Addison-Wesley, 1981).

bility, that they are in control, and that the contribution of workers is marginal. As one manager who was interviewed stated: "I've worked my ass off for fifteen years to get where I am. Why should I give it up? Why should I help some guy who hasn't known the tough times I have to do my job and make me look bad?" As a consequence, they tend to resist introduction of any participatory management.

What can be done to overcome this? A number of ideas come to mind:

1. Fear occurs because of misunderstanding. Thorough training in the philosophy and the process will remove some of the insecurity.

2. Thorough training in quality circle skills needs to be provided for these managers. This will mean that they will be as qualified as are the circle members.

Presently, in most factories, rank-and-file workers learn basic technical skills which assist them in performing their production tasks. They are not trained in problem solving or statistical analysis. This training is reserved (if done at all) for members of the specialized quality control department and for managers.

When circles begin to function, "quality control disciplines" are required. As a consequence, plant workers have the opportunity to learn these techniques. Supervisors, however, are often ignored. The superior knowledge of the workers often adds to the insecurity of the supervisory group.

3. Middle management and engineering staff can be trained for and assume new challenges, jobs and responsibilities. Numerous researchers have shown that power within an organization is not finite.[14] In fact, executives have discovered that the more responsibility they ask subordinates to assume and the more authority they give them, the more powerful and respected they themselves become.[15] The process, of course, must start at the top.

4. Middle management should be encouraged to form its own quality circles.

5. Senior management can make a commitment that no one will be terminated because of quality circle improvements.

Adversarial Relationship Between Management and Union

Management maintains that it is using quality circles in order to humanize the workplace. Unions, however, are nervous and skeptical of this claim. At least four factors, in the past, have impeded labour-management cooperation. First, most older union executive members remember the broken promises of the past. They also are committed to familiar ways and dislike change which threatens their power. Second, they believe managing the company is management's business. In this sense, leaders feel it best to remain aloof from management because unions have no real control over final decisions. Third, in the fear that they will be seen as being "in management's pocket" and fail to win re-election, union leaders are discouraged from establishing too close or too compatible a relationship with management. Fourth, most unions feel that improving productivity implies line "speed-up" and hence layoffs and decreased union membership. Finally, the popularity of quality of working life (QWL) programs with many non-union corporations has reinforced the feeling that keeping unions out is the real "hidden agenda" of QWL and QC programs. Typically, most American managers have shown little concern for their employees. As observers of labour-management issues often note: "The two sides of the American industrial equation are workers to be exploited by managers and managers to be sabotaged by workers." In this atmosphere, it is extremely difficult, but necessary, to promote a harmonious relationship and a feeling of trust. Management, because company well-being is its responsibility, has the onus of establishing open communications between management, workers and the worker representatives.

Implementation Process

Other reasons why quality circles experience problems have to do with the implementation process:

1. The training of members in analytical skills and, more importantly, in interpersonal skills, is superficial. Sometimes, an organization makes the mistake of training only leaders. It then expects the leaders to train circle members. The ability to train and to prepare educational materials are specialized skills. This, for the majority of individuals, requires many years to develop. Confidence is difficult to attain. Circle leaders generally do not have these skills. The leader must also know when to provide training. If the leader provides it at a time when it is not needed, he or she is "hogging the show"; if, on the other hand, it is to be provided at the exact time that it is required, the leader must be infinitely ready—a task which is viewed with misgivings by even professional trainers!

2. Training of management is at the orientation level, and these members do not understand the process or the difficulties. If management is truly committed, it can show this by being willing to participate in the full training program. It must be remembered that, in Japan, presidents and rank-and-file employees, even of large corporations, study the same topics. This suggestion is not as unreasonable or time-consuming

as it might seem. Members of management, because they are more experienced and better educated, require a much shorter time to learn the same skills.

3. A poor choice of facilitator is made. The facilitator must be the type of person who is capable of training and developing people. The preferred individual is one who can assist in the "processes" and leave "content" to those who are more closely associated with the problem. Also, facilitators may become overextended. There may be too many circles within the organization for one facilitator to coordinate. To make matters worse, because of their skills, these people are invited to become external consultants to suppliers and consumers of the organization.

The conflict-of-interest issue may be one problem. A second one is that the overextended facilitator is not available when required and is unable, physically and emotionally, to provide the type of assistance and support that a circle leader and members may require.

4. A poor choice of members for the steering committee is made. As pointed out previously, the steering committee is key to the success of the program. It follows therefore that the members must be committed to its philosophy and concepts and that all major interested parties must be represented. If the union and the shop-floor workers participate in top-level decisions that affect them, they will feel more committed to the process.[16]

An interesting and novel approach to this problem has been adopted by Cumis Insurance Company, of Burlington, Ontario. Ernie Long, the company's former facilitator, reports:

> We have provided some flexibility in the membership of the steering committee. Each circle elects one representative to sit on the committee. With five permanent members, this may appear cumbersome. In reality, it works well; the actual size of the committee rarely exceeds ten. Circle members tend to go to a committee meeting only when they have a vested interest in the agenda. The advantage, however, is that each circle knows that it can influence decisions insofar as they could be affected by the decisions.[17]

Lack of Readiness

Some external consultants, particularly those who have been trained in quality of working life methodology, insist that an organization must be "ready"—that an atmosphere of trust and willingness to cooperate must exist before a quality circle program is started. Of course, the probability that a program will succeed is enhanced when these preconditions exist. As the study, reported later in this book, of Ford Motor Co. of Canada indicates, improvement in relationships and cost-saving benefits can occur even if the organizational climate is not ideal.[18] Key management, union personnel and circle participants must be willing, however, to expend the time and effort required to make quality circles work. Without either climate or commitment, the circle program will be in difficulty.

Objectives and Roles

A frequently heard complaint of circle members is that the organization has not implemented problem solutions that have been suggested. Generally, however, there is another side to the story. The quality circle has extended itself beyond its authority and boundaries and has made decisions regarding work and practices which were not directly within its control and of which it had little first-hand knowledge. The issue is further complicated by the fact that those who were not only most knowledgeable but also most affected by the decision were not consulted. Such a solution can lead only to disappointment and disillusionment with the process; it cannot be implemented.

To avoid problems of this type, it should not be assumed that circle members can set objectives and roles that are compatible with quality circle principles. Of course, they can be taught to do so. At the beginning, however, circle objectives and roles, together with guidelines, should be clarified and clearly communicated prior to the inauguration of the first circle. If these are broad in scope, they will not be stifling or overly restrictive and will permit the circles to learn and grow on their own. Generally, this is the role of the steering committee. The facilitator may be required to explain tactfully why a circle cannot ''solve'' a particular problem or to ensure that appropriate steps are taken to include those who will be affected by the decision. In the long run, each circle should be permitted to determine its own roles and objectives within the broader organizational framework which has been determined by the steering committee.

Feedback

A recent study of a large Michigan heavy equipment firm[19] indicates that a quality circle program within the company can be extremely successful but may not be perceived as successful. In this company, substantial cost savings were occurring, quality was improving, and attitudes toward the organization of those who were participating in quality circles had improved. Suggestions were also being implemented. Of course QC members knew about the success of their own limited improvements. Since they did not hear otherwise, they assumed that the activities of their circle were the only benefit to the company and that the program was not a company-wide success. Unfortunately, because of a lack of recognition and because the program did not appear to be important to the company, a number of participants became discouraged and stopped attending meetings.

Management, in this case, made a deliberate decision not to publicize QC improvements. The company wanted to play down the quantitative aspects of the success and preferred that attitudinal changes evolve slowly. Of course, there is merit in this viewpoint. In this case, however, employees within the firm, other than those who were involved in quality circles, were not aware that a quality circles program existed.

What has been described is a frequent problem. The steering committee and the facilitator are so busy making the program function satisfactorily that they forget that feedback and recognition also are important to the success of their efforts.

FACTORS WHICH CONTRIBUTE TO PROBLEMS

Lack of senior management commitment. For success:
- Management must believe employees want to do and can do a responsible job.
- Money is required.
- Executive time is required.
- Patience is required.

Lack of middle management support. To overcome this:
- Thorough training is needed.
- New challenges should be assigned to this group.
- A promise should be made that there will be no terminations because of quality circle improvements.
- Management should receive training similar to that which quality circle members receive.
- Management should be encouraged to form its own quality circles.

Management has responsibility to improve the adversarial relationship which exists between management and union. Reasons for distrust on the part of the union include:
- Past trickery.
- Old habits.
- Role differences.
- Fear of not being re-elected.
- Feeling that quality circles are just another method for obtaining increased productivity without benefit to workers.

Implementation process is poor. Present practices should be improved. These include:
- Training of circle participants is minimal.
- Training of management is at orientation level.
- Poor choice of facilitator is made.
- Poor choice of members for steering committee is made.
- Lack of readiness.
- Feedback inadequate.
- Objectives and roles are unspecified.

FOUR

A COMPARISON OF JAPAN AND NORTH AMERICA

DIFFERENCES AND SIMILARITIES

Before a system that works in one culture can be transferred and translated into a second culture, it is important to understand the differences and similarities between the two cultures. The Japanese culture is fundamentally a paternalistic one; the American culture is based on middle-class entrepreneurial values. The dominant goal of the key elite in Japan is the preservation of the traditional society; in America, it is individual self-advancement.

It must be remembered also that, for the most part, the Japanese people are radically homogeneous. This contrasts with the American melting pot of nations. Many Americans retain the national cultures and values of their immigrant ancestors. Superimposed on this are dominant racial groups. In the United States, people of black and of Spanish ancestry have distinct cultures. In particular geographical areas, these cultures are the majority. Canada has its French and native cultures. Heterogeneity means that there exists a large variety, not only of different cultures and values, but of very different methods and argots. Even communication can be a problem.

Values and Human Relations

There are important value differences between the American and Japanese cultures. Japanese firms are people centered, not task centered. This does not mean that production is unimportant. On the contrary: the paternalism, the group values and the company dependency of employees ensures that the company and its productivity are uppermost in the minds of employees (See Table 4–1).

Also, Japan is a small nation with a large population. People live in relatively crowded quarters. Because of this, group and community interests are paramount, and cooperation and harmony are stressed. In addition, the extended family and the traditional benevolence of Japanese firms provides greater security and less necessity for a keenly competitive individual work orientation. As one writer explains:

TABLE 4–1
A Comparison of Japanese and American Systems

Values and Human Relations

Japanese	*American*
Basic value and strategy of key people is preservation of traditional society.	Basic value and strategy of key people is individual self-advancement.
Homogeneous race of people.	Heterogeneous peoples.
Extended family system.	Nuclear family system.
Education system is very specialist oriented and geared to life's work; education is key to access of prestige and initial position.	Education system is liberal in nature; education is key to vertical mobility.
Closed social system; class structure is rigid.	Open social system; class structure is fluid.

Social and economic status are dependent on traditional organization standards. Organization for which one works and "school ties" are extremely important. Little job mobility.	Social and economic status are dependent on size of organization and on hierarchical level attained. "School ties" of some importance. Through ability and entrepreneurship can attain wealth and prestige; therefore intense individual competition.
Company interests supersede family interests.	Purpose of life resides in the family and in leisure.
Groupism, i.e., the group comes first; the individual is devoted and loyal to the group. Mutual dependence and *schicksalgemeinschaft* consciousness.	Individualism, i.e., ultimate value is on the individual; devotion and loyalty to the group are weak.
Blending of the firm's goals and the individual's life goals. Sense of being, prestige, security and morale tied to company and to company's prestige and prosperity.	To the individual, the firm is nothing more than a means to obtain wages. To the firm, the individual is a resource similar to machinery or raw materials.
Stress on harmony in human relations (emphasis on warm human relations, mutual consent of all members, and community relationships).	Human relations are artificial relations for work purposes; cease outside the company.
Egalitarianism in substance (little chance for class discrimination; small earnings differentials).	Egalitarianism in theory (strong class consiousness; competition for equal opportunity).

chial management in Japan retains the socially re-
able characteristic of the traditional kinship system.
Although it gives little encouragement to individualists and
indeed individualism is frowned upon if not actually punished, each member of the organization is regarded as an
integral and important cog in the functioning of the whole
enterprise. Conformity to the purpose of the unit rests
upon fostering and structuring the situation to achieve
complete identification between superior and subordinate.[1]

Japanese people accept their role within society. The social
system is closed, and the class structure is rigid. Education,
therefore, is important in assisting an individual to obtain a
managerial position with the most prestigious government
organizations, banks and companies.[2] This keen competitiveness begins with kindergarten. If one goes to the best kindergarten and is successful, one can go to the best primary
school, to the best junior school, the best high school, and the
high-status universities such as Tokyo Imperial University.
The high suicide rate among the young has been directly
attributed to the competitiveness of the educational system
and of family expectations.[3]

In North America, by contrast, the nuclear family is important and life is directed toward the family. An open social
system exists and, except in the minds of the "old families,"
is extremely fluid. Instant status and prestige can be achieved
by becoming "nouveau riche" through ability and through
entrepreneurship. Also, America is a relatively new nation
which was built on the rugged individualism of its pioneers.
Individual accomplishment has always been glorified and rewarded. There is little incentive for group-mindedness. Equal
opportunity, at least in theory, is available to each person
within the North American system.

The wage system also rewards individualism. Unions have
ensured that the worker is paid relatively well and that the
work is not too difficult. Incentive and bonus systems, except
at upper echelons of an organization, are not common. Group
incentives are seldom paid. As a consequence, no reason
exists for employees to cooperate and to work together.

The education system prepares people, in the English tradition, not to be workers, but, through its general approach, to
be leaders and managers. The education system itself is not

highly competitive; instead, the self-fulfillment and development of the individual is stressed. Funding, through loans and grants, is available to help all who have demonstrated minimal qualifications to attend a university or a college.

Company management also has a different value orientation regarding employees—they are considered a replaceable and dispensable resource, just one cog in a multi-cog production process. It is not surprising therefore that relationships established between employees within the company are work related and not social in nature. The company is a place to obtain wages to purchase more valued commodities.

In summary, the Japanese system tries to preserve the existing society. Groupism and stress on harmony in human relations is important. The mutual dependence and the group-value consciousness means that individual goals and organizational goals blend. In North America, acceptance of the firm's goals by employees is rare. There is a stress on the individual, and on improving one's own well-being. The social system is fluid, and "school ties" are of only minor importance.

VALUE SYSTEMS

	Japan	*North America*
Key strategy	Paternalism	Entrepreneurship
People	Homogeneous	Heterogeneous
Basic concern	People	Tasks
Orientation	Group and harmony	Individual
Social system	Closed and rigid	Open and fluid
Family	Extended	Nuclear
Education	Specialized	Liberal
Employees' feelings about firm	Oneness with firm	Place to earn money

Management Relations
...ս Personnel Systems

What do these values and human relations practices mean in terms of labour-management relations and the personnel systems that exist?

Labour-Management Relations. In Japan, unions are company unions (Table 4–2). For the most part, there is cooperation between the executive members and management. Conflict is abhorred, and the union assumes the role of keeping workers in line. The union also organizes social functions. Wage negotiations do not cause problems at the workplace; negotiations occur on a national basis during the *Shunto* (spring wage offensive). Strikes are political in nature and of short duration, and occur during employees' lunch hours or in their own time after work. Few work rules are written into the "collective agreement"; because management has all the rights, only general rules exist. Trust between union executive members and management and between management and workers is nurtured. This means that there is a desire to experiment, to innovate and to learn together. In short, in the majority of manufacturing companies, Japanese unions do not impose a constraint on management.

For North American managers, this approach on the part of unions would be akin to paradise. North American unions are organized by craft, industry or discipline, and generally there is more than one union (or at least more than one local branch of a union) in each company. Each union or local protects its own members and its own work territory. Strikes, when they occur, are directed against the management of the organization and tend to close the plant. After a strike begins, the union-management relationship tends to deteriorate, and bargaining positions become more rigid. As a consequence, strikes in North America tend to be of long duration. Some have lasted six months, eight months or even a year.

The union may organize social functions; its primary purpose, however, is to attain a reasonable portion of the gains in productivity and to protect individual rights. Since conflict between union and management is expected, a set of ground rules has been established by which both parties agree to abide. Negotiations are conducted at a national or local level—if the company is large, at both levels. To protect the rights of workers, a grievance and arbitration process exists. To ensure equity at the workplace, a detailed set of rules has been established. Most of these are negotiated, but management, through the "residual rights of management," can specify additional regulations. If the union believes these regulations are unjust, it can grieve them. Bargaining power, game playing, and "fishmarket haggling" strategies create an adversarial relationship where suspicion and distrust abound. Unions do impose a constraint on management (Table 4–2).

TABLE 4–2
A Comparison of Japanese and American Systems

Personnel Systems and Labour-Management Relations

Japanese	*American*
In the large firms, there is lifelong employment, i.e., there are no layoffs. Flexibility is gained through part-time and temporary employees.	Employment of people only at times when needed; layoffs in recessionary times.
Seniority-based promotion system. Evaluations for promotions are comprehensive and stress not only work results but incentive, effort and perceived capability.	Seniority system at times of promotion and layoffs at lower levels. Political system in promotion at upper management levels.
Career progress is slow.	Career progress rapid in early years.
Wage system is based on seniority and age. About one-third of wages are based on bonus system which depends on profitability of the company.	Wages are based on classification, position, negotiating ability and power. Incentive systems are rare.

(con'td)

Japanese	*American*
Enterprise assumes obligation for welfare and benefits.	Pension and welfare plans regulated by government and subject to negotiation.
Extensive mobility within organization. Little mobility to different organizations; individual is dependent on company.	Extensive mobility; individual is independent of company.
Extensive employee training and education; training is work directed.	Training and education is primarily responsibility of the individual; reimbursement of expenditures often possible.
Employees are generalists.	Employees are specialists.
Acceptance of robots, innovation and decreases in number of employees.	Resistance to robotics, innovation and decrease in number of employees.
Labour unions are organized by company; cooperation between labour and management.	Labour unions are organized by craft and job type; unions safeguard the rights of the individual.
Role of unions—social functions, keeping workers in line; little constraint on management.	Role of unions—political in nature, keeps management honest at the local level; protects rights of individual worker; considerable constraint on management.
Nature of conflict—political strikes, of short duration, on worker's own time.	Nature of conflict—strikes against enterprise to gain concessions; could be lengthy in nature.
Conflict abhorred; unions participate in management through labour-management councils, etc.	Conflict accepted within rules of game; much tension in labour-management relationships.

Japanese	*American*
Spring wage offensive (*Shunto*) at a national level.	Negotiations every 1 to 3 years at national and local level.
General rules at workplace.	Detailed rules at workplace mostly specified in the collective agreement.
Trust nurtured.	Adversarial relationship nurtured.
Desire to experiment and learn together.	Games of one-upmanship.

Personnel Systems. In large companies in Japan, there is lifelong employment; that is, permanent employees are not laid off or terminated. Incompetent employees are given less desirable and less challenging tasks or assigned to smaller firms. Flexibility is gained through the use of part-time and temporary workers. Usually, workers over the age of fifty-five (fifty-seven in some firms) and women are temporary workers.

Large Japanese industries practice a just-in-time inventory policy, that is, they minimize the

> time from initial entry of parts and raw materials to their actual use. As much as possible, in-process stocks [are] eliminated or reduced to the absolute minimum. Both inventory costs and labor time on materials handling are considered as surplus and thus waste.[4]

This means that fewer people are hired in materials management, and that employees in small or supplier firms could be subject to greater employment variability depending on the needs of the large firm.

Career progress is slow. Evaluation of employees is lifelong and promotion is based on work results, employee incentive and effort, perceived capability and seniority. Older workers are given preference over young workers for promotion. This leads to some dissatisfaction among the younger men. In spite of this, there is no mobility of managerial employees to competitive organizations and little from one large firm to another large firm. The mobility that does occur is among younger employees who transfer from the large enterprise to smaller firms—usually subsidiaries of the parent company.

This does not mean that employees become narrowly specialized. There are extensive training and education programs within the enterprise. Transfers from one functional area to another functional area within the company are frequent. Employees therefore become generalist, knowing a great amount about the entire organization, rather than specialists, who know almost everything about a particular aspect of operations. When jobs are eliminated, workers are retrained and placed in new positions.

Japan is also unique in its approach to compensation. The employees' welfare and benefits are the responsibility of the enterprise. Wages are based on seniority, position, age and need. About one-third of the wages are dependent on the company bonus system. The bonus system depends, in turn, on the profitability of the firm. This means that the financial well-being of the employee's family, its self-esteem and its prestige depend upon the success of the firm.

It is not surprising in this environment that employees should accept organizational goals, robotics and innovation and not resist the elimination of jobs and the retraining of employees.

In contrast, in North America the Protestant work ethic is important. Workers are given the opportunity to work and to receive wages that will provide them with a life of dignity and comfort. They are, however, engaged on a contractual basis and are retained on the payroll only as long as the company is profitable and their services are required.

Career progress is relatively rapid in the early years. Promotion is on the basis of seniority at lower levels, and on a political basis at the upper levels. While performance appraisals exist, these are subjective in nature and often lack validity and reliability. Their usefulness is therefore limited. As a result, selection for promotion is based on the key organizations which the individual has joined, the activities which have been performed and a variety of personal characteristics such as the ability to enhance the career of some senior official.

Dissatisfied employees join competitor firms and other allied companies. Training and education are the responsibility of the individual. Companies do have some internal training programs, and unions have negotiated for reimbursement of educational expenditures. Generally, specialized training is important and employees tend to remain in one, perhaps two, specialized disciplines during their career with an organization.

Wages are based on classification, on position within the hierarchy and on the individual's or union's negotiating ability and power. Benefits and pension plans are regulated by governments and are subject to negotiation between management and the union.

Unions make the argument that a resistance to innovation and change (for example, the use of robotics) is built into this "dog-eat-dog" system. Productivity increases through technology or innovation generally come at the expense of jobs. As one manager so aptly put it, "Oh, we don't want the [products] to be defect free. If there aren't enough repairs, we'll lose employees. Already we have lost two this year."

Summary. Japanese unions cooperate with enterprise management. Trust is nurtured. The relationship between North American unions and management is more likely to be adversarial in nature.

The personnel systems of the two countries are also very different. Career progress is slow in Japan, rapid in North America. Promotions in Japan are based on a lifelong evaluation system; in North America, they are based on political considerations. Wages in Japan are a combination of salary (based on seniority, age, need and position) and bonus. In North America, salary is based on discipline, level within the organization, seniority and negotiating ability and power. Japanese enterprises train their workers; in North America, training is each person's own responsibility. While Japanese employees accept innovations, robotics and retraining, North American employees, perceiving that their jobs will be threatened, resist them.

Organizational Structure and Managerial Practices

The organizational structure and the managerial philosophy in Japan are different from those of North America (see Table 4–3).

LABOUR-MANAGEMENT RELATIONS

	Japan	*North America*
Union	Company	Craft, industrial, by discipline
Conflict	Abhorred	Expected within rules of game
Role	Keep workers in line	Protect work of members
	Plan social functions	Protect rights of individuals
		Obtain gains of productivity
Wage negotiations	National	National and local
Strikes	Limited	Prolonged
	Political	Against management
	On workers' own time	Close plant
Rules at workplace	General	Detailed
Trust	Extended and nurtured	At times and in certain organizations, non-existent
Strategy	Build trust	Power and game playing
Constraint on management	No	Yes

PERSONNEL SYSTEMS

	Japan	*North America*
Employment	Lifelong for permanent employees Temporary work force	Contractual
Career progress	Slow	Fast
Mobility to other firms	Minimal	Considerable
Mobility between functions	Considerable	Limited
Orientation	Generalist	Specialist
Wages	Salary and bonus	Salary; based on negotiating power
Training	Extensive programs	Responsibility of individual

TABLE 4–3
A Comparison of Japanese and American Systems (Organizational Structure and Managerial Principles)

Japanese	*American*
Organizational Structure	
Organization is people centered, not functionalism centered.	Organization is production oriented. People are a dispensable commodity.
Firm is a partnership among shareholders, managers and workers. Stress is on cooperative teamwork.	Work system is based upon individual input. Jobs are specialized through design, and each individual does only own job.
Indeterminate and fluid job descriptions; a generalist orientation.	Clearly defined job descriptions, authority and responsibility; specialist orientation.
Every worker is an inspector.	Inspection teams are built into the work staff.
Japanese-style adaptation of modern bureaucracy. Few staff resources which are isolated from line functions. "Desk" jobs integrated fully into line management. First-line supervisors report directly to plant managers.	Pyramid-shaped bureaucracy. Many staff departments and "desk" jobs. Supervisors never report directly to plant managers.
Key managerial positions are preserved for family members or "the school" graduates.	Key managerial positions are political in nature.
Managerial Practices	
Management has long time horizons.	Management has short time horizons.

(cont'd)

71

Japanese	*American*
Long-range planning. Labour is a fixed cost, therefore production and marketing strategy must be carefully determined.	Many fire-fighting and crisis-coping techniques.
Harmony and stability emphasized.	Creativity and environmental coping emphasized.
At workplace, worker is treated as an equal. Kept informed of prices, technological advances, competition.	Management feels that shop-floor worker lacks intelligence, is incapable of contributing and is unwilling to do so.
Paternalistic concern for welfare of subordinates and ensuring that individuals can "save face."	Concern for self-preservation (colloquially known as "covering your ass").
Emphasis on production— cost economy, quality control and product simplicity.	Emphasis on marketing and creating a changing consumer need.
Experience curves and product cycles are linked.	Experience curves are a marketing tool.
Quantity of suggestions is important. Training assists employees to improve suggestions. Ninety percent are usable.	Quality of suggestions is important. Few suggestions are used.
"Work smarter, nor harder" philosophy.	Work hard and be consistently perfect.

The Japanese firm is a partnership among shareholders, managers and workers. People are important. They in turn ensure that productivity occurs. Few employees work in a purely staff function; the "desk" jobs have been integrated

72

fully into line management. Job descriptions are very fluid; every worker shares responsibility for all the jobs that must be done. A good example of this is the fact that every worker is an inspector. Also the formal organizational hierarchy is much flatter; the first level supervisor reports directly to the plant manager.

North American firms, by contrast, are production oriented. Employees are dispensable. The structure is tall and pyramid-shaped. This bureaucracy has many staff positions and "desk" jobs. Responsibility, authority, and jobs are clearly defined. Too, jobs are highly specialized. Each employee therefore feels responsible only for his or her own task. Inspection teams and quality control units try to ensure that standards are maintained.

Managerial principles under which companies in the two countries function are in many ways bipolar. In Japan, harmony and stability in operations are emphasized. The Japanese also have a longer-term outlook. Because labour is a fixed cost, a production and marketing strategy that maximizes this resource over the long run must be determined. At the workplace, workers are treated as partners. They are kept informed of technological advances, competitors' strategies, prices and other marketing and production matters which concern "their" product.

The suggestion systems is vital to productivity goals. Quantity, not importance, of suggestions is stressed. As a consequence, the number of suggestions received is high. Toyota, for example, received 17.9 suggestions per employee in 1980 and adopted close to 90 percent of these. This compares to a meagre 0.84 suggestions per employee per year and an adoption rate of 23 percent for General Motors Corporation. In Japan, financial incentives for suggestions are small (ranging from a few dollars to less than five hundred dollars). In 1980, for example, for 25 million suggestions worth 10 billion dollars annually, companies paid only four billion dollars.[5]

At Nissan Chemical, for the first five years in which an *Ai* (all members' ideas) movement has been in operation, the return on investment has been considerable. For the first three years, the movement produced 928 suggestions for a total cost savings of 600 million yen ($2,400,000 U.S.). The implementation cost was only 125 million yen ($500,000 U.S.)—an ROI of 5:1. In 1981, 987 proposals realized a cost savings of 630 million yen ($2,520,000 U.S.) on an expenditure of 160 million yen ($640,000 U.S.). This ROI was better than 4:1. At the time of writing, management's target cost savings for 1982 was the equivalent of $4 million on an investment of $800,000. It appears that suggestion systems are good business in Japan.[6]

Production, with its corresponding emphasis on cost economy, quality control, and product simplicity, is more important than marketing. One of the techniques used for this purpose links product life cycle and economies of scale. McMillan explains this concept (experience curves) thus:

> . . . indicates that not only do total average costs per unit decline logarithmically with each doubling of output, but also that fast growth produces a learning effect . . . there is more widespread understanding . . . [that] aggressive marketing in foreign markets can improve productivity and unit cost structures.[7]

The Japanese management philosophy can be summed up in two mottos, "be prepared for the future" and "work smarter, not harder."

North American management normally has short time horizons and emphasizes creativity and coping. A large amount of managerial time is spent fire fighting and managing crises. Because responsibility lies with one individual, in some companies considerable time is spent in self-preservation (i.e., in ensuring that if something goes wrong, the manager cannot be blamed for it).

The marketing department is key in any consumer-oriented organization. An emphasis is placed on creating consumer demand for a current product and ensuring that this preference changes as the product changes.

Since management frequently believes that shop-floor workers lack intelligence, are incapable of contributing to improving the company, and, in any event, are unwilling to do so, the idea is that workers should work mechanically—hard, consistently and accurately. The following statement by a young training director is typical of this attitude: "Those dumb girls can't be taught anything; they do nothing right." Many of those "dumb girls" were thirty-five to fifty-five years old, ran successful households, managed investment portfolios, had responsible positions within community clubs and projects, had worked with the company for many years and probably knew more about the company than the young training director did. It did not occur to the company that employees at all levels require an opportunity to express an opinion and have a decision-making role in the work they do.

So, the prince found Cinderella (well, quality circles) and everyone lived happily ever after? No. Unfortunately, the management of that large, successful, well-known company, whose net profits are dropping, and the management of many other companies are still convinced that their management people have all the answers and that their shop-floor people do not understand the problem and could not and would not contribute to its solution if they did.

Perhaps a more receptive suggestion system might help. In North America, substantial compensation (e.g., a new car; up to $20,000) can be received for a quality suggestion. In spite of this, most companies receive relatively few usable suggestions. The organizational structure and process often hinder suggestion submission. One young man expressed the feelings of many North American employees with this story:

> My suggestion was accepted. I received $5,000 in company shares or in a bond—my choice. Wow, was I happy—until the end of the month. I had chosen a bond but discovered that I could not cash it for six months. In the meantime, income tax deductions for the additional $5,000 of income were being taken from my paycheque. I'll never write another suggestion!

The stories and the reasons differ but the conclusion is the same: No more suggestions!

It is unlikely that the Japanese have more intelligent and conscientious employees than can be found in North America. It is more likely that the Japanese have a structure and managerial practices that encourage employees to be concerned and contribute to the company. North American systems appear to encourage the opposite—apathy and lack of commitment.

Decision Making

In Japan, collective, bottom-up consensus decision making occurs. Everyone who is affected by the decision studies the problem and the implications. There is a shared search for information and optimal solutions. A great deal of behind-the-scenes manoeuvring occurs. Since harmony is valued, compromises are made. This is most visible in the collusive type of relationship that exists between government, business and labour. Although the study of a problem takes a considerable length of time, once the decision has been made, implementation occurs quickly.

In North America, strategy, policies and goals are determined at the upper echelons of the organization. The goals of the more senior levels are then accomplished in an end-means chain: the end (assignment) of the senior level becomes the means (tasks to be accomplished) of the lower level.

Power, nature and scope of decision making increase as position within the hierarchy becomes more senior. At the shop-floor and first supervisory levels, the individuals are responsible only for their specific tasks. Design engineers, who may or may not be familiar with the work tasks, have simplified these jobs so that there is a need to perform and not make decisions. The decision to implement an innovation is relatively rapid; the change process itself often meets with considerable resistance. Greater detail regarding decision making is given in Table 4–4.

TABLE 4–4

A Comparison of Japanese and American Systems (Decision Making and Communication)

Japanese	*American*
Collective decision making (bottom-up consensus-type decision making as seen in the *ringi* system, proposal system, etc.).	Top-down decision making and one-way orders. Little consideration given to opinions at the lower echelons; end-means chain.

76

Verbal and nonverbal communication (*nemawashi* or behind-the-scenes manoeuvres; information transmitted by implicit understanding, gut decisions, etc.).

Autocratic authority of the top; expanded power of the bureaucracy.

Collective work performance systems (common room system; total membership participation and planning).

Individual work performance.

Exemption from responsibility (seat of authority is obscure; no one and everyone takes responsibility).

Individual responsibility and scapegoating.

Separation of ownership and management. Real power lies with operatives.

Strong owner pressure. The company president is a hired hand who can be terminated.

Shared search for information and optimal solutions.

Segregated responsibility for information search and optimal solutions.

"Japan, Inc." (collusive relationship of government, business and labour).

Insistence on and protection of individual rights through all means, including legal.

MANAGEMENT AND THE ORGANIZATION

	Japan	*North America*
Job descriptions	Fluid	Rigid
	Worker responsible for all jobs	Worker responsible for one job

(con'd)

	Japan	*North America*
Structure	Flat bureaucracy	Tall pyramidal bureaucracy
	Few desk jobs	Desk jobs often exceed production jobs
Outlook	Long term	Fire fighting
	Production stressed	Marketing stressed
Worker	Partner in production	Poor substitute for a machine
Suggestions	Quantity encouraged	Quality stressed
	Little financial incentive	Large financial incentives
	Many received	Few received
	Majority implemented	Few implemented

DECISION MAKING

	Japan	*North America*
Process of deciding	Bottom-up	Top-down
	All who are affected are involved	
	Slow	Rapid
Implementation	Rapid	Difficult

DEMING'S PRINCIPLES

No discussion of what American industry can learn from the Japanese would be complete without reference to the fourteen principles established by the father of the quality control movement, Dr. W. Edwards Deming (see Table 4–5).

Deming feels that managers must learn to plan for the future. The company must know where it wishes to be in ten, twenty or more years and must be willing to reallocate resources and to be innovative in using these resources. Part of the reallocation involves a new philosophy regarding what is acceptable. No company, to be competitive, can function with the level of mistakes, defects, unsuitable materials, untrained employees, incompetent management and antiquated training methods that have been acceptable in the past. A second part of this reallocation involves the elimination of quality control offices. Instead, Deming suggests, every employee should be trained in statistical process control. A third part of this reallocation involves suppliers. The number of companies which provide the same part or material to the company must be minimized. Only those suppliers who have accepted the new philosophy and who apply statistical process control should be retained.

The reallocation cannot occur without recognizing certain fundamentals. First, two sources of problems exist. The system contributes 85 percent of these and employees contribute 15 percent. It makes sense, therefore, to concentrate on the "important many instead of the trivial few." Second, a new emphasis on thorough job-related training and on modern training techniques is required. This massive training of all employees must be general in nature and must emphasize statistical techniques and good supervision. And retraining must ensure that employees do not become obsolete and they can keep up with changes in materials, methods, styles, models and new equipment.

TABLE 4–5
Fourteen Obligations of Top Management (Dr. W. Edwards Deming)

---

1. Innovate and allocate resources to fulfill the long-range needs of the company and customer rather than short-term profitability.

2. Discard the old philosophy of accepting defective products.

3. Eliminate dependence on mass inspection for quality control; instead depend on process control, through statistical techniques.

4. Reduce the number of multiple source suppliers. Price has no meaning without an integral consideration for quality. Encourage suppliers to use statistical process control.

(cont'd)

5. Use statistical techniques to identify the two sources of waste—the system (85 percent) and local faults (15 percent); strive to constantly reduce this waste.

6. Institute more thorough, better job-related training.

7. Provide supervision with knowledge of statistical methods; encourage use of these methods to identify which defects should be investigated for solution.

8. Reduce fear throughout the organization by encouraging open, two-way, nonpunitive communication. The economic loss resulting from fear to ask questions or report trouble is appalling.

9. Help reduce waste by encouraging design, research and sales people to learn more about the problems of production.

10. Eliminate the use of goals and slogans to encourage productivity, unless training and management support is also provided.

11. Closely examine the impact of work standards. Do they consider quality or help anyone do a better job? They often act as an impediment to productivity improvement.

12. Institute rudimentary statistical training on a broad scale.

13. Institute a vigorous program for retraining people in new skills, to keep up with changes in materials, methods, product designs, and machinery.

14. Make maximum use of statistical knowledge and talent in your company.

Summarized by Ford Product Quality Office Manufacturing Staff, April 28, 1981.

As a consequence of the new emphasis on training, statistics can be used to determine whether the fault lies with the system or the worker, and supervisors can have time to help employees to do the job for which they were hired. People must also be made to feel secure rather than afraid. Deming maintains that in American industry at the present time, employees, even those in management, do not understand what their job is, how to do it correctly, or who to ask. Many, in fact, are afraid to ask questions or to report trouble. The training of generalists, rather than specialists, is important because employees need to understand the problems of other departments and of the organization as a whole rather than just the problems of one department.

A third fundamental which management must recognize is that the work standards within the organization must be examined carefully to ensure that quality has top emphasis. Numerical goals, slogans and posters do not accomplish this and should be eliminated. In fact, states Deming, these are just indications of managerial incompetence.

In summary, Deming feels that management must create the type of work environment that ensures that employees who have the statistical and work skills that are needed are permitted and assisted in doing the work for which they are employed.

SUMMARY

In summary, what can be learned from the Japanese and what role can quality circles play in bringing about changes to assist North American industries, if not to re-establish market supremacy, at least to be competitive?

First, Japanese methods cannot and must not be accepted without adapting them to North American culture and circumstances.

Second, managerial attitudes toward quality control and shop-floor and other blue- and white-collar workers must change. Management must recognize that each worker, even if only in some small way, can contribute to solving problems that affect the company and him or her directly. The quality circle approach is a good beginning.

Third, large companies must accept the responsibility of better training their employees and the challenge of assisting educational institutions in the education of graduates in workplace human relations and human resource management.

Fourth, a careful examination must be made of the collective bargaining process. The old adversarial methods may have been adequate in the days when workers were uneducated and the issues were simple. It does not appear to be the answer today. This is not to suggest that unions must make the concessions. That would not work; owners and managers of many companies have a history of dishonest manipulations. The alternative is that companies should make concessions. That is a possibility, but short-term gains may mean long-term losses. The failure to remain competitive may mean that the company will fail and all jobs will be lost. The key, then, is for the parties to develop trust and to search for solutions that are in both their best interests.

But developing trust is no easy chore. Perhaps it may be accomplished only by changing attitudes, values, and philosophies and by changing structures. On the other hand, perhaps trust can be accomplished more simply—by getting to know each other and by setting aside the stereotypes that are held. By working together, by solving problems together, by helping one another, opportunities arise to understand each other. Quality circles can assist this process.

Unfortunately, there is no cookbook formula and no right answers. The direction is one which each organization and its employees must choose. For many companies and their workers, however, there is a wrong answer—to continue in the present manner. Continuation will bring the inevitable—the inability to remain competitive and to keep jobs.[8]

PART II

THE
IMPLEMENTATION
PROCESS

FIVE

IMPLEMENTATION

In Chapter 3 some of the problems that can be experienced because of poor implementation were addressed. This chapter outlines additional steps in a successful implementation. Before circles are initiated, commitment should be secured, existing threats alleviated, and the establishment of the groups set in motion. The first step, however, is to decide whether to employ an external consultant.

THE EXTERNAL CONSULTANT

The employment of an external consultant to assist in the implementation of the program is optional. All the work is done internally by employees. There are advantages and disadvantages to using an external person.

First, external consultants generally have a broader theoretical and practical background, either because they have observed a greater variety of circles in operation or because they have had a greater opportunity to study the available research. For this reason, they are able to present a greater variety of options, alternatives and ideas. This also means that they will be more conscious of inconsistencies between practice and the goals and objectives of the organization.

Second, because they are external to the organization, they are relatively immune to the power structure and can view the organization and the quality circle program more objectively. Because of this, they are in a better position than the internal consultant to challenge the established behavioural patterns of senior and middle management, and the information and insights which they present are viewed as being more neutral and more credible.

Third, generally they can gain access to key people within the organization more readily—after all, consultants do cost money. They also can be influential in behind-the-scenes manoeuvring should this become necessary.

Fourth, a good external quality circles consultant can aid in changing the climate of the organization. Individuals generally are afraid to try new techniques and behaviours. Consultants can encourage experimentation and can assist individuals in successful personal adaptations. They can also nurture positive changes in attitudes and, through feedback, can discourage negative ones. Consultants can aid the process even more by modelling constructive communications. In one instance, for example, middle managers, during a training seminar, were helped in perceiving the existing attitudes and viewpoints within the organization by making a collage (a series of posters) about the climate of the organization.

Sometimes middle and senior managers require a "support system"—particularly one that is external to the organization—or just someone on whom they can try ideas. Consultants can perform that function and be that sounding board.

Perhaps one of the most important purposes of external agents is to retain the momentum. As circles continue to function, the initial excitement, attention and glamour tend to diminish. Furthermore, it is not always possible for the organization to implement the solutions which have been suggested. The circle members may begin to feel disappointed, frustrated, resentful and manipulated. Consultants can provide support, encouragement and counsel. They can coach and educate members. But more important, they can be good listeners and can assure the circle members they are on the right track and that the problems which they are experiencing are expected or are the usual type of difficulties. To overcome some of the unanticipated or negative outcomes which cause disllusionment, external consultants can lead the steering committee and others through "anticipatory planning" and in periodic re-evaluations of the circle processes. Again, external consultants can be a source of new ideas and alternatives.

Consultants, however, are expensive and generally do not, and cannot, do the detailed planning and required work. They also can be insensitive to the organization and its needs, the unofficial power structures and the organizational chart. Often, they are too busy and, at least in Canada, located too far away for frequent and easy consultation. Consequently, there are many large organizations that do not utilize externals.

If the organization decides to hire an external consultant, the choice of individual or company should be made before any work is done. He or she then can assume some responsibility for obtaining commitment, providing initial explanations, seeing that training programs are developed, and ensuring that adequate training occurs. This individual is extremely important to the success of the program, and care must be taken to select a person who is mature, sensitive to people's feelings, supportive and approachable. If the company is unionized, an individual who is perceived to be sympathetic, or at least neutral, to the union movement can give credibility to the program and help union executive and rank-and-file members to feel greater trust regarding management personnel with whom they must work.

There are other traits which the consultant should possess. The organization will want a generalist—someone who understands the structure and purposes of the organization, as well as the external environment in which, and the constraints under which, the organization operates. Certainly, too, a specialist is required—someone who understands quality circles and has the necessary interpersonal, process and statistical skills.

Of course, the consultant should not have a vested interest in improving the status of a particular group—management, labour, or any other. He or she should be open and be willing to confront conflict, even when senior management is involved. The person should have an awareness of practice, research and theory and be experienced in a variety of consulting situations instead of having worked in the same type of situation over and over again.

Other characteristics of good consultants include flexibility, the willingness to listen and to tailor existing informational and training materials to the needs of the organization, the ability and desire to train others, the willingness to work themselves out of a job, and last, but most important, to be available when required.

Not all external consultants are trained in interpersonal skills, basic statistical techniques and group processes. Different consultants have different expertise. With the popularity of quality circles, many management consulting firms, both large and small, have embraced the concept by purchasing one of the commercial packages which are readily available. In evaluating the credentials of external people, organizations should be leery of a smooth polished approach which is based on ''have canned package, will implement'' and assure themselves that the consulting firm or individuals have the requisite skills needed to advise about and implement quality circles.

EXTERNAL CONSULTANTS

Advantages
- more ideas, options and alternatives
- immune to power structure
- better access to key people
- help employees experiment with new behaviour
- provide support system
- retain momentum

Disadvantages
- expensive
- do not do the work
- sometimes insensitive
- busy

Required characteristics
- mature
- sensitive to people's feelings
- supportive
- approachable
- credibility with union
- generalist
- specialist in quality circles
- willing to confront conflict
- flexible

PRELIMINARY COMMITMENT AND PLANNING

Five issues must be addressed before quality circles are instituted:
1. Senior management should be committed to the endeavour.
2. Union involvement and commitment should be assured.
3. Threats felt by middle management should be anticipated and programs developed to neutralize them.
4. Plans should be established to overcome the threat of empire building by quality circle leaders or facilitators.
5. An analysis of the organizational climate should be made.

Senior Management Involvement

Often in the implementation of a change program, it seems sensible to start small and build to bigger and better things. This is not appropriate for quality circles; the commitment that is required from senior management is crucial to the success of the program. First, either release time from duties or payment for time spent working on quality circles (if one of these methods is chosen) must be approved. Resources must be redeployed, not for the next month or the next year, but for many years to come. The results of the deliberations of each of the circles must be presented not only to appropriate technical and middle management groups but also to affected senior management personnel. The reception which these presentations receive will influence the enthusiasm and willingness which the circles show for continued problem solving. And finally, changes suggested by quality circles must be implemented. This often requires an unanticipated utilization of resources. Because of these involvements, upper management commitment is mandatory.

It is important too to have the commitment of more than one individual of the senior management group. Where only one person is committed to the concept, that person's promotion, illness or other fortune or misfortune may adversely affect the circles.

Union Involvement

Mentioned earlier was the fact that union executives are often very suspicious of management and feel that quality circles are one more in a long series of methods to extract greater productivity from the workers. Furthermore, there is considerable fear that this concept, if successful, will lead to the dismissal of great numbers of employees and make the union unnecessary in the representation of workers' interests. To assist in overcoming these feelings, it is necessary to:

1. Contact the members of the union executive in the very early stages of discussion.
2. Consult with union representatives at every step.
3. Place influential union members on the steering committee.
4. Refuse to consider issues which properly belong in the collective agreement and within the grievance procedure.
5. Not permit the union to make gains as the price of members' participation. Because of the nature of the union and its legitimate activities, it is not unusual for the union executive to place conditions or to make demands in exchange for the promise of members' participation. Such demands generally do not improve the relationship and should not be a condition of participation.

Middle Management

In the traditional system of management, a hierarchical structure exists. Individuals who, after many years, have "made it" to middle management have subordinates who report to them and over whom they exercise a certain degree of legitimate reward and coercive power. Issues and problems are reported, after screening, through the hierarchy to more senior management; line people seldom meet or formally express their concerns directly to anyone except their supervisor.

Quality circles change this relationship and structure. First, members of senior management who are concerned with the particular improvement are included in presentations. Second, middle management often perceives that circles have assumed a substantial portion of their unique problem-solving role. In the eyes of the first-level supervisors, circles also appear to be doing work which rightfully belongs to the supervisor. Additionally, line people may use the direct link with senior administration as a lever over their bosses.

To assist these two groups, the new role expectations which the organization has should be clarified. But more is needed. It should be demonstrated, through explicit actions, that quality circles do not threaten, but do enhance, these individuals' roles and positions. One of the best methods to overcome the insecurity which the supervisor may feel is to make that person the quality circle leader. But before this occurs, extensive training is required to teach this person to behave as a leader rather than as a boss. In short, if these managers are educated in the new management system and in the philosophy of managing human resources and taught how to function in their new roles, there should be little resistance to the perceived encroachment on their power.

No matter how adequately the pre-planning has been done, and how carefully the changes have been implemented, some managers will oppose quality circles either vocally or surreptitiously. There must be an office or official (perhaps the steering committee) which can detect and respond to opposition and any acts of sabotage that may occur.

Empire Building

Because facilitators and leaders are organizational members, there could be a tendency on their part to use their positions to further their visibility and career. Consequently, facilitators may establish circles, not because they are desired or necessary, but because they increase their own prestige and status. Leaders have been known to build empires too—particularly when the leader is a line person and the members wish to discredit a supervisor.

The story is told of a quality circle that was extremely successful and was the pride of senior management. Through threats and bullying, the circle members made life miserable for supervisors and middle management. Tremendous hostility was created within the shop. Needless to say, at the first opportunity, middle management made it impossible for the circle to function; it died a premature death.

The problem of empire building must be foreseen and a contingency plan developed to deal with it.

The Organizational Climate

If the organization is committed to the implementation of quality circles, it is wise to organize these in the most advantageous area first. For this reason, it is better that an organizational climate analysis be conducted. But climate surveys have other advantages too. They indicate the attitudes and perceptions which employees have regarding such organizational processes as motivation, communication, decision making, goal setting, leadership, control and the level of trust and interaction which exists within the various units. The initial climate survey also serves as a basis of comparison when improvements occur in the future. Lastly, it provides busy managers with feedback regarding their own interpersonal skills.

In reality, however, it may be necessary to begin "where the system is," that is, to proceed with the implementation of quality circles in a particular designated area rather than beginning with a climate diagnosis. Facilitators, for example, do not have a choice; their instructions often are top-down. Additionally, organizational units do not necessarily like being "diagnosed"; the budget will not permit it; senior management does not believe it is necessary; and members are intimidated by the expected results. There are many reasons. Even if it is impossible to do a survey, it is necessary for those charged with quality circle implementation to understand the organization and the people who function within it. To do this, rapport has to be established so that employees at all levels can be questioned frequently, in an empathetic manner, to elicit their responses and attitudes.

INITIATING THE CIRCLES

A five-step process will help quality circles to get off on the right foot. The five steps are:

1. An explanation of quality circles to all levels of the organization.
2. Participation in training programs by management, supervisors, leaders, facilitators, coordinators and union personnel.
3. The development of a procedure for implementing circle suggestions.
4. The development of evaluation programs for measuring the impact of the suggestions which are implemented.
5. The establishment of required structures.

A discussion of these five steps follows.

Explanation About Quality Circles

After approval has been obtained, the next step is to explain the quality circle concept to all those who are interested and may be participating. The purpose of this explanation is to provide facts about the circles and how they operate. More importantly, however, the explanation illustrates to prospective participants that the concept has merit and that it will help the organization and its members to grow without threatening the job or position of any person. This means that the fears and apprehensions which employees have must be anticipated and dispelled.

As noted previously, the idea of worker contribution frequently poses a threat to middle management and first-level supervisory staff, who feel that quality circles will be doing their work, making them look incompetent and rendering their positions unnecessary. In dealing with this perceived threat, a number of issues can be addressed. First, members at all levels within the organization should understand that collective thinking is better than that of the individual or the sum of the individuals. Second, most operations are extremely complex; even the simplest of actions can affect many other departments and people. This system of interrelationships can be better visualized if the organization is compared to a labyrinth in which all the units are connected by elastic bands (see Figure 5–1). When the slightest pressure is placed on the maze—by changing the shape or size of the units or by pulling on any one of the elastic bands—the entire system changes. Employees should have an input into those changes that affect them. Third, the new role of first-level and middle management, as true leaders and managers, should be not only communicated, but also carefully planned and taught. Furthermore, opportunities should be provided to practise this new role in non-threatening circumstances and suitable positive reinforcement should be offered when these new behaviours are displayed. Lastly, fears should be alleviated if policies are determined, strategies are developed and promises are kept which ensure that no person is laid off as a result of any circle implementation but is assisted in growing to full potential within the organization.

Both management and union should be aware that the success of quality circles will change employees and management. By experiencing an opportunity to work together, each group is better able to understand and empathize with the attitudes and requirements of the other. Because of this, employees are able to cooperate to preserve customers and

FIGURE 5–1
Change in Organizational Relationships When Pressure Applied at Any Position

markets and hence jobs and positions within the company.

Financial success, however, is seldom immediate. It is not unusual for very few tangible results to occur for the first two or three years of a program. A more realistic time frame is three to five years.

Finally, the explanation must include the fact that quality circles are not a means by which union or management can make gains that they have not achieved at the bargaining table. Bargaining continues as usual; those issues that belong at the bargaining table or within the grievance process do not belong in a quality circle meeting. Also, participants should be aware that quality circles are not a panacea or a cure for one or more ills of the company. Indeed, they will not be given a fair trial if they are perceived only in terms of being the cure to a specific ailment.

In addition to the explanation, participants could be allowed to visit another company and have an opportunity to observe a successful circle in operation. Alternately, external employees, who perform the same type of work and have participated in a successful quality circle in another organization, could explain the benefits and what quality circles have accomplished within the organization for which they work.

In summary, the quality circle should be so well explained, with free and open discussion permitted, that there are no surprises for any of the participating groups. All participants, particularly those in management, should be aware that their philosophy of management may have to change. For one thing, quality circles can be successful only if management believes that workers can and want to make a contribution. Secondly, it follows that as a result of quality circles, an improvement in things like quality, productivity and scrap loss may occur. These gains, however, are not the primary purpose of a circle; the primary purpose is to provide employees with an opportunity to contribute in the decision-making process in those fields or areas of knowledge where they have the expertise. Management will be required not only to encourage these contributions but to seek active ways to elicit them.

Training Programs

Seven groups of people require training or orientation. These are:
1. Senior and middle management.
2. Union executive members.
3. First-line supervisors.
4. Steering committee.
5. Facilitators.
6. Leaders.
7. Members of the circles.

Comments have been made throughout this book regarding the training and orientation that is required for the first three groups. This final section addresses the training of those in the last four categories, that is, the people involved in the actual operation of the circle. Sample training programs are shown in Appendix 1.

Steering Committee. The immediate training of the members of the steering committee is general in nature. Certainly they need to understand the quality circle concept, how management philosophy must be adapted, the benefits that can be attained as a result of employee participation, the activities and techniques used by the circles, as well as their role as policy makers (and not circle participants). They also require interpersonal skills. Although information is always advantageous, because of time and money constraints, much of the practical day-to-day information which will not be immediately useful to members can be postponed.

Facilitators. The most vital person in the quality circle program is the facilitator. This individual is the liaison among the various groups. It follows that his or her ability and the education provided determines the direction and success of the program. The exact training, however, is difficult to specify; personal qualities are more important than factual information.

Perhaps the only way in which magnitude and intensity of the training can be understood is by examining the role which these individuals play. They:
1. Sit and advise the steering committee.

2. Develop or assist in developing training materials.
3. Train or assist in training the other six groups.
4. Attend some meetings or portions of meetings for each circle that operates.
5. Actively promote circles.
6. Arrange for visits to other plants and for visitors to speak to quality circles at their home base.
7. Coordinate activities of all circles.
8. Help circles to prepare reports and presentations.
9. Provide support and assistance as required.

From this description it should be obvious that facilitators are not developed through a few days of training. Instead, they have been educated in the required skills over a long period of time—generally at a university, with another company, or in another function in the same organization. Graduates who might have these skills could come from extremely diverse fields such as business administration, education, industrial engineering, or the social sciences.

Leaders. Just as the coordinator is the key person in the quality circle movement within the company, leaders are the key people to the individual circles. Leaders generally are first-line supervisors. In that role, they have learned how to be bosses and how to get production out. Quality circles require a very different role, and considerable time must be spent teaching leaders the new role and providing an opportunity for them to practice it. The training that occurs will be in five main categories:

1. Human resource management.
2. Team building models and techniques.
3. Organizational climate.
4. Statistical procedures.
5. Conducting meetings.

As pointed out previously, quality circles are built on the philosophy of the worth of the human being and on the assumptions that employees can and wish to participate in decisions that affect them and that they have needs and motives which they want to satisfy in the workplace. Leaders need skills that will enable them to assist employees who wish to contribute to do so.

Many organizations have found that teams which work together well have better productivity and quality records.

Increased effectiveness in brainstorming, offering suggestions, feedback, criticism, group decision making and negotiating increases team cohesiveness. Leaders need the ability to build these skills in others. Also, an ability to interpret and react to non-verbal communication assists them in sensing covert deviations.

Leaders, even when they function as first-line supervisors, have a responsibility to members of the group to ensure that the environment is conducive to excellent work. The key to this is the degree of trust that exists and the system, methods and philosophy of work, including that regarding the chain of command, information requirements and access, idea receptiveness, promotional opportunities, flexibility, planning, decision making and control. Some methods are better for improving the climate of the workplace than are others. Because of this, leaders should examine key ideas that have been developed. At the minimum, they should understand the processes, structures, philosophies and power bases within the company.

The statistical procedures which leaders require and need to reteach to circle members include cause and effect diagrams, sampling, control charts and a wide variety of graphing techniques including histograms, scattergrams and Pareto diagrams. (These are explained in Chapter 9.) Leaders need to be able to explain the techniques and to know why, when and how each should be utilized.

One of a leader's most important skills is the ability to chair meetings. Chairing, in the broad sense, involves more than conducting the circle meeting. Part of the responsibilities include budgeting time, starting and stopping on time, ensuring that each member is provided with agendas well in advance of the meeting, ensuring that each member participates, ensuring that records are kept and pre-planning for a successful meeeting.

To top it off, leaders must jog memories, ensure that work is completed on time, promote the quality circle concept, recruit new members, train, and be pleasant and enthusiastic through it all. The training of leaders therefore must be a continuous process; the preliminary few days are a beginning. At that time only the philosophy and some of the basic skills can be imparted.

Members of the Circles. Work must be done in a cooperative manner, and all members should participate in problem solving. For this reason, members need interpersonal and technical skills (brainstorming, statistics, graphing, etc.) and a sense of responsibility (attending meetings on time, keeping within rules and procedures, completing work assigned to them, etc.). Because members promote the circle and recruit new members, they should also have promotional and public relations skills.

Quality circle members also require training in group team work, new roles and behaviour, and in interpersonal skills. Many books are available which address the best approaches; reference librarians can assist interested members in locating one or two of these. Generally, personnel within the company, particularly the training and development department and the quality circle facilitator, can develop or assist in developing programs to accomplish these aims. Various commercial companies also sell pre-packaged materials.

Suggestions

Very early in the initiation process, guidelines should be established to determine some methods and techniques by which suggestions can be brought before the appropriate quality circles and implemented. Since this involves policy, the steering committee is probably in the best position to formulate these guidelines.

Measuring the Impact

Methods, too, must be established for deciding whether a circle has been successful. This usually means that some *a priori* measures and standards must exist and some measurement must occur at varying intervals after circles have been established. Generally, in a manufacturing firm, these types of measures are fairly easy to obtain—a job is done more easily, in less time, with less waste. In service institutions, such as libraries and educational institutions, the impact of the change is more difficult to observe and to measure. At times the only available means of measurement are attitude surveys at varying points in time. One such survey is shown in Chapter 11.

ESTABLISHING THE STRUCTURE

After commitment has been secured and quality circles have been explained to those who are concerned or interested,

quality circle structures are required. These involve:
1. The establishment of a steering committee.
2. The naming or hiring of a facilitator.
3. Staffing the circle.
4. Arranging for meeting rooms and times of meeting.
5. Setting up operating rules and procedures.

The Steering Committee

Members of the steering committee are selected from a cross-section of levels and departments. At the minimum, senior management, middle management, each of the unions, first-level supervisory staff, the operating core, support staff and technostructure personnel such as design engineers and quality control are represented. This is the policy-making group; it does not become involved in day-to-day activities but determines general guidelines. Responsibilities of the steering committee include:

1. Establishing general policies regarding the structures and processes of the circles.
2. Determining the channels of reporting. Some examples include guidelines concerning minutes of meetings, publicity and opportunities to report findings and recommendations to functional areas and to concerned senior management.
3. Determining the number of circles that is appropriate for the company. If only one circle operates, a considerable amount of pressure for success is placed on the members of that circle. Furthermore, if it should fail, the whole concept fails. If the circle is perceived to be too successful, members may feel they are entitled to special treatment. Resentment tends to arise because of this, and an underground movement could develop to sabotage the circle concept. The steering committee therefore should think in terms of numerous circles. Costs, of course, are a constraint.
4. Determining the selection methods and the final membership of the circles. Sometimes there are too many volunteers for one circle; other times there are too few, and other individuals must be encouraged to volunteer. There have even been occasions when only a buddy group has come forward and used strong-arm tactics to keep others from doing so.

Policies should exist that facilitate easy access to a circle for all employees who are interested.

5. Determining whether circles will meet on company time or on individuals' free time. Is one method better than the other? Perhaps, but evidence is sparse. Some evidence indicates that both methods of participation can exist side by side. In the Ford Motor Company, for example, depending on the plant, employees meet either on company time or on their own time. Both types of circles have met with equal success. If the decision is made to meet on company time, the steering committee should facilitate the release from work for employees who are participating. In most companies it is customary for the meetings to occur during work hours.

6. Determining how suggestions from the general work force might be solicited and implemented.

7. Establishing guidelines governing the reward system that is appropriate for improvements which result from the efforts of the circles.

The steering committee is a standing committee that meets once every one or two months. As new problems arise, new policies are formulated.

Facilitators

When more than one quality circle exists, an individual is required to coordinate and facilitate the activities of the circles and to perform those roles which have been outlined earlier in the chapter. Depending on the number of circles, this responsibility is delegated to one or more persons. As the circles increase in number, a coordinator of the facilitators may be necessary.

The facilitator attends at least one meeting of each circle. While at the meeting, he or she does not interfere with the circle activities, but listens and provides assistance if requested. In addition, the facilitator assists and trains leaders when this assistance is requested or when the need to offer guidance becomes evident. Generally the facilitator is not a volunteer, but should be someone who is interested in this type of work, who is willing to work hard and who has been trained in the required skills.

In a unionized company, the choice of a facilitator can be a thorny issue. Management typically feels this person should be someone from managerial ranks. If the choice is made arbitrarily, the union may use the appointment to argue that the program is "another management effort to gain greater productivity from employees." To overcome this, some organizations have decided on two facilitators—a union person and a management person. But this avoids the real issue and forces a difficult role upon the two facilitators—particularly if the union uses its appointee to undermine the program. It is probably better to resolve the situation through discussion and compromise. The union can assist in selecting a person who has been a respected union official or who has the necessary personal characteristics and high credibility with union members.

Staffing

Quality circles are staffed by volunteers. Membership can range from three to twenty persons. Usually seven to ten is an ideal number. If the membership is too small, an insufficient number of ideas are advanced; if the membership is too large, some people feel intimidated and do not contribute to their fullest potential.

One member of the circle is usually the leader. A leader can be any member. Generally it is the first-line supervisor, who has been trained in the techniques of conducting a meeting, in encouraging others to participate, and in brainstorming techniques and the new non-authoritarian role that this position requires.

There are a number of reasons why the first-line supervisor should be chosen as leader:

1. If this person is not chosen, she or he may feel threatened.
2. If the circle is successful, employees, because they have direct access to management, may intimidate and blackmail the supervisor.
3. The most thankless and difficult job is that of the first-line supervisor. This individual is a buffer. Being a successful leader generally enhances the self-image of the supervisor and the respect that the workers feel toward this person.

The Meeting

Quality circles usually meet once a week in a conference

room away from the work area. Meeting times are always pre-determined, and the agenda for the coming week and reminders of the responsibilities undertaken are sent well in advance of the meeting to all members. Minutes are kept and are circulated to the members, the facilitator and the steering committee.

Shift work presents a problem for circles. To cope with the different times when members are available, two methods have been used successfully for scheduling meetings: (1) A quality circle for each shift can function with a linking pin (one or two people who attend all meetings) being the coordinating mechanism. (2) The second method involves scheduling. For one week, the circle meets one hour before quitting time for the first shift; the next week the circle meets for the first hour of the second shift. If three shifts exist, the same type of rotation pattern can occur. There is a fourth alternative: each shift can form its own circle which is independent of other circles in the unit.

Operating Rules and Procedures

The circle determines its own operating rules and procedures. Decisions are made through consensus rather than by a majority vote or by a dominant member forcing his or her opinion on the group.

Circle members should be pre-trained in consensus decision making. The process involves assuming that every suggestion that is offered, until proven inadequate, will help to solve the problem. In other words, better decisions are made when members:

1. Listen carefully to what others are saying without judging the statement.
2. Examine each proposal in detail.
3. Ask for clarification of unclear and hazy details.
4. Avoid dominating or forcing their opinions on other members of the group.
5. Provide support and acknowledgment to others and their ideas.
6. Build on others' ideas by adding to them.
7. Originate new ideas and approaches when the time is appropriate. So that members do not spend group discussion time determining the best method to present their own ideas,

103

a thinking and organization break can occur—two or three minutes when members can, without interruption, think through ideas and jot these down for later presentation.

8. Confront differences that occur by: (a) Specifying where the differences lie. Sometimes issues become clarified through a restatement of the problem or the tangential issues. (b) Questioning the assumptions underlying the solutions or alternatives given. (c) Pointing out details and facts that may have been forgotten or overlooked. Personal attacks or evaluative judgments generally detract from a consensual solution.

SUMMARY

In summary, what are the actual steps in the process of implementing quality circles?

External Consultant

1. A decision is made whether to use only the internal organizational development department or specialist, if the company is large enough to have one, or an external consultant to assist in the implementation.

Obtaining Commitment

The next step in the process is obtaining the commitment of the major parties who are concerned. To do this:

2. An off-site seminar is held at which members of senior management are introduced to the concept of quality circles. Usually a short review of motivational and leadership issues, the advantages of circles, the need for their commitment, the required new role and management philosophy, and similar topics are discussed. Appendix 1 gives a sample program.

Seminars can be held on company premises, but the proximity of offices and work distractions may hinder the training.

3. Senior management evaluates the approach and makes a decision as to whether or not the concept should be intro-

duced to middle management. Senior management may decide at this stage to proceed with implementation or to establish a study group to investigate and report. There are advantages, however, to waiting until input is received from middle management.

Although a decision made by the more senior group can be implemented quickly, the involvement of middle management provides an opportunity for clarification of organizational goals and contingencies and for feedback and information exchange. The information disseminated is more accurate, therefore there are fewer speculative rumours. But input by middle management provides these individuals not only with greater input, but also with greater control over the process. As a consequence, they are more committed and ensure that implementation proceeds more quickly and with minimal disruption. Researchers argue that another advantage exists. By allowing participation in the decision-making process, senior management gains the acceptance of middle management and, through group norms and group influence, attains a greater control over their actions.

4. Off-site seminars are held for middle management and union executive members.

5. Both middle management and the union executive make independent analyses of the program, its advantages and disadvantages, their new roles and whether or not to actively support the first steps in the implementation process.

Setting Up the Circle Structure

6. Senior management announces to the employees within the organization that it intends to proceed with the implementation of the quality circle program, the reasons for the decision and the perceived future benefits to the company and to the employees.

Depending on the management style of key personnel, the number of unions involved, and the existing union-management relationship, this communication could originate with both senior management and then union executive.

7. A steering committee is established.

8. A facilitator is selected by the steering committee. This person becomes an additional member of that committee.

Getting the Program off on the Right Foot

9. The steering committee, together with the consultant, if there is one, establish guidelines and principles. At the minimum, this must include such items as release time, the incorporation of the present suggestion plan into the quality circle program, the evaluation of the impact which circles have, and the remuneration system to be used.

10. The facilitator holds informational meetings and training seminars on quality circles and QC processes for members of the human resources department and other supervisory staff. An example of the content that can be included is given in Appendix 1.

11. The facilitator holds informational meetings for rank-and-file workers. Among the issues which are explained are the concept of quality circles itself, what advantages it has for the company and for the employees, the broad framework and guidelines within which circles are to function, the structure, the reporting relationships and the process and activities of the circles.

12. The facilitator, steering committee and external consultant, if there is one, develop an "anticipatory planning" program. The idea is to anticipate the problems, negative behaviours and attitudes that may occur, and the consequences of these for participants and for the organization. Response patterns are developed that can be utilized; this avoids fire fighting if the problems do materialize.

13. A request is made for volunteers by sending each member of the organization a pre-printed form to complete. To ensure the success of the initial program, managers in some companies, on an informal basis, may ask specific rank-and-file workers to volunteer. If there are more members than required, the selection is made by drawing names.

14. The facilitator, together with the supervisory committee, select team leaders from first-level supervisory ranks.

15. The facilitator develops training programs for team leaders and trains them.

16. Team members are trained.

17. Each circle begins to function.

18. The facilitator develops training programs and assists team leaders in developing mini-training sessions which address the circles' needs for the coming week. For example,

when circles have begun to function, a mini-session may concentrate on the process of setting goals and objectives. During the first weeks, a review of brainstorming and the Ishikawa diagram may be appropriate. Later each circle needs to learn about statistical techniques and evaluation. Examples of all these are given in this book and may be used as a guide. It is best, however, if each circle develops its own criteria and those forms it wishes to use well in advance of the time that they are needed. In this way it can feel ownership, a pride in the creativity and a greater commitment to the decisions which are reached.

IMPLEMENTATION

External consultant?
Commitment
• senior management
• middle management
• union

Setting up the structure
• announcement made
• steering committee established
• facilitator named

Off on the best foot
• guidelines, principles and objectives established
• managerial informational meeting held
• rank-and-file informational meeting held
• anticipatory planning programs developed
• volunteers requested and circles established
• team leaders selected
• leaders trained
• other training programs developed
• circle members trained
• circles begin to function
• leaders continue training of circle members

SIX

THE CIRCLE BEGINS TO FUNCTION

IDENTIFYING AND SOLVING A PROBLEM

Beginning circles often have difficulty knowing where and how to begin. The procedure, however, is common sense: the completed activity suggests the subsequent requirement. As a guide, suggested procedures for identifying and solving problems used by one quality circle follow.

Extensive informational search has been included in the procedure. In many cases, these (observation of the work situation for potential problems and for sub-causes of a problem) will be unnecessary. Because employees are extremely familiar with their work situations, they will be able to recall irregularities or dysfunctional aspects quite readily.

Before a step-by-step procedure can be explored, five terms, because they are used in a somewhat different context than usual, should be understood: ''problem'' or ''effect,'' ''cause,'' ''sub-cause,'' ''verify the sub-cause'' and ''solution.'' Also, certain processes and techniques—brainstorming, consensus decision making, delphi technique, fishbone diagram, action plan, checklist and sheets—are basic to the process of identifying and explaining a problem. These also are defined and an explanation is given regarding their use.

The Terms Defined

The terms "problem to be solved" and "effect to be solved" are used interchangeably to indicate a broad area of difficulty or activity or inactivity that exists. Problems or effects in the hotel industry could be complaints about quality and price of food, customer theft, late deliveries, damage to parked cars, noise and rowdy guests.

A *cause* contributes to a problem. In quality circles, the cause-and-effect diagram (commonly known as the fishbone diagram) is always used, and the word "cause" refers to the names that are given to the fishbones protruding from the main skeletal structure (backbone). For convenience, most people think in terms of four causes that contribute to the effect—materials, equipment, methods and personnel. Other names for these fishbones can be used; the names are not important to the process.

Sub-causes are the specific issues, difficulties and activities that have been identified as contributing to the problem. For example, in the hotel industry, if the selected objective of a particular circle is to increase the number of hotel dining room customers, and one of the problems or effects that must be solved is "poor service," some of the sub-causes could be:

Regarding Materials:
• frozen food—poor quality, unappetizing appearance, discoloration
• food types—inadequate selection
• table service—chipped, faded
• liquor—poor selection
• uniforms—unattractive colours, need repair, unattractive style, improper fit

Regarding Methods:
• cleanliness of utensils
• reservations
• payment procedure for food bill
• problems with tips

When a circle member *verifies* the sub-causes of the problem (does an analysis of the sub-causes), that individual examines the various facets of the sub-cause through methods such as observation, surveys, time studies, frequency studies and motion studies. The process includes graphing (particularly with Pareto diagrams) and charting the activities. For example, if "reservations" was one identified sub-cause, a member might want to determine and graph:

- the number of times that the telephone was not answered promptly compared to the number of times the telephone rang
- the reasons for the unanswered telephone
- the length of time that parties who had a reservation were kept waiting
- the number of patrons who could not be accommodated satisfactorily (together with the reasons, the day of the week and the hour)
- the extent of use of alternate arrangements or facilities (e.g., bar)
- the manner in which the telephone was answered
- the occurrence of the many additional service activities that affect whether or not the system of reservations works to the advantage of the hotel dining room

The *solution* goes beyond improvement in the reservation system and other sub-causes and addresses the initial problem. In the example given, solutions are suggested for "poor service."

Brainstorming is used at any time that the circle feels that many new ideas are needed. At the minimum, brainstorming is needed at the time the circle is beginning to function and is attempting to find problems within the organization that should be solved. The technique also is used in generating sub-causes and in generating solutions to sub-causes which have been verified as contributing to the problem. The brainstorming procedure is extremely simple—circle members spend a few minutes suggesting ideas as quickly as they can think of them or when their turn occurs.

Consensus decision making is another way of saying that everyone agrees (or at least does not disagree too strongly) with the option that has been selected. Generally this occurs after the advantages and disadvantages of all options have been discussed. Circles always attempt to arrive at decisions and options through consensus.

The Delphi technique is a procedure that assists in the evaluation of two or more alternatives (if members were not successful, through the process of consensus decision making, in selecting the best alternative).

Generally each person rates the importance of an evaluative

factor (e.g., cost) on a specified scale. The ratings of all members on each factor are averaged and this becomes the new "weight" for the importance of that specific item or factor. Each member then rates how well, in his or her opinion, the particular sub-cause satisfies the evaluative factor (e.g., cost—a high cost would score low; a reasonable cost would score high). Again all ratings for each item are averaged. Finally the two averages for each item are multiplied together. The highest (or lowest) total score determines the most acceptable alternative.

Three terms—"cause and effect diagram," "fishbone diagram" and "Ishikawa diagram"—are used interchangeably. The fishbone diagram is a structured method to list the sub-causes of a problem or the solutions to a sub-cause and to organize the ideas so that relationships that exist are perceived more quickly. Circle members concentrate, through brainstorming, on one cause or solution (e.g., methods). When no member has any further suggestions about the first cause or solution, the circle does the same thing for the second cause or solution (e.g., materials) until all ideas have been written on the diagram.

Action plans and *checklists* are usually used together and specify work that must be done to verify a sub-cause or to determine a solution to a sub-cause or to a problem. An action plan outlines the necessary activities in broad terms, their order, and specifies the person who has responsibility for the action. A checklist or checksheet lists the specific items for each action that must be examined to verify if a sub-cause is contributing to the problem or if a suggested solution eliminates or improves a sub-cause or problem.

The Steps in the Process

The steps in the process, which are shown schematically in Figures 6–1a to 6–1f, and the suggested time intervals are:
1. *The initial meeting* is held (Week 1). At this meeting, eight activities occur: (*a*) Members introduce themselves and talk about their specific tasks, their work and external interests, and their expertise. This is generally beneficial even if all individuals of the circle are members of the same unit; employees know surprisingly little about their co-workers.

111

(*b*) A team leader is elected (if one has not been appointed previously).

(*c*) The circle members give their circle a name.

(*d*) A secretary is elected. This person keeps the minutes, looks after circulation of agendas and does other necessary paper work.

(*e*) The necessary supplies or a working kit are given to all members.

What is in the "kit" depends on the unit itself. When supplies are freely available within the unit (an engineering circle), the dispensing of supplies is unnecessary. For a shop-floor group this is more important; these employees do not have the same access to supplies and equipment.

One firm gave each member who had joined a plant circle his or her own briefcase (personalized), complete with QC logo, pens, pencils, ruler, coloured pencils, transparency materials, three-ring binder, looseleaf paper, graph paper, note-book, writing pad, appropriate readings and "how to" reminders, calendar, file folders and carrying folders. Although relatively minimal, some cost was involved. The benefit obtained, however, far exceeded the cost. Members showed

---

FIGURE 6–1a
Flow Chart Showing Overview of Process for Identifying and Solving a Problem

---

FIGURE 6–1b
Flow Chart Outlining Preliminary Activity

considerable pride in their briefcases; the boost in morale and commitment was significant; and the gesture was a catalyst for a larger number of volunteers and more circles.

(*f*) The goals and objectives of the company are reviewed. Usually this is a good opportunity for one of the senior managers or a member of the steering committee to meet with the circle, to show personal interest and to establish rapport. Since the goals and objectives of the company have been outlined during the training sessions held prior to the establishment of the circles, only a short review is necessary.

g) The unit or department supervisor (and others) share with circle members those problems areas within the unit or department which are affecting productivity adversely, such as quality and down-time. This is an excellent opportunity to review such things as production, sales figures, trends, environmental constraints, gross margin, unit expenses and overhead.

h) Before the meeting breaks up, circle members are asked to think about goals and objectives for the circle itself. These will be established at the next meeting.

2. *The next meeting* (Weeks 2-3). Through consensus decision making, the circle sets specific goals and objectives for itself (e.g., decrease waste by 5 percent; improve quality so that there are 20 percent fewer rejects; decrease costs by 5

FIGURE 6–1c
Flow Chart Outlining Selection of Critical Problem

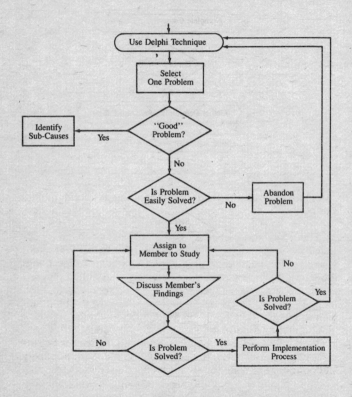

percent). To keep members on the right track, leaders sometimes review the problem areas within the unit which were
outlined during the previous week. Important goals and
objectives include not only quantitative measures but also
qualitative ones—circle recognition and an opportunity for members to learn new skills and improve their working conditions.

FIGURE 6–1d
Flow Chart Showing Process for Identifying Sub-Causes

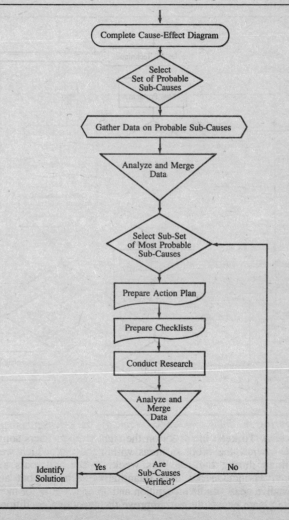

FIGURE 6-1e
Flow Chart for Process of Identifying Solutions to Selected Problem

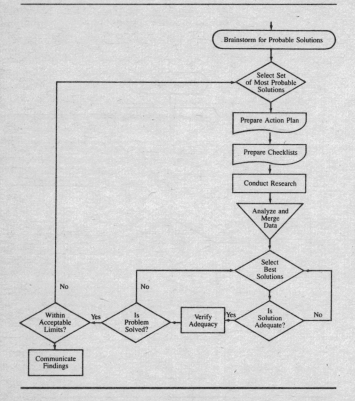

3. *During the following week* (Week 4), the circle members brainstorm for possible problems. Circle members may find it advantageous to observe and jot down specific problem areas within the unit during the week prior to the brainstorming session. The process of brainstorming should be reviewed at the beginning of the meeting.

4. *The analyses of the advantages,* disadvantages and prob-

FIGURE 6–1f
Flow Chart Showing Implementation Process

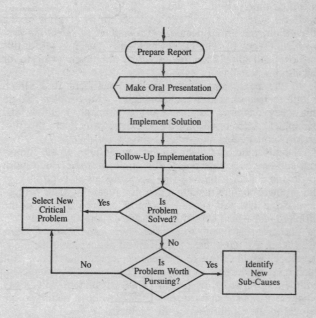

lems in implementing each of the suggestions is usually left for the next meeting (Week 5). This has several advantages: circle members will have forgotten who offered the initial suggestions, new problems may have surfaced during the week, and members also can use the delay to study each of the problems.

117

5. *Difficult problems are eliminated.* These include those which do not assist in fulfilling circle and goals and objectives, those for which the circle will not receive credit, those for which information is not available and those which other organizational groups are studying. Also, each problem that can be easily analyzed and rectified is assigned to one group member for study. The member is asked to report within a specified time period.

6. If no agreement on a problem occurs as a result of the discussion, the group decides on a *method to select the best problem* (Week 6). The Delphi method is a useful tool for this purpose and should be reviewed by the team prior to or during this session.

7. In the next step of the process, members first search within their work setting for *sub-causes of the problem*. To do this, they examine the materials, equipment, methods and personnel. After reviewing the Ishikawa principles, this diagram is constructed showing all sub-causes (Week 7).

8. Usually members have similar *perceptions* of the important sub-causes at this point. The circle, however, may wish to do more data gathering (on how sub-causes contribute to the problem) before making a decision regarding their perception of the few that account for most of the variation in the problem and which should be examined more thoroughly.

9. The group is finally to *use the seven basic tools of statistics* (Week 9). After these are reviewed and a plan of action is developed by the circle (e.g., observe scrap, rejects, rework), each member accepts an assignment and agrees to complete it within a specified time period. This assignment will verify whether or not the sub-causes which have been identified are critical to the elimination of the problem.

Generally, a checklist or checksheet for each sub-cause, procedure or technique that must be observed and charted is also developed.

10. Each member of the circle *performs the assigned work* and prepares charts, graphs and Pareto diagrams (in subsequent weeks). Each week while the research is continuing, members make progress reports to the circle.

11. Also, during the time period when members are conducting their research on an individual basis, the *circle determines the criteria* that are to be utilized, if necessary, to determine if a problem (effect) can be "solved" by eliminating or

improving the specified sub-causes. Such factors as cost, availability of materials and political considerations are specified.

12. The results of the individual analyses, together with the Pareto diagrams, are *presented to the circle meeting* and the findings are discussed.

13. Often sub-causes that must be improved, eliminated or adapted will be obvious after this presentation. If not, the circle members, using the criteria previously developed and the modified Delphi technique, *select* these.

14. At this point, the circle has only identified certain sub-causes that are contributing to the problem. *Solutions to the sub-causes* are suggested by use of brainstorming. (Some circles, however, like to use the fishbone diagram).

15. *An action plan and checklists* are developed specifying the activities and procedures that must be examined.

16. *The results* of the individual analyses, together with charts and graphs, are presented to the circle meeting and the findings are discussed.

17. *The circle selects* the "best" solutions.

18. *Solutions are implemented,* if possible at this stage, on a small trial basis and the effects of the implementation are observed.

19. *Observations are discussed* by the circle.

20. When the circle feels it has information that should be shared with management and technical staff, or when it cannot proceed without approval or funding of its plans, it *prepares a report* outlining its research and its conclusions. In the process of preparing the report, data gathering again occurs. At this stage, this information search should provide confirmation of the previous conclusions.

21. Circle members make an *oral presentation* to appropriate technical and managerial personnel.

22. *Members participate in the implementation* of the recommended solutions and in analyzing and solving unforeseen events that occur.

23. A check is made that the problem has been eliminated or resolved. If it has, the circle begins again with a new problem.

The Process in Detail

Considerably greater detail is given in this and the following chapters. Brainstorming and the Delphi technique are described in the latter portion of this chapter. In Chapter 7, the Ishikawa diagram, the use of statistical tools and the selection of criteria for analyzing solutions are explained. In Chapter 8, suggestions for preparing professional reports and oral presentations are given.

REQUIRED DEFINITIONS

Problem

Cause

Sub-cause

Verifying the sub-causes

Solutions

Brainstorming

Delphi technique

Ishikawa/fishbone/cause-and-effect diagram

Action plans

Checklists and checksheets

THE STEPS IN THE PROCESS

Initial meeting
- Introductions
- Team leader selected
- Circle named
- Secretary elected
- Working kit provided
- Goals of company reviewed
- Productivity record reviewed

Circle goals and objectives established

Brainstorming for problems to be solved

Discussion of problem suggestions

Selection of one problem

Completion of fishbone diagram

Selection of sub-causes *perceived* to be most crucial to problem elimination

Development of action plans, checksheets and checklists to assist in sub-cause analyses

Assignment of activities to individual members for purpose of verifying sub-causes

Presentation to circle of verification (results of analyses, Pareto charts, etc.)

Selection of sub-causes *shown* to be most crucial to problem elimination or improvement

Brainstorming for solutions to identified sub-causes

Selection of most probable solutions

Development of action plans, checksheets and checklists to assist in analyses of solution

Assignment of activities to individual members for purposes of investigating and verifying solutions.

Selection of best solutions

Preparation of report

Oral presentation to members of technical and managerial staff

Implementation follow-through

New problem selected

SELECTING A PROBLEM

Brainstorming

The first task of the circle is to generate problems; the second is to choose one problem from the many alternatives that have been generated. One method by which problem ideas can be produced is through brainstorming.

Brainstorming is a thought-generating session. The aim is to provoke as many ideas as possible in the time available. No thought is given to the practicality of the suggestions or the changes that may be required to implement them. All ideas are simply jotted down without appraisal. Appraisal as to advantages, disadvantages and problems in implementing occurs only after all ideas have been generated. Two examples of a problem list generated through brainstorming are given in Figures 6–2 and 6–3. Five other variations can also be used. These are: (1) the Gordon approach,[1] (2) the black box technique,[2] (3) the synetics system,[3] (4) the collective notebook method.[4] and (5) the Phillips 66 buzz session.[5]

The Gordon Approach. The Gordon approach is very similar to brainstorming, but there is one difference: the specific reason for the brainstorming is not revealed to the members. Members participate in suggesting problems or issues which they have observed.

FIGURE 6–2
Results of Brainstorming in a Medical Laboratory

Brainstorming for Problems: Medical Laboratory
1. Excessive removal of supplies by non-lab personnel
2. Stat abuse, especially on holidays
3. Lack of orientation for doctors
4. Broken drawers
5. Holiday weekend scheduling
6. Improperly filled-out requisitions
7. Mislabelled specimens
8. Getting admission results on charts

9. Specimens dumped en masse on the lab by nurses at the end of their shift
10. Excessive phone calls for results
11. Slick floors outside histology
12. Inadequate directions to help patients find the lab
13. Time wasted on multiple trips to the copying machine
14. Bad connections on phone calls from reference lab
15. Unnecessary ordering of tests
16. Coverage of clerk's phone when clerk is out
17. Insufficient recognition for jobs well done
18. Excessive memoranda
19. Too much noise made by maintenance workers
20. Abuse of beeper paging

Source: Sybil A. Wellstood and Linda Wright, "Using Quality Circles to Solve Lab Problems," *Medical Laboratory Observer*, February 1983: 34.

Gordon, who originated this concept, felt that brainstorming had certain drawbacks. Often, when members feel that they have suggested the correct answer (problem idea, in this case), they lose interest in the process and concentrate instead on how to sell their idea at the evaluation stage.

The Black Box Technique. The black box technique solves problems through graphic presentations. Generally two situations are presented and the question that is asked is "What common problems could be causing this situation?" or "How can these two situations (machines, designs, structures) be made more compatible?" or "How can they function more harmoniously?"

The Synetics System. The synetics system is mentioned here even though it may be more useful in generating solutions than in problem ideas. There are three basic steps which involve an analysis of PAG (problem as given by the leader) and PAU (problem as understood by each of the members of the circle). When this analysis is completed, certain generalizations are reached. On the basis of the generalizations, model building occurs. The last phase involves extensive research and exchanges of thoughts and ideas, not only by members of the circle, but also by outside experts who may have expertise to help in the solution of the problem.

FIGURE 6–3

Results of Brainstorming for Problems Within a Prestigious Hotel*

Brainstorming for Problems: Hotel Industry

Complaints about staff

Linens

Poor-quality food

Leaky faucets

Bad supplies

Customer theft (towels, jewelry, pictures, ash trays, keys)

Dirty windows

Deliveries late and incomplete

High-priced food

Damage to vehicles in parking lot

Theft of contents of vehicles in parking lot

Valet abuse

Poor air conditioning and heating

Poor sales of desserts in dining room

Tea badly made

Poor elevator service

Slow or poor room service

Excessive noise and rowdy guests

Slow busboys

Lack of pest control

Lack of timely snow removal

Overbooking

Shortage of accommodation, couches, cribs

Complaints about child care

Inadequate advertising and promotion

Pool water too cold

TV reception inadequate

Insufficient use of conference rooms

Poor information desk and tour guides

Music in bars

Weak drinks

Inadequate security and safety

Bookings and reservations

Poor service in dining room

Inconvenient parking facilities

* This brainstorming problem list is a composite of lists developed by Central Michigan University students in the MSA 620 course (Organizational Behavior and Human Effectiveness) during October 1983.

Collective Notebook. For the collective notebook technique, each member is provided with a pocket-sized notebook. Participants record in the notebook all problem ideas as they observe them during a one- or two-week period and present them at the circle meeting. All ideas are subsequently discussed and evaluated. More frequently, notebooks are collected by the leader or the facilitator and are summarized for the next meeting.

Brainstorming is an excellent idea, but there is a tendency for members to evaluate the source of the idea rather than the suggestion itself. Under the collective notebook system, ownership of an idea is ambiguous; the responsibility of presenting and arguing for the concept is that of the leader or facilitator. This individual can clarify ambiguities prior to the meeting. To enhance participation and make threatened members feel more effective, she or he can obtain support for ideas from more dominant members of the circle.

Phillips 66 Buzz Session. The Phillips 66 buzz session uses a sub-group of six people who generate problem ideas for six minutes (6,6). Each group selects a recording secretary who reports the ideas to the larger group.

BRAINSTORMING

Thought-generating session.

Ideas flow freely.

No appraisal occurs.

Variations:
• Gordon approach
• black box technique
• synetics system
• collective notebook method
• Phillips 66 buzz session

Choosing One Problem

Many problem ideas will be generated at the brainstorming session. Many of them can be solved within a week or two because the causes are readily identifiable, because the information needed is readily available or can be obtained by the group and because the resources to complete the solution are within the control of the group. These types of problems are categorized as "immediate action," and one person is given the responsibility for seeking the additional information that is needed to resolve each issue and for implementing the solution.

This type of problem is illustrated by the following: An employee tried for many years to have the stool on which he sat moved eight inches to the right so that he could more easily reach his work area without standing. All requests failed; the man finally gave up. When he joined the quality circle, this was a top priority item. The circle designated it for immediate action, ascertained through research that the move had no additional consequences, and had the stool shifted immediately. The man was sold on circles!

The group problem which is chosen should be a more complex one, that is one which appears to have no apparent or discernible solution. These require further analysis. If more than one problem idea of this type has been generated through brainstorming, the group must choose the most appropriate and acceptable one. This choice may be difficult because members sometimes feel committed to their own suggestions. A process of eliminating less desirable problem ideas is required. Generally, a three-pronged approach is useful. This includes:
1. Elimination of all problems which do not relate to or complement the established objectives of the unit.
2. Elimination of additional problems which do not meet pre-established operational criteria which the circle has set for itself.
3. The application of a modified Delphi technique to determine the one best problem.

On the Basis of Goals and Objectives. Prior to brainstorming for problem ideas, the circle usually sets some general objectives for improving the unit, that is, goals that the members feel should be attained. Generally, objectives that are set are very general in nature and can be such things as less machine down-time, lower scrap costs, better quality, improved cleanliness, better scheduling, etc.

Before selecting the objectives or goals, the circle can ask the production superintendent or quality control department to review the performance data for the unit and the objectives of the department and the company with them. The circle also may wish to set additional criteria by which the problem can be judged. Some of these criteria might be:
1. Is the implementation of the problem within the control of the unit? A problem suggesting that the company should be

reorganized might be desirable, but the unit cannot control the implementation of this.

2. Is a solution attainable by the circle?

3. Does the problem provide sufficient challenge to the team and is it reasonably difficult?

4. When it is accomplished, can the results be measured?

5. Is the problem acceptable to each member of the team (or at least not objectionable)?

6. Is it within the unit work area?

7. Is it congruent with goals and objectives which the circle has established?

8. Is the opportunity cost that will be incurred to achieve success reasonable? Opportunity cost may include finding information, spending time in doing analyses, or giving up other opportunities.

These criteria, of course, are suggestive. The circle may feel that they do not need criteria for judging problems, that a different set are needed, or that they want to modify some existing set. Sometimes, it is better for the facilitator or leader to establish a set of criteria independently for himself or herself and call attention to particular ones that may cause the circle difficulty.

What purpose do these criteria have? The first, and the one of immediate interest, is that problem ideas can be eliminated from further discussion if they do not tie in with or complement the circle's established objectives.

On the Basis of Operational Criteria. A number of complex problems will be eliminated because they do not fit the goals which the circle has determined for the unit. Additional practical issues must be addressed, however, to eliminate other problem ideas. Of importance are:

1. Whether the problem lies within the area or unit. If the answer is no, the problem, at least for beginning circles, should be postponed. Circles, when they first begin to function, are extremely eager and feel that they would like to solve problems of considerable significance to the organization—that is, problems that are created for them in other units within the organization or external to the organization. There are some dangers in this approach.

First, external problems require a considerably longer time to solve. It is important that the circle experience early success. If the project takes too long, some members might become discouraged.

Second, the circle may be accused of meddling in other units' affairs. This may result in a lack of cooperation from those units. Considerable pressure may be placed on middle and senior management to disband the circle or to "clip its wings." External hostility always makes it difficult, if not impossible, for a circle to solve the problems that it has set for itself.

Third, because the problem lies elsewhere, the circle will lose control of methods to implement the solution. If that happens, other departments receive credit for the solutions determined by the circle.

2. The information requirements. An evaluation is made of how much outside help is needed, from whom, if each of these people or units are willing to cooperate, and if not, whether other sources of information or methods of getting this information are available. Obviously, if the information cannot be procured easily, that problem should be abandoned.

3. Timing. An estimate is made regarding the time that will be required to complete an analysis and to implement it. An ideal time span for a beginning circle to solve its first problem is approximately three months.

4. Effectiveness. Some thought is given to the benefits that can accrue to the organization and to individuals and how these improvements can be measured.

The group discusses each of these issues and generally is able to come to a consensus that certain problems should not be investigated because they are too difficult in terms of the benefits attained.

Using the Modified Delphi Technique. If more than one problem suggestion remains after discussion of the relationship to goals and the practicality of each, the modified Delphi technique can be used to reach a final decision.

In using this technique, members first discuss the merits and the importance of each of the outstanding problem ideas. After everyone has provided input, each member of the group ranks each of the remaining problems according to his or her preference (from 1 to the number of problems which remain) and assigns it a rating according to his or her perception of the importance of the problem to the organization (on a scale of 1 for most important to 10 for least important). The two rankings are multiplied together. Members' rankings for each problem idea are totalled. The one with the lowest score is chosen. Figures 6–4 and 6–5 illustrate the use of the modified Delphi technique. Figure 6–4 shows that the chosen problem is C—to try to eliminate the noise level; in Figure 6–5, Computer A is selected.

Should a number of problems receive almost identical scores, the group may wish to discuss the issues again and to rank and rate once more those which remain.

By Decree. A problem can also be selected by decree of the steering committee, the production superintendent or another party. The big advantages to this method are that circle members can begin work on a problem immediately and that the problem is pertinent to the organization. The main disadvantages are that the problem may not be important to the circle, that the circle members may feel used and manipulated, and that they will not approach the analysis and solution with the same dedication as they would for a problem selected by the circle. Nevertheless, it is probably the method that is most widely used with beginning groups.

There are many reasons for this. Members of the steering committee feel that they know the problems of the organization better, that the process is too complicated for rank-and-file workers, that it wastes too much time, that circle members cannot be trusted to choose suitable problems, that they do not know the problems, or that it is necessary to go slowly. Each of these beliefs violates the basic management philosophy and concept on which quality circles are based.

On the other hand, there can be considerable advantage to the circle in having the facilitator or steering committee assign a problem that is vital to the organization. First, when circles start out, the process can be extremely confusing; there are many new ideas and concepts and a new role is expected of members. Some of the confusion can be eliminated by having a ready-made problem. Second, problem delineation can be an extremely difficult and frustrating experience. The circle members, at the beginning, have not tested the problem selection skills which they have learned and have not yet established successful work-team relationships. Third, a problem selected by a senior group is one that is important to the organization. When the problem is resolved, greater recogni-

FIGURE 6–4
Use of the Modified Delphi Technique to Choose Among Problems Generated Through Brainstorming

Circle	A			B			C			D			E			F		
Members	P	I	T	P	I	T	P	I	T	P	I	T	P	I	T	P	I	T
Mary	6	1	6	3	10	30	1	1	1	2	1	2	5	6	30	4	3	12
	(6 × 1 = 6)			(3 × 10 = 30)														
John	4	4	16	2	2	4	1	6	6	3	1	3	5	2	10	6	3	18
Peter	1	3	3	2	6	12	3	7	21	4	1	4	5	5	25	6	5	30
Louise	2	3	6	1	9	9	3	1	3	4	7	28	5	6	30	6	5	30
Hilda	5	6	30	2	8	16	1	1	1	3	8	24	4	6	24	6	4	24
Brenda	4	8	32	1	6	6	2	5	10	3	4	12	6	6	36	5	8	40
Irene	6	1	6	5	7	35	4	1	4	3	1	3	2	4	8	1	2	2
Will	2	7	14	1	8	8	3	4	12	6	10	60	5	8	40	4	9	36
Total for problem idea			113			120			58			136			203			192

Problems which remain (lettered for convenience):

A Slick floors outside histology   D Mislabelled specimens
B Coverage of clerk's phone when clerk is out   E Specimens dumped
C Too much noise   F Excessive phone calls

P = Preference on a scale of 1–6 (there are 6 items); 1 signifies high preference for solving this problem; 6 indicates a low preference.

I = Importance on a scale of 1–10; 1 indicates that its solution would be highly important to the unit; 10 indicates that the solution would have a low effect.

T = Total (Rank multiplied by Importance).

FIGURE 6–5

Computer Comparison Worksheet* Used in Modified Delphi Technique Decision Making

| | Average Weight (Importance of Factor) | Perception of "Goodness" of Each Computer on Given Factor | | | | | |
| | | Average Raw Score | | | Average Weighted Score** | | |
		A	B	C	A	B	C
Cost	7						
Initial	4	8.0	6.7	7.3	32.0	26.8	29.2
Add on	1	0.0	0.0	0.5	0.0	0.0	0.5
Maintenance	2	8.0	7.0	6.0	16.0	14.0	12.0
Performance	7						
CAD	4	7.3	7.7	7.5	29.2	30.8	30.0
Other Academic	3	6.0	7.5	7.3	18.0	22.5	21.9
Function	10						
CAD Workstations							
CAD Analysis	5	9.0	6.0	7.5	45.0	30.0	37.5
CAM Interface							
Academic							
• Cobol							
• Fortran							
• Basic	3.5	7.2	7.1	7.0	25.2	24.9	24.5
• PL1							
• RPG II							
• IBM Assembler							

(cont'd)

THE IMPLEMENTATION PROCESS

Applications Software							
Micro Communications							
Alternate Operating Systems	1.5		7.0	5.7	5.0	10.5	8.6	7.5
Networking Capability							
Operating System		3	8.5	6.0	7.0	25.5	18.0	21.0
Resource Control Facilities	0.75							
Conversion	0.5							
Ease of Maintenance	0.75							
Ease of Use	1.0							
Growth Capability		3	5.3	7.2	5.0	15.9	21.6	15.0
CAD CAM	1							
Interactive Terminals	1							
Processing	1							
Product Growth Capability	4	4	7.0	6.8	5.9	28.0	27.2	23.6
Vendor Support	3	3	2.0	6.8	9.0	6.0	20.4	27.0
Compatibility with current equipment		2						
Backup	1		4.0	0.0	0.0	4.0	0.0	0.0
Peripheral Mass Storage Sharing	1		4.0	0.0	0.0	4.0	0.0	0.0
							259.3	244.8	249.7

*This Delphi worksheet for the comparison of computers was developed at St. Clair College of Applied Arts and Technology under the guidance of Mr. Bruce McAusland, President, and Mr. Tom McCarthy, Executive Director of Educational Planning.

**Each member of the computer evaluation team would make two sets of evaluations. The first set weights the importance of the factor (cost, performance, etc.) to the purchaser/user. The second set describes the perception of the committee member of how adequately each computer would satisfy the criteria specified. The *average* response for the importance of the factor appears in columns 1 and 2; the *average* response of the adequacy of each factor for each computer appears in columns 3, 4, and 5. Columns 6, 7, and 8 are the product of the first two sets of columns, i.e., the average weighted score is obtained by multiplying the average factor weight by the average raw score. Numbers given are hypothetical. In this case, the highest number signifies the highest importance or the highest adequacy.

CHOOSING THE ONE PROBLEM

Criteria
It is congruent with unit objectives.

It is practical.
• Lies within the unit.
• Has obtainable information requirements.
• Can be completed within a reasonable time.
• Will benefit organization or individuals.

Procedure
By decree.

By modified Delphi technique.
• Discussion.
• Each member ranks problem ideas according to preference.
• Each member rates problem ideas according to importance to organization.
• Rank score is multiplied by importance score for each person and each item.
• Scores of all members for each problem area are added together.
• The idea with the lowest score is chosen.

---

tion results. Fourth, senior groups, because they have more decision-making experience, are more likely to select a problem that can be analyzed and resolved within a relatively short period of time. Fast progress will hold the member's interest. The circle therefore should think seriously about requesting that the first problem be assigned.

SEVEN

PROBLEM (EFFECT) ANALYSIS

After the problem (effect that will be analyzed) has been selected, the activities of the circle centre around four main activities:

1. Suggesting possible sub-causes of the effect (problem) by analyzing the situation from a materials, equipment, methods and personnel perspective.

2. Investigating or verifying each probable sub-cause. This is generally accomplished by gathering and analyzing information and by obtaining input from experts who have the necessary knowledge.

3. Deciding on a course of action to eliminate or improve the most crucial sub-cause deficiency.

4. Preparing a report and making a presentation to senior and functional management who can authorize implementation of the ideas.

Three of these activities are discussed in this chapter; the last is discussed in the next chapter.

ANALYSIS OF THE PROBLEM

After there is agreement on one problem, there is a need to define that problem more precisely and to verify it. This is done by:

1. Determining how it is affecting the operations of the unit or company.
2 Determining what is the sub-cause of the problem through cause and effect analysis.
3. Verifying the diagnosis through checksheets, sampling, graphs and Pareto analysis.

The details of sampling, preparing graphs, and doing Pareto analysis are described in Chapter 9. The other two issues are discussed here.

How Is the Problem Affecting Operations?

The first issue that must be decided is how and to what extent the problem that has been selected is affecting the operation of the unit and company. This information is generally easily available from such sources as the rejects and repair sheets. If the problem selected has no significant impact on the company, it probably should not be tackled no matter how interesting it sounds or how interested individual members are in pursuing it. It will be extremely difficult to justify later and will give the circle little opportunity for interacting with technical people and middle and senior management, or for gaining credibility.

The Cause of the Problem

Two main methods exist by which an analysis of the causes of the effect can be made: cause-and-effect diagrams and process analysis or flow diagrams. Both types are similar and differ only in the method of construction.

A cause-and-effect diagram is a sequence of lines and symbols which illustrate the relationship between an effect (the problem that has been selected) and its causes. The flow diagram achieves the same purpose through a series of steps or boxes.

The cause-and-effect diagram is also known as a fishbone analysis or Ishikawa diagram (after Professor Kaoru Ishikawa of the University of Tokyo, who first used this method at the Fukiai iron works in 1953). It starts with a skeleton such as

135

that shown in Figure 7–1. The head of the fish is the problem that the circle is attempting to solve (i.e., the effect that has been observed).

FIGURE 7–1
Fishbone Diagram

Four main areas in which the deficiency could occur are the *Materials*, the *Equipment*, the *Methods* or the *Personnel*. Circle members, through brainstorming, examine each of these four areas one at a time. At the same time, they suggest possible sub-causes. As each person makes a suggestion in turn (or passes), the idea is placed on the fishbone (see Figure 7–2). Finally the group as a whole decides on the most likely sub-causes—those that will be investigated further—and these are circled (see Figure 7–3).

After the sub-causes are discussed, if a consensus decision has not been reached, the group can either vote on those which are most likely or decide that additional analysis needs to be done. Additional analysis answers such questions as: Does the same sub-cause occur under more than one classification? Are there deviations? Is there consistency or does it change? Does it occur all the time? Some of the time? At the end, an action plan is developed for the purpose of determining whether each of the identified sub-causes is at fault and as

FIGURE 7–2
Completed Fishbone

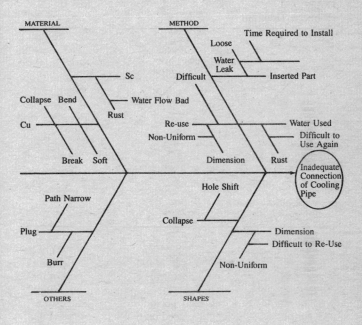

Source: Ford Casting Division Japanese Productivity Study Group, *Report on the Japanese Automotive Foundry Industry*, December 1980, unpaginated.

a written record of who is to do the work. Figures 7–4 and 7–5 are two different types of action plans.

Process analysis is very much like fishbone analysis. At the beginning of the process is the effect we have noticed (that is, the problem we have chosen to analyze). Each of the activities or steps in the process is retraced, beginning with the most recent and working backwards (Figure 7–6). Each of the steps

FIGURE 7–3
Completed Fishbone With Most Likely Causes Circled

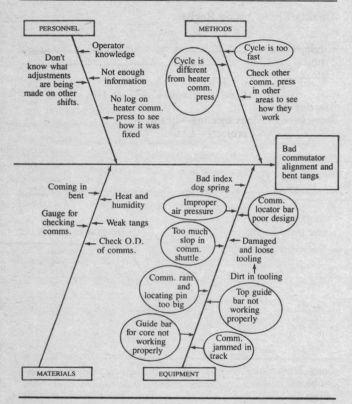

Source: R. A. Ball and S.P. Barney, *Quality Circle Project Manual* (Dearborn, MI: Ford Motor Co.): 23. "Comm." = commutator.

or activities is then examined for possible sub-causes. Again, all ideas are jotted down, interrelationships are indicated, and sub-causes are analyzed to determine the ones that are most probable.

138

FIGURE 7–4
Action Register

Quality Circle Action Register

Circle Name_____   Circle Area_____
Problem Selected_____
Date_____

Meeting Agenda
Review of previous meeting—Leader
Status update on projects—Leader
Follow-up report of implementation of projects—Facilitator
Analysis of current problem(s)—Circle members
Assignment of action items—Leader and members

Action Items (Immediate problems):
Assignment or problem
to be investigated   Responsible member
1.
2.
3.
4.
5.
6.
7.
8.

Long-Term Items:
Problems currently
being analyzed   Responsible member
1.
2.
3.
4.
5.
6.
7.

FIGURE 7–5
Action Plan

Action Plan (to tie objectives with established timetable)

Target Area: _____   Date: _____
Shop: _____   Facilitator: _____
Section: _____   Circle Leader: _____

Tactics	Assigned to	Scheduled Completion Date
1.		
2.		
3.		
4.		
5.		
6.		
7.		
8.		

Prepared by: _____
Date: _____

Constructing the Cause-and-Effect Diagram

Cause-and-effect diagrams are the key method of problem analysis. As a consequence, every circle member needs to be able to construct the fishbone without hesitation. To review the process again:

1. Goals, measurement criteria and time limits are established.
2. The problem to be solved is identified (effect). Steps 1 and 2 have been discussed in some detail earlier.
3. The cause-and-effect diagram starts with a basic fishbone in which the specific effect is indicated with an arrow. An arrow leads to the effect or the "head of the fish" (Figure 7–7).
4. The four words "materials," "equipment," "methods,"

and "personnel" are placed on the bones of the fish. These are the causes of the effect (see Figure 7–8). Other items such as "shapes" and "design" also may be used.

5. The circle starts with one of the causes, such as "Equipment." Each member, in turn, suggests a sub-cause. These are written on the fishbone. No evaluation, comment or criticism occurs at this stage. Also, there are no "bad" ideas; even false or "dumb" ideas can inspire other circle members to identify the true sub-cause.

6. The leader continues to call on each member, in turn, until all ideas are written on the diagram (Figure 7–9).

7. The diagram is posted on the wall of the unit until the next meeting. During the week, members who have additional ideas can add these. Also the various sub-causes can be observed for a week. A major advantage of postponing discussion is that members will forget who originated the idea. As a consequence, they will be more comfortable criticizing the idea and will not feel they are criticizing the person who suggested the idea.

8. Members analyze each of the sub-causes in an attempt to find the most likely or "true" causes. As these are identified, they are circled.

9. The diagram is left on the wall. It may be necessary to determine new "true" causes if analysis indicates that those which have been selected contribute to the effect in only a limited way.

10. Each of the circled sub-causes is analyzed by the circle group to determine how investigation and verification can be conducted.

11. Members select or the leader assigns each of the sub-causes to one or more members of the group for investigation.

12. Members conduct research on each sub-cause and report, presenting charts and graphs, at the next meeting.

VERIFYING THE SUB-CAUSES OF THE PROBLEM THROUGH DATA COLLECTION

When suspected sub-causes have been identified, a follow-up of each is required to determine if it is contributing to the problem. This is the data-gathering and analysis part of the

FIGURE 7–6
Process Analysis or Flow Diagram with Verifications

*Corrective actions are italicized.
Source: R.A. Ball and S.P. Barney, *Quality Circles Project Manual* (Dearborn, MI: Ford Motor Co.): 23.

FIGURE 7–7
Fishbone Diagram

FIGURE 7–8
Fishbone Diagram

FIGURE 7–9
A Completed Fishbone Diagram for In-House Cafeteria

Source: This cause-and-effect diagram was contributed by Central Michigan University students Jane McGlauflin, John Kern, V. Joyce Milton and Jim Young.

diagnosis. Four techniques can assist in the gathering of data:
1. using checklists or sheets.
2. drawing graphs—line, bar or circle graphs, histograms or scatter diagrams

3. doing Pareto analysis
4. carrying out sampling and statistical analyses

The use of all techniques is discussed here; the introduction to the construction of graphs and to sampling is left to Chapters 9 and 10.

Checklists and Checksheets

Everyone uses checklists. For example, a checklist shows the groceries that must be purchased at the store or the activities that must be completed during a specified time period. As each item is purchased or as each activity is completed, it is checked off or crossed off the list (see Figure 7–10). In the same way, the circle members use the checklist as a guide to the processes and activities which they must observe and analyze.

A checksheet is just a checklist that is a bit more complicated. It specifies what action is to be taken, when it is to be done, by whom, the tools that will be used, and the specific standards or cautions (Figure 7–11).

The items that go on a checklist or sheet are agreed to by circle members. Frequently the responsibility for constructing the checklist or sheet is given to an individual member; in that case, additional items are added later by the group. After the members have agreed to the items on the checklist or sheet, the responsibility for carrying out the actions specified is assigned to individual team members.

FIGURE 7–10
Checklist Regarding Situation Which Exists in a Shop

Checklist—Situation Analysis

Circle_____	Date_____
Shop and Section_____	Circle Leader_____
Target Area_____	Facilitator_____
Circle Members_____	_____
_____	_____

(cont'd)

_____ _____
_____ _____
_____ _____

Repair Method
☐ Appropriate shop tools and machinery
☐ Availability of unrepaired product
☐ Capital alignment
☐ Excessive wait time
☐ Junking of material
☐ Line balance
☐ Material availability to operator
☐ Material flow
☐ Repetitive motions
☐ Shop inventory of material
☐ Use of modern technology
☐ Appropriate use of floor space
☐ Wasted motions
☐ Working conditions and environment

Utilization of Human Resources
☐ Employee application
☐ Employees have proper skills and training
☐ Labour relations
☐ Safety
☐ Supervisory management

Other Items (Write these out)
☐
☐

Graphs

Someone once said that a picture is worth a thousand words. Graphs are visual representations of what is occurring. Their purpose is to illustrate connections or interrelationships among two or more elements (such as variables and causes). Also, well-constructed graphs save time and make explanation easier. For these reasons, circle members should graph as many of their observations and analyses as possible.

FIGURE 7-11
Checksheet

Maintenance Check Sheet

Systems: Cupola
Maintenance ranking: A

Checking Items	Checking Cycles	Checkpoints and Standards	Checked By	Tools	Reference
1. Outer shell of melting zone	Every 3 months	• Thin spots on outer shell • When a thin spot is found, the thickness is checked with a small run through hole. • Minimum limit: 3 mm	Melt Foreman	Hammer	Melting one is replaced every 2 years.
2. Pre-heat zone	"	"	"	"	Pre-heat zone is replaced every 2 years

(cont'd)

Checking Items	Checking Cycles	Checkpoints and Standards	Checked By	Tools	Reference
3. Tuyere	Every day	• Thin spots, hollows, water leaks • Hollows are filled by welding	"		
4. Cooling condition in melting zone and tuyere	More than 3 times a day	• Checking and cleaning of cooling water nozzle holes • No foreign body allowed	"		In case of many foreign bodies, checking cycle is shortened to every 3 hours
	Every month	• Foreign body in tuyere cooling water box • No foreign body allowed.	"	Specified tool	
5. Recuperator	Every 5 shifts	• Dust removing • Checking outer shell • Checking and mending of lining	"	Wire brush Broom	Replace interval • Secondary recuperator Upper part—2 years Lower part—4 years • Primary recuperator—6 years

6. Corrosion on chimney	Every 3 months	• Tapping test	"	Hammer	
7. Air leak	"	• Duct joints, recuperators • No air leak at all	"		

Systems: Dust Collector
Maintenance ranking: A

Checking Items	Checking Cycles	Checkpoints and Standards	Checked By	Tools	Reference
1. Filter	Every month	• All damaged filters are replaced	Foreman	"CONEX 5055U" by "Nakao Filter"	
2. Dust bag	Every 3–4 hrs.	• Replace bag when full	"		
3. Duct fan motor	Every year	• Grease	"		
4. Duct fan	Every 3–4 hrs.	• Thermo color tape on bearings "White"	"	Eye check	When the temperature rises over 70°C, the color tape turns from white to red

(cont'd)

Checking Items	Checking Cycles	Checkpoints and Standards	Checked By	Tools	Reference
	Every year	• Grease the bearings	"		
	Every 3 months	• Impelor —Endusting —No deposit is allowed	"	Specified tool	
5. Rotary valves	Every 6 months	• Motor oil replacement	Maintenance people		
	Every year	• Grease the bearings	Foreman		
	Every month	• Chain tension check and oiling	"		
6. Dust remover	Every month	• V-belt tension check	"		Wear in V-belts and pulleys are also checked
	"	• Grease the worm speed reducer	"		
	"	• Oil pan cleaning	"		

Source: Ford Casting Division Japanese Productivity Study Group, *A Report on the Japanese Automotive Foundry Industry* (Windsor, Ont., unpaginated).

There are many types of graphs. Among the simplest are bar graphs, line graphs, circle graphs and pie graphs. Often these four are all that are necessary. If more sophisticated graphs are desired, then histograms, scattergrams and the widely publicized Pareto diagram can be used.

As circle members become more experienced in graph construction, they may wish to show comparisons and relationships through cumulative frequency polygons, geometric line charts, ogive curves and Lorenz curves, and through the use of various types of logarithmic graph paper.

Graphs are extremely easy to construct, and members of circles should not hesitate to use even the most complex-sounding of these. Generally, the most awesome part of a graph is the name that has been given to it. Usually graphs are easier to read if they are drawn on graph paper or on grids. Colour coding and labels may be used if desired. Instructions are given in Chapter 9 for the most commonly used types of graphs.

Pareto Diagrams

The Pareto diagram is named after the Italian economist and sociologist Vilfredo Pareto (1848–1923). Pareto first used the illustration to show the number of people in various income classes and added the numbers in these groups from poorest to richest. Today, Pareto diagrams are used to identify sub-causes which contribute to a particular effect. The most important sub-causes are shown first on the graph so that the greatest amount of attention and resources can be directed to correcting these first.

While this section refers to showing sub-causes using the Pareto diagram, causes and effects can be shown just as well. In fact, these diagrams are usually constructed on the basis of many variables, including defect, shift, machine and operation.

Pareto diagrams are used to indicate how one particular element or sub-cause contributes to the entire problem. These diagrams are particularly useful in showing improvement. When a particular sub-cause is identified and corrected, its occurrence and contribution to the total number of defects should decrease. It is not unusual for circle members to start

151

their problem diagnosis with Pareto diagrams, then brainstorm, construct cause-and-effect diagrams and finally construct additional Pareto diagrams.

This graph combines bar graphs and a line graph. The bar graph illustrates the amount which each sub-cause contributes to the whole, and the line graph illustrates the whole or total problem.

Sampling

Probably the most difficult decisions that circle members make are those concerning sampling. Sampling involves a process where a small number or proportion of items (or people) is selected from the entire population for detailed examination and analysis in order that decisions (estimates) can be made about the quality or the nature of the whole population or the entire product being produced.

In the factory or plant, sampling is relatively easy. The quality control centre is already engaged in this activity. Individuals from this centre, therefore, can be most helpful in explaining the methods which they use.

The two simplest methods of sampling are to choose a specified number of items are random (without concern for time, machine, operator, etc.; in other words, in the same way that numbers are chosen from a hat) or at varying intervals. When varying interval sampling is utilized, a few items are selected every half-hour, or at some specified interval, and are analyzed or compared to predetermined standards. On the basis of the chosen sample, conclusions are made about the entire production process.

"How big should the sample be?" is a question that is often asked. For beginning circles, a good common-sense rule is to take as large a sample as is needed to feel reasonably comfortable with the decision that has to be made. Sampling, however, is costly, and caution must be exercised. Frequently the quality control department can assist in this decision. The question also is discussed in Chapter 10.

COMPLETING THE PROCESS: ELIMINATING SUB-CAUSES

After the sub-causes of the effect have been analyzed and it has been determined with some reasonable certainty that some sub-causes are more important than others, some type of closure is necessary. In other words, because of the expense, a decision must be made to seek solutions for only one or two of the most important sub-causes. To do this, the verified sub-causes are listed and the available data, complete with observations, charts and graphs, are reviewed. Finally, fol-

---

FIGURE 7–12
Analysis Sheet: Does Solution Meet Established Criteria?

Circle_____	Department_____
The Problem_____	Cause No._____

To What Extent Does/Is Solution

Possible Solution and Causes	Solve Problem?	Implementation Possible?	Effective?	Acceptable?	Require Resources? Available?	Provide Credit for Our QC?

lowing a team discussion, solutions to the selected sub-causes are suggested and a selection of the one or two most suitable solutions is made (after additional observations and analyses) using criteria which are developed by the circle.

Examples of such common-sense criteria include:
1. Does it solve the problem?
2. Is implementation possible?
3. Is it the cheapest and most effective method?

FIGURE 7–13
Control Chart

Circle_____   Department_____

Target Selection Area_____

General Objectives

1. _____   3. _____

2. _____   4. _____

Actions

1. _____   4. _____

2. _____   5. _____

3. _____   6. _____

Progress on Objectives/Actions

Date   Monitored By   Results   Additional Problems/Actions

_____
_____
_____
_____
_____
_____
_____
_____

---

4. Is the solution acceptable to the main parties?
5. Are the resources available or could they be made available without upsetting the organization?
6. Will the quality circle receive credit for it? If not, is there an equally good solution that can solve the problem and for which the quality circle will get credit?

Criteria can be developed if desired through brainstorming; generally this is unnecessary. Circles which do prefer to formalize their evaluation process can develop a useful device similar to the matrix that is shown in Figure 7–12 for analyzing whether the solution meets the established criteria.

Finally, the solutions that receive the highest rating, that is, those which will contribute most to the elimination of the problem and which best satisfy the established criteria, are selected and, after approval, are implemented. Implementation requires that an action plan be developed. This plan specifies what will be done, who will do the work, by what deadline, how they will do it, what assistance or resources are needed, and the standards that must be met.

MONITORING RESULTS

Solutions that have been implemented are monitored. There are five reasons for this:
1. To ensure that the problem really has been solved.
2. To measure improvement.
3. To modify any ancillary effects that might not have been anticipated in the implementation which could detract from the solution.
4. To assist employees in accepting the change.
5. For quality circle prestige and recognition.

Two instruments are required for monitoring results—a checklist of activities that are required and observations that are to be made and control charts. The checklist information is already available on the action sheet and can be transferred easily. Control sheets show the progress on a daily or weekly basis. An example is shown in Figure 7–13.

To conclude the project, new graphs may have to be drawn, a new sample selected, and additional statistical calculations may have to be done.

FIGURE 7–14
Reminder Sheet Regarding Goals and Objectives

Circle Name_____   Department_____

Goals which the group has selected

1. _____

2. _____

3. _____

4. _____

Current Performance   Desired Standard Benefits to be Realized

1. _____

_____

_____

2. _____

_____

_____

3. _____

_____

_____

4. _____

_____

_____

Progress on goals (activity and information about progress)

The circle also will wish to record the progress that has been made toward the goals and objectives that have been set. A large wall chart, similar to the one shown in Figure 7–14, can be used.

A final word of caution is in order. Many techniques and forms have been provided in this chapter. They are suggestive in nature. *It is always better for the circle to develop its own criteria, its own methods and its own forms, if and when they are required*. The illustrations indicate the type of format and the terms that can be used.

PROBLEM ANALYSIS AND SOLUTION

Problem (effect) defined.

Causes of the problem are MEMP:
• materials
• equipment
• methods
• personnel

All probable sub-causes identified by use of fishbone or process analysis.

Sub-causes investigated through use of:
• checklists and checksheets
• graphs
• Pareto analysis
• sampling

Preferred sub-causes identified.

Possible solutions to identified sub-causes investigated.

Preferred solutions identified.

Actions required to implement preferred solution identified.

Action plan and checklist developed.

Action implemented.

Implementation monitored to:
• ensure problem solved
• measure improvement
• modify unexpected effects
• explain the change
• for prestige and recognition

(cont'd)

THE IMPLEMENTATION PROCESS

Report written and oral presentation made.

CONSTRUCTING AND USING CAUSE-AND-EFFECT DIAGRAMS

Goals Set
Use of Ishikawa (fishbone) diagram.
• problem identified
• basic fishbone drawn
• fishbone labelled
• sub-causes identified, written on fishbone

Members conduct research and report.
• "true" causes identified and circled
• circle determines *how* investigation of sub-causes can be done
• members select sub-causes to investigate
• final sub-cause selected

EIGHT

THE FINAL DETAILS: THE REPORT AND THE PRESENTATION

WRITING THE FORMAL REPORT

When the circle has completed its investigation and made some decisions, it writes a formal report presenting its findings to the technical experts and senior management. This report serves at least five purposes:

1. It assists readers in understanding the problem and the facts.
2. It convinces readers that the information is trustworthy.
3. It assists readers in reaching a decision.
4. It assists readers in evaluating the competence and ability of those who wrote the report.
5. It provides a permanent record of the work and the recommendations. To accomplish these objectives, it is necessary to:

1. Follow a conventional style in organizing the report.
2. Answer specific questions that the reader may have.
3. Know the audience who will be reading the report.
4. Prepare the report in a technical format that will be psychologically appealing and easy for the reader to follow.
5. Distribute the document.

A further analysis is made of each of these details.

Organization

By convention, reports have at least four sections. The first section explains the problem, why it was undertaken and the possible benefits that improvements were perceived to have. The second portion explains the methodology—what the circle members did and how they gathered information. A third part includes a presentation of the findings, that is, the cause-and-effect relationships. These generally are in both text and quantitative data format. The fourth section includes the conclusions, the recommendations, the cost-benefit analyses and/or the results of the monitoring process. Recommendations address *what, who, where, when* and *why:* issues of what is to be done, who is to do it, where it should be done, at what time or within what duration it should be done and why it is recommended.

Findings in Text Format. The text describes, in words, the results of the investigation that circle members conducted. It should be written in short simple sentences, without the unnecessary use of technical or difficult words. It is better to impress others with the thoroughness and high quality of the analyses than by the use of long complicated-sounding words. Indeed, these may make it more difficult for others to understand the substance of the problem and the recommendations. Care should be taken to arrange topics and facts in logical order.

Headings and subheadings are important in the organization of the data. The most important heading is usually in capital letters and centered. The lesser heading is centered, in normal typing and underlined. A more subordinate heading is in normal typing, appears at the left-hand side and is underlined. Each company, however, has its own style, and circle members should consult other reports which have been prepared by executives (and their staffs) within the organization. It goes without saying that the report focuses on the practical, is complete. is honest and is highly readable. Readability can be accomplished by attention to grammatical style and technical detail.

Presenting Quantitative Data. Bosses usually want the facts (numbers) together with what these numbers mean (conclusions) and what should be done about them (recommendations). This means that special care must be taken to make statistical sections not only accurate and precise, but also interesting. Certain guidelines are generally followed:

1. All numbers are checked for accuracy.

2. A generous number of *useful* charts, graphs and tables are included, particularly small or "spot" tables (these highlight parts of larger tables). The use of spot tables avoids cluttering the writing with too many figures.

Because most readers find it annoying to have to flip back and forth, supporting information is placed as close to the discussion as possible. It also can be placed at the end of the report or in the appendices. If the table or illustration is large and only marginally relevant, or if only certain parts of it are relevant to the topic under discussion, it is common for the table to appear in the appendices. Of course, the text must report that the figure or table exists and its function. Furthermore, the figure or table, if placed in the text, appears after (not before) it is mentioned.

3. Each table and figure should be so well labelled that it can stand alone, without the text. At any time in the future, it should be possible to determine what it represents and the point in time at which the study was done. Headings therefore must be very complete.

4. Many readers find it difficult to interpret charts, graphs and tables. It therefore is necessary to talk, within the text, about the contents of supporting information.

5. The use of too many or too large numbers can intimidate readers. Figures can be made more meaningful if they are related to the whole or to another variable, by the use of percentages, ratios, ranges, averages and trends, or if very large numbers are rounded off. (For example, $2,556,789.34 is more easily understood if, in the text, it is given as two and one-half million dollars).

6. Each table, illustration and appendix begins on a new page.

Questions

Readers generally want the following seven questions answered:

1. What is the problem?

2. What is the best or necessary way for the problem to be resolved?
3. On what basis has this decision been made?
4. Is the implementation feasible? How?
5. What pitfalls exist as a result of implementation?
6. What alternate actions are available and what are the costs and benefits of each of these?
7. What costs and benefits (both financial and personal) result because of the implementation?

The report attempts to answer these questions. In doing so, it considers the temperaments and personalities of the key readers. Some readers prefer extensive quantitative data, while others want none at all. The circle members should determine who the key readers will be and what those readers' preferences are.

Generally, most readers expect the report to be accurate, reliable, unprejudiced and clear. They also expect conclusions to be objective (based on fact) rather than emotional. That is not to say that subjective judgments (feelings and impressions of the circle members) cannot be used. They can, but they must be clearly identified as such.

In answering the questions, documentation is provided to back up what is said. Here the observations, charts and graphs play a major part.

Technical Details

A good report has a cover, title page, table of contents, table of illustrations, list of tables and executive summary. All start on a new page. If other authors' work has been used in preparing the report, or if such information is paraphrased, a bibliography is also necessary. Other preliminary material that is included within a specific organization can be observed by examining reports which are on file.

The cover merely protects the remainder of the report. Most organizations have guidelines regarding the type of cover page or cover that should be used. The title page specifies the name of the study and its nature and purpose, to whom the study is being presented, who has prepared the report, and the date. Tables of contents and lists of tables and illustrations enumerate the respective items and the page on which each item is located. The executive summary is a one- or two-page abstract of the report. It is necessary because it gives a quick view of what the report is about, because executives are busy people and generally will not read a full report, and because an executive summary is cheaper to distribute—especially if a large number of people must know the essence of the report but do not need the entire copy. The executive summary is placed after the title page.

Finally, nothing makes a report look shabbier and less credible than a bad typing job. Unless circle members have considerable report-typing skills, this task should be delegated to a competent secretary. The facilitator has the responsibility of ensuring that support services of this type are available.

Distribution

One last question remains. To whom should the project report be sent? First, all circle members, the facilitator and the members of the steering committee receive a copy. Second, it is distributed at the oral presentation to all those who are present. Unless participants are required to examine the report during the presentation itself (this should be unnecessary), it is given out following the oral session. In this way, participants are not distracted and can concentrate on the oral presentation itself.

Following this (and not before), the document may be distributed to all others who are interested or concerned. Most circles seek as wide a distribution as possible—keeping in mind the formal hierarchical structure of the organization and the fact that reporting channels do exist.

A Different Type of Report

A report that was prepared by a Japanese quality control circle is illustrated in Figure 8–1. Interesting to note are the details:
1. Signatures of the members.
2. Details regarding the membership and the history of the circle.

3. Reasons for the selection of the project.
4. Analysis of the present situation.
5. Details of countermeasures (causes and improvements).
6. Details of the follow-up.
7. Results and impression of the improvements.

This particular report was reduced to one $8\frac{1}{2}'' \times 11''$ page—a very handy format. (Perhaps U.S. and Canadian organizations should ask quality circles to suggest ways in which organizational reports here could be reduced to similar size!)

Has the work of the circle concerning the project been completed at this point? No. Circle members also should make one or more presentations. The next section assists members in preparing for this.

FIGURE 8–1
A Japanese Quality Circle Report

Report on "MQ" Circle Activity Results	Date_____ Signatures Chief Q.C. Foreman C. Leader

Dept. Name: 2nd Casting Group, 1st Sect Circle Name: Kin (plane) Circle Circle Leader: Susumu Kaneichi Content of Project: Transfer from molding to cleaning operations Activity Theme: Improve the rate of operation by counter-measure or planning Goal of Project: Number of trouble should be reduced by 70% Project duration: March to August 1980	*Members* Members: 6 Average Age: 43 Yr. Oldest Age: 50 Yr. Youngest Age: 33 Yr. Circle Formation: Oct. 1975 Meeting Time: Approx. 5 Hr. No. of Meeting: 4 Times Project History: Eleventh

(cont'd)

Reasons for Selecting Project

1. In order to challenge on the model line, this theme should be tackled.
2. It makes operations easier.
3. Do not block molding line process.

Analysis of Present Situation

Equipment and Number of Breakdowns at Product Transfer

Project Planning Table (1980/83)

Execution Item	*Person in Charge*
Selection of theme	All member
Analysis of present condition	
Pickup of problem points	
Study of counter-measure	
Implement counter-measure	
Certification of results	
Drag or brake	All member

Analysis of Main Causes

Problem Points				*Main Causes*
Trouble of dam breakdown equipment	No breakdown	No dag under impact	Position cannot be determined	Position of product is shifted sideways

(cont'd)

165

Trouble on transfer equipment	Does not catch products	No product under clamp	Position determination is poor	Product is shifted when dam is broken
Hanger exchange equipment	Hanger of S.M.B. cannot be in position	Not at the center of receiver	Product moves	The receiving stage is not stable
Hanger lowering equipment	Casting does not slide from a slide	Product is stuck	Metal overflows at pouring cup	Too much metal flow

Details of Counter-measures (Itemize all and please write in detail the following);
Who was in charge.
Designation of responsibility to members.
Date of meetings and schedules.

Major Cause

Trouble of dam rupture equipment

Position of product shifted sideway on plate

Counter-measure and Improvement

Counter-measure 1—Install Y-shaped receiver on the surface plate
Result—The products bump into the receiver Failure

Counter-measure 2—Install stopper on slide
Result—There was a slippage depending on the type of machine

Counter-measure 3—Installation of guide—A guide was installed along the sides of the support on the surface place

Result—The problem of side sliding was eliminated 397 cases—> 33 cases

        Big Success

Trouble in transfer equipment	*Counter-measure 4*—Installation of guide plate against pusher to determine position
When broken, the product position is shifted	*Result*—Very effective for small slide 218 cases—>173 cases
	Counter-measure 5—Installed thick rubber sheet of 10mm in thickness to hold products when dam was broken
	Result—No effect
	Counter-measure 6—Installed an additional metal piece to hold product in addition to the counter-measure 5
	Result—Position shifts by the reaction of the dam rupture was decreased 173 cases—>47 cases
Trouble in hanger change equipment	*Counter-measure 7*—Manufactured a larger size receiving stage, which include crank for all types of machine with different shapes
*All type of machine is not stable on the receiving stage uniformly	*Result*—Most of them are stable on the receiving stage 109 cases—>42 cases

(cont'd)

Trouble in hanger lowering equipment	*Counter-measure 8*—Present situations were reported and cooperation was requested to man in charge of melt
*Overflow hot metal stays some part of slide	*Result* 67 cases—>11 cases

Follow-Up

3 check items were added to daily "PM check list" and the items were checked and confirmed before operation.
1. Adjustment of guide plate.
2. Adjust and wear of rubber sheet and support metal piece.
3. Adjust the receiving stage.

Results (as specific as possible)	1. 658 case out of 803 case of (choko-tei) cases are obtained and thus the result of 82% was successful, which is far above our goal of 70%. (803 cases/mo. − 145 cases/mo.) × 0.5 min./case × 9 men/line = 49 H/mo.; Labor Cost Reduction By this improvement, the rate of operation of the total line was increased by 1.5%.
—Amount of money (yen/mo.)	
—Amount of labour (EH/mo.)	
—Number of technical suggestions	
—If possible, amount of money and amount of labour should be recorded to obtain the results	
	2. Number of suggestions —>120 cases applied (Ward 4 cases) Amount of money and labor to obtain the above result: Money—about 50,000 yen Labor—48H

Impression of the Result: (Section chief or foreman should describe it)

The results are reflected on the reduction of standard time.

Impression of the foreman
(must be written)

Impression of section chief
(Must be written)

There have been a large number of problems in the old equipment, which had to be improved by means of schedule change and decrease in slags. This is the result: that all members of the circle understood the operation of equipment and worked hard to solve the problems.

The results obtained here are exceptionally great by implementing each countermeasure, by analyzing in detail on the cases and details of (choko-tei). I would like to evaluate the results very highly, because the result is directly related to the reduction of manpower on the [in Japanese].

Source: Ford Casting Division Japanese Productivity Study Group. *A Report on the Japanese Automotive Foundry Industry* (Windsor, Ont., December 1980), unpaginated; diagrams and Japanese script have been omitted.

THE WRITTEN REPORT

Purposes
• Helps in understanding.
• Documents that information is trustworthy.
• Helps in decision making.
• Used in performance evaluation.
• Is a permanent record.

Organization
• Part I: The Problem
• Part II: How Solved and the Difficulties
• Part III: Findings
• Part IV: Conclusions and Recommendations

Questions that are answered
• What is the problem?
• Best way to resolve?
• Why?
• Is it feasible?
• Pitfalls?

(cont'd)

• Alternate actions?
• Costs and benefits?

Distribution
• Members, facilitator, members of steering committee.
• All those who attend oral presentation.
• Others who are interested through formal channels.

MAKING THE ORAL PRESENTATION[1]

Presentations by quality circle members to functional areas and to middle and senior management who are affected by the improvement are used to:
1. Persuade these groups that the recommended solution should be implemented.
2. Report the results of a successful implementation.
3. Show management that quality circles are successful and money allocated to the program is being well spent.

A good presentation is a show-and-tell. It has many of the features of a good report, namely:
1. Facts are presented—why the problem was selected, the methods that were utilized in analyzing and solving the problem, the solution, the monitoring process, the improvements and benefits that have been or will be attained, the costs involved, problems in implementation and how these have been or will be overcome and the recommendations.

The report should not be overloaded with facts. There should be enough to cover the subject but not so many that the reader will lose interest.
2. A variety of audio-visual materials can be used, including graphs, charts, diagrams, overhead transparencies, slides, flip charts and the blackboard. Visual aids increase audience interest and result in greater learning.

Visual aids can, however, be used badly. Some steps to make the presentation more professional include:
a) For maximum visibility, print on audio-visual materials should be large, clear and legible. A very limited amount of material should be presented on each "aid."
b) Diagrams are more visible when large and heavy lines in black, red, blue or green are used. Colours such as brown,

pink, orange and yellow are good for highlighting but are more difficult to see. A variety of coloured backgrounds helps to break the monotony of one colour.

c) Materials should be prepared so clearly and legibly that turning out lights is unnecessary.

d) If possible, materials should be tested ahead of time in the room where the presentation is to be held.

e) "Aids" should be checked to ensure that they are in the correct sequence. They then should be numbered and the same number written in the appropriate position in the notes.

f) To ensure that the audience's view of the material is not blocked, a pointer should be used.

g) One problem experienced by most beginning presenters is the tendency to speak to the visual aid rather than to the audience. To overcome this, a deliberate effort must be made to "look the audience in the eye" throughout the presentation.

3. The talk should be given from an outline or from notes and should *never* be read verbatim. The presentation has to sound spontaneous and exciting. To achieve this, circle members should maintain eye contract with the audience.

4. Appropriate humour should be used. A technical presentation can be extremely boring—particularly if it goes on for a long time. Appropriate jokes or cartoons help the audience to relax and to participate in the presentation.

5. Time should be set aside for questions. The question period is an important time for gaining audience rapport and for convincing reluctant members. It helps to:

a) Look directly at the person who is asking the question but answer to the entire audience. In this way, everyone is included in the answer. Otherwise, some feel left out and lose interest.

b) If one person asks two or three questions, jot them down as a reminder and answer each question separately, stating the question prior to the answer. This keeps the audience from becoming confused.

c) If a question is unclear, the presenter or circle leader should request clarification. The question then is answered, as are all questions, briefly and with specifics. If the answer is not known, circle members offer to find the answer.

d) The voice and body gestures of audience members often reveal the content and the intent of their questions. Good speakers learn to watch for the messages.

e) Finally, and most important, questions that could be asked are anticipated prior to the presentation, and suitable answers are prepared.

6. The presentation begins with interesting opening comments. These are given in such a way as to arouse interest in spite of the fact that they tell the audience the purpose of the presentation and what will be covered.

7. Equally interesting closing remarks are made. The closing leaves a final thought—a summary of ideas, a restatement of the main points, a poem, a quotation, a story or a joke. The closing is probably the part of the presentation that will be remembered longest.

8. Finally, circle members acknowledge all those who participated in solving the problem and all those who have attended the presentation.

Prior to the presentation, considerable preparation and planning occurs. First, circle members decide who should attend and which circle members are to be involved in the presentation and to what extent. A detailed agenda is prepared, including a suggested time schedule and key speakers. This and an invitation to attend are circulated to all expected participants. Generally circle members enjoy the opportunity of presenting the details of their work to members of the technical staff and to management. Each member who wishes to do so should be given an opportunity to participate at some point in the presentation.

Participation, however, requires preparation. Part of this preparation includes writing out what is going to be said, having it typed with double or triple spacing and then highlighting it with a red pen. Highlights mark the statements that have to be emphasized and the places where extra-long pauses should occur, the various visual aids are to be introduced and the jokes are to be told. Practising out loud and trying to make the presentation sound spontaneous and interesting is important. This practice, in front of the mirror and using a tape recorder, or before other circle members, should continue until the material is known so well that it can be "read" while looking at the audience, that is, presented using the manuscript as a guide only.

Some reluctant circle members hesitate to volunteer for presentations because they are "too nervous in front of a group." Nervousness is very natural; most good speakers are nervous before a presentation. In fact, some nervousness is needed to do a good job. There are, however, techniques that can be used to control excessive nervousness. These include:

a) Acting natural. The presentation is being made to a group of friends. After all, each person has the same interests—the best for the company.

b) Practising before colleagues and in front of a mirror with a tape recorder until the results are pleasing.

c) A few deep breaths just prior to beginning the presentation help the speaker to relax. A sip or two of water keeps the throat and mouth moist so coughing or choking does not occur.

d) Most important, of course, is the pep talk to oneself—the positive thinking that states, "Of course I can do an excellent job."

The final step in the presentation is to arrange for a follow-up meeting so that a response by management can be provided, particularly if recommendations and not a completed project are being presented.

In summary, the presentation is a SPEECH:

Subject
Point
Enthusiasm
Exhibits
Conciseness
Humour

That is, the *s*ubject chosen is delivered in a manner that is to the *p*oint, with *e*nthusiasm and *e*xhibits, *c*oncisely, and *h*umorously.

A sample of the written portion of a quality circle presentation is given in Figure 8–2.

FIGURE 8–2
Japanese Quality Control Circle Presentation and Agenda

15th Improvement Activity Presentation Within Company

Outline of Presentation Content

December 1, 1980

1. *Presentation title*: "Improvement of Gauge Supervision Method"

(cont'd)

2. *Name of speaker*: Kensaku Kawazoe, Metal Mold Plant, Metal Mold Section
Name of circle: Asai Group Circle *Number of members*: 4 persons.

3. *Present situation and reasons to select this theme*:
Up-to-date supervision of all gauges has been done locally in the east side of the Metal Mold Building. Thus, in order to take out a gauge, traffic of employees has been increased. and when we take out a particular gauge, it has been very difficult to find the gauge because of the tremendous increase of number of gauges.

Thus, this circle decided to select this situation to eliminate the problem to make it more efficient.

4. *Goal*:
a) When to complete: end of November *b*) What problem: checkout of gauge *c*) How to improve: to be able to check out within 5 minutes.

5. *Approach*:
"Why," "what," "when," "who," "what method"—these are passwords for our group to ask and find answers by ourselves. Based on the QC method, at the meetings we repeated to collect our ideas to make progress in this theme.

6. *Counter-measure* (solution):
We have had several meetings together and discussed how to make gauge checkout and walking distance to be simpler and shorter. We did not have any good ideas for a while. Then our suggestion was "The best way is to have gauges closest to where they are needed." If we can condense our idea, the essence was that the gauges should be controlled where the gauges are used most frequently by local control (eliminate central control). Thus, we may reduce employee traffic. We are agreed on the idea. By the result of the above study, we planned to find a method of localized control.

7. *Results*:
The following results are obtained
a) Re-arrangement of gauges: unnecessary gauges were discarded and number and types of gauges were reduced from 434 to 317.
b) Local Control: Walking distances were shortened by spreading the control to locations, such as finishing process, lathe, electrode, outside request, etc.
c) Color Coded: All gauges were color coded to make checkout easier.

8. *Effect*:

a) (Items which cannot be indicated by number or money)

    i. Cooperative structure was enforced among the circle members.

    ii. We recognized once again the importance of positive action by the members and this result helped to make us more positive in our daily activity

b) (Money and Number)

    i. Now the gauge checkout time was reduced to within 3 minutes

    Before improvement: 15 minutes

    $(15 - 3) \times 13$ persons $\times$ 23 days = 59.8 hours per month thus reduction of 209,300 yen.

9. *Problems*:

Location of gauges, changes in installation, supervision of accuracy—how did we decide?

a) Location of gauge—map will be distributed to all workers.

b) Change in installation—once a drawing is made, it should be decided by a route from section chief [to] foreman [to] circle leader.

c) Supervision of accuracy—accuracy should be checked twice a month by man in charge.

10. *Future Plan*:

We have to otain confidence for future circle activity by this experience to solve problems of gauge administration. There are many problems left for further improvement. We would like to utilize this valuable experience and to make further improvements.

Source: Ford Casting Division Japanese Productivity Study Group, *A Report on the Japanese Automotive Foundry Industry* (Windsor, Ont., December 1980), unpaginated.

Audio-visual materials:
- large, clear, legible
- better if lights do not have to be turned off
- black, red, blue and green diagrams are seen more clearly
- pre-tested in presentation room
- in correct sequence

(cont'd)

- pointer used so view is not blocked

Presentation is *never* read word for word.

Humour helps.

Time is set aside for questions. Presenter
- looks at person asking question
- answers to the audience
- answers one question at a time
- gives specific but brief answer

Circle anticipates questions prior to presentation.

Interesting opening statement.

Interesting closing statement.

Acknowledgment.

Pre-preparation:
- full talk typed and highlighted
- talk practised

Overcome nervousness by:
- acting natural
- practising
- taking deep breaths
- taking sips of water
- positive thinking: "I can do an excellent job"

Follow-up meeting arranged.

SPEECH:
- *S*ubject
- *P*oint
- *E*nthusiasm
- *E*xhibit
- *C*onciseness
- *H*umour

PART III

STATISTICAL ANALYSIS AND EVALUATION

NINE

ANALYZING PROBLEM CAUSES USING GRAPHS AND STATISTICS

This chapter outlines the use and construction of the remaining most important tools needed for the analysis of causes. This includes line, bar, circle and pie graphs, histograms, scattergrams and Pareto diagrams.

GRAPHS[1]

Line Graphs

A line graph shows an event that has occurred. If the following data regarding defects were plotted as line graphs, they would appear as shown in Figure 9–1c.

Cause of defect	No. of defects previous week	No. of defects this week
Porosity	21	15
Opening too narrow	9	4
Opening too wide	6	6
Calibration	12	3
Leakage	15	6
Off centre	12	2

STATISTICAL ANALYSIS AND EVALUATION

By convention, the Y-axis of a graph is the vertical one and the X-axis is horizontal. Appropriate scales or labelling are placed on the two axes. In this illustration, the scale representing the number of defects (from 0 to 30; where possible, graphs always begin at 0) is placed on the Y-axis and the sub-cause or defect is placed on the X-axis.

A dot is placed at 21 for porosity, at 9 for opening too narrow, at 6 for opening too wide, etc. (see Figure 9–1a). When dots have been placed which correspond to the number of defects for all sub-causes, the dots are joined (see Figure 9–1b). This line represents the number of defects for a particular time period. The title on the graph is so complete that it will be identifiable many years in the future.

FIGURE 9–1a
First Step in Drawing a Line Graph

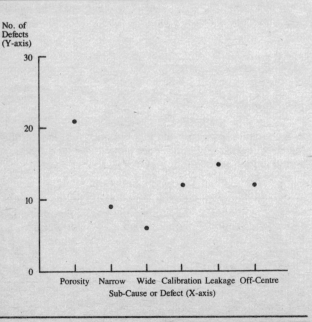

Line graphs are extremely useful for comparisons. Figure 9–1c compares the defects made before and after the implementation of a quality circle suggestion. Figure 9–2 illustrates a different type of line graph comparison—warehouse productivity (as an index) compared to total productivity (on the same index).

Bar Graphs

A bar graph is very similar to and is used for the same

FIGURE 9-1b
Line Graphs Showing Defects in Widget Department (L) by
Sub-Cause During Week of April 8, 198X to April 12, 198X

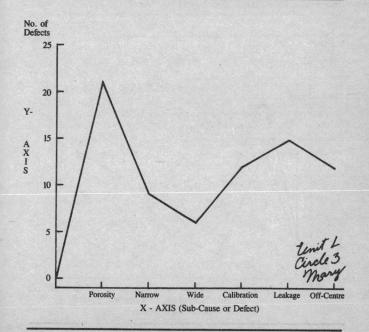

No. of Defects

Y-AXIS

X - AXIS (Sub-Cause or Defect)

Porosity   Narrow   Wide   Calibration   Leakage   Off-Centre

*Unit L
Circle 3
Mary*

purposes as a line graph (see Figure 9–3 and 9–4). The only difference is that bars are drawn instead of lines.

Circle Graphs

Circle graphs show the percentage of one item as a percentage of the whole. They are more difficult to construct because measurements must be exact. A protractor and a compass are required.

The procedure for constructing a circle graph is as follows:
1. Observations are made on the sub-causes of the effect in

FIGURE 9-1c
Line Graph Comparing Defects in Widget Department (L) for the Week of April 8, 198X and the Week of April 15, 198X

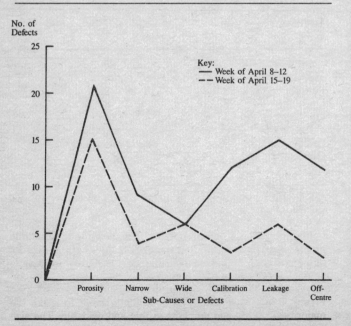

question. For example, a quality circle member observes that of seventy-five defects that occurred on a particular machine, twenty-one were attributable to porosity, nine to a too-narrow opening, six to a too-wide opening, twelve to improper calibration and fifteen to leakages. Twelve were off-centre.

2. The actual number of occurrences are translated into percentage form by dividing the actual number of occurrences that are attributable to the problem in question (21 for porosity) by the total number of defects (75) and multiplying by 100 (percent). In the above example, this would mean that 28 percent of the defects were attributable to porosity, 12 percent to a too-narrow opening, 8 percent to an opening that was too wide, 16 percent to improper calibration and 20 percent to leakage. The remaining 16 percent were off-centre.

3. To find the number of degrees (out of 360, the number of degrees in a circle) which each percentage represents, each percentage is multipled by 3.6. (Divide by 100 (percent) and multiply by 360 degrees). The figure that is obtained is the proportion of 360 which each cause (defect) represents. To illustrate:

Sub-cause	No. of Defects	Percentage	Degrees (Angle)
Porosity	21	28*	100.8*
Opening too narrow	9	12	43.2
Opening too wide	6	8	28.8
Calibration	12	16	57.6
Leakage	15	20	72.0
Off centre	12	16	57.6
	75	100	360.0

*21 divided by 75 multiplied by 100 = 28; 28 divided by 100 and multiplied by 360 or 28 times 3.6 = 100.8.

In other words, when defects are shown on the circle graph, an angle is drawn that shows porosity as 100.8 degrees of the 360 degrees that are available; the too-narrow opening is an angle of 43.2 degrees, and so on.

4. A circle of desired size is drawn using a compass (see Figure 9-5a). This usually is sufficiently large to make the majority of labels and numbers visible and readable. The size

usually does not exceed half a page unless a large graph is required for a group presentation.

5. A straight line is drawn from the centre point of the circle to the edge of the circle, usually horizontally (see Figure 9-5b).

6. Using the midpoint of the circle and the straight line as a base, the required angle is measured with a protractor.

7. A line is drawn from the midpoint to the edge of the circle to represent the required angle (see Figure 9-5c).

8. For each of the other defects, using the midpoint of the circle and any straight line as a base, the required angle is measured and a straight line is drawn to enclose the angle. The completed circle graph is shown in Figure 9-5d.

By this means, a visual diagram is constructed which shows each part (cause of the defect, etc.) as a proportion of the whole.

Pie Graphs

A "pie chart" is a circle graph from which one section has been partially removed to emphasize the importance of that particular event or cause. Figure 9-6 shows a pie graph or chart in which the defects caused by porosity (twenty-one of seventy-five, or 28 percent) have been accentuated.

Histograms

A histogram is used for two purposes. First, it shows the frequency (in number or as a percentage) with which an event occurs and helps to determine whether the problem that has been identified occurs more frequently during a specified interval (such as at a particular time, at a particular calibration). The second purpose of the histogram is to compare the shape of the distribution itself with some known distribution. For example, when a particular machine operates for more than eight hours without maintenance, defects increase by 10 percent every two hours. Quality circle members observe the machine and note the actual number of defects. This actual occurrence is compared with the expected distribution. To better illustrate this, the two distributions are plotted on the same graph paper using different colours or shading. In the

FIGURE 9–2
Line Graph—Warehouse and Total Productivity Based on PPP
Index Without Buybacks

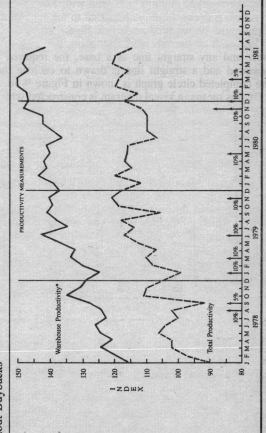

*PPP Index Without Buybacks

FIGURE 9–3
Vertical Bar Graph Showing Defects in Widget Department (L) by Sub-Cause During the Week of April 8, 198X to April 12, 198X

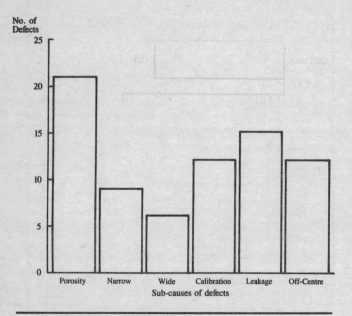

same way, two or more machines, systems or operators can be compared.

A histogram is easy to construct. The following procedure can be used:

1. An observation is made, or available information is analyzed, to determine how frequently each sub-cause (defect, etc.) occurs at each point in time, at each calibration, and so on.

2. A *continuous interval* of measurement (such as time or calibration) is decided on, and this is shown on the X-axis (horizontal axis) with equal distances between each number. For example, a quality circle on an automobile assembly line

FIGURE 9–4
Horizontal Bar Graph Showing Defects in Widget Department (L) by Sub-Cause During the Week of April 8, 198X to April 12, 198X

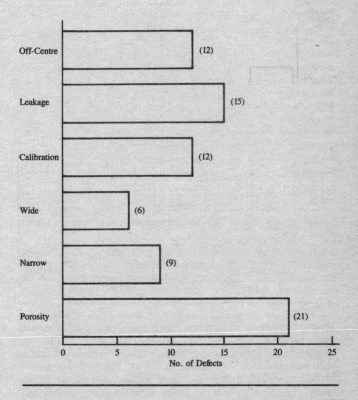

observed that the seventy-five defects mentioned previously occurred irregularly during the week as shown:

Day of week*	Time of day*	No. of defects
Monday	6:00 a.m. to 12:00 a.m.	10
Monday	12:00 a.m. to 6:00 p.m.	8
Monday	6:00 p.m. to 12:00 p.m.	4
Monday	12:00 p.m. to 6:00 a.m.	5
Tuesday	6:00 a.m. to 12:00 a.m.	3
Tuesday	12:00 a.m. to 6:00 p.m.	2
Tuesday	6:00 p.m. to 12:00 p.m.	2
Tuesday	12:00 p.m. to 6:00 a.m.	5
Wednesday	6:00 a.m. to 12:00 a.m.	1
Wednesday	12:00 a.m. to 6:00 p.m.	1
Wednesday	6:00 p.m. to 12:00 p.m.	1
Wednesday	12:00 p.m. to 6:00 a.m.	2
Thursday	6:00 a.m. to 12:00 a.m.	2
Thursday	12:00 p.m. to 6:00 a.m.	1
Thursday	6:00 a.m. to 12:00 a.m.	2
Thursday	12:00 p.m. to 6:00 p.m.	3
Friday	6:00 a.m. to 12:00 a.m.	5
Friday	12:00 a.m. to 6:00 p.m.	3
Friday	6:00 p.m. to 12:00 p.m.	7
Friday	12:00 p.m. to 6:00 a.m.	8

*In this instance, the X-axis is labelled with the days of the week and the time periods.

3. The number of occurrences (or percentages) is shown on the Y-axis (vertical axis) with an equal distance between each number. In this illustration, since defects range from 1 to 10, the numbers 0 to 10 are placed on the Y-axis (a graph begins at 0, if possible).

4. A vertical bar graph is drawn to show this. The bars are always adjacent to each other, that is, no space is left between them because time (or other variable chosen) is continuous. Generally the lines between the bars are not drawn but that is unimportant—it is convenient to do so. Figure 9-7 shows a histogram of the number of defects which occurred during the week of April 8 to April 12 in the Widget Department at four different time periods of each day.

Pareto Diagrams

The Pareto diagram is based on the Pareto principle, which states that any effect is the result of a variety of causes which can be added together to produce the total effect and that, in many instances, only one or two causes, categories or sub-processes are dominant, i.e., contribute more than one-half to the total effect that occurs.

FIGURE 9–5
Steps in Drawing a Circle Graph

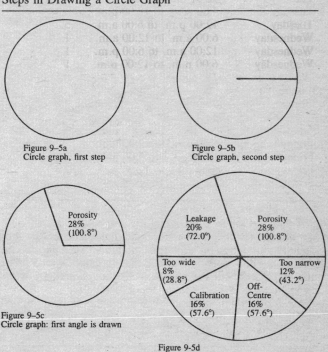

Figure 9–5a
Circle graph, first step

Figure 9–5b
Circle graph, second step

Figure 9–5c
Circle graph: first angle is drawn

Porosity
28%
(100.8°)

Leakage
20%
(72.0°)

Porosity
28%
(100.8°)

Too wide
8%
(28.8°)

Too narrow
12%
(43.2°)

Calibration
16%
(57.6°)

Off-
Centre
16%
(57.6°)

Figure 9-5d
Complete circle graph showing defects in
Widget Department (L) by sub-cause during
the week of April 8, 198X to April 12, 198X.

The diagram can indicate:
1. The degree to which one element or cause contributes to a problem.
2. Whether improvements have occurred.

FIGURE 9-6
Pie Graph Showing Defects in Widget Depart (L) by Sub-Cause and Emphasizing Defects Because of Porosity During the Week of April 8, 198X to April 12, 198X.

A Pareto diagram is two graphs in one—a line graph and a bar graph. The bar graph illustrates the variation, by frequency, percentage or cost, that occurs in one variable in each of the different forms which that variable can take. The line graph indicates the effect of all these variations, when cumulated one at a time from largest to smallest.

An example will illustrate: The effect that is being examined is the number of breakdowns caused by defects. These breakdowns occur seventy-five times in total as shown:

	No. of defects	Cumulative breakdowns
Porosity	21	21
Leakage	15	36
Calibration	12	48
Off-centre	12	60
Opening too narrow	9	69
Opening too wide	6	75

FIGURE 9–7

Histogram Showing Number of Defects in Widget Department (L) During Four Time Periods Each Day for the Week of April 8, 198X to April 12, 198X

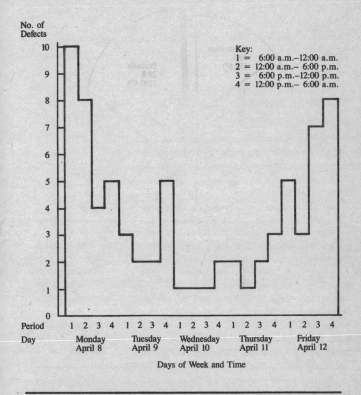

Figure 9–8a illustrates the Pareto diagram (the line and bar graphs) that shows these relationships. The bar graph indicates the number of times each breakdown occurs and the types of defect which cause that breakdown. The line graph shows the cumulation of each of these breakdowns.

FIGURE 9–8a
Pareto Diagram Showing Contribution of Sub-Causes to Breakdown in Widget Department (L) for the Week of April 8, 198X to April 12, 198X

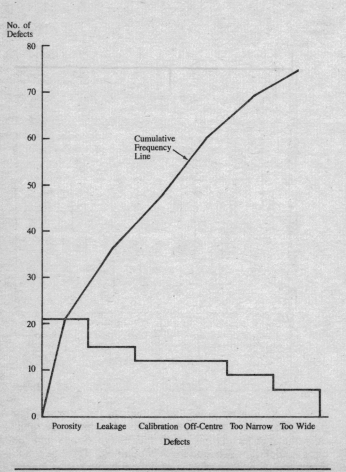

FIGURE 9–8b
Pareto Diagram Showing Contribution of Sub-Causes to Breakdown in Widget Depart (L) for the Week of April 8, 198X to April 12, 198X

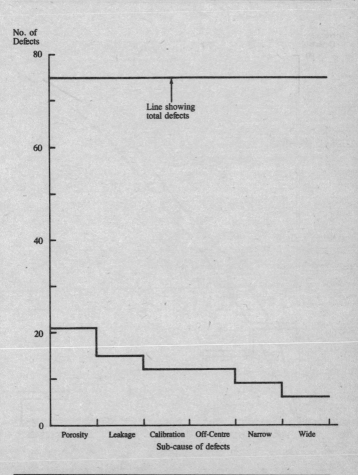

FIGURE 9–8c
Pareto Diagram Showing Contribution of Sub-Causes to Breakdown in Widget Department (L) for the Week of April 8, 198X to April 12, 198X

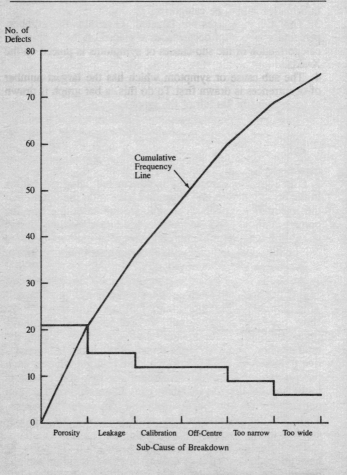

No. of Defects

Cumulative Frequency Line

Sub-Cause of Breakdown

Porosity   Leakage   Calibration   Off-Centre   Too narrow   Too wide

Pareto diagrams, which are easy to construct and interpret, are drawn as follows:

1. Possible sub-causes of an effect are identified using a fishbone diagram.

2. Information is gathered about a particular effect and its apparent sub-causes. A decision is made as to how this information should be categorized.

3. The X and Y axes are labelled. Generally the number, percentage or cost of occurrences is placed on the Y-axis; the categorization of the sub-causes or symptoms is placed on the X-axis.

4. The sub-cause or symptom which has the largest number of occurrences is drawn first. To do this. a bar graph is drawn at the origin (the far left of the graph).

5. Beside the first bar, a second bar is drawn to illustrate the sub-cause, symptom or defect which has the second greatest number of occurrences.

6. This process continues until all sub-causes, symptoms or defects are illustrated by bars.

7. The cumulative frequency is determined using sub-causes in the order in which they have been drawn on the graph, and the line indicating this is drawn. In this case, the line for porosity shows twenty-one defects; leakage is shown as thirty-six; calibration as forty-eight, and so on.

By convention, the cumulative line graph is generally drawn at the midpoint of each interval or bar graph (Figure 9–8a). When this is done, the cumulative frequency line is extended so that it begins at the origin (at 0 on both the X and Y axes). This, however, is not important, and Figures 9–8b and 9–8c show the same Pareto graph. In the first, the cumulative frequency line graph is drawn as a straight line, indicating the total number of defects; in the second illustration, the cumulative frequency corresponds to the extreme right edge of each bar graph. The technical details are not important; what is important is that circle members use one method or that each understands what is being illustrated. Through experience, study and training sessions, members become more sophisticated in the techniques that are used.

The three illustrations of the Pareto diagram (Figure 9–8) have utilized the number of defects. A Pareto diagram can use percentages, for example:

Cause of defect	No. of defects	Cumulative breakdowns
Porosity	28	28
Leakage	20	48
Calibration	16	64
Off-centre	16	80
Too-narrow opening	12	92
Too-wide opening	8	100

This illustration is shown in Figure 9–9.

Costs also could be used, for example:

Cause of defect	No. of defects	Unit cost of repair	Total repair cost	Cumulative costs
Porosity	21	$30	$630	$ 630
Calibration	12	20	240	870
Too-wide opening	6	30	180	1,050
Leakage	15	5	75	1,125
Off-centre	15	3	45	1,170
Too-narrow opening	9	3	27	1,197

This Pareto diagram is illustrated in Figure 9–10. It is a very different diagram from the other four. Defects attributable to some causes are very difficult to repair, and, while there may be few of them (too wide an opening, for example), the cost to the firm may be quite high. Quality circles should observe and illustrate the same problem from as many different perspectives as possible.

Although it is not noticeable in these examples because the same data is used to illustrate all cases, Pareto diagrams in the "real world" show that very few items contribute almost all of the value or variation. In fact, even in the above example of costs, three of the six items (porosity, calibration, too wide an opening) contribute about 88 percent of the value or variation. It is these "vital few" items that a quality circle analyzes and improves first.

Scattergrams

Scattergrams are utilized when it is believed that two occurrences are related to each other. If, for example, it is believed that raw material of a certain porosity causes the calibration of a particular part to vary excessively, a good way to examine this would be through the use of a scattergram. By examining the cluster of dots, it is possible to determine whether a relationship exists, whether this relationship differs as the variable changes, and whether certain conditions create or contribute to a deficiency. By examining the pattern of dots, as shown in Figure 9–11c, for example, it is not difficult to draw the conclusion that porous materials (porosity of 241, 242 and 243) tend to produce products that are calibrated improperly (at .0001, .0002, .0007, and .0008).

How is a scattergram constructed?

1. Observations are made over a period of time (hourly for a week, for example) of two or more variables or elements, one of which is suspected of causing the other, or both of which might be caused by a third as yet unidentified cause.

2. Figures, representing the respective number of occurrences of each element, are placed on the two axes of the graph and the axes are labelled. (Porosities of 236 to 243 have been placed on the Y-axis and calibrations of .0001 to .0008 have been placed on the X-axis).

3. A dot is placed for each joint occurrence. Ten parts were produced on a particular day when the porosity of raw material is 237 and ten parts cause calibrations of .0001, .0001, .0002, .0005, .0003, .0008, .0004, .0005, .0005 and .0004 (see Figure 9–11a). Porosity changed to 243 and three parts were produced with calibrations of .0008, .0007 and .0008 (see Figure 9–11b).

As pointed out earlier, Figure 9–11c shows that as the raw material becomes more porous, proper calibration becomes more difficult.

A FEW FINAL WORDS

Graphs are easy to understand and easy to draw. Because the relationship can be visualized, circle members can more clearly understand the causes that produce a particular effect.

FIGURE 9–9
Pareto Diagram Showing Contribution of Sub-Causes to Breakdown, by Percentage, in Widget Department (L) for the Week
of April 8, 198X to April 12, 198X

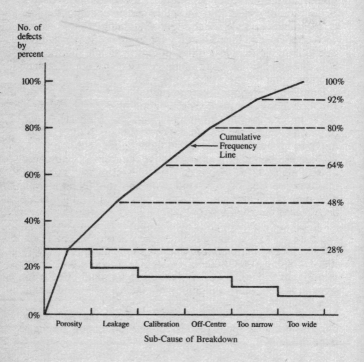

FIGURE 9–10
Pareto Diagram Showing Contribution of Sub-Causes to Breakdown, by Cost, in Widget Department (L) for the Week of April 8, 198X to April 12, 198X

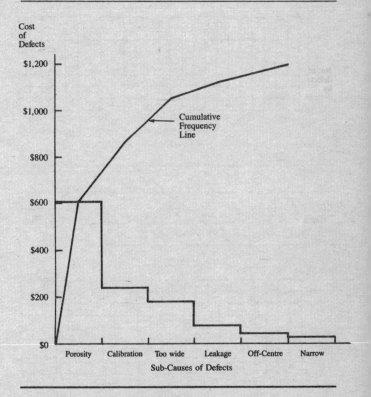

Some conventions exist that standardize what is done and help to better visualize the relationships that exist:
1. Generally graphs are placed on graph paper or grid paper.
2. The X and Y axes are always labelled. The X-axis is always horizontal; the Y-axis is always vertical.
3. A descriptive title is included with the graph. This title

199

FIGURE 9–11a
Effect of Porosity of 237 on Calibration. Observations Taken
April 8, 198X to April 12 198X

FIGURE 9–11b
Effect of Porosity of 237 and 243 on Calibration. Observations Taken April 8, 198X to April 12 198X

always includes a date and is so complete that the graph is immediately identifiable—even several years later.
4. Often graphs are initialled or signed by the person who

researched the data and drew the graph. In that way, the individual assumes responsibility for the correctness of the information and illustration.

FIGURE 9–11c
Effects of Porosity on Calibration. Observations Taken April 8, 198X to April 12, 198X

Porosity

KNOW HOW TO CONSTRUCT:
Graphs
• line graph
• horizontal bar graphs
• vertical bar graphs

Circle graphs
• pie chart

Histogram

Pareto diagram can be drawn on basis of:
• number of defects
• percentages
• costs

Scattergram

TEN

SAMPLING AND STATISTICS

Sampling is a process in which a small number of items are selected from an entire population for detailed examination and statistical analyses, because they are representative of that population. This is done so that decisions can be made about the characteristics of the whole population.

Before sampling or statistical procedures can be discussed in any detail, certain terms that are commonly used must be understood, such as: random sample, systematic sample, stratified sample, duster sample, mean, mode, median, frequency distribution, cumulative frequency distribution, normal curve, kurtosis, skewness, area under the curve, dispersion, standard deviation and variance. It is also important to know how to sample and how many to sample, and to check whether the sample is representative of the population.

SAMPLING

Researchers may draw a random sample. a systematic random sample, a stratified sample, or a cluster sample. These terms simply refer to the method that has been chosen to select the units which will be examined in greater detail.

Random Sampling

When random sampling occurs, the units are selected without specifying any characteristics which the units must have or time intervals in which they must be selected (except that they are produced by the machine, operators or section of interest). If sampling is *systematic*, units are selected at regular intervals—for instance, every third, tenth or twentieth unit or one every fifteen minutes, half hour or hour. In other words, there is some system or pattern for selecting the units.

Stratified Sampling

A stratified sample is chosen when there is a desire to examine certain groups in detail and it is necessary to ensure that there are enough units in each of the groups. In the plant, stratified sampling is used when the quality circle decides that it will examine four units each day which are produced on each of four lathes by each of twelve operators for a one-week period. (The number of units selected during the week is 4 (units) × 4 (lathes) × 12 (operators) × 5 (days) = 960 units.) Under this selection process, it is relatively easy to give estimates of adequate or inadequate performance for (1) each day of the week, (2) each of the four machines, and (3) each of the twelve operators. To do this, however, 960 units, assuming a five-day week, would have to be selected and examined.

This differs from random sampling because the machine and person have been specified. In random sampling, selection would be made at the end of the line without regard to operator or machine.

In using stratified sampling, it is necessary to decide on the number of groupings (strata) that are to be examined, whether the same proportion of units will be selected from each group or whether proportionately more units will be selected from some groupings than from others, and the total number of items or elements that is required.

Taking a larger sample from one group than from others may be justified because the group consists of a larger number (five units are made on Lathe 2 during the same time that one unit is made on Lathe 1 and on Lathe 3); because there is more variability (Lathe 2 appears to malfunction more frequently); or because it is cheaper to sample one group (for example: In order to sample and examine a unit, it must be destroyed. Lathe 3 and Lathe 1 produce parts which are made using an expensive alloy; Lathe 2 uses alloys that can be recycled). Under these circumstances, more Lathe 2 units are selected than Lathe 1 or Lathe 3 units.

Many formulas are given for selecting the number of units that will be examined and the total number of units. As circle members become more experienced, they will want to learn about these. At the beginning, some common-sense rules will suffice:

1. Enough units from one grouping must be examined so that circle members feel they have a reasonable knowledge of how a machine or operator is performing.

2. *As few units in each grouping as possible* should be selected. Sampling costs money because:

- Someone has to take time to examine each unit and do the analyses.
- It is often necessary to destroy the unit.
- Units which have been taken for the purpose of examination are not available for production purposes.

In short, because information costs money, it is never possible to be 100 percent certain about how an operation is proceeding. Because of this, small samples are taken and estimates about the characteristics of the entire population (such as quality) are made.

Cluster Sampling

In cluster sampling, the population is divided into sub-groups (for example, three lathes and twelve operators give thirty-six sub-groups or clusters). Not all thirty-six groups are examined if cluster sampling is used. Instead only specific sub-groups which are perceived to be typical of the others are chosen (for example, Operators 3, 5 and 11 who work on Lathe 2; Operator 1 on Lathe 1; Operator 7 on Lathe 3). A large number of units, however, are selected from each of these five sub-groups. On the basis of examination of the selected units, conclusions are made about the characteristics of the parts produced on all three lathes by all twelve operators.

Cluster sampling is especially useful if clusters are homogeneous (the work done on all lathes by all operators is of the same quality). Decisions that must be made concern the size of each cluster, whether an equal or unequal number of units should be selected from each of the sub-groups, and the total number of units that are to be selected.

Logical reasons must exist for selecting particular clusters. If there are none: clusters and units selected are chosen randomly.

The same common-sense rules of thumb can be used in cluster sampling—as few units as possible but a sufficient number so that some confidence can be placed in the estimates that are made.

STATISTICAL MEASURES

Statistics can be extremely simple or extremely complex. Percentages, frequencies and cumulative frequencies are the simplest of statistical measures and describe the number of items that have been observed in a particular category. Other methods of describing a relationship, in statistical terms, are centrality measures and the normal curve.

Distributions

To describe a number of proportion of items which are in a specific category or grouping, the term "frequency distribution" is used. When the number of items in several categories are added together (summated or cumulated), the term "cumulative frequency distribution" is used.

For example:

	No. of Defects	*Cumulative Frequency*
Machine A	3	3
Machine B	6	9
Machine C	9	18
Machine D	2	20
Machine E	5	25

The numbers 3, 6, 9, 2 and 5 represent the frequency or frequency distribution of defects by machine and the numbers 3, 9, 18, 20 and 25 represent the cumulative frequency distribution.

Centrality Measures

Centrality measures are those which indicate the centre, the middle or the average. Three measures are used most commonly—mean, mode and median.

Mean. The mean is the average of a group of numbers. If a worker wants to know his or her mean (average) monthly salary for the past year, he or she would add the value of all cheques received and divide by 12 (because there are 12 months).

Mode. Mode means fashionable, popular or chosen most frequently; it is the item, value, etc. that occurs the greatest number of times in a given series of observations. If the mode concerning defects produced on a particular machine is required and defects are examined on a daily basis for a month, the numbers from 0 to the largest number of defects which occur are written in a column. Each day a check mark is placed beside the number of defects that occur that day. The number with the most checks at the end of the month is the mode.

Median. A third measure of centrality is the median. If a worker wants to know the median salary which was received in the forty-nine weeks of the year in which he or she worked (three weeks were holidays), the salaries received in each of the weeks are arranged in order from smallest to largest or vice versa. The employee then counts to the half-way point (twenty-five in this case). The twenty-fifth number in the list is the median. If an even number of items appears in the list (say, the median salary for all fifty-two weeks), the employee again counts to the halfway point (in this case, between the twenty-sixth and the twenty-seventh items). The salaries which appear twenty-sixth and twenty-seventh are added together and are divided by two. The figure so obtained is the median.

The Normal Curve

Statisticians have determined, through experience, that any time thirty or more people or units are selected randomly and

FIGURE 10–1a
Normal Curve

are examined on any one chracteristic that can be measured on a continuous scale (height or weight, for instance) that there are some people who are very low on this characteristic and some that are very high. The majority are somewhere between very low and very high.

Through the examination of many such samples, statisticians have determined that the curve of the distribution of these characteristics is bell-shaped, as shown in Figure 10-1a. This distribution has become known as the normal curve.

The concept may be easier to understand by examining the manner in which a normal curve is constructed. The area under the curve represents very small bar graphs, each of which is drawn to represent the actual characteristics of the units under study. In other words, in drawing the normal curve of the heights of the entire population (or a large representative sample thereof) the frequency of all people from the shortest to the tallest, in one-quarter inch (or five-millimeter) intervals, is calculated. These frequencies are each drawn as vertical bar graphs. The bar graphs, when squeezed together, assume the shape of the normal curve.

Mean, standard deviation, kurtosis and skewness are terms which describe the characteristics or properties of a distribution that can be shown by drawing a normal curve.

Kurtosis. What is kurtosis? Samples can be drawn from many types of groups. If a random sample of the general population is drawn and the heights of all the people are measured, the distribution appears like the one that is shown in Figure 10–1a. If, however, the sample is drawn only from professional basketball players, there is relatively little difference between the heights, and the majority are grouped in very small range. The normal curve of this group is shown at the left in Figure 10–1b. If almost an equal number of people are selected at each height, the normal curve is much flatter, similar to that shown at the right in Figure 10–1b. Kurtosis, then, is the relative degree of curvature near the mode of a normal curve.

Skewness. Normal curves can also be skewed, that is, have the largest portion to the right or left of centre, as shown in Figure 10–1c. In other words, using the example of height, although a random sample is drawn, the majority of the people that are selected in the sample are very tall or very short. Skewness is the state of being asymmetric or distorted.

Both kurtosis and skewness indicate that the sample which has been drawn varies from the usual or normal.

Mean. The mean (written as x̄) can be calculated by adding together all the numbers which represent the characteristic in question (all the various heights, for example) and dividing by the number of units or people.

FIGURE 10–1b
Kurtosis

FIGURE 10–1c
Skewness

Standard Deviation. The mean is not the only measure that is needed to describe a normal distribution. As explained earlier, some normal curves are tall and some are very flat. For convenience, statisticians decided to draw a line under the curve and to divide this line into six approximately equal parts. They called the distance between each of these six parts a standard deviation. Three of the standard deviations are to the left of the mean (and hence represent people or units who have less of the characteristics that the mean person or unit has (for exmaple, they are shorter than the average person). Three standard deviations are to the right of the mean. In Figure 10–1d, A and D are one standard deviation away from the mean; and B and E are two standard deviations away from the mean. Statistical textbooks give formulas for calculating standard deviation and variance. The variance formula appears like this: $\Sigma(x_i - \bar{x})^2/N$. Standard deviation is the square root of the variance.

To illustrate: A machine is observed for eight days. In those eight days, the following number of defects occur: 12, 10, 10, 9, 8, 7, 5 and 3. The mean number of defects for the eight days is $12 + 10 + 10 + 9 + 8 + 7 + 5 + 3$ divided by number of items (8) or 64 divided by $8 = 8$ defects.

The variance is calculated as follows:

x_i	Mean ($\bar{x}$)	$x_i - \bar{x}$	$(x_i - \bar{x})^2$
12	8	4	16
10	8	2	4
10	8	2	4
9	8	1	1

x_i	Mean ($\bar{x}$)	$x_i - \bar{x}$	$(x_i - \bar{x})^2$
8	8	0	0
7	8	-1	1
5	8	-3	9
3	8	-5	25
		$\Sigma(x_i - \bar{x})^2 =$	60

Variance = 60 divided by 8 or 7.5.
Standard deviation is the square root of 60/8 or 2.739.

What the formula is saying is that the mean is subtracted from each of the observations. This gives $(x_i - \bar{x})$. Each of these numbers is then squared $(x_i - \bar{x})^2$ and added together $\Sigma(x_i - \bar{x})^2$. (In statistics, the Greek letter sigma (Σ) indicates "to summate" or "to add together.") Finally, this value is divided by N (the number of observations). This is the value for variance. To obtain the standard deviation, it is necessary to take the square root of the variance.

Of course, it is not necessary to calculate the mean or the standard deviation manually; a computer can do it.

INTERPRETING STATISTICS

The area of any closed figure, such as a square, circle, triangle or octagon, can be calculated. A line under the curve makes the normal curve a "closed figure" and its area can be calculated. It may be redundant to say but important to do so: A triangle has 100 percent of its area within the triangle; the same is true for a square, a circle, and the area under the normal curve.

Statisticians have arbitrarily divided the line under the curve into six equal parts. They have called the distance between each of these one-sixth divisions a *standard deviation*. Because the area under the normal curve represents many bar graphs that are squeezed together, it is possible to select the specific bar graphs that fall at exactly the mean and at one and two standard deviations to the left or the right of the mean (or any other point). In Figure 10—1d, these are shown as $\bar{x}$I, DH, AJ, EG and BK.

FIGURE 10–1d
Relationship Between Normal Curve and Standard Deviation
(SD)

By examining many samples, statisticians have also determined that 2.3 percent of the area under the curve is to the left and to the right of the bar graphs which indicate the location of the second standard deviation from the mean, that is, the area circumscribed by FEG and by CBK.

Statisticians have also determined that the area under the curve which is bounded by the first and second standard deviations (EGHD and BKJA) is 13.6 percent of the whole of the area under the curve. Additionally, the area under the curve which is bounded by the mean and the first standard deviation to the left or to the right of the mean (x̄IHD and x̄IJA) is 34.1 percent of the whole of the area under the curve.

Why is this important?

If a unit (such as a machine or a person) in a particular sample has a certain amount of a characteristic and the amount of that characteristic is described as being one standard deviation to the left of the mean, that unit possesses more of the characteristic than 15.9 percent (2.3 percent plus 13.6 percent) of the other units in the sample. If a second unit has a certain amount of a characteristic and the amount of that characteristic is described as being one standard deviation to the right of the mean, the unit possesses more of that characteristic than 84.1 percent (2.3 + 13.6 + 34.1 + 34.1) of the other units in the sample.

FIGURE 10–1e
Relationship Between Standard Deviation and Area Under
Curve

An example may illustrate. A quality circle records the number of defects produced by one hundred machines at hourly intervals over a one-month period. A computer calculates the mean ($\bar{x}$ is 10) and the standard deviation (SD is 2) for the entire sample. It also calculates the mean number of defects for each machine. For six machines the data given or calculated by members is as follows:

Average

Machine	Number of Defects	Standard Deviation
B1	6	2 (to the left)
L3	8	1 (to the left)
M6	10	0
P2	12	1 (to the right)
R9	14	2 (to the right)
W3	16	3 (to the right)

When the number of defects for all 100 machines are shown as bar graphs as a normal curve, Machine B1 can be described as being (6 – 10)/2 or 2 SD to the left of the mean. For Machine M6, this is (10 – 10)/2 or 0 deviations from the mean. For Machine W3, this is (16 – 10)/2 or 3 standard deviations to the right of the mean.

In other words, Machine B1 is a "good" machine; only 2.3 percent of the machines produced less defects than this machine did. Machine M6 is an average machine, but both R9 and W3 produced more than their share of defects. In the case of R9, it produced more defects than 84.1 percent of the machines in the sample. W3 is the worst machine; all 99 other machines produced less defects.

Within the work situation, it is necessary to correct a situation which produces or where there are too many deviants (for example, it is necessary to fix or replace a machine that produces to many defects). The mean and standard deviation also assist quality circle members in making decisions by allowing them to compare their findings with known or previously calculated standards through the use of statistical tests such as the t-test, analysis of variance or the chi-square (χ^2) goodness-of-fit test. Most companies have statistical packages for the computer which are used to compute these tests. All that is usually necessary is for quality circle members to list the results of observations and the known or previously calculated mean and standard deviation.

The numbers chosen in this sample make the decision process very easy. Calculations are not required to reach the decision that Machine W3 is producing too many defects and should be replaced. If, however, a company can replace only one machine but must decide between three machines with means and standard deviations of:

Machine A ($\bar{x} = 10.369$, SD = 2.613),
Machine B ($\bar{x} = 9.763$, SD = 0.215), and
Machine C ($\bar{x} = 10.637$, SD = 1.200), the decision is more difficult and the appropriate calculations and tests must be made.

SUMMARY

In this chapter, three types of sampling and the concept of the normal curve and frequency distributions have been described. These statistics are sufficient to conduct the majority of analyses that will be required by circle members. The concepts are simple; the terminology that is used makes these appear more difficult than they really are. Circle members should be encouraged to learn and use statistical tools. As experience grows, more complex methods can be studied and the nuances can be appropriately interpreted.

STATISTICS
Sampling
• random
• systematic
• stratified
• cluster

Statistical measures
• percentages, frequencies, cumulative frequencies
• centrality measures: mean, mode, median
• normal curve
• standard deviation and variance

Normal curve
• kurtosis
• skewness
• area under the curve

ELEVEN

EVALUATING THE CIRCLE

After circles have been in operation for some time, even the most patient senior management will want assurances that money invested in this concept has been well spent. To show this, three types of measurements are necessary: objective productivity-type measures, subjective attitudinal measures regarding the impact that the circle has had on the organization, and an analysis of the internal processes of the circles.

PRODUCTIVITY MEASURES

The easiest way to measure success is through objective measures, that is, the concrete improvements which have occurred because of the work of quality circles. For this purpose, records are kept of improvements throughout the year. Additionally, one or two meetings are set aside at which past suggestions are examined and an action plan is set to investigate the long-range impact that the suggestions have had. Finally, a report is written by each quality circle outlining these benefits and improvements—placing, where possible, actual dollar figures on the savings that have accrued.

This objective productivity improvement analysis might address some of the following issues:

1. Better quality as measured by a reduction in rejects, fewer defective products, fewer recalls and fewer products which require work.

2. Less scrap or waste.

3. Greater quantity of production.

4. Decrease in direct marginal cost (the cost of producing one unit).

5. Decrease in overhead or fixed costs.

6. Better equipment, machine and facility utilization.

7. Decrease in number and seriousness of accidents and more concern for safety and wearing of safety equipment.

8. Decrease in expenditures for maintenance of plant and equipment.

9. Less down time.

10. Increase in clients and customers, both in numbers and in value of purchases.

11. Greater customer satisfaction as shown by fewer customer complaints, less hostility and less office time allocated to problem solving.

12. For some or all employees, task procedures that have been simplified or improved.

No circle should feel, and no management should feel, that a circle has failed if there is little or no improvement in productivity—particularly in the first two or three years of circle operation. Even after the circle has become well established, improvement occurs in only one or two of the areas mentioned.

A more formal evaluation sheet used in Japan by Suzuki Motor Company is shown in Figure 11–1. Of interest are the eight criteria used and the weightings assigned to teach:

- Number of suggestions made

  2 points for each suggestion

- Length of time for which the circle meets

  3 - 13 points times the number of meetings per month

- Attendance rate

  2 - 5 points

- Money saved or the rank given the suggestion

  10 points for suggestions up to 9,999 yen ($450); 170 points for suggestions of 200,000 yen ($2,000) or more

- Standards corrected

  1 - 5 points for each correction

- Report presented at conference   40 points for each presentation
- Report published   40 points for each publication
- Standards violation   Deduction of 10 or 15 points for each violation

Each company and the circles in that company must decide whether such a formal evaluation serves a purpose. If the scheme is useful, the point system should be reached by a process of consensus decision making. Also, the system may have to change depending on the age of the circles and the unit or department in which they operate.

RELATIONSHIP-ORIENTED MEASURES

Relationships, satisfaction, trust and cooperation are much more difficult to measure than productivity. Many problems exist in trying to quantify these aspects of organizational life and to prove, not only that there has been an improvement, but also that the improvement was attributable to circle operation. Relationships are long term in nature; U.S. and Canadian management, however, tends to be oriented to short-term results. Generally, no a priori measurements are made prior to circle introduction. External factors too affect internal processes. It is very difficult, for example, for trust to exist when the economy is in a severe downturn and massive layoffs are occurring or are imminent. Additionally, the validity of attitudinal surveys and organizational climate surveys has been questioned.

For those who may find it useful, a questionnaire developed to measure changes in attitudes which may result when quality circles are used is given at the end of this chapter. The questionnaire has five sections:
1. Questions about the circle and training.
2. Questions about circle processes.
3. Questions about the perceived effectiveness of the circle, namely which groups contribute to the success.
4. Questions concerning attitudes regarding the circle and the organization.
5. Questions about the respondent.

FIGURE 11–1
Quality Circle Evaluation Sheet of Suzuki Motor Company

Month	Section Chief			
Section	Circle	Leader		
Item	Evaluation item		Weight	Points
Number of suggestions made	Number of improvements, ideas, opinions, and suggestions presented (Limited to Quality Circle suggestions)		2 ×	(cases)
Times circle met	15–29 minutes		3 ×	(times)
	30–59 minutes		7 ×	(times)
	60–89 minutes		10 ×	(times)
	90 + minutes		13 ×	(times)
Attendance	–59 percent		2 ×	(times)
	60–79 percent		3 ×	(times)
	80 + percent		5 ×	(times)
Money saved	to 9,999 yen or 5th rank		10 ×	(cases)
	10,000–49,999 yen or 4th rank		30 ×	(cases)
	50,000–99,000 yen or 3rd rank		70 ×	(cases)
	100,000–199,999 yen or 2nd rank		100 ×	(cases)
	200,000 yen or 1st rank		170 ×	(cases)
SOS SIS	Correction of errors		1 ×	(cases)
	Formulation, revision		5 ×	(cases)
Report given at Quality Circle conference			40 ×	(cases)
Report published in			40 ×	(cases)

Registered members

Remarks

File Number

Type of suggestion

(Data)	(Data)	(Data)	(Data)

(Data)	(Data)	(Data)	(Data)

Type of suggestion	File number	Money saved or suggestions for one case a month

Conference name

Name of magazine, issue

(cont'd)

SOS SIS violation	Standard is correct but not conformed to	– 15 × (cases)
	Standard not correct and could not be conformed to	– 10 × (cases)
	TOTAL	
Details	SOS, SIS Division New No. Entry error	

Note: 1. When the Quality Circle meets, this list must be submitted before the 10th of the following month. (If it is not submitted, the circle meeting will not be recognized as such.)
2. For the money saved in (4), supporting materials in written form

The questions about the circle processes centre on fifteen elements that play a part in circle success. These are examined to determine which are important. An additional nine statements attempt to determine the perceived purpose of the circle.

The attitudinal questions in Section 4 examine the feelings which members have about the circle, the work attitudes that exist, and whether members feel they are making a contribution. The last part of this section deals with commitment and loyalty to the organization, effort which the member would exert for the company, and the similarity in values which exists between company management and circle members.

The last section asks questions regarding age, gender, education, employment with the company and similar industries, position, department, union activities, participation as a member in and as a leader of a circle, and reasons for joining the circle.

Since the entire questionnaire is somewhat long, sections and questions should be selected carefully, depending on the desired purpose that a researcher has in mind. Several studies using this questionnaire are reported later in the book.

As relationships and trust improve, the amount of time that managers must spend resolving internal problems decreases. Interviews with managers in key positions therefore may also be useful in determining that attitudes have improved.

How can improvements be indicated to management? A

One check in three months	

Revision	Enforcement

must be submitted with this evaluation list (except for suggestions).
Source: Tadao Koguri, "Providing Incentives of the QC Circle Through an Evaluation System," *Japan Quality Control Circles* (Tokyo: Asian Productivity Organization, 1982): 170.

section in the annual report of the circle always illustrates the manner in which at least some of the nine improvements listed below have occurred:

1. Greater trust and cooperation among employees, and particularly between management and rank-and-file employees, and between union executive members and company officials.
2. More open and meaningful communication, including better feedback and managerial responsiveness.
3. Better employee attitudes toward the company, toward management, and particularly toward the first-line supervisor.

FIGURE 11–2
Circle Meeting Assessment

Structure	Never Sometimes Usually Often Always
The group skips from subject to subject.	
Members of the group raise concerns and questions that are off the subject.	
Members know during the meeting where the meeting is on the agenda.	
So much information is discussed that group	(cont'd)

members become over-
whelmed. _____

Members come to the meeting
knowing the purpose and/or
agenda. _____

Group members come and go
at will during the meeting. _____

The rules by which the
meeting is conducted are
clear. _____

Discussions seem to go on
endlessly. _____

Influence

Chosen solutions are what the
leader wants rather than
what the group wants. _____

Participation by group members is encouraged. _____

The leader power plays or
rams decisions through. _____

Most members of the group
participate in discussions. _____

Some members have concerns
or ideas that never get on
the agenda. _____

All sides of an issue get aired. _____

The same few members tend
to monopolize discussion. _____

Problem Solving

The group divides or
stalemates on issues. _____

The group proposes solutions
before thoroughly identifying causes. _____

The same problems repeatedly
emerge over the span of
several meetings. _____

Various alternatives are aired
before a decision is
reached. _____

There is disagreement over the
real issue or problem which
is being considered. _____

The problem under discussion
is guise for another
under-the-surface problem. _____

Openness

Members tell the leader what
he or she wants to hear. _____

Members are willing to
express their real feelings
about problems or issues. _____

Disagreement or discord is
ignored or avoided. _____

Members are subject to
personal attack. _____

Members are open and willing
to be critical. _____

Follow-Through

There is confusion about who
is going to make the
decision or have the final say. _____

When a decision is reached,
appropriate action is taken. _____

The records of the meeting are
available before the next
meeting. _____

There is confusion after the
meeting over who was to
get things done and what was
to be done. _____

Adapted from: Steven Barney, *Quality Circles: Adapting Materials and Training to Organizational Needs* (unpublished paper prepared for Central Michigan University under the direction of Dr. Olga L. Crocker, December 1982).

4. Fewer short or suspect absences.

5. More interpersonal problems being worked out among employees so that there are fewer formal complaints and grievances.

6. More people being trained in company-needed skills on their own initiative and greater opportunities occurring for employees to use these skills.

7. Increase in number of employees who are interested in becoming members of quality circles.

8. Greater personal satisfaction regarding work, and feelings that the job offers opportunities to use abilities and skills and to perform work that is important, challenging and responsible.

9. Problems that quality circles are solving are increasing in number and in complexity.

QUALITY CIRCLE PROCESSES

Finally, some soul searching is in order. Members must analyze how effectively they have worked as a team. This analysis could include such things as the structure of the circle, the influence which the group and individual members have, their openness, follow-through, and problem-solving ability. Members may want to construct their own evaluation form; the thirty-item questionnaire developed by Barney (1982) may be helpful in this procedure (Figure 11-2).

After the questionnaires are completed, results must be analyzed. The circle must weigh the pros and cons of doing this internally or having the quality circle office do it for them. If the office does the analysis, members may be more honest in answering the questions because they are assured of the anonymity of their responses. On the other hand, circle members may learn more by bringing any differences of opinion into the open immediately. Some members could, however, feel intimidated and therefore not be willing to express their true opinions. Under either method, circle members must discuss problem areas and methods by which the internal processes can be improved.

Last but most important, after circle members have carried out objective, subjective, and process analyses, three things remain—self-congratulations, a pat on the back for fellow members, and a celebration for a job well done!

EVALUATION SHOULD INCLUDE IMPROVEMENTS IN:

Productivity
• quality
• scrap
• quantity
• marginal cost
• overhead
• equipment
• safety and accidents
• maintenance
• down-time
• sales

- customer satisfaction
- tasks

Attitude and relationships

- trust
- communication
- subordinate-supervisor relationships
- absenteeism
- complaints and grievances
- use of skills
- membership of circles
- personal satisfaction
- type and number of problems solved

Circle processes

- structure
- influence
- problem solving
- openness
- follow-through

A Questionnaire About Quality Circles

I. *Questions about the Technical Aspects of the Circle*

A. Check the correct answer.
1. To what type of circle or team do you presently belong?
___ shop-floor
___ clerical/office/white-collar
___ technical
___ professional
___ managerial
___ other (specify)
2. How often does the circle meet?
___ daily
___ more than once a week, but not daily
___ once a week
___ twice a month
___ once a month
___ less than once a month
3. How often would you like the circle to meet?
___ daily

(cont'd)

___ more than once a week, but not daily
___ once a week
___ twice a month
___ once a month
___ less than once a month

4. Do you think the circle should meet:
___ on company time
___ after work but at time-and-a-half pay, double-time pay, etc.
___ after work at regular compensation
___ after work without compensation
___ a combination of without compensation and one of the others

5. For what length of time does the circle meet?
___ less than an hour
___ approximately one hour
___ between one and two hours
___ more than two hours
___ length of time varies

B. Prior to joining the circle, how adequately were you trained in each of the following skills? Please answer by selecting the correct option according to the following scale:

        1 not at all
        2 very little
        3 somewhat
        4 considerably
        5 more than adequately

___6 decision making
___7 fishbone analysis
___8 graphs
___9 statistics
___10 conducting a meeting
___11 team and interpersonal interaction
___12 managerial philosophy
___13 goal-setting processes
___14 On a scale of 1 (low) to 5 (high), overall how would you rate your training prior to joining the circle?

C. Since joining the circle, how adequately have you been trained in each of the following skills?
___15 decision making
___16 fishbone/process analysis
___17 graphs

____18 statistics

____19 conducting a meeting

____20 team and interpersonal interaction

____21 managerial philosophy

____22 goal-setting processes

____23 writing a report

____24 making an oral presentation

____25 On a scale of 1 (low) to 5 (high), overall how would you rate your training since joining the circle?

II. *Questions about Circle Processes*

D. Following are a number of factors which determine how successfully the circle is able to solve problems. Which of these have been important to your circle? Please answer by selecting the correct option according to the following scale:

> 1 extremely unimportant
> 2 somewhat unimportant
> 3 neither unimportant nor important
> 4 somewhat important
> 5 extremely important

____26 Commitment to and participation in the circle by members

____27 Aggressiveness of the members

____28 Ability of the members

____29 Ability and commitment of the leader

____30 Ability and commitment of the facilitator

____31 Knowledge of the job by the members

____32 Effort of circle members and leader

____33 Cooperation among circle team

____34 Training received by members

____35 Technical assistance received

____36 Managerial attitude, support and responsiveness

____37 Managerial recognition of the circle

____38 Feedback provided

____39 Difficulty of the problem chosen

____40 Good luck

E. Rate each of the following statements according to how well the item describes the purpose of the circle of which you are a member:

> 1 extremely unimportant
> 2 somewhat unimportant

(cont'd)

3 neither unimportant nor important
4 somewhat important
5 extremely important

___41 to increase productivity
___42 to increase quality
___43 to decrease the number of defective parts
___44 to increase communication between workers and management
___45 to become competitive in national or world markets
___46 to improve the quality of work life for employees
___47 to increase employee participation
___48 to allow employees to use their intelligence, expertise and innovative ability
___49 to make employees think they are important
___50 to make management or the company look good.

III. *Questions about the Effectiveness of the Circle*

F. How effective the circle is depends upon many people, In your opinion, what is the contribution that each of the following make to the success of your circle? Rate each according to the following scale:
1 no contribution
2 very little contribution
3 moderate contribution
4 considerable contribution
5 a tremendous contribution

___51 You, yourself
___52 Other circle members
___53 Circle leader
___54 Facilitator
___55 Steering committee
___56 Unit supervisor
___57 Plant management
___58 Corporate management
___59 Union/union executive
___60 To what extent have improvements suggested by your quality circle been implemented? Choose the right answer from among the following:
1 not at all

2 a little
3 moderately
4 considerably
5 to a great extent
6 every suggestion has been implemented

IV. *Questions Concerning Feelings about the Circle and the Organization*

G. Following are statements which have been made about the operation of other circles. Based on your own experiences as a circle member, how strongly do you agree or disagree with each statement? Answer according to the following scale:

1 strongly disagree
2 somewhat disagree
3 neither disagree or agree
4 somewhat agree
5 strongly agree

___61 I enjoy being a member of the circle.

___62 I would join another circle if I was moved to another unit or area of work responsibility.

___63 I would recommend to my friends that they join a circle.

___64 My experiences with the circle have been unpleasant and frustrating.

___65 I communicate with supervisors more easily than I did in the past.

___66 My relationship with my work group is better than it has been in the past.

___67 Our circle is doing important work.

___68 Our circle has made a worthwhile contribution to the organization.

___69 The company has profited financially from our circles' efforts.

___70 Our efforts are appreciated within this company.

H. Following are statements that have often been made by employees about the company for which they work. Based on your own experience with this company, how strongly do you agree or disagree with each statement? Use the 1 to 5 scale described above to give your answer.

___71 I am happy to put in extra effort for this company.

(cont'd)

___72 I tell my neighbors and friends that this company is an excellent employer.

___73 This company is important to me.

___74 I would quit my job tomorrow if I could get an equal or better job.

___75 I do my best every day for the company.

___76 The goals and values that I have are similar to those of company management.

___77 I disagree with the company's policies and regulations.

___78 I am sorry that I went to work for this company.

___79 I would do any task or work which I was asked to do in order to remain with the company.

V. *Some Questions about You*

I. Please check the right answer.
1. Age
___ Less than 20 years of age
___ 20–25 years of age
___ 26–30 years of age
___ 31–35 years of age
___ 36–40 years of age
___ 41–45 years of age
___ 46–50 years of age
___ 51–55 years of age
___ 56–60 years of age
___ 61 + years of age
2. Gender ___Male ___Female
3. Education Level
___ Grade 8 or less
___ Grade 9 to 11
___ Completed high school (grade 12 or 13)
___ Some college training or education
___ Some university education
___ Received a diploma from a college
___ Awarded a degree
___ Awarded a master's degree
___ Awarded a doctoral degree
4. Length of employment with the company
___ Less than six months
___ 7 months to 12 months
___ 1 to 2 years

___ 3 to 5 years
___ 6 to 10 years
___ 11 to 20 years
___ more than 20 years

5. Length of employment in a similar industry (include employment for present company in the total)
___ Less than six months
___ 7 months to 12 months
___ 1 to 2 years
___ 3 to 5 years
___ 6 to 10 years
___ 11 to 20 years

6. Your position in this firm is:
___ Production worker (hourly pay)
___ Production worker (salaried)
___ Office worker (hourly pay)
___ Office worker (salaried)
___ Supervisory/first-line management
___ Middle management
___ Senior management
___ Technical
___ Professional
___ Other (specify) _____

7. The department in which you are employed is:
___ Production
___ Sales
___ Marketing
___ Finance
___ Accounting
___ Purchasing
___ Personnel/industrial relations
___ Design/research and/or development
___ Services to other employees (mailroom, cafeteria, etc.)
___ Other (specify) _____

8. How long have you participated in a circle or team?
___ Not at all
___ Less than 6 months
___ 7 to 12 months
___ 13 to 18 months
___ 19 to 24 months
___ 25 to 30 months

(cont'd)

STATISTICAL ANALYSIS AND EVALUATION

___ 30 to 60 months
___ More than 5 years

J. Why did you join the circle? Check all answers which apply:
___ 9. to get time off from work
___10. to meet or influence members of management
___11. because a friend, acquaintance or person with whom you share a ride did
___12. as a joke
___13. union asked/told me to do so
___14. management or supervisor asked/told me to do so
___15. for personal recognition
___16. because of peer pressure
___17. monetary reward
___18. to get some problems straightened out
___19. to help the company
___20. to keep my job (or jobs in general)

K. Select the three most important reasons. Place the number of the items (from 9 to 20) below.
21.___
22.___
23.___

L. Check the best answer
24. Do you enjoy being the team leader?
___ Yes
___ No
___ Not a team leader presently
25. If you are a leader or have been one in the past, what is the total period of time you have been/were a leader?
___ Not at all
___ Less than 6 months
___ 7 to 12 months
___ 13 to 18 months
___ 19 to 24 months
___ 25 to 30 months
___ 30 to 60 months
___ More than 5 years
26. If you are not presently a circle leader, would you like to be one?

___ Yes
___ No
___ Am presently a circle leader

27. The union that represents blue-collar workers in the firm can be described as being:
___ Extremely militant
___ Somewhat militant
___ In between militant and not militant
___ Somewhat non-militant
___ Extremely non-militant
___ Not applicable

28. The union that represents clerical workers in the firm can be described as being:
___ Extremely militant
___ Somewhat militant
___ In between militant and not militant
___ Somewhat non-militant
___ Extremely non-militant
___ Not applicable

(If this survey is being done in a variety of organizations):

29. The type of industry in which you are employed is:
___ Production/manufacturing
___ Professional (accounting, law, education, etc.)
___ Medical services
___ Civil service
___ Retail/wholesale sector
___ High technology
___ Service industry
___ Finance, insurance or real estate
___ Primary resource or basic industries (steel, coal, etc.)
___ Other (specify)_____

30. How many employees normally work in your company?
___ 20 or less
___ 21–100
___ 101–500
___ 501–1,000
___ 1,001–10,000
___ Over 10,000
___ Not applicable
___ Self-employed and only employee
___ Other

PART IV

CASE STUDIES
AND CONCLUSION

TWELVE

FORD MOTOR CO.
OF CANADA

The Ford Motor Co. of Canada, in Windsor, Ontario, is an excellent example of how a company can involve employees in the decision-making process in an effort to increase operating effectiveness and to improve employee working conditions.[1]

The Employee Involvement (EI) process originated in the United States during the 1979 national negotiations when Ford and the United Auto Workers (UAW) affirmed their intentions to jointly support an effort to increase employee participation on the shop floor. Operationalization of these intentions was initiated by establishment of the National Joint Committee of Employee Involvement (NJCEI).

Senior executives of both the company and the union have shown their commitment by being personally involved. The NJCEI, for example, was formerly chaired jointly by Donald F. Ephlin, UAW Vice-President and Director of the Ford Department (now Dennis Yokich), and by Peter J. Pestillo, Vice-President of Labor Relations, Ford Motor Company.

A quality circle structure has been suggested which management and union can establish at the local level (Figure 12–1). Reporting to the NJCEI (at least in the United States; a similar body does not exist in Canada) is the local plant steering committee. in Canada, EI coordinators assist problem-solving groups in shop-floor decision making.

The Employee Involvement concept has flourished. Presently, there are an estimated 10,000 employees who are participating actively in approximately eight hundred EI teams at sixty plants in Canada and the United States. Not only has operating performance risen, but employee attitudes and perceptions of the company have improved. Rank-and-file workers, for the most part, are positive and enthusiastic about the program.

This attitude is new. The climate at Ford Motor in the United States has been anything but conducive to cooperation. Historically the relationship between management and the union has been adversarial and hostile. Suspicion and distrust date back to the early and middle 1940s, when Henry Ford refused to recognize the UAW as the representative of the workers, and sit-down strikes were not only the rule but were characterized by bloodshed. The situation was no different in Canada. In fact, more recently, in 1979, labour-management relationships were strained because of revised practices that were implemented by management at the new Essex Engine Plant. As a consequence, at this plant, the union initially refused to support EI efforts because it felt that this was another method by which the company could take advantage of employees.

With the deepening recession, however, the situation changed. In order to stem the level of worker layoffs and the mounting threat of foreign competition, both sides, during the 1982 negotiations, agreed to cooperate. As Jerry Steele, Industrial Relations Manager for both the Windsor and Essex plants, points out: "We were not competitive from a cost, productivity, or quality standpoint; in all the indicators or barometers of our industry, we were not competitive. We had to change." Ray Wakeman, President of UAW Local 200, which represents all Ford blue-collar employees in the city of Windsor, also admits that: "we have to look at all the avenues because [the union's] primary function is to do things that would secure the workers a better place to work and not jeopardize their employment."[2] Both union executive members and management agree, however, that EI is not a substitute for negotiations and that it does not infringe on issues that are negotiable.

As a result of these types of attitude changes, during the 1982 negotiations, Ford and the UAW agreed to establish a joint employee involvement program. As a consequence, a set of guidelines and structures were initiated. In the Windsor area there are six operations—Windsor Engine Plant #1 (WEP #1), Windsor Engine Plant #2 (WEP #2), Essex Engine

238

FIGURE 12–1
Ford's Quality Circle Organization

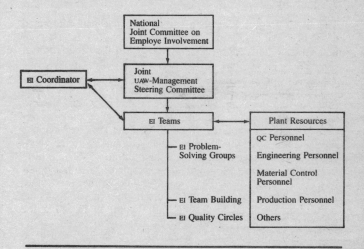

Source: Adapted from *A Handbook on the UAW-Ford Process for Local Unions and Management* (Dearborn, MI: UAW-Ford National Joint Committee on Employee Involvement, 1980): 26.

Plant (EEP), Essex Aluminum Plant, Windsor Casting Plant (WCP), and Windsor Export Supply. Employee Involvement groups function in the first five operations. The WEP #1, WEP #2 and EEP have retained the name "Employee Involvement"; the WCP has TOPP—"Total Opportunity for People Participation." At the Aluminum Plant, four groups are tackling quality problems, and the groundwork is being laid to move to problem-solving teams. The last group—the all-salary employees at Export Supply—are being trained, and it is probable that in the near future a white-collar employee involvement team will begin to function.

The early negativism in the EEP makes it particularly interesting to examine. If quality circles (Employee Involvement) could make a difference in an organizational climate that was so far from ideal, it certainly has possibilities for firms where a more cooperative stance is taken by unions and management.

THE ESSEX ENGINE PLANT

The Essex Engine Plant is a capital-intensive and automated assembly line operation. Approximately 1,400 hourly-paid and 400 salaried employees are engaged in the production of standard V-6 engines which are used in the Cougar, the Thunderbird and other Ford models.

The plant did not begin operations until April 13, 1981. Later in that year, the EI concept was initiated—and discontinued. Unfortunately, the climate at that time was not conducive to cooperate ventures. Not until after the 1982 negotiations did EI teams officially begin to function again—with the blessing of both management and the plant union.

Plant management followed the example of Ford headquarters (U.S.) executives. Plant manager Leo Brown (and other plant officers), for example, endorsed the process from the outset and provided leadership and support in initiating the program. Today they continue to be actively involved.

Both the company and the union have chosen well-liked and respected people for the key positions. Company/Union appointees are: Gary Lesperance, EI coordinator for the Windsor operations (now Pat McKrow); Gene Gadzos, EI Facilitator for the EEP; John Rivard, Hourly Facilitator for the two WEPs; and Ken Gouin, TOPP Coordinator at the WCP. All have extensive labour relations backgrounds. More importantly, however, according to at least one blue-collar employee, they also "are great guys and are easy to work with."

EI teams at EEP are organized largely by work units on the basis of tasks which are performed. For example, each area has its problem-solving team which consists of eight to ten hourly-paid and salaried workers. The teams communicate with the Steering Committee and report their progress and problems on a regular basis. The Committee provides direction and assists teams on difficult projects. Most important of all, it publicizes the team's accomplishments (see Figure 12–1).

The Steering Committee is central to the organization and the implementation of EI. It consists of both company and union representatives. Curtis Davidson, Plant Union Chair-

FIGURE 12–2
Eight Basic Steps in Launching EI

1. Union and Management Involvement and Support	• Management/Union awareness and briefing • Formulation of commitment • Budget and consultant considerations • Develop objectives and plans
2. Establishment of Steering Committee	• Committee membership and education • Establishing roles and relationship (EI Administrator & Committee) • Formulation of structure and direction of EI Process • Committee meeting coordination, minutes, secretary, etc.
3. Diagnosis of the Organization	• Education of Committee on methods (e.g., EIQ, Interviews) • Formulating and recommending a strategy • Consultant considerations • Data ownership and feedback
4. Selection of Pilot Area	• Selecting optimum organizational unit • Formulating an implementation strategy • Type of project, cost, operating considerations, etc. • Supervision and Union support
5. Preparation of the Organization	• Communicating EI (e.g., newsletters, bulletin boards, etc.) • EI awareness training, management and Union
6. Establishment of Local Pilot Project	• Voluntary support and participation • Determine target group(s) • Training to supervisors & group members (problem-solving, group techniques, presentations, EI Process, etc.)
7. Evaluation and Fine Tuning	• Determining measurements & objectives • Reporting considerations • Maintaining records • Making adjustments
8. Generalization and Extension	• Extension to: – new groups – new locations

Memo: It is important to note that this is a dynamic "non-linear" process, thus elements of any step will occur throughout the process.

Source: *A Handbook on the* UAW—*Ford Process for Local Unions and Management* (Dearborn, MI: UAW—Ford National Joint Committee on Employee Involvement, 1980): 18

person, and Frank Morand, Bruce Magee and Sid Chase, UAW Committee, represent the union. Leo Brown, Plant Manager, Gifford Brown, Area Manager, Mel Rowe, Quality Control Manager, James Barry, Manufacturing and Plant Engineering Manager, and Jerry Steele, Industrial Relations Manager, represent the company. Working closely with the Committee are the coordinators and facilitators who act as the resource persons and who maintain liaison with all levels to ensure that communications are open and that the teams are functioning smoothly.

The program was implemented through an eight-step process (Figure 12–2) that was in two phases. Phase one focused on orientation and the promotion and acceptance of the EI concept. Managers and union representatives were thoroughly trained in the philosophy, the application, and the team processes involved in EI. Feasibility studies and needs assessments were conducted.

Following this managerial and union executive orientation, the second phase was implemented and the concept was introduced to rank-and-file workers. They responded with enthusiasm; a request for volunteers resulted in over 150 applications. Twenty-nine employees were selected, by random draw, to participate in a twenty-hour training program. While many employees were disappointed that they were not chosen, they perceived that participation was not only a privilege, but one which carried with it considerable responsibility.

Training consisted of units of the plant organization and on Employee Involvement. In addition, a variety of skills and processes such as leadership effectiveness, motivational theories, personality styles, group dynamics, decision-making processes, communication skills "nuts and bolts" issues such as problem identification, problem specification and resolution, and presentation techniques were learned (Figure 12–3). To assist the teams, an EI centre was established. The centre houses the facilitator's office, meeting facilities, information about EI, and audio-visual aids. In short, anyone who wants to know what is happening in EI can learn about it at the centre.

Currently, the training program is being expanded. In addition to EI training, Ford in Windsor has instituted substance abuse awareness training, a twenty-hour upgrading (on company time) in statistical process control safety, work practices, etc., and a five-evening pre-employment orientation program in which prospective employees (and other interested persons)

FIGURE 12–3
Typical Training Program for EI Team Members

ENGINE DIVISION PARTICIPATIVE PROBLEM SOLVING GROUP TRAINING

Objective	**Content**
Topic: Introduction Plant Organization	*Time* = .5 hours
Provide employees with an understanding of the plant organization and its products.	Introduction Structure Functions Responsibilities Building an Engine
Topic: Communications	*Time* = 3.5 hours
Emphasize the importance of listening and its impact on group participation.	Exercise "Group Listening" Film "Power of Listening" Discussion
Develop skills in active listening.	Exercise "One-Way vs. Two-Way Communication"
Increase the employee's awareness and skills for using two-way communication.	Discussion/Critique
Topic: Motivation	*Time* = 1.5 hours
Provide employees with an assessment of their own needs in the work environment.	Exercise "Motivation Feedback Opinionnaire." Discussion of Maslow, Herzberg
Create an understanding of motivation and its impact on group participation.	
Provide employees with an understanding of employee involvement and the conditions necessary for the successful implementation of problem-solving groups.	

(cont'd)

CASE STUDIES AND CONCLUSION

Topic: Leadership
Provide employees with group leadership concepts and techniques.

Develop an awareness of leadership styles and their impact on group participation.

Time = 2.5 hours
Discussion of McGregor
Discussion of Blake/Mouton
Case Study: "Mallard Airplane Company"
Discussion and summary of communications, motivation

Topic: Group Techniques
Develop an awareness of techniques that assist in the group decision-making process.

Develop skills for making more effective group decisions and recommendations.

Time = 3.0 hours
Handouts and discussion of group dynamics
Exercise "Subarctic Survival"
Discussion/Critique

Topic: Problem Identification
Identify Quality Control Measuring Techniques and Reports.

Develop the ability/skill to identify and separate problems in their work areas.

Time = 2.0 hours
QC Measuring Techniques
Discussion on QC Measuring Techniques

Stairstepping Techniques
Practice Discussion

Topic: Problem Specification and Resolution
Develop the ability and skills to more accurately define problems and identify their cause or causes.

Develop skills for making recommendations to management and/or Steering Committee for problem resolution.

Time = 5.0 hours
Systematic Problem-Solving Techniques
Practice Discussion
Case Study
Discussion Critique
Brainstorming Techniques
Practice Discussion

Topic: Presentation Techniques Develop an awareness of the use of charts and graphics for effective presentations. Develop effective presentation skills.	*Time* = 2.0 hours Use of Visuals Practice Discussion Platform Skills Practice Discussion

---

are given the opportunity to hear about the company, safety and work practices, and where EI is thoroughly explained.

In addition, EI teams and middle management personnel have taken the initiative in sharing their expertise and knowledge not only with academics but with other firms in the Windsor community. As one union member stated, "This program makes us feel like people; we want to share that feeling with others."

The Process

To review, the complete eight-step process (shown in Figure 12–2) included:
1. The involvement of union and management personnel and their indication of support.
2. The establishment of the steering committee.
3. The diagnosis of the organization. This included establishing a committee on methods to be utilized, the formulation of a strategy, a discussion of the interrelationship between EI and Ford's existing suggestion system.
4. The selection of the pilot area. This involved an analysis of costs and benefits, the extent of supervisory and union support and finally the formulation of an implementation strategy.
5. The preparation of the members of the organization for EI.
6. The establishment of the local pilot project.
7. The evaluation and fine tuning of the program.
8. Generalizing the program and extending it to other locations within the plant.

The Results

EI has been a success. Currently, the EEP has seven teams in which 55 employees participate. At the WEP and the EEP,

sixteen teams are functioning and 160 employees are involved. Problems which have been resolved through EI include:
• reduction in kerosene usage in the Block Department at WEP #1
• quality and cost improvements in WEP #2
• energy savings at both WEPs
• reduction of rejects and improved efficiency in the testing areas at EEP

This last was an interesting problem. A stopper at the end of a vacuum tube sometimes became dislodged in testing. Since the tube then was drawing air, the part was rejected. This meant that it had to be sent to "repair," fitted with the plug and retested. Considerable tension between employees in repair and those who handled the part resulted because of the so-called "stupidity and carelessness" of that unit. The EI team determined that plugs, not employees, were at fault. A variety of solutions were tried: golf tees worked but had other drawbacks: taping was messy and time consuming. The solution: a longer plug. The result: a 17 percent increase in effectiveness of that unit.

Projects still in process include a number of improvements in materials, methods, quality and costs in all areas. Colour coding, instead of numbering, appears to be the solution to the matching problem that involves piston and bore size. Two hundred pairs of a new type of glove, which has a longer life and is cheaper and more flexible, have been ordered and will be examined during the next few weeks. Of great interest to team members is a van-pooling scheme. One team of employees is determined to resolve difficulties that have occurred in the past.

No company can long afford to sustain a loser. Employee Involvement is growing because it is not a cost burden; groups generate sufficient high-calibre ideas and suggestions to justify their existence. "They love solving problems," Gary Lesperance, EI coordinator, states. "Not the big ones— just the little ones; the kind that everybody used to walk by and say 'Somebody should do something about that.' " EI teams are doing that something. But more importantly, the barriers between plant employees and office employees are being broken down. The two groups are working together; engineers and managers are requesting assistance from shop-floor personnel to solve problems which they experience.

And from a labour relations point of view—Bill Johnston,

Manager of Labour Relations and Hourly Personnel, Windsor Operations, has this to say: "EI is not a single program but a changing way to do business. It is one of a number of Ford programs aimed at communications, openness and an interest in our employees, not as a means to complete production schedules, but as people." When pressed, Johnston admits that grievances have dropped about 25 percent. This has resulted in considerable cost savings for the company and faster grievance resolution for the union in spite of the fact that 1,100 additional employees have been hired.

Unlike its U.S. Ford organization, the Essex Engine plant did not use outside consultants during the institutionalization of the change process. Instead, it mobilized only internal resources. Both union and company officials attribute much of the initial success to the need for cooperation between the two in resolving day-by-day EI problems.

An external study of the success of the EI program in this plant, conducted by the authors of this book, with the assistance of Local 200 of the UAW, is reported in the next chapter.

"SOS"

The 255 engine, which had been produced by Windsor Engine Plant #2, was being phased out in 1982, and the plant, which was down to eighty-three employees and which the company said was unprofitable, was about to be closed. The employees, however, were determined to keep it open. To meet the challenge, a "Save Our Stampings" (SOS) team was established. Union and management working together

spearheaded improvements in productivity and quality control that turned the operation around. It is now efficient and profitable. The SOS team saved their own jobs, and created new jobs. (Editorial *Windsor Star*, September 16, 1983)

Union and management are proud of the successes that have been accomplished. Some of these include: the plant is cleaner; lighting has been improved; a heated blow-off has been installed on the washer so that stamp parts dry and do not have to be derusted; there is improved cutting and stacking of oil pan blanks. Scrap has decreased from 18 percent to 2 percent; quality too has improved.

Plant Manager Leo Brown quickly agrees that employee team efforts have meant that the plant has continued to operate rather than being shut down. Furthermore, Brown says, "These efforts exemplify the kind of team action between employees, union and management which is necessary to keep our plants viable." The teams have been directly responsible for new business—the 3.8 litre rocker-arm cover press, assembly and paint operations. Recently production of the 3.02 five-litre engine was moved to this plant.

Employees and the union, too, are proud of their efforts. So enthusiastic is the SOS team that they have developed a presentation about their circle which they proudly deliver at other plants and organizations and to other groups that are interested. John Rivard, Hourly SOS Facilitator, proudly states that, "Our aim is no scrap and no rejects. We are determined to keep our plant open." Just recently, the team consisting of Henry (Hank) Hunt, Charlie Warner, Frank Ferrari, Charlie Cloutier, Joe Clemente, Ray Bolton and Bob Davis was one of five groups recognized for "outstanding business achievement" by the Ontario Chamber of Commerce.

THE FUTURE OF EI

In spite of its success, both management and union continue to take a cautious approach to EI. It appears that senior management has not yet clarified the new role behaviours that they will be required to adopt—that of policy makers and not decision makers on day-to-day issues. This will be necessary if EI is to permeate the company.

There are reservations too. The economy and car sales have improved. The question which no one wants to voice is whether prosperity will work to the detriment of EI. Will the lessons of the past be forgotten by both management and the union? Both groups are quick to respond to this query. "EI is here to stay. The foundation has been carefully laid."

FORD MOTOR CO. OF CANADA

History
* relationships between union and management extremely poor
* 1979—National Joint Committee of Employee Involvement established
* 1982—Canadian EI established

Engine Plants
* steering committee of union and management members
* eight-step process of implementation
* twenty-hour training program
* additional twenty-hour training program in other facets for all employees
* sixteen teams and 160 employees participate at present
* many cost-saving improvements
* attitudes improved

SOS
* EI saved plant from being closed down

THIRTEEN

UAW—FORD EMPLOYEE INVOLVEMENT SURVEY

Generally, because of the underlying philosophy of quality circles, workers have a sense of participation at the shop-floor level. Through QCs, they can contribute their ingenuity, creativity, skills and talents to the attainment of organizational goals. In most cases, participants are intrinsically motivated because of the opportunities for self-development and accomplishment. It is not surprising, therefore, that most companies find a substantial improvement in worker attitudes and an increase in productivity after the introduction of quality circles.

Indeed, most of the literature has postulated that worker participation improves job satisfaction and productivity and that it stimulates psychological involvement. Blumberg (1968) reviewing the literature on this subject, stated:

> There is hardly a study in the entire literature which fails to demonstrate that satisfaction in work is enhanced or that other generally acknowledged beneficial consequences accrue from a genuine increase in workers' decision-making power. Such consistency of findings . . . is rare in social research. (123)

Likewise, Locke and Schweiger (1979), following an examination of the subsequent literature, concluded that:

> The benefits alleged the result from PDM (participation in decision making) by workers fall into two major categories. The first includes *increased morale and job satisfaction*

and their frequent concomitants, reduced turnover, absenteeism, and conflict. The second category includes outcomes pertaining directly to *productive efficiency*, e.g. higher production, better decision quality, better production quality, and reduced conflict (again) and costs. (277)

Are the above comments true for the Windsor and Essex Engine Plants? A study conducted by Chiu and Crocker with the assistance of members of UAW Local 200 attempted to analyze the level of effectiveness of the UAW-Ford Employee Involvement Program.

Using an earlier version of the questionnaire shown in Chapter 11, data were obtained from two sources. First thirty-six employees of the Windsor and Essex Engine Plants responded. The second sample consisted of thirty-one employees from Canadian automotive and automotive parts manufacturing assembly line firms. All respondents in the second sample stated that they were not participating in an employee decision-making program.

Questionnaires for the Engine Plants were administered randomly by the union to EI members. The second set of questionnaires were administered to participants in a stress seminar and to students prior to night classes at a local college of applied arts and technology.

The demographic characteristics of the two samples do not differ significantly. All participants are male auto workers, predominantly in the thirty-one to fifty age group. Employees of both groups are, for the most part, shop floor workers. Both groups are also relatively well educated. Of the Engine Plant group, 63.9 percent reported that they had completed at least high school. Of the second group, 74.2 percent had completed at least high school. Almost all employees from both groups had more than ten years of seniority with their employers.

The study utilized a five-part questionnaire. One part requested personal and demographic information—age, sex, educational level, length of employment with the company and degree of participation in shop-floor decision making or employee involvement. A second section, which was omitted by non-Engine plant employees, requested that participants give their opinions concerning the EI process by ranking twelve factors in order of their importance in assisting team members to solve problems. The twelve factors were: effort, training, ability of members, technical assistance from engineers, management responsiveness, cooperation among the circle members, active participation of members, recognition by the company, feedback, task difficulty, luck and use of job knowledge. In this section respondents also indicated, on a 5-point scale ranging from 1 (low) to 5 (high), their opinions with respect to those individuals who are responsible for the effectiveness of the circle or team.

In a third part of the questionnaire, the respondents were asked to indicate their experiences and perceptions with the circle or team. The items in a fourth section, which both sample groups answered, measured the degree to which respondents feel committed to the employing organization (Porter, 1974: 603–9). The nine items are divided into three categories: three items relate to the individual's involvement and satisfaction with the organization; three items relate to the individual's willingness to exert effort to achieve organizational goals, and the other three items relate to the individual's willingness to accept organizational values and policies.

The final section of the questionnaire provided respondents with the opportunity of making open-ended comments. These are given in Appendix 8.

THE FINDINGS

At the time of the study (April 1983), two-thirds of the Engine Plants' respondents had been participating in a circle or team for less than six months. A substantial group (ten of thirty-six, or 27.8 percent) had been involved for a period ranging from thirteen to twenty-four months. One person had participated for a period of seven to twelve months and one person was involved for more than twenty-four months.

Each circle or team member was involved in a shop-floor team which met weekly. Ten persons reported that they were currently leaders or had been leaders in the past. Of those who were not currently team leaders, eight of twenty-six (30.8 percent) stated that they did not wish to assume the leader's role. Each of the remaining eighteen (69.2 percent) would like to be a team leader.

All but one respondent felt that the circle or team should meet on company time. This other respondent indicated a desire to meet after work but with compensation. It must be pointed out, however, that EI teams do meet on company time; respondents may have been indicating that this arrangement was satisfactory.

Exactly one-half of the respondents felt that the purpose of EI was to improve quality. The next most popular response to the question regarding purpose was to improve communication (six replies or 16.67 percent). Five others (13.9 percent) responded that all seven items which were stated (to increase quality, productivity, quality of working life, communication and worker creativity, to decrease defects and to meet the Japanese challenge) were purposes of EI.

Why did participants join the teams? To what extent were the teams' suggestions implemented? To what extent did members feel that pre-training had been adequate? In answer to the first question—why the member had joined—fourteen (38.9 percent) did so for personal recognition. Another twenty-two reported other reasons for joining. Among the reasons given were being asked to do so, because buddies were joining, to improve the company, because of peer pressure, for monetary considerations and because it meant time off from work.

Interestingly, sixteen of the thirty-six respondents (44.4 percent) felt that the team's suggestions had been implemented to a great extent to a very great extent. An additional thirteen of the thirty-six (36.1 percent) felt that suggestions had been implemented to some extent. Six respondents (16.7 percent) felt suggestions had been implemented to only a very slight extent.

Respondents split down the middle on the matter of training. Eighteen felt that pre-training was limited and eighteen felt that considerable pre-training had occurred. It was thought that perceptions of adequacy of pre-training would be a function of involvement time in a circle or team and whether the respondent was a leader or not. The results showed that time in the program did not significantly change perceptions of the adequacy of pre-training (chi-square = 1.33, degrees of freedom = 1, not significant). The data concerning leadership was more interesting. Of those respondents who were or had been leaders, eight of ten (80.0 percent) felt they had adequate pre-training; two of ten (20.0 percent) felt that they did not. Of the 18 who wanted to be future leaders, eleven (61.1 percent) did not feel that their training had been adequate. Seven of the eighteen thought pre-training had been adequate.

CASE STUDIES AND CONCLUSION

The results are very similar for those eight respondents who did not wish to assume the leader's role. Five (62.5 percent) felt their pre-training had been inadequate; three (37.5 percent) felt it had been adequate. When the chi-square test of goodness was applied to these results, the differences were statistically significant; that is, results such as these could occur by chance once in each eleven times (chi-square = 5.00, degrees of freedom = 2, p = 0.09). This is sufficiently infrequent to conclude that the steering committee should carefully examine its pre-training programs, especially the training of rank-and-file workers. It appears that these employees perceive this aspect of the EI program is inadequate.

Who contributes to the greatest extent to the effectiveness of the circle or team? The results are summarized in Table 13–1. Not surprisingly, the majority of respondents felt that group members, the team leader, and they themselves contributed the greatest amount. The behind-the-scenes roles of both the steering committee and the union executive, generally speaking, were unrecognized. Only eleven of thirty-six persons (30.6 percent), in each case, felt that a substantial contribution was made by either of these two groups.

Twelve factors were named, and respondents were asked to

TABLE 13–1
Extent to Which Members of the Organization are Responsible for Circle or Team Success

Participant	Value Assigned*					Total
	1	2	3	4	5	
Yourself	0	1	16	11	8	134
Group Members	0	0	7	18	11	148
Team Leader	1	2	12	10	11	136
Facilitator	2	5	13	10	6	121
Steering Committee	7	9	9	7	4	100
Union Executive	7	7	11	10	1	99
Plant Management	5	2	8	14	7	124
Corporate Management	6	4	10	9	7	115

*According to contribution; 1 = little; 5 = great. Total possible score for any item is 180 (36 subjects times a high score of 5).

rank each factor, in descending order of importance, regarding the circle's or team's ability to solve problems. Table 13–2 gives this summary in terms of number of responses together with the median.[1] The most important factors are job knowledge (median is 2.0), effort (median is 3.5), training (median is 4.0), ability of members (median is 4.5), cooperation (median is 5.0), and active participation (median is 5.0).

Two-thirds of respondents had extremely positive feelings regarding the teams or circles. Six persons (16.7 percent), however, had relatively negative or neutral feelings toward the teams. Did any similarities exist among the members of this group and did they differ from other members? The negative/neutral group was similar to the positive group in age, education, experience and length of participation in the EI program. The group included one leader, one individual who did not wish to assume a leader role and four persons

---

TABLE 13–2

Factors Contributing to Teams' Abilities to Handle Problems, as Ranked by EI Participants (In descending order of importance)

Factors	*Ratings By Number of Respondents*					*Median Value**
	1	2	3	4	5	
1. Use of job knowledge	11	8	3	2	2	2.0
2. Effort	3	5	10	5	2	3.5
3. Training	3	6	7	3	4	4.0
4. Ability of members	4	8	2	4	6	4.5
5. Cooperation	5	2	2	5	5	5.0
6. Active participation	4	2	5	5	5	5.0
7. Technical assistance	0	1	1	8	1	6.5
8. Management responsiveness	0	0	2	1	6	8.0
9. Recognition	1	0	1	1	3	9.0
10. Feedback	1	1	2	2	1	9.0
11. Task	1	1	1	0	1	10.0
12. Luck	2	0	0	0	0	12.0

*The median is the rating (ranking) on each item given by the ''middle'' person. In this case, it is the average of the ranking given by the eighteenth and nineteenth respondents.

who would accept this role if they were asked. These six people differed from the more positive group in their responses to the question on success of implementation of the team's suggestions (four of six felt that implementation was inadequate) and in their reasons for participating in the EI program. Four indicated that they had joined for ''other'' reasons but gave no clarification of that reason. One had joined to get two hours off from work; a second had joined to improve conditions at work. Again, if there is a message in these six responses, it may be that the steering committee or Engine Plants' management should be sensitive to the need for ensuring that implementation of teams' suggestions occurs, or, if it cannot, to better communicate the reasons for any delay or rejection.

The last objective section of the questionnaire was answered by Engine Plant and by non–Engine Plant employees. The nine items measure:
• involvement of the individual and satisfaction with the company (questions 72, 73, 74 of questionnaire given in Chapter 11)
• a willingness to exert effort to achieve company goals (questions 71, 75, 79)
• a willingness to accept organizational values and policies (questions 76, 77, and 78).

How do employees of the Engine Plants who are participating in EI feel about their organization as a place to work? How do their feelings compare to those of other employees who are not involved in a quality circle or similar program?

Responses to the items concerning the Windsor Essex Engine Plants as a place to work indicate that generally the plant is considered to be a good place to work (mean = 3.942, SD = 0.51). (The number ''1'' signifies strong disagreement with the positive statements and the number ''5'' indicates strong agreement with these same statements).) EI participants, however, are less willing to expend effort to achieve organizational goals (mean = 3.556, SD = 0.745) and are even less willing to adopt organizational values and policies (mean = 2.833, SD = 1.000).

Interestingly, however, the dispersion (standard deviation) is much greater for the items concerning effort and values. This indicates that much greater variability in responses exists, that is, that some members of the group agree very

TABLE 13–3
Comparisons of Responses—Ford Engine Plants (EI involvement) vs. Plants Not Involved in Quality Circles

	Engine Plant		Non–Engine Plant		t-test	Probability
	Mean	SD	Mean	SD		
Good place to work	3.942	0.515	3.624	0.479	2.602	0.008
Expend effort	3.556	0.745	3.779	0.572	1.357	NS
Accept values	2.833	1.000	2.349	0.776	2.177	0.020

*The mean is the average of all the scores; standard deviation (SD) has been explained in Chapter 9.

strongly with the positive statements while others disagree very strongly with the same statements. In other words, some members are extremely willing to expend effort for the company; others are not. Also some members are extremely willing to adopt organizational values; others are strongly opposed to this.

Are these three averages significantly different from average responses given by the automotive and automotive parts respondents who are not involved in employee decision making? A summary table of the relevant information and the statistical tests is given in Table 13–3. The data indicate that the non–Engine Plants group had a mean = 3.624 (SD = 0.479) for satisfaction; a mean of 3.779 (SD = 0.572) for effort; and a mean of 2.349 (SD = 0.776) for acceptance of values and policies.

From this analysis it can be concluded that the two groups are significantly different in their perceptions of their company as a good place to work and in their willingness to accept the values of the organization. There is no statistically significant difference in their willingness to expend effort for their organization. In other words, the findings indicate that Ford employees who are participating in EI are significantly more satisfied with their organzation and are significantly more willing to accept the values and policies of the company than are people who do not work for Ford and who are not involved in shop-floor problem solving (if our samples were representative of each group).

TABLE 13–4
Comparison of Responses Group which Perceives EI Positively vs. Group which Perceives EI Negatively

	Positive Group ($N_1 = 30$)		Negative Group ($N_2 = 6$)		t-test	Probability
	Mean	SD	Mean	SD		
Good place to work	3.980	0.496	3.750	0.610	1.000	NS
Expend effort	4.119	0.753	3.056	0.705	3.186	0.001
Accept values	2.983	1.043	2.084	0.783	1.995	0.020

Previously, it was pointed out that six persons had negative or neutral feelings about circles or teams. Responses of these six employees were compared to the other thirty Ford employees. The results are given in Table 13–4. The data indicate that there is no difference between the two groups in their perception of Ford Motor Co. of Canada as a place to work. Both groups are relatively satisfied. The negative/neutral group, however, is significantly less willing to expend effort to achieve the goals of the organization or to accept the organizational values than is the group which perceives EI more favourably.

SUMMARY

In summary, the statistical analysis has indicated that:
1. The majority of respondents have been or are or would like to be a team leader.
2. Half of the respondents felt that the purpose of EI was to improve quality, suggesting that they are quality conscious. Others felt that EI was directed toward improving communication. Still others felt that the purpose could not be defined in one statement and chose instead all available categories.
3. Participants join the EI program for a variety of reasons. Most important is personal recognition.
4. Less than one-half of respondents felt that teams' suggestions are implemented reasonably frequently. One-sixth of the respondents felt implementation was "slight" or "very slight."
5. Leaders of teams perceive that they have been reasonably

well trained prior to the introduction of EI. Rank-and-file employees, however, did not feel that they had been well trained.

6. Generally, EI participants felt that members, the leader and they themselves personally contribute most to the effectiveness of the team. The contributions of the union executive and the steering commitee were less well recognized.

7. The ability to solve problems depends mainly on members' job knowledge, effort, training, ability and active participation, and on cooperation within the groups.

8. The majority of workers feel positive about EI.

9. Only six persons of the thirty-six sampled had negative or neutral feelings about EI. They also were less satisfied with the implementation process and most had joined the group for other, but unspecified, reasons. Furthermore, on the average, this group of six was less willing to expend effort to accomplish the goals of the company and was less willing to accept organizational values and policies.

10. The EI implementation appears to be proceeding smoothly.

11. Participants in EI programs are more likely to perceive that their company is a good place to work than are non-participants. They are, on the average, also more willing to accept organizational values. The mean score for non-Ford workers on willingness to expend effort is somewhat higher than that of Ford employees; the difference is not significant.

CONCLUSIONS AND RECOMMENDATIONS

Survey results suggest that EI has some impact on worker attitudes. EI participants are positive about the program and are willing to work with management to achieve corporate goals, that is, to improve the company's competitive position by increasing product quality and operating efficiency. It is important to remember that EI at the Essex Engine Plant has been in operation for less than a year and that generally even more positive results are experienced in the long run. Other Ford studies, namely the 1982 UAW–Ford Employee Involvement survey,[2] confirm that, since the introduction of EI, Ford employees have shown substantial improvement in attitudes concerning problem-solving, supervisory practices, job satisfaction, product quality and cost consciousness. This is in keeping with other research on quality circles. Northrup Corporation, Aircraft Division, for example, based on pre- and post-implementation data, also found that worker attitudes improved positively after QC participation.[3] Honeywell Corporation, in a 1982 survey, found that QC participants appeared psychologically committed to the company and that their perceptions and reactions were positive.[4] Quality circles do affect worker attitudes in a positive direction.

The findings of this study, however, point out two areas of weakness: the steering committee might do well to examine both the training program and the process and record of implementation of teams' suggestions.

One result in the findings was especially surprising. EI participants did not feel more willing to exert effort to achieve company goals than did employees from other auto-related firms that did not have a quality circle approach. A number of explanations come to mind. First, the EI program at the Essex Engine Plant is relatively new. Second, the previous few years have demanded substantial sacrifice from all employees in all automobile-related industries. Employees of other firms may not yet feel that their companies are economically secure. This could mean that greater effort continues to be required on their part to secure their own jobs. A third reason comes to mind. It is possible that employees feel that they had little or no part in determining the goals and values of the organization and that these do not represent them. If this is the case, as EI matures and the employees become more experienced at decision making. Ford management might wish to involve shop-floor people in strategic decision making—the setting of organizational goals and values. Participation should increase commitment and the willingness to exert greater effort and to internalize the values of the company.

FINDINGS

Majority of members would like to be leaders.

Employees are quality conscious.

Many join EI teams for personal recognition.

Most feel suggestions are implemented reasonably frequently.

Leaders feel they are well trained.

Members feel they are not well trained.

Leaders, members, and individuals contribute most to EI success.

Union and steering committee perceived to contribute least to EI success.

Ability to solve problems depends on:
• job knowledge
• effort
• training
• ability
• active participation
• cooperation

Most members are positive about EI.

Only six respondents of the thirty-six sampled are not positive about EI.
• feel implementation process is unsatisfactory
• joined for other unspecified reasons
• feel training inadequate

EI participants feel:
• Ford of Canada is a good place to work
• less positive about willingness to expend effort
• even less positive about accepting organizational values
• significantly more positive regarding company and accepting organizational values than non-EI participants in other companies.

FOURTEEN

"PSI":
VICKERS INCORPORATED
WORLD HEADQUARTERS

> With a core philosophy that emphasizes the dignity, self-worth, and contributions of employees, a company cannot help but succeed. Without such a philosophy, a company cannot hope to succeed.

These sentences, posted in the office of a member of the middle management team, express the philosophy and values of Vickers Incorporated World Headquarters management.

Vickers Incorporated operates in such diverse high technology growth industries as computer systems, farm equipment, aircraft and marine guidance and control, and fluid power. Vickers develops and manufactures hydraulic and pneumatic products and systems which provide power and control for industrial machinery, mobile vehicles, aircraft, ships, and land defense systems. Its products include hydraulic pumps, valves, motors, power units, transmissions, packaged systems, accessories, pneumatic products, solenoid valves, winches and planetary gear drives. The company employs 7,000 people and operates in forty-four countries, including Canada. World Headquarters (WHQ) is located in Troy, Michigan.

Vickers's quality circle teams are named PSI (an acronym for "pounds per square inch," adapted to stand for "People Seeking Improvement"). The PSI program began when the company was up for sale during a period of deepest decline. Personnel at the plants (and two at WHQ) were being put on indefinite layoffs; others, and this included the headquarters staff, were being encouraged to take early retirement. Employees were impressed that a company at such a time would budget the funding necessary; this, to them, was proof of the commitments to PSI that exists.

Vickers's PSI groups are unique. While there are a few departmental teams, the majority of the fourteen circles, each with five to eight members (predominantly engineers), are cross-functional. No pilot project was established. Programs at various Vickers U.S. plants pioneered the way for quality circle implementation at WHQ. At these plants, teams have been in operation for over four years.

Vickers's management felt that productivity in the non-manufacturing sector had to be improved because:

1. A substantial portion of the cost of a product is attributable to overhead. It made little sense to streamline plant operations only to lose these gains in office areas—whether it was through the work of clerks or general managers.

2. In most industrial firms in North America, the number of people engaged in administrative duties is steadily increasing while the number of employees engaged in production is decreasing. Vickers is no exception. If this trend continues, the manufacturing labour segment could be too small to offset the administrative cost increases.

3. Office activity is labour-intensive. In addition, long-established, traditional methods exist for each function.

4. New types of machines in office operations are often inappropriate or are improperly used (e.g., computer output).

5. Savings attributable to improvements are difficult to quantify. If visible cost reductions are to be achieved, a continuous generation of ideas is required.

Management also recognized that, in addition to the usual resistance to change, other key problems had to be addressed:

1. If PSI groups were to quantify improvements, standards and output measurements would be required for office activities. Because these are more difficult to define than in manufacturing, few exist.

2. The setting of standards and of measurements would be perceived as regimentation or a taking away of individual freedom. Considerable resistance could be anticipated.

3. Certain aspects of administrative work depend upon "knowledge," and specially qualified people are hired for these jobs. A substantial portion of their time, however, is spent on work

263

FIGURE 14–1
Plan for Implementing PSI at Vickers

activities that are clerical in nature and which could be done by lower-paid personnel. A resistance to a redistribution of these tasks could occur.

4. The PSI concept would be perceived as a threat by middle managers. This group undoubtedly would perceive that employees would be assuming their decision-making role, usurping their position within the hierarchy, and that they (the

managers) would be required to share their authority and power.
5. The heterogeneous, company-wide PSI teams would have
a tendency, at least in the early experimental stages, to want to
address problems in which their expertise and knowledge was
limited and which other employees would have to implement
(e.g., personnel policies).

These problems were discussed and plans and actions were
taken to overcome their negative impact. Finally, an administrative plan for implementing the program was formulated
(see Figures 14–1 and 14–2).

ORGANIZATION

The structure for PSI which was agreed upon was a three-tier
type, that is, it had a steering committee, an operating committee, and task groups (circles).

Steering Committee

The general manager is chairperson of the steering committee
which includes the department heads in charge of: manufacturing, marketing, engineering, finance, management and information systems, planning and product management, the
corporate vice-president—personnel and the program facilitator. Figure 14–3 shows this structure in greater detail.

The steering committee appoints members to the operating
committee, sets overall policy, assigns resources, arbitrates
problems, provides backing and support to the program and
the circles and, at times, establishes priorities.

Operating Committee

The operating committee has the key role in PSI success. It
consists of nine employees, mostly middle managers, each
representing a different department, and nine others, who are
alternates. The program facilitator is chairperson. The term
of office for this group has not yet been determined, and members are changed periodically but not more than once a year.

FIGURE 14–2
Program Launch—Productivity/Quality Improvement

Business Plan Milestone Report

Symbols:
x - milestone target
☐ - milestone complete
x - x revised target

Business Plan

Milestones

Weeks

	1	2	3	4	5	6	7	8	9	10	11	12	13	14	15	16	17	18	19	20	21	22

VP-General Manager
1. Approve implementation — x
2. Appoint program coordinator — x

Program Coordinator
1. Arrange for training program — x
2. Publish start of program — x
3. Attend meetings — (. . . . . all meetings . . . . .)

Management Development
1. Prepare training program — x

Milestones	1	2	3	4	5	6	7	8	9	10	11	12	13	14	15	16	17	18	19	20	21	22
2. Conduct sessions											x	x										
Steering Committee																						
1. First meeting		x																				
2. Appoint operating committee		x																				
3. Approve task group leaders				x																		
4. Approve task group organization						x																
5. Approve group goals									x													
6. Approve group plans														x								
Operating Committee																						
1. First Meeting				x																		
2. Appoint group leaders				x																		
3. Training sessions					x	x																
4. Appoint task group members					x																	
5. Assist in setting goals								x														
6. Approve task group goals								x														

(cont'd)

Weeks	1	2	3	4	5	6	7	8	9	10	11	12	13	14	15	16	17	18	19	20	21	22
Milestones																						
7. Approve task group plans												x										
8. Write MBO's for goals														x								
9. Summary report to steering committee																	x					
Task Groups																						
1. Initial meeting				x																		
2. Training sessions						x	x	x														
3. Set goals								x	x													
4. Write plan											x											
5. Start investigation/research																						
6. Progress reports—monthly															x		x					

Comments:

FIGURE 14–3
Vickers Productivity Quality Improvement Organization

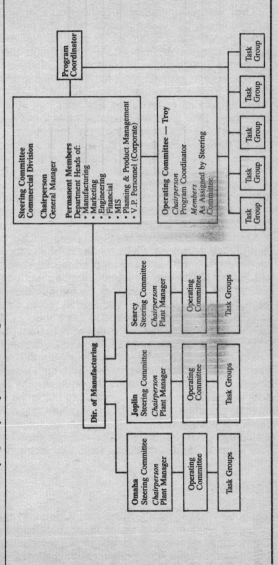

This committee establishes procedures; approves projects; reviews and approves the group's goals and procedures; provides guidance and direction for areas of cost reduction or productivity improvement to the task groups; monitors the progress of, and directs and controls, the activities of the task groups; reviews claimed successes and results; provides assistance as required to task groups; resolves cross-functional conflicts relating to credit for cost reduction improvements; contributes ideas for non-financial rewards for the task groups; and establishes annual goals for each department.

The operating committee, in general, is a communication vehicle. One member of this committee is the liaison to each of the teams. Most attend occasional meetings of their PSI circle(s), all are available as sounding boards and in an advisory capacity. To ensure adequate communication up the hierarchy, one member is assigned as a liaison to each member of the steering committee.

Quality circle methods are new. There is little experience and few guidelines on which to draw. As a consequence, as in the majority of companies, top management was committed but not sufficiently prepared regarding the long-term nature of PSI. This has meant that the top management group, because they are pragmatic, has wanted results for expended monies. The operating committee must manage this impatience, must ensure that top management makes itself available for presentations, and that top executives really listen.

The operating committee must also ensure that circle members do not become discouraged. PSI circle members are impatient with the discussion, the research, the inability to structure solutions to (what appeared to be, at the beginning) very simple problems. "One of our [the operating committee's] more important tasks," says a committee member, "is to encourage circle members and to keep up their enthusiasm. Our job is to see that decisions get made quickly."

Facilitator

The job of the program facilitator, in addition to chairing the operating committee and acting as an ex-officio member of the steering committee, is to: coordinate communications between all committees and groups; ensure that training of circle captains and members occurs; act as liaison between PSI groups and the two committees; provide and monitor the record-keeping and reporting systems; and ascertain the progress (or lack of progress) which PSI groups are experiencing.

Captains

In some groups, captains (leaders) were appointed by the steering committee. The criteria which were used included personality, innovativeness, flexibility, willingness to take risks, aggressiveness, demonstrated leadership ability and a willingness to listen, to use peer participation and to allow freedom to members. In other circles, members elected their own captains. The majority of captains are those who have been subjected to considerable "baptism under fire"—the unit supervisors.

What role does the team captain have? According to the captain of PSI Team 8, this individual: organizes activities and logistics, monitors the meetings and ensures that all members of the team are participating, communicates with and assists team members between meetings, is careful not to impose his or her own ideas on the group and assists in monitoring implementation. Circles which are experiencing the greatest success are those which rotate secretarial and chairing responsibilities. In these circles, agendas are circulated in advance, and minutes are recorded and circulated. This is not true for all teams.

Operation

Each PSI circle meets for one hour each week on company time. (One circle holds meetings during the lunch hour.) Members are volunteers; each person who indicated a desire to participate was assigned by the steering committee to one of the heterogeneous PSI groups. New members also may join. Designated members may drop out if they wish; few have done so.

One of the first issues which each circle faced was how to select the problem that would be studied. The procedure varied among circles. Generally, following a brainstorming session in which many ideas were generated, each idea was discussed and evaluated. In some cases, a consensus approach was used to decide on the one problem. In other cases, a nucleus of problems was desired, so members were given the required number of votes, and democracy ruled. The most successful groups (about one-third, at this point) took on "bite-sized" problems.

TRAINING

Leader training sessions include:
• an explanation of the program and its objectives and why it is necessary
• what teams are expected to do and how they are related to the steering committee and the operating committee
• logistics and procedures such as chairing meetings, agendas, minutes, types of reports and forms that can be developed and used
• how to establish goals
• value engineering concepts (cost benefit analysis to help the groups identify areas where productivity improvement could occur
• calculation of and recognition of savings
• motivation of employees
• recognition

The training program was limited to these topics because the assumption was made that employees at WHQ, who are mostly professionals with degrees or post–high school training, had the necessary skills and knowledge that PSI required. Nothing could have been further from the truth, and the operating committee is currently attempting to develop more comprehensive training units.

PROJECTS UNDERTAKEN AND IMPLEMENTED

Among the projects that have been undertaken and which presently are under study are:
• improving the quality and reliability of all products
• improving heat treating
• modifying performance and developing review forms
• reviewing of inter-office magazine circulation
• updating of job posting procedures

- examining mail and small packages transfer procedures, including mail to employees' homes and the usage of "confidential" envelopes
- reducing the number of in-house manuals
- providing a directory and information guide and refining the telephone directory
- providing recorded response to incoming calls during facility shutdown
- reducing proliferation of "unit model" releases
- reducing or eliminating rented cafeterias and their maintenance
- providing markers to assist in the relocation of removed microfilm records
- improving paper flow of shipper notifications
- assessing actions necessary to reduce tardiness and unauthorized early departures
- educating personnel to the features and benefits of the word processor
- improving computer terminal availability
- revising the processing and distribution of computer-produced invoices
- computerizing energy consumption and cost reports
- reducing the monthly phone expense, with a 5 percent reduction goal
- minimizing distractions within the workplace
- reducing employee time spent on scanning or reading bulletin boards.
- improving copying services
- reviewing coffee-break procedures

About one-third of the circles, to date, have made suggestions which have been implemented. Completed projects include:

- modification of order procedures; savings of $600
- modification of "impending change" notices; savings of $24,000
- engineers trained in computer utilization; savings of $52,800 or 0.55 engineering person-years gained
- transfer of parts and service drawings; savings of $10,200 annually
- increased productivity of team members by holding team meetings on personal time rather than on company-paid time; potential savings are $4,050
- improved mailroom efficiency; three stages have been implemented to date with a resulting savings of $27,800

273

• reduction of electrical energy used by turning off one of two cooling system pumps; savings of $20,000 annually
• printing of graph paper in-house; savings of $553 annually
• review of engineering cost reporting system; projected mininum annual savings of $22,000
• expedition of "release pending" procedures; savings of $3,000 annually
• implementation of a standard engineering project filing system; potential cost savings of $50,000 to $70,000 annually

Figure 14–4 illustrates the cost savings report form that is currently being used by quality circles within the manufacturing operations. Discussions at WHQ are continuing as to whether or not PSI teams want a similar format.

FIGURE 14–4
Monthly Status Report

**Monthly Status Report
of Achievement**

Team Identification_____	Steering Committee Approvals:
Team Leader_____	Project Nos. Approved_____
Month of_____	Project Nos. Rejected_____

Project Identification Annual Goal   Achievements_____

1. Current Month	$ _____
Year to Date	$ _____
Percent of Project Goal:	
Current Month	_____
Yeart to Date	_____

| 0 | 25 | 50 | 75 | 100 |

2. Current Month	$ _____
Year to Date	$ _____
Percent of Project Goal:	
Current Month	_____
Year to Date	_____

| 0 | 25 | 50 | 75 | 100 |

(cont'd)

Team Total Current Month	$ _____
Year to Date	$ _____
Percent of Project Goal:	
Current Month	_____
Year to Date	_____

| 0 | 25 | 50 | 75 | 100 |

RECOGNITION OF CIRCLES

Incentives for participation are necessary. These, however, do not have to be monetary in nature. In the manufacturing plants, monetary recognition includes savings bonds, small prizes for the best team each month, trips for very significant achievements or ideas (or the best in a particular quarter). Non-monetary forms of recognition include dinners and baseball or football games for team employees and their spouses. A more "risky" activity includes a raffle for a number of prizes. A raffle ticket is given to the circle for each idea which is submitted during the month. The more tickets, of course, the better are the chances of winning.

FIGURE 14–5
Letter Regarding an Accepted Proposal

Date: _____

To:
c/o Dept:
From:
Subject: *Quality & Cost Improvement Proposal—Accepted*
　　　Group # _____
　　　Team # _____
　　　Proposal # _____

Your proposal has been reviewed and approved by the Operating and Steering Committees.
A record of the annual savings amount of $ —— will be placed in your personnel file. The Steering Committee wishes to thank you for your participation and encourages you to submit additional cost improvement proposals in the future.
Attachment: Copy of Proposal

FIGURE 14–6
Letter Regarding an Unaccepted Proposal

Date: _____

To:
c/o Dept:
From:
Subject: *Quality & Cost Improvement Proposal—Not Accepted*
    Group # _____
    Team # _____
    Proposal # _____

Your proposal has been reviewed by the Operating and Steering Committees and was not accepted: [reasons are given.]

The Steering Committee wishes to thank you for your participation and encourages you to continue to submit other ideas and suggestions to reduce our operating costs.
Attachment: Copy of Proposal

These ideas have not been adopted at WHQ. Non-monetary recognition, however, is frequent and includes direct personal recognition by top departmental and divisional management and wall plaques for contributions made.

Additionally, achievement is noted in the employees' personnel records. Immediate feedback also is provided by acknowledging in writing the suggestion that has been made and the anticipated cost savings (See Figures 14–5 and 14–6).

IN RETROSPECT

Progress to date has not been easy. With the PSI concept, WHQ management is in the early stages of a pioneering project; for them there are few guidelines and a continuous variety of different types of problems. Of course, everyone knew that the process would not fall into place immediately, and that there would be a very frustrating, painful growing period. "But," the facilitator reflects, "we underestimated how lengthy and frustrating that period would be. And we did make some mistakes." The mistakes were attributable to lack of knowledge and a desire to help teams accomplish early successes.

One of these mistakes was the setting of organizational goals for the groups. In an effort to help, management established goals, which, unfortunately, were perceived as being financial and qualitative in nature only, that is, they were cost-cutting targets. Resentment occurred. Again, in retrospect, a senior member of management muses, "If we had to do it all over again? First, we would avoid setting goals. You need to build harmony among the teams; they need a history of working together and of achieving success. Because there was no previous experience, our goals were set unrealistically high. Teams could not help but fall short. Management too had higher expectations. It was a no-win situation—a situation in which disappointment was programmed into the process."

Second, the training program for captains, which consisted of six sessions of one to one-and-a-half hours, and the indoctrination program for management were inadequate. The initial captain training program included familiarization with the PSI concept, the goals of the organization, the fundamentals of the change process, how to conduct a meeting, and techniques of problem solving. One middle manager, a member of the operating committee, states, "We were venturing into a new untried area. We had no history to fall back on and so were unable to anticipate all of the problems." Presently, Vickers is considering instituting periodic training sessions—on a continuing basis—mostly in additional techniques of group interaction and problem solving.

A third problem, was experienced in the early stages. Circles were enthusiastic and felt that, at last, an opportunity was available which could help in eliminating the problems and bottlenecks. Projects selected, at times, tended to be difficult and far-reaching, and encompassed many departments of the organization. Circles generally underestimated the time that was required and the difficulty of conducting research and reaching consensus. In future, most of the circles will take on smaller, more manageable problems.

Lack of time to pursue circle activities has been a problem. Each circle is anxious to do an excellent job and to make the organization a better place to work and ensure that it remains competitive. This is not easy. Because of the adverse economic times, each person has had to assume additional functional duties and responsibilities. The lack of time to conduct required research is extremely frustrating.

A fourth problem concerns management style. Like that of other organizations that had their beginnings in the 1940s and

1950s, Vickers's management group is mature, and for the majority, the Theory-X style of management has worked well. The Theory-Z style requires considerable flexibility and adaptibility. "No matter how hard a manager tries," states one member, "it is easy to slip back into the old ways."

In addition to problems, there have been many advantages. Among the most important is the tendency of circle members to believe that everything can be accomplished. They do not accept excuses and reasons; they just do it! To accomplish goals, protocol and organizational formality are ignored. The result has been a better communication system and a flattening of the hierarchy of the organization.

Management too has responded with enthusiasm. They are determined that this will be a grass-roots movement—loose, flexible and responsive. The direction and success will come from the members themselves. To this end, they are determined to avoid formalization and bureaucratic trappings. It is formalization and bureaucracy, says one senior management member, that "undermine incentive, thought and creativity. We have exceptional employees and are confident PSI teams will be successful."

PSI—PEOPLE SEEKING IMPROVEMENT

Why quality circles in an office situation?
• overhead contributes substantially to costs
• administrative staff increasing while production staff decreasing
• long-established practices exist
• machines used improperly
• savings for each suggestion difficult to quantify

Key problems:
• no standards or output measurements
• resistance to establishing these
• highly qualified people doing clerical work
• middle management apprehensive
• fear that teams would overextend their authority and expertise

PSI structure:
• steering committee

- operating committee—key to PSI group success
- facilitator
- fourteen PSI groups of five to eight members each
- cross-functional membership of groups

Annual cost savings of $250,000 currently achieved.
Incentives and recognition:
- acknowledgement letter
- notation in personnel file
- savings bonds
- trips for outstanding ideas
- wall plaques
- social events
- raffle

In retrospect:
- management set goals; this was a mistake
- training inadequate
- problems selected were too difficult
- lack of time
- management style

Circles believe they can make anything happen.

Management has been responsive.

FIFTEEN

IN CONCLUSION: QCs—SUCCESS OR FAILURE?

Are quality circles the answer to motivational and other problems which face the North American industrial world in the 1980s? The quality control circle and small group concept have assisted Japan in becoming the world trading nation that it is today. These activities, according to a survey done by the Kansai Productivity Centre, increase communication among members, make the workplace more humane and pleasant, provide workers with greater self-realization, decrease defects, increase efficiency and productivity, develop worker knowledge and skill; increase the number of group suggestions; decrease accidents, decrease production costs, increase product quality, and decrease absenteeism.[1]

Studies indicate that in North America, too, there have been benefits. For companies, QCs have resulted in: financial gain because of employees' concern for quality, their problem solving and their suggestions regarding the improvement of production processes and methods for decreasing costs; financial gain because of increased productivity; better union-management and employer–employee relationships; and fewer grievances and fewer conflicts. For employees, QCs have meant increased development of skills and abilities, greater challenges and learning opportunities and greater satisfaction.[2] Quality circles can assist both the organization and the employees. Why, then, are some applications of the method successful while others are not?

Japanese writers claim that the humanization of the workplace is the key to success:

Human beings . . . must become the central focus of the workplace. Despotic exercise of authority denies a worker an independent personality, turns him into a "cogwheel" or a "pebble." It inhibits productivity, results in the misuse of authority and naturally leads to the self-destruction of the company.[3]

But Japanese and American cultures and systems are very different, and the techniques that work in a company in Japan will not work—without adaptation—here. One vital idea, however, can be carried over: the way to humanize the workplace is to allow workers to participate in decision making in those areas which affect them and in which they have the expertise. "What the workers want most, as more than 100 studies in the last 20 years show, is to become masters of their immediate environments and to feel that their work and they themselves are important—the twin ingredients of self-esteem."[4] A people-building process performs miracles.

Quality circles are people-builders. They allow employees to be human and not just robots or appendages of machines. Circles require workers to use their intelligence, creativity and ingenuity, not merely their physical efforts.

Second, quality circles present workers with challenge. This means that skill and abilities which they have learned are utilized. This, in turn, results in the need for new skills and knowledge and for additional training.

Third, quality circles increase communication between company employees. No longer does the company abdicate to the union the right to talk to its own workers. Management, engineers, and other white-collar employees solve problems with shop-floor workers. In doing so, they eliminate established stereotypes. Workers are no longer perceived as being illiterate, stupid people who are incapable of thinking and incapable of understanding instructions. Instead, they are individuals who love football, baseball and the latest hit tunes and movies, who live in the same environment and have the same problems, concerns and interests as managers have. The eye-openers works both ways—blue-collar workers discover that office personnel do not fritter away their time and that they do not intentionally try to make life miserable for those who "do the work." More importantly, blue-collar workers discover how inflexible the hierarchy is and how difficult it is to implement change. Circle members gain an understanding of the difficulties face by supervisors and a new respect for this group. The communication process results in a better understanding of different groups within the organization, which in turns results in less conflict, higher self-esteem, better morale and a greater commitment to the organization.

Are QCs the key to all motivational problems? Although they have been used for these purposes, the degree of their influence on worker motivation cannot be determined. Motivation is an abstract construct; it is difficult to define and more difficult to measure. Eysenck explains it this way:

> [N]o aspect of human behavior has proved more resistant to analysis and measurement. The effort of psychologists to grapple with drive and motivation has evoked a remarkable variety of unsatisfactory solutions, ranging from purely semantic exercises to psuedo-mathematical treatment of non-existent data. As a result there is still no generally accepted method of measuring the degree of motivation under which a person is working at any particular time.[5]

Only time will tell if quality circles are the missing link which, in the American environment, can inspire employees to put in a forty-hour week for forty hours of pay. The more important issue, however, is that it cannot hurt an organization to ensure that employees function in an environment that provides them with an opportunity to give their best efforts.

STEPS TO ENSURE FAILURE

Will quality circles be a success or a failure? Only the personnel within an organization can determine this. Ten steps will help to ensure failure:

1. Management should have a hidden agenda in initiating circles. Failure will be ensured if management thinks of QCs as an easy way to make a buck without spending too much money, or as a union-busting technique. Another method that will assist failure is to make numerous promises to ensure that the union cooperates at the beginning, and then break the promises. Of course, there will be a special delight when the rug is pulled out and the union realizes that it has been

tricked, that its members have been gullible, and that it was easy to "put one over on them." If there is no union, the hidden agenda can be that QCs are a good way to keep unions out.

One last method will guarantee that QCs fail. Management can use every opportunity to "screw" employees. Fishmarket haggling tactics are good for this purpose—even when the employee is right, has something coming and has been treated unjustly. This will show that management is really clever. Workers understand and respect that!

2. If failure is desired, management can rush into the program with a minimum of planning but insist that everyone, or only one pilot project, participate—at minimal cost, of course. In presenting the program, lots of flip charts and booklets should be used—in four colours. People, their problems, and listening to what they have to say are not important.

3. Very little time should be spent on training. After all, training takes money, and it means that people are away from their regular duties. All that talk about quality circles being successful because of training and techniques used is just a lot of rubbish. Employees will catch on after a while—the important thing is that there is communication. Good old "rap sessions" are the key.

4. Management should also expect large dollar returns very quickly. After all, the name implies that there is going to be quality and, by implication, fast profits. If results are not coming quickly enough, pressure should be put on the circles. One good way to do this is to threaten to cancel the program. That will show everyone that the company means business.

5. Bureaucratization of the concept will help ensure failure. Lots and lots of paperwork is needed. If everything is written down, if paper flows up the organization, something is really happening. For failure, it is best to have a precise structure, to ensure that everyone understands this and does not deviate from it, and that there is an emphasis on bureaucracy and following the proper channels.

6. Management should permit circles to work only on problems which emphasize quality control and cost savings. After all, these are "quality" circles, and quality and cost are the only things that are important to the company.

7. The supervisor and other members of middle management are not important in the process—except that they should do a good job of quality circle management with little or no time

from other duties. Besides, they are better educated; they already know these things and are paid to adjust quickly.

8. Non-responsiveness to circles helps to ensure failure. Circle suggestions that are costly or that management thinks are unnecessary should not be implemented. If circle suggestions are too good to turn down, slow response time will achieve the same purpose. Good day-to-day operating techniques include finding reasons for the circle to postpone its meetings or arranging work schedules in such a way that it will be difficult for all circle members to be present. Also, circles should not make presentations and send their reports to senior management; that violates the chain of command. If presentations are planned, members of management can make it a point to have something "come up" so that they do not attend the sessions.

9. When QC suggestions in a unit result in a need for fewer employee workhours, people should be laid off.

10. The best way to ensure failure is to assume that quality circles will not work in North America. After all, this is a Japanese concept, and the Japanese are disciplined from childhood and will do everything that they are told.

STEPS TO ENSURE SUCCESS

Just as the personnel within the organization can ensure that quality circles are a failure, they also have the power to ensure that they are a success. The steps are:

1. The quality circle concept is a people-building, not a people-using, philosophy. Open and trusting communication with employees and the union is required. If membership is voluntary, if the union is consulted, and if it shares the gains and the limelight, the union executive cannot object to quality circles.

2. Development should start slowly and the movement should be allowed to grow naturally. Extensive planning is needed before quality circles are launched. At first, it is very difficult for employees who in the past were expected only to "do" (as they were told) to begin thinking, talking, listening and caring as members of a circle. Also, care must be used in selecting steering committee members, the facilitator and circle leaders.

3. Training should be emphasized and re-emphasized. Communication and "rap sessions" are great, but a goal and a direction give purpose to the meetings. Success really does lie

in the techniques—the ability of the group to organize a project, to gather and analyze data through brainstorming, cause-and-effect or process diagrams, statistical methods and the delphi technique. These give structure and direction to a circle's activities. They also remove the politicking.

4. Progress in the beginning stages is very slow. Circle members must learn the techniques and how to work with each other. When circle members are unable to meet established objectives, they become frustrated. Unrealistic expectations also create a feeling among management members that circles have not been successful. Success, not failure, should be programmed into the process.

5. The emphasis should be on people solving problems and not on hierarchical pyramids or paperwork.

6. The other "quality"—quality of working life—is extremely important, and employees should be encouraged to solve problems that will mean added personal and group satisfaction.

7. The supervisor's role and that of other middle management members must change as the circle develops. Possible role expansion includes goal setting and policy making, training and mentoring, and being allowed to make those day-to-day decisions that affect their work area without consulting superiors. This means that these people's skills must be adequately developed, that a reward system which recognizes team and circle development must be in place, and that supervisory support systems must be built. Additionally, management must know how to positively reinforce participative behaviours. Time must be allocated into schedules to permit this group to perform activities that are expected of them. Quality circles work best if they are treated as a line, rather than a staff, responsibility.

In other words, circles must be part of a total organizational effort. Everyone including senior management, middle management and supervisory staff, must be committted and involved. Crucial to success is the sharing of information that must occur among units and departments and hierarchical levels.

8. As many suggestions as possible should be implemented as quickly as possible. If this cannot be done, feedback should be provided to the circle regarding the reasons for the delay or the non-implementation. Also, senior management, as well as technical people, must be involved in presentations and must read and comment on the reports which are submitted.

9. Management should advertise its commitment that no employee will be laid off because of the implementation of quality circle suggestions. Instead, the organization should undertake to retrain employees and to reassign them to new jobs.

10. The idea that quality circles will not work in North America is nonsense. QCs will work in Canada and in the United States, and there are countless cases which show that they do (see lists in appendices). It is necessary, however, to adapt the concept to North American culture and to the specific organization.

There is nothing in the quality circle idea that is not applicable within the North American context. And there is much that is—the recognition of employees as people, the self-fulfilment, the knowledge that one is needed; these are the foundations of the Canadian and U.S. individualistic systems.

The quality control concept is not a Japanese idea. It is an American idea that was brought to Japan by Deming, Juran and others who followed. But even if it were a Japanese concept, multiculturalism has prepared people to learn from others, to take and adapt a wide variety of concepts and to build that new, better and bolder mousetrap or quality circle.

And so, in conclusion, if the proper people-developing philosophy exists, and if ideas to further it are followed thoughtfully and deliberately, managers may be surprised to discover in five, ten or fifteen years that success will come. That success involves all employees. Rank-and-file workers will be concerned about the well-being of the company and will solve problems and accomplish goals without management supervision and prodding. Management, on the other hand, will be willing and able to provide guidance, encouragement and support. Furthermore managers, engineers and white-collar and blue-collar employees, unionized and non-unionized, will cooperate to ensure that the company remains competitive, and that each employee has a rewarding and desirable job. On to the twenty-first century; quality circles are here!

Quality circles:
• Effect financial savings.
• Improve union–management relationships.
• Increase employee motivation and productivity.

- Increase individual development.
- Improve morale.

Because they:
- Are people builders.
- Present workers with challenge.
- Increase communication among employees.

Cure to motivational problems?
- Perhaps; but motivation is an abstract concept which is difficult to define and measure.

To ensure QCs are a failure:
- Use them as a union-busting technique.
- Do minimal pre-planning.
- Have minimal training.
- Expect large dollar returns quickly.
- Demand lots of paperwork.
- Allow circles to work only on quality and cost-savings problems.
- Ignore needs of supervisors and middle management personnel.
- Implement few suggestions, and those slowly.
- Lay off employees because of suggestion implementation.
- Believe that QCs won't work.

To ensure that QCs are a success:
- Use them to build people.
- Start slowly and let the movement grow naturally.
- Emphasize training.
- Be patient and expect little in the early stages.
- Emphasize people and people problems.
- Quality of working life is important and circles should address these types of problems.
- Plan new roles for supervisors and middle managers.
- Implement improvements quickly or provide feedback regarding the difficulties.
- Retrain and reassign employees who have become redundant because of circle idea implementation.
- Believe they do work and can work.

APPENDICES

Training Programs

Length of Training Session

1. Top executives	2 days
2. Middle management	3 days
3. Union executive	3 days
4. Steering or advisory committee	4 days
5. Facilitators	10 days
6. Circle Leaders	8 days
7. Circle members	5 days

Length of Initial Training Session by Topic

	Time in Hours						
Group (as numbered above)	1	2	3	4	5	6	7
Introduction to Organization/Circles	1.0	1.0	1.0	1.0	1.0	1.0	1.0
a) Roles	.5	1.0	1.0	3.0	1.0	2.0	.5
b) Implementation process	.5	1.5	1.5	2.0	4.0	1.0	1.0
c) Cautions	.5	.5	.5	.5	.5	.5	.5
Human Resource Management							
a) Motivation	1.5	2.5	2.5	2.5	6.5	2.0	—
b) Leadership	1.5	2.5	2.5	2.5	6.5	3.0	—
c) Communication	1.5	3.5	3.5	4.0	6.5	3.5	3.5
d) Feedback	.5	1.0	1.0	1.5	1.5	1.0	1.0
Group Processes							
a) Group techniques	.5	1.5	1.5	2.5	6.5	3.0	3.0

(cont'd)

	1	2	3	4	5	6	7
b) Brainstorming	1.5	1.5	1.5	1.5	2.0	1.5	1.5
c) Decision Making	1.0	1.0	1.0	1.0	3.0	1.0	1.0
Circle Skills (Appendix 1 cont'd)							
a) Problem identification	1.0	1.0	1.0	1.0	6.5	6.5	6.5
b) Problem specification	1.0	.5	.5	.5	13.0	13.0	10.0
c) Presentation skills	.5	.5	.5	.5	4.5	6.5	1.5
d) Meeting logistics	—	—	—	—	2.0	6.5	1.5
TOTAL	13.0	19.5	19.5	24.0	65.0	52.0	32.5

Content of Initial Seminars and Emphasis on Topics

Orientation	1	2	3	4	5	6	7
What is a quality circle?	H	H	H	H	H	H	H
Costs and benefits	H	H	H	M	M	H	H
Philosophy of human resource management under QC's	H	H	H	H	H	H	L
Differences between Canada/U.S. and Japan	M	M	M	L	L	L	L
Union involvement	M	M	H	H	H	M	M
Threats posed to middle management and supervisors	H	H	—	H	H	H	—
Case studies of results achieved by QCs	M	M	M	M	M	M	M
Structure and responsibilities	H	H	M	H	H	—	—
Roles							
Executive	M	L	L	M	L	L	L
Middle management	H	H	L	H	M	L	—
Union executive	H	H	H	H	M	M	M
Steering (advisory) committee	H	H	M	H	H	H	H
Facilitators	H	H	M	H	H	H	H
Circle Leaders	L	M	M	H	H	H	H
Circle members	L	L	M	L	H	H	H
Implementing a Circle and Carrying out Recommendations							
Setting up objectives	L	L	L	M	H	H	H
Setting up a steering committee	M	M	M	—	—	—	—
Deciding on the number of quality circles	M	—	—	H	—	—	—
Choosing participants—steering committee	L	L	M	—	—	—	—
—facilitators	M	M	M	H	—	—	—
—leaders	L	M	M	H	—	—	—
—members	L	—	M	M	H	—	—
Getting involvement from the participants	M	M	M	H	H	—	—
Skills required	M	L	L	M	H	H	—
Selecting problems and issues	L	—	—	H	H	H	H
Analyzing costs/benefits of projects	H	—	—	H	H	H	H
Implementing recommendations	H	L	L	H	H	M	L
Some cautions							
Steps to ensure that QCs are a success	H	M	M	M	M	M	—
Steps to ensure that QCs process functions well	—	—	—	M	H	H	H

Motivation

Theoretical background—hierarchical, two-factor, equity and expectancy	M	M	M	M	H	M	—
Reinforcement theory	M	M	M	M	H	M	—
Assessing personal needs and motives	M	M	M	M	H	M	—
Relationship of participation to motivation	H	H	H	L	H	H	—
Assessing environment	H	M	M	L	H	H	—

Leadership

Theoretical background—Theories X and Y; Theory Z	M	M	M	M	H	H	—
Theoretical—situational and contingency theory	M	M	M	M	H	M	—
Assessment of own leadership style	M	M	M	M	M	H	—
Awareness of leadership styles and their impact on group participation and performance	M	M	M	M	H	H	—
Group leadership concepts and techniques	M	M	M	M	H	H	—

Communication

Importance of listening and its impact on group participation	H	M	M	M	H	H	H
Development of active listening skills	H	M	M	M	H	H	H
Non-verbal communication	H	M	M	M	H	H	H
Skills required for meaningful two-way communication	H	M	M	M	H	H	H

Feedback, suggestions and criticism

Functional and dysfunctional types	H	M	M	M	H	H	H
Knowledge of results	H	M	M	M	H	H	H
Sources of performance feedback	H	L	L	L	H	H	H
Impact of goals and feedback on performance	H	M	M	M	M	H	H
Used as a managerial tool	H	M	—	M	H	H	—

Group dynamics and processes

Theory of group dynamics	H	H	H	H	H	H	H
Positive, neutral and negative modes of interaction	H	H	H	H	H	H	H
Negotiating skills	H	H	H	H	H	H	H
Arriving at consensus decision making	H	H	H	H	H	H	H
Brainstorming	H	H	H	H	H	H	H

Circle skills

Problem identification	L	L	L	M	H	H	H
Problem specification and resolution	L	L	L	M	H	H	H
Statistics: Techniques	L	L	L	M	H	H	H
Statistics: When to use	L	L	L	M	H	H	H
Statistics: How to construct and use	L	L	L	M	H	H	H
Report preparation	L	L	L	H	H	H	L
Oral presentations	L	L	L	M	H	H	L

Meeting Logistics

Chairing a meeting	—	—	—	—	H	H	L
Encouraging participation	—	—	—	—	H	H	M
Agendas	—	—	—	—	H	H	H

(cont'd)

APPENDICES

Keeping minutes of meetings	—	—	—	—	H	H	H
Other logistics	—	—	—	H	H	H	H

H means high content in this area.
M means moderate content in this area.
L means that, in the beginning stages, content in this area can be low.

QC Education and Training Courses Promoted by Toyota Group

Courses	Frequency	Number of Participants
Middle Management		
Toyota QC Middle Management Course (51 hours)	once a year	198
Toyota Reliability Engineering Middle Management Course (30 hours)	once a year	176
QC Staff		
Toyota QC Basic Course (138 hours)	once a year	525
Toyota Reliability Engineering Basic Course (60 hours)	twice a year	657
Toyota Design of Experiments Course (78 hours)	twice a year	177
Superintendents		
Toyota QC Circle Promoter's Course (36 hours)	twice a year	276
Foremen and Group Leader		
Toyota QC Foremen's Problem-Solving Course (27 hours)	once a year	121

Source: *the wheel extended: A Toyota Quarterly Review* (Tokyo), Spring 1980, p. 26.

U.S. Companies Using Quality Circles

The application of quality circles spans a wide variety of American industry. Among the organizations reportedly using circles are:

Abbott Labs (IL)
Advanced Micro Devices
Aerojet Ordnance
Alcan Aluminum Corporation
Allstate Insurance Company
American Airlines
American Biltrite, Inc.
American Can Co.
American Express
American Hoechst Corp.
AMF–Harley Davidson Corp.
AMP, Inc.
Anja Engineering Corp.
Applied Magnetics
Arco Sola, Inc. (CA)
Armco, Inc.
Automatic Electric Co.
Babcock & Wilcox Co.
Bank of America, San Francisco
Bank of California
Barber-Colman Co.
Bell Northern Research, Inc.
Bethlehem Steel

Blue Cross (WA, AK)
Wm. L. Bonnell Co.
Borg Warner—Spring Division
Braceland Bros. (PA)
Canadian Appliance Mfg. Co. Ltd.
C.B. Fleet Co. (VA)
Centerline Circuits (CO)
Central Pacific Bank (HI)
Champion Spark Plug Co.
Chase Manhattan Bank (NY)
Chemical Bank of New York
Chicago Title & Trust Co.
Citibank, N.A.
Continental Illinois National Bank
Copperweld Steel Co.
Cordis Dow Corp.
Corning Glass Works (PA)
Crocker Bank
Dana Corporation (IN)
Datapoint Corp.
Davidson Rubber Inc. (GA)
Dayton Tire & Rubber Co., Oklahoma City, OK

Dover Corporation
Duncan Industries
E .G. & G. Torque Systems
E.I. DuPont de Nemours Co.
Eaton Corporation
Estee Lauder Inc. (NY)
Eaton Engine Components Plant (MI)
Exxon Co.—Nuclear Division
Fairchild Bipolar LSI
Fairchild Digital Division
Fairchild Weston Controls
Federal Products Co.
Firemen's Fund Insurance Companies
First & Merchants National Bank
Fleetguard
Ford Motor Co.
Frolic Footwear Division, Wolverine
Galigher Company
Gates Learjet Corp. (KS)
G. E. Glass Plant (UT)
General Electric (RI)
General Motors Corporation
Gleason Works—Machine Div., Rochester, NY
Golden State Sanwa Bank
Goodrich Chemical Company
Graco, Inc.
Great Lakes Steel (MI)
Grove Valve, Oakland, CA
GTE Automatic Electric Company
Harper Wyman Co.
Hawaiian Dredging & Construction
Hazeltine Corporation
Hertz Corporation (CA)
Holiday Inn (FN)
Honeywell Inc.
Houston National Bank
Hughes Aircraft Co.
IBM (FL)
Ingersoll-Rand Research, Inc.
Intel Corporation
I.T.T. (MS, NJ, NY, TN)
I.T.T. Royal Electric Division (RI)
International Paper Co.

International Rectifier
Johnson & Johnson Products Inc.
Koppers World (MD)
The Kroger Co.
J. B. Lansing Sound Co.
Lincoln National Life Insurance Co.
Litton—Data Systems Division
Lockheed Missile & Space Corporation
Lumisistemas CM, S.A., Mexico
Marine Midland Bank
Marlin Rockwell—Division of TRW
Martin-Marietta Aerospace
Martin Marietta Chemicals Division (NC)
Massey Ferguson (MI)
McGraw-Edison (IL, NY)
Mellon Bank, N.A. (PA)
Memorex Corporation
Metropolitan Transit Authority (New York City)
Mid-Florida Technical Institute (FL)
Monsanto Chemical Co.
Morton Chemical Co.
Motorola
Mt. Sinai Medical Center of Greater Miami
Naval Air Rework Facility/No Island, San Diego, CA
New York Port Authority
C.A. Norgren Co.
Norris Industries—Vernon Division
Northern Telecom (NC)
Northrop Corporation
Oak Switch Systems, Inc. (IL)
Olin Brass Co.
Olin Paper & Film Group
Peabody Floway
Pentel of America
Pet Food Co.
Phelps Dodge Wire Magnet (IN, KY, OH)
Philips ECG (NY, OH)
Pittsburgh National Bank (PA)
Polaroid Corporation, Norwood, MA

(cont'd)

297

Poly Chrome Corporation

Precision Shooting Equipment

Ralston Purina Co.

RCA—Distribution & Special Products Division

Robinson Brick & Tile

Rockford Products

Rockwell International Collins Communications Systems Division

Rockwell International Specifications Systems Group, Seal Beach, CA

Sacramento County, CA

Santa Clara Unified School District (CA)

Sargent and Lundy

Schering Plough, Kenilworth NJ

Sealy Mattress Co. (MD, IL)

Security Pacific National Bank (CA)

Sennett Steel Corporation

Sherwin Williams Co. (CA)

Simplex Time Recorder

Smith Corona (NY)

Smith Kline Instruments, Inc.

Solar Turbines International

Spectrum Inc.

Sperry Gyroscope

Sperry Vickers

Standyne Distribution Center (IN)

Standyne Western (OH)

Sundstrand

Tektronix

Texize

Thor Electronics

3M Company, St. Paul, MN

Timex

Trane Air Conditioning—Lexington Manufacturing Division

The Trane Company, LaCrosse, WI

Tungsten Carbide Manufacturing

U.N.C.—National Automatic Tools

Unicore Federal Prison Industries, Inc. (NY)

Union Bank

Union Carbide, Greenville, SC

United California Bank

U.S. Department of the Army (CO)

U.S. Naval Aviation Logistics Center

U.S. Naval Ordnance Center, Louisville, KY

U.S. Naval Weapons Support Center

USA DARCOM Automated Logistics

The Upjohn Company—Varian Micro Tube Division

Verbatim

Vickers, Inc.

Voss Industries, Inc.

Warner-Lambert Co.—Consumer Products Group

Waters Associates

Waugh Controls Corporation

Western Wheel Corporation

Westinghouse Electric Corporation

Woodward-Governor Co.

Xerox Corporation

Yolo County, California

Canadian Companies Using Quality Circles

Name and Address of Company	Date Initiated	No. of Circles	Contact Person
Aetna Canada Aetna Canada Centre 145 King Street West Toronto, Ontario M5H 3T7	June 1982	12	Brenda Butler Manager General Planning
Air BC 4680 Cowley Crescent Richmond, B.C. V7B 1C1	May 1983	8	Donna M. Hornsby Secretary
Allis Chambers 155 Dawson Road Guelph, Ontario N1H 1A4	July 1982	1	Peter Leslie Supervisor Employee Relations
Anca Inc. 111 Consumers Drive Whitby, Ontario	1982	2	Tessa Hogewaard
B.C. Tel. 3777 Kingsway Vancouver, B.C. V5H 3Z7	1981	40	Sue Knot Personnel Manager Viki MacMillan QC Coordinator

APPENDICES

Bell Canada   1982   30   Ron Deaken
393 University Ave., 9th Floor   Section Manager
Toronto, Ontario M5G 1W9   Organization
                              Development

Bonar Packaging Ltd.   March 1983   14   Zenon Onufryk
2380 McDonnell Road
Burlington, Ontario L7R 4A1

Burroughs   1982   20   Carol Postineks
51 Burmac Road   Manager
Winnipeg, Manitoba R3C 2P7   Training and
                              Development

C.I.L.   Michael Damphousse,
Box 10   H.R. Development
Montreal, Quebec H3C 2R3   Manager

CUNA of Ontario   2   Ann Allan
895 Brand Street   Facilitator
Burlington, Ontario

Cardinal Meat Specialist   1983   4   Jack Boulet
    Ltd.   Controller
2396 Stanfield Road
Mississauga, Ontario L4Y 1S1

Champion Road   1981   16   Elgin Fisher
    Machinery   Facilitator
P.O. Box 10
Goderich, Ontario N7A 3Y6

City Bank Leasing   Richard P. Tailor
P.O. Box 5060, South
    Service Road
Burlington, Ontario

Claude Neon   7   Michel Bergeron
1855 Hymus   Sales Supervisor
Dorval, Quebec H9P 1J8

Claude Neon   1983   8   Tom Badani
555 Ellesmere Road   Facilitator
Scarborough, Ontario M1R 4E8

Constellation Assurance Company	December 1983	2	Jan Shuckard Asst. Vice-President Corporate Services
26 Wellington Street East Toronto, Ontario M5E 1J6			

Control Data Canada 1982 22 William P. Murphy
1855 Minnesota Court
Mississauga, Ontario L5N 1K7

Courtesy Chevrolet 1982 Don Bannerman
3131 Main Street General Manager
Vancouver, B.C. V5T 3G8

Crush Canada, Inc. March 1983 3 E. L. Marr
1590 O'Connor Drive QC Facilitator
Toronto, Ontario M4B 2V4

Cumis Insurance March 1981 11 Anne Wright
P. O. Box 5065 Training Specialist
Burlington, Ontario

Cyanamid Canada Inc. 1984 Jim Sands
2255 Sheppard Avenue Director, H.R.
  East
Willowdale, Ontario M2J 4Y5

Dominion Directory 1983 5 Doug Gavin
4400 Dominion Street
Burnaby, B.C. V5G 4G4

Dominion Life March 1983 33 Linda Lehtonew
Assurance Co. Ltd. QC Coordinator
111 Westmount Road
  South
Waterloo, Ontario
N2J 4C6

Dover Corp. (Canada) 1981 3 K. McCullough
Ltd. Manager of
Dover Elevator   Engineering
126 John Street *or* D. Powers
Toronto, Ontario Supervisor of Quality
M5V 2E3   Control

(cont'd)

APPENDICES

Duracel Inc.   1981   4   Dwight S. Cameron
2333 North Sheridan Way   QC Manager
Mississauga, Ontario
L5K 1A7

EDP Industries   1983   2   John Fysh
1313 Main Street
Vancouver, B.C.
V5T 3G8

Equitable Insurance   1983   3   Nicole Elbaz
  Company   Supervisor
200 Rue St-Jacques
Montreal, Quebec
H2Y 1M2

Esso Chemical Canada   1980   1   R. W. Tully
P. O. Box 3004   PVC Operations
Sarnia, Ontario N7T 7M5

Fisher Controls Co.   1981   7   Rick DeVleeschower
  of Canada
1039 Dundas Street
Woodstock, Ontario
N4S 7Z6

Foothills Hospital   April 1983 5   Michael Oakes
1403—29 Street, N. W.   Staff Development
Calgary, Alberta T2N 2T9   Officer

Ford Motor Company   Fall 1982   16   Pat McKrow
  of Canada   QC Coordinator
No. 1 Quality Way
Windsor, Ontario

General Foods   1983   2   Wendy Vinegar
95 Moatfield Drive   Supervisor H.R.
Don Mills, Ontario   Development and
M3B 3L6   Recruitment

Gould Outdoor Signs   2   Paula McKay
Brantford, Ontario

Great West Life   March 1982 30   Ed. J. Taylor
60 Osborne Street North   Associate Manager
Winnipeg, Manitoba   Productivity Services
R3C 3A5

Hewlett Packard Canada Ltd. 6877 Goreway Drive Mississauga, Ontario L4V 1M8	June 1981	13	John T. Rooney Commercial Services Manager *or* Mark Borkowski Personnel Representative
Hiram Walker P. O. Box 250 Winfield, B.C. V0H 2C0	1982	3	Gene Levesque
Hook Signs 2335—30th Avenue N.E. Calgary, Alberta T2E 7C7	1983	6	Randy Otto
Hostess Chips P. O. Box 250 Kentville, N.S.	1983	8	Marlene McFarlane Personnel Manager
Hostess Food Products Ltd. 1001 Bishop Street North Cambridge, Ontario	March 1983	17	S. Cairns Vice President Operations
Hussman Store Equipment Limited P.O. Box 550 Brantford, Ontario N3T 5R2	February 1983	11	J. Al. Spence President
IBM Canada 3500 Steeles Avenue East Toronto, Ontario L3R 2Z1		700	Dennis Makepeace Program Manager Quality
Kaufman Footwear 410 King Street West Kitchener, Ontario N2G 4J8	1982	3	Phil Hendly Personnel Manager
Knape & Vogt Canada Inc. 340 Carlingview Drive Rexdale, Ontario M9W 5G5	1983	4	Joe Teixeira Distribution Manager

(cont'd)

Lucerne Safeway 9256-198 Street Langley, B.C.	1982	2	Norm Reeve Director, Marketing
Mainland Magazine 9453-198th Street Langley, B.C. V3A 4P8	October 1982	4	Norm Reeve
McCain Foods P.O. Box 540 Hartland, N.B. E0J 1N0	1984	1	Ken Nichols V.P. Personnel and Training
Motorways P. O. Box 738 60 Eagle Drive Winnipeg, Manitoba R3C 2L8	December 1983		Don L. White Vice President Operations
Mountain City News P. O. Box 768 Hamilton, Ontario L8N 3N2	1983	2	Roli Pitalik
Nashua Canada Ltd. 550 Braidwood Avenue Peterborough, Ontario K9J 6X4	July 1979	10	J. J. Zeyen Vice President Manufacturing
Neon Products Box 2063 Vancouver, B.C. V6B 3F4	1982	8	Babs Babcock
New Balance 72 St. Leger Street Kitchener, Ontario N2H 6R7	1983	7	Margot Baird Facilitator
Northern Telecom Canada Ltd. (various locations)	1984	15	Sam Barnes Manager, Manufacturing and Training
Omark Canada Ltd. 505 Edinburgh Road North Guelph, Ontario N1H 6L 4	February 1983	12	Al Rogers Training Manager

Otis Elevator McCaul Street Toronto, Ontario	1983		Dave Rhodes
Overwaitea Foods P. O. Box 7200 Vancouver, B.C. V6B 4E4	October 1982	17	Art Van Pelt Employee Relations Manager
Jim Pattison Pontiac Buick 3434 Main Street Vancouver, B.C. V5V 3N2	1983	3	Don Bannerman V.P.
Provincial News 14436-121A Avenue Edmonton, Alberta T5L 4L2	1983	2	Peter Kiernan Director, Marketing
Seaboard Advertising 1885 Clark Drive Vancouver, B.C. V6B 3S4	1982	8	Mike Jefferson
Toronto-Dominion Bank 55 King St. W. & Bay Street Toronto, Ontario M5K 1A2	Spring 1982	15	Ron Sinclair Coordinator Quality Program
Trans Ad 48 St. Clair Avenue West Toronto, Ontario M4V 2Z2			
Tridon Limited 2190 South Service Road, W. Oakville, Ontario, L6L 5T8	October 1983	1	Ed Artuso QCC Facilitator
Vanguard P. O. Box 280 Winfield, B.C. V0H 2C0	1982	6	Jim Molyneaux
Venturetrans Manufacturing P. O. Box 100, Station A Kingston, Ontario	1983	3	Al Charlton

(cont'd)

Weldwood of Canada Ltd. 1055 West Hastings Street Vancouver. B.C.	1984		Randy Schaeffer Manager, Labour Relations
Westinghouse Canada Inc. P. O. Box 510 Hamilton, Ontario L8N 3K2	January 1980	57	R. McCormick Director Corporate Productivity Services
Wilfrid Laurier University 75 University Avenue, West Waterloo, Ontario N2L 3C5	March 1983	4	Dr. J. Alex Murray Dean School of Business & Economics

Canadian Companies Which Have Reportedly Instituted Quality Circles

Alberta Children's Hospital	North American Life
Alcan Aluminum	Ontario Hydro
Excelsior Insurance	University of Calgary
McDonnell Douglas Corp.	

Selected List of Canadian Management Consultants in Quality Circles, and Organizations Promoting QC/QWL in Canada

E & L Enterprises
(Ernie Long)
447 Patricia Drive
Burlington, Ontario L7T 1J9
Tel.: 1-416-525-2375

K. D. Frey & Associates
R. R. 2
Rockwood, Ontario N0B 2K0
Tel.: 1-519-856-9727

Institut National de Productivité
(Fernand Gauthier, Director-
  Général)
1 Complexe Desjardins, Tour Sud
C. P. 157, Suite 1509
Montréal, Québec, Canada
H5B 1B5
Tel: 1-514-873-7601

Ontario Quality of Working Life
  Centre
(Hugh Auld)
400 University Avenue
Toronto, Ontario M7A 1T7
Tel.: 1-416-965-5958

Personnel and Productivity
Management
(O. L. Crocker)
Faculty of Business Administration
University of Windsor
Windsor, Ontario N9B 3P4
Tel.: 1-519-253-4232;
  1-519-734-7648

Qualitran Professional Services
(L. M. Galicinski)
Stroud, Ontario
Tel.: 1-705-722-8550

Thorne, Stevenson & Kellogg
(Cyril Charney)
2300 Yonge Street
Toronto, Ontario M4P 1G2
Tel.: 1-416-483-4313

Woods Gordon Management
  Consultants
(Dr. Pierre DuBois)
630, boul. Dorchester ouest
Montréal, Québec, Canada
H3B 1T9
Tel.: 1-514-875-5835

(cont'd)

APPENDICES

Woods Gordon Management
   Consultants
(Colin Lockie)
Royal Trust Tower
Toronto, Ontario
Tel.: 1-416-864-1212

APPENDIX 6
Consultants in Quality Circles in the United States

There are several sources of information and/or consulting on the quality circle application in the U.S. They are:

Ann Arbor Consulting Assoc.
Philip Alexander
5204 Jackson Road
Ann Arbor, MI 48103
(313) 995-2404

American Quality Institute
4567 Gatetree Circle
Pleasanton, CA 94566
(415) 462-0493

Consulting Associates Inc.
Ron Kregoski & Ed Yaeger
21333 Haggerty Rd., Suite 311
Novi, MI 48050
(313) 348-0001

William Golombewski & Assoc.
593 Van Buren St.
Chicago, IL 60605
(312) 922-5985

Growing Organizations Unlimited
Carter Taylor
467 Tarrington Road
Rochester, NY 14609
(716) 482-1629

Juran Enterprises Inc.
Dr. Joseph Juran
866 United Nations Plaza
New York, NY 10017
(212) 832-3127

Organizational Dynamics
16 New England Exec. Park
Burlington, MA 01803
(617) 272-8040

Participative Systems, Inc.
Sidney Rubinstein
909 State Road, P.O. Box 18
Princeton, NJ 08540
(609) 452-1244

(cont'd)

Productivity Quality Assoc.
Michael Clearey
7718 Normandy Lane
Dayton, OH 45459
(513) 274-7817

Quality Circle Institute
Donald Dewar
1425 Vista Way
Airport Industrial Park
P.O. Box Q
Red Bluff, CA 96080
(916) 527-6970

Quality Circle Systems
21 Tilton Lane
Andover, MA 01810
(617) 475-9563

Quest Associates Ltd.
P.O. Box 182
Park Forest, IL 60466
(312) 747-3663

Rath and Strong Inc.
Chuck Carter Jr.
P.O. Box 5001
Richardson, TX 75080
(214) 235-0210

Reddy, Berger, Rosen and Woods,
    Inc.
Jack Reddy
2406 Massachusetts Ave.
Lexington, MA 02173
(617) 862-8888

Quality Control Circles Inc.
Wayne Rieker
Higgins and Root Bldg.
400 Blossom Hill Rd.
Los Gatos, CA 95030
(408) 358-2711

Stat-A-Matrix Inc.
Stanley Marash
P.O. Box 2152
Menlo Park Station
Edison, NJ 08817
(201) 548-0600

Robert Tate
1456 Tuscany Way
Germantown, TN 38138
(901) 754-6376

Training & Business Analysis
Gloria O'Meara
P.O. Box 24322, Edina Station
Minneapolis, MN 55424
(612) 478-6287

Visser Quality Assoc.
3 Mitchelle Ave.
New Brunswick, NJ 08816
(201) 828-2964

Wag and Assoc.
Eugene Lee
681 Market St., Ste. 1049
San Franciso, CA 94105
(415) 543-5262

APPENDIX 7
Organizations Promoting Quality Circles in the United States

American Management Association
Charles Ferris, Program Director
135 West 50th Street
New York NY 10020
Tel.: 1-212-586-8100

American Productivity Center
Jack Grayson, Chairman of the
   Board
123 North Post Oak Lane
Houston, TX 77024
Tel.: 1-713-681-4020

American Quality Institute
Paul Plum
4567 Gatetree Circle
Pleasanton, CA 94566
Tel.: 1-408-253-3038 or
1-408-462-0493

American Society for Quality
   Control
Quality Circles Committee
Dr. Robert T. Amsden, Chairman
Suite 7000
2300 West Well Street
Milwaukee, WI 53203
Tel.: 1-414-272-8575

International Association of Quality
   Circles
801-B West Eighth Street, Ste. 301
Cincinnati, OH 45203
Tel.: 1-513-381-1959

International City Management
   Association
1120 G Street, N.W.
Washington, DC 20005
Tel.: 1-202-626-4600

Technological Transfer Institute
One Penn Plaza
Suite 1411
250 West 34th Street
New York, NY 10119
Tel.: 1-212-947-2648

Open-Ended Comments of Ford EI Participants in Survey

"More effort in job. Management in quality before quantity. More feedback."

"Circle teams provide an outlet for creativity. It may be the only way to go in the future. It is an improvement from continual confrontation."

"I have seen results from stamping team, Plant 2, and block team, Plant 1. So I know they are doing a fine job. I believe the union should be more informed and involved in employee involvement as it will benefit us all."

"I believe that our team is really trying. But in my opinion we take leadership towards picking out a worthwhile task."

"I feel the concept is a good idea. I have found that in actual practice the management does not want to change the system, therefore, the employee involvement teams are doomed to fail."

"The team idea is a positive attitude in which the company gives its employees a chance to better the jobs and quality."

"Quality Circle Team Concept helps the company to solve some problems which it can't see or solve."

"The quality circle team (Ford's is Problem Solving Teams) is effective in improving quality, productivity and a better work environment because it utilizes the company's greatest asset—people. Every worker is given the opportunity to become involved in the general product. These are basic needs being answered, and job security is improved as a quality product improves sales, etc.''

"Not enough important problems referred to our EI team from either management, our facilitator, union, or other. I don't think enough people on the floor are being trained in EI and therefore have negative reactions towards something they haven't experienced!''

"It works well.''

"EI is an exceptional way of voicing your opinions as far workers' attitudes on job performance, boredom on line, changing management's opinion of quantity first instead of quality in most instances. If we are going to compete with the Japanese we must do something to keep our warranty down, e.g., changing machine drills in ''x'' amount of hours regardless of worn out or not, but not wait till tool's bit is worn or broken as most times happens now.''

"If everyone pitches in and contributes, the EI concept can make our jobs easier as well as perpetuate them.''

"I think it's a good idea and more people should be involved in it.''

"We work as a team, to find out all kinds of quality problems on the engine line. We discuss and solve together, try to make more fun-loving, so people can come to work every day.''

"The Circle Team Concept could be a vital tool if used properly. Only *bad* management can be the master link between success and failure.''

"I agree wholeheartedly, with the quality circle team concept. In practice something is obviously lacking. Certain areas feel the ''Team's'' efforts overlap their responsibility, thereby misinterpreting our intent, thus resulting initially in certain members losing interest and eventually resigning.''

"I feel this type of team concept in the workplace is long overdue. To allow the workers to exchange information and ideas should benefit both workers and company. However, in a factory setting, the continuity of a group is a very hard thing to accomplish. As the group members move from job to job, plant to plant, area to area, maintaining the same members is quite impossible. The ability of these groups (with proper company support) to effect changes increasing both productivity and quality are limitless. While I feel all this is very positive, it should be carried further into the areas of re-educating the work force, i.e. instead of drawing skilled people out of school, draw a small percentage, say 5–10%, from existing workers through retraining.''

Quality Circle (Partners in Progress) Newsletter—American Motors Corporation and United Auto Workers

Volume II, no. 1   January 10, 1983

Why P.I.P.

When we are in the plant on P.I.P business, many employees stop us and ask how the P.I.P. process is developing and whether or not it is succeeding. During these conversations, we find that many employees do not understand the process and quite frankly are skeptical about its chances for success. In this regard, perhaps it would be appropriate to answer a few questions that hopefully will help you develop a better understanding of Partners in Progress.

Many changes have taken place within the society, the workforce and the industry over the last ten to twenty years. One only has to look at the automobile market to find the reasons for these changes.

The oil embargo probably had the greatest impact on the automobile market by causing consumers to search out and find a car that would give them greater gas mileage. This resulted in the great influx of foreign automobiles into our country. Additionally, the fluctuating economy caused people to become more quality conscious resulting in their search for greater utility for their dollar. In an effort to attain an even greater degree of product quality. Management began to put more emphasis on utilizing the expertise of their employees.

314

Thus, as a result of a sagging economy and a search by the consumer for increased quality and reliability, many companies and unions have re-evaluated their management philosophy and a new pattern of management within the United States is developing. The new patterns vary from company to company but basically they emphasize greater employee participation in dealing with the day-to-day problems and the decisions that are required to resolve them.

In order for American industries to remain competitive, changes in Management and Union philosophy should parallel changes in consumer attitudes. The Partners in Progress process is a step in the right direction because it gives employees the opportunity to voluntarily become involved in solving the problems that affect them and their work. This results in greater operational efficiency and improved product quality and reliability.

The primary key to a successful process, however, is communication and cooperation. We all recognize that when Management and the Union communicate and work together in a cooperative spirit, we begin to understand each other and through better understanding, we can build a more effective operation.

The Partners in Progress Coordinators and Editor of the Newsletter would like to help answer any questions you may have concerning the P.I.P. process. Therefore, please feel free to contact Gerry Wade, Bob Ludwig, Jerry Costello or Pat Mike at 7071, 7072 or 7073 and we will try to answer these questions by way of the P.I.P. Newsletter.

Dept. 808—Press Room 1/5

Each member received a fact sheet containing PIP guidelines. The minutes from the last meeting were read and approved. The group then discussed who the next alternate admitted to the group would be. It was the consensus of the group that Jim Kane representing the die setters would be the next member admitted.

Reports
Sleeves

John Walauskis reported on difficulty in obtaining information. Coordinator Jerry Costello will find out who the purchasing agent is for the group. A sample of sleeves now being used in Milwaukee was inspected by the group. The group felt that the sleeves presently being used in the department are better than the sleeves being used in Milwaukee. The group will submit a sample of the most popular type of sleeves to the purchasing agent to aid in determining worker preference.

New Problems

Tony Perry will pursue the possibility of having in-plant television operating during the half hour breaks on weekends. There is special interest in sporting events.

(cont'd)

315

Bad steel was then discussed. The group questioned why so much scrap is run before the load of steel is finally rejected. John Holland and Lenny Peden will investigate and report back at the next meeting. Tony Perry was welcomed as a new member of the group.

Dept. 1828—Final Assembly 1/5

Coordinator Bob Ludwig reported that the communications from the group had been delivered to Mr. Austin and the Steering Committee. The next Steering Committee meeting will be on January 10, 1983. Action on the letters should be taken at that time.

Dan Vaccaro presented a new problem to the group. It is #56—Fascia containers which do not stack properly. After discussing the rear suspension bolt problem, the group decided to keep it on hold for further monitoring. The group then discussed the condition of the restrooms within the department. Wes Schutz will contact Joe Zabrauskus about what can be done to clean them up. Problem #5—Too many supervisors was considered solved as of 1/5/83.

The group then polled for a new problem. They decided that the only criteria to be applied to their decision was that the problem should concern product quality. It was decided to work on Problem #44—Sealer–Brake Line Bracket, (Front Flex). The Coordinator was requested to find

out which department and area is involved with this problem at Lakefront. They will make personal contact to investigate. It was felt that the group may go to Lakefront to try to find out what is causing the problem or send representatives to one of the Lakefront Group's meetings to discuss.

Dept. 2836—Body Metal 1/6

Part of the group went to Dept. 808 to investigate the problem having to do with the dent in the rear quarter panel. The group felt that perhaps it was originating in Dept. 808.

It was reported to the group that at this time there will be no alteration in the ventilation of Bldg. 101 2nd Floor. The group will monitor the problem and tests will be run to further investigate the situation.

The group also discussed the response they had received from Mr. Herrendeen concerning problems with the Gilman.

Dept. 2837—Body Paint 12/14

Dave King, Fire Marshall was present to discuss the emergency aid system at AMC Lakefront plant. The group agreed that everything that can presently be done is being done. It was further decided that the group could not influence this situation so the problem was dropped for now.

The group brainstormed for new problems to handle. Problem #16—Job Setups was added to the list.

12/21

The meeting began with a report by Mavis Wakefield from Dept. 2838. She stated that she had been shown several areas where they are having problems with excess sealer blocking holes. She gave the report to Jon Sebestyen. Improvements have been made but the group will continue to work on this.

Work was continued on new problem #12—Eye wash in sealer area. It was decided to combine problems #11 and #12. Problem #11 concerns eye glass cleaning station. It was the consensus to have Jon contact the safety man on December 22 to see what can be done about these problems.

It was decided to work on Problem #10 No time bell. Bill Petit will contact Mr. Wheeler on this subject to see how long a bell has been on order.

The group also decided to work on Problem #15—Gaps in seams. Jon will talk to Mr. Batassa to find out which is the worst and most recurring water leak.

1/14

There was a consensus to invite Mr. Visintainer to the next meeting to get a report on the door latch situation.

Dept. 2838—Body Trim 1/5

Ken Hughes asked to be dropped from the Partners in Progress

Program. Richard Foster will be the next person to enter the program. Carol Luciani was elected Recording Secretary for the group.

The group was notified that the women's washroom will be installed in Bldg. 190—1st floor in the near future.

Al Ellis reported on the sealer problems from the Paint Dept. The problem has improved very much but we will continue to monitor the problem from time to time.

Lorin Lichterman attended the meeting to observe the Partners in Progress Program in action.

12/22

Terry Keller has been installed as Facilitator with Elaine Janicek as Co-Facilitator.

The safety rail in the cushion room has not been completed as of this date. This will be followed up by the Committee.

It was decided that further investigation is needed to evaluate the need or desire for fixtures on scuff molding jobs. The committee will follow up and report back to the group.

Regarding water leaks in the trunk area, sealer problems still need monitoring and contact with 2836 and 2837. (Some improvements have been made but not on everything.)

Mavis Wakefield, Bill Petit and Dave Ruhl of 2837 P.I.P. group are helping solve some of the sealer problems.

NOTES

Chapter 1

1. This introduction is paraphrased from Eugene Guizzetti, *What Is Quality of Work Life?* (M.B.A. major paper prepared under the direction of Dr. Olga L. Crocker, Faculty of Business Administration, University of Windsor, Windsor, Ontario, 1983.

2. Masaaki Imai, "Quality Control and Small Group Activities: The Key to Improved Productivity," *When in Japan: An Introduction for Doing Business in and with Japan,* Vol. 3 (Tokyo: Planning and Promotion Division, Hotel Okura, April 20, 1982): 17.

3. Robert R. Rehder, "What American and Japanese Managers Are Learning from Each Other," *Business Horizons* 24 (March–April 1981): 68.

4. R. Lozano and Philip C. Thompson, "QC Implementation in the Space Shuttle External Tank Program at the Michoud Marietta Corporation," *ASQC 34th Annual Technical Conference Transactions,* 1980.

5. James Thompson, *Organizations in Action* (New York: McGraw-Hill, 1967): 151.

NOTES

Chapter 2

1. Bando Satoshi, "Qualitative Change in the Labor Movement," *Japan Echo* 8 (1981): 30–37.

2. Hitoshi Kume, "Quality Control in Japan's Industries," *the wheel extended: A Toyota Quarterly Review* (Tokyo), Spring 1980, p. 21.

3. Upon the recommendation of JUSE Managing Director Dr. K. Koyanagi, who had received a donation from Dr. Deming of the royalties from the published transcripts of his lectures, the Board of Directors of JUSE approved setting up a fund for the Deming Prize. Subsequently, Dr. Deming again donated a portion of the royalties from the Japanese edition of his work *Some Theories of Sampling* to this fund.

4. *JSA Technical Reports*, nos. 1–4 (Japanese Standards Association, 1963–1969).

5. JUSE did not define the term "pan-industrial," but seems to have used it to mean "including all industries."

6. "QC Circle Activities and the Suggestion System," *Japan Labor Bulletin*, January 1982, p. 5.

7. J. M. Juran, "International Significance of the QC Circle Movement," *Quality Progress,* November 1980, pp. 18–19.

8. Patricia Fisher Foley and Thomas J. McGuire, eds., *World Almanac and Book of Facts* (New York: Newspaper Enterprise Association, 1983), p. 151.

9. Kaoru Ishikawa, "QC Circle Activities," *QC in Japan Series No. 1* (Tokyo: Union of Japanese Scientists and Engineers, April 1968).

10. Itajime Karatsu, *Quality Control to Extend a Company: From Top Management to the Factory Floor* (Tokyo, 1966), p. 132.

11. Masaaki Imai, "Policy Development: Japanese Management's New Strategic Tool." *The Japan Economic Journal*, February 22, 1983, p. 12.

12. Robert E. Cole, *Work, Mobility and Participation* (Berkeley, CA: University of California Press, 1979), p. 138.

13. J. M. Juran, "Product Quality: A Prescription for the West. Part II: Upper Management Leadership and Employee Relations," *Management Review* 70 (June 1981): 58.

14. "U.S. Executives Look at Japanese QC," *Quality Progress* 13 (February 1980): 8.

15. Susumu Takamiya, "The Characteristics of Japanese Management," *Management Japan* 14 (Summer 1981): 8.

16. George A. De Vos, "Apprenticeship and Paternalism." In *Modern Japanese Organization and Decision-Making*, edited by Ezra F. Vogel (Berkeley, CA: University of California Press, 1975), p. 217.

17. Edwin D. Reischauer, *The Japanese* (Cambridge, MA: Harvard University Press, 1977), pp. 131–32.

18. Chie Nakane, *Japanese Society* (Berkeley, CA: University of California Press, 1970), p. 19.

19. "QC Circle Activities and the Suggestion System," *Japan Labor Bulletin*, January 1982, p. 5.

20. Peter F. Drucker, "Behind Japan's Success," *Harvard Business Review* 59 (January–February 1981): 83–90.

21. Tadashi Hanami, *Labour Relations in Japan Today* (Tokyo: Kodansha, 1981), p. 92.

22. Except for the fact that women are generally temporary rather than permanent employees, little mention is made in the literature regarding their role in industry. It is therefore not clear whether women have supervisory positions.

23. William Bowen, "Japanese Managers Tell How Their System Works," *Fortune*, November 1977, p. 128.

24. Yoshi Tsurumi and Rebecca Tsurumi, "A Closer Look at Japan's 'Lifetime' Employment System," *Pacific Basin Quarterly* 8 (Fall 1982): 5.

25. Ibid.

26. Conversation with Japanese trade consulate officials.

27. Christopher Byron, "How Japan Does It," *Time*, March 30, 1981, pp. 44–50.

28. Bando Satoshi, "Qualitative Change in the Labor Movement," *Japan Echo* 8 (1981): 30–37.

29. Kiyoaki Murata, "What Makes Japan Tick," *The Japan Times Weekly*, February 27, 1982, p. 3.

30. Yoshitaka Fujita, "The Workers' Autonomous Small Group Activities and Productivity in Japan," *Management Japan* 14 (Summer 1981): 18.

31. Masaaki Imai, "Small Group Activities: The Key to Improved Productivity," *The Japan Economic Journal*, February 23, 1982, p. 12.

32. Charles J. McMillan, "Production Planning and Organization Design at Toyota," *Business Quarterly*, Winter 1981, pp. 22–30.

33. The word *kanban* means "signboard" or "label." In production processes, such as Toyota's engine plant, a *kanban* is attached to each unit. When the unit has been processed at a particular stage in the production process, the *kanban* is returned and serves as a reorder instruction. There is no warehouse of supplies and raw materials in large Japanese production companies. Instead suppliers deliver goods on demand, that is, just in time to be used in production. The *kanban* indicates that another unit (or units) is needed.

34. Masaaki Imai, "Quality Control and Small Group Activities: The Key to Improved Productivity," *When in Japan: An Introduction for Doing Business in and with Japan*, Vol. 3 (Tokyo: Planning and Promotion Division, Hotel Okura, April 20, 1982), p. 17.

35. Yoshinobu Nayatani as quoted by Masaaki Imai, "Policy Deployment: Japanese Management's New Strategic Tool," *When in Japan: An Introduction for Doing Business in and with Japan*, Vol. 4 (Tokyo: Planning and Promotion Division, Hotel Okura, February 14, 1983), p. 26.

36. Robert E. Cole, *Industry at the Crossroads, Michigan Papers in Japanese Studies*, no. 7 (Center for Japanese Studies, University of Michigan, 1982), pp. 100–101.

37. Yoshitaka Fujita, "Participative Work Practices in the Japanese Auto Industry: Some Neglected Considerations," in *Industry at the Crossroads, Michigan Papers in Japanese Studies*, No. 7, edited by Robert E. Cole (Ann Arbor, MI: University of Michigan, Center for Japanese Studies, 1982), p. 84.

38. Tadao Koguri, "Providing Incentives to the QC Circle Through an Evaluation System." *Japan Quality Control Circles* (Tokyo: Asian Productivity Organization, 1982), p. 170.

Chapter 3

1. Edgar H. Schein, "SMR Forum: Does Japanese Management Style Have a Message for American Managers?" *Sloan Management Review* 23 (Fall 1981): 55.

2. "Talking in Circles Improves Quality," *Industry Week*, February 14, 1977, p. 62.

3. Ibid. and *Quality Circles at Honeywell: A Study of Partici-*

pant Perceptions (Minnetonka, MN: Corporate Human Resources Development Department, Corporate Conference Center), unpaginated.

4. *Quality Circles at Honeywell.*

5. Barry A. Stein and Rosabeth M. Kanter, "Building the Parallel Organization: Creating Mechanisms for Permanent Quality of Work Life," *The Journal of Applied Behavioral Science* 16 (1980): 371–86.

6. Frank M. Gryna, Jr., *Quality Circles: A Team Approach to Problem Solving* (New York: AMACOM, a division of American Management Association, 1981), p. 45.

7. *Toronto-Dominion Quality Programme Introductory Kit* (Toronto: Toronto-Dominion Bank of Canada, 1982), p. 10.

8. Mignon Mazique, "The Quality Circle Transplant," *Issues & Observation*, May 1981, p. 2.

9. David Soyka, "Honeywell Pioneers in Quality Circle Movement," *World of Work Report*, September 1981, p. 66.

10. A recent survey by the American Management Association indicated that 65 percent of companies had employed consultants to help on a portion or on all of the circle activity. Morris (1981) also reports that 70 percent of the thirty-three organizations surveyed had received assistance from consultants and that half of them had contracted for total implementation packages.

11. Joyce MacDonald and Carol Robinson, "Concept for Management," *The Quality Circles Journal* 4 (November 1981): 13–15.

12. Douglas McGregor, *The Human Side of Enterprise* (New York: McGraw-Hill, 1960); idem, *The Professional Manager* (New York: McGraw-Hill, 1967). For completeness, it should be pointed out that two additional views exist: the "blank state" theory and the view that "there is no such thing as human nature." The first dismisses any inherent characteristics as myths. Those who subscribe to this theory maintain that characteristics which exist are a product of environment and circumstance. The second view is that of behaviourists (a philosophy originated by B.F. Skinner). Basically, behaviourists repudiate the concept of human nature, attitudes, needs, and other internal aspects of human nature with the assumption that "If you can't see it, it isn't there."

13. William Ouchi, *Theory Z: How American Business Can*

Meet the Japanese Challenge (Reading, MA: Addison-Wesley, 1981).

14. See for example: R. R. Blake and Jane S. Mouton, "The Dynamics of Influence and Concern," *International Journal of Social Psychiatry* 2 (1957): 263–65; A. C. Filley and A. J. Grimes, "The Bases of Power in Decision Processes," in *Academy of Management Proceedings: 27th Annual Meeting*, edited by R. W. Millman and M. P. Hottenstein (1967): 133–60; and C. J. Lammers, "Power and Participation in Decision Making in Formal Organizations," *American Journal of Sociology* 73 (1967): 201–16.

15. See for example: H. C. Kelman, "Compliance, Identification and Internalization: Three Processes of Attitude Change," *Journal of Conflict Resolution* 2 (1958): 51–60; Ronald J. Ebert and Terence R. Mitchell, *Organizational Decision Processes: Concepts and Analysis* (New York: Crane, Russak & Company, 1975), pp. 239–40; and A. Zander and T. Curtis, "Effects of Social Power on Aspiration Setting and Striving," *Journal of Abnormal and Social Psychology* 64 (1962): 63–74.

16. See any organizational behaviour textbook. Two examples are: R. Dennis Middlemist and Michael A. Hitt, *Organizational Behavior: Applied Concepts* (Palo Alto, CA: Science Research Associates, 1981); and Terence R. Mitchell, *People in Organizations: Understanding Their Behavior* (New York: McGraw-Hill, 1978).

17. Conversation with Ernie Long, formerly with Cumis Insurance Co., Burlington Ontario.

18. The United Auto Workers, which represents employees at Ford of Canada, has in the past taken a stand against quality circle implementation. At this point, the union has left the decision to the union local which represents employees of each plant. Also, in the days of Henry Ford, the relationship between the union and management was not always pleasant. Today, the aftermath of this relationship exists.

19. Paper prepared for Central Michigan University by Michael Nastanski under the direction of Dr. Olga L. Crocker, October 1983.

NOTES

Chapter 4

1. Solomon B. Levine, *Industrial Relations in Postwar Japan* (Urbana, IL: University of Illinois Press, 1958), p. 36.
2. Kubota, Akira," Japan: Social Structure and Work Ethic," *Asia Pacific Community* 20 (Spring 1983): 8.
3. Ibid., p. 7.
4. Charles J. McMillan, "Production Planning and Organization Design at Toyota," *Business Quarterly*, Winter 1981, p. 24.
5. Charles J. McMillan, "From Quality Control to Quality Management: Lessons from Japan," *Business Quarterly*, Spring 1982, pp. 37, 38.
6. Masaaki Imai, "Small Group Activities—Five Times ROI? The Case of Nissan Chemical Industries," *When in Japan: An Introduction for Doing Business in and with Japan,* Vol. 4 (Tokyo, Japan: Planning and Promotion Division, Hotel Okura, June 14, 1982), p. 17.
7. Charles J. McMillan, "Is Japanese Management Really So Different?" *Business Quarterly*, Autumn 1980, pp. 27–28.
8. In addition to references previously cited, comparative Japanese information which is given here is based on: "The New Economy," *Time*, May 30, 1983; Tadashi Hanami, *Labor Relations in Japan Today* (Tokyo: Kodansha International Ltd., 1981); M. Sumiya, "The Emergence of Modern Japan," in *Workers and Employers in Japan: The Japanese Employment Relations System*, edited by K. O. Kochi, B. Karsh, and S. B. Levine (Princeton, NJ: Princeton University Press, 1974); Clark Kerr, John T. Dunlop, Frederick Harbison, and Charles A. Myers, *Industrialism and Industrial Man* (New York: Oxford University Press, 1964); and John W. Bennett and Iwao Ishino, "Paternalistic Economic Organizations and Japanese Society," in *Paternalism in the Japanese Economy: Anthropological Studies of Oyabun-Kabun Patterns*, edited by Bennett and Ishino (Minneapolis: University of Minnesota Press, 1963), p. 243.

Chapter 6

1. William J. Gordon, "An Operational Approach to Cre-

ativity," *Harvard Business Review* 34 (November–December 1956); 41–51.

2. Sydney Dauer and Alice Dauer, "A New Approach to Creative Thinking and Idea Development," *IBM Engineering Seminar*, 1956.

3. Tom Alexander, "Synetics: Inventing by the Madness Method," *Fortune*, August 1965.

4. John W. Haefele, *Creativity and Innovation* (New York: Van Nostrand Reinhold, 1962), p. 151.

5. Carl E. Gregory, *Management of Intelligence* (New York: McGraw-Hill, 1967), p. 200.

Chapter 8

1. Some good books for those who wish to know more about reports and oral presentations are: Ronald Adler, *Communicating at Work: Principles and Practices for Business and the Professions* (Mississauga, Ont.: Random House, 1983); Abne M. Eisenberg, *Understanding Communication in Business and the Professions* (New York: Macmillan, 1978); Jerry W. Koehler, Karl W. E. Anatol, and Ronald L. Applbaum, *Public Communication: Behavioral Perspectives* (New York: Macmillan, 1978); Raymond V. Lesikar, *Basic Business Communication* (Georgetown, Ont.: Richard D. Irwin, Inc., 1979); John J. Makay, *Speaking with an Audience: Communicating Ideas and Atittudes* (New York: Crowell, 1977); J. H. Menning, C. W. Wilkinson, and Peter B. Clarke, *Communicating Through Letters and Reports* (Georgetown, Ont.: Richard D. Irwin, Inc., 1979); Robert L. Montgomery, *A Master Guide to Public Speaking* (New York: Harper & Row, 1979); and Don B. Morlan and George E. Tuttle, Jr., *An Introduction to Effective Oral Communication* (Indianapolis, IN: Bobbs-Merrill, 1976).

Chapter 9

1. A book which is very practical and which explains graphs succinctly is Vernon Clover and Howard Balsley, *Business Research Methods* (Columbus, OH: Grid, Inc., 1974).

Chapter 12

1. The content material given in this chapter is based on interviews conducted by Dr. Olga Crocker or Johnny Sik Leung Chiu with: Mr. Curtis Davidson, UAW Plant Chairperson of Essex Engine Plant and other union members; Mr. Gary Lesperance, former Coordinator of EI Programs, Windsor Operations; and Mr. Bill Johnston, former Manager of Labor Relations and Hourly Personnel, Windsor Operations; and on information provided in "Guidelines for Implementing UAW-Ford Employee Involvement Programs" (Dearborn, MI: UAW-Ford National Joint Committee on Employee Involvement, September 1980; and *A Handbook on the UAW-Ford Process for Local Unions and Management* (Dearborn, MI: UAW—For National Joint Committee on Employee Involvement, 1980.

2. *The Windsor Star*, March 3, 1982.

Chapter 13

1. The median is obtained by placing all responses for each factor in order from 1 to 12, and counting to the mid-point and looking the response which this individual has given. For example, for the second item in the table, effort, all responses were ranked (placed in a column in order) from 1 to 12. Halfway down our column was between the eighteenth and nineteenth responses (there are thirty-six in total). The eighteenth respondent had answered 3; the nineteenth respondent had answered 4. The median therefore is 3.5.

2. *UAW—Ford Employee Involvement: A Special Survey Report* (Dearborn, MI: UAW—Ford National Development and Training Center, March 1983).

3. Robert I. Patchin, *Quality Control Circles in an Office Environment* (Northrup Corporation, Aircraft Division, April 1981), p. 5.

4. *Quality Circles at Honeywell: A Study of Participant Perceptions* (Minnetonka, MN: Corporate Human Resource Development Department, Honeywell, Inc., July 1982).

Chapter 14

1. The information for this chapter is based on interviews by Dr. Olga L. Crocker with: Mr. Donald Young, Coordinator of the PSI Program; Mr. John Olaja, Director of Advertising; Mr. Derek Millet, engineer; Mr. Bob Brown; Mr. Bob Immel; and other individuals with the company who asked that they not be identified. Two Vickers publications also were utilized: *Plan for Productivity/Quality Improvement, Commercial Division* (Troy, MI: July 1980) and *Quality Power Components and Systems to Meet Industry's Needs, the World Over* (Troy, MI: n.d.).

Chapter 15

1. Yoshitaka Fujita, "The Workers' Autonomous Small Group Activities and Productivity in Japan," *Management Japan* 14 (Summer 1981): 17.
2. Zane K. Quible, "Quality Circles: A Well Rounded Approach to Employee Involvement," *Management World*, September 1981, p. 10.
3. J. E. Struthers, *Canada–Japan Essay: Long Road Back* (Canada–Japan Council, Summer 1981), p. 6.
4. *Work in America*, Report of a Special Task Force to the Secretary of Health, Education and Welfare (Cambridge, MA: The MIT Press, 1973).
4. H. J. Eysenck, "The Measurement of Motivation," *Scientific American* 208 (May 1963): 130.

BIBLIOGRAPHY

ABEGGLEN, JAMES C. *Management and Worker: The Japanese Solution*. Tokyo: Kodansha International, 1973.

ABERNATHY, WILLAIM J., and KIM B. CLARK. "Notes on a Trip to Japan: Concepts and Interpretations," In *Industry at the Crossroads*, Michigan Papers in Japanese Studies No. 7, edited by Robert E. Cole. Ann Arbor: University of Michigan, Center for Japanese Studies, 1982.

ABRAMS, JIM. "What You Train Is What You Get." *The Japan Times Weekly*, March 5, 1983: 3.

"Action Exchange." *American Libraries* (December 1982): 714.

ALEXANDER, C. PHILIP. "Learning from the Japanese." *Personnel Journal* 60 (August 1981): 616–19.

ALEXANDER, TOM. "Synetics: Inventing by the Madness Method." *Fortune*, August 1965.

AMSDEN, DAVIDA M., and ROBERT T. AMSDEN. "Problem-Solving Comparisons: QC Circles, KT, ZD, and Others." *ASQC 32nd Annual Technical Conference Transactions*. Milwaukee: American Society for Quality Control, 1978.

AMSDEN, DAVIDA M., and ROBERT T. AMSDEN, eds. *QC Circles: Applications, Tools, and Theory*. Milwaukee: American Society for Quality Control, 1976.

AMSDEN, DAVIDA M., and ROBERT T. AMSDEN. "The Research Aspects of QC Circles." *IAQC 1st Annual Conference Transactions*. Cincinnati: International Association of Quality Circles, 1979.

BIBLIOGRAPHY

AMSDEN, DAVIDA M., and ROBERT T. AMSDEN. "Results of Research on QC Circles." *ASQC 34th Annual Technical Conference Transactions*. Milwaukee: American Society for Quality Control, 1980.

AMSDEN, DAVIDA M., and ROBERT T. AMSDEN. "Statistics Applied to and by QC Circles." *ASQC 32nd Annual Technical Conference Transactions*. Milwaukee: American Society for Quality Control, 1978.

AMSDEN, ROBERT T., and DAVIDA M. AMSDEN. "A Look at QC Circles." *Tooling & Production*, June 1980.

"An Aging Work Force Strains Japan's Traditions." *Business Week*, April 20, 1981: 72–85.

ANTILLA, SUSAN. "East Meets West: The Quality Circle." *Working Woman*, October 1981: 88–91.

AOUNUMA, YOSHIMATSU. "The Japanese and the Organization." *the wheel extended: A Toyota Quarterly Review* 9 (Tokyo), Spring 1980, pp. 9–19.

AUBREY, CHARLES A. II, and LAWRENCE A. ELDRIDGE. "Banking on High Quality." *Quality Progress* 14 (December 1981): 14–19.

AUBREY, CHARLES A. II, and WENDY CAROL FENCL. "Management, Professional and Clerical Quality Circles." *ASQC 36th Annual Technical Conference and Exposition Transactions*. Milwaukee: American Society for Quality Control, 1982: 54–61.

AZUMI, KOYA, and CHARLES MCMILLAN. "Worker Sentiment in the Japanese Factory: Its Organizational Determinants." In *Japan: The Paradox of Progress,* edited by Lewis Austin. New Haven: Yale University Press, 1976.

BABBIT, ROBERT C. "One Company's Approach to Quality Circles." *Quality Progress* 14 (October 1981): 28–29.

BALDWIN, DAVID, and DAVID GROMES. "EI at Canton Forge." *Work Life Review* 2 (March 1983): 17–21.

BALL, R. A., and S. P. BARNEY. *Quality Circle Project Manual*. Rawsonville, MI: UAW—Ford Employee Involvement, 1982.

BANDO, SATOSHI. "Qualitative Change in the Labor Movement." *Japan Echo* 8 (Spring 1981): 30–37.

BARNEY, STEPHEN. *Quality Circles: Adapting Materials and Training to Organizational Needs*. Unpublished paper, Central Michigan University, December 1982.

BARRA, RALPH J. *Putting Quality Circles to Work: A Practical Strategy for Boosting Productivity and Profits*. New York: McGraw-Hill, 1983.

BEARDSLEY, JEFFERSON F. "Ingredients of Successful Quality Circles." *IAQC 2nd Annual Conference Transactions*. Cincinnati: International Association of Quality Circles, 1980.

BEARDSLEY, J. F. "The Quality Circle Steering Committee." *The Quality Circles Quarterly* 1 (Fourth Quarter 1978): 26–30.

BEARDSLEY, J. F. "Training is the Heart of the Lockheed QC Circle Program." In *ASQC 30th Annual Technical Conference Transactions*. Milwaukee: American Society for Quality Control, 1976.

BENEDICT, RUTH. *The Chrysanthemum and the Sword: Patterns of Japanese Culture*. New York: New American Library, 1967.

BENNETT, J. W., and IWAO ISHINO. "Paternalistic Economic Organizations and Japanese Society." In *Paternalism in the Japanese Economy*. Minneapolis: University of Minnesota Press, 1963.

BIEBER, OWEN. "UAW Views Circles: Not Bad at All." *The Quality Circles Journal* 5 (August 1982): 6.

BINSTOCK, S. L. "Americans Express Dissatisfaction with Quality of U.S. Goods." *Quality Progress* 14 (January 1981): 12–14.

BIRD, ALLAN. "A Comparison of Japanese and Western Management." *Management Japan* 15 (Autumn 1982): 21–24.

BLAKE, R. R., and JANE S. MOUTON. "The Dynamics of Influence and Concern." *International Journal of Social Psychiatry* 2 (1957): 263–65,

BLUESTONE, IRVING. "Labor's Stake in Improving the Quality of Work Life." *International Conference on the Quality of Working Life*, Toronto, 1981. Available from Work in America Institute, Scarsdale, NY.

BLUMBERG, PAUL. *Industrial Democracy: The Sociology of Participation*. New York: Shocken, Books, 1969.

BOCKER, HANS J., and HERMAN O. OVERGAARD. *Quality Circles: Answer to the Productivity Challenge*. Research Paper Series No. 3281. Waterloo, Ontario: Wilfrid Laurier University, 1982.

BOCKER, HANS J., and HERMAN O. OVERGAARD. *Quality Circles: A Managerial Response to the Productivity Problem*. Research Paper Series No. 3381. Waterloo, Ontario: Wilfrid Laurier University, 1982.

BIBLIOGRAPHY

BROOKE, KEITH A. "QC Circles' Success Depends on Management Readiness to Support Workers' Involvement." *Industrial Engineering* 14 (January 1982): 76–79.

BRUCE-BRIGGS. B. "The Dangerous Folly Called Theory Z." *Fortune*, May 17, 1982.

BRUNET, LUCIE. "Quality Circles: Can They Improve QWL?" *The Canadian Scene* 4 (1981): 1–2.

BRYANT, STEPHEN, and JOSEPH KEARNS. " 'Workers' Brains as Well as Their Bodies': Quality Circles in a Federal Facility." *Public Administration Review* 42 (March–April 1982): 144–50.

BUBACK, KENNETH, and JAROSLAV I. DUTKEWYCH. "Quality Circles in Health Care: The Henry Ford Hospital Experience." *IAQC 4th Annual Conference Transactions*. Cincinnati: International Association of Quality Circles, 1982.

BYRON, CHRISTOPHER. "How Japan Does It." *Time*, March 30, 1981.

CANDY, WARREN L. "Maintenance Groups Make and Implement Own Suggestions for Improving Productivity." *Industrial Engineering* 14 (February 1982): 44–48.

CLARK, GREGORY. "Western Reindustrialization and Japan: Why Japan Works (1)." *The Japan Economic Journal*, March 9, 1982: 24.

CLARK, RODNEY. *The Japanese Company*. New Haven: Yale University Press, 1979.

CLELAND, D.I. "Matrix Management (Part II): A Kaleidoscope of Organizational Systems." *Management Review* 70 (December 1981): 48–56.

CLINE, NANCY, and DALIA PALAU. "Quality Circles in the Recovery Room." *Nursing and Health Care* 3 (November 1982): 494–96.

CLOVER, VERNON, and HOWARD BALSLEY. *Business Research Methods*. Columbus, OH: Grid, Inc., 1974.

COLE, ROBERT E. "Common Misconceptions of Japanese QC Circles." *ASQC 35th Annual Technical Conference and Exposition Transactions*. Milwaukee: American Society for Quality Control, 1981.

COLE, ROBERT E. "Diffusion of New Work Structures in Japan." *IAQC 1st Annual Conference Transactions*. Cincinnati: International Association of Quality Circles, 1979.

COLE, ROBERT E. *Japanese Blue Collar: The Changing Tradition*. Los Angeles: University of California Press, 1971.

COLE, ROBERT E. "Japanese Quality Control Circles: Are They Exportable to U.S. Firms?" *World of Work Report* 4 (June 1979): 42, 46.

COLE, ROBERT E. "Learning from the Japanese: Prospects and Pitfalls." *Management Review* 69 (September 1980) 22–28.

COLE, ROBERT E. "Made in Japan—Quality Control Circles." *Across the Board* 16 (November 1979): 72–78.

COLE, ROBERT E. "Made in Japan: A Spur to U.S. Productivity." *ASIA Magazine,* May–June 1979, pp. 18–24.

COLE, ROBERT E. "QC Warning Voiced by U.S. Expert on Japanese Circles." *World of Work Report* 6 (July 1981): 49–51.

COLE, ROBERT E. "Quality Control Practices in the Auto Industry: United States and Japan Compared," *Ann Arbor Observer,* February 1982: 27–28.

COLE, ROBERT E. *Industry at the Crossroads. Michigan Papers in Japanese Studies, No. 7.* Ann Arbor: University of Michigan, Center for Japanese Studies, 1982.

COLE, ROBERT E. "Rationale for Financial Incentives for Quality Circle Members." *The Quality Circles Journal* 4 (February 1981): 8.

COLE, ROBERT E. "Will QC Circles Work in the U.S.?" *Quality Progress* 13 (July 1980): 30–33.

COLE, ROBERT E. *Work, Mobility, and Participation: A Comparative Study of American and Japanese Industry.* Los Angeles: University of California Press, 1979.

COLE, ROBERT E., and ANDREW G. WALDER. *Structural Diffusion: The Politics of Participative Work Structures in China, Japan, Sweden, and the United States.* Ann Arbor: University of Michigan, Center for Research on Social Organizations, 1981.

COLLARD, R. "The Quality Circle in Context." *Personnel Management* (U.K.) 13 (September 1981): 26–30, 51.

COMSTOCK, VIVIAN C., and GERALD E. SWARTZ. "Predictable Developmental States in the Evolution of a Quality Circle." *IAQC 2nd Annual Conference Transactions.* Cincinnati: International Association of Quality Circles, 1980.

COURTRIGHT, WILLIAM. "Hughes Circles: An Update." *The Quality Circles Journal* 4 (August 1981): 30-34.

CUTTS, ROBERT E. "The Productivity Proposition: Notes on the Japanese Approach." *Japan Airlines Travel Magazine,* October 1980: 4.

DAILEY, JOHN J. JR., and RUDOLPH L. KAGERER. "A Primer on Quality Circles," *Supervisory Management* 27 (June 1982): 40–43.

DAVIDSON, WILLIAM H. "Small Group Activity at Musashi Semiconductor Works." *Sloan Management Review* 23 (Spring 1982): 3–14.

DAUER, SYDNEY, and ALICE DAUER. *A New Approach to Creative Thinking and Idea Development*. Syracuse: IBM Engineering Seminar, 1956.

DEMING, W. EDWARDS. "Improvement of Quality and Productivity Through Action by Management." *National Productivity Review* 1 (Winter 1981–82): 12–22.

DEMING, W. EDWARDS. "On Some Statistical Aids Towards Economic Production." *Interfaces* 5 (August 1975): 1–15.

"Dr. W. Edwards Deming—The Statistical Control of Quality, Part I." *Quality*, February 1980: 38–41.

"Dr. W. Edwards Deming—The Statistical Control of Quality, Part II." *Quality*, March 1980: 34–36.

DE VOS, GEORGE, A. "Apprenticeship and Paternalism." In *Modern Japanese Organization and Decision-Making*, edited by Ezra F. Vogel. Berkeley: University of California Press, 1975.

DEWAR, D. *The Quality Circle Handbook*. Red Bluff, CA: Quality Circle Institute, 1982.

DEWAR, DONALD L. "If Japan Can—We Can Too." *IAQC 3rd Annual Conference Transactions*. Cincinnati: International Association of Quality Circles, 1981.

DEWAR, DONALD L. "Implementing Quality Circles in Your Organization." *IAQC 2nd Annaual Conference Transactions*. Cincinnati: International Association of Quality Circles, 1980.

DEWAR, DONALD L. "Measurement of Results—Lockheed QC Circles." *ASQC 30th Annual Technical Conference Transactions*. Milwaukee: American Society for Quality Control, 1976.

DEWAR, DONALD L. *The Quality Circle Guide to Participation Management*. Englewood Cliffs, NJ: Prentice-Hall, 1982.

DI GEORGIO, BRENT S. "Management and Labor Cooperate to Increase Productivity." *Supervision* 43 (January 1981); 5–7.

DOI, TAKEO. *The Anatomy of Dependence*. Translated from the Japanese by John Bester. Tokyo: Kodansha International, 1973.

DONOVAN, J. MICHAEL. "Building Management Support for Quality Circle Programs." In *IAQC 3rd Annual Conference Transactions*. Cincinnati: International Association of Quality Circles, 1981.

DONOVAN, J. MICHAEL. "New Tools For Problem Solving in Quality Circles." *IAQC 3rd Annual Conference Transactions*. Cincinnati: International Association of Quality Circles, 1981.

DONOVAN, J. MICHAEL. "Quality Circles—Goldmine or Fad? Skillfull Management of the Program Can Make the Difference." *IAQC 1st Annual Conference Transactions*. Cincinnati: International Association of Quality Circles, 1979.

DONOVAN, J. MICHAEL. "Quality Circles Help School Through Financial Crises." *The Quality Circles Journal* 2 (Third Quarter 1979): 14–17.

DONOVAN, J. MICHAEL. "A Roadmap for Solving Problems in Quality Circles." *The Quality Circles Journal* 2 (Fourth Quarter 1979): 16–22.

DONOVAN, J. MICHAEL. "Skillful Management of the Program Can Make the Difference." *IAQC 2nd Annual International Conference Transactions*. Cincinnati: International Association of Quality Circles, 1980.

DONOVAN, J. M., and WINGATE SIKES. "QC Circles: An Explosive Formula for Cutting Costs." *The Quality Circles Journal* 1 (Fourth Quarter 1978): 19–22.

DORE, RONALD. *British Factory—Japanese Factory: The Origins of National Diversity in Industrial Relations*. London: Alden & Mowbray, 1973.

DRUCKER, PETER F. "Behind Japan's Success." *Harvard Business Review* 59 (January–February 1981): 83–90.

DUBOIS, PIERRE. "Quality Circles: A Valuable Tool for Effective Management." *Canadian Banker and ICB Review* 90 (April 1983): 38–43.

East Asian Studies Program, Ohio State University. *Business and Society in Japan: Fundamentals for the Businessman*. Bradley M. Richardson, ed. New York: Praeger, 1981.

EBERT, RONALD J., and TERENCE R. MITCHELL. *Organizational Decision Processes: Concepts and Analysis*. New York: Crane, Russak & Company, 1975.

EI UAW-Ford Employe Involvement. *A Handbook On the UAW-Ford Prcoess for Local Unions and Management*. Dearborn, MI: UAW—Ford National Joint Committee on Employe Involvement, 1980.

EISENBERG, ABNÉ. *Understanding Communication in Business and the Professions*. New York: Macmillan, 1978.

EMORY, C. WILLIAM. *Business Research Methods*. Homewood, IL: Richard D. Irwin, Inc., 1980.

Employe Involvement Process Workshop. Dearborn, MI: UAW—Ford National Development and Training Center, March 1983.

EPSTEIN, EUGENE. *People and Productivity: A Challenge to Corporate America. A Study from the New York Stock Exchange, Office of Economic Research*. New York: New York Stock Exchange, 1982.

ERICKSON, TOM, and JANICE G. SPROUL. "How Do You Know You Have Arrived at Where You Thought You Were Going?" *IAQC 1st Annual Conference Transactions*. Cincinnati: International Association of Quality Circles, 1979.

EYSENCK, H. J. "The Measurement of Motivation." *Scientific American* 208 (May 1963): 130–40.

"Father of Quality Control Circles Doubts Their Long-Term Viability in the West." *International Management*, August 1982: 23–25.

FENNEY, E. "Quality Circles: Using Pooled Effort to Promote Excellence." *Training and Human Resource Development*, January 1980.

FILLEY, A. C., and A. J. GRIMES. "The Bases of Power in Decision Processes." In *Academy of Management Proceedings: 27th Annual Meeting*, 1967, edited by R. W. Millman and M. P. Hottenstein: 133–60.

FITZGERALD, LAURIE, and JOSEPH MURPHY. *Installing Quality Circles: A Strategic Approach*. San Diego, California: University Associates, 1982.

FOLEY, PATRICIA FISHER, and THOMAS J. MCGUIRE, eds. *The World Almanac and Book of Facts*. New York: Newspaper Enterprise Association, 1983.

Ford Casting Division Japanese Productivity Study Group. *A Report on the Japanese Automotive Foundry Industry*. Windsor, Ont.: December 1980.

FUJITA, YOSHITAKA. "Participative Work Practices in the Japanese Auto Industry: Some Neglected Considerations." In *Industry at the Crossroads*, edited by Robert E. Cole.

Michigan Papers in Japanese Studies No. 7. Ann Arbor: University of Michigan, Center for Japanese Studies, 1982: 75–86.

FUJITA, YOSHITAKA. "The Workers' Autonomous Small Group Activities and Productivity in Japan." *Management Japan* 14 (Summer 1981): 16–18.

FUKADA, RYUJI. "Japanese Management Not Magic, But Science." *The Japan Times Weekly*, March 13, 1982: 5.

GELINAS, MARY V. "A Systems Approach to Quality Circles." *IAQC 4th Annual Conference Transactions*. Cincinnati: International Association of Quality Circles, 1982.

General Electric Company. *Quality Circles Leadings and Facilitating Manual*. Bridgeport, CT: General Electric Company Quality Projects, 1981.

GIBSON, PRICE. "Assess Readiness, Measure Change and Survive." *The Quality Circles Journal* 5 (May 1982): 19–31.

GIBSON, PRICE. "Challenges for Quality Circles and Quality of Work Life." *IAQC 4th Annual Conference Transactions*. Cincinnati: International Association of Quality Circles, 1982.

GIBSON, PRICE. "Full-Time Facilitation." *The Quality Circles Journal* 4 (August 1981): 9.

GIBSON, PRICE. *Quality Circles: One Approach to Productivity Improvement*. Work in American Institute Studies in Productivity. New York: Pergamon, 1982.

GIBSON, PRICE. *Quality Circles Facilitator Education and Development Needs. A Report on Research Conducted in Northeastern Ohio Organizations*. Kent, OH: Kent State University, College of Special Programs, March 1981.

GIBSON, PRICE. "Questions and Challenges for Quality Circles Implementors." *Creativity Week V Proceedings*. Greensboro, NC: Center for Creative Leadership, 1982: 60–77.

GIBSON, PRICE. "Short-Term Fad or Long-Term Fundamental? The Need for Research into the Quality Circle Process." *The Quality Circles Journal* 4 (May 1981): 25–26.

GOODFELLOW, MATTHEW. "Quality Control Circle Programs— What Works and What Doesn't." *Quality Progress* 14 (August 1981): 32–33.

GORDON, WILLIAM J. "Operational Approach to Creativity."

Harvard Business Review 34 (November–December 1956): 41–51.

GOW, ERNEST. "Would Our Use of the Japanese 'Quality Circle' Bring Cost Savings?" *Management Accounting* 58 (February 1980): 18.

GREEN, R.R. "Productivity Improvements for J. C. Penney Catalog." *AIIE Proceedings,* Spring 1981: 489–93.

GREGORY, CARL E. *Management of Intelligence: Scientific Problem Solving and Creativity.* New York: McGraw-Hill, 1967.

GRYNA, FRANK M., JR. *Quality Circles: A Team Approach to Problem Solving.* New York: AMACOM, A Division of the American Management Association, 1981.

GUEST, ROBERT H. "Quality of Work Life: Learning from Tarrytown." *Harvard Business Reviews* 57 (July–August 1979): 76–87.

Guidelines for Implementing UAW—Ford Employe Involvement Programs. UAW—Ford National Joint Committee on Employe Involvement. September 1980.

GUIZZETTI, EUGENE. "What is Quality of Work Life?" M.B.A. major paper, University of Windsor, 1983.

HAEFELE, JOHN W. *Creativity and Innovation.* New York: Van Nostrand Reinhold, 1962.

HALL, FRANK. "Made in Japan." *Plastics Engineering,* November 1980: 38–48.

HALL, FRANK. "Participation Improves Quality . . . Because it Changes Attitudes." *Machinery,* July 1971: 46–50.

HALL, JAMES L., and JOE K. LEIDECKER. "Is Japanese-Style Management Anything New? A Comparison of Japanese-Style Management with U.S. Participative Models." *Human Resource Management* 20 (Winter 1981): 14–21.

HANAMI, TADASHI. *Labor Relations in Japan Today.* Tokyo: Kodansha International, 1982.

Handbook on the UAW—Ford Process for Local Unions and Management. UAW Ford National Joint Committee on Employe Involvement, 1980.

HANLEY, JOSEPH. "Our Experience with Quality Circles." *Quality Progress* 13 (February 1980): 22–24.

HATTRUP, COLLEEN. "The Changing Roles of Participants in a Self-Facilitation Mode." *IAQC 4th Annual Conference Transactions. Cincinnati: International Association of Quality Circles, 1982.*

HATVANY, NINA, and VLADIMIR PUCIK. "Japanese Management Practices and Productivity." *Organization Dynamics* 9 (Spring 1981): 4–21.

HAZAMA, HIROSHI. "Characteristics of Japanese Corporate Management." *the wheel extended: A Toyota Quarterly Review* (Tokyo), Special Supplement, Winter 1979, pp. 1–8.

HAYES, ROBERT H. "Reflections on Japanese Factory Management." *Harvard Business School Working Paper*, January 1981.

HAYES, ROBERT H. "Why Japanese Factories Work." *Harvard Business Review* 59 (July–August 1981): 56–66.

HEGLAND, RONALD E. "Quality Circles: Key to Productivity with Quality." *Production Engineering*, June 1981: 26–31.

HERIP, WALTER M. "Forging Ahead." *The Quality Circles Journal* 5 (November 1982).

HERZENBERG, STEPHAN A., and WILLIAM A. SCHWARTZ. "UAW: Loosening the Chains." *The Harvard Crimson* 21 (February 21, 1979): 3.

HILL, C., and W. CARTWRIGHT. "Quality Circles Work." *The Quality Circles Journal* 1 (Third Quarter 1978): 27–36.

HOFFMAN, FRANK O. "A Quality Atmosphere: Quality Circles Demand a Supportive Business Philosophy." *Management World* 12 (January 1983) 44.

"Honeywell Quality Circles: Part of a Growing American Trend." *Journal of Organizational and Behavior Management* 3 (1981–82): 97–101.

HOWARD, NIGEL, and YOSHIYA TERAMOTO. "The Really Important Difference Between Japanese and Western Management." *Management International Review* 21 (February 1981): 19–30.

HUNT, BONNIE. "Measuring Results in a Quality Circle Pilot Test." *Quality Circles Journal* 4 (August 1981): 26–29.

HUTCHINS, DAVID. "How Quality Goes Round in Circles." *Management Today*, January 1981: 27–28.

IMAI, MASAAKI. "Plant-Wide Campaigns: Voluntary Activities Extended Beyond Small Group." *The Japan Economic Journal*, July 27, 1982: 12.

IMAI, MASAAKI. "Policy Development: Japanese Management's New Strategic Tool." *The Japan Economic Journal*, February 22, 1983: 12.

IMAI, MASAAKI. "Productivity in Disarray: Its 'Hard' and 'Soft'

Aspects.'' *The Japan Economic Journal*, January 26, 1982: 12.

IMAI, MASAAKI. "Quality Control and Small Group Activities: The Key to Improved Productivity." *The Japan Economic Journal*, April 27, 1982: 12.

IMAI, MASAAKI. "Small Group Activities—Five Times ROI? The Case of Nissan Chemical Industries." *The Japan Economic Journal*, June 14, 1982: 12.

IMAI, MASAAKI. "Small Group Activities: The Key to Improved Productivity." *The Japan Economic Journal*, February 23, 1982: 12–13.

IMAI, MASAAKI. "From Taylor to Ford to Toyota: 'Kanban' System—Another Challenge from Japan." *The Japan Economic Journal*, March 30, 1982: 12.

IMAI, MASAAKI. "Total Quality Control as Corporate Strategy." *The Japan Economic Journal*, December 28, 1982: 12.

IMBERMAN, WOODRUFF. "Why Quality Control Circles Don't Work." *Canadian Business*, May 1982: 103–6.

INGLE, SUD. *Quality Circles Master Guide: Increasing Productivity with People Power*. New York: Prentice-Hall, 1982.

INGLE, SUD. "How to Avoid Quality Circle Failure in Your Company." *Training and Development Journal* 36 (June 1982): 54–59.

IRVING, ROBERT R. "QC Circles Spur Productivity, Improve Product Quality." *Iron Age* 221 (June 5, 1978): 61–63.

IRVING, ROBERT R. "QC Payoff Attracts Top Management." *Iron Age* 222 (August 20, 1979): 64–65.

ISHIKAWA, KAORU. "Cause and Effect Diagram—CE Diagram—Tokusei Yo-In Zu-Ishikawa Diagram." In *QC Circles: Applications, Tools, and Theory*, edited by Davida M. Amsden and Robert T. Amsden. Milwaukee: American Society for Quality Control, 1976: 91–94.

ISHIKAWA, KAORU. *Guide to Quality Control*. Tokyo: Asian Productivity Organization, 1976.

ISHIKAWA, KAORU. *QC Circle Activities: QC in Japan*. Series No. 1, Tokyo: Japanese Union of Scientists and Engineers, April 1968.

ISHIKAWA, KAORU. "Quality In Japan: QC Circle Activities." *Quality*, May 1980: 97.

JACKSON, MICHAEL. *Productivity Improvement:* A Study of Selected Approaches. M.B.A. major paper, University of Windsor, May 1982.

Japan Quality Control Circles. Tokyo: Asian Productivity Organization, 1982.

"Japanese Managers Tell How Their System Works." *Fortune*, November 1977: 126–38.

Japanese Standards Association. *JSA Technical Reports*, No. 104, 1963–1969.

"Japan's High-Tech Challenge." *Newsweek*, August 9, 1982: 48–54.

"Japan's Industrial Competitiveness: The Human Factor." *Japan Labor Bulletin*, May 1982: 5–8.

JENKINS, K. M. and J. SHIMADA. "Quality Circles in the Service Sector." *Supervisory Management* 26 (August 1981): 2–7.

JOCH, ALAN. "Quality Circles: The Key to Better Management?" *Metal Center News*, June 1982: 64–69.

JOHNSON, BRYAN. "Brave New World of Nissan—U.S.A." *The Globe and Mail*, June 18, 1983.

JOHNSON, RICHARD TANNER, and WILLIAM G. OUCHI. "Made in America (Under Japanese Management.)" *Harvard Business Review* 52 (September–October 1974): 61–69.

JEUCHTER, W. MATTHEW, and TOM UTNE. "Wellness: Addressing the 'Whole' Person." *Training and Development Journal* 36 (May 1982): 112–16.

JURAN, JOSEPH M. "International Significance of the QC Circle Movement." *Quality Progress* 13 (November 1980): 18–22.

JURAN, JOSEPH M. "Japanese and Western Quality: A Contrast." *Quality Progress* 11 (December 1978): 10–18.

JURAN, JOSEPH M. "Product Quality—A Prescription for the West. Part I: Training and Improvement Programs," *Management Review* 6 (June 1981): 9–14.

JURAN, JOSEPH M. "Product Quality—A Prescription for the West. Part II: Upper-Management Leadership and Employee Relations." *Management Review* 7 (July 1981): 57–61.

JURAN, JOSEPH M. "Quality Control of Service—the 1974 Japanese Symposium." *Quality Progress* 8 (April 1975): 10–13.

KARATSU, HAJIME. *Quality Control to Extend a Company: From Top Management to the Factory Floor*. Tokyo: Japan, 1966.

BIBLIOGRAPHY

KARATSU, HAJIME. "What Makes Japanese Products Better?" *SAM Advanced Management Journal* 47 (Spring 1982): 4–7.

KEEFE, JOHN P. "Part-Time Facilitation." *The Quality Circles Journal* 4 (August 1981): 8.

KEEFE, JOHN, and WILLIAM A. KRAUS. *Building Effective Quality Circles: A Research Report*. Hendersonville, NC: General Electric Company Quality Projects, 1982.

KELLMAN, H. C. "Compliance, Identification and Internalization: Three Processes of Attitude Change." *Journal of Conflict Resolution* 2 (March 1958): 51–60.

KERR, CLARK, JOHN T. DUNLOP, FREDERICK HARBISON, and CHARLES A. MYERS. *Industrialism and Industrial Man*. New York: Oxford University Press, 1964.

KIDA, HIROSHI. "Life-Long Learning: Education for All People at All Ages." *Look Japan*, December 10, 1981: 1–3.

KIKUCHI, SEIICHI. "Japanese Quality Control Method Increasingly Finds Its Way Abroad." *The Japan Economic Journal*, June 1, 1982: 11

KLEIN, GERALD D. "Implementing Quality Circles: A Hard Look at Some of the Realities." *Personnel* 58 (November–December 1981): 11–21.

KLEIN, WALTER F., and THOM SCHAMBERGER. "Part-Time Facilitators and Quality Control Circles in the Hospital Environment." In *IAQC 4th Annual Conference Transactions*. International Association of Quality Circles, 1982: 528–40.

KNIGHT, L. J. "Quality Circles in Action: A Canadian Experience:" *CTM: The Human Element*, February 1983, 20–21.

KOEHLER, JERRY W., KARL W. E. ANATOL, and RONALD L. APPLBAUM. *Public Communication: Behavioral Perspectives*. New York: Macmillan, 1978.

KOGURI, TADAO. "Providing Incentives to the QC Circle Through an Evaluation System." *Japan Quality Control Circles*. Tokyo: Asian Productivity Organization, 1982.

KONARICK, RONALD B., and WAYNE REED. "A Military Approach: Work Environment Improvement Teams." *The Quality Circles Journal* 4 (August 1981): 35–40.

KONDO, YOSHIO. "Company-Wide Quality Control in Japanese Industries and its Impact on Quality of Work Life." *International Conference on the Quality of Working Life*. Scarsdale, NY: Work in America Institute, 1981.

KONDO, YOSHIO. "The Role of Managers in QC Circle Movement." In *QC Circles: Applications, Tools, and Theory*, edited by Davida M. Amsden and Robert T. Amsden. Milwaukee: American Society for Quality Control, 1976: 41–54.

KONZ, STEPHAN. "Quality Circles: Japanese Success Story." *Industrial Engineering* 11 (October 1979): 24–26.

KONZ, STEPHAN. "Quality Circles; An Annotated Bibliography." *Quality Progress* 14, (April 1981): 30–35.

KOSHIRO, KAZUYOSHI. "The Quality of Working Life." *the wheel extended: A Toyota Quarterly Review* (Tokyo), Special Supplement, June 1981, pp. 1–8.

KRAAR, LOUIS. "The Japanese Are Coming—With Their Own Style of Management." *Fortune*, March 1975: 116–21, 160–64.

KUBOTA, AKIRA. "Japan: Social Structure and Work Ethic." *Asia Pacific Community* 20 (Spring 1983).

KUME, HITOSHI. "Quality Control in Japan's Industries." *the wheel extended: A Toyota Quarterly Review* 9 (Tokyo), Spring 1980.

LAMMERS, C. J. "Power and Participation in Decision Making in Formal Organizations." *American Journal of Sociology* 73 (1967): 201–16.

LANCIANESE, F. W. "Small Plant's Safety Success Formula." *Occupational Hazards* 43 (July 1981): 45–48.

LAW, JOE M. "Quality Circles at a Naval Shipyard: Employee Involvement Ups Productivity." *World of Work Report* 6 (January 1981): 3–4.

LEE, YONG Y., and LARRY W. FEGLEY. "How QC Circles Were Started in AMP, Inc." In *IAQC 1st Annual Conference Transactions*. Cincinnati: International Association of Quality Circles, 1979.

LESIKAR, RAYMOND V. *Basic Business Communication*. Homewood, IL: Richard D. Irwin, Inc., 1979.

"Lessons from Japan, Inc." *Newsweek*, September 8, 1980: 61–62.

LEVIN, SOLOMON B. *Industrial Relations in Postwar Japan*. Urbana, IL: University of Illinois Press, 1958.

LINDSAY, WILLIAM M. "Can Quality Circles Bridge the Japanese/American Culture Gap?" In *IAQC 4th Annual Conference Transactions*. Cincinnati: International Association of Quality Circles, 1982.

BIBLIOGRAPHY

LOCKE, E. A., and D. M. SCHWEIGER. "Participation in Decision Making: One More Look." In *Research in Organizational Behavior*, edited by B. M. Staw, Greenwich, CT: JAI Press, Inc., 1979.

LOHR, STEVE "Overhauling American's Business Management." *The New York Times*, January 4, 1981: VI, 15. For letters about this article, see February 15, 1981: VI, 102.

LOZANO, ROBERT. "Quality Circles—Blue-Collar, White-Collar and Other Hues." In *ASQC 36th Annual Technical Conference Transactions*. Milwaukee: American Society for Quality Control, 1982.

LOZANO, ROBERT, and PHILIP C. THOMPSON. "QC Circle Implementation in the Space Shuttle External Tank Program at the Michoud Marietta Corp." In *ASQC 34th Annual Technical Conference Transactions*. Milwaukee: American Society for Quality Control, 1980.

MACDONALD, JOYCE, and CAROL ROBINSON. "Concept for Management." *The Quality Circles Journal* 4 (November 1981): 13–15.

MAGUIRE, MARY A., and RICHARD T. PASCALE. "Communication, Decision Making and Implementation Among Managers in Japanese and American Managed Companies in the United States." *Sociology and Social Research* 63 (1978): 1–23.

MAIN, JEREMY. "The Battle for Quality Begins." *Fortune*. December 29, 1980, 28–33.

MARKS, MITCHELL LEE. "Conducting an Employee Attitude Survey." *Personnel Journal* 61 (September 1982): 684–91.

MARSH, ROBERT M., and HIROSHI MANNARI. *Modernization and the Japanese Factory*. Princeton, NJ: Princeton University Press, 1976.

MARTIN, WALLACE. "What Management Can *Expect* From an Employee Attitude Survey." *Personnel Administrator,* July 1981: 75–79.

MASER, MARJORIE. "Mount Sinai Invests in Quality Circles." *Health Services Manager* 14 (February 1982): 44–48.

MAZIQUE, MIGNON. "The Quality Circle Transplant." *Issues and Observation* 1 (May 1981): 1–3.

MCCLENAHAN, J. S. "Bringing Home Japan's Lessons." *Industry Week* 208 (February 23, 1981): 69–73.

MCGREGOR, DOUGLAS. *The Human Side of Enterprise*. New York: McGraw-Hill, 1960.

MCGREGOR, DOUGLAS. *The Professional Manager*. New York: McGraw-Hill, 1967.

MCMILLAN, CHARLES J. "From Quality Control to Quality Management: Lessons from Japan." *Business Quarterly* 47 (Spring 1982): 31–40.

MCMILLAN, CHARLES. "Is Japanese Management Really So Different?" *Business Quarterly* 45 (Autumn 1980): 26–31.

MCMILLAN, CHARLES J. "Production Planning and Organization Design at Toyota." *Business Quarterly* 46 (Winter 1981): 22–30.

MENNING J. H., C. W. WILKINSON, and PETER B. CLARKE. *Communicating Through Letters and Reports*. Homewood, IL: Richard D. Irwin, Inc., 1976.

METZ, EDMUND, J. "Diagnosing Readiness." *The Quality Circles Journal* 4 (November 1981): 16–20.

METZ, EDMUND J. "The Verteam Circle." *Training and Development Journal* 35 (December 1981): 78–85.

MEYER, ROBERT P. "Marriage of Your P's and Q's Through Quality Circles." In *ASQC 36th Annual Technical Conference Transactions*. Milwaukee: American Society for Quality Control, 1982.

MIDDLEMIST, R. DENNIS, and MICHAEL A. HITT. *Organizational Behavior: Applied Concepts*. Palo Alto, CA: Science Research Associates, 1981.

MILLS, TED. "Human Resources: Why The New Concern?" *Harvard Business Review* 53 (March–April 1975): 120–34.

MITCHELL, TERENCE R. *People in Organizations: Understanding Their Behavior*. New York: McGraw-Hill, 1978.

MITO, TADASHI. "The Internationalization of Japanese Management," *the wheel extended: A Toyota Quarterly Review* 9 (Tokyo), Summer 1981, pp. 2–9.

MONTGOMERY, ROBERT L. *A Master Guide to Public Speaking*. New York: Harper & Row, 1979.

MORLAND, JULIA. *Quality Circles*. London: Industrial Society, 1981.

MORRIS, ROSEMARY. *Quality Circles Consulting: Marketing Survey and Industrial Analysis*. San Jose, CA: FMC Corporation, Ordnance Division Engineering, 1981.

MURATA, KIYOAKI. "What Makes Japan Tick?" *The Japan Times Weekly*, February 27, 1982: 3.

The Motorola Participative Management Program. Corporate Offices, Motorola Inc., 1983.

BIBLIOGRAPHY

NAKANE, CHIE. *Japanese Society*. Berkeley: University of California Press, 1970.

NAKAYAMA, ICHIRO. *Industrialization and Labor—Management Relations in Japan*. Translated by Ross E. Mouer. Tokyo: The Japan Institute of Labor, 1975.

NAYATANI, YOSHINOBU. As quoted by Masaaki Imai. "Policy Deployment: Japanese Management's New Strategic Tool." *When in Japan: An Introduction for Doing Business in and with Japan*. Vol. 4. Tokyo, Japan: Planning and Promotion Division, Hotel Okura, February 14, 1983: 24–26.

National League for Nursing. "The Quality Circle Process." *Nursing and Health Care* 3 (November 1982): 492–93.

"The New Economy," *Time*, May 30, 1983.

"The New Industrial Relations." *Business Week*, May 11, 1981: 85–87, 89–90, 92–93, 96, 98.

ODAKA, KUNIO. *Toward Industrial Democracy: Management and Workers in Modern Japan*. Cambridge, MA: Harvard University Press, 1975.

OISHI, O. "The Concept of Perfect Production." *CTM: The Human Element*, February 1981: 14–16.

ORBAUGH, PAMELA K., and TIM ORBAUGH. "Is Your Lab Ready for Quality Circles?" *Medical Laboratory Observer*, February 1983: 41–45.

ORFAN, CONSTANTINE. "In-Process and End-Product Goals of Quality Circles." *The Quality Circles Journal* 4 (February (1981): 26–27.

OUCHI, WILLIAM. *Theory Z: How American Business Can Meet the Japanese Challenge*. Reading, MA: Addison-Wesley, 1981.

OZAWA, TERUTOMO. *People and Productivity in Japan*. Work in America Institute Studies in Productivity. New York: Pergamon Press, 1982.

PABST, WILLIAM R. JR. "Motivating People in Japan." *Quality Progress* 5 (October 1972): 14–18.

PASCALE, RICHARD T., and ANTHONY G. ATHOS. *The Art of Japanese Management: Applications for American Executives*. New York: Simon & Schuster, 1981.

PASCARELLA, PERRY. "Fad or Philosophy? QCs May Have Become Too Popular." *Industry Week*, March 22, 1981: 23–24.

PASCARELLA, PERRY, *Industry Week's Guide to Tomorrow's*

Executive: Human Management in the Future Corporation. New York: Van Nostrand Reinhold, 1981.

PASCARELLA, PERRY. "Quality Circles: Just Another Management Headache?" *Industry Week*, June 26, 1982: 50–55.

PATCHIN, ROBERT I. "Consultants: Good and Bad." *The Quality Circles Journal* 4 (May 1981): 11–12.

PATCHIN, ROBERT I. "Facilitators, Facilitation and Ownership." *The Quality Circles Journal* 4 (February 1981): 13–14.

PATCHIN, ROBERT I. "Stairway to the Stars." *The Quality Circles Journal* 5 (February 1981): 10–15.

PATCHIN, ROBERT I., and ROBERT CUNNINGHAM. *The Management and Maintenance of Quality Circles*. Homewood, IL: Dow Jones–Irwin, 1983.

PERRY, BERNARD J. "Problem Identification: What's the Best Way." *IAQC 2nd Annual Conference Transactions*. Cincinnati: International Association of Quality Circles, February 1980.

PETERS, THOMAS J. "Putting Excellence Into Management." *Business Week*, July 21, 1980: 196–205.

Plan for Productivity/Quality Improvement, Commercial Division. Sperry-Vickers Corp., July 1980.

PORTER, L. W., R. M. STEERS, R. T. MOWDAY and P. V. BOULIAN. "Organizational Commitment, Job Satisfaction, and Turnover Among Psychiatric Technicians." *Journal of Applied Psychology* 59 (1974): 603–9.

Productivity and Quality Control: The Japanese Experience. Tokyo: Japan External Trade Organization, 1980.

"QC Circle Activities and the Suggestion System." *Japan Labor Bulletin*, January 1982: 5–8.

"Quality Circle Boom Part of Growing American Trend." *Supervision* 43 (September 1981): 8–11.

Quality Circles at Honeywell: A Study of Participant Perceptions. Minnetonka, MN: Corporate Human Resource Development Department, Honeywell Inc., July 1982.

Quality Fluid Power Components and Systems to Meet Industry's Needs, the World Over. Troy, MI: Sperry Vickers Corp., n.d.

"Quality and Productivity: America's Revitilization." *Business Week*, November 8, 1982: 19–20, 25–26, 30.

"Quality: The U.S. Drives to Catch Up." *Business Week*, November 1, 1982: 66–69, 70, 77, 80.

BIBLIOGRAPHY

QUIBLE, ZANE K. "Quality Circles: A Well-Rounded Approach to Employee Involvement." *Management World* 10 (September 1981): 10–11, 38.

REED, THOMAS W., and MARK R. OLSON. "Circle Quality—Members Remembered." In *IAQC 4th Annual Conference Transactions*. Cincinnati: International Association of Quality Circles, 1982.

REHDER, ROBERT R. "What American and Japanese Managers Are Learning From Each Other." *Business Horizons* 24 (March–April 1981): 63–70.

REHDER, ROBERT R. "Japan's Synergistic Society: How It Works and Its Implications for the United States." *Management Review* 70 (October 1981): 64–66.

REID, LAURA. "Nashua: Using Statistics to Solve Hidden Problems." *The Financial Times of Canada*, November 22, 1982: 11–13.

REISCHAUER, EDWIN O. *The Japanese*. Cambridge, MA: Harvard University Press, 1977.

RENDALL, ELAINE. "Quality Circles: A 'Third Wave' Intervention." *Training and Development Journal* 35 (March 1981): 28–31.

RENDALL, ELAINE, and MARJORIE MASER. "Using Quality Circles in the Health Service." *Human Resource Development* 4 (June 1980): 12–14.

Report on the Survey of Labor-Management Consultation Systems at Work as of 1980. Tokyo: Japan Productivity Center, April 1981.

REIKER, WAYNE S. "Management's Role in QC Circles." In *IAQC 2nd Annual Conference Transactions*. Cincinnati: International Association of Quality Circles, February 1980.

RIEKER, WAYNE S. "The QC Circle Phenomenon: An Update." In *ASQC 33rd Annual Technical Conference Transactions*. Milwaukee: American Society for Quality Control, 1979.

RIEKER, WAYNE S. "What Is the Lockheed Quality Control Circle Program?" In *ASQC 30th Annual Technical Conference Transactions*. Milwaukee: American Society for Quality Control, 1976.

RIEKER, WAYNE S., and SHAUN J. SULLIVAN. "Can the Effectiveness of QC Circles Be Measured?" *The Quality Circles Journal* 4 (May 1981): 29!-31.

RINGLE, WILLIAM M. "The American Who Remade Made in Japan." *Nation's Business* 69 (February 1981): 67–70.

ROHLEN, THOMAS P. "The Company Work Group." *In Modern Japanese Organization and Decision-Making*, edited by Ezra F. Vogel, Berkeley: University of California Press, 1975: 185–209.

ROLLAND, I., and R. JANSON. "Total Involvement as a Productivity Strategy." *California Management Review* 24 (Winter 1981): 40–48.

ROSOW, JEROME M. "Productivity and the Blue-Collar Blues." *American Management Associations Annual Conference Transactions*. New York: American Management Association, February 1971.

ROSS, JOEL E., and WILLIAM C. ROSS. *Japanese Quality Circles & Productivity*. Reston, VA: Reston Publishing Company, 1982.

Royal Bank of Canada. *The Communication of Ideas. A Collection of Monthly Letters*. Montreal, 1972.

RUBENSTEIN, SIDNEY P. "New Management Concepts From Japan: A Tale of Two Conferences." *Paperboard Packaging*, January 1970: 44–45.

RUBINSTEIN, SIDNEY P. "Participative Quality Control." *Quality Progress* 4 (January 1971): 24–27.

RUBINSTEIN, SIDNEY P. "QC Circles and U.S. Participative Movements." In *QC Circles: Applications, Tools, and Theory*, edited by Davida M. Amsden and Robert T. Amsden. Milwaukee: American Society for Quality Control, 1976: 157–62.

RUBINSTEIN, SIDNEY P. "QWL and the Technical Societies." *Training and Development Journal* 34 (August 1980): 76–81.

SANDHOLM, LENNART. "Japanese Quality Circles—A Remedy for the West's Quality Problems?" *Quality Progress* 16 (February 1983): 20–23.

SATO, KINKO. "More & More Japanese Women are Hoping to Get Lifetime Jobs." *The Japan Economic Journal*, March 30, 1982: 11.

SCHEIN, EDGAR H. "SMR Forum: Does Japanese Management Style Have a Message for American Managers?" *Sloan Management Review* 23 (Fall 1981): 55–68.

SCHMIDT, JERRY L. "Participative Management—Challenge to Competition." *ASQC 34th Annual Technical Conference Transactions*. Milwaukee: American Society for Quality Control, 1980.

SCHMITT, G. A., N. P. PRESTON, and B. S. MITCHELL. "Successful Application of a Quality Circle Program in a Utility Environment." *AIIE Proceedings, Fall Annual Conference*, Fall 1980: 365–71.

SEDAM, SCOTT M. "QC Circle Training Process Should Cover Relating, Supporting, Problem Solving Skills." *Industrial Engineering* 14 (January 1982): 70–74.

SEDERBERG, GEORGE W. "The Role of the Steering Committee." In *IAQC 4th Annual Conference Transactions*. Cincinnati: International Association of Quality Circles, 1982.

SEELYE, H. NED, EDWARD C. P. STEWART, and JOYCE A. SWEEN. *Evaluating Quality Circles in U.S. Industry: A Feasibility Study*. Arlington, VA: U.S. Department of Defense, Office of Naval Research, 1982.

SHAW, ROBERT J. "Middle Management's Role in Quality Circles." *Management Focus* 29 (May–June 1982): 34–36.

SHEARMAN, ROBERT W. "How Can America Increase Productivity in the Next Decade?" *Quality Progress* 12 (January 1979): 22–26.

SIEGEL, IRVING H. *Productivity Measurement: An Evolving Art*. New York: Pergamon, 1982.

SINGLETON, JACK. "Quality Circles in a State Psychiatric Hospital." In *IAQC 4th Annual Conference Transactions*. Cincinnati: International Association of Quality Circles, 1982.

SOKOL, MARC, and V. HURWITZ. "Evaluation Equals Growth and Survival." *The Quality Circles Journal* 5 (August 1982): 15–20.

SORGE, MARJORIE. "Work Smarter, Not Harder, Advises Quality Consultant." *Automotive News*, July 27, 1981: 6.

SOYKA, DAVID. "Honeywell Pioneers in Quality Circle Movement." *World of Work Report* 6 (September 1981): 65–67.

SPROW, EUGENE E. "Made in USA." *Tooling and Production*, February 1982: 73–80.

SPROW, EUGENE E. "The Quality Commitment." *Tooling and Production*, March 1982: 73–80.

STANSBURY, JAMES F. "Financial Incentives For Circles?" *The Quality Circles Journal* 4 (February 1981): 7.

STEIN, BARRY A., and ROSABETH MOSS KANTER. "Building the Parallel Organization: Creating Mechanisms for Permanent Quality of Work Life." *The Journal of Applied Behavioral Science* 16 (1980): 371–86.

STRUTHERS, J. E. *Canada–Japan Essay: Long Road Back*. Canada–Japan Council, February 1981: 6–10.

SUGIMOTO, YASUO. "The Advancing QC Circle Movement." *Japan Quality Control Circles*. Tokyo: Asian Productivity Organization, 1972.

SUMIYA, M. "The Emergence of Modern Japan." In *Workers and Employers in Japan: The Japanese Employment Relations System*, edited by K. Ōkochi, B. Karsh, and S.B. Levine. Princeton, NJ: Princeton University Press, 1974.

SWARTZ, GERALD E., and VIVIAN C. COMSTOCK. "One Firm's Experience with Quality Circles." *Quality Progress* 12 (September 1979): 14–16.

TAGLIAFERRI, L. E. "As Quality Circles Fade, a Bank Tries Top Down Teamwork." *ABA Banking Journal* 74 (July 1982): 98–100.

TAKAMIYA, SUSUMU. "The Characteristics of Japanese Management," *Management Japan* 14 (Summer 1981): 6–9.

TAKEDA, YUTAKA. *Autonomous Self-Management Activity: A Key to High Productivity at Nippon Steel Corporation*. A paper presented at the Japan Society, May 9, 1980.

TAKEUCHI, H. "Productivity: Learning form the Japanese." *California Management Review* 23 (Summer 1981): 5–19.

"Talking in Circles Improves Quality." *Industry Week* 192 (February 14, 1977): 62–64.

TAVERNIER, GERARD. "Awakening a Sleeping Giant: Ford's Employee Involvement Program." *Management Review* 70 (June 1981): 15–20.

TAYLOR, FREDERICK W. *Scientific Management*. New York: Harper & Row, 1911, 1947.

TAYLOR, MARK. "BankCal Quality Circles." In *IAQC 4th Annual Conference Transactions*. Cincinnati: International Association of Quality Circles, March 1982.

THOMPSON, JAMES. *Organizations in Action*. New York: McGraw-Hill, 1967.

THOMPSON, PHILIP C. "Management Circles—No!" *The Quality Circles Journal* 4 (November 1981): 7.

THOMPSON, PHILIP C. *Quality Circles: How To Make Them Work in America*. New York: AMACOM, a Division of American Management Association, 1982.

THOMPSON, PHILIP C. "Voluntary Circles." *The Quality Circles Journal* 4 (May 1981): 9.

BIBLIOGRAPHY

Toronto-Dominion Quality Programme Introductory Kit. Toronto: Toronto Dominion Bank of Canada, 1982.

TORTORICH, R., R., THOMPSON, C. ORFAN, D. LAYFIELD, C. DREYFUS, and M. KELLY. "Measuring Organizational Impact of Quality Circles." *The Quality Circles Journal* 4 (November 1981): 26–33.

TOWNSHEND, ROLPH. "Why the Japanese Are So Successful." *Management Review* 69 (October 1980): 29–47.

TSURUMI, YOSHI, and REBECCA TSURUMI. "A Closer Look at Japan's Lifetime Employment System." *Pacific Basin Quarterly* 8 (Fall 1982): 5–6.

TUTTLE, HOWARD C. "The Shortest Distance to Employee Ideas is a Circle." *Production*, June 1971, pp. 73–74.

UAW—Ford Employe Involvement: A Special Survey Report. Dearborn, MI: UAW—Ford National Development and Training Center, March 1983.

"U.S. Executives Look at Japanese QC." *Quality Progress* 13 (February 1980): 8.

VARLEY, PAUL H. "An Inquiry Into the Chrysanthemum and the Sword of Japanese Civilization." *Look Japan*, March 10, 1982, pp. 10–11.

VOGEL, EZRA. *Japan as Number One: Lessons for America*. Cambridge, MA: Harvard University, Press, 1979.

VOGEL, EZRA, ed. *Modern Japanese Organization and Decision-Making*. Berkeley and Los Angeles; University of California Press, 1975.

WELLSTOOD, SYBIL A., and LINDA WRIGHT. "Using Quality Circles to Spot and Solve Lab Problems." *Medical Laboratory Observer*, February 1983: 32–37.

WERTNER, WILLIAM B., JR. "Quality Circles: Key Executive Issues." *Journal of Contemporary Business* 11 (Second Quarter 1982): 17–26.

"Why Industrial Productivity Is as Important as Military Arms." *Government Executive* 13 (October 1981): 38–40.

WIDTFELDT, JAMES R. "How IES Can Contribute to, Gain from a Quality Circle." *Industrial Engineering* 14 (January 1982): 64–68.

"Will the Slide Kill Quality Circles?" *Business Week*, January 11, 1982: 108–9.

Windsor Star, March 3, 1983.

Work in America. Report of a Special Task Force to the

Secretary of Health, Education and Welfare. Cambridge, MA: MIT Press, 1973.

"Worker Motivation in Japan (II)." *Japan Labor Bulletin,* March 1982: 5–8.

YAGER, ED. "Examining the Quality Control Circle." *Personnel Journal* 58 (October 1979): 682–84, 708.

YAGER, ED. "Quality Circle: A Tool for the '80s," *Training and Development Journal* 34 (August 1980): 60–63.

YAGER, EDWIN G. "The Quality Control Circle Explosion." *Training and Development Journal* 35 (April 1981): 98–105.

YAKABE, KATSUMI. Labor Relations in Japan: Fundamental Characteristics. Tokyo: International Society for Educational Information, 1974.

YAMADA, MITSUHIKO. "Japanese-Style Management in America: Merits and Difficulties." *Japanese Economic Studies* 10 (Fall 1981): 1–31.

YANG, CHARLES Y. "Management Styles: American Vis-a-Vis Japanese." *Columbia Journal of World Business* 12 (Fall 1977): 23–31.

YANKELOVICH, DANIEL. *New Rules: Searching for Self-Fulfillment in a World Turned Upside Down.* New York: Random House, 1981.

YOSHIDA, MITSUKUNI. "The Concept of 'Labor' in Japan." *the wheel extended: A Toyota Quarterly Review* (Tokyo), Spring 1980, 2–8.

YOSHINO, M. Y. *Japan's Managerial System: Tradition and Innovation.* Cambridge, MA: MIT Press, 1968.

YOST, JOHN C. "Quality Circles: Is Everybody Ready and Willing?" In *IAQC 1st Annual Conference Transactions.* Cincinnati: International Association of Quality Circles, February 1979.

YUKOSAWA, TOSHIHARU. "The QC Circle Movement Applied to Shop Requirement." *Japan Quality Control Circles.* Tokyo: Asian Productivity Organization, 1983.

ZAGER, ROBERT, and MICHAEL P. ROSOW, eds. *The Innovative Organization: Productivity Programs in Action.* New York: Pergamon Press, 1982.

ZANDER, A., and T. CURTIS. "Effects of Social Power on Aspiration Setting and Striving." *Journal of Abnormal and Social Psychology* 64 (1962): 63–74.

ZEMKE, RON. Quality Circles: "Can They Work in the U.S.?"

Journal of Applied Management 5 (September–October 1980): 16–21.

ZWEIG, PHILIP D. "Quality Circles—A Kind of Employee Brainstorming—Helping Banks Solve Problems, Improve Performance." *American Banker* 146 (January 19, 1981): 1–4.

INDEX

Page references in italics are to tables and figures.

27 million Americans can't read a bedtime story to a child.

It's because 27 million adults in this country simply can't read.

Functional illiteracy has reached one out of five Americans. It robs them of even the simplest of human pleasures, like reading a fairy tale to a child.

You can change all this by joining the fight against illiteracy.

Call the Coalition for Literacy at toll-free **1-800-228-8813** and volunteer.

Volunteer Against Illiteracy. The only degree you need is a degree of caring.